Between Hume and Mill

AN ANTHOLOGY OF BRITISH PHILOSOPHY, 1749–1843

Between Hume and Mill

AN ANTHOLOGY OF BRITISH PHILOSOPHY, 1749–1843

Selected Readings from Hartley to Ferrier

EDITED BY

ROBERT BROWN

THE MODERN LIBRARY

NEW YORK

CONTENTS

THOMAS REID

JOSEPH PRIESTLEY

JOSEPH PRIESTLEY AND
RICHARD PRICE

DUGALD STEWART

JAMES FREDERICK FERRIER

INTRODUCTION

None of the philosophers represented in this collection is read much now, although some of them were once highly valued for their achievements. Priestley, Price, and James Mill were men of international reputation in their time. And among educated people, such names as Hartley, Reid, Stewart, and Brown commanded a respect now reserved for economic advisors to major governments. The eclipse of most of these philosophers dates from the middle of the last century. Thus Tucker's work has not been reprinted since 1848; James Mill's book was last edited in 1869 by his son; the writings of Thomas Brown, though they passed quickly through many editions, have not been reprinted in substantial form since 1860; and the works of Reid, Stewart, and Ferrier have not been re-edited since the same period. Of the remaining men, the exchange between Priestley and Price last appeared in 1832, and Hartley's views were kept alive to the extent that James Mill's book was read.

An editor who flies in the face of such devaluation ought to be able to give good reasons why others should follow him. But doing this is not always the same as answering the question which, for many readers, is their first line of defence: "Why should I (or anyone) read these particular writers?" For this question sometimes challenges the editor in too general a way. It sometimes asks him to provide a reason for every possible reader; and there is no such statable set of reasons. We do not know now who these contemporary readers are or who they will be in the future. Nor do we know in advance which topics will interest them and which problems they will think most important. So the question "Why should I read this?" resembles the question "Why should I eat this?" Neither question has a general answer. If you are not hungry perhaps you ought not to eat this; and if you have no taste for truth obtained by honest means, then you certainly ought not to read these philosophers. Yet once this much has been said, it is still reasonable to ask what claim the philosophers represented in this volume have on our attention today. Why not abandon their works to the scholar and the specialist?

One conventional, but nevertheless correct, answer needs only to be mentioned. It is that much of the origins of John Stuart Mill's thought—hence much of the origins of nineteenth-century liberal thought—lies within these writings. Much of it does not, of course, because this volume excludes ethical and political philosophy. However, it does include most of the epistemological, and even metaphysical, underpinnings which British thinkers of this period contributed to the political liberalism of the nineteenth century. Another answer, equally conventional but equally correct, is that the influence of Locke, Berkeley, and Hume on British thinkers of the later nineteenth century cannot be understood if we are ignorant of the impact these three men had upon their contemporaries and immediate successors in the eighteenth century. This ignorance is illustrated whenever we visualize the century between the publication of the last volume of Hume's *Treatise on Human Nature* (1740) and the appearance of John Stuart Mill's *A System of Logic* (1843) as an era in which British philosophy simply marked time. We then think of Mill as a man who reached back across a vacant century to reestablish the work begun by Berkeley and Hume, quite forgetting for the moment that there was a chain of distinguished intermediaries. It was, after all, Mill's father, James, who was strongly influenced by Thomas Brown and David Hartley, and they, in turn, by Hume and Locke respectively. The results of this intervening century of hard work by many philosophers were available to Mill when he began writing his *Logic*. But the very success of that book contributed to the neglect of its predecessors. For by amply fulfilling Mill's hope that it would "cement together the detached fragments of a subject never yet treated as a whole," the *Logic* seemed to make unnecessary the reading of those detached fragments.

However, there is an additional reason for their neglect over the past century. It is that the Neo-Hegelianism introduced into the English-speaking world by the Scot, J. H. Stirling, in his book *The Secret of Hegel* (1865), had first to run a long course which greatly modified the earlier British tradition. The arrival of Scottish Hegelianism has a religious origin: in his Introduction Stirling wrote that "Spiritualism seems dying out in England, and . . . more and more numerous voices daily cry hail to the new God, matter—matter, too, independent of any law . . . pliant only to the moulding influence of *contingent* conditions." This reference to the malevolent influence of Darwin's theory of natural selection explains the use to which it was hoped that Hegel's philosophy could be put. It was to defend "the existence of God, the freedom of the will, and the immortality of the soul" against Darwinism. (Late in life, Stirling attacked his enemy in a book with that very title, arguing that Darwin had failed to show that there was no principle of design in nature.) Once introduced, Hegelianism—understood as one version of the view that the material world is entirely constructed by minds and is spiritual throughout—had a highly varied and influential career in Britain. It strongly affected men as diverse as Edward Caird, T. H. Green, Bernard Bosanquet, F. H. Bradley, and J. M. McTaggart. Not until the dominance of these thinkers had been effectively challenged by such opponents of Idealism as William James, G. E. Moore, and Bertrand Russell, could the writings of the earlier empiricists regain our attention.

But while the philosophical interests of past generations do not give us good reason for continuing to ignore certain thinkers today, neither do such past interests justify our revaluing the contributions of those men. In order to do that we must have some grounds for claiming that the writers concerned are worth reading independently of the stature of the people whom they influenced. In the present case such grounds are easily supplied. It was, for example, the intermediaries between Hume and J. S. Mill who produced the invariable sequence theory of causation (Brown), made the first serious modern attack on the representative theory of perception and thinking (Reid), and explored the Humean distinction between sense impressions and ideas (Reid, Stewart, Price, Brown). These intermediaries also gave us the modern formulation of such problems as that of the existence of other minds and the proof of an external world. They gave us, in addition, the definitional view of mathematics (Stewart), the falsifiability theory of induction (Hartley), and the first statement of the principles of common sense (Reid). Modern materialism owes something to Priestley's reliance on Boscovich's physics, and modern psychology owes its origin, in some important respects, to Hartley. Present day opponents of free will should be grateful to both men. Brown made clear the significance of the kinesthetic sense in our construction of reality; James Mill the importance and logic of relation-terms in its description; Ferrier the necessity for correlating different kinds of sense-impressions in the obtaining of self-knowledge. Taken together these are substantial and exciting achievements, whereas taken separately they are likely to be lost in what we now see as the increasing velocity of the accumulation of learning from the time of Hume to that of J. S. Mill. This is one argument in favor of what the present volume attempts to provide: a selection of these authors' best and most characteristic work in the fields of epistemology, metaphysics, and philosophy of science.

It is true, of course, that considered as a group these thinkers do not have many detailed views in common, though certain topics are to be found in the writings of most of them. Thus most have something to say about the relations between sensations and the sensory mechanisms, especially the relations concerning sight and touch; the relation between sense-impressions and ideas; the relationships holding between will, desire, and motive; something on free will and necessity; on pleasure; on memory; on imagination. But to list some of their topics in common is merely to list topics bequeathed from earlier writers and passed on to this day. There is nothing in these general topics which is distinctive to this period. Whatever is distinctive in their treatment is common only to sub-groups of the larger one. Hartley, Priestley, and Mill, for example, held much the same doctrine concerning the association of sensations and ideas, while Reid and Stewart shared the same view concerning the role played by the principles of common sense in human action.

However, it is possible to divide almost all the thinkers whose work is given here into two opposing camps which illustrate, in brief, the crucial intellectual allegiances of that time. On one side are those philosophers who believe in mechanistic explanations of mental operations (thinking matter), as shown, for example, in the production of complex ideas from simple ones by the process of association; who believe in the unknowability of the external world except by the indirect means of certain mental states; who think that the will is completely determined causally; and who hold that our basic common sense beliefs about matter, minds, space, and time need important corrections. Into this camp fall Hartley, Tucker, Priestley, Brown, and Mill. On the other side are those who are not mental mechanists, not supporters of the doctrine of the association of ideas in its more extended applications, do not hold a representative theory of perception, do not believe that so-called free choices are entirely determined, and do think that the fundamental common sense beliefs about the world can be known by us to be true. This subgroup includes Reid, Price, and Stewart. The remaining man, Ferrier, is a transition figure, as the sharp division between his earlier and later work indicates, and he falls outside this scheme of classification.

The deepest difference between the two sets of philosophers is that, in general, the former hold the procedural principle that every event, state, or process must have a causal explanation, ultimately a physical one. The latter group denies this. Since the use of a procedural principle is justified (or attacked) on the basis of its successes and failures, there is no quick way in philosophy of forcing either the adoption or abandonment of such a principle. Opinions may differ as to its successes and failures. The approximately one hundred years of British philosophy represented here shows quite well how the supporters and opponents of such a basic principle of procedure employ it on a wide variety of problems until all interesting differences of view seem to stand revealed. When the use of the principle no longer discloses new questions, it falls from the forefront of discussion as though by the common consent of its advocates and critics.

Yet while this absence of unanimous conclusions is not a reasonable ground for ignoring these writers, it does make clear that the philosophers of this period have at least one reason in common for claiming our attention today. It is that the same division of loyalties exists within contemporary philosophy. A substantial number of philosophers now believe that all human thought and behavior can be explained as the causal product of a society of goal-directed animals. These philosophers also believe that the self-maintaining features of such a society account both for the presence of social conventions and for the growth of individual self-awareness. An equally substantial number of philosophers reject this view. They believe that complex purposive behavior is explicable only in a non-causal way: that if, for example, a person could have the causal knowledge required to predict correctly his own actions, he could never decide to perform those actions. For, so the argument runs, it is logically impossible for us to decide to do what we have already predicted that we will do. On grounds such as these, they try to defend freedom of the will and the irreducibility of the notion of human purpose against the encroachments of the causal explanations put forward by the new scientific materialists. It is not surprising that there is a familiar tone to these arguments. Any reader of the exchange between Price and Priestley, or of Reid's critical remarks on Hartley, will find encapsulated there a similar disagreement about the appropriate limits of scientific explanation. It is a disagreement which flourishes after every major change in the body of scientific knowledge. To the extent that we live in a period of permanent scientific revolution we also live in one of permanent disagreement as to its suitable boundaries.

The details of the selection in this volume have been guided by the usual mixture of considerations. Ethics has been excluded because the period from Hobbes to Bentham is well represented by the two volumes of selections in L. A. Selby-Bigge's *British Moralists,* now reissued under the editorship of D. D. Raphael. Technical logic is ruled out because it is a field of its own; the connection between pure logic and philosophy is often slight. In any case, with the exception of Augustus De Morgan's *Essay on Probabilities* (1838), little was contributed to the subject by British writers of this period. Within the remaining fields of philosophy, the chief figure not represented is William Whewell. His interesting and influential work, *Philosophy of the Inductive Sciences, Founded upon their History,* first appeared in 1840. But this book underwent considerable alterations in later editions (the third edition appeared in 1858), and it is debatable that the first edition best gives Whewell's considered views. More important, however, is the fact that Whewell's ideas on induction are based, quite consciously and explicitly, on his examination of the history of the natural sciences. Because of the length of his examination, it is very difficult in a selection to present Whewell's philosophical arguments independently of the mass of historical detail within which they are embedded. It has seemed prudent not to try.

There are three other men whose work may be missed from this volume. They are Sir William Hamilton, Samuel Bailey, and Richard Whateley. The reputation of Hamilton, once great, has never recovered from Mill's pungent and thorough criticism in *An Examination of Sir William Hamilton's Philosophy* (1865). Many philosophers today would think this obscurity quite justified. Hamilton's stupifying style and the battalions of footnotes he marshalled in support of his rather tenuous arguments are not likely to lead to his resurrection. Nevertheless, his two early papers from the *Edinburgh Review,* "On The Philosophy of the Unconditioned; In Reference to Cousin's Infinito-Absolute" (1829) and "Philosophy of Perception" (1830)—the latter being an extended review of Jouffroy's French edition of Reid's *Works* —were important historically. The reason they have not been included here is one which has been used throughout the editing of this volume. It is that no selection is included merely because of its historical interest, however great that may be. If a philosopher's thought obtains its interest for us today chiefly by borrowed means, then his views have been taken to belong to the history of the subject and to have no useful role in current controversies. Hamilton's two papers do not pass this test. The one on the philosophy of the unconditioned does not succeed in asserting much more than that, in Hamilton's words, "the mind can conceive, and consequently can know, only the *limited, and the conditionally limited.*" In its uninteresting form this assertion is trivially true, and in its more interesting interpretation obviously false. Hamilton's other paper incorporates his replies to Brown's criticism of Reid and some of Hamilton's own corrections of Reid. The substance of much of this appeared later in Hamilton's notes and appendices to his edition of Reid's *Works*.

Samuel Bailey is a more appealing figure. His *Essays on the Pursuit of Truth and on the Progress of Knowledge* (1829) is both lucid and sensible. It does not, however, make any substantial advance on the contributions of some of the earlier philosophers included here, such as Reid, Stewart, and Brown. For that reason Bailey has been excluded. Richard Whateley's amusing and cogent reply to Hume's sceptical writings on the possible occurrence of miracles is contained in his essay "Historic Doubts Relative to Napoleon Buonaparte" (1819). Since no other selections on either ethics or religion have been included here, it has seemed best not to introduce an essay which, though of considerable logical interest, has its origin in the philosophy of religion.

Whenever feasible, the selections are given without internal alteration. In some places, however, omissions have seemed to be desirable because of the author's prolixity, unnecessary repetition of examples, or divergence from the philosophical argument of interest to us today. These omissions are indicated in the text by three dots for brief omissions and five dots for longer ones. In no case is the author's argument adversely affected. To the original footnotes of the various authors have been added a large number by the present editor. In addition, some of the original footnotes have been supplemented or corrected. These changes enable the reader to identify historical figures and the sources used by the authors. Cross references have been given in a number of places, and quotations and phrases in foreign languages have been translated. Many footnotes in the original texts have been dropped silently because they are inessential. In some passages these footnotes have been replaced by the editor with what is hoped will be more useful ones of his own. All these additions and changes are placed in square brackets with the abbreviation "Ed." printed after them. The wording of the texts themselves has not been altered except for the correction of a few obvious misprints. Since no modern critical edition of any of these texts has yet been produced, use has been made of the available editions best suited to the present purpose.

ROBERT BROWN

ACKNOWLEDGMENTS

Professor John Passmore has made many useful suggestions concerning the contents of this book, and I am grateful for his help. Mr. A. D. Barker generously translated a number of passages for me. I owe to him also the sources of several quotations. The library staff of the Institute of Advanced Studies, Australian National University, have been indefatigable on my behalf. Mrs. Mavis Rose and Mrs. Glenda McIntyre have given typing aid when it was most needed and when appreciation was least likely to be expressed. I express it now with pleasure.

R. B.

Between Hume and Mill

*AN ANTHOLOGY OF
BRITISH PHILOSOPHY,
1749–1843*

DAVID HARTLEY

1705–1757

The son of a needy vicar in Yorkshire, Hartley graduated from Jesus College, Cambridge, in 1726, received the M.A. in the following year, and later became a Fellow of the College. He gave up his original intention of entering the Church because of reservations concerning the Thirty-nine articles, but remained a devout member of the Church of England all his life. Establishing himself as a successful physician, although without a medical degree, he wrote in favor of inoculation for smallpox and, less commendably, in favor of Mrs. Stephen's medicine for "the stone." Twice married, the second time to a woman of means, he became the friend of such eminent men as Bishops Butler, Law, and Stillingfleet, William Cheselden, the surgeon, and Stephen Hales, the botanist. He was made a Fellow of the Royal Society and retained an interest in logic, mathematics, physiology, and theology. Not long before his death, at his home in Bath, he corresponded with his young admirer Joseph Priestley, who thirty years later was to make Hartley's work more widely known.

The philosophical writings of Hartley consist of an early short essay in Latin, "Conjecturae quaedam de sensu, motu, et idearum generatione" (1731?) [Some Speculations about Sensation, Movement, and the Generation of Ideas] and the two-part volume, *Observations on Man, His Frame, His Duty and His Expectations* (1749), on which he worked from about 1730. In addition, the long, anonymous essay entitled "An Enquiry into the Origin of the Human Appetites and Affections, Shewing How Each Arises from Association" (1747) is sometimes attributed to him, although the *Dictionary of Anonymous and Pseudonymous English Literature* (Edinburgh, 1926) ascribes it to either Rev. John Barr, otherwise unknown, or to James Long, equally unknown.

It is Hartley's observations on man's frame in Part I of *Observations on Man*, and not his views on ethics and religion in Part II, which have chiefly preserved his interest for both psychologists and philosophers. To the former Hartley is known as the father of physiological psychology—he brought the very word "psychology" into English—and as the first systematic exponent, though not originator, of the doctrine of the association of ideas. To philosophers Hartley is known for his deep influence on James Mill, and through him John Stuart Mill and Alexander Bain, as well as for a more remote influence on Herbert Spencer and William James. To philosophers Hartley is also known for an ambition very similar to that of David Hume: to account for all the operations of the human mind in terms analogous to those employed by Newton in explaining the behavior of material bodies by means of the law of gravity.

However, Hartley differed from Hume in giving the analogy a physiological interpretation. Vibrations occurring on the surface of the nerves and in the brain cause simple sensations in the mind. The physical vestiges of these vibrations are little vibrations (vibratiuncles) which cause ideas of sensation to arise. These two sorts of vibrations are not only the physical correlates of simple sensations and ideas of sensation; it is the vibrations themselves that become associated by joint occurrence, so that eventually the occurrence of one produces a disposition for another to occur. When this association is established, the correlated sensations and ideas are also aroused in accordance with the same universal law of association. Sensations and their residual ideas, then, are the building blocks of the mind. The law of association holds them together, just as the law of gravity holds particles of matter together. But the mental structure has a tangible foundation in the fibrils of the nerves, spinal marrow, and brain. Without their operation there would be no mental life, although their operation is not identical with it.

Critics of Hartley have often been scornful of the theory of vibrations despite the tentative way in which he put it forward. Yet as a piece of physiological speculation—"vibrations are motions backwards and forwards of the small particles . . . exceedingly short and small"—it is a vast improvement on the water-pipe theory of Hartley's day, such as that held by Hermann Boerhaave (1668–1738). This theory assumed that the nerves were tubes filled with a fluid which moved back and forth to extend or contract the muscles. More importantly, the doctrine of vibrations enabled Hartley to be clear about the nature of scientific hypotheses and also suggested to him a whole series of testable genetic hypotheses about human behavior: his accounts of the development of speech and of voluntary movement are obvious examples. For this reason I have included, in the selection below, as much of the doctrine of vibrations as seems necessary to support and explain Hartley's later remarks on such topics as assent, memory, and free will.

Hartley's philosophical views are of considerable interest today, and it is a mistake to complain, as some philosophers have, that Hartley is a man chiefly concerned with the psychological or physiological origins of behavior, and that therefore he offers little to the purely philosophical reader. For, to take only one example, if Hartley had not been concerned with the way in which complex behavior is built up, in law-governed fashion, from simpler responses, he could not have justified his grading of intellectual pleasures as better (more pleasant) than merely sensual pleasures in the way that he did. Because intellectual pleasures have so many associations with the original pleasures of sense, the number of gratifiable desires is greatly increased. Hence an intellectual pleasure gratifies more desires than do merely sensual ones, though it develops from and is supported by them. But the grading of different kinds of pleasures is an ancient topic in philosophy; and if Hartley is correct in his genetic account, he has explained why we should rank intellectual pleasures higher, since they give us more associated pleasures. If he is not correct, he has tried to explain why we should rank thusly and has failed. Thus Hartley's psychology bears directly and interestingly on his philosophical conclusions.

SELECTIONS FROM

Observations on Man, Part I *

*

The Doctrines of Vibrations
and Association in General

CHAPTER I

THE GENERAL LAWS ACCORDING TO WHICH THE
SENSATIONS AND MOTIONS ARE PERFORMED,
AND OUR IDEAS GENERATED

My chief design in the following chapter is briefly to explain, establish, and apply the doctrines of *vibrations* and *association*. The first of these doctrines is taken from the hints concerning the performance of sensation and motion, which Sir Isaac Newton has given at the end of his Principia, and in the Questions annexed to his Optics; the last

* 6th edition, Thomas Tegg and Son, London, 1834.

from what Mr. Locke, and other ingenious persons since his time, have delivered concerning the influence of *association* over our opinions and affections, and its use in explaining those things in an accurate and precise way, which are commonly referred to the power of habit and custom, in a general and indeterminate one.

The doctrine of *vibrations* may appear at first sight to have no connexion with that of *association;* however, if these doctrines be found in fact to contain the laws of the bodily and mental powers respectively, they must be related to each other, since the body and mind are. One may expect, that *vibrations* should infer *association* as their effect, and *association* point to *vibrations* as its cause. I will endeavour, in the present chapter, to trace out this mutual relation.

The proper method of philosophizing seems to be, to discover and establish the general laws of action, affecting the subject under consideration, from certain select, well-defined, and well-attested phænomena, and then to explain and predict the other phænomena by these laws. This is the method of analysis and synthesis recommended and followed by Sir Isaac Newton.

I shall not be able to execute, with any accuracy, what the reader might expect of this kind, in respect of the doctrines of *vibrations* and *association,* and their general laws, on account of the great intricacy, extensiveness, and novelty of the subject. However, I will attempt a sketch in the best manner I can, for the service of future inquirers.

SECTION I

THE DOCTRINE OF VIBRATIONS, AND
ITS USE FOR EXPLAINING THE SENSATIONS

PROP. I: *The white medullary Substance of the Brain, spinal Marrow, and the Nerves proceeding from them, is the immediate Instrument of Sensation and Motion.*

Under the word *brain,* in these observations, I comprehend all that lies within the cavity of the skull, *i. e.* the *cerebrum,* or *brain* properly so called, the *cerebellum,* and the *medulla oblongata.*

This proposition seems to be sufficiently proved in the writings of physicians and anatomists; from the structure and functions of the several organs of the human body; from experiments on living animals; from the symptoms of diseases, and from dissections of morbid bodies. Sensibility, and the power of motion, seem to be conveyed to all the parts, in their natural state, from the brain and spinal marrow, along the nerves. These arise from the medullary, not the cortical part, every where, and are themselves of a white medullary substance. When the nerves of any part are cut, tied, or compressed in any considerable degree, the functions of that part are either entirely destroyed, or much impaired. When the spinal marrow is compressed by a dislocation of the *vertebræ* of the back, all the parts, whose nerves arise below the place of dislocation, become paralytic. When any considerable injury is done to the medullary substance of the brain, sensation, voluntary motion, memory, and intellect, are either entirely lost, or much impaired; and if the injury be very great, this extends immediately to the vital motions also, *viz.* to those of the heart, and organs of respiration, so as to occasion death. But this does not hold equally in respect of the cortical substance of the brain; perhaps not at all, unless as far as injuries done to it extend themselves to the medullary substance. In dissections after apoplexies, palsies, epilepsies, and other distempers affecting the sensations and motions, it is usual to find some great disorder in the brain, from preternatural tumours, from blood, matter, or serum, lying upon the brain, or in its ventricles, &c. This may suffice as general evidence for the present. The particular reasons of some of these phænomena, with more definite evidences, will offer themselves in the course of these observations.

PROP. II: *The white medullary Substance of the Brain is also the immediate Instrument, by which Ideas are presented to the Mind: or, in other words, whatever Changes are made in this Substance, corresponding Changes are made in our Ideas; and vice versâ.*

The evidence for this proposition is also to be taken from the writings of physicians and anatomists; but especially from those parts of these writings which treat of the faculties of memory, attention, imagination, &c. and of mental disorders. It is sufficiently manifest from hence, that the perfection of our mental faculties depends upon the perfection of this substance; that all injuries done to it affect the trains of ideas proportionably; and that these cannot be restored to their natural course till such injuries be repaired. Poisons, spirituous liquors, opiates, fevers, blows upon the head, &c. all plainly affect the mind, by first disordering the medullary substance. And evacuations, rest, medicines, time, &c. as plainly restore the mind to its former state, by reversing the foregoing steps. But there will be more and more definite evidence offered in the course of these observations.

PROP. III: *The Sensations remain in the Mind for a short time after the sensible Objects are removed.*

This is very evident in the sensations impressed on the eye. Thus, to use Sir Isaac Newton's words, "If a burning coal be nimbly moved round in a circle, with gyrations continually repeated, the whole circle will appear like fire; the reason of which is, that the sensation of the coal, in the several places of that circle, remains impressed on the *sensorium* until the coal return again to the same place. And so in a quick consecution of the colours," (*viz.* red, yellow, green, blue, and purple, mentioned in the experiment, whence this passage is taken,) "the impression of every colour remains on the *sensorium* until a revolution of all the colours be completed, and that first colour return again. The impressions therefore of all the successive colours are at once in the *sensorium*—and beget a sensation of white." *Opt.* b. I. p. 2. Experiment 10.[1]

Thus also, when a person has had a candle, a window, or any other lucid and well-defined object, before his eyes for a considerable time, he may perceive a very clear and precise image thereof to be left in the *sensorium,* fancy, or mind (for these I consider as equivalent expressions in our entrance upon these disquisitions,) for some time after he has closed his eyes. At least this will happen frequently to persons who are attentive to these things in a gentle way; for, as this appearance escapes the notice of those who are entirely inattentive, so too earnest a desire and attention prevents it, by introducing another state of mind or fancy.

To these may be referred the appearance mentioned by Sir Isaac Newton, *Opt.* Qu. 16. *viz.* "When a man in the dark presses either corner of his eye with his finger, and turns his eye away from his finger, he will see a circle of colours like those in the feather of a peacock's tail. And this appearance continues about a second of time after the eye and finger have remained quiet." The sensation continues therefore in the mind about a second of time after its cause ceases to act.

The same continuance of the sensations is also evident in the ear. For the sounds which we hear are reflected by the neighbouring bodies, and therefore consist of a variety of sounds, succeeding each other at different distances of time, according to the distances of the several reflecting bodies; which yet causes no confusion or apparent complexity of sound, unless the distance of the reflecting bodies be very considerable, as in spacious buildings. Much less are we able to distinguish the successive pulses of the air, even in the gravest sounds.

As to the senses of taste and smell, there seems to be no clear direct evidence for the continuance of their sensations after the proper objects are removed. But analogy would incline one to believe, that they must resemble the senses of sight and hearing in this particular, though the continuance cannot be perceived distinctly, on account of the shortness of it, or other circumstances. For the sensations must be supposed to bear such an analogy to each other, and so to depend in common upon the brain, that all evidences for the continuance of sensations in any one sense, will extend themselves to the rest. Thus all the senses may be considered as so many kinds of feeling; the taste is

---

[1] See Newton's *Opticks* (Dover, New York, 1952), p. 141. Ed.

nearly allied to the feeling, the smell to the taste, and the sight and hearing to each other. All which analogies will offer themselves to view when we come to examine each of these senses in particular.

In the sense of feeling, the continuance of heat, after the heating body is removed, and that of the smart of a wound, after the instant of infliction, seem to be of the same kind with the appearances taken notice of in the eye and ear.

But the greatest part of the sensations of this sense resemble those of taste and smell, and vanish to appearance as soon as the objects are removed.

PROP. IV: *External Objects impressed upon the Senses occasion, first in the Nerves on which they are impressed, and then in the Brain, Vibrations of the small, and as one may say, infinitesimal, medullary Particles.*

These vibrations are motions backwards and forwards of the small particles; of the same kind with the oscillations of pendulums, and the tremblings of the particles of sounding bodies. They must be conceived to be exceedingly short and small, so as not to have the least efficacy to disturb or move the whole bodies of the nerves or brain. For that the nerves themselves should vibrate like musical strings, is highly absurd; nor was it ever asserted by Sir Isaac Newton, or any of those who have embraced his notion of the performance of sensation and motion, by means of *vibrations*.

In like manner we are to suppose the particles which vibrate, to be of the inferior orders, and not those biggest particles, on which the operations in chemistry, and the colours of natural bodies, depend, according to the opinion of Sir Isaac Newton. Hence, in the *proposition,* I term the medullary particles, which vibrate, *infinitesimal.*

Now that external objects impress vibratory motions upon the medullary substance of the nerves and brain (which is the immediate instrument of sensation, according to the first proposition) appears from the continuance of the sensations mentioned in the third; since no motion, besides a vibratory one, can reside in any part for the least moment of time. External objects, being corporeal, can act upon the nerves and brain, which are also corporeal, by nothing but impressing motion on them. A vibrating motion may continue for a short time in the small medullary particles of the nerves and brain, without disturbing them, and after a short time would cease; and so would correspond to the above-mentioned short continuance of the sensations; and there seems to be no other species of motion that can correspond thereto.

COR. As this proposition is deduced from the foregoing, so if it could be established upon independent principles, (of which I shall treat under the next,) the foregoing might be deduced from it. And on this supposition there would be an argument for the continuance of the sensations, after the removal of their objects; which would extend to the senses of feeling, taste, and smell, in the same manner as to those of sight and hearing.

.   .   .   .   .

SECTION II

OF IDEAS, THEIR GENERATION AND ASSOCIATIONS; AND
OF THE AGREEMENT OF THE DOCTRINE OF VIBRATIONS
WITH THE PHAENOMENA OF IDEAS

PROP. VIII: *Sensations, by being often repeated, leave certain Vestiges, Types, or Images, of themselves, which may be called, Simple Ideas of Sensation.*

I took notice in the Introduction, that those ideas which resemble sensations were called ideas of sensation; and also that they might be called *simple* ideas, in respect of the intellectual ones which are formed from them, and of whose very essence it is to be *complex*. But the ideas of sensation are not entirely simple, since they must consist of parts both co-existent and successive, as the generating sensations themselves do.

Now, that the simple ideas of sensation are thus generated, agreeably to the proposition, appears, because the most vivid of these ideas are those where the corresponding sensations are most vigorously impressed, or most frequently renewed; whereas, if the sensation be faint, or uncommon, the generated idea is also faint in proportion, and, in extreme cases, evanescent and imperceptible. The exact observance of the order of place in visible ideas, and of the order of time in audible ones, may likewise serve to shew, that these ideas are copies and offsprings of the impressions made on the eye and ear, in which the same orders were observed respectively. And though it happens, that trains of visible and audible ideas are presented in sallies of the fancy, and in dreams, in which the order of time and place is different from that of any former impressions, yet the small component parts of these trains are copies of former impressions; and reasons may be given for the varieties of their compositions.

It is also to be observed, that this proposition bears a great resemblance to the third; and that, by this resemblance, they somewhat confirm and illustrate one another. According to the third proposition, sensations remain for a short time after the impression is removed; and these remaining sensations grow feebler and feebler, till they vanish. They are therefore, in some part of their declension, of about the same strength with ideas, and in their first state, are intermediate between sensations and ideas. And it seems reasonable to expect, that, if a single sensation can leave a perceptible effect, trace, or vestige, for a short time, a sufficient repetition of a sensation may leave a perceptible effect of the same kind, but of a more permanent nature, *i. e.* an idea, which shall recur occasionally, at long distances of time, from the impression of the corresponding sensation, and *vice versâ*. As to the occasions and causes, which make ideas recur, they will be considered in the next proposition but one.

The method of reasoning used in the last paragraph is farther confirmed by the following circumstance; *viz.* that both the diminutive declining sensations, which remain for a short space after the impressions of the objects cease, and the ideas, which are the copies of such impressions, are far more distinct and vivid, in respect of visible and audible impressions, than of any others. To which it may be added, that, after travelling, hearing music, &c. trains of vivid ideas are very apt to recur, which correspond very exactly to the late impressions, and which are of an intermediate nature between the remaining sensations of the third proposition, in their greatest vigour, and the ideas mentioned in this.

The sensations of feeling, taste, and smell, can scarce be said to leave ideas, unless very indistinct and obscure ones. However, as analogy leads one to suppose that these sensations may leave traces of the same kind, though not in the same degree, as those of sight and hearing; so the readiness with which we reconnoitre sensations of feeling, taste, and smell, that have been often impressed, is an evidence that they do so; and these generated traces or dispositions of mind may be called the ideas of feeling, taste, and smell. In sleep, when all our ideas are magnified, those of feeling, taste, and smell, are often sufficiently vivid and distinct; and the same thing happens in some few cases of vigilance.

PROP. IX: *Sensory Vibrations, by being often repeated, beget, in the medullary Substance of the Brain, a Disposition to diminutive Vibrations, which may also be called Vibratiuncles, and Miniatures, corresponding to themselves respectively.*

This correspondence of the diminutive vibrations to the original sensory ones, consists in this, that they agree in kind, place, and line of direction; and differ only in being more feeble, *i. e.* in degree.

This proposition follows from the foregoing. For since sensations, by being often repeated, beget ideas, it cannot but be that those vibrations, which accompany sensations, should beget something which may accompany ideas in like manner; and this can be nothing but feebler vibrations, agreeing with the sensory generating vibrations in kind, place, and line of direction.

Or thus: By the first proposition it appears, that some motion must be excited in the medullary substance, during each sensation; by the fourth, this motion is determined to be a vibratory one: since therefore some motion must also, by the second, be excited in the medullary substance during the presence of each idea, this motion cannot be any other than a vibratory one: else how should it proceed from the original vibration attending the sensation, in the same manner as the idea does from the sensation itself? It must also agree in kind, place, and line of direction, with the generating vibration. A vibratory motion, which recurs *t* times in a second, cannot beget a diminutive one that recurs ½ *t,* or 2 *t* times; nor one originally impressed on the region of the brain corresponding to the auditory nerves, beget diminutive vibrations in the region corresponding to the optic nerves; and so of the rest. The line of direction must likewise be the same in the original and derivative vibrations. It remains therefore, that each simple idea of sensation be attended by diminutive vibrations of the same kind, place, and line of direction, with the original vibrations attending the sensation itself: or, in the words of the proposition, that sensory vibrations, by being frequently repeated, beget a disposition to diminutive vibrations corresponding to themselves respectively. We may add, that the vibratory nature of the motion which attends ideas, may be inferred from the continuance of some ideas, visible ones for instance, in the fancy for a few moments.

This proof of the present proposition from the foregoing appears to be incontestable, admitting the fourth: however, it will much establish and illustrate the doctrines of vibrations and association, to deduce it directly, if we can, from the nature of vibratory motions, and of an animal body; and not only from the relation between sensations and ideas. Let us see, therefore, what progress we can make in such an attempt.

First, then, if we admit vibrations of the medullary particles at all, we must conceive, that some take place in the *fœtus in utero,* both on account of the warmth in which it lies, and of the pulsation of those considerable arteries, which pass through the medullary substance, and which consequently must compress and agitate it upon every contraction of the heart. And these vibrations are probably either uniform in kind and degree, if we consider short spaces of time; or, if long ones, increase in a slow uniform manner, and that in degree only, as the *fœtus in utero* increases in bulk and strength. They are also probably the same in all the different regions of the medullary substance. Let these vibrations be called the *natural vibrations.*

Secondly, As soon as the child is born, external objects act upon it violently, and excite vibrations in the medullary substance, which differ from the natural ones, and from each other, in degree, kind, place, and line of direction. We may also conceive that each region of the medullary substance has such a texture as to receive, with the greatest facility, the several specific vibrations, which the objects corresponding respectively to these regions, *i. e.* to their nerves, are most disposed to excite. Let these vibrations be, for the present, called *preternatural* ones, in contradistinction to those which we just now called *natural ones.*

Thirdly, Representing now the natural vibrations by *N,* and the preternatural ones, from various objects, by *A, B, C, &c.* let us suppose the first object to impress the vibrations *A,* and then to be removed. It is evident from the nature of vibratory motions, that the medullary substance will not, immediately upon the removal of this object, return to its natural state *N,* but will remain, for a short space of time, in the preternatural state *A,* and pass gradually from *A* to *N.* Suppose the same object to be impressed again and again, for a sufficient number of times, and it seems to follow, that the medullary substance will be longer in passing from *A* to *N,* after the second impression than after the first, after the third impression than second, &c. till, at last, it will not return to its natural original state of vibration *N* at all, but remain in the preternatural state *A,* after the vibrations have fallen to a diminutive pitch, their kind and place, or chief seat, and their line of directions, continuing the same. This state may therefore be fitly denoted by *a,* and, being now in the place of the natural state *N,* it will be kept up by the heat of the medullary substance, and the pulsation of its arteries. All this seems to follow from the above-mentioned disposition of animal bodies to accommodate themselves to, and continue in, almost any state that is often impressed; which is evident from innumerable both common and medical observations, whatever be determined concerning the manner of explaining and accounting for these facts. For the alterations which habit, custom, frequent impression, &c. make in the small constituent particles, can scarce be anything besides alterations of the distances, and mutual actions, of these particles; and these last alterations must alter the natural tendency to vibrate. We must, however, here resume the supposition made in the last paragraph, *viz.* that the several regions of the brain have such a texture as disposes them to those specific vibrations, which are to be impressed by the proper objects in the events of life. And this will much facilitate and accelerate the transition of the state *N* into *a;* since we are to suppose a predisposition to the state *A,* or *a.*

It will somewhat illustrate and confirm this reasoning, to remark, that musical strings always accommodate themselves to, and lean towards the state into which they were last put. Thus the tone of a musical string either rises or falls upon altering its tension, according as the preceding tension was greater or less than its present tension. Now the small component parts of a musical string must recede from, and approach to, each other, *i. e.* must oscillate lengthways, during every transverse oscillation of the string. And this must arise from the mutual influences of the component particles tending to their last superinduced state. Let us suppose something analogous to this to take place in the component molecules of the brain, the molecules of the molecules, &c. and it will follow, that *A* may overpower *N,* and *a* become the natural state. Now, since the human body is composed of the same matter as the external world, it is reasonable to expect, that its component particles should be subjected to the same subtle laws. And the exquisite structure of animal bodies in so many other respects, makes it easier to conceive, that the organ of organs, *viz.* the medullary substance, should be endued with a proper subtle ultimate structure, for the purpose of retaining a state that is frequently impressed. One may guess also, that it is better suited to this purpose during its growth, *i. e.* in passing from infancy to adult age, than afterwards; as this would be very agreeable to the phænomena.

Fourthly, Suppose now the vibrations *A, B, C, D,* &c. belonging to each of the senses, to be excited, and repeated in such order and manner as usually happens to the new-born infant upon its entrance into this new scene of things. It is evident, that these will have a greater power to overrule the natural state *N,* than the vibrations *A* from one single object could have: for *A* affected only one region of the medullary substance primarily; whereas *A, B, C, D,* &c. affect all the regions primarily in their turn. It is evident also, that the secondary vibrations, or those which are propagated from the region of the medullary substance primarily affected into the rest, will be overruled, in great measure, in each region, by the primary vibrations peculiar to that region. Lastly, It is evident, that of the vibrations which are excited in each region, no one can prevail over all the rest, but each must leave an effect, in proportion to its strength and frequency. We may conceive, therefore, that each region of the medullary substance will have a tendency generated in it to vibrate with vibrations of the same frequency (but weaker in degree) as those which the several appropriated objects impress upon it respectively; and that diminutive vibrations resembling them will rise in succession in each region. For each region may easily be conceived to lean sometimes to the vibrations from one object, sometimes to those from another, according to the strength, frequency, and novelty of the impression, the then present disposition of the nervous system, association (of which in the two next propositions), and other such-like causes. And for the same reason, as in every sense the idea of some one object of that sense must prevail over all the rest, we may conclude, that sometimes the ideas belonging to one sense, sometimes those belonging to another, will prevail over the rest.

Or thus: Some vibrations there must always be in the medullary substance, on account of its heat, and the pulsation of the arteries which pass through it. These cannot be the natural ones *N*, because they will soon be overruled by the great force and variety of impressions made on the new-born infant, which must also dispose each region of the brain to lean to some or other of those vibrations which are excited in it primarily. Hence we may conceive, that a very complex set of vibrations, arising from the mixture and combinations of degree, kind, place, and line of direction, exists always in the medullary substance, being kept up by its heat, and the pulsation of its arteries, when other causes are wanting, almost in the same manner as in a concert of music the air is agitated by vibrations of a very complex kind. But then, as in a concert, some one instrument generally strikes the ear more than the rest, so of the complex vibrations which exist in the medullary substance, some one part will prevail over the rest, and present the corresponding idea to the mind. Some region must be disposed, at each instant, to vibrate stronger than the rest; and of the specific vibrations which are generally impressed upon this region, some one will have a more favourable concurrence of circumstances than the rest. And thus it will follow, according to the terms of the proposition, that sensory vibrations, by being sufficiently repeated, will beget a disposition to miniature vibrations corresponding to them respectively; or, using the appellations above assumed, that *A, B, C,* &c. will beget *a, b, c,* &c.

If we allow the proof of this proposition thus deduced from the nature of vibratory motions, and of an animal body, the foregoing proposition will follow from it, and hold equally, in respect of the senses of feeling, taste, and smell, as of sight and hearing. Or, in other words, if we allow that original impressed vibratory motions leave a tendency to miniature ones of the same kind, place, and line of direction, it will follow, that sensations must beget ideas, and that not only in the senses of sight and hearing, where the ideas are sufficiently vivid and distinct, but in the three others, since their sensations are also conveyed to the mind by means of vibratory motions. We may also perhaps discover hereafter, from the nature of vibratory motions, and of the human brain, compared with the circumstances of life, why the ideas of one sense are more vivid and distinct than those of another.

PROP. X: *Any Sensations* A, B, C, *&c. by being associated with one another a sufficient Number of Times, get such a Power over the corresponding Ideas* a, b, c, *&c. that any one of the Sensations* A, *when impressed alone, shall be able to excite in the Mind,* b, c, *&c. the Ideas of the rest.*

Sensations may be said to be associated together, when their impressions are either made precisely at the same instant of time, or in the contiguous successive instants. We may therefore distinguish association into two sorts, the synchronous, and the successive.

The influence of association over our ideas, opinions, and affections, is so great and obvious, as scarcely to have escaped the notice
of any writer who has treated of these, though the word *association,* in
the particular sense here affixed to it, was first brought into use by Mr.
Locke. But all that has been delivered by the ancients and moderns,
concerning the power of habit, custom, example, education, authority,
party-prejudice, the manner of learning the manual and liberal arts,
&c. goes upon this doctrine as its foundation, and may be considered
as the detail of it, in various circumstances. I here begin with the
simplest case, and shall proceed to more and more complex ones continually, till I have exhausted what has occurred to me upon this subject.

This proposition, or first and simplest case of association, is manifest from innumerable common observations. Thus, the names,
smells, tastes, and tangible qualities of natural bodies, suggest their
visible appearances to the fancy, *i. e.* excite their visible ideas; and,
vice versâ, their visible appearances impressed on the eye raise up
those powers of reconnoitring their names, smells, tastes, and tangible
qualities, which may not improperly be called their ideas, as above
noted; and in some cases raise up ideas, which may be compared with
visible ones, in respect of vividness. All which is plainly owing to the
association of the several sensible qualities of bodies with their names,
and with each other. It is remarkable, however, as being agreeable to
the superior vividness of visible and audible ideas, before taken notice
of, that the suggestion of the visible appearance from the name is the
most ready of any other; and, next to this, that of the name from the
visible appearance; in which last case, the reality of the audible idea,
when not evident to the fancy, may be inferred from the ready pronunciation of the name. For it will be shewn hereafter, that the audible idea is most commonly a previous requisite to pronunciation.
Other instances of power of association may be taken from compound
visible and audible impressions. Thus the sight of part of a large building suggests the idea of the rest instantaneously; and the sound of the
words which begin a familiar sentence, brings the remaining part to
our memories in order, the association of the parts being synchronous
in the first case, and successive in the last.

It is to be observed, that, in successive associations, the power of
raising the ideas is only exerted according to the order in which the
association is made. Thus, if the impressions *A, B, C,* be always made
in the order of the alphabet, *B* impressed alone will not raise *a,* but *c*
only. Agreeably to which it is easy to repeat familiar sentences in the
order in which they always occur, but impossible to do it readily in an
inverted one. The reason of this is, that the compound idea, *c, b, a,*
corresponds to the compound sensation *C, B, A;* and therefore requires the impression of *C, B, A,* in the same manner as *a, b, c,* does

that of *A, B, C*. This will, however, be more evident, when we come to consider the associations of vibratory motions, in the next proposition.

It is also to be observed, that the power of association grows feebler, as the number either of synchronous or successive impressions is increased, and does not extend, with due force, to more than a small one, in the first and simplest cases. But, in complex cases, or the associations of associations, of which the memory, in its full extent, consists, the powers of the mind, deducible from this source, will be found much greater than any person, upon his first entrance on these inquiries, could well imagine.

PROP. XI: *Any Vibrations*, A, B, C, &c. *by being associated together a sufficient Number of Times, get such a Power over* a, b, c, &c. *the corresponding Miniature Vibrations, that any of the Vibrations* A, *when impressed alone, shall be able to excite* b, c, &c. *the Miniatures of the rest.*

This proposition may be deduced from the foregoing, in the same manner as the ninth has been from the eighth.

But it seems also deducible from the nature of vibrations, and of an animal body. Let *A* and *B* be two vibrations, associated synchronically. Now, it is evident, that the vibration *A* (for I will, in this proposition, speak of *A* and *B* in the singular number, for the sake of greater clearness) will, by endeavouring to diffuse itself into those parts of the medullary substance which are affected primarily by the vibration *B*, in some measure modify and change *B*, so as to make *B* a little different from what it would be, if impressed alone. For the same reasons the vibration *A* will be a little affected, even in its primary seat, by the endeavour of *B* to diffuse itself all over the medullary substance. Suppose now the vibrations *A* and *B* to be impressed at the same instant, for a thousand times; it follows, from the ninth proposition, that they will first overcome the disposition to the natural vibrations *N,* and then leave a tendency to themselves, which will now occupy the place of the original natural tendency to vibrations. When therefore the vibration *A* is impressed alone, it cannot be entirely such as the object would excite of itself, but must lean, even in its primary seat, to the modifications and changes induced by *B,* during their thousand joint impressions; and therefore much more, in receding from this primary seat, will it lean that way; and when it comes to the seat of *B,* it will excite *B*'s miniature a little modified and changed by itself.

Or thus: When *A* is impressed alone, some vibration must take place in the primary seat of *B,* both on account of the heat and pulsation of the arteries, and because *A* will endeavour to diffuse itself over the whole medullary substance. This cannot be that part of the natural vibrations *N,* which belongs to this region, because it is supposed to be overruled already. It cannot be that which *A* impressed alone would have propagated into this region, because that has always hitherto been overruled, and converted into *B;* and therefore cannot have begotten a tendency to itself. It cannot be any full vivid vibration, such as *B, C, D,* &c. belonging to this region, because all full vibrations require the actual impression of an object upon the corresponding external organ. And of miniature vibrations belonging to this region, such as *b, c, d,* &c. it is evident, that *b* has the preference, since *A* leans to it a little, even in its own primary seat, more and more, in receding from this, and almost entirely, when it comes to the primary seat of *B*. For the same reasons *B* impressed alone will excite *a;* and, in general, if *A, B, C,* &c. be vibrations synchronically impressed on different regions of the medullary substance, *A* impressed alone will at last excite *b, c,* &c. according to the proposition.

If *A* and *B* be vibrations impressed successively, then will the latter part of *A, viz.* that part which, according to the third and fourth propositions, remains, after the impression of the object ceases, be modified and altered by *B*, at the same time that it will a little modify and alter it, till at last it be quite overpowered by it, and end in it. It follows therefore, by a like method of reasoning, that the successive impression of *A* and *B,* sufficiently repeated, will so alter the medullary substance, as that when *A* is impressed alone, its latter part shall not be such as the sole impression of *A* requires, but lean towards *B,* and end in *b* at last. But *B* will not excite *a* in a retrograde order; since, by supposition, the latter part of *B* was not modified and altered by *A,* but by some other vibration, such as *C* or *D*. And as *B,* by being followed by *C,* may at last raise *c;* so *b,* when raised by *A,* in the method here proposed, may be also sufficient to raise *c;* inasmuch as the miniature *c* being a feeble motion, not stronger, perhaps, than the natural vibrations *N,* requires only to have its kind, place, and line of direction, determined by association, the heat and arterial pulsation conveying to it the requisite degree of strength. And thus *A* impressed alone will raise *b, c,* &c. in successive associations, as well as in synchronous ones, according to the proposition.

It seems also, that the influence of *A* may, in some degree, reach through *B* to *C;* so that *A* of itself may have some effect to raise *c,* as well as by means of *b*. However, it is evident, that this chain must break off, at last, in long successions; and that sooner or later, according to the number and vigour of the repeated impressions. The power of miniature vibrations to raise other miniatures may, perhaps, be made clearer to mathematicians, by hinting, that the efficacy of any vibration to raise any other, is not in the simple ratio of its vividness, but as some power thereof less than unity; for thus *b* may raise *c,* a weaker vibration than *b, c* may raise *d,* &c. with more facility than if the efficacy was in the simple ratio of the vividness, and yet so that the series shall break off at last.

If the ninth proposition be allowed, we may prove this in somewhat a shorter and easier manner, as follows. Since the vibrations A and B are impressed together, they must, from the diffusion necessary to vibratory motions, run into one vibration; and consequently, after a number of impressions sufficiently repeated, will leave a trace, or miniature, of themselves, as one vibration, which will recur every now and then, from slight causes. Much rather, therefore, may the part b of the compound miniature $a + b$ recur, when the part A of the compound original vibration $A + B$ is impressed.

And as the ninth proposition may be thus made to prove the present, so it ought to be acknowledged and remarked here, that unless the ninth be allowed, the present cannot be proved, or that the power of association is founded upon, and necessarily requires, the previous power of forming ideas, and miniature vibrations. For ideas, and miniature vibrations, must first be generated, according to the eighth and ninth propositions, before they can be associated, according to the tenth and this eleventh. But then (which is very remarkable) this power of forming ideas, and their corresponding miniature vibrations, does equally presuppose the power of association. For since all sensations and vibrations are infinitely divisible, in respect of time and place, they could not leave any traces or images of themselves, *i. e.* any ideas, or miniature vibrations, unless their infinitesimal parts did cohere together through joint impression, *i. e.* association. Thus, to mention a gross instance, we could have no proper idea of a horse, unless the particular ideas of the head, neck, body, legs, and tail, peculiar to this animal, stuck to each other in the fancy, from frequent joint impression. And, therefore, in dreams, where complex associations are much weakened, and various parcels of visible ideas, not joined in nature, start up together in the fancy, contiguous to each other, we often see monsters, chimeras, and combinations, which have never been actually presented.

Association seems also necessary to dispose the medullary substance to this or that miniature vibration, in succession, after the miniatures of a large number of original vibrations have been generated.

Nor does there seem to be any precise limit which can be set to this mutual dependence of the powers of generating miniatures, and of association upon each other: however they may both take place together, as the heart and brain are supposed to do, or both depend upon one simple principle; for it seems impossible, that they should imply one another *ad infinitum*. There is no greater difficulty here than in many other cases of mutual indefinite implication, known and allowed by all. Nay, one may almost deduce some presumption in favour of the hypothesis here produced, from this mutual indefinite implication of its parts so agreeable to the tenor of nature in other things. And it is certainly a presumption in its favour, that a less power of generating miniatures will be a foundation for a larger of association, and *vice versâ,* till, at last, the whole superstructure of ideas and associations observable in human life may, by proceeding upwards according to analysis, and downwards according to synthesis, be built upon as small a foundation as we please. Thus we may observe, that neither does this eleventh proposition necessarily require the ninth, in its full extent, not *vice versâ,* for their demonstration. The least miniatures, with the feeblest cohesions of their parts, will, by degrees, run into larger, with stronger cohesions, from the same principles; nor are there any visible limits to the influence and extent of these powers, supposing the natural faculties of the being under consideration sufficiently extended.

Let me add, that the generation of sensible ideas from sensations, and the power of raising them from association, when considered as faculties of the mind, are evident and unquestionable. Since therefore sensations are conveyed to the mind, by the efficiency of corporeal causes of the medullary substance, as is acknowledged by all physiologists and physicians, it seems to me, that the powers of generating ideas, and raising them by association, must also arise from corporeal causes, and consequently admit of an explication from the subtle influences of the small parts of matter upon each other, as soon as these are sufficiently understood; which is farther evinced from the manifest influences of material causes upon our ideas and associations, taken notice of under the second proposition. And as a vibratory motion is more suitable to the nature of sensation than any other species of motion, so does it seem also more suitable to the powers of generating ideas, and raising them by association. However, these powers are evident independently, as just now observed; so that the doctrine of association may be laid down as a certain foundation, and a clew to direct our future inquiries, whatever becomes of that of vibrations.

PROP. XII: *Simple Ideas will run into complex ones, by Means of Association.*

In order to explain and prove this proposition, it will be requisite to give some previous account of the manner in which simple ideas of sensation may be associated together.

Case 1. Let the sensation *A* be often associated with each of the sensations *B, C, D,* &c. *i. e.* at certain times with *B,* at certain other times with *C,* &c. it is evident, from the tenth proposition, that *A,* impressed alone, will, at last, raise *b, c, d,* &c. all together, *i. e.* associate them with one another, provided they belong to different regions of the medullary substance; for if any two, or more, belong to the same region, since they cannot exist together in their distinct forms, *A* will raise something intermediate between them.

Case 2. If the sensations *A, B, C, D,* &c. be associated together, according to various combinations of twos, or even threes, fours, &c. then will *A* raise *b, c, d,* &c. also *B* raise *a, c, d,* &c. as in case the first.

It may happen, indeed, in both cases, that *A* may raise a particular miniature, as *b,* preferably to any of the rest, from its being more associated with *B,* from the novelty of the impression of *B,* from a tendency in the medullary substance to favour *b,* &c. and in like manner, that *b* may raise *c* or *d* preferably to the rest. However, all this will be over-ruled, at last, by the recurrency of the associations; so that any one of the sensations will excite the ideas of the rest at the same instant, *i. e.* associate them together.

Case 3. Let *A, B, C, D,* &c. represent successive impressions, it follows from the tenth and eleventh propositions, that *A* will raise *b, c, d,* &c. *B* raise *c, d,* &c. And though the ideas do not, in this case, rise precisely at the same instant, yet they come nearer together than the sensations themselves did in their original impression; so that these ideas are associated almost synchronically at last, and successively from the first. The ideas come nearer to one another than the sensations, on account of their diminutive nature, by which all that appertains to them is contracted. And this seems to be as agreeable to observation as to theory.

Case 4. All compound impressions *A + B + C + D,* &c. after sufficient repetition leave compound miniatures *a + b + c + d,* &c. which recur every now and then from slight causes, as well such as depend on association, as some which are different from it. Now, in these recurrences of compound miniatures, the parts are farther associated, and approach perpetually nearer to each other, agreeably to what was just now observed; *i. e.* the association becomes perpetually more close and intimate.

Case 5. When the ideas, *a, b, c, d,* &c. have been sufficiently associated in any one or more of the foregoing ways, if we suppose any single idea of these, *a* for instance, to be raised by the tendency of the medullary substance that way, by the association of *A* with a foreign sensation or idea *X* or *x,* &c. this idea *a,* thus raised, will frequently bring in all the rest, *b, c, d,* &c. and so associate all of them together still farther.

And upon the whole, it may appear to the reader, that the simple ideas of sensation must run into clusters and combinations, by association; and that each of these will, at last, coalesce into one complex idea, by the approach and commixture of the several compounding parts.

It appears also from observation, that many of our intellectual ideas, such as those that belong to the heads of beauty, honour, moral qualities, &c. are, in fact, thus composed of parts, which, by degrees, coalesce into one complex idea.

And as this coalescence of simple ideas into complex ones is thus evinced, both by the foregoing theory, and by observation, so it may be illustrated, and farther confirmed, by the similar coalescence of letters into syllables and words, in which association is likewise a chief instrument. I shall mention some of the most remarkable particulars, relating to this coalescence of simple ideas into complex ones, in the following corollaries.

COR. I. If the number of simple ideas which compose the complex one be very great, it may happen, that the complex idea shall not appear to bear any relation to these its compounding parts, nor to the external senses upon which the original sensations, which gave birth to the compounding ideas, were impressed. The reason of this is, that each single idea is overpowered by the sum of all the rest, as soon as they are all intimately united together. Thus in very compound medicines the several tastes and flavours of the separate ingredients are lost and overpowered by the complex one of the whole mass: so that this has a taste and flavour of its own, which appears to be simple and original, and like that of a natural body. Thus also, white is vulgarly thought to be the simplest and most uncompounded of all colours, while yet it really arises from a certain proportion of the seven primary colours, with their several shades or degrees. And to resume the illustration above-mentioned, taken from language, it does not at all appear to persons ignorant of the arts of reading and writing, that the great variety of complex words of languages can be analysed up to a few simple sounds.

COR. II. One may hope, therefore, that, by pursuing and perfecting the doctrine of association, we may some time or other be enabled to analyse all that vast variety of complex ideas, which pass under the name of ideas of reflection, and intellectual ideas, into their simple compounding parts, i. e. into the simple ideas of sensation, of which they consist. This would be greatly analogous to the arts of writing, and resolving the colour of the sun's light, or natural bodies, into their primary constituent ones. The complex ideas which I here speak of, are generally excited by words, or visible objects; but they are also connected with other external impressions, and depend upon them, as upon symbols. In whatever way we consider them, the trains of them which are presented to the mind seem to depend upon the then present state of the body, the external impressions, and the remaining influence of prior impressions and associations taken together.

COR. III. It would afford great light and clearness to the art of logic, thus to determine the precise nature and composition of the ideas affixed to those words which have complex ideas, in a proper sense, *i. e.* which excite any combinations of simple ideas united intimately by association; also to explain, upon this foundation, the proper use of those words, which have no ideas. For there are many words which are mere substitutes for other words, and many which are only auxiliaries. Now it cannot be said, that either of these have ideas, properly so called. And though it may seem an infinite and impossible task, thus to analyse the significations and uses of words, yet, I suppose, this would not be more difficult, with the present philological and philosophical helps to such a work, than the first making of dictionaries and grammars, in the infancy of philology. Perhaps it may not be amiss just to hint, in this place, that the four following classes comprise all the possible kinds into which words can be distinguished, agreeably to the plan here proposed:

1. Words which have ideas, but no definitions.
2. Words which have both ideas and definitions.
3. Words which have definitions, but no ideas.
4. Words which have neither ideas nor definitions.

It is quite manifest, that words seen or heard, can raise no ideas in the mind, or vibrations in the brain, distinct from their visible and audible impressions, except as far as they get new powers from associations, either incidental ones or arising from express design, as in definitions; and therefore, that all other ways of considering words, besides what is here suggested, are either false or imperfect.

Cor. IV. As simple ideas run into complex ones by association, so complex ideas run into decomplex ones by the same. But here the varieties of the associations, which increase with the complexity, hinder particular ones from being so close and permanent, between the complex parts of decomplex ideas, as between the simple parts of complex ones: to which it is analogous, in languages, that the letters of words adhere closer together than the words of sentences, both in writing and speaking.

Cor. V. The simple ideas of sensation are not all equally and uniformly concerned in forming complex and decomplex ideas: *i. e.* these do not result from all the possible combinations of twos, threes, fours, &c. of all the simple ideas; but, on the contrary, some simple ideas occur in the complex and decomplex ones much oftener than others; and the same holds of particular combinations by twos, threes, &c. and innumerable combinations never occur at all in real life, and, consequently, are never associated into complex or decomplex ideas. All which corresponds to what happens in real languages; some letters, and combinations of letters, occur much more frequently than others, and some combinations never occur at all.

Cor. VI. As persons who speak the same language have, however, a different use and extent of words, so, though mankind, in all ages and nations, agree, in general, in their complex and decomplex ideas, yet there are many particular differences in them; and these differences are greater or less, according to the difference, or resemblance, in age, constitution, education, profession, country, age of the world, &c. *i. e.* in their impressions and associations.

COR. VII. When a variety of ideas are associated together, the visible idea, being more glaring and distinct than the rest, performs the office of a symbol to all the rest, suggests them, and connects them together. In this it somewhat resembles the first letter of a word, or first word of a sentence, which are often made use of to bring all the rest to mind.

COR. VIII. When objects and ideas, with their most common combinations, have been often presented to the mind, a train of them, of a considerable length, may, by once occurring, leave such a trace, as to recur in imagination, and in miniature, in nearly the same order and proportion as in this single occurrence. For, since each of the particular impressions and ideas is familiar, there will want little more for their recurrency, than a few connecting links; and even these may be, in some measure, supplied by former similar instances. These considerations, when duly unfolded, seem to me sufficient to explain the chief phænomena of memory; and it will be easily seen from them, that the memory of adults, and masters in any science, ought to be much more ready and certain than that of children and novices, as it is found to be in fact.

COR. IX. When the pleasure or pain attending any sensations and ideas is great, all the associations belonging to them are much accelerated and strengthened. For the violent vibrations excited in such cases, soon overrule the natural vibrations, and leave in the brain a strong tendency to themselves, from a few impressions. The associations will therefore be cemented sooner and stronger than in common cases; which is found agreeable to the fact.

COR. X. As many words have complex ideas annexed to them, so sentences, which are collections of words, have collections of complex ideas, *i. e.* have decomplex ideas. And it happens, in most cases, that the decomplex idea belonging to any sentence is not compounded merely of the complex ideas belonging to the words of it; but that there are also many variations, some oppositions, and numberless additions. Thus, propositions, in particular, excite, as soon as heard, assent or dissent; which assent and dissent consist chiefly of additional complex ideas, not included in the terms of the proposition. And it would be of the greatest use, both in the sciences and in common life, thoroughly to analyse the matter, to shew in what manner, and by what steps, *i. e.* by what impressions and associations, our assent and dissent, both in scientifical and moral subjects, is formed.

PROP. XIII: *When simple Ideas run into a complex one, according to the foregoing Proposition, we are to suppose, that the simple miniature Vibrations corresponding to those simple Ideas, run in like manner, into a complex miniature Vibration, corresponding to the resulting complex Idea.*

This proposition is analogous to the ninth and eleventh, and may be deduced from the last, as they are from the eighth and tenth respectively. It is also an evidence and illustration of the second; shewing, not only that the state of the medullary substance is changed, according to the several natures of the ideas which are presented to the mind; but also shewing, in general, of what kind this change is, and in what manner it is effected.

PROP. XIV: *It is reasonable to think, that some of the complex Vibrations attending upon complex Ideas, according to the last Proposition, may be as vivid as any of the sensory Vibrations excited by the direct Action of Objects.*

For these complex vibrations may consist of so many parts co-existent and successive, and these parts may so alter and exalt one another, as that the resulting agitations in the medullary substance may no longer be miniature vibrations, but vivid ones equal to those excited by objects impressed on the senses. This process may be farther favoured by a mixture of vivid real impressions among the ideas, by the irritability of the medullary substance, by a previous disposition to the vibrations to be excited, &c.

COR. I. When the complex miniature vibrations are thus exalted in degree, we are to conceive, that the corresponding complex ideas are proportionally exalted, and so pass into intellectual affections and passions. We are therefore to deduce the origin of the intellectual pleasures and pains, which are the objects of these affections and passions, from the source here laid open.

COR. II. Since the present proposition unfolds the nature of affections and will, in the same manner, and from the same principles, as the twelfth does that of ideas, intellect, memory, and fancy; it follows, that all these are of the same original and consideration, and differ only in degree, or some accidental circumstances. They are all deducible from the external impressions made upon the senses, the vestiges or ideas of these, and their mutual connexions by means of association, taken together and operating on one another.

COR. III. It follows also from this proposition, that the intellectual pleasures and pains may be greater, equal, or less, than the sensible ones, according as each person unites more or fewer, more vivid or more languid, miniature vibrations in the formation of his intellectual pleasures and pains, &c.

COR. IV. It is evident, that all the vibrations which belong to ideas, and intellectual affections, must reside in the brain, or even in the most internal parts of it, not in the spinal marrow or nerves. The brain is therefore the seat of the rational soul, *i. e.* of the soul, as far as it is influenced by reasons and moral motives, even though we should admit, that the spinal marrow and nerves, are, in part, the sensorium, or the seat of the sensitive soul; which is some argument, that this ought not to be admitted, but that the sensorium, in men at least, ought to be placed in the internal parts of the brain.

COR. V. It is of the utmost consequence to morality and religion, that the affections and passions should be analysed into their simple compounding parts, by reversing the steps of the associations which concur to form them. For thus we may learn how to cherish and improve good ones, check and root out such as are mischievous and immoral, and how suit our manner of life, in some tolerable measure, to our intellectual and religious wants. And as this holds, in respect of persons of all ages, so it is particularly true, and worthy of consideration, in respect of children and youth. The world is, indeed, sufficiently stocked with general precepts for this purpose, grounded on experience; and whosoever will follow these faithfully, may expect good general success. However, the doctrine of association, when traced up to the first rudiments of understanding and affection, unfolds such a scene as cannot fail both to instruct and alarm all such as have any degree of interested concern for themselves, or of a benevolent one for others. It ought to be added here, that the doctrine of association explains also the rise and progress of those voluntary and semi-voluntary powers, which we exert over our ideas, affections, and bodily motions (as I shall shew hereafter, Prop. XXI.) and by doing this, teaches us how to regulate and improve these powers.

COR. VI. If beings of the same nature, but whose affections and passions are, at present, in different proportions to each other, be exposed for an indefinite time to the same impressions and associations, all their particular differences will, at last, be overruled, and they will become perfectly similar, or even equal. They may also be made perfectly similar, in a finite time, by a proper adjustment of the impressions and associations.

COR. VII. Our original bodily make, and the impressions and associations which affect us in passing through life, are so much alike, and yet not the same, that there must be both a great general resemblance amongst mankind, in respect to their intellectual affections, and also many particular differences.

COR. VIII. Some degree of spirituality is the necessary consequence of passing through life. The sensible pleasures and pains must be transferred by association more and more every day, upon things that afford neither sensible pleasure nor sensible pain in themselves, and so beget the intellectual pleasures and pains.

COR. IX. Let the letters *a, b, c, d, e,* &c. represent the sensible pleasures; x, y, and z, the sensible pains, supposed to be only three in number; and let us suppose all these, both pleasures and pains, to be equal to one another: If now the ideas of these sensible pleasures and pains be associated together, according to all the possible varieties, in order to form intellectual pleasures and pains, it is plain, that pleasure must prevail in all the combinations of seven or more letters; and also, that when the several parts of these complex pleasures are sufficiently united by association, the pains which enter their composition will no longer be distinguished separately, but the resulting mixed and complex pleasures appear to be pure and simple ones, equal in quantity to the excess of pleasure above pain, in each combination. Thus association would convert a state in which pleasure and pain were both perceived by turns, into one in which pure pleasure alone would be perceived; at least, would cause the beings who were under its influence to an indefinite degree, to approach to this last state nearer than by any definite difference. Or, in other words, association, under the supposition of this corollary, has a tendency to reduce the state of those who have eaten of the tree of the knowledge of good and evil, back again to a paradisiacal one. Now, though the circumstances of mankind are not the same with those supposed in this corollary, yet they bear a remarkable resemblance thereto, during that part of our existence which is exposed to our observation. For our sensible pleasures are far more numerous than our sensible pains; and though the pains be, in general, greater than the pleasures, yet the sum total of these seems to be greater than that of those; whence the remainder, after the destruction of the pains by the opposite and equal pleasures, will be pure pleasure.

Cor. X. The intellectual pleasures and pains are as real as the sensible ones, being, as we have seen, nothing but the sensible ones variously mixed and compounded together. The intellectual pleasures and pains are also all equally of a factitious and acquired nature. We must therefore estimate all our pleasures equally, by their magnitude, permanency, and tendency to procure others; and our pains in like manner.

Cor. XI. The sensible pleasures and pains have a greater tendency to destroy the body, than the intellectual ones; for they are of a particular local nature, and so bear hard upon the organs which convey them. But the destruction of any one considerable part of the body is the destruction of the whole, from the sympathy of the parts; whereas the intellectual pleasures and pains, being collected from all quarters, do not much injure any organ particularly, but rather bring on an equable gradual decay of the whole medullary substance, and all the parts thereon depending.

·   ·   ·   ·   ·

PROP. XX: *All that has been delivered above, concerning the Derivation of ideal Vibratiuncles from sensory Vibrations, and concerning their Associations, may be fitly applied to motory Vibrations and Vibratiuncles.*

This proposition is the immediate consequence of admitting the doctrines of vibrations and association, in the manner in which they have been asserted in the foregoing propositions. It contains the theory of the voluntary and semi-voluntary motions; to facilitate the application of which theory in the next proposition, I shall deliver the principal cases of this, in the following corollaries.

COR. I. The motory vibrations of the five classes mentioned Prop. XVIII. will generate a propensity to corresponding motory vibratiuncles.

COR. II. These motory vibratiuncles will affect the brain, as well as the motory nerves along which they descend; and, indeed, their descent along the motory nerves will be principally owing to their being first excited in the brain. This is sufficiently evident in the motory vibratiuncles which are derived from the motory vibrations of the second and third classes. As to the motory vibrations of the other classes, it is evident, that the brain is strongly affected by the sensory vibrations which give birth to them, and consequently, that a proportional affection of the brain must take place in the motory vibratiuncles derived from them.

COR. III. The motory vibratiuncles will cohere to one another, by associations both synchronous and successive. Hence the simple parts, of which complex and decomplex motions are compounded, may cohere closely, and succeed readily to each other.

COR. IV. The motory vibratiuncles will also cohere to ideal ones by association. Common ideas may therefore excite motory vibratiuncles, and consequently be able to contract the muscles, provided the active powers lodged in their fibres and blood globules be sufficiently exalted for this purpose.

COR. V. If we suppose the ideal vibratiuncles to be so much increased from the causes mentioned, Prop. XIV. as to be equal in strength to the usual sensory vibrations, the motory vibratiuncles connected with them by association must be supposed to be increased proportionably. Hence ideas may occasion muscular motions of the same strength with the automatic motions.

COR. VI. The third and last connexion of the motory vibratiuncles is that with sensory vibrations, foreign to them, *i. e.* such as had no share in generating the motory vibratiuncles under consideration. Particular motions of the body may therefore by association be made to depend upon sensations, with which they have no natural and original connexion.

COR. I. As muscular motion has three connexions deducible from association, *viz.* those mentioned in the third, fourth, and sixth corollaries, so the sensations and ideas have the same three connexions. Hence the whole doctrine of association may be comprised in the following theorem, *viz.*

If any sensation A, *idea* B, *or muscular motion* C, *be associated for a sufficient number of times with any other sensation* D, *idea* E, *or muscular motion* F, *it will, at last, excite* d, *the simple idea belonging to the sensation* D, *the very idea* E, *or the very muscular motion* F.

The reader will observe, that association cannot excite the real sensation D, because the impression of the sensible object is necessary for this purpose. However, in certain morbid cases, the idea is magnified so as to equal, or even overpower, sensible impressions.

PROP. XXI: *The voluntary and semi-voluntary Motions are deducible from Association, in the Manner laid down in the last Proposition.*

In order to verify this proposition, it is necessary to inquire, what connexions each automatic motion has gained by association with other motions, with ideas, or with foreign sensations, according to the third, fourth, and sixth corollaries of the last proposition, so as to depend upon them, *i. e.* so as to be excited no longer, in the automatic manner described in the nineteenth proposition, but merely by the previous introduction of the associated motion, idea, or sensation. If it follow that idea, or state of mind (*i. e.* set of compound vibratiuncles), which we term the will, directly, and without our perceiving the intervention of any other idea, or of any sensation or motion, it may be called voluntary, in the highest sense of this word. If the intervention of other ideas, or of sensations and motions (all which we are to suppose to follow the will directly), be necessary, it is imperfectly voluntary; yet still it will be called voluntary, in the language of mankind, if it follow certainly and readily upon the intervention of a single sensation, idea, or motion, excited by the power of the will: but if more than one of these be required, or if the motion do not follow with certainty and facility, it is to be esteemed less and less voluntary, semi-voluntary, or scarce voluntary at all, agreeably to the circumstances. Now, if it be found, upon a careful and impartial inquiry, that the motions which occur every day in common life, and which follow the idea called the will, immediately or mediately, perfectly or imperfectly, do this, in proportion to the number and degree of strength in the associations, this will be sufficient authority for ascribing all which we call voluntary in actions to association, agreeably to the purport of this proposition. And this, I think, may be verified from facts, as far as it is reasonable to expect, in a subject of inquiry so novel and intricate.

In the same manner as any action may be rendered voluntary, the cessation from any, or a forcible restraint upon any, may be also, *viz.*

by proper associations with the feeble vibrations in which inactivity consists, or with the strong action of the antagonist muscles.

After the actions, which are most perfectly voluntary, have been rendered so by one set of associations, they may, by another, be made to depend upon the most diminutive sensations, ideas, and motions, such as the mind scarce regards, or is conscious of; and which therefore it can scarce recollect the moment after the action is over. Hence it follows, that association not only converts automatic actions into voluntary, but voluntary ones into automatic. For these actions, of which the mind is scarce conscious, and which follow mechanically, as it were, some precedent diminutive sensation, idea or motion, and without any effort of the mind, are rather to be ascribed to the body than the mind, *i. e.* are to be referred to the head of automatic motions. I shall call them automatic motions of the secondary kind, to distinguish them both from those which are originally automatic, and from the voluntary ones; and shall now give a few instances of this double transmutation of motions, *viz.* of automatic into voluntary, and of voluntary into automatic.

The fingers of young children bend upon almost every impression which is made upon the palm of the hand, thus performing the action of grasping in the original automatic manner. After a sufficient repetition of the motory vibrations which concur in this action, their vibratiuncles are generated, and associated strongly with other vibrations or vibratiuncles, the most common of which, I suppose, are those excited by the sight of a favourite plaything which the child uses to grasp, and hold in his hand. He ought, therefore, according to the doctrine of association, to perform and repeat the action of grasping, upon having such a plaything presented to his sight. But it is a known fact, that children do this. By pursuing the same method of reasoning, we may see how, after a sufficient repetition of the proper associations, the sound of the words *grasp, take hold,* &c. the sight of the nurse's hand in a state of contraction, the idea of a hand, and particularly of the child's own hand, in that state, and innumerable other associated circumstances, *i. e.* sensations, ideas, and motions, will put the child upon grasping, till, at last, that idea, or state of mind which we may call the will to grasp, is generated and sufficiently associated with the action to produce it instantaneously. It is therefore perfectly voluntary in this case; and by the innumerable repetitions of it in this perfectly voluntary state, it comes, at last, to obtain a sufficient connexion with so many diminutive sensations, ideas, and motions, as to follow them in the same manner, as originally automatic actions do the corresponding sensations, and consequently to be automatic secondarily. And in the same manner, may all the actions performed with the hands be explained, all those that are very familiar in life passing from the original automatic state through the several degrees of voluntariness till they become perfectly voluntary, and then repassing through the same degrees in an inverted order, till they become secondarily automatic on many occasions, though still perfectly voluntary on some, *viz.* whensoever an express act of the will is exerted.

I will, in the next place, give a short account of the manner in which we learn to speak, as it may be deduced from the foregoing proposition. The new-born child is not able to produce a sound at all, unless the muscles of the trunk and larynx be stimulated thereto by the impression of pain on some part of the body. As the child advances in age, the frequent returns of this action facilitate it; so that it recurs from less and less pains, from pleasures, from mere sensations, and lastly from slight associated circumstances, in the manner already explained. About the same time that this process is thus far advanced, the muscles of speech act occasionally, in various combinations, according to the associations of the motory vibratiuncles with each other. Suppose now the muscles of speech to act in these combinations at the same time that sound is produced from some agreeable impression, a mere sensation, or a slight associated cause, which must be supposed to be often the case, since it is so observable, that young children, when in a state of health and pleasure, exert a variety of actions at the same time. It is evident, that an articulate sound, or one approaching thereto, will sometimes be produced by this conjoint action of the muscles of the trunk, larynx, tongue, and lips; and that both these articulate sounds, and inarticulate ones, will often recur, from the recurrence of the same accidental causes. After they have recurred a sufficient number of times, the impression, which these sounds, articulate and inarticulate, make upon the ear, will become an associated circumstance (for the child always hears himself speak, at the same time that he exerts the action) sufficient to produce a repetition of them. And thus it is, that children repeat the same sounds over and over again, for many successions, the impression of the last sound upon the ear exciting a fresh one, and so on, till the organs be tired. It follows, therefore, that if any of the attendants make any of the sounds familiar to the child, he will be excited from this impression, considered as an associated circumstance, to return it. But the attendants make articulate sounds chiefly; there will therefore be a considerable balance in favour of such, and that of a growing nature: so that the child's articulate sounds will be more and more frequent every day—his inarticulate ones grow into disuse. Suppose now, that he compounds these simple articulate sounds, making complex ones, which approach to familiar words at some times, at others such as are quite foreign to the words of his native language, and that the first get an ever-growing balance in their favour, from the cause just now taken notice of: also, that they are associated with visible objects, actions, &c. and it will be easily seen, that the young child ought, from the nature of association, to learn to speak much in the same manner as he is found in fact to do. Speech will also become a perfectly voluntary action, *i. e.* the child will be able to utter any word or sentence proposed to him by others, or by himself, from a mere exertion of the will, as much as to grasp: only here the introductory circumstance, *viz.* the impression of the sound on the ear, the idea of this sound, or the preceding motion in pronouncing the preceding word is evident; and therefore makes it probable, that the same thing takes place in other cases. In like manner, speech, after it has been voluntary for a due time, will become secondarily automatic, *i. e.* will follow associated circumstances, without any express exertion of the will.

From the account here given of the actions of handling and speaking, we may understand in what manner the first rudiments are laid of that faculty of imitation, which is so observable in young children. They see the actions of their own hands, and hear themselves pronounce. Hence the impressions made by themselves on their own eyes and ears become associated circumstances, and consequently must, in due time, excite to the repetition of the actions. Hence like impressions made on their eyes and ears by others will have the same effect; or, in other words, they will learn to imitate the actions which they see, and the sounds which they hear.

In the same manner may be explained the evident powers which the will has over the actions of swallowing, breathing, coughing, and expelling the urine and fæces, as well as the feeble and imperfect ones over sneezing, hiccoughing, and vomiting. As to the motion of the heart, and peristaltic motion of the bowels, since they are constant, they must be equally associated with every thing, *i. e.* peculiarly so with nothing, a few extraordinary cases excepted. They will therefore continue to move solely in the original automatic manner, during the whole course of our lives. However, association may, perhaps, have some share in keeping these motions, and that of respiration, up for a time, when the usual automatic causes are deficient in any measure; and may thus contribute to their equability and constancy. It seems certain, at least, that where unequable and irregular motions of the heart and bowels are generated, and made to recur for a sufficient number of times, from their peculiar causes, in full quantity, a less degree of the same causes, or even an associated circumstance, will suffice to introduce them afterwards. And the same thing may be observed of hysteric and epileptic fits. These recur from less and less causes perpetually, in the same manner, and for the same reasons, as original automatic motions are converted into voluntary ones.

I will add one instance more of the transition of voluntary actions into automatic ones of the secondary kind, in order to make that process clearer, by having it singly in view. Suppose a person who has a perfectly voluntary command over his fingers, to begin to learn to play upon the harpsichord; the first step is to move his fingers from key to key, with a slow motion, looking at the notes, and exerting an express act of volition in every motion. By degrees the motions cling to one another, and to the impressions of the notes, in the way of association so often mentioned, the acts of volition growing less and less express all the time, till at last they become evanescent and imperceptible. For an expert performer will play from notes, or ideas laid up in the memory, or from the connexion of the several complex parts of the decomplex motions, some or all; and, at the same time, carry on a quite different train of thoughts in his mind, or even hold a conversation with another. Whence we may conclude, that the passage from the sensory, ideal, or motory vibrations which precede, to those motory ones which follow, is as ready and direct, as from the sensory vibrations to the original automatic motions corresponding to them; and consequently, that there is no intervention of the idea, or state of mind, called will. At least, the doctrine of association favours this, and the fact shews, that there is no perceptible intervention, none of which we are conscious.

And thus, from the present proposition, and the nineteenth taken together, we are enabled to account for all the motions of the human body, upon principles which, though they may be fictitious, are, at least, clear and intelligible. The doctrine of vibrations explains all the original automatic motions, that of association the voluntary and secondarily automatic ones. And if the doctrine of association be founded in, and deducible from, that of vibrations, in the manner delivered above, then all the sensations, ideas, and motions, of all animals, will be conducted according to the vibrations of the small medullary particles. Let the reader examine this hypothesis by the facts, and judge for himself. There are innumerable things, which, when properly discussed, will be sufficient tests of it. It will be necessary, in examining the motions, carefully to distinguish the automatic state from the voluntary one, and to remember, that the first is not to be found pure, except in the motions of the new-born infant, or such as are excited by some violent irritation or pain.

Cor. I. The brain, not the spinal marrow, or nerves, is the seat of the soul, as far as it presides over the voluntary motions. For, by Cor. II. of the last proposition, the efficacy of the motory vibratiuncles depends chiefly on that part of them which is excited within the brain.

Cor. II. The hypothesis here proposed is diametrically opposite to that of Stahl,[1] and his followers. They suppose all animal motions to be voluntary in their original state, whereas this hypothesis supposes them all to be automatic at first, *i. e.* involuntary, and to become

---

[1] Georg Ernst Stahl (1660–1734), German physician and chemist, best known for his work on the chemical theory of combustion, was also the author of *Theoria medica vera* (Halle, 1707), concerning mind and body. Ed.

voluntary afterwards by degrees. However, the Stahlians agree with me concerning the near relation of these two sorts of motion to each other, as also concerning the transition (or rather return, according to my hypothesis) of voluntary motions into involuntary ones, or into those which I call secondarily automatic. As to final causes, which are the chief subject of inquiry amongst the Stahlians, they are, without doubt, every where consulted, in the structure and functions of the parts; they are also of great use for discovering the efficient ones. But then they ought not to be put in the place of the efficient ones; nor should the search after the efficient be banished from the study of physic, since the power of the physician, such as it is, extends to these alone. Not to mention, that the knowledge of the efficient causes is equally useful for discovering the final, as may appear from many parts of these observations.

Cor. III. It may afford the reader some entertainment, to compare my hypothesis with what Des Cartes and Leibnitz have advanced, concerning animal motion, and the connexion between the soul and body. My general plan bears a near relation to theirs. And it seems not improbable to me, that Des Cartes might have had success in the execution of his, as proposed in the beginning of his Treatise on Man,[1] had he been furnished with a proper assemblage of facts from anatomy, physiology, pathology, and philosophy, in general. Both Leibnitz's preestablished harmony, and Malebranche's system of occasional causes, are free from that great difficulty of supposing, according to the scholastic system, that the soul, an immaterial substance, exerts and receives a real physical influence upon and from the body, a material substance. And the reader may observe, that the hypothesis here proposed stands clear also of this difficulty. If he admit the simple case of the connexion between the soul and body, in respect of sensation, as it is laid down in the first proposition, and only suppose, that there is a change made in the medullary substance, proportional and correspondent to every change in the sensations, the doctrine of vibrations, as here delivered, undertakes to account for all the rest, the origin of our ideas and motions, and the manner in which both the sensations and these are performed.

Cor. IV. I will here add Sir Isaac Newton's words, concerning sensation and voluntary motion, as they occur at the end of his Principia,[2] both because they first led me into this hypothesis, and because they flow from it as a corollary. He affirms then, "both that all sensation is performed, and also the limbs of animals moved in a voluntary manner, by the power and actions of a certain very subtle spirit, *i. e.* by the vibrations of this spirit, propagated through the solid

---

[1] *Traité de l'Homme* in *Oeuvres de Descartes,* Vol. XI, edited by C. Adam and P. Tannery (Paris, 1909). Ed.

[2] *Mathematical Principles of Natural Philosophy,* Book III, last paragraph. Ed.

capillaments of the nerves from the external organs of the senses to the brain, and from the brain into the muscles."

Cor. V. It follows, from the account here given of the voluntary and semi-voluntary motions, that we must get every day voluntary and semi-voluntary powers, in respect of our ideas and affections. Now this consequence of the doctrine of association is also agreeable to the fact. Thus we have a voluntary power of attending to an idea for a short time, of recalling one, of recollecting a name, a fact, &c. a semi-voluntary one of quickening or restraining affections already in motion, and a most perfectly voluntary one of exciting moral motives, by reading, reflection, &c.

PROP. XXII: *It follows, from the Hypothesis here proposed, concerning the voluntary Motions, that a Power of obtaining Pleasure, and removing Pain, will be generated early in Children, and increase afterwards every Day.*

For the motions which are previous and subservient to the obtaining of pleasure, and the removal of pain, will be much more frequent, from the very instant of birth, than those which occasion pain. The number also of the first will be perpetually increasing, of the last decreasing. Both which positions may be evinced by the following arguments:

First, The pleasures are much more numerous than the pains. Hence the motions which are subservient to them are much more numerous also.

Secondly, The associated circumstances of the pleasures are many more in number than the pleasures themselves. But these circumstances, after a sufficient association, will be able to excite the motions subservient to the pleasures, as well as these themselves. And this will greatly augment the methods of obtaining pleasure.

Thirdly, It favours the position here advanced, that the motions subservient to pleasure are of a moderate nature; and therefore, that they can be excited with the more ease, both in an automatic and voluntary manner.

Fourthly, The pains, and consequently the motions subservient to them, are few, and of a violent nature. These motions are also various, and therefore cannot be united to objects and ideas with constancy and steadiness; and, which is most to be regarded, they end, at last, from the very make of the body, in that species of motion which contributes most to remove or assuage the pain. This species therefore, since it recurs the most frequently, and continues longest, must be confirmed by association, to the exclusion of the rest.

Cor. I. Many changes in the actions of young children, very difficult to be explained, according to the usual methods of considering human actions, appear to admit of a solution from this proposition.

These changes are such as tend to the ease, convenience, pleasure, of the young child; and they are sufficiently observable in the transition of the originally automatic actions into voluntary ones, as matters of fact, whatever be determined concerning their cause. I shall therefore refer to them occasionally, in the course of these papers, as allowed matters of fact.

COR. II. It seems also, that many very complex propensities and pursuits in adults, by which they seek their own pleasure and happiness, both explicitly and implicitly, may be accounted for, upon the same, or such-like principles.

COR. III. To similar causes we must also refer that propensity to excite and cherish grateful ideas and affections, and trains of these, which is so observable in all mankind. However, this does not hold in so strict a manner, but that ungrateful trains will present themselves, and recur on many occasions, and particularly whenever there is a morbid, and somewhat painful, state of the medullary substance.

COR. IV. Since God is the source of all good, and consequently must at last appear to be so, *i. e.* be associated with all our pleasures, it seems to follow, even from this proposition, that the idea of God, and of the ways by which his goodness and happiness are made manifest, must, at last, take place of, and absorb all other ideas, and he himself become, according to the language of the Scriptures, *All in all.*

COR. V. This proposition, and its corollaries, afford some very general, and perhaps new, instances of the coincidence of efficient and final causes.

COR. VI. The agreement of the doctrines of vibrations and association, both with each other, and with so great a variety of the phænomena of the body and mind, may be reckoned a strong argument for their truth.

CHAPTER III

CONTAINING A PARTICULAR APPLICATION OF THE
FOREGOING THEORY TO THE PHAENOMENA OF IDEAS,
OR OF UNDERSTANDING, AFFECTION, MEMORY, AND IMAGINATION

SECTION I

WORDS, AND THE IDEAS ASSOCIATED WITH THEM

PROP. LXXIX: *Words and Phrases must excite Ideas in us by Association, and they excite Ideas in us by no other Means.*

Words may be considered in four lights.

First, As impressions made upon the ear.

Secondly, As the actions of the organs of speech.

Thirdly, As impressions made upon the eye by characters.

Fourthly, As the actions of the hand in writing.

We learn the use of them in the order here set down. For children first get an imperfect knowledge of the meaning of the words of others; then learn to speak themselves; then to read; and, lastly, to write.

Now it is evident, that in the first of these ways many sensible impressions, and internal feelings, are associated with particular words and phrases, so as to give these the power of raising the corresponding ideas; and that the three following ways increase and improve this power, with some additions to and variations of the ideas. The second is the reverse of the first, and the fourth of the third. The first ascertains the ideas belonging to words and phrases in a gross manner, according to their usage in common life. The second fixes this, and makes it ready and accurate; having the same use here as the solution of the inverse problem has in other cases in respect of the direct one. The third has the same effect as the second; and also extends the ideas and significations of words and phrases, by new associations; and particularly by associations with other words, as in definitions, descriptions, &c. The advancement of the arts and sciences is chiefly carried on by the new significations given to words in this third way. The fourth by converting the reader into a writer, helps him to be expert in distinguishing, quick in recollecting, and faithful in retaining, these new significations of words, being the inverse of the third method, as just now remarked. The reader will easily see, that the action of the hand is not an essential in this fourth method. Composition by persons born blind has nearly the same effect. I mention it as being the common attendant upon composition, as having a considerable use deducible from association, and as making the analogy between the four methods more conspicuous and complete.

This may suffice, for the present, to prove the first part of the proposition; *viz.* that words and phrases must excite ideas in us by association. The second part, or that they excite ideas in us by no other means, may appear at the same time, as it may be found upon reflection and examination, that all the ideas which any word does excite are deducible from some of the four sources above-mentioned, most commonly from the first or third.

It may appear also from the instances of the words of unknown languages, terms of art not yet explained, barbarous words, &c. of which we either have no ideas, or only such as some fancied resemblance, or prior association, suggests.

It is highly worthy of remark here, that articulate sounds are by their variety, number, and ready use, particularly suited to signify and suggest, by association, both our simple ideas, and the complex ones formed from them, according to the twelfth proposition.

Cor. It follows from this proposition, that the arts of logic and rational grammar depend entirely on the doctrine of association. For logic, considered as the art of thinking or reasoning, treats only of such ideas as are annexed to words; and, as the art of discoursing, it teaches the proper use of words in a general way, as grammar does in a more minute and particular one.

PROP. LXXX: *To describe the Manner in which Ideas are associated with Words, beginning from Childhood.*

This may be done by applying the doctrine of association, as laid down in the first chapter, to words, considered in the four lights mentioned under the last proposition.

First, then, The association of the names of visible objects, with the impressions which these objects make upon the eye, seems to take place more early than any other, and to be effected in the following manner: the name of the visible object, the nurse, for instance, is pronounced and repeated by the attendants to the child, more frequently when his eye is fixed upon the nurse, than when upon other objects, and much more so than when upon any particular one. The word *nurse* is also sounded in an emphatical manner, when the child's eye is directed to the nurse with earnestness and desire. The association therefore of the sound *nurse,* with the picture of the nurse upon the *retina,* will be far stronger than that with any other visible impression, and thus overpower all the other accidental associations, which will also themselves contribute to the same end by opposing one another. And when the child has gained so much voluntary power over his motions, as to direct his head and eyes towards the nurse upon hearing her name, this process will go on with an accelerated velocity. And thus, at last, the word will excite the visible idea readily and certainly.

The same association of the picture of the nurse in the eye with the sound *nurse,* will, by degrees, overpower all the accidental associations of this picture with other words, and be so firmly cemented at last, that the picture will excite the audible idea of the word. But this is not to our present purpose. I mention it here as taking place at the same time with the foregoing process, and contributing to illustrate and confirm it. Both together afford a complete instance for the tenth and eleventh propositions, *i. e.* they shew, that when the impressions A and B are sufficiently associated, A impressed alone will excite b, B impressed alone will excite a.

Secondly, This association of words with visible appearances, being made under many particular circumstances, must affect the visible ideas with a like particularity. Thus the nurse's dress, and the situation of the fire in the child's nursery, make part of the child's ideas of his nurse and fire. But then as the nurse often changes her dress, and the child often sees a fire in a different place, and surrounded by different visible objects, these opposite associations must be less strong than the part which is common to them all; and consequently we may suppose, that while his idea of that part which is common, and which we may call essential, continues the same, that of the particularities, circumstances, and adjuncts, varies. For he cannot have any idea, but with some particularities in the non-essentials.

Thirdly, When the visible objects impress other vivid sensations besides those of sight, such as grateful or ungrateful tastes, smells, warmth, or coldness, with sufficient frequency, it follows from the foregoing theory that these sensations must leave traces, or ideas, which will be associated with the names of the objects, so as to depend upon them. Thus an idea, or nascent perception, of the sweetness of the nurse's milk will rise up in that part of the child's brain which corresponds to the nerves of taste, upon his hearing her name. And hence the whole idea belonging to the word *nurse* now begins to be complex, as consisting of a visible idea, and an idea of taste. And these two ideas will be associated together, not only because the word raises them both, but also because the original sensations are. The strongest may therefore assist in raising the weakest. Now, in common cases the visible idea is strongest, or occurs most readily at least; but, in the present instance, it seems to be otherwise. We might proceed in like manner to shew the generation of ideas more and more complex, and the various ways by which their parts are cemented together, and all made to depend on the respective names of the visible objects. But what has been said may suffice to shew what ideas the names of visible objects, proper and appellative, raise in us.

Fourthly, We must, however, observe, in respect of appellatives, that sometimes the idea is the common compound result of all the sensible impressions received from the several objects comprised under the general appellation; sometimes the particular idea of some one of these, in great measure at least, *viz.* when the impressions arising from some one are more novel, frequent, and vivid, than those from the rest.

Fifthly, The words denoting sensible qualities, whether substantive or adjective, such as *whiteness, white, &c.* get their ideas in a manner which will be easily understood from what has been already delivered. Thus the word *white,* being associated with the visible appearance of milk, linen, paper, gets a stable power of exciting the idea of what is common to all, and a variable one, in respect of the particularities, circumstances, and adjuncts. And so of other sensible qualities.

Sixthly, The names of visible actions, as walking, striking, &c. raise the proper visible ideas by a like process. Other ideas may likewise adhere in certain cases, as in those of tasting, feeling, speaking, &c. Sensible perceptions, in which no visible action is concerned, as hearing, may also leave ideas dependent on words. However, some visible ideas generally intermix themselves here. These actions and perceptions are generally denoted by verbs, though sometimes by substantives.

And we may now see in what manner ideas are associated with nouns, proper and appellative, substantive and adjective, and with verbs, supposing that they denote sensible things only. Pronouns and particles remain to be considered. Now, in order to know their ideas and uses, we must observe,

Seventhly, That as children may learn to read words not only in an elementary way, *viz.* by learning the letters and syllables of which they are composed, but also in a summary one, *viz.* by associating the sound of entire words, with their pictures, in the eye; and must, in some cases, be taught in the last way, *i. e.* wheresoever the sound of the word deviates from that of its elements; so both children and adults learn the ideas belonging to whole sentences many times in a summary way, and not by adding together the ideas of the several words in the sentence. And wherever words occur, which, separately taken, have no proper ideas, their use can be learnt in no other way but this. Now pronouns and particles, and many other words, are of this kind. They answer, in some measure, to *x, y,* and *z,* or the unknown quantities in algebra, being determinable and decypherable, as one may say, only by means of the known words with which they are joined.

Thus *I walk* is associated at different times with the same visible impression as *nurse walks, brother walks,* &c. and therefore can suggest nothing permanently for a long time but the action of walking. However the pronoun *I,* in this and innumerable other short sentences, being always associated with the person speaking, as *thou* is with the person spoken to, and *he* with the person spoken of, the frequent recurrency of this teaches the child the use of the pronouns, *i. e.* teaches him what difference he is to expect in his sensible impressions according as this or that pronoun is used; the infinite number of instances, as one may say, making up for the infinitely small quantity of information, which each, singly taken, conveys.

In like manner, different particles, *i. e.* adverbs, conjunctions, and prepositions, being used in sentences, where the substantives, adjectives, and verbs, are the same, and the same particles, where these are different, in an endless recurrency, teach children the use of the particles in a gross general way. For it may be observed, that children are much at a loss for the true use of the pronouns and particles for some years, and that they often repeat the proper name of the person instead of the pronoun; which confirms the foregoing reasoning. Some of the inferior parts or particles of speech make scarce any alteration in the sense of the sentence, and therefore are called expletives. The several terminations of the Greek and Latin nouns and verbs are of the nature of pronouns and particles.

Eighthly, The attempts which children make to express their own wants, perceptions, pains, &c. in words, and the corrections and suggestions of the attendants, are of the greatest use in all the steps that we have hitherto considered, and especially in the last, regarding the pronouns and particles.

Ninthly, Learning to read helps children much in the same respects; especially as it teaches them to separate sentences into the several words which compound them; which those who cannot read are scarce able to do, even when arrived at adult age.

Thus we may see, how children and others are enabled to understand a continued discourse relating to sensible impressions only, and how the words in passing over the ear must raise up trains of visible and other ideas by the power of association. Our next inquiry must be concerning the words that denote either intellectual things, or collections of other words.

Tenthly, The words that relate to the several passions of love, hatred, hope, fear, anger, &c. being applied to the child at the times when he is under the influence of these passions, get the power of raising the miniatures or ideas of these passions, and also of the usual associated circumstances. The application of the same words to others helps also to annex the ideas of the associated circumstances to them, and even of the passions themselves, both from the infectiousness of our natures, and from the power of associated circumstances to raise the passions. However, it is to be noted, that the words denoting the passions do not, for the most part, raise up in us any degree of the passions themselves, but only the ideas of the associated circumstances. We are supposed to understand the continued discourses into which these words enter sufficiently, when we form true notions of the actions, particularly the visible ones attending them.

Eleventhly, The names of intellectual and moral qualities and operations, such as fancy, memory, wit, dulness, virtue, vice, conscience, approbation, disapprobation, &c. stand for a description of these qualities and operations; and therefore, if dwelt upon, excite such ideas as these descriptions in all their particular circumstances do. But the common sentences, which these words enter, pass over the mind too quick, for the most part, to allow of such a delay. They are acknowledged as familiar and true, and suggest certain associated visible ideas, and nascent internal feelings, taken from the descriptions of these names, or from the words, which are usually joined with them in discourses or writings.

Twelfthly, There are many terms of art in all the branches of learning, which are defined by other words, and which therefore are only compendious substitutes for them. The same holds in common life in numberless instances. Thus riches, honours, pleasures, are put for the several kinds of each. Such words sometimes suggest the words of their definitions, sometimes the ideas of these words, sometimes a particular species comprehended under the general term, &c. But, whatever they suggest, it may be easily seen, that they derive the power of doing this from association.

Thirteenthly, There are many words used in abstract sciences, which can scarce be defined or described by any other words; and yet, by their grammatical form, seem to be excluded from the class of particles. Such are identity, existence, &c. The use of these must therefore be learnt as that of the particles is. And indeed children learn their first imperfect notions of all the words considered in this and the three last paragraphs chiefly in this way; and come to precise and explicit ones only by means of books, as they advance to adult age, or by endeavouring to use them properly in their own deliberate compositions.

This is by no means a full or satisfactory account of the ideas which adhere to words by association. For the author perceives himself to be still a mere novice in these speculations; and it is difficult to explain words to the bottom by words; perhaps impossible. The reader will receive some addition of light and evidence in the course of this section; also in the next, in which I shall treat of propositions and assent. For our assent to propositions, and the influence which they have over our affections and actions, make part of the ideas that adhere to words by association; which part, however, could not properly be considered in this section.

COR. I. It follows from this proposition, that words may be distinguished into the four classes mentioned under the twelfth proposition.

1. Such as have ideas only.
2. Such as have both ideas and definitions.
3. Such as have definitions only.
4. Such as have neither ideas nor definitions.

Under definition I here include description, or any other way of explaining a word by other words, excepting that by a mere synonymous term; and I exclude from the number of ideas the visible idea of the character of a word, and the audible one of its sound; it being evident, that every word heard may thus excite a visible idea, and every word seen an audible one. I exclude also all ideas that are either extremely faint, or extremely variable.

It is difficult to fix precise limits to these four classes, so as to determine accurately where each ends, and the next begins; and, if we consider these things in the most general way, there is perhaps no word which has not both an idea and a definition, *i. e.* which is not attended by some one or more internal feelings occasionally, and which may not be explained, in some imperfect manner at least, by other words. I will give some instances of words which have the fairest right to each class.

The names of simple sensible qualities are of the first class. Thus *white, sweet,* &c. excite ideas; but cannot be defined. It is to be observed here, that this class of words stands only for the stable part of the ideas respectively, not for the several variable particularities, circumstances, and adjuncts, which intermix themselves here.

The names of natural bodies, animal, vegetable, mineral, are of the second class; for they excite aggregates of sensible ideas, and at the same time may be defined (as appears from the writings of natural historians) by an enumeration of their properties and characteristics. Thus likewise geometrical figures have both ideas and definitions. The definitions in both cases are so contrived as to leave out all the variable particularities of the ideas, and to be also more full and precise, than the ideas generally are in the parts that are of the permanent nature.

Algebraic quantities, such as roots, powers, surds, &c. belong to the third class, and have definitions only. The same may be said of scientifical terms of art, and of most abstract general terms, moral, metaphysical, vulgar: however, mental emotions are apt to attend some of these even in passing slightly over the ear; and these emotions may be considered as ideas belonging to the terms respectively. Thus the very words, *gratitude, mercy, cruelty, treachery,* &c. separately taken, affect the mind; and yet, since all reasoning upon them is to be founded on their definitions, as will be seen hereafter, it seems best to refer them to this third class.

Lastly, the particles *the, of, to, for, but,* &c. have neither definitions nor ideas.

COR. II. This matter may be illustrated by comparing language to geometry and algebra, the two general methods of expounding quantity, and investigating all its varieties from previous *data.*

Words of the first class answer to propositions purely geometrical, *i. e.* to such as are too simple to admit of algebra; of which kind we may reckon that concerning the equality of the angles at the basis of an Isosceles triangle.

Words of the second class answer to that part of geometry which may be demonstrated either synthetically or analytically; either so that the learner's imagination shall go along with every step of the process painting out each line, angle, &c. according to the method of demonstration used by the ancient mathematicians; or so that he shall operate entirely by algebraic quantities and methods, and only represent the conclusion to his imagination, when he is arrived at it, by examining then what geometrical quantities the ultimately resulting algebraical ones denote. The first method is in both cases the most satisfactory and affecting, the last the most expeditious, and not less certain, where due care is taken. A blind mathematician must use words in the last of these methods, when he reasons upon colours.

Words of the third class answer to such problems concerning quadratures, and rectifications of curves, chances, equations of the higher orders, &c. as are too perplexed to be treated geometrically.

Lastly, words of the fourth class answer to the algebraic signs for addition, subtraction, &c. to indexes, coefficients, &c. These are not algebraic quantities themselves; but they alter the import of the letters that are; just as particles vary the sense of the principal words of a sentence, and yet signify nothing of themselves.

Geometrical figures may be considered as representing all the modes of extension in the same manner as visible ideas do visible objects; and consequently the names of geometrical figures answer to the names of these ideas. Now, as all kinds of problems relating to quantity might be expounded by modes of extension, and solved thereby, were our faculties sufficiently exalted, so it appears possible to represent most kinds of ideas by visible ones, and to pursue them in this way through all their varieties and combinations. But as it seems best in the first case to confine geometry to problems, where extension, and motion, which implies extension, are concerned, using algebraic methods for investigating all other kinds of quantity, so it seems best also to use visible ideas only for visible objects and qualities, of which they are the natural representatives, and to denote all other qualities by words considered as arbitrary signs. And yet the representation of other quantities by geometrical ones, and of other ideas by visible ones, is apt to make a more vivid impression upon the fancy, and a more lasting one upon the memory. In similes, fables, parables, allegories, visible ideas are used for this reason to denote general and intellectual ones.

Since words may be compared to the letters used in algebra, language itself may be termed one species of algebra; and, conversely, algebra is nothing more than the language which is peculiarly fitted to explain quantity of all kinds. As the letters, which in algebra stand immediately for quantities, answer to the words which are immediate representatives of ideas, and the algebraic signs for addition, &c. to the particles, so the single letters, which are sometimes used by algebraists to denote sums or differences, powers or roots universal of other letters, for brevity and convenience, answer to such words as have long definitions, to terms of art, &c. which are introduced into the sciences for the sake of compendiousness. Now, if every thing relating to language had something analogous to it in algebra, one might hope to explain the difficulties and perplexities attending the theory of language by the corresponding particulars in algebra, where every thing is clear, and acknowledged by all that have made it their study. However, we have here no independent point whereon to stand, since, if a person be disposed to call the rules of algebra in question, we have no way of demonstrating them to him, but by using words, the things to be explained by algebra for that purpose. If we suppose indeed the sceptical person to allow only that simple language, which is necessary for demonstrating the rules of algebra, the thing would be done; and, as I observed just now, it seems impossible to become acquainted with this, and at the same time to disallow it.

Cor. III. It will easily appear, from the observations here made upon words, and the associations which adhere to them, that the languages of different ages and nations must bear a great general resemblance to each other, and yet have considerable particular differences; whence any one may be translated into any other, so as to convey the same ideas in general, and yet not with perfect precision and exactness. They must resemble one another, because the phænomena of nature, which they are all intended to express, and the uses and exigences of human life, to which they minister, have a general resemblance. But then, as the bodily make and genius of each people, the air, soil, and climate, commerce, arts, sciences, religion, &c. make considerable differences in different ages and nations, it is natural to expect that the languages should have proportionable differences in respect of each other.

Where languages have rules of etymology and syntax, that differ greatly, which is the case of the Hebrew compared with Greek or Latin, this will become a new source of difformity. For the rules of etymology and syntax determine the application and purport of words in many cases. Agreeably to which we see that children, while yet unacquainted with that propriety of words and phrases which custom establishes, often make new words and constructions, which, though improper according to common usage, are yet very analogous to the tenor of the language in which they speak.

The modern languages of this western part of the world answer better to the Latin, than according to their original Gothic plans, on this account; inasmuch as not only great numbers of words are adopted by all of them from the Latin, but also because reading the Latin authors, and learning the Latin grammar, have disposed learned men and writers to mould their own languages in some measure after the Latin. And, conversely, each nation moulds the Latin after the idiom of its own language, the effect being reciprocal in all such cases.

In learning a new language, the words of it are at first substitutes for those of our native language; *i. e.* they are associated, by means of these, with the proper objects and ideas. When this association is sufficiently strong, the middle bond is dropped, and the words of the

new language become substitutes for, and suggest directly and immediately, objects and ideas; also clusters of other words in the same
language.

In learning a new language, it is much easier to translate from it
into the native one, than back again; just as young children are much
better able to understand the expressions of others, than to express
their own conceptions. And the reason is the same in both cases.
Young children learn at first to go from the words of others; and those
who learn a new language, from the words of that language, to the
things signified. And the reverse of this, *viz.* to go from the things
signified to the words, must be difficult for a time, from what is delivered concerning successive associations under the tenth and eleventh
propositions. It is to be added here, that the nature and connexions of
the things signified often determine the import of sentences, though
their grammatical analysis is not understood; and that we suppose the
person who attempts to translate from a new language is sufficiently
expert in the inverse problem of passing from the things signified to
the corresponding words of his own language. The power of association is every where conspicuous in these remarks.

COR. IV. It follows also from the reasoning of this proposition, that
persons who speak the same language cannot always mean the same
things by the same words; but must mistake each other's meaning.
This confusion and uncertainty arises from the different associations
transferred upon the same words by the difference in the accidents
and events of our lives. It is, however, much more common in discourses concerning abstract matters, where the terms stand for collections of other terms, sometimes at the pleasure of the speaker or
writer, than in the common and necessary affairs of life. For here
frequent use, and the constancy of the phænomena of nature, intended to be expressed by words, have rendered their sense determinate and certain. However, it seems possible, and even not very difficult, for two truly candid and intelligent persons to understand each
other upon any subject.

That we may enter more particularly into the causes of this confusion, and consequently be the better enabled to prevent it, let us consider words according to the four classes above-mentioned.

Now mistakes will happen in the words of the first class, *viz.* such
as have ideas only, where the persons have associated these words
with different impressions. And the method to rectify any mistake of
this kind is for each person to shew with what actual impressions he
has associated the word in question. But mistakes here are not common.

In words of the second class, *viz.* such as have both ideas and definitions, it often happens, that one person's knowledge is much more
full than another's, and, consequently, his idea and definition much

more extensive. This must cause a misapprehension on one side, which yet may easily be rectified by recurring to the definition. It happens also sometimes in words of this class, that a man's ideas, *i. e.* the miniatures excited in his nervous system by the word, are not always suitable to his definition, *i. e.* are not the same with those which the words of the definition would excite. If then this person should pretend, or even design, to reason from his definition, and yet reason from his idea, a misapprehension will arise in the hearer, who supposes him to reason from his definition merely.

In words of the third class, which have definitions only, and no immediate ideas, mistakes generally arise through want of fixed definitions mutually acknowledged, and kept to. However, as imperfect fluctuating ideas, that have little relation to the definitions, are often apt to adhere to the words of this class, mistakes must arise from this cause also.

As to the words of the fourth class, or those which have neither ideas nor definitions, it is easy to ascertain their use by inserting them in sentences, whose import is known and acknowledged; this being the method in which children learn to decypher them: so that mistakes could not arise in the words of this class, did we use moderate care and candour. And, indeed, since children learn the uses of words most evidently without having any *data,* any fixed point at all, it is to be hoped, that philosophers, and candid persons, may learn at last to understand one another with facility and certainty; and get to the very bottom of the connexion between words and ideas.

It seems practicable to make a dictionary of any language, in which the words of that language shall all be explained with precision by words of the same language, to persons who have no more than a gross knowledge of that language. Now this also shews, that, with care and candour, we might come to understand one another perfectly. Thus sensible qualities might be fixed by the bodies, in which they are most eminent and distinct; the names of a sufficient number of these bodies being very well known. After this, these very bodies, and all others, might be defined by their sensible properties; and these two processes would help each other indefinitely, actions might be described from animals already defined, also from the modes of extension, abstract terms defined, and the peculiar use of particles ascertained. And such a dictionary would, in some measure, be a real as well as a nominal one, and extend to things themselves. The writer of every new and difficult work may execute that part of such a dictionary which belongs to his subject; at least in the instances where he apprehends the reader is likely to want it.

COR. V. When words have acquired any considerable power of exciting pleasant or painful vibrations in the nervous system, by being often associated with such things as do this, they may transfer a part of these pleasures and pains upon indifferent things, by being at other times often associated with such. This is one of the principal sources of the several factitious pleasures and pains of human life. Thus, to give an instance from childhood, the words *sweet, good, pretty, fine,* &c., on the one hand, and the words *bad, ugly, frightful,* &c., on the other, being applied by the nurse and attendants in the young child's hearing almost promiscuously, and without those restrictions that are observed in correct speaking, the one to all the pleasures, the other to all the pains of the several senses, must by association raise up general pleasant and painful vibrations, in which no one part can be distinguished above the rest; and when applied by farther associations to objects of a neutral kind, they must transfer a general pleasure or pain upon them.

All the words associated with pleasures must also affect each other by this promiscuous application. And the same holds in respect of the words associated with pains. However, since both the original and the transferred pleasures and pains heaped upon different words are different, and in some cases widely so, every remarkable word will have a peculiar internal feeling, or sentiment, belonging to it; and there will be the same relations of affinity, disparity, and opposition, between these internal sentiments, *i. e.* ideas, belonging to words, as between the several *genera* and *species* of natural bodies, between tastes, smells, colours, &c. Many of these ideas, though affording considerable pleasure at first, must sink into the limits of indifference; and some of those which afforded pain at first, into the limits of pleasure. What is here said of words, belongs to clusters of them, as well as to separate words. And the ideas of all may still retain their peculiarities, by which they are distinguished from each other, after they have fallen below the limits of pleasure into indifference, just as obscure colours, or faint tastes do.

It is observable, that the mere transit of words expressing strong ideas over the ears of children affects them; and the same thing is true of adults, in a less degree. However, the last have learnt from experience and habit to regard them chiefly, as they afford a rational expectation of pleasure and pain. This cannot be discussed fully, till we come to consider the nature of assent; but it may give some light and evidence to the reasoning of this corollary, just to have mentioned the manner, in which we are at first affected by words.

COR. VI. Since words thus collect ideas from various quarters, unite them together, and transfer them both upon other words, and upon foreign objects, it is evident, that the use of words adds much to the number and complexness of our ideas, and is the principal means by which we make intellectual and moral improvements. This is verified abundantly by the observations that are made upon persons born deaf, and continuing so. It is probable, however, that these persons make use of some symbols to assist the memory, and fix the fancy: and they must have a great variety of pleasures and pains transferred upon visible objects from their associations with one another, and with sensible pleasures of all the kinds; but they are very deficient in this, upon the whole, through the want of the associations of visible objects, and states of mind, &c., with words. Learning to read must add greatly to their mental improvement; yet still their intellectual capacities cannot but remain very narrow.

Persons blind from birth must proceed in a manner different from that described in this proposition, in the first ideas which they affix to words. As the visible ones are wanting, the others, particularly the tangible and audible ones, must compose the aggregates which are annexed to words. However, as they are capable of learning and re- taining as great a variety of words as others, or perhaps a greater, *cæteris paribus,* and can associate with them pleasures and pains from the four remaining senses, also use them as algebraists do the letters that represent quantities, they fall little or nothing short of others in intellectual accomplishments, and may arrive even at a greater degree of spirituality and abstraction in their complex ideas.

COR. VII. It follows from this proposition, that, when children or others first learn to read, the view of the words excites ideas only by the mediation of their sounds, with which alone their ideas have hith- erto been associated. And thus it is that children and illiterate persons understand what they read best by reading aloud. By degrees, the in- termediate link being left out, the written or printed characters suggest the ideas directly and instantaneously; so that learned men understand more readily by passing over the words with the eye only, since this method, by being more expeditious, brings the ideas closer together. However, all men, both learned and unlearned, are peculiarly affected by words pronounced in a manner suitable to their sense and design; which is still an associated influence.

COR. VIII. As persons, before they learn to read, must have very imperfect notions of the distinction of words, and can only understand language in a gross general way, taking whole clusters of words for one undivided sound, so much less can they be supposed to have any conceptions concerning the nature or use of letters. Now all mankind must have been in this state before the invention of letters. Nay, they must have been farther removed from all conceptions of letters, than the most unlearned persons amongst us, since these have at least heard of letters, and know that words may be written and read by means of them. And this makes it difficult to trace out by what steps alphabeti- cal writing was invented; or is even some presumption that it is not a human invention. To which is to be added, that the analyzing complex articulate sounds into their simple component parts appears to be a problem of too difficult and perplexed a nature for the rude early ages, occupied in getting necessaries, and defending themselves from external injuries, and not aware of the great use of it, even though they had known the solution to be possible and practicable. However, I shall mention some presumptions of a contrary nature under the next proposition.

PROP. LXXXI: *To explain the Nature of Characters intended to represent Objects and Ideas immediately, and without the Intervention of Words.*

Since characters made by the hand are capable of the greatest varieties, they might be fitted by proper associations to suggest objects and ideas immediately, in the same manner as articulate sounds do. And there are some instances of it in common use, which may serve to verify this, and to lead us into the nature of characters standing immediately for objects and ideas. Thus the numeral figures, and the letters in algebra, represent objects, ideas, words, and clusters of words, directly and immediately; the pronunciation of them being of no use, or necessity, in the operations to be performed by them. Thus also musical characters represent sounds and combinations of sounds, without the intervention of words, and are a much more compendious and ready representation than any words can be.

Characters seem to have an advantage over articulate sounds in the representation of visible objects, inasmuch as they might, by their resemblance, even though only a gross one, become rather natural, than mere arbitrary representatives.

They had also an advantage as representatives in general, before the invention of alphabetical writing, since persons could by this means convey their thoughts to each other at a distance.

If we suppose characters to be improved to all that variety and multiplicity which is necessary for representing objects, ideas, and clusters of characters, in the same manner as words represent objects, ideas, and clusters of words, still they might be resolved into simple component parts, and rendered pronunciable by affixing some simple or short sound to each of these simple component parts; just as articulate sounds are painted by being first resolved into their simple component parts, and then having each of these represented by a simple mark or character.

If we suppose the most common visible objects to be denoted both by short articulate sounds, and by short characters bearing some real, or fancied, imperfect resemblance to them, it is evident, that the sound and mark, by being both associated with the visible object, would also be associated with one another; and consequently that the sound would be the name of the mark, and the mark the picture of the sound. And this last circumstance seems to lead to the denoting all sounds by marks, and therefore perhaps to alphabetical writing.

At the same time it must be observed, that the marks would bear different relations of similarity and dissimilarity to one another from those which the corresponding sounds did.

This would happen, according to whatever law the marks were made, but especially if they were resemblances of visible objects. And this, as it seems, would occasion some difficulty and perplexity in representing sounds by marks, or marks by sounds.

PROP. LXXXII: *To explain the Nature of figurative Words and Phrases, and of Analogy, from the foregoing Theory.*

A figure is a word, which, first representing the object or idea *A,* is afterwards made to represent *B,* on account of the relation which these bear to each other.

The principal relation, which gives rise to figures, is that of likeness; and this may be either a likeness in shape, and visible appearance, or one in application, use, &c. Now it is very evident from the nature of association, that objects which are like to a given one in visible appearance, will draw to themselves the word by which this is expressed. And indeed this is the foundation upon which appellatives are made to stand for so great a number of particulars. Let the word *man* be applied to the particular persons *A, B, C,* &c. till it be sufficiently associated with them, and it will follow, that the appearance of the new particular person *D* will suggest the word, and be denoted by it. But here there is no figure, because the word *man* is associated with different particular persons from the first, and that equally or nearly so.

In like manner, the corresponding parts of different animals, *i. e.* the eyes, mouth, breast, belly, legs, lungs, heart, &c. have the same names applied in a literal sense, partly from the likeness of shape, partly from that of use and application. And it is evident, that if we suppose a people so rude in language and knowledge, as to have names only for the parts of the human body, and not to have attended to the parts of the brute creatures, association would lead them to apply the same names to the parts of the brute creatures, as soon as they became acquainted with them. Now here this application would at first have the nature of a figure; but when by degrees any of these words, the eye for instance, became equally applied from the first to the eyes of men and brutes, it would cease to be a figure, and become an appellative name, as just now remarked.

But when the original application of the word is obvious, and remains distinct from the secondary one, as when we say the mouth or ear of a vessel, or the foot of a chair or table, the expression is figurative.

Hence it is plain, that the various resemblances which nature and art afford are the principal sources of figures. However, many figures are also derived from other relations, such as those of cause, effect, opposition, derivation, generality, particularity; and language itself, by its resemblances, oppositions, &c. becomes a new source of figures, distinct from the relations of things.

Most metaphors, *i. e.* figures taken from likeness, imply a likeness in more particulars than one, else they would not be sufficiently definite, nor affect the imagination in a due manner. If the likeness extend to many particulars, the figure becomes implicitly a simile, fable, parable, or allegory.

Many or most common figures pass so far into literal expressions by use, *i. e.* association, that we do not attend at all to their figurative nature. And thus by degrees figurative senses become a foundation for successive figures, in the same manner as originally literal senses.

It is evident, that if a language be narrow, and much confined to sensible things, it will have great occasion of figures: these will naturally occur in the common intercourses of life, and will in their turn, as they become literal expressions in the secondary senses, much augment and improve the language, and assist the invention. All this is manifest from the growth of modern languages, in those parts where they were heretofore particularly defective.

We come now to the consideration of analogy. Now things are said to be analogous to one another, in the strict mathematical sense of the word *analogy,* when the corresponding parts are all in the same ratio to each other. Thus if the several parts of the body in different persons be supposed exactly proportional to the whole bodies, they might be said to be analogous in the original mathematical sense of that word. But as this restrained sense is not applicable to things, as they really exist, another of a more enlarged and practical nature has been adopted, which may be thus defined. Analogy is that resemblance, and in some cases sameness, of the parts, properties, functions, uses, &c. any or all, of *A* to *B,* whereby our knowledge, concerning *A,* and the language expressing this knowledge, may be applied in the whole, or in part, to *B,* without any sensible, or, at least, any important practical error. Now analogies, in this sense of the word, some more exact and extensive, some less so, present themselves to us every where in natural and artificial things; and thus whole groups of figurative phrases, which seem at first only to answer the purposes of convenience in affording names for new objects, and of pleasing the fancy in the way to be hereafter mentioned, pass into analogical reasoning, and become a guide in the search after truth, and an evidence for it in some degree. I will here set down some instances of analogies of various degrees and kinds.

The bodies of men, women, and children, are highly analogous to each other. This holds equally in respect of every other species of animals; also of the several corresponding parts of animals of the same species, as their flesh, blood, bones, fat, &c. and their properties.

Here the words applied to the several analogous things are used in a sense equally literal in respect of all. And the analogy is in most cases so close, as rather to be esteemed a coincidence, or sameness.

In comparing animals of different kinds the analogy grows perpetually less and less, as we take in a greater compass; and consequently our language more and more harsh, when considered as literal, whilst yet it cannot well be figurative in some things, and literal in others; so that new words are generally assigned to those parts which do not sufficiently resemble the corresponding ones. Thus the fore-legs of men and fowls, as we might call them in a harsh, literal, or a highly figurative way, are termed hands and wings respectively. However, in some cases, the same word is used, and considered as a figure; as when the cries of birds and beasts are termed their language. We may also observe, that every part in every animal may, from its resemblance in shape and use to the corresponding parts in several other animals, have a just right to a name, which shall be common to it and them.

What has been said of animals of the same and different kinds holds equally in respect of vegetables. Those of the same kind have the same names applied to the corresponding parts in a literal sense. Those of different kinds have many names common to all used in a literal sense, some new ones peculiar to certain kinds, and some that may be considered as so harsh in a literal sense, that we may rather call them figurative terms.

The same may be said of the mineral kingdom, considered also according to its genera and species.

Animals are also analogous to vegetables in many things, and vegetables to minerals: so that there seems to be a perpetual thread of analogy continued from the most perfect animal to the most imperfect mineral, even till we come to elementary bodies themselves.

Suppose the several particulars of the three kingdoms to be represented by the letters of an alphabet sufficiently large for that purpose. Then we are to conceive, that any two contiguous species, as A and B, M and N, are more analogous than A and C, M and O, which have one between them. However, since A and B, M and N, are not perfectly analogous, this deficiency may be supplied in some things from C and O, in others from D and P, &c. so that M can have no part, property, &c. but what shall have something quite analogous to it in some species, near or remote, above it or below it, and even in several species. And in cases where the parts, properties, &c. are not rigorously exact in resemblance, there is, however, an imperfect one, which justifies the application of the same word to both: if it approach to perfection, the word may be said to be used in a literal sense; if it be very imperfect, in a figurative one. Thus when the names of parts, properties, &c. are taken from the animal kingdom, and applied to the vegetable, or *vice versâ,* they are more frequently considered as figurative, than when transferred from one part of the animal kingdom to another.

In like manner, there seems to be a gradation of analogies respecting the earth, moon, planets, comets, sun, and fixed stars, compared with one another. Or if we descend to the several parts of individuals, animals, vegetables, or minerals, the several organs of sensation are evidently analogous to each other; also the glands, the muscles, the parts of generation, in the different sexes of the same kind, &c. &c. without limits. For the more any one looks into the external natural world, the more analogies, general or particular, perfect or imperfect, will he find every where.

Numbers, geometrical figures, and algebraic quantities, are also mutually analogous without limits. And here there is the exactest uniformity, joined with an endless variety, so that it is always certain and evident how far the analogy holds, and where it becomes a disparity or opposition on one hand, or a coincidence on the other. There is no room for figures here; but the terms must be disparate, opposite, or the same, in a strictly literal sense respectively.

The several words of each particular language, the languages themselves, the idioms, figures, &c. abound also with numerous analogies of various kinds and degrees.

Analogies are likewise introduced into artificial things, houses, gardens, furniture, dress, arts, &c.

The body politic, the body natural, the world natural, the universe; —The human mind, the minds of brutes on one hand, and of superior beings on the other, and even the Infinite Mind himself;—the appellations of father, governor, judge, king, architect, &c. referred to God; —the ages of man, the ages of the world, the seasons of the year, the times of the day;—the offices, professions, and trades, of different persons, statesmen, generals, divines, lawyers, physicians, merchants; —the terms night, sleep, death, chaos, darkness, &c. also light, life, happiness, &c. compared with each other respectively; life and death, as applied in different senses to animals, vegetables, liquors, &c.— earthquakes, storms, battles, tumults, fermentations of liquors, lawsuit, games, &c. families, bodies politic lesser and greater, their laws, natural religion, revealed religion, &c. &c. afford endless instances of analogies natural and artificial. For the mind being once initiated into the method of discovering analogies, and expressing them, does by association persevere in this method, and even force things into its system by concealing disparities, magnifying resemblances, and accommodating language thereto. It is easy to see, that in the instances last alleged, the terms used are for the most part literal only in one sense, and figurative in all their other applications. They are literal in the sense which was their primary one, and figurative in many or most of the rest. Similes, fables, parables, allegories, &c. are all instances of natural analogies improved and set off by art. And they have this in common to them all, that the properties, beauties, perfections, desires, or defects and aversions, which adhere by association to the simile, parable or emblem of any kind, are insensibly, as it were, transferred upon the thing represented. Hence the passions are moved to good or to evil. Speculation is turned into practice, and either some important truth felt and realized, or some error and vice gilded over and recommended.

.   .   .   .   .

SECTION II

OF PROPOSITIONS, AND THE NATURE OF ASSENT

PROP. LXXXVI: *To explain the Nature of Assent and Dissent, and to shew from what Causes they arise.*

It appears, from the whole tenor of the last Section, that assent and dissent, whatever their precise and particular nature may be, must come under the notion of ideas, being only those very complex internal feelings, which adhere by association to such clusters of words as are called *propositions* in general, or affirmations and negations in particular. The same thing is remarked in the 10th corollary to the 12th proposition.

But in order to penetrate farther into this difficult and important point, I will distinguish assent (and by consequence its opposite, dissent) into two kinds, rational and practical; and define each of these.

Rational assent then to any proposition, may be defined, a readiness to affirm it to be true, proceeding from a close association of the ideas suggested by the proposition, with the idea, or internal feeling, belonging to the word truth; or of the terms of the proposition with the word truth. Rational dissent is the opposite to this. This assent might be called verbal; but as every person supposes himself always to have sufficient reason for such readiness to affirm or deny, I rather choose to call it rational.

Practical assent is a readiness to act in such manner as the frequent vivid recurrency of the rational assent disposes us to act; and practical dissent the contrary.

Practical assent is therefore the natural and necessary consequence of rational, when sufficiently impressed. There are, however, two cautions to be subjoined here, *viz.* first, that some propositions, mathematical ones for instance, admit only of a rational assent, the practical not being applied to them in common cases. Secondly, that the practical assent is sometimes generated, and arrives at a high degree of strength, without any previous rational assent, and by methods that have little or no connexion with it. Yet still it is in general much influenced by it, and, conversely, exerts a great influence upon it. All this will appear more clearly when we come to the instances.

Let us next inquire into the causes of rational and practical assent, beginning with that given to mathematical conclusions.

Now the cause that a person affirms the truth of the proposition *twice two is four,* is the entire coincidence of the visible or tangible idea of twice two with that of four, as impressed upon the mind by various objects. We see every where, that twice two and four are only different names for the same impression. And it is mere association which appropriates the word truth, its definition, or its internal feeling, to this coincidence.

Where the numbers are so large, that we are not able to form any distinct visible ideas of them, as when we say that 12 times 12 is equal to 144; a coincidence of the words arising from some method of reckoning up 12 times 12, so as to conclude with 144, and resembling the coincidence of words which attends the just-mentioned coincidence of ideas in the simpler numerical propositions, is the foundation of our rational assent. For we often do, and might always, verify the simplest numerical propositions, by reckoning up the numbers. The operations of addition, subtraction, multiplication, division, and extraction of roots, with all the most complex ones relating to algebraic quantities, considered as the exponents of numbers, are no more than methods of producing this coincidence of words, founded upon and rising above one another. And it is mere association again, which appropriates the word truth to the coincidence of the words, or symbols, that denote the numbers.

It is to be remarked, however, that this coincidence of words is by those who look deeper into things, supposed to be a certain argument, that the visible ideas of the numbers under consideration, as of 12 times 12, and 144, would coincide as much as the visible ideas of twice two and four, were they as clear and distinct. And thus the real and absolute truth is said by such persons to be as great in complex numerical propositions, as in the simplest. All this agrees with what Mr. Locke has observed concerning numbers, *viz.* that their names are necessary in order to our obtaining distinct ideas of them; for by distinct ideas he must be understood to mean proper methods of distinguishing them from one another, so as to reason justly upon them. He cannot mean distinct visible ideas.

In geometry there is a like coincidence of lines, angles, spaces, and solid contents, in order to prove them equal in simple cases. Afterwards in complex cases, we substitute the terms whereby equal things are denoted for each other, also the coincidence of the terms, for that of the visible ideas, except in the new step advanced in the proposition; and thus get a new equality, denoted by a new coincidence of terms. This resembles the addition of unity to any number, in order to make the next, as of 1 to 20, in order to make 21. We have no distinct visible idea, either of 20 or 21; but we have of the difference between them, by fancying to ourselves a confused heap of things supposed or called 20 in number; and then farther fancying 1 to be added to it. By a like process in geometry we arrive at the demonstration of the most complex propositions.

The properties of numbers are applied to geometry in many cases, as when we demonstrate a line or space to be half or double of any other, or in any other rational proportion to it.

And as in arithmetic words stand for indistinct ideas, in order to help us to reason upon them as accurately as if they were distinct; also cyphers for words, and letters for cyphers, both for the same purpose; so letters are put for geometrical quantities also, and the agreements of the first for those of the last. And thus we see the foundation upon which the whole doctrine of quantity is built; for all quantity is expounded either by number or extension, and their common and sole exponent is algebra. The coincidence of ideas is the foundation of the rational assent in simple cases; and that of ideas and terms together, or of terms alone, in complex ones. This is upon supposition that the quantities under consideration are to be proved equal. But if they are to be proved unequal, the want of coincidence answers the same purpose. If they are in any numeral ratio, this is only the introduction of a new coincidence. Thus, if, instead of proving *A* to be equal to *B,* we are to prove it equal to half *B,* the two parts of *B* must coincide with each other, either in idea or terms, and *A* with one.

And thus it appears, that the use of words is necessary for geometrical and algebraical reasonings, as well as for arithmetical.

We may see also that association prevails in every part of the processes hitherto described.

But these are not the only causes of giving rational assent to mathematical propositions, as this is defined above. The memory of having once examined and assented to each step of a demonstration, the authority of an approved writer, &c. are sufficient to gain our assent, though we understand no more than the import of the proposition; nay, even though we do not proceed so far as this. Now this is mere association again; this memory, authority, &c. being, in innumerable instances, associated with the before-mentioned coincidence of ideas and terms.

But here a new circumstance arises. For memory and authority are sometimes found to mislead; and this opposite coincidence of terms puts the mind into a state of doubt, so that sometimes truth may recur, and unite itself with the proposition under consideration, sometimes falsehood, according as the memory, authority, &c. in all their peculiar circumstances, have been associated with truth or falsehood. However, the foundation of assent is still the same. I here describe the fact only. And yet, since this fact must always follow from the fixed immutable laws of our frame, the obligation to assent (whatever be meant by this phrase) must coincide with the fact.

And thus a mathematical proposition, with the rational assent or dissent arising in the mind, as soon as it is presented to it, is nothing more than a group of ideas, united by association, *i. e.* than a very complex idea, as was affirmed above of propositions in general. And this idea is not merely the sum of the ideas belonging to the terms of the proposition, but also includes the ideas, or internal feelings, whatever they be, which belong to equality, coincidence, truth, and in some cases, those of utility, importance, &c.

For mathematical propositions are, in some cases, attended with a practical assent, in the proper sense of these words; as when a person takes this or that method of executing a projected design, in consequence of some mathematical proposition assented to from his own examination, or on the authority of others. Now, that which produces the train of voluntary actions, here denoting the practical assent, is the frequent recurrency of ideas of utility and importance. These operate according to the method laid down in the 20th proposition, *i. e.* by association; and though the rational assent be a previous requisite, yet the degree of the practical assent is proportional to the vividness of these ideas; and in most cases they strengthen the rational assent by a reflex operation.

Propositions concerning natural bodies are of two kinds, vulgar and scientifical. Of the first kind are, *that milk is white, gold yellow, that a dog barks,* &c. These are evidently nothing but forming the present complex idea belonging to material objects into a proposition, or adding some of its common associates, so as to make it more complex. There is scarce room for dissent in such propositions, they being all taken from common appearances. Or, if any doubt should arise, the matter must be considered scientifically. The assent given to these propositions arises from the associations of the terms, as well as of the ideas denoted by them.

In scientifical propositions concerning natural bodies, a definition is made, as of gold from its properties, suppose its colour, and specific gravity, and another property or power joined to them, as a constant or common associate. Thus gold is said to be ductile, fixed, or soluble in *aqua regia.* Now to persons who have made the proper experiments a sufficient number of times, these words suggest the ideas which occur in those experiments, and, conversely, are suggested by them, in the same manner as the vulgar propositions above-mentioned suggest and are suggested by common appearances. But then, if they be scientifical persons, their readiness to affirm that gold is soluble in *aqua regia* universally, arises also from the experiments of others, and from their own and others' observations on the constancy and tenor of nature. They know, that the colour, and specific gravity, or almost any two or three remarkable qualities of any natural body, infer the rest, being never found without them. This is a general truth; and as these general terms are observed to coincide, in fact, in a great variety of instances, so they coincide at once in the imagination, when applied to gold, or any other natural body, in particular. The coincidence of general terms is also observed to infer that of the particular cases in many instances, besides those of natural bodies; and this unites the subject and predicate of the proposition, *gold is soluble in aqua regia,* farther in those who penetrate still deeper into abstract speculations. And hence we may see, as before, First, That terms or words are absolutely necessary to the art of reasoning: Secondly, That our assent is here also, in every step of the process, deducible from association.

The propositions formed concerning natural bodies are often attended with a high degree of practical assent, arising chiefly from some supposed utility and importance, and which is no ways proportionable to the foregoing, or other such like allowed causes of rational assent. And in some cases the practical assent takes place before the rational. But then, after some time the rational assent is generated and cemented most firmly by the prevalence of the practical. This process is particularly observable in the regards paid to medicines, *i. e.* in the rational and practical assent to the propositions concerning their virtues.

It is to be observed, that children, novices, unlearned persons, &c. give, in many cases, a practical assent upon a single instance; and that this arises from the first and simplest of the associations here considered. The influence of the practical assent over the rational arises plainly from their being joined together in so many cases. The vividness of the ideas arising from the supposed utility, importance, &c. does also unite the subject and predicate sooner and closer, agreeably to what has been observed in the general account of association.

The evidences for past facts are a man's own memory, and the authority of others. These are the usual associates of true past facts, under proper restrictions, and therefore beget the readiness to affirm a past fact to be true, *i. e.* the rational assent. The integrity and knowledge of the witnesses, being the principal restriction, or requisite, in the accounts of past facts, become principal associates to the assent to them; and the contrary qualities to dissent.

If it be asked, how a narration of an event supposed to be certainly true, supposed doubtful, or supposed entirely fictitious, differs in its effect upon the mind, in the three circumstances here alleged, the words being the same in each, I answer, first, in having the terms *true, doubtful,* and *fictitious,* with a variety of usual associates to these, and the corresponding internal feelings of respect, anxiety, dislike, &c. connected with them respectively; whence the whole effects, exerted by each upon the mind, will differ considerably from one another. Secondly, If the event be of an interesting nature, as a great advantage accruing, the death of a near friend, the affecting related ideas will recur oftener, and by so recurring agitate the mind more, in proportion to the supposed truth of the event. And it confirms this, that the frequent recurrency of an interesting event, supposed doubtful, or even fictitious, does, by degrees, make it appear like a real one, as in reveries, reading romances, seeing plays, &c. This affection of mind may be called the practical assent to past facts; and it frequently draws after it the rational, as in the other instances above alleged.

The evidence for future facts is of the same kind with that for the propositions concerning natural bodies, being like it, taken from induction and analogy. This is the cause of the rational assent. The practical depends upon the recurrency of the ideas, and the degree of agitation produced by them in the mind. Hence reflection makes the practical assent grow for a long time after the rational is arisen to its height; or if the practical arise without the rational, in any considerable degree, which is often the case, it will generate the rational. Thus the sanguine are apt to believe and assert what they hope, and the timorous what they fear.

There are many speculative abstracted propositions in logic, metaphysics, ethics, controversial divinity, &c. the evidence for which is the coincidence or analogy of the abstract terms, in certain particular applications of them, or as considered in their grammatical relations. This causes the rational assent. As to the practical assent or dissent, it arises from the ideas of importance, reverence, piety, duty, ambition, jealousy, envy, self-interest, &c. which intermix themselves in these subjects, and, by doing so, in some cases add great strength to the rational assent; in others destroy it, and convert it into its opposite.

And thus it appears, that rational assent has different causes in propositions of different kinds, and practical likewise; that the causes of rational are also different from those of practical; that there is, however, a great affinity, and general resemblance, in all the causes; that rational and practical assent exert a perpetual reciprocal effect upon one another; and consequently, that the ideas belonging to assent and dissent, and their equivalents and relatives, are highly complex ones, unless in the cases of very simple propositions, such as mathematical ones. For besides the coincidence of ideas and terms, they include, in other cases, ideas of utility, importance, respect, disrespect, ridicule, religious affections, hope, fear, &c. and bear some gross general proportion to the vividness of these ideas.

Cor. I. When a person says, *video meliora proboque, deteriora se-*

quor[1]; it shews that the rational and practical assent are at variance, that they have opposite causes, and that neither of these has yet destroyed the other.

COR. II. The rational and practical faith in religious matters are excellent means of begetting each other.

COR. III. Vicious men, *i. e.* all persons who want practical faith, must be prejudiced against the historical and other rational evidences in favour of revealed religion.

COR. IV. It is impossible any person should be so sceptical, as not to have the complex ideas denoted by assent and dissent associated with a great variety of propositions, in the same manner, as in other persons; just as he must have the same ideas in general affixed to the words of his native language, as other men have. A pretended sceptic is therefore no more than a person who varies from the common usage in his application of a certain set of words, *viz.* truth, certainty, assent, dissent, &c.

COR. V. As there is a foundation for unity amongst mankind in the use and application of words, so there is for an unity in the assent, or complex ideas belonging to propositions; and a philosophical language, or any other method of bringing about the first unity, would much conduce to this. A careful examination of things, of the world natural, the human mind, the Scriptures, would conduce much also. But candour, simplicity, and an humble sense of our own ignorance, which may be called a religious or christian scepticism, is the principal requisite, and that without which this part of the confusion at Babel can never be remedied. When religion has equally and fully absorbed different persons, so that God is, in respect of them, all in all, as far as the present condition of mortality will permit, their practical assent must be the same; and therefore their rational cannot differ long or widely.

The ideas and internal feelings which arise in the mind, from words and propositions, may be compared to, and illustrated by, those which the appearances of different persons excite. Suppose two persons, *A* and *B,* to go together into a crowd, and there each of them to see a variety of persons whom he knew in different degrees, as well as many utter strangers. *A* would not have the same ideas and associations raised in him from viewing the several faces, dresses, &c. of the persons in the crowd, as *B,* partly from his having a different knowledge of, and acquaintance with them, partly from different predispositions to approve and disapprove. But let *A* and *B* become equally acquainted with them, and acquire, by education and association, the same predispositions of mind, and then they will at last make the same judgment of each of the persons whom they see.

1 "I see what is better and approve it, yet I pursue what is worst." Ovid, *Metamorphoses,* VIII, 20. Ed.

Cor. VI. Religious controversies concerning abstract propositions arise generally from the different degrees of respect paid to terms and phrases, which conduce little or nothing to the generation of practical faith, or of love to God, and trust in Him through Christ.

PROP. LXXXVII: *To deduce Rules for the Ascertainment of Truth, and Advancement of Knowledge, from the Mathematical Methods of considering Quantity.*

This is done in the doctrine of chances, with respect to the events there considered. And though we seldom have such precise *data,* in mixed sciences, as are there assumed, yet there are two remarks, of very general use and application, deducible from the doctrine of chances.

Thus, first, If the evidences brought for any proposition, fact, &c. be dependent on each other, so that the first is required to support the second, the second to support the third, &c. *i. e.* if a failure of any one of the evidences renders all the rest of no value, the separate probability of each evidence must be very great, in order to make the proposition credible; and this holds so much the more, as the dependent evidences are more numerous. For instance, if the value of each evidence be $\frac{1}{a}$, and the number of evidences be in n, then will the resulting probability be $\frac{1}{a^n}$. I here suppose absolute certainty to be denoted by 1; and consequently, that a can never be less than 1. Now it is evident, that $\frac{1}{a^n}$ decreases with every increase both of a and n.

Secondly, If the evidences brought for any proposition, fact, &c. be independent on each other, *i. e.* if they be not necessary to support each other, but concur, and can, each of them, when established upon its own proper evidences, be applied directly to establish the proposition, fact, &c. in question, the deficiency in the probability of each must be very great, in order to render the proposition perceptibly doubtful; and this holds so much the more, as the evidences are more numerous. For instance, if the evidences be all equal, and the common deficiency in each be $\frac{1}{a}$, if also the number of evidences be n as before, the deficiency of the resulting probability will be no more than $\frac{1}{a^n}$, which is practically nothing, where a and n are considerable. Thus if a and n be each equal to 10, $\frac{1}{a^n}$ will be $\frac{1}{10,000,000,000}$, or only one in ten thousand millions; a deficiency from certainty, which is utterly imperceptible to the human mind.

It is indeed evident, without having recourse to the doctrine of

chances, that the dependency of evidences makes the resulting probability weak, their independency strong. Thus a report passing from
one original author through a variety of successive hands loses much
of its credibility, and one attested by a variety of original witnesses
gains, in both cases, according to the number of successive reporters,
and original witnesses, though by no means proportionably thereto.
This is the common judgment of mankind, verified by observation and
experience. But the mathematical method of considering these things
is much more precise and satisfactory, and differs from the common
one, just as the judgment made of the degrees of heat by the thermometer does from that made by the hand.

We may thus also see in a shorter and simpler way that the resulting
probability may be sufficiently strong in dependent evidences, and of
little value in independent ones according as the separate probability
of each evidence is greater or less. Thus the principal facts of ancient
history are not less probable practically now, than ten or fifteen centuries ago, nor less so then, than in the times immediately succeeding;
because the diminution of evidence in each century is imperceptible.
For, if $\frac{1}{a}$ be equal to 1, $\frac{1}{a^n}$ will be equal to 1 also; and if the deficiency of $\frac{1}{a}$ from 1 be extremely small, that of $\frac{1}{a^n}$ will be extremely
small also, unless n be extremely great. And for the same reason a
large number of weak arguments proves little; for $\frac{1}{a}$ the deficiency of
each argument, being extremely great, $\frac{1}{a^n}$ the resulting deficiency of
independent evidences, will be extremely great also.

It appears likewise, that the inequality of the separate evidences
does not much affect this reasoning. In like manner, if the number of
evidences, dependent or independent, be great, we may make great
concessions as to the separate values of each. Again, a strong evidence in dependent ones can add nothing, but must weaken a little;
and, after a point is well settled by a number of independent ones, all
that come afterwards are useless, because they can do no more than
remove the imperceptible remaining deficiency, &c. And it will be of
great use to pursue these and such like deductions, both mathematically, and by applying them to proper instances selected from the sciences, and from common life, in order to remove certain prejudices,
which the use of general terms, and ways of speaking, with the various
associations adhering to them, is apt to introduce and fix upon the
mind. It cannot but assist us in the art of reasoning, thus to take to
pieces, recompose, and ascertain our evidences.

If it be asked, upon what authority absolute certainty is represented by unity, and the several degrees of probability by fractions less than unity, in the doctrine of chances? also, upon what authority the reasoning used in that doctrine is transferred to other subjects, and made general, as here proposed? I answer, that no person who weighs these matters carefully, can avoid giving his assent; and that this precludes all objections. No sceptic would, in fact, be so absurd as to lay two to one, where the doctrine of chances determines the probability to be equal on each side; and therefore we may be sure, that he gives a practical assent at least to the doctrine of chances.

M. De Moivre[1] has shewn, that where the causes of the happening of an event bear a fixed ratio to those of its failure, the happenings must bear nearly the same ratio to the failures, if the number of trials be sufficient; and that the last ratio approaches to the first indefinitely, as the number of trials increases. This may be considered as an elegant method of accounting for that order and proportion, which we every where see in the phænomena of nature. The determinate shapes, sizes, and mutual actions of the constituent particles of matter, fix the ratios between the causes for the happenings, and the failures; and therefore it is highly probable, and even necessary, as one may say, that the happenings and failures should perpetually recur in the same ratio to each other nearly, while the circumstances are the same. When the circumstances are altered, then new causes take place; and consequently there must be a new, but fixed ratio, between the happenings and the failures. Let the first circumstances be called A, the new ones B. If now the supposition be made so general, as equally to take in both A and B, the ratio of the happenings and failures will not be such as either A or B required. But still it will tend to a preciseness, just as they did, since the sum of the causes of the happenings must bear a fixed ratio to the sum of the causes of the failures.

An ingenious friend has communicated to me a solution of the inverse problem, in which he has shewn what the expectation is, when an event has happened p times, and failed q times, that the original ratio of the causes for the happening or failing of an event should deviate in any given degree from that of p to q. And it appears from this solution, that where the number of trials is very great, the deviation must be inconsiderable; which shews that we may hope to determine the proportions, and, by degrees, the whole nature, of unknown causes, by a sufficient observation of their effects.

The inferences here drawn from these two problems are evident to attentive persons, in a gross general way, from common methods of reasoning.

Let us, in the next place, consider the Newtonian differential

---

1 Abraham de Moivre (1667–1754), the French mathematician who fled to England in 1688, published *The Doctrine of Chances; or A Method of Calculating the Probabilities of Events in Play* (London, 1718). Ed.

method, and compare it with that of arguing from experiments and observations, by induction and analogy. This differential method teaches, having a certain number of the ordinates of any unknown curve given with the points of the absciss on which they stand, to find out such a general law for this curve, *i. e.* such an equation expressing the relation of an ordinate and absciss in all magnitudes of the absciss, as will suit the ordinates and points of the absciss given, in the unknown curve under consideration. Now here we may suppose the given ordinates standing upon given points to be analogous to effects, or the results of various experiments in given circumstances, the absciss analogous to all possible circumstances, and the equation afforded by the differential method to that law of action, which, being supposed to take place in the given circumstances, produces the given effects. And as the use of the differential method is to find the lengths of ordinates not given, standing upon points of the absciss that are given, by means of the equation, so the use of attempts to make general conclusions by induction and analogy, from particular effects or phænomena, in different given circumstances, by applying the general law conclusion to these circumstances.

This parallel is the more pertinent and instructive, inasmuch as the mathematical conclusion drawn by the differential method, though formed in a way that is strictly just, and so as to have the greatest possible probability in its favour, is, however, liable to the same uncertainties, both in kind and degree, as the general maxims of natural philosophy drawn from natural history, experiments, &c.

If many ordinates be given; if the distances of the points of the absciss, on which they stand, be equal and small; if the ordinate required lie amongst them, or near them; and if there be reason to think, that the curve itself is formed according to some simple, though unknown law; then may we conclude, that the new ordinate, determined by the equation, does not vary far from the truth. And if the resulting equation be simple, and always the same, from whatever given ordinates it be extracted, there is the greatest reason to think this to be the real original law or equation of the curve; and consequently that all its points and properties may be determined with perfect exactness by means of it: whereas, if the given ordinates be few, their distances great or unequal, the ordinate required considerably distant from many or most of them, the unknown curve be a line drawn at hazard, and the resulting equation different, where different ordinates are given, though their number be the same, there will be little probability of determining the new ordinate with exactness; however, still the differential method affords us the greatest probability which the *data* permit in such cases.

In like manner, if the experiments or observations be many, their circumstances nearly related to each other, and in a regular series, the circumstances of the effect to be investigated nearly related to them; also, if the real cause may be supposed to produce these effects, by the varieties of some simple law, the method of induction and analogy will carry great probability with it. And if the general conclusion or law be simple, and always the same, from whatever phænomena it be deduced, such as the three laws of nature, the doctrines of gravitation, and of the different refrangibility of light; or to go still higher, by taking a mathematical instance, the law for finding the coefficients of the integral powers of a binomial, deduced from mere trials in various powers; there can scarce remain any doubt, but that we are in possession of the true law inquired after, so as to be able to predict with certainty, in all cases where we are masters of the method of computation, or applying it; and have no reason to suspect, that other unknown laws interfere. But, if the given phænomena be few, their circumstances very different from each other, and from those of the effect to be predicted; if there be reason to suppose, that many causes concur in the producing these phænomena, so that the law of their production must be very complex; if a new hypothesis be required to account for every new combination of these phænomena; or, at least, one that differs considerably from itself; the best hypothesis which we can form, *i. e.* the hypothesis which is most conformable to all the phænomena, will amount to no more than an uncertain conjecture; and yet still it ought to be preferred to all others, as being the best that we can form.

That instantaneous and necessary coalescence of ideas, which makes intuitive evidence, may be considered as the highest kind of induction, and as amounting to a perfect coincidence of the effect concluded with those from which it is concluded. This takes place only in mathematics. Thus we infer, that 2 and 2 make 4, only from prior instances of having actually perceived this, and from the necessary coincidence of all these instances with all other possible ones of 2 and 2. Mathematical demonstrations are made up of a number of these, as was observed above.

Where the instances from whence the induction is made are alike, as far as we know, to that under consideration, at least in all things that affect the present inquiry, it affords the highest probability, and may be termed induction, in the proper sense of the word. Thus we infer, that the bread before us is nutritive and wholesome, because its smell, taste, ingredients, manner of composition, &c. are the same as those of other bread, which has often before been experienced to be so.

But, if the instance under consideration be in some respects like the foregoing ones, in others not, this kind of proof is generally termed one taken from analogy. Thus, if we argue from the use and action of the stomach in one animal to those in another, supposed to be unknown, there will be a probable hazard of being mistaken, proportional in general to the known difference of the two animals, as well as a probable evidence for the truth of part, at least, of what is advanced, proportional to the general resemblance of the two animals. But if, upon examination, the stomach, way of feeding, &c. of the second animal should be found, to sense, the same as in the first, the analogy might be considered as an induction properly so called, at least as approaching to it; for precise limits cannot be fixed here. If the second animal be of the same species, also of the same age, sex, &c. with the first, the induction becomes perpetually of a higher and a higher order, approaching more and more to the coincidence, which obtains in mathematical evidences, and yet never being able entirely to arrive at it. But then the difference, being only an infinitesimal fraction, as it were, becomes nothing to all practical purposes whatsoever. And if a man considers farther, that it would be hard to find a demonstration, that he does not mistake the plainest truths; this lessens the difference theoretically also.

It is often in our power to obtain an analogy where we cannot have an induction; in which case reasoning from analogy ought to be admitted; however, with all that uncertainty which properly belongs to it, considered as more or less distant from induction, as built upon more or fewer dependent or independent evidences, &c. Analogy may also, in all cases, be made use of as a guide to the invention. But coincidence in mathematical matters, and induction in others, wherever they can be had, must be sought for as the only certain tests of truth. However, induction seems to be a very sufficient evidence in some mathematical points, affording at least as much evidence there as in natural philosophy; and may be safely relied on in perplexed cases, such as complex series, till satisfactory demonstrations can be had.

The analogous natures of all the things about us are a great assistance in deciphering their properties, powers, laws, &c. inasmuch as what is minute or obscure in one may be explained and illustrated by the analogous particular in another, where it is large and clear. And thus all things become comments on each other in an endless reciprocation.

When there are various arguments for the same thing taken from induction or analogy, they may all be considered as supporting one another in the same manner as independent evidences. Thus, if it could be shewed, that the human understanding is entirely dependent on association, (as is remarked in this and the last section,) the many analogies and connexions between the understanding and affections, as these terms are commonly understood and contradistinguished by writers, would make it very probable, that association presides in the same manner in the generation of the affections; and *vice versâ*. And the more analogies, and mutual connexions, between the understanding and affections, were produced, so many more independent or concurrent evidences would there be for this prevalence of association in one, admitting it in the other. But, if now it be shewn farther, that the understanding and affections are not really distinct things, but only different names, which we give to the same kind of motions in the nervous system, on account of a difference in degree, and other differences which it would be tedious here to enumerate, but which make no difference in respect of the power of association, then all the arguments from analogy are transformed into one of induction; which, however, is stronger than the united force of them all. For now it may be shewed, that association must prevail in each motion in the brain, by which affection is expounded, from a large induction of particulars, in which it prevails in the generation of ideas, or of the motions by which they are expounded, and which we suppose to be proved to be of the same kind with those that expound the affections. Thus also inductions may be taken from the smell and taste of bread, to prove it wholesome; which would both be transformed into one simple argument stronger than both, could we see the internal constitution of the small parts of the bread, from whence its smell, and taste, and wholesomeness, are all derived. Thus, again, all the arguments of induction for the manner of extracting the square root in numbers vanish into the single demonstrative proof, as soon as this is produced. And the great business in all branches of knowledge is thus to reduce, unite, and simplify our evidences; so as that the one resulting proof, by being of a higher order, shall be more than equal in force to all the concurrent ones of the inferior orders.

Having now considered in what manner the doctrine of chances, and the Newtonian differential method, may serve to shew in general the value of dependent and independent or concurrent evidences, and the probability of general conclusions formed by induction and analogy; let us next inquire by what means we are to form these general conclusions, and discover their evidences. Now the different methods of doing this may be said to resemble respectively the rule of false in common arithmetic; the algebraic methods of bringing the unknown quantity into an equation, under a form capable of all the algebraic operations, addition, subtraction, &c.; the algebraic methods of finding the roots of equations of the higher orders by approximation; and the art of decyphering: all which four methods bear also a considerable resemblance to each other. I will consider them in order, and endeavour to shew how analogous methods may be introduced into the sciences in general to advantage.

First, then, As according to the rule of false, the arithmetician supposes a certain number to be that which is sought for; treats it as if it was that; and finding the deficiency or overplus in the conclusion, rectifies the error of his first position by a proportional addition or subtraction, and thus solves the problem; so it is useful in inquiries of all kinds to try all such suppositions as occur with any appearance of probability, to endeavour to deduce the real phænomena from them; and if they do not answer in some tolerable measure, to reject them at once; or if they do, to add, expunge, correct, and improve, till we have brought the hypothesis as near as we can to an agreement with nature. After this it must be left to be farther corrected and improved, or entirely disproved, by the light and evidence reflected upon it from the contiguous, and even, in some measure, from the remote branches of other sciences.

Were this method commonly used, we might soon expect a great advancement in the sciences. It would much abate that unreasonable fondness, which those who make few or no distinct hypotheses, have for such confused ones as occur accidentally to their imaginations, and recur afterwards by association. For the ideas, words, and reasonings, belonging to the favourite hypothesis, by recurring, and being much agitated in the brain, heat it, unite with each other, and so coalesce in the same manner, as genuine truths do from induction and analogy. Verbal and grammatical analogies and coincidences are advanced into real ones; and the words which pass often over the ear, in the form of subject and predicate, are from the influence of other associations made to adhere together insensibly, like subjects and predicates, that have a natural connexion. It is in vain to bid an inquirer form no hypothesis. Every phænomenon will suggest something of this kind: and, if he do not take care to state such as occur fully and fairly, and adjust them one to another, he may entertain a confused inconsistent mixture of all, of fictitious and real, possible and impossible: and become so persuaded of it, as that counter-associations shall not be able to break the unnatural bond. But he that forms hypotheses from the first, and tries them by the facts, soon rejects the most unlikely ones; and, being freed from these, is better qualified for the examination of those that are probable. He will also confute his own positions so often, as to fluctuate in equilibrio, in respect of prejudices, and so be at perfect liberty to follow the strongest evidences.

In like manner, the frequent attempts to make an hypothesis that shall suit the phænomena, must improve a man in the method of doing this; and beget in him by degrees an imperfect practical art, just as algebraists and decypherers, that are much versed in practice, are possessed of innumerable subordinate artifices, besides the principal general ones, that are taught by the established rules of their arts; and these, though of the greatest use to themselves, can scarce be explained or communicated to others. These artifices may properly be referred to the head of factitious sagacity, being the result of experience, and of impressions often repeated, with small variations from the general resemblance.

Lastly, The frequent making of hypotheses, and arguing from them synthetically, according to the several variations and combinations of which they are capable, would suggest numerous phænomena, that otherwise escape notice, and lead to *experimenta crucis,* not only in respect of the hypothesis under consideration, but of many others. The variations and combinations just mentioned suggest things to the invention, which the imagination unassisted is far unequal to; just as it would be impossible for a man to write down all the changes upon eight bells, unless he had some method to direct him.

But this method of making definite hypotheses, and trying them, is far too laborious and mortifying for us to hope that inquirers will in general pursue it. It would be of great use to such as intend to pursue it, to make hypotheses for the phænomena, whose theories are well ascertained; such as those of the circulation of the blood, of the pressure of the air, of the different refrangibility of the rays of light, &c. and see how they are gradually compelled into the right road, even from wrong suppositions fairly compared with the phænomena. This would habituate the mind to a right method, and beget the factitious sagacity above-mentioned.

The second of the four methods proposed is, that of bringing the unknown quantity to an equation, and putting it into a form susceptible of all the algebraic operations. Now to this answers, in philosophy, the art of giving names, expressing nothing definite, as to manner, quantity, &c. and then inserting these names, or indefinite terms, in all the enunciations of the phænomena, to see whether, from a comparison of these enunciations with each other, where the terms are used in the greatest latitude, some restrictions, something definite in manner, degree, or mutual relation, will not result. Things that are quite unknown have often fixed relations to one another, and sometimes relations to things known, which, though not determinable with certainty and precision, may yet be determined in some probable manner, or within certain limits. Now as in algebra it is impossible to express the relation of the unknown quantity to other quantities known or unknown, till it has a symbol assigned to it of the same kind with those that denote the others; so in philosophy we must give names to unknown quantities, qualities, causes, &c. not in order to rest in them, as the Aristotelians did, but to have a fixed expression, under which to treasure up all that can be known of the unknown cause, &c. in the imagination and memory, or in writing for future inquirers.

But then it is necessary, for the same reasons, that these terms should have no more of secondary ideas from prior associations, than the terms *x* and *y* in algebra.—Whence, if we use old terms excluding the old associations, the reader should be made aware of this at first, and incidentally reminded of it afterwards. Sir Isaac Newton has used the words *æther, attraction,* and some others, in this way, not resting in them, but enumerating a great variety of phænomena; from the due comparison of which with each other, and with such as farther observation and experiments shall suggest, their laws and action will, perhaps, be discovered hereafter; so that we may be able to predict the phænomena. There is also an instance of the proper manner of reasoning concerning the knowable relations of unknown things in Mr. Mede's *Clavis Apocalyptica*.[1]

The third method is that of approximating to the roots of equations. Here a first position is obtained, which, though not accurate, approaches, however, to the truth. From this, applied to the equations, a second position is deduced, which approaches nearer to the truth than the first; from the second, a third, &c. till the analyst obtains the true root, or such an approximation as is practically equivalent, every preceding discovery being made the foundation for a subsequent one, and the equation resolving itself, as it were, gradually. Now this is indeed the way, in which all advances in science are carried on; and scientific persons are in general aware, that it is and must be so. However, I thought it not improper to illustrate this general process by a parallel taken from algebra, in which there is great exactness and beauty. Besides, writers do not often dispose their arguments and approximations in this way, though for want of it they lose much of their clearness and force; and, where the writer does this, the reader is frequently apt to overlook the order of proofs and positions.

Sir Isaac Newton's Optics, Chronology, and Comment on Daniel, abound with instances to this purpose: and it is probable, that his great abilities and practice in algebraic investigations led him to it insensibly. In his Chronology he first shews in gross, that the technical chronology of the ancient Greeks led them to carry their authorities higher than the truth; and then, that the time of the Sesostris mentioned by the Greek historians was near that of Sesac mentioned in the Old Testament; whence it follows, that these two persons were the same; and consequently, that the exact time of Sesostris's expedition may now be fixed by the Old Testament. And now, having two points absolutely fixed, *viz.* the expeditions of Sesostris and Xerxes, he fixes all the most remarkable intermediate events; and these being also fixed, he goes on to the less remarkable ones in the Greek history. And the chronology of the Greeks being rectified, he makes use of it to rectify the contemporary affairs of the Egyptians, Assyrians, Babylonians,

[1] Joseph Mede (1586–1638), an encyclopedic theologian, Biblical scholar and classicist of Christ's College, Cambridge, published his study of the Apocalypse in London, 1627; he was particularly interested in allegorical interpretations of the Bible. Ed.

Medes, and Persians, making use of the preceding step every where, for the determination of the subsequent one. He does also, in many cases, cast light and evidence back from the subsequent ones upon the precedent. But the other is his own order of proof, and ought to be that in which those who call his chronology in question should proceed to inquire into it.

The fourth and last method is that used by decypherers, in investigating words written in unknown characters, or in known ones substituted for one another, according to secret and complex laws. The particular methods by which this is done are only known to those who study and practise this art: however, it is manifest in general, that it is an algebra of its own kind, and that it bears a great resemblance to the three foregoing methods; also, that it may be said, with justness and propriety in general, that philosophy is the art of decyphering the mysteries of nature; that criticism bears an obvious relation to decyphering; and that every theory which can explain all the phænomena, has all the same evidence in its favour, that it is possible the key of a cypher can have from its explaining that cypher. And if the cause assigned by the theory have also its real existence proved, it may be compared to the explanation of a cypher; which may be verified by the evidence of the person who writes in that cypher.

These speculations may seem uncouth to those who are not conversant in mathematical inquiries; but to me they appear to cast light and evidence upon the methods of pursuing knowledge in other matters, to sharpen the natural sagacity, and to furnish *loci* for invention. It appears also not impossible, that future generations should put all kinds of evidences and inquiries into mathematical forms; and, as it were, reduce Aristotle's ten Categories, and Bishop Wilkins's forty *Summa Genera*,[1] to the head of quantity alone, so as to make mathematics and logic, natural history and civil history, natural philosophy and philosophy of all other kinds, coincide *omni ex parte*.

.   .   .   .   .

OF LOGIC

It is the purport of this and the foregoing section, to give imperfect rudiments of such an art of logic, as is defined above, *i. e.* as should make use of words in the way of mathematical symbols, and proceed by mathematical methods of investigation and computation in inquiries of all sorts. Not that the *data* in the sciences are as yet, in general, ripe for such methods; but they seem to tend to this more and more perpetually, in particular branches, so that it cannot be amiss to prepare ourselves, in some measure, previously.

1 John Wilkins (1614–1672), Bishop of Chester and Fellow of the Royal Society, was the author of *An Essay Towards a Real Character and a Philosophical Language* (London, 1688). Hartley's reference is to Chapter I, Second Part. Ed.

Logic, and metaphysics, which are nearly allied to logic, seem more involved in obscurity and perplexity, than any other part of science. This has probably been the chief source of scepticism, since it appears necessary, that that part of knowledge, which is the basis of all others, which is to shew wherein certainty, probability, possibility, improbability, and impossibility, consist, should itself be free from all doubt and uncertainty.

It seems also, that as logic is required for the basis of the other sciences, so a logic of a second order is required for a basis to that of the first, of a third for that of a second, and so on *sine limite:* which, if it were true, would, from the nature of dependent evidences, prove that logic is either absolutely certain, or absolutely void of all probability. For, if the evidence for it be ever so little inferior to unity, it will, by the continual infinite multiplication required in dependent evidences infinitely continued, bring itself down to nothing. Therefore, *e converso,* since no one can say, that the rules of logic are void of all probability, the *summum genus* of them must be certain. This *summum genus* is the necessary coalescence of the subject with the predicate. But the argument here alleged is merely one *ad hominem,* and not the natural way of treating the subject. The necessary coalescence just spoken of carries its own evidence with it. It is necessary from the nature of the brain, and that in the most confirmed sceptic, as well as in any other person. And we need only inquire into the history of the brain, and the physiological influences of words and symbols upon it by association, in order to see this. I am also inclined to believe, that the method here proposed of considering words and sentences as impressions, whose influence upon the mind is entirely to be determined by the associations heaped upon them in the intercourses of life, and endeavouring to determine these associations, both analytically and synthetically, will cast much light upon logical subjects, and cut off the sources of many doubts and differences.

As the theories of all other arts and sciences must be extracted from them, so logic, which contains the theory of all these theories, must be extracted from these theories; and yet this is not to reason in a circle in either case, since the theory is first extracted from self-evident or allowed particulars, and then applied to particulars not yet known, in order to discover and prove them.

It may not be amiss here to take notice how far the theory of these papers has led me to differ in respect of logic, from Mr. Locke's excellent *Essay on Human Understanding,* to which the world are so much indebted for removing prejudices and incumbrances, and advancing real and useful knowledge.

First, then, It appears to me, that all the most complex ideas arise from sensation; and that reflection is not a distinct source, as Mr. Locke makes it.

Secondly, Mr. Locke ascribes ideas to many words, which, as I have defined idea, cannot be said to have any immediate and precise ones; but only to admit of definitions. However, let definition be substituted instead of idea, in these cases, and then all Mr. Locke's excellent rules concerning words, delivered in his third book, will suit the theory of these papers.

As to the first difference, which I think may be called an error in Mr. Locke, it is, however, of little consequence. We may conceive, that he called such ideas as he could analyse up to sensation, ideas of sensation; the rest ideas of reflection, using reflection, as a term of art, denoting an unknown quantity. Besides which, it may be remarked, that the words which, according to him, stand for ideas of reflection, are in general words, that, according to the theory of these papers, have no ideas, but definitions only. And thus the first difference is, as it were, taken away by the second; for, if these words have no immediate ideas, there will be no occasion to have recourse to reflection as a source of ideas; and, upon the whole, there is no material repugnancy between the consequences of this theory, and any thing advanced by Mr. Locke.

The ingenious Bishop Berkeley has justly observed against Mr. Locke, that there can be no such thing as abstract ideas, in the proper sense of the word idea. However, this does not seem to vitiate any considerable part of Mr. Locke's reasoning. Substitute definition for idea in the proper places, and his conclusions will hold good in general.

.   .   .   .   .

SECTION IV

OF MEMORY

PROP. XC: *To examine how far the Phænomena of Memory are agreeable to the foregoing Theory.*

Memory was defined in the introduction to be that faculty by which traces of sensations and ideas recur, or are recalled, in the same order and proportion, accurately or nearly, as they were once presented.

Now here we may observe,

First, That memory depends entirely or chiefly on the state of the brain. For diseases, concussions of the brain, spirituous liquors, and some poisons, impair or destroy it; and it generally returns again with the return of health, from the use of proper medicines and methods. And all this is peculiarly suitable to the notion of vibrations. If sensations and ideas arise from peculiar vibrations, and dispositions to vibrate, in the medullary substance of the brain, it is easy to conceive, that the causes above alleged may so confound the sensations and ideas, as that the usual order and proportion of the idea shall be destroyed.

Secondly, The rudiments of memory are laid in the perpetual recurrency of the same impressions, and clusters of impressions. How these leave traces, in which the order is preserved, may be understood from the eighth, ninth, tenth, and eleventh propositions.

The traces which letters, and words, *i. e.* clusters of letters, leave, afford an instance and example of this. And, as in languages the letters are fewer than the syllables, the syllables than the words, and the words than the sentences, so the single sensible impressions, and the small clusters of them, are comparatively few in respect of the large clusters; and, being so, they must recur more frequently, so as the sooner to beget those traces which I call the rudiments or elements of memory. When these traces or ideas begin to recur frequently, this also contributes to fix them, and their order, in the memory, in the same manner as the frequent impression of the objects themselves.

Thirdly, Suppose now a person so far advanced in life, as that he has learnt all these rudiments, *i. e.* that he has ideas of the common appearances and occurrences of life, under a considerable variety of subordinate circumstances, which recur to his imagination from the slightest causes, and with the most perfect facility; and let us ask, how he can be able to remember or recollect a past fact, consisting of one thousand single particulars, or of one hundred such clusters as are called the rudiments of memory; ten single particulars being supposed to constitute a rudiment? First, then, We may observe, that there are only one hundred links wanting in the chain; for he has already learnt considerable exactness in the subordinate circumstances of the one hundred clusters; and perfect exactness is not to be supposed or required.—Secondly, The one hundred clusters recur again and again to the imagination for some time after the fact, in a quick and transient manner, as those who attend sufficiently to what passes in their own minds may perceive; and this both makes the impression a little deeper, and also serves to preserve the order. If the person attempts to recollect soon after the impression, the effect remaining in the brain is sufficient to enable him to do this with the accuracy required and experienced; if a longer time intervene, before he attempts to recollect, still the number of involuntary recurrences makes up in some measure for the want of this voluntary recollection. However, the power of recollection declines in general, and is entirely lost by degrees. It confirms this reasoning, that a new set of strong impressions destroys this power of recollection. For this must both obliterate the effects of the foregoing impressions, and prevent the recurrency of the ideas.— Thirdly, As the single impressions, which make the small clusters, are not combined together at hazard, but according to a general tenor in nature, so the clusters which make facts succeed each other according to some general tenor likewise. Now this both lessens the number of varieties, and shews that the association between many of the clusters, or rudiments, or one hundred links supposed to be wanting, is cemented already. This may be both illustrated and exemplified by the observation, that it is difficult to remember even well-known words that have no connexion with each other, and more so to remember collections of barbarous terms; whereas adepts in any science remember the things of that science with a surprising exactness and facility. —Fourthly, Some clusters are excluded from succeeding others, by ideas of inconsistency, impossibility, and by the methods of reasoning, of which we become masters as we advance in life.—Fifthly, The visible impressions which concur in the past fact, by being vivid, and preserving the order of place, often contribute greatly to preserve the order of time, and to suggest the clusters which may be wanting. —Sixthly, It is to be observed, that as we think in words, both the impressions and the recurrences of ideas will be attended with words; and these words, from the great use and familiarity of language, will fix themselves strongly in the fancy, and by so doing bring up the associated trains of ideas in the proper order, accurately or nearly. And thus, when a person relates a past fact, the ideas do in some cases suggest the words, whilst in others the words suggest the ideas. Hence illiterate persons do not remember nearly so well as others, *cæteris paribus*. And I suppose the same is true of deaf persons in a still greater degree. But it arises hence also, that many mistakes in the subordinate circumstances are committed in the relations of past facts, if the relater descend to minute particulars. For the same reasons these mistakes will be so associated with the true facts after a few relations, that the relater himself shall believe that he remembers them distinctly.—Seventhly, The mistakes which are committed both on the foregoing account and others, make considerable abatements in the difficulty here to be solved.

Fourthly, Let it now be asked, in what the recollection of a past fact, consisting of one hundred clusters, as above, differs from the transit of the same one hundred clusters, over the fancy, in the way of a reverie? I answer, partly in the vividness of the clusters, partly and principally in the readiness and strength of the associations, by which they are cemented together. This follows from what has been already delivered; but it may be confirmed also by many other observations. —Thus, first, Many persons are known by relating the same false story over and over again, *i. e.* by magnifying the ideas, and their associations, at last to believe that they remember it. It makes as vivid an impression upon them, and hangs as closely together, as an assemblage of past facts recollected by memory.—Secondly, All men are sometimes at a loss to know whether clusters of ideas that strike the fancy strongly, and succeed each other readily and immediately, be recollections, or mere reveries. And the more they agitate the matter in the mind, the more does the reverie appear like a recollection. It resembles this, that if in endeavouring to recollect a verse, a wrong word, suiting the place, first occurs, and afterwards the right one, it is difficult during the then present agitation to distinguish the right one. But afterwards, when this agitation is subsided, the right word easily regains its place. Persons of irritable nervous systems are more subject to such fallacies than others. And madmen often impose upon themselves in this way, *viz.* from the vividness of their ideas and associations, produced by bodily causes. The same thing often happens in dreams. The vividness of the new scene often makes it appear like one that we remember and are well acquainted with.—Thirdly, If the specific nature of memory consist in the great vigour of the ideas, and their associations, then, as this vigour abates, it ought to suggest to us a length of time elapsed; and *vice versâ*, if it be kept up, the distance of time ought to appear contracted. Now this last is the case: for the death of a friend, or any interesting event, often recollected and related, appears to have happened but yesterday, as we term it, *viz.* on account of the vividness of the clusters, and their associations, corresponding to the nature of a recent event.—Fourthly, It is not, however, to be here supposed, that we have not many other ways of distinguishing real recollections from mere reveries. For the first are supported by their connexion with known and allowed facts, by various methods of reasoning, and having been related as real recollections, &c.

Fifthly, In like manner we distinguish a new place, book, person, &c. from one which we remember, supposing both to be presented in like circumstances. The parts, associates, &c. of that which we remember, strike us more strongly, are suggested by each other, and hang together, which does not hold of the new. The old does also suggest many associates, which a new one in like circumstances would not. And if from the then state of fancy, the distance of time, &c. there be any doubt of these things either with respect to the old or new, a like doubt arises in respect of the memory. An attentive person may observe, that he determines of such things, whether they be old or new, by the vividness of the ideas, and their power of suggesting each other, and foreign associates.

Some persons seem to suppose, that the soul surveys one object, the old for instance, and comparing it with the impressions which a similar new one would excite, calls the old one an object remembered. But this is like supposing an eye within the eye to view the pictures made by objects upon the *retina*. Not to mention, that the soul cannot in the same instant, during the same τὸ νῦν[1] survey both the old and new, and compare them together; nor is there any evidence, that this is done in fact. A person who inquires into the nature of memory, may indeed endeavour to state the difference between the impressions of old and new, as I have done here; but this is a speculation that few persons concern themselves with, whereas all remember and apply the words relative to memory just as they do other words. We may conclude therefore, that the difference of vividness and connexion in the ideas, with the other associates of recollections, are a sufficient foundation for the proper use of the words relative to the memory, just as in other like cases.

Sixthly, The peculiar imperfection of the memory in children tallies with the foregoing account of this faculty; and indeed this account may be considered as a gross general history of the successive growth of the memory, in passing from childhood to adult age. Children must learn by degrees the ideas of single impressions, the clusters which I call rudiments, and the most usual connexions and combinations of these. They have also the use of words, and of objects and incidents, as signs and symbols, with the proper method of reasoning upon them, to learn; and during their noviciate in these things their memories must labour under great imperfections. It appears also, that the imperfections peculiar to children correspond in kind as well as degree to the reasons here assigned for them. Their not being able to digest past facts in order of time is, in great measure, owing to their not having the proper use of the symbols, whereby time is denoted.

Seventhly, The peculiar imperfection of the memory in aged persons tallies also with the foregoing account. The vibrations, and dispositions to vibrate, in the small medullary particles, and their associations, are all so fixed by the callosity of the medullary substance, and by repeated impressions and recurrences, that new impressions can scarce enter, that they recur seldom, and that the parts which do recur bring in old trains from established associations, instead of continuing those which were lately impressed. Hence one may almost predict what very old persons will say or do upon common occurrences. Which is also the case frequently with persons of strong passions, for reasons that are not very unlike. When old persons relate the incidents of their youth with great precision, it is rather owing to the memory of many preceding memories, recollections, and relations, than to the memory of the thing itself.

Eighthly, In recovering from concussions, and other disorders of the brain, it is usual for the patient to recover the power of remembering the then present common incidents for minutes, hours, and days, by degrees; also the power of recalling the events of his life preceding

1 "Instant" or "indivisible unit of time." Ed.

his illness. At length he recovers this last power perfectly, and at the same time forgets almost all that passed in his illness, even those things which he remembered, at first, for a day or two. Now the reason of this I take to be, that upon a perfect recovery the brain recovers its natural state, *i. e.* all its former dispositions to vibrate; but that such as took place during the preternatural state of the brain, *i. e.* during his illness, are all obliterated by the return of the natural state. In like manner dreams, which happen in a peculiar state of the brain, *i. e.* in sleep, vanish, as soon as vigilance, a different state, takes place. But if they be recollected immediately upon waking, and thus connected with the state of vigilance, they may be remembered. But I shall have occasion to be more explicit on this head in the next Section.

Ninthly, It is very difficult to make any plausible conjectures why some persons of very weak judgments, not much below idiots, are endued with a peculiar extraordinary memory. This memory is generally the power of recollecting a large group of words, suppose, as those of a sermon, in a short time after they are heard, with wonderful exactness and readiness; but then the whole is obliterated, after a longer time, much more completely than in persons of common memories and judgments. One may perhaps conjecture, that the brain receives all dispositions to vibrate sooner in these persons, and lets them go sooner, than in others. And the last may contribute to the first: for, new impressions may take place more deeply and precisely, if there be few old ones to oppose them. The most perfect memory is that which can both receive most readily, and retain most durably. But we may suppose, that there are limits, beyond which these two different powers cannot consist with each other.

Tenthly, When a person desires to recollect a thing that has escaped him, suppose the name of a person, or visible object, he recalls the visible idea, or some other associate, again and again, by a voluntary power, the desire generally magnifying all the ideas and associations; and thus bringing in the association and idea wanted, at last. However, if the desire be great, it changes the state of the brain, and has an opposite effect; so that the desired idea does not recur, till all has subsided; perhaps not even then.

Eleventhly, All our voluntary powers are of the nature of memory; as may be easily seen from the foregoing account of it, compared with the account of the voluntary powers given in the first chapter. And it agrees remarkably with this, that, in morbid affections of the memory, the voluntary actions suffer a like change and imperfection.

Twelfthly, For the same reasons the whole powers of the soul may be referred to the memory, when taken in a large sense. Hence, though some persons may have strong memories with weak judgments, yet no man can have a strong judgment with a weak original power of retaining and remembering.

SECTION V

OF IMAGINATION, REVERIES, AND DREAMS

PROP. XCI: *To examine how far the Phœnomena of Imagination, Reveries, and Dreams, are agreeable to the foregoing Theory.*

The recurrence of ideas, especially visible and audible ones, in a vivid manner, but without any regard to the order observed in past facts, is ascribed to the power of imagination or fancy. Now here we may observe, that every succeeding thought is the result either of some new impression, or of an association with the preceding. And this is the common opinion. It is impossible indeed to attend so minutely to the succession of our ideas, as to distinguish and remember for a sufficient time the very impression or association which gave birth to each thought; but we can do this as far as it can be expected to be done, and in so great a variety of instances, that our argument for the prevalence of the foregoing principle of association in all instances, except those of new impressions, may be esteemed a complete induction.

A reverie differs from imagination only in that the person being more attentive to his own thoughts, and less disturbed by foreign objects, more of his ideas are deducible from association, and fewer from new impressions.

It is to be observed, however, that in all the cases of imagination and reverie, the thoughts depend, in part, upon the then state of body or mind. A pleasurable or painful state of the stomach or brain, joy or grief, will make all the thoughts warp their own way, little or much. But this exception is as agreeable to the foregoing theory, as the general prevalence of association just laid down.

We come next to dreams. I say then, that dreams are nothing but the imaginations, fancies, or reveries of a sleeping man; and that they are deducible from the three following causes; *viz.* First, The impressions and ideas lately received, and particularly those of the preceding day. Secondly, The state of the body, particularly of the stomach and brain. And, thirdly, Association.

That dreams are, in part, deducible from the impression and ideas of the preceding day, appears from the frequent recurrence of these in greater or lesser clusters, and especially of the visible ones, in our dreams. We sometimes take in ideas of longer date, in part, on account of their recency: however, in general, ideas that have not affected the mind for some days, recur in dreams only from the second or third cause here assigned.

That the state of the body affects our dreams, is evident from the dreams of sick persons, and of those who labour under indigestions, spasms, and flatulencies.

Lastly, We may perceive ourselves to be carried on from one thing to another in our dreams partly by association.

It is also highly agreeable to the foregoing theory to expect, that each of the three foregoing causes should have an influence upon the trains of ideas that are presented in dreams.

Let us now see how we can solve the most usual phænomena of dreams upon these principles.

First, then, The scenes which present themselves are taken to be real. We do not consider them as the work of the fancy; but suppose ourselves present, and actually seeing and hearing what passes. Now this happens, First, Because we have no other reality to oppose to the ideas which offer themselves, whereas in the common fictions of the fancy, while we are awake, there is always a set of real external objects striking some of our senses, and precluding a like mistake there: or, if we become quite inattentive to external objects, the reverie does so far put on the nature of a dream, as to appear a reality. Secondly, The trains of visible ideas, which occur in dreams, are far more vivid than common visible ideas; and therefore may the more easily be taken for actual impressions. For what reasons these ideas should be so much more vivid, I cannot presume to say. I guess, that the exclusion of real impressions has some share, and the increased heat of the brain may have some likewise. The fact is most observable in the first approaches of sleep; all the visible ideas beginning then to be more than usually glaring.

Secondly, There is a great wildness and inconsistency in our dreams. For the brain, during sleep, is in a state so different from that in which the usual associations were formed, that they can by no means take place as they do during vigilance. On the contrary, the state of the body suggests such ideas, amongst those that have been lately impressed, as are most suitable to the various kinds and degrees of pleasant and painful vibrations excited in the stomach, brain, or some other part. Thus a person who has taken opium, sees either gay scenes, or ghastly ones, according as the opium excites pleasant or painful vibrations in the stomach. Hence it will follow, that ideas will rise successively in dreams, which have no such connexion as takes place in nature, in actual impressions, nor any such as is deducible from association. And yet, if they rise up quick and vividly one after another, as subjects, predicates, and other associates use to do, they will be affirmed of each other, and appear to hang together. Thus the same person appears in two places at the same time; two persons appearing successively in the same place coalesce into one; a brute is supposed to speak (when the idea of voice comes from that quarter), or to handle; any idea, qualification, office, &c. coinciding in the instant of time with the idea of one's self, or of another person, adheres immediately, &c. &c.

Thirdly, We do not take notice of, or are offended at, these inconsistencies; but pass on from one to another. For the associations, which should lead us thus to take notice, and be offended, are, as it were, asleep; the bodily causes also hurrying us on to new and new trains successively. But if the bodily state be such as favours ideas of anxiety and perplexity, then the inconsistency and apparent impossibility, occurring in dreams, are apt to give great disturbance and uneasiness. It is to be observed likewise, that we forget the several parts of our dreams very fast in passing from one to another; and that this lessens the apparent inconsistencies, and their influences.

Fourthly, It is common in dreams for persons to appear to themselves to be transferred from one place to another, by a kind of sailing or flying motion. This arises from the change of the apparent magnitude and position of the images excited in the brain, this change being such as a change of distance and position in ourselves would have occasioned. Whatever the reasons be, for which visible images are excited in sleep, like to the objects with which we converse when awake, the same reasons will hold for changes of apparent magnitude and position also; and these changes in fixed objects, being constantly associated with motions in ourselves when awake, will infer these motions when asleep. But then we cannot have the idea of the *vis inertiæ* of our own bodies, answering to the impressions in walking; because the nerves of the muscles either do not admit of such miniature vibrations in sleep; or do not transmit ideas to the mind in consequence thereof; whence we appear to sail, fly, or ride. Yet sometimes a person seems to walk, and even to strike, just as in other cases he seems to feel the impression of a foreign body on his skin.

Those who walk and talk in their sleep, have evidently the nerves of the muscles concerned so free, as that vibrations can descend from the internal parts of the brain, the peculiar residence of ideas, into them. At the same time the brain itself is so oppressed, that they have scarce any memory. Persons who read inattentively, *i. e.* see and speak almost without remembering, also those who labour under such a morbid loss of memory, as that though they see, hear, speak, and act, *pro re nata,* from moment to moment, yet they forget all immediately, somewhat resemble the persons who walk and talk in sleep.

Fifthly, Dreams consist chiefly of visible imagery. This agrees remarkably with the perpetual impressions made upon the optic nerves and corresponding parts of the brain during vigilance, and with the distinctness and vividness of the images impressed.

We may observe also, that the visible imagery in dreams is composed, in a considerable degree, of fragments of visible appearances lately impressed. For the disposition to these vibrations must be greater than to others, *cæteris paribus,* at the same time that by the imperfection and interruption of the associations, only fragments, not whole images, will generally appear. The fragments are so small, and so intermixed with other fragments and appearances, that it is difficult to trace them up to the preceding day; the shortness of our memory contributing also not a little thereto.

It happens in dreams, that the same fictitious places are presented again and again at the distance of weeks and months, perhaps during the whole course of life. These places are, I suppose, compounded at first, probably early in youth, of fragments of real places, which we have seen. They afterwards recur in dreams, because the same state of brain recurs; and when this has happened for some successions, they may be expected to recur at intervals during life. But they may also admit of variations, especially before frequent recurrency has established and fixed them.

Sixthly, It has been observed already, that many of the things which are presented in dreams, appear to be remembered by us, or, at least, as familiar to us; and that this may be solved by the readiness with which they start up, and succeed one another, in the fancy.

Seventhly, It has also been remarked, that dreams ought to be soon forgotten, as they are in fact; because the state of the brain suffers great changes in passing from sleep to vigilance. The wildness and inconsistency of our dreams render them still more liable to be forgotten. It is said that a man may remember his dreams best by continuing in the same posture in which he dreamt; which, if true, would be a remarkable confirmation of the doctrine of vibrations; since those which take place in the medullary substance of the brain would be least disturbed and obliterated by this means.

Eighthly, the dreams which are presented in the first part of the night are, for the most part, much more confused, irregular, and difficult to be remembered, than those which we dream towards the morning; and these last are often rational to a considerable degree, and regulated according to the usual course of our associations. For the brain begins then to approach to the state of vigilance, or that in which the usual associations were formed and cemented. However, association has some power even in wild and inconsistent dreams.

COR. I. As the prophecies were, many of them, communicated in the way of divine visions, trances, or dreams, so they bear many of the foregoing marks of dreams. Thus they deal chiefly in visible imagery; they abound with apparent impossibilities, and deviations from common life, of which yet the prophets take not the least notice: they speak of new things as of familiar ones: they are carried in the spirit from place to place; things requiring a long series of time in real life are transacted in the prophetical visions as soon as seen; they ascribe to themselves and others new names, offices, &c.; every thing has a real existence conferred upon it; there are singular combinations of fragments of visible appearances; and God himself is represented in a visible shape, which of all other things must be most offensive to a pious Jew. And it seems to me that these and such like criterions might establish the genuineness of the prophecies, exclusively of all other evidences.

COR. II. The wildness of our dreams seems to be of singular use to us, by interrupting and breaking the course of our associations. For, if we were always awake, some accidental associations would be so much cemented by continuance, as that nothing could afterwards disjoin them; which would be madness.

COR. III. A person may form a judgment of the state of his bodily health, and of his temperance, by the general pleasantness or unpleasantness of his dreams. There are also many useful hints relating to the strength of our passion deducible from them.

CONCLUSION

CONTAINING SOME REMARKS ON THE MECHANISM OF THE HUMAN MIND

Besides the consequences flowing from the doctrine of association, which are delivered in the corollaries to the fourteenth proposition, there is another, which is thought by many to have a pernicious tendency in respect of morality and religion; and which therefore it will be proper that I should consider particularly.

The consequence I mean is that of the mechanism or necessity of human actions, in opposition to what is generally termed free-will. Here then I will,

First, State my notion of the mechanism or necessity of human actions.

Secondly, Give such reasons as induce me to embrace the opinion of the mechanism of human actions.

Thirdly, Consider the objections and difficulties attending this opinion.

And, lastly, Allege some presumptions in favour of it from its consequences.

By the mechanism of human actions I mean, that each action results from the previous circumstances of body and mind, in the same manner, and with the same certainty, as other effects do from their mechanical causes; so that a person cannot do indifferently either of the actions A, and its contrary a, while the previous circumstances are the same; but is under an absolute necessity of doing one of them, and that only. Agreeably to this I suppose, that by free-will is meant a power of doing either the action *A,* or its contrary *a;* while the previous circumstances remain the same.

If by free-will be meant a power of beginning motion, this will come to the same thing; since, according to the opinion of mechanism, as here explained, man has no such power; but every action, or bodily motion, arises from previous circumstances, or bodily motions, already existing in the brain, *i. e.* from vibrations, which are either the immediate effect of impressions then made, or the remote compound effect of former impressions, or both.

But if by free-will be meant any thing different from these two definitions of it, it may not perhaps be inconsistent with the mechanism of the mind here laid down. Thus, if free-will be defined the power of doing what a person desires or wills to do, of deliberating, suspending, choosing, &c. or of resisting the motives of sensuality, ambition, resentment, &c. Free-will, under certain limitations, is not only consistent with the doctrine of mechanism, but even flows from it; since it appears from the foregoing theory, that voluntary and semi-voluntary powers of calling up ideas, of exciting and restraining affections, and of performing and suspending actions, arise from the mechanism of our natures. This may be called free-will in the popular and practical sense, in contradistinction to that which is opposed to mechanism, and which may be called free-will in the philosophical sense.

I proceed now to the arguments which favour the opinion of mechanism.

First, then, it is evident to, and allowed by all, that the actions of mankind proceed, in many cases, from motives, *i. e.* from the influence which the pleasures and pains of sensation, imagination, ambition, self-interest, sympathy, theopathy, and the moral sense, have over them. And these motives seem to act like all other causes. When the motive is strong, the action is performed with vigour; when weak, feebly. When a contrary motive intervenes, it checks or over-rules, in proportion to its relative strength, as far as one can judge. So that where the motives are the same, the actions cannot be different; where the motives are different, the actions cannot be the same. And it is matter of common observation, that this is the case in fact, in the principal actions of life, and such where the motives are of a magnitude sufficient to be evident. It is reasonable therefore to interpret the obscure cases by the evident ones; and to infer, that there are in all instances motives of a proper kind and degree, which generate each action; though they are sometimes not seen through their minuteness, or through the inattention or ignorance of the observer. Agreeably to which, those persons, who study the causes and motives of human actions, may decypher them much more completely, both in themselves, and those with whom they converse, than others can.

Suppose now a person able to decypher all his own actions in this way, so as to shew that they corresponded in kind and degree to the motives arising from the seven classes of pleasures and pains considered in this theory; also able to decypher the principal actions of others in the same way: this would be as good evidence, that motives were the mechanical causes of actions, as natural phænomena are for the mechanical operation of heat, diet, or medicines. Or if he could not proceed so far, but was able only to decypher most of his own actions, and many of the principal ones of others, still the evidence would scarce be diminished thereby, if the deficiency was no more than is reasonably to be expected from our ignorance and inattention, in respect to ourselves and others. Let the reader make the trial, especially upon himself, since such a self-examination cannot but be profitable, and may perhaps be pleasant; and that either according to the seven classes of pleasures and pains here laid down, or any other division, and judge as he thinks fit upon mature deliberation.

It may be of use in such an inquiry into a man's self, as I here propose, for him to consider in a short time after any material action is past, whether, if he was once more put into the same rigidly exact circumstances, he could possibly do otherwise than as he did. Here the power of imagination will intervene, and be apt to deceive the inquirer, unless he be cautious. For in this review, other motives, besides those which did actually influence him, will start up; and that especially if the action be such as he wishes to have been performed with more vigour or less, or not to have been performed at all. But when these foreign motives are set aside, and the imagination confined to those which did in fact take place, it will appear impossible, as it seems to me, that the person should have done otherwise than the very thing which he did.

Secondly, According to the theory here laid down, all human actions proceed from vibrations in the nerves of the muscles, and these from others, which are either evidently of a mechanical nature, as in the automatic motions; or else have been shewn to be so in the account given of the voluntary motions.

And if the doctrine of vibrations be rejected, and sensation and muscular motion be supposed to be performed by some other kind of motion in the nervous parts; still it seems probable, that the same method of reasoning might be applied to this other kind of motion.

Lastly, To suppose, that the action A, or its contrary a, can equally follow previous circumstances, that are exactly the same, appears to me the same thing, as affirming that one or both of them might start up into being without any cause; which, if admitted, appears to me to destroy the foundation of all general abstract reasoning; and particularly of that whereby the existence of the First Cause is proved.

One of the principal objections to the opinion of mechanism is that deduced from the existence of the moral sense, whose history I have just given. But it appears from that history, that God has so formed the world, and perhaps (with reverence be it spoken) was obliged by his moral perfections so to form it, as that virtue must have amiable and pleasing ideas affixed to it; vice, odious ones. The moral sense is therefore generated necessarily and mechanically. And it remains to be inquired, whether the amiable and odious ideas above shewed to be necessarily affixed to virtue and vice respectively, though differently, according to the different events of each person's life, do not answer all the purposes of making us ultimately happy in the love of God, and of our neighbour; and whether they are not, *cæteris paribus,* the same entirely, or at least in all material respects, in those who believe mechanism, who believe free-will, and who have not entered into the discussion of the question at all; or if there be a difference, whether the associations arising from the opinion of necessity, do not tend more to accelerate us in our progress to the love of God, our only true happiness. It appears to me, that the difference is in general very small; also that this difference, whatever it be, is of such a nature as to be a presumption in favour of the doctrine of necessity, all things being duly considered.

When a person first changes his opinion from free-will to mechanism, or, more properly, first sees part of the mechanism of the mind, and believes the rest from analogy, he is just as much affected by his wonted pleasures and pains, hopes and fears, as before, by the moral and religious ones, as by others. And the being persuaded, that certain things have a necessary influence to change his mind for the better or the worse, *i. e.* so as to receive more sensible, sympathetic, religious pleasures, or otherwise, will force him still more strongly upon the right method, *i. e.* put him upon inquiring after and pursuing this method.

If it be objected, That the moral sense supposes, that we refer actions to ourselves and others, whereas the opinion of mechanism annihilates all those associations, by which we refer actions to ourselves or others; I answer, that it does this just as the belief of the reality and infinite value of the things of another world annihilates all the regards of this world. Both have a tendency to these respective ends, which are indeed one and the same at the bottom; but both require time, in order to produce their full effects. When religion has made any one indifferent to this world, its pleasures and pains, then the kingdom of God, or pure unmixed happiness, comes in respect of him; so that he may then well refer all to God. However, a man may be thoroughly satisfied in a cool deliberate way, that honours, riches, &c. can afford no solid happiness; and yet desire them at certain times, eagerly perhaps, from former associations. But such a thorough general conviction applied previously to the particular instances, is a great help in a time of temptation, and will gradually destroy the wrong associations.

In like manner, the opinion that God is the one only cause of all things, has a tendency to beget the most absolute resignation, and must be a great support in grievous trials and sufferings.

We may shew by a like method of reasoning, that the affections of gratitude and resentment, which are intimately connected with the moral sense, remain notwithstanding the doctrine of mechanism. For it appears from the account of resentment above delivered, that this, and by consequence gratitude, in their nascent state, are equally exerted towards all things, animate and inanimate, that are equally connected with pleasure and pain. By degrees all succeeding circumstances are left out, and our love and hatred confined to preceding ones, which we consider as the only causes. We then leave out inanimate objects entirely, brutes and children in most circumstances, and adults in some. All which is chiefly done, because acknowledgments, rewards, threatenings, and punishments, with the other associated circumstances of gratitude and resentment, can have no use but with respect to living intelligent beings. By farther degrees we learn such a use of the words cause and effect as to call nothing a cause, whose cause, or preceding circumstance, we can see, denominating all such things mere effects, all others causes. And thus, because the secret springs of action in men are frequently concealed, both from the bystander, and even from the agent himself, or not attended to, we consider men in certain circumstances as real causes; and intelligent beings as the only ones that can be real causes; and thus confine our gratitude and resentment to them: whence it seems to follow, that as soon as we discover created intelligent beings not to be real causes, we should cease to make them the objects either of gratitude or resentment. But this is, in great measure, speculation; for it will appear to every attentive person, that benevolence, compassion, &c. are amiable, and the objects of gratitude, envy, and malice, the contrary, from whatever causes they proceed; *i. e.* he will find his mind so formed already by association, that he cannot withhold his gratitude or resentment: and it has been my business in the foregoing analysis of the affections, to point out the several methods by which this and such like things are brought about. And, for the same reasons, a person must ascribe merit and demerit, which are also intimately connected with the moral sense, to created intelligent beings, though he may have a full persuasion, that they are not real causes.

It does indeed appear, that this is owing to our present imperfect state, in which we begin with the idolatry of the creature, with the worship of every associated circumstance; and that as we advance in perfection, the associations relating to the one only, Ultimate, Infinite Cause, must at last overpower all the rest; that we shall pay no regards but to God alone; and that all resentment, demerit, sin, and misery, will be utterly annihilated and absorbed by his infinite happiness and perfections. For our associations being in this, as in many other cases, inconsistent with each other, our first gross and transitory ones must yield to those which succeed and remain.

While any degree of resentment, or unpleasing affection, is left, it may be shewn, that the same associations which keep it up, will turn it upon the creatures, and particularly upon ourselves. And, on the other hand, when the consideration of the Ultimate Cause seems ready to turn it from ourselves, it will also shew that it ought to be annihilated.

These may be considered as general remarks, tending to remove the difficulties arising from the consideration of the moral sense. I will now state the principal objections to the opinion of mechanism, in a direct, but short way, adding such hints as appear to me to afford a solution of them.

First, then, It may be said, that a man may prove his own free-will by internal feeling. This is true, if by free-will be meant the power of doing what a man wills or desires; or of resisting the motives of sensuality, ambition, &c. *i. e.* free-will in the popular and practical sense. Every person may easily recollect instances, where he has done these several things. But then these are entirely foreign to the present question. To prove that a man has free-will in the sense opposite to mechanism, he ought to feel that he can do different things, while the motives remain precisely the same: and here I apprehend the internal feelings are entirely against free-will, where the motives are of a sufficient magnitude to be evident; where they are not, nothing can be proved.

Secondly, It may be said, that unless a man have free-will, he is not an agent. I answer, that this is true, if agency be so defined as to include free-will. But if agency have its sense determined, like other words, from the associated appearances, the objection falls at once. A man may speak, handle, love, fear, &c. entirely by mechanism.

Thirdly, It may be said, that the denial of free-will in man is the denial of it in God also. But to this it may be answered, that one does not know how to put the question in respect of God, supposing free-will to mean the power of doing different things, the previous circumstances remaining the same, without gross anthropomorphitism. It does not at all follow, however, because man is subject to a necessity ordained by God, that God is subject to a prior necessity. On the contrary, according to the doctrine of mechanism, God is the cause of causes, the one only source of all power.

Fourthly, It may be said, that men are perpetually imposed upon, unless they have free-will, since they think they have. But here again free-will is put for the power of doing what a man wills or desires, &c. for, in the sense opposite to mechanism, few persons have ever entered into the discussion of the point at all; and those who do with sufficient attention, cannot but determine against free-will, as it seems to me.

Fifthly, It may be said, that the doctrine of mechanism destroys the notion of a particular providence altering the course of nature so as to suit it to the actions of men. I answer, that laying down philosophical free-will, such an alteration in the course of nature may perhaps be necessary. But if man's actions, and the course of nature, be both fixed, they may be suited to each other in the best possible manner; which is all that can be required, in order to vindicate God's attributes, as well as all that man can desire.

Sixthly, It may be said, that all motives to good actions, and particularly to prayer, are taken away by denying free-will. I answer, that according to the mechanical system, prayer and good actions are the means for obtaining happiness; and that the belief of this is the strongest of motives to impel men to prayer and good works.

Seventhly, It may be said, that the denial of free-will destroys the distinction between virtue and vice. I answer, that this is according as these words are defined. If free-will be included in the definition of virtue, then there can be no virtue without free-will. But if virtue be defined obedience to the will of God, a course of action proceeding from the love of God, or from benevolence, &c. free-will is not at all necessary; since these affections and actions may be brought about mechanically.

A solution analogous to this may be given to the objection taken from the notions of merit and demerit. Let the words be defined, and they will either include free-will, or, not including it, will not require it; so that the proposition, *merit implies free-will*, will either be identical, or false.

Eighthly, It may be said, that the doctrine of mechanism makes God the author of sin. I answer, that till we arrive at self-annihilation, sin always will, and ought to, appear to arise from ourselves; and that, when we are arrived thither, sin and evil of every kind vanish. I answer also, that the doctrine of philosophical free-will does not remove our difficulties and perplexities, in respect of the moral attributes of God, unless by transferring them upon the natural ones; *i. e.* by our supposing that some prior necessity compelled God to bestow free-will on his creatures. It seems equally difficult, in every way, to account for the origin of evil, natural or moral, consistently with the infinity of the power, knowledge, and goodness of God. If we suppose that all tends to happiness ultimately, this removes the difficulty so far as to produce acquiescence in the will of God, and thankfulness to him; and that just as much upon the system of mechanism as that of free-will. Moral evil has no difficulty in it, besides what arises from the natural evil attending it.

Ninthly, It may be said, that the exhortations of the Scriptures presuppose free-will. I answer, that they are to be considered as motives impelling the will, and contributing, as far as they are attended to, to rectify it. A parent who believes the doctrine of mechanism may, consistently with it, or rather must necessarily, in consequence of this belief, exhort his child. Therefore God, who is pleased to call himself our heavenly father, may do the same. And if we embrace the opinion of universal restoration, then all the exhortations contained both in the word and works of God, will produce their genuine effect, and concur to work in us dispositions fit to receive happiness ultimately.

I come now to hint some consequences of the doctrine of mechanism, which seem to me to be strong presumptions in its favour.

First, then, It entirely removes the great difficulty of reconciling the prescience of God with the free-will of man. For it takes away philosophical free-will, and the practical is consistent with God's prescience.

Secondly, It has a tendency to beget the most profound humility and self-annihilation; since, according to this, we are entirely destitute of all power and perfection in ourselves, and are what we are entirely by the grace and goodness of God.

Thirdly, It has a tendency to abate all resentment against men. Since all that they do against us is by the appointment of God, it is rebellion against him to be offended with them.

Fourthly, It greatly favours the doctrine of universal restoration. Since all that is done is by the appointment of God, it cannot but end well at last.

Fifthly, It has a tendency to make us labour more earnestly with ourselves and others, particularly children, from the greater certainty attending all endeavours that operate in a mechanical way.

Lastly, There are many well-known passages of Scripture, which cannot be reconciled to the doctrine of philosophical free-will, without the greatest harshness of interpretation.

It may also be objected to the whole foregoing theory, as well as to the doctrine of vibrations in particular, that it is unfavourable to the immateriality of the soul; and, by consequence, to its immortality. But to this I answer, that I am reduced to the necessity of making a *postulatum* at the entrance of my inquiries; which precludes all possibility of proving the materiality of the soul from this theory afterwards. Thus I suppose, or postulate, in my first proposition, that sensations arise in the soul from motions excited in the medullary substance of the brain. I do indeed bring some arguments from physiology and pathology, to shew this to be a reasonable *postulatum,* when understood in a general sense; for it is all one to the purpose of the foregoing theory, whether the motions in the medullary substance be the physical cause of the sensations, according to the system of the schools; or the occasional cause, according to Malbranche; or only an adjunct, according to Leibnitz. However, this is not supposing matter to be endued with sensation, or any way explaining what the soul is; but only taking its existence and connexion with the bodily organs in the most simple case, for granted, in order to make farther inquiries. Agreeably to which I immediately proceed to determine the species of the motion, and by determining it, to cast light on some important and obscure points relating to the connexion between the body and the soul in complex cases.

It does indeed follow from this theory, that matter, if it could be endued with the most simple kinds of sensation, might also arrive at all that intelligence of which the human mind is possessed: whence this theory must be allowed to overturn all the arguments which are usually brought for the immateriality of the soul from the subtlety of the internal senses, and of the rational faculty. But I no ways presume to determine whether matter can be endued with sensation or no. This is a point foreign to the purpose of my inquiries. It is sufficient for me, that there is a certain connexion, of one kind or other, between the sensations of the soul, and the motions excited in the medullary substance of the brain; which is what all physicians and philosophers allow.

I would not therefore be any way interpreted so as to oppose the immateriality of the soul. On the contrary, I see clearly, and acknowledge readily, that matter and motion, however subtilely divided, or reasoned upon, yield nothing more than matter and motion still. But then neither would I affirm, that this consideration affords a proof of the soul's immateriality. In like manner the unity of consciousness seems to me an inconclusive argument. For consciousness is a mental perception; and if perception be a monad, then every inseparable adjunct of it must be so too, *i. e.* vibrations, according to this theory, which is evidently false. Not to mention, that it is difficult to know what is meant by the unity of consciousness.

But it is most worthy of notice, that the immateriality of the soul has little or no connexion with its immortality; and that we ought to depend upon Him who first breathed into man the breath of the present life, for our resurrection to a better. All live unto him. And if we depend upon any thing else besides him, for any blessing, we may be said so far to renounce our allegiance to him, and to idolize that upon which we depend.

HARTLEY'S WRITINGS

There is no standard, or even modern, edition of Hartley's writings. The third edition of *Observations on Man,* with notes by H. Pistorius and Edited by David Hartley, the younger, appears in 3 vol. (London, 1791). The complete work has not been edited since then. The two essays, "Conjecturae quaédam de sensu" and "An Enquiry into the Origin of the Human Appetites" appear in *Metaphysical Tracts by English Philosophers of the Eighteenth Century,* Edited by Samuel Parr (London, 1837). Joseph Priestley produced an abridged version of *Observations on Man* under the title *Hartley's Theory of the Human Mind* (London, 1775); he excised the doctrine of vibrations and the theology, prefixing three expository essays of his own. William Hazlitt published an abridged edition, *An Essay on the Principles of Human Action* in 1805 with a highly critical essay entitled "Remarks on the Systems of Hartley and Helvetius." The essay is reprinted in Hazlitt's *Works,* Vol. I, Edited by P. R. Howe (London and Toronto, 1930).

WRITINGS ON HARTLEY

The most systematic exposition in English of Hartley's views is that given by G. S. Bower in *Hartley and James Mill* (London, 1881). It is not a critical account, however. Basil Willey's chapter on Hartley in *The Eighteenth-Century Background* (London, 1940), is sympathetic and lucid. A much harsher verdict is offered in Ernest Albee's *A History of English Utilitarianism* (London, 1901). The short treatment in Th. Ribot's *English Psychology* (London, 1889), contains some remarks of interest as does the chapter in *Dissertation on the Progress of Ethical Philosophy* by Sir James Mackintosh (Edinburgh, 1838). But in many ways the two best general summaries remain those in *Brett's History of Psychology,* Edited by R. S. Peters (London, 1953), and in *A History of Association Psychology* by H. C. Warren (New York, 1921). For an interesting estimate by a psychologist, see R. C. Oldfield, "Hartley's 'Observations on Man'" in *Annals of Science,* Vol. 7 (London, 1951). There are also references to Hartley worth noting in: Elie Halévy, *The Growth of Philosophical Radicalism* (London, 1952); William James, *The Principles of Psychology,* Vol. I (New York, 1890); and Leslie Stephen, *History of English Thought in the Eighteenth Century,* 2 vol. (London, 1876). For readers of German, there are substantial accounts of Hartley in M. Heider, *Studien über David Hartley* (Bonn, 1913); and in B. Schoenlank's *Hartley und Priestley, die Begründer des Assoziationismus in England* (Halle, 1882).

ABRAHAM TUCKER

1705–1774

The "Montaigne of metaphysics," as Tucker has been called, was the son of a well-to-do London merchant; having lost his parents while still a child, he was reared by an uncle. Tucker entered Merton College, Oxford, in 1721, and after having studied philosophy and mathematics, Italian and French, he read law at Inner Temple, although he never practiced except as a Justice of the Peace. In 1727, having bought the estate of Betchworth Castle near Dorking, he set himself to learn agriculture and to live as a country gentleman. He was married nine years later to the daughter of a neighboring land owner. Tucker spent most months of each year managing his estate, devoting the remaining time to life in London. His circle of friends was appreciative but not eminent, and he was unknown to the general educated public.

His wife died in 1754, leaving him to look after their two daughters. He apparently began writing only after her death, publishing, in addition to his few writings on philosophy, an article on political societies "by a country gentleman to his son" and printing privately a paper on a phonetic alphabet and vocal sounds. Tucker became blind three years before his death but invented a writing machine that allowed his elder daughter, Judith, to continue working with him. She later became his literary editor. The younger daughter's son, Sir H. P. St. John Mildmay, was the author of the appreciative "Life" prefixed to the second edition (1805) of *The Light of Nature Pursued.* This preface is our chief source of biographical information about Tucker.

Tucker began writing *The Light of Nature Pursued,* his only substantial work, about 1756, and did not finish it until 1774, the year of his death. The first four volumes he published himself in 1768 under the pseudonym Edward Search. The last three volumes were edited by his daughter Judith, and appeared in 1778. The work went through seven printings before 1850. Tucker also published an essay entitled "Freewill, Foreknowledge, and Fate, by Edward Search" in 1763. It was attacked in the *Monthly Review* in July of that year, and Tucker promptly replied in another pamphlet, "Man in Quest of Himself by Cuthbert Comment" (1763). He seems to have published nothing else on philosophy.

Tucker is now read, when he is read at all, either as an early utilitarian in the history of ethics or as an unwilling follower of Hartley in the development of associationist psychology. Yet his influence on successive generations of Cambridge students throughout the nineteenth century was considerable: he strongly affected the argument of William Paley's *Principles of Moral and Political Philosophy* (1785), a book which was widely used as a text at Cambridge University and elsewhere for many years. Paley himself was generous in his praise of Tucker, saying in the preface to *Principles,* "I have found in this writer more original thinking and observation upon the several subjects that he has taken in hand than in any other, not to say than in all others put together. His talent also for illustration is unrivalled."

When we set aside these historical interests, however, Tucker remains a writer of some originality in the philosophy of mind. Though he refers to himself as always "averse to differing from Mr. Locke," Tucker's chapter, Satisfaction, criticizes Locke's view that desire is constantly accompanied by uneasiness. The first explicit description of the fusion of elementary ideas into a single complex one seems to have been Tucker's, and he distinguishes this process from ordinary association of ideas. Moreover, he goes on to suggest how "trains" of ideas arise: these are regular successions of ideas which bear on "some one purpose retained in view"; after the ideas have been linked together by various means some of them are eventually forgotten through lack of attention. We are then left with the important conclusions alone, having lost the supporting evidence. When that happens we mistakenly think that we are born with innate beliefs, and we then manufacture a variety of inherited faculties, like that of the moral sense, to explain their presence. Thus Tucker, like Hartley, tries to account for our knowledge of nonempirical beliefs in terms of their disguised origin in experience. But the two men differ in their description of how the disguise becomes effective.

No writer gains more from severe editing than does Tucker, and few writers lend themselves so well to prudent selection. The general structure of *The Light of Nature Pursued* is so loose that the question of the consistency of a continuous argument hardly arises. Large stretches are idly fanciful; indeed, some of the later chapters, such as those on the Mundane Soul and The Vision, consist largely of speculations on the properties of the disembodied soul and the composition of the Soul of the World. However, the chapters below are all drawn from Part I (Human Nature), and nothing could be less fanciful than Tucker's remarks, contained in these selections, on the definition of an action or on forbearance to act; nor could one provide a better instance of shrewd, patient examination of a problem than his treatment of Locke's view that uneasiness is "the sole incitement constantly spurring to action." These chapters stand on their own as examples of analysis. And if we take examples in philosophy as seriously as Wittgenstein urged us to, then Tucker's homely illustrations often raise issues which carry us well beyond the scope of Tucker's own argument.

SELECTIONS FROM

The Light of Nature Pursued*

*

CHAPTER II

ACTION

I have heard of a formal old gentleman who, finding his horse uneasy under the saddle, alighted and called to his servant in the following manner. Tom, take off the saddle which is upon my bay horse and lay it upon the ground, then take the saddle from thy grey horse, and put it upon my bay horse, lastly, put the other saddle upon thy grey horse. The fellow gaped all this while at this long peachment, and at last cried out, Lackaday, Sir, could not you have said at once, Change the saddles? We see here how many actions are comprised under those three little words, Change the saddles, and yet the master, for all his exactness, did not particularize the tenth part of them; lifting up the flap of the saddle, pulling the strap, raising the tongue, drawing out the buckle, taking up the saddle, pulling it towards him, stooping to lay it down, lifting up his body again, and so forth. But had he stayed to enumerate all the steps his man must take in executing his orders, they would not have got home by dinner time. Therefore expedience recommends compendious forms of speech for common use, and puts us often upon expressing a long course of action by a single word, else we could make no dispatch in our discourses with one another: for were we to describe all the motions we make in any business transacted, we must spend more time in the narrative than we did in the performance.

* 3rd edition, Vol. I, Thomas Tegg and Son, London, 1834.

But our horseman, though by far too minute and circumstantial for the fine gentleman, was not enough so for the philosopher. Whoever would penetrate into the nature of things, must not take them in the lump, but examine their several parts and operations separately. The anatomist, when he would teach you the structure of the human body, does not content himself with telling you it has head, limbs, body, and bowels, for this you knew before and was knowledge enough for common occasions: he lays open the muscles, injects the veins, traces the nerves, examines the glands, their strainers, vessels, and tunicles. And the naturalist goes further, he describes the little bladders whereof every fibre consists, their communication with one another, the nitro-aerious fluid pervading them, distending their coats, thereby shortening the string and producing muscular motion.

Thus to become intimately acquainted with our mind we must, as I may say, dissect it, that is, analyze action into its first constituent parts. The action of the Drama or Epopee, the critics say must be one and entire, or the performance will prove defective. To that of a play they allow the compass of a natural day; that of the Iliad takes in, I think, twenty-nine days, and that of the Æneid six years. We may look upon actions of this enormous bulk till we are tired without learning anything from thence concerning the structure of the mind: let us therefore consider what is truly and properly a single action, and try how far that will help us in our researches.

2. A single action I take to be so much as we can perform at once, for the present moment only lies in our power nor does our activity reach any farther. What our future actions shall be, depends upon our future volitions; we may determine and resolve long beforehand, but it is well known our resolutions frequently change, and when the time of execution comes, we shall do what is then in our minds, not what we had there before, if the two happen to differ.

I will not pretend to calculate how many actions we may perform in any given space of time, as some have computed how many particles of air would lie in an inch: but certainly the motions of our mind are extremely quick. When upon finding yourself thirsty in a sultry day you snatch up a cup of liquor, if after you have gotten it half way up, you espy a wasp floating on the surface, you thrust it instantly from you; which shows that one volition is not sufficient to lift your hand to your mouth, for you see the mind may take a contrary turn in that little interval. How nimble are the motions of the fencer and the tennis player! the hand perpetually follows the eye and moves as fast as the objects can strike upon that; but between every impulse of the object and every motion of the hand, an entire perception and volition must intervene. How readily do our words occur to us in discourse, and as readily find utterance at the tongue the moment they present themselves! The tongue does not move mechanically like a clock, which once wound up will go for a month, but receives every motion and forms every modulation of voice by particular direction from the mind. Objects and ideas rise continually in view; they pass without ceasing before us, vary, appear and vanish; for what is so quick as thought? Yet volition keeps pace with perception and sometimes perhaps out-strips it: for in speaking the word Mind the whole idea seems to present in one perception, but there must be four several volitions to guide the tongue successively in pronouncing the four different letters. Not that volition runs more ground than perception, but follows close with unequal steps, like young Julus after his father: for when you read you see the whole word together, and consequently the D before you pronounce the M.

3. In very nice works we lie under a necessity of spinning very fine, but though we are obliged sometimes to split the hair we need not quarter it. Therefore I shall call one action so much as passes between each perception and the next, although this action produce several contemporary motions. And anybody may see with half an eye that our larger actions, such as we speak of in common conversation, consist of those under actions: for as days, months, years, and all measurable portions of time are made up of moments, so all our performances and transactions are made up of momentary acts. A walk consists of steps, a game at chess of moves, a description of particulars, a narration of circumstances, and discourse in general, whether serious or trifling, labored or careless, of words and syllables, each whereof must have its distinct volition to give it effect.

Nor does there need much penetration to observe how sociably the two faculties lead one another, as I may say hand in hand, not only in entering upon our works but through all the steps necessary to complete them. If you would walk to any place, it is not enough to use your understanding before you set out in choosing the nearest or most commodious way, but you must use your eyes all along to conduct your steps: for should you shut them a moment, you might chance to run against a post, or tread beside the path. If you are to discourse on any subject, when you have chosen your matter and settled your form, the business is not all done; you must consult your judgment from time to time during the delivery for proper expressions and proper tones of voice. Even your perpetual gabblers, who let their tongues run before their wits, cannot proceed with one faculty alone, for though they talk without thinking, they do not talk without perceiving: their ideas draw through their imagination in a string, though it proves indeed only a rope of sand without pertinence and without coherence.

4. But these single acts, though confined to a moment of time, may contain several coexistent parts. For we make many motions together by one and the same exertion of our activity; we may reach out our

hands, step with our feet, look with our eyes, speak and think at once. And the like may be said of perception, for we can see, hear, feel, discern, remember, all at the same instant. I know not whether I may have occasion hereafter to consider the parts of action, but for the present I stick to my definition before laid down, terming the whole scene of ideas presented together to our view one perception, and the whole exertion of our activity, upon how many subjects soever operating, one volition, which though without duration may have a large scope: just as your mathematical surfaces which, though void of thickness, may extend to a very spacious circumference.

The not observing the shortness of action, has given occasion I believe to the notion mentioned at the end of the last chapter concerning distinct agents and various powers in the mind: for by help of this clue we may unravel the mystery, and discover that what was esteemed the act of several agents, was indeed successive acts of the mind exerting her two faculties at different times. When several ideas present themselves together, the mind cannot always judge immediately between them, for their colours change for a while, fading and glowing alternately, or the scales of judgment and inclination rise and fall by turns; the mind being sensible of this, sees nothing better than to hold them in her attention until the colours settle or the balance fixes; as soon as that happens she perceives which of them is the stronger, and this some people fancy done by an elective power, wherewith the Will gives a preference of its own, because the preference follows in consequence of a voluntary attention. Or perhaps a new colour sparkles out unperceived before, or a new weight falls into the scale: and this they call creating a preference. When the preference becomes visible, the mind instantly discerns it, and pronounces the object good whereon it alights; and having now no further use for contemplation, she looks out for proper measures of execution, which as soon as they occur she puts immediately in practice.

5. Nor will it be useless to take notice that in common speech we confine action to outward motions and exercises of our bodily powers: as when we distinguish between an active and a sedentary life, between seasons of action and seasons of deliberation: which expressions look as if we thought ourselves totally inactive in the latter, and so indeed we naturally may at first sight because we can show no effects of our activity, But every volition produces some effect, although not always discernible; and every production of our own, be it of a fleeting thought or a permanent work, springs from our volition. If a man retires from business into his closet, we cannot necessarily conclude he does nothing there; for whatever indolent posture he may throw his body into, his mind may find constant employment all the while. Now the mind has only one active power to serve her upon all occasions; therefore acting and thinking are the same with respect to

the power enabling us to go through them; they differ only in the subjects operated upon. When the mind withdraws from the world, she may roam about her own habitation; when she ceases to act upon the limbs, she may nevertheless act upon herself, that is, raise ideas to pass in review before her.

6. There is another division of action I find made by Mr. Locke[1] into action properly so called, and forbearance, which latter he seems to think requires the interposition of the Will as much as the former: thus if a man asks his friend to take a walk, it is equally an exertion of his Will whether he refuses or accepts the offer. But I cannot readily understand how a mere forbearance to act is any exercise of our active power at all: it seems to me rather a discernment of the other faculty that we do not like the thing proposed, which discernment or dislike we have seen before is frequently taken for our Will. What we call a forbearance I apprehend to be generally a choice of some other action. We will not walk because we had rather ride, or talk, or think, or do something else: we forbear to act because we would consider first what is proper to be done; or we forbear to deliberate any longer because the time of action is at hand. When we make several motions together, we may forbear one and continue the rest, for while walking and discoursing with a companion we may point at some distant object, which after he has seen we may let our hand fall to our side: but this I do not look upon as any volition of ours, it is rather a ceasing of volition with respect to the arm, which falls down by its gravity, not by our power, and would do the same were we at that instant utterly to lose our active faculty. Nevertheless it must be owned that forbearance is sometimes the sole point we set our minds upon and take pains to effect. When Rich sits as an equestrian statue in one of his pantomines, we take him for the very marble he represents, for he moves neither head nor body nor limbs, he wags neither eye nor finger, but continues wholly inactive; what he thinks of all the while, whether of the audience or profits of the house, neither you nor I can tell, but if any such thoughts rove in his fancy their rovings are accidental, his mind being intent on nothing else but forbearance from all manner of motion. We cannot deny this attention to be an effort of the mind, but then it is not a forbearance; it is an actual watching of the ideas as they rise, and excluding such as would prompt him to motion. Perhaps his face itches, or the stirrup presses against his ancle, and he wants to relieve himself, but checks those desires as fast as they start up, and if by this care he can avoid every volition to move, his purpose is answered without anything further to be done. For our limbs do not move of themselves, nor unless we will to move them: therefore that they remain motionless is not owing to volition, but to the absence of volition.

[1] *In an Essay Concerning Human Understanding,* Book II, Chapter XXI, 5. Ed.

Should we think the limbs do not move because we will Not to move them, this would be sliding back into the vulgar sense of the word Will, wherein it stands for inclination or judgment: for a Will not to move is an act of the other faculty, being no more than a dislike to motion, or a discernment of its impropriety, which produces no volition nor exertion of our activity at all upon the object so discerned.

7. Some immovable postures we keep ourselves in by a continual effort of the mind. If our statue holds up a truncheon in the right hand, he must keep his arm in that position by his own strength: but this cannot, in any light, be deemed a forbearance, for if he forbears to exert himself but for a moment, the arm will fall downwards by its own weight.

If there is any such thing as a total forbearance of action, I conceive it must be in reverie after a fatigue, or when we lie down in order to sleep. Ideas run to and fro in our fancy uncalled, without attention, without preference or rejection of anything occurring, and the mind seems to remain entirely passive. But since whatever passes does not proceed from volition, where shall we find marks of any volition at all? Were we to suppose the mind utterly divested of her active power just at her entrance upon the scene, I do not see how anything could fall out otherwise than it does.

8. But we very rarely find a necessity of considering action so minutely as to distinguish the restraining those workings of imagination, which would excite us inadvertently to motions we choose to avoid, from the forbearance consequent thereupon: and since forbearance often requires a stronger effort of the mind than action itself, for it will cost us more pains to forbear cutting faces, swearing, or any other foolish habit we have got than to practise them, therefore I shall not scruple to ascribe forbearance to volition, for so it may be remotely though not directly; and after the example of Mr. Locke, to include that together with any actual exercise of our powers under the general name of action.

9. One remark more shall conclude the chapter. In speaking of action, besides the several co-existent motions and several successive volitions before-mentioned, we ordinarily comprehend several operations of other agents acting in a series towards completing the purpose we had in view, provided we conceive them necessarily consequent upon our volition. Thus when Roger shot the hawk hovering over his master's dove-house, he only pulled the trigger, the action of the spring drove down the flint, the action of the flint struck fire into the pan, the action of the fire set the powder in a blaze, that of the powder forced out the shot, that of the shot wounded the bird, and that of gravity brought her to the ground. But all this we ascribe to Roger, for we say he brought down the felon; and if we think the shot a nice one, applaud him for having done a clever feat. So likewise we claim the

actions of other persons for our own, whenever we expect they will certainly follow as we shall direct. When Squire Peremptory distrained his tenant for rent, perhaps he did no more than write his orders in a letter, this his servant carried to the post, the postman conveyed it into the country, where it was delivered to the steward, who sent his clerk to make the distress. Yet we ascribe the whole to the Squire's own doing, for we say he distrained his tenant, and call it a prudent or a cruel act, according as we think of the circumstances of the case.

Hence the law maxim, he that does a thing by another, does it himself; which though valid in Westminster-hall will not hold good in the school of metaphysics, for there we shall find nothing an act of the mind that is not the immediate product of her volition. But for the uses of prudence and morality we must recur back again to the common language, because we cannot judge of the merits of men's doings without taking the consequences into our idea of the action. Pulling a trigger, or drawing characters upon paper, are neither good nor bad, right nor wrong, considered in themselves: but as the trigger so pulled shall occasion the slaughter of a man, or of some vermin, or only a bounce in the air; as the characters so drawn shall tend to the necessary security of our property, or to bring a hardship upon our neighbour, or shall carry no meaning at all, we pronounce the action prudent or idle, moral or wicked.

CHAPTER V

MOTIVES

Having in my list of causes assigned a particular class to the final, I shall treat of them distinctly, though in reality they are a species of the ideal, as the latter are of our ideas in general. For many ideas pass in review before us which have no share at all in our actions: and many serve us for a guidance in our conduct which yet did not prompt us to pursue it. While we stand talking at a window, passengers may go by without drawing our attention; we see them move along, but do nothing different nor in a different manner from what we should have done had they not appeared; the sight of our companion and our knowledge of language direct us which way to turn our head and how to express ourselves: these ideas perhaps we had before we entered upon our discourse, which we do not begin till another idea arises, probably of entertainment or of giving or receiving some information. When a man walks, he may see bushes growing by the way side, cows grazing in the field, birds flying in the air, without regarding or making any use of the notices they offer: these then are part of his ideas, but not ideal causes, which are the shape of his path and several marks whereby he knows his way; yet neither are these the final cause, but health, exercise, diversion, business, or some other end, he proposes to himself in walking.

This final cause we commonly style the Motive, by a metaphor taken from mechanical engines which cannot play without some spring or other mover to set them at work: and because we find action usually follows upon the suggestion of proper motives, therefore we conceive them moving the mind to exert herself. Thus, by a light figure, we hear her frequently compared to a balance, and the motives to weights hanging in either scale. But if we will apply this comparison to the mind, I think it suits her better in the exercises of her understanding than in her volitions; for it is the judgment poises the motives in its scale to try which of them preponderate, nor does volition ensue until the weight be determined.

Some there are who will not allow the mind to act upon motives at all, or at least assign her a limited power which she exercises sometimes of acting against or without them, or of giving them a weight which does not naturally belong to them; they say, she plays tricks with her balance, like a juggling shopkeeper who slides his little finger slily along one side of the beam, and by pressing upon it, makes twelve ounces of plums draw up a pound of lead. It must be owned, to our shame, that we too frequently practise these scurvy tricks to cheat those who have dealings with us, and what is more fatal, to cheat ourselves into error and mischief: but I hope to make it appear in due time that this is done, not by a free will of indifference overpowering the force of our motives, but by privately slipping in or stealing out the weights in either scale, which we often get a habit of doing so covertly that we are not aware of the fraud ourselves.

2. Now how shall we manage to steer safely between two opposite extremes? The doctors Hartley and Berkeley would not allow the mind an efficient cause of her own actions: the maintainers of indifference[1] make her not only the efficient cause of her actions but of their causes too, for they will have it that her activity supplies the place of final causes, or gives force to motives.

I shall remark, in the first place, that they distinguish between acting and choosing, to which latter only they ascribe the privilege of indifference. Whether such distinction has any foundation in nature I have already suggested some reasons to question, and may canvass the point more thoroughly hereafter when a proper occasion shall offer. But since they admit we never proceed to action without motives, that our choice sometimes arises from the decision of our judgment without our interposition, and that motives often operate so forcibly we cannot resist them: this is going a great way, and it will be but one

[1] See Richard Price's *On the Doctrine of Necessity* reprinted in this volume. Ed.

little step further to show that acting upon our ideas is acting as well as upon our limbs: which will entitle us to inquire upon the subject of those choices we make in consequence of something done by ourselves, whether some motive does not influence us in everything we do towards bringing on the determination.

In the next place, I would beg leave to ask them, how they become so well acquainted with their own actions beforehand as to lay schemes and plans for their future conduct, and depend upon their adherence thereto? I suppose they do not pretend to the spirit of prophecy, and without that, I do not see how we can know any future event, otherwise than by our knowledge of the causes: for an event, independent on antecedent causes, must remain absolutely contingent until it comes to pass. Yet do they lay claim to commendation for their steadiness in adhering to their plan: the mind then must remain indifferent during the whole time of such adherence, else they would forfeit their claim which they rest solely upon the right exercise of this privilege. For did not the mind retain her freewill of indifference either to keep or to break a resolution already taken, how much soever we might applaud them for resolving, we could owe them no applause for performing.

Then as to their resting the merit of actions solely upon the due use of this freedom of indifference, without which, say they, we shall have no room to praise or blame, to reward or punish: have patience, and perhaps in the sequel of these inquiries we may find other sources of distributive justice besides this privilege. What if we should discover approbation and censure so little inconsistent with the efficacy of motives that they act themselves as such, and become due solely for the influence they are likely to have upon our behaviour?

But as I find the work of improving my own knowledge much more agreeable to my taste than that of battling the opinions of others, I shall leave my antagonists in possession of their indifference for the present, if they still think fit to claim it after all the evidence produced against their title by Mr. Locke; and shall proceed in my consideration of final causes, in hopes thereby to kill two birds with one stone. For while in pursuit of my journey, minding only my own business, I may happen to discover motives for every species of action, and then indifference must quit the field of course, as having nothing to do there. Nor can we take a better method for the recovery of our right than by enclosing the whole contested ground, piece by piece, until there be not a spot left whereon the liberty of indifference may rest its foot.

3. To prevent mistakes, when I speak of the efficacy of motives and of their moving the mind to exert herself, I desire it may be understood that these are figurative expressions; and I do not mean thereby to deny the efficacy of the mind, or to assert any motion,

force, or impulse imparted to her from the motives, as there is to one billiard ball from another upon their striking; but only to observe that motives give occasion to the mind to exert her endeavours in attaining whatever they invite her to, which she does by her own inherent activity, not by any power derived from them. And all mankind understand the matter so, except perhaps some few persons of uncommon sense and superfine understandings. When the poet makes Belinda ask, What mov'd my mind with youthful lords to roam? would he have you believe that vanity, pleasure, desire of conquest, hope of an advantageous match, or any other motive you can assign, made all those motions contained in the idea of roaming? No, surely—it was the lady herself by her own vigour and sprightliness. When she sits down to her toilet, unnumbered treasures ope at once. What opes the treasures? Why the maid, with her hands, not with her desire of tiffing out her mistress in a killing attire. And it is this agency of the mind which denominates an action ours, for whatever proceeds from other efficient causes does not belong to us. Therefore you see, when the maid had sylphs to work for her, he describes the performance, though done by her hands, to them instead of her, And Betty's prais'd for labours not her own.

Nobody will deny that we sometimes act upon motives, that we follow where they lead us, and that we should have acted otherwise had they not presented or had other motives appeared in the opposite scale to outweigh them. How many people flock to hear Handel play upon the organ! they follow him to the Haymarket, to Covent Garden, to the Foundling Hospital; had he not been to perform they never would have stirred from home, but if their doctor had told them that going abroad might prove fatal to their health, they would have forborne. Therefore motives have a natural efficacy to put us upon action, and we need no other spring to move us so long as we have store of them; nor need we fear the want of a continual supply, when we consider how many occasions of life, of amusement, of business, we have to provide for, and how many idle fancies to gratify.

But we run into frequent mistakes concerning the operation of motives, for want of first settling accurately with ourselves what they be. A motive I conceive is the prospect of some end actually in view of the mind at the time of action and urging to attain it: whereas we are apt to take for motives any reasons we can allege in justification of our conduct. If any body should ask why you make your stated meals at breakfast, dinner, and supper, every day, I warrant you would answer, Why, I could not live without eating. But reflect a little with yourself. Do you think of starving every time you run down stairs to dinner? Do not you go because you are hungry, because you like the victuals, because you will not make the family wait, because it is your usual hour? How then can the preservation of life, which is the farthest of anything from your thoughts, be your motive of eating? If you would dissuade a debauchee from his courses, you tell him of the discredit he will bring upon himself from all wise and judicious persons: yet he still goes on as before, and this you call acting against a powerful motive. But is it so in fact with him? Perhaps the approbation of your musty sober fellows weighs nothing in his estimation; he feels no other weight in his scale besides the gratification of appetite: therefore he follows the only motive inclining him to action.

4. But as Hermogenes was a singer even when he did not sing; and the cobbler retains his appellation after he has shut up his stall and sits among his fellow topers at the two-penny club; so motives still preserve their character with us while they lie dormant in the box and do not operate in the scale. If we know a man has covetousness or ambition, we impute all his actions to that motive; so that a politician cannot take an airing but we suppose him going on some deep design, nor a miser step into his closet but we conclude him counting over his bags. But besides our general motives of conduct, we have many little desires and whimsies which come in every now and then for a share of our motions; and unless we get acquainted with these, we cannot account for a man's behavior in particular instances.

Few of us I hope are without some prudential motives in store, and those being the most creditable, we would willingly ascribe all our motions to them, not observing what other inducements may slip in unawares to weigh down the scale or so cover it as to leave no admittance for anything else: for inclination and humour so mimic the garb and gestures of reason that we take them for her very self. Sometimes two motives occur together both inciting to the same action, and in this case we cannot rightly tell to which it belongs: because we can judge the efficacy of causes no otherwise than by their effects. This last deceit is greatly promoted by that aptness of inclination to draw reason after her, not as a friend to consult with, but as an advocate to support her cause: for reason, which ought always to keep upon the bench, too often descends to the bar, and then we take her arguments for judgments of court, and applaud ourselves for having paid them a due obedience. When the minister labours to extend the prerogative which he has under his own management, he thinks himself all the while pursuing the public good: when the parson vexes his parishioners with lawsuits, he, good man, would be contented with his present income, but he must not injure his successors: when the young girl chooses her mate for black eyes, white teeth, a frolic air and sprightly prattle, she despises all mercenary views, and pays regard only to solid merit and happiness.

In short, we shall find it extremely difficult with our utmost care and circumspection to know our real motives, as well in general, what stock of them we have, as what weighed with us upon every particular occasion. For we seldom attend to our motive at the instant of its operation, and if we go to recall if afterwards to our reflection, another shall start up in its place. Nor do we know the true weight of our motives before trial. While we hold them in the scale of contemplation they feel exceeding heavy, whereupon we confidently form resolutions of bearing pain, encountering dangers and surmounting difficulties, supposing that our motive fastened thereto, like lead to a bludgeon, will give it a force that shall bear down all opposition; but when the time of action comes, they are found wanting in the balance, and lie lighter than a feather.

There is a vulgar saying, That we measure other folks' corn by our own bushel: therefore we wonder at their proceeding when running in a different channel from our own, because we judge of their sentiments by those we feel ourselves. One is apt to cry, I should have done otherwise had I been in such an one's place, that is, had you had the same materials, abilities, or opportunities as he: but are you sure you should have acted otherwise had you had the same notions, ways of thinking, and motives too, without any mixture of those you now possess? For our desires vary as much as our faces, and what works powerfully upon one, may have no influence at all upon another. If we see a person bringing great damage upon one who has never offended him, without any inducement either of pleasure or profit to himself, we stand in astonishment that anybody can behave so absurdly without the least motive to urge him; and ascribe his procedure to mere perverseness of will. For we find no motives in our own storehouse that could engage him: resentment, gratification of some appetite or self-interest, may have surprised us sometimes into unwarrantable actions, but we feel no temptation to do mischief for mischief's sake, and therefore can conceive no such in another. But there are tempers with whom mischief itself acts as a powerful motive; some dispositions there are utterly void of humanity, whose place is supplied by a love of injustice and cruelty: even freak and wantonness may do much upon a mind where there is no consideration either of benevolence or prudence to weigh against them.

5. Motives frequently introduce and give life to one another. Your coachman entered into your service for a livelihood; this led him to obey your orders, which directed him to take care of your horses; this put him upon providing hay for them, and that induced him to inquire where the best was to be had. While on his way to the market, he thinks of nothing but the shortest road to get thither; this therefore is the sole motive he has now in view: but if the prior motives had not operated, none of the subsequent would have had any influence upon him.

For the most part we portion our time into large actions tending to some distant end not presently accomplished, which consists of under parts, and admits many bye actions not belonging to the principal. He that travels to York, goes most likely upon some business: he divides his journey into several stages, and while upon each, thinks of nothing but getting well to his inn: this then is his motive for the time. On the road he finds himself weary and alights, or thirsty and stops at the door of some public house, or perhaps he enters into discourse with the passengers in going along, or stands still to look at some magnificent building. All these have separate motives of their own; refreshment, thirst, amusement, or curiosity, which bear no relation to his main design.

While we work, or study, or converse, we often change our posture, turn our eyes, and make many side motions having no connexion with the purpose we are about. But have we not motives for those excrescences of action? We feel ourselves uneasy in one posture, and therefore exchange it for another; we look out for new objects because those before us have cloyed our eyes; we find some trifling amusement in every exercise of our activity. For employment seldom so totally engages us as to fill up all the spaces of our time, but restlessness, whimsy, or habit, come in to supply the vacancies. The busy mind of man cannot lie a moment inactive: she works incessantly with both her faculties while awake, and if her weightier motives suspend their action ever so little, some lighter will slip in to keep her in play: for she has often been compared to an exceeding fine balance, that will turn with the slightest hair when nothing lies in the opposite scale; and she has her drawers stocked with the grains of fancy as well as the pounds of reason.

While one motive urges to action, another may model the shape of it. When a grave divine and powdered fop enter the room together, civility prompts them alike to pay their compliments to the company, but decency leads one to a sober manly deportment, and affectation drives the other into a mincing step, a fantastic air, and an over-delicacy of expression.

The designs that generate our larger actions take time in the forming, we see them grow by degrees to maturity, and have leisure to contemplate them: but the ideas causing our lesser motions, like lightning, flash, strike, and vanish; they pass so swiftly we cannot get a look at them nor remember their existence. Besides, our weighty motives having the largest influence upon our lives, deserve our greatest regard, and we commonly apply our whole attention to them, overlooking all the rest so far as scarce to know we have any such belonging to us, or to mistake them for something else. Therefore we say, The motive of prudence, but the impulse of fancy, the force of habit, or the sally of imagination: and sometimes term the motion of these latter mechanical, supposing volition had no share in them, or at other times ascribe them to the privilege of indifference for want of discerning the motive that made a difference between one idle motion and another. But whoever desires a thorough acquaintance with the mind, ought to bestow some thoughts upon her little motives, since they have so considerable a share in our actions, and if we are not aware of them, will so cover the scale as to prevent the weighty motive from reentering, or slip in at improper times, thereby producing a total avocation from the business in hand, or at least an interruption of our proceedings.

6. Nor must I omit to take notice of a certain magic that seems to alter the condition of our motives; they fluctuate and vary unaccountably, fading and regaining their colours, losing and retrieving their weight. An idea, that yesterday appeared vivid and strong, shall today show no sign of vigour at all; we still see it in the same form and position of parts as before, but it looks pale and lifeless, and feels as nothing in our hand. A thing we were extremely fond of at one time, we care not a pin for at another; what we admire this hour, we despise the next. Even virtue and pleasure have their seasons of engaging; not only as they appear or disappear to our thoughts, but when we have a full and distinct view of their features, we do not always find them strike upon us with equal allurement.

This fluctuation of our motives I believe has opened another door to the notion of a freewill of indifference; for observing that the mind does not always proceed to action instantly upon the suggestion of motives, that others of them oftener prevail than we should expect, that she resists the strongest passions and breaks through the firmest resolutions; we conclude she has an authority of her own independent of the motives, so that they cannot act until having first received her royal assent, but she can give any of them a preference without regard to their respective weights, and by taking part with inclination, can give it strength to overpower judgment, or by siding with the latter enable it to master the former. But all this may as well be accounted for by the variable quality of motives: while they continue changing their colours the balance keeps nodding to and fro, the mind perceives she has not a just estimation of their weights, and this is a motive with her to suspend action until the balance settles, and then it is the preponderating weight, not the mind, that sinks down the scale. When you have formed a resolution, so long as the considerations inducing you to make it retain their original vigour, and those you rejected their original weakness, and no new matter not taken at first into consideration interferes, you will surely adhere to your resolution: but if the tables turn, if that which was strongest becomes weakest, or fresh inducements not provided against before fall into the opposite scale, you will as surely break it. And that such accidents frequently happen, every one may satisfy himself who will attend carefully to the difference there is in our ideas of a thing between the time of resolving and the time of executing.

'Tis true we do sometimes play tricks with our balance, making it incline to either side as we please; but then this is done by art, not by strength or authority, and always brought about by the application of motives. For we have a power over our ideas, as has been remarked before, by stopping some of their channels to turn them into what other courses we like best, thereby excluding some ideas, and calling up others to our thoughts. We may close our ears against the admonitions of wisdom, or may hear them without attending, or may fill our imagination with something else that shall hinder them from entering; but it impeaches not the weight of a motive, nor shows your superior strength, that it does not operate when you will not let it come into the scale. And whoever watches himself narrowly when he practises this juggling, may always discern some motive of prejudice, favour, wilfulness, or shame of being overcome, which puts him upon the artifice; so that the mind will be found not so perfectly indifferent as she pretends in the very exercise of her indifference.

7. Here I shall take the liberty to stop a moment while I recommend it to every man to study diligently his motives of action; to examine what stock he has, as well of the permanent as of the transient kind, as well of his grand undertakings as of his sudden motions and manners of proceeding; what are their respective weights, either absolutely or comparatively, with one another; to remark how they introduce or mutually affect each other, how they fluctuate, their seasons of vigour and faintness; to distinguish what motive actually swayed with him upon every particular occasion. If he can do all this completely, he will discover the impositions of others, and what is better, will avoid imposing upon himself, which is the worst of all deceits. As the world goes, we lie under the necessity sometimes of alleging specious motives which did not influence us. A man asks you to lend him money which you have reason to think he will not repay, but you dare not tell him so, then you must put him off with excuses: but you ought always to know your own real motive. If the mind ever exerts a power of willing as well as acting, she performs that work by the instrumentality of motives, for therein lies her whole strength. When she perfectly knows her tools, where they lie, what they will do, and when they are in proper order, she may take her measures surely with respect to her moral and prudential conduct, and attain what the poet calls a life unacquainted with disappointment. In short, I look upon the study of our motives as conducing more than any one thing to that most useful of all sciences, The knowledge of oneself.

8. We have seen how the same considerations do not weigh alike with different persons, nor with the same person at different times; how they fluctuate and vary, their colours change to and fro, their weight diminishes, vanishes, and returns again, their form and parts continuing all along the same. Hence it appears that motives are com-

pound ideas, containing something whereon the force of the whole and its title to be deemed a final cause depends, which when wanting it loses its essence: for a motive having lost its force is no motive at all, nor the cause of anything. It remains then that we turn our thoughts to seek for that ingredient which gives efficacy to the compound, and denominates it a motive.

CHAPTER VI

SATISFACTION

Pleasure seems at first sight to bid the fairest for being that ingredient which gives weight to our motives, and we find by experience in multitudes of instances that it proves a sufficient inducement with us to act, for we perform many of our actions because we like them. And perhaps this may be the thing according to some notions of pleasure, for the word is not always taken precisely in the same sense. But it is the safest way to settle the meaning of our words by the standard of custom, and if we understand the term as it is commonly understood, we shall find pleasure often insufficient to perform the office of a motive, for we do many things against our liking. Pleasure in vulgar estimation stands opposed to business, duty, works of use, and necessity: yet in all these we feel some engagement, self-approbation, or complacence of mind, that carries us through with them. Pleasures, usually so called, often lose their gust, they satiate and cloy upon repetition, and nauseate instead of inviting. Therefore Mr. Locke has fixed upon the term Satisfaction,[1] as being more extensive, comprehending all that complacence we feel as well in business as diversion, as well in the works of prudence as in the starts of fancy. I cannot follow a better authority, especially as I find nothing within my own experience or observation to contradict it: therefore shall adopt his term Satisfaction to express that vivifying ingredient which gives life and vigour to our motives. But to prevent misapprehension, I think it necessary to subjoin a few remarks, in order to ascertain what I conceive we both understand by Satisfaction.

2. In the first place, I scarce need to take notice of what is obvious to every one, that we are not always in so happy a situation as to choose between enjoyments which we will prefer; we are sometimes reduced to the hard necessity of choosing between evils, which of them we judge the lightest. The pleuretic lying on his left side does not expect pleasure by turning to the other; he has no more in view than a diminution of pain. Mischief and displeasure seize upon us unawares, and we think of nothing but how to deliver ourselves from

1 A somewhat misleading claim. See *Essay*, Book II, Chapter VII, 2. Ed.

them: dangers threaten, and our care tends solely to escape them. Now in all these cases we are prompted to what we do by uneasiness, therefore uneasiness has an efficacy to set us at work as well as satisfaction; and accordingly Mr. Locke has given them both for distinct principles of action, though I have blended them together into one. But this I do not from any variance in opinion, but for convenience and shortness sake: and I think the junction may be made without any violence, for as a penny saved is a penny gotten, and the miser looks upon it as an actual gain if he can produce the abatement of a payment, so every diminution or avoidance of uneasiness is an approach towards satisfaction. Therefore, though I may speak of them apart, whenever necessity shall so require, yet for the generality I shall consider satisfaction only, and hope what I say of this will, with very little variation, be found applicable to the other.

3. In the second place, if any man desires to know what satisfaction is, he must not expect to learn it by definition from me; I can help him no further than by pointing out where he may find it himself. Let him reflect on what he feels when anything happens that pleases him, when he sits down to a well furnished table with a good appetite, when he reads a diverting book, when he receives news of some desirable event, when he looks back upon some performance for which he can applaud himself. Nor let him stop here, but carry on his contemplation to the common occurrences of life: when he applies to the business of his profession, or gives orders to his servant, or hears a newspaper, or takes his hat off the pin to go abroad, he will find that complacence in his most ordinary actions which renders life valuable. For bare existence has no other worth than as it serves for a basis to happiness, for we cannot be happy without being at all; but we all value our lives at a high rate, which we could not do, considering how thinly pleasures are scattered in the world, unless we found something satisfactory in almost everything we do upon the most trifling occasions. Some men live contentedly without pleasure, as that stands in the vulgar sense for an intense degree of enjoyment; but your melancholic persons, after having lost that glee which others feel in every common exercise of their powers, quickly grow weary of life. Therefore we must look upon satisfaction as the general term, containing under it joy, delight, pleasure, amusement, complacence, engagement, content, as the several stages. The lowest degree of satisfaction suffices to put us in motion when no higher intervenes; in our idle hours or vacant spaces of time we turn our eyes to look at a butterfly, or put down our hands to remove the flap of our waistcoat that had gotten between us and the chair. For the mind uses a nicer balance than the master of the mint: a cobweb will draw down the scale when nothing offers to counterpoise. Her understanding indeed is liable to mistake, being ill served by its ideas, which exhibit things frequently

under wrong appearances, but her volition follows exactly according to her apprehension of things.

4. When the mind has no grand purpose in view, she can fully content herself with any little trifle that presents; if she finds herself easy, and pleasure does not solicit, nor business urge, nor danger threaten, she rests perfectly satisfied with her condition, desiring nothing further. Which induced Hyeronymus to place happiness in vacuity or absence of pain, that is, in mere ease; supposing the sweetest pleasures engage us no otherwise than by creating a want of themselves, which fills us with an uneasiness we cannot remove without attaining them. But I may venture to refer it to the first man you meet in the street, whether there is not a real and sensible difference between actual pleasure and the bare absence of pain: for if this were sufficient to constitute happiness, we must be happy during every sound nap or fainting fit; because while the senses are gone so that we feel nothing, we certainly do not feel pain.

The same consideration I suppose led Epicurus to maintain that all pleasures were equal in degree, and differed only in kind, for the lowest of them satisfies the mind, and the highest can do no more: therefore a man finds as complete satisfaction in pulling up the heel of his slipper in the morning, as he does in recovering his only child that had been stolen away last week by a gipsy. But this contradicts daily experience, which testifies that we find a much greater relish in some pleasures than we do in others. A man may sit picking his fingers after dinner with perfect tranquillity of mind, but this is nothing to compare with the joy he feels on hearing the voice of an intimate friend at the door. Nor is it true that the mind can satisfy herself with little pleasures, unless when greater are not to be had or not apprehended in the imagination; who would not leave his trifling amusements upon being invited to a diversion he is extremely fond of, if no prudential or other motive withhold him? Why need the mind ever suspend her choice between two pleasures proposed until she has determined which is the greater, if either of them would answer her purpose alike? Therefore when several satisfactions offer together, that apprehended the greatest always prevails and carries away volition from the rest: nor can it be said to do so by the uneasiness of wanting it; for though we sometimes would forego an opportunity but that we fear we shall blame ourselves for having slipped it yet this is not always the case; we frequently quit a lesser pleasure for a greater instantly upon summons, without the least thought of what we might suffer by a self-denial. There is the like difference of degree in uneasiness; when several accost us at once, we fly that which presses the hardest. So if satisfaction pulls one way and uneasiness drives another, whichever is the strongest overpowers the other and gives the turn to our motion.

Happy is it for us that we can content ourselves with a small pittance of satisfaction, for else our lives would pass most uncomfortably: poignant pleasures and high delights rarely come in our way, and we should have nothing but uneasiness to fill up the large intervals between them. How miserably would the shopkeeper and the artizan spend their days, if they could work no longer than while the dread of starving hung over them! This perhaps might drive them into their several occupations at first, but their work furnishes them with an amusement that wholly engages their thoughts, and while they content themselves with finishing their tasks, they remove the evil without having it perpetually stare them in the face. What enterprize of moment could we perform; what business requiring a length of time could we complete, if we might never stir without some very powerful incitement to spur us? How many useful acquirements should we miss, if the apprehension of their being useful were not enough to move us, without having some particular signal service they will do us under contemplation? our dearest pleasures seldom drop into our mouths, but we must do many things to prepare for their reception, and what we do preparatory thereto partakes of the nature of business. For how lively expectations soever we may entertain at our entrance upon an undertaking, they cannot keep up their vigour during the course of a long work, which we pursue with that quiet complacency accompanying our ordinary motions. It has been commonly observed that a man can never succeed in any science, art, or profession, unless he takes a liking to it, but the liking here requisite need not arise to that high pitch as to render the fatigues of profession an uninterrupted scene of transport or delight. Hence we find that our gentle satisfactions, taken together in their whole amount, are much more valuable than our higher enjoyments; as exceeding them greatly in number, as furnishing us principally with employment for our time, and as serving us in our most useful and important occasions.

5. In the third place I shall remark, that although I have assigned satisfaction for the active ingredient of our motive, yet, if we examine the matter strictly, it is not very satisfaction but the prospect or idea of it; for these are different: one may have the full idea of a toothache one does not feel, and of a diversion one does not partake of. Now we do not use to enter upon action but for some end, which end is some satisfactory perception attainable thereby. Even when we walk for walking sake, it is not the bare motion, but the pleasant feel of our limbs, or of the air, that excites us. But this perception follows upon the action, and had no existence at the instant when the motive operated.—Therefore it is not the substance, but the prospect or expectance of satisfaction, which makes that part of the compound rendering it a motive. And this expectance, though sometimes fallacious, suffices to put us in motion: the child, that went to play with the candle, expected pleasure but found only smart; and the coward, who

runs away from his own shadow, expected a mischief that would not have attacked him.

Since, then, expectation is not the same with the thing expected, it follows that we may pursue satisfaction without being in a state of enjoyment, and fly uneasiness without being in a state of suffering. The former does not often happen, because, being founded upon delusion, we soon discover our expectations to be delusive upon trial, which then changes our prospect, and we change our measures accordingly. Yet it does happen sometimes; for those who have made pleasures their constant employment, quickly cloy themselves with the frequent repetition of them, yet still pursue them with delusive hopes of the same relish they used to find heretofore, and run from diversion to diversion, in restless expectation of an enjoyment they cannot attain. But uneasiness exciting us to avoid it, may continue to operate without delusion: for if we find our endeavours upon trial effectual to ward off a mischief, this will encourage us to repeat them as often as the danger presents, and so long as we can keep evil aloof, we shall not fall into a state of suffering. If two old acquaintances, who had not met for some years before, were to espy one another on the opposite sides of the Haymarket, probably they would run together into the middle of the street, if the weather were fine and the ground dry, where they would join in an agreeable conversation: in the midst of their discourse they see a coach fifty yards off driving directly towards them, I suppose they would remove out of the way to one side or other, still continuing their talk. What then is it puts them upon this action? not satisfaction, for they propose no addition to that by changing their ground: it is no other than the uneasiness of being trampled upon by the horses, which, because they can avoid without trouble, makes no interruption of their enjoyment. He that walks along Cheapside must turn and wind perpetually to avoid jostling the other passengers; the prospect of uneasiness he would feel upon running against people, induces him to all those motions, which yet makes no abatement of any satisfaction he may have in the errand he goes upon, nor throws him into a state of suffering.

6. For my fourth remark, I shall observe that present satisfaction is the end we constantly have in view on proceeding to action. Nor does this contradict what I have just been endeavouring to prove, for by present satisfaction I would not be understood so strictly as to mean the satisfaction we actually have at the instant of acting: for this is no subject of action, nor can receive alteration thereby. We cannot unfeel the pain we feel by any effort of ours, nor does the pleasure we now have need an effort to procure it. But the satisfaction we propose in every exertion of our activity is that of the moment next immediately ensuing, and this may be called present satisfaction without any impropriety of speech. For we are constantly told the present time

only is in our power, the past being gone and the future lying out of our reach: but this present time is in reality the next succeeding instant, that alone being the subject of our power, for we do not act in order to obtain what we have already. Perceptions flow in upon us without intermission, and we generally have a foresight of them before they come, as also a power many times to alter their course by the proper application of objects or management of our organs: therefore we keep constantly upon the look out; while we see that such perceptions as we like will rise of their own accord, we have nothing to do, when they will not, we use our activity to procure them. In all action there are three things to be considered, the prospect or expectation, the action itself, and the perception to be introduced thereby: the first has no other value than as it directs us what action to pursue, nor the second than as it tends to procure the third, so that our business lies in helping ourselves to procure satisfactory or escape uneasy perceptions. But as we must every instant have some perception or other, we must provide for the next ensuing perception, and as soon as that is had, another to follow immediately after furnishes us with the like employment; so that our wants, starting up successively without intermission, require a continual supply; which confines our cares to the present moment, leaving the provision for future moments to our subsequent endeavours.

This accounts for what Mr. Locke has fully proved to be fact, that good, the greater good acknowledged and apprehended to be such, does not always determine the Will: and I may add, it never does, unless by means of the satisfaction we feel in making advances towards it; for if any distant advantage can raise in us a desire of attaining it, the gratification of this desire will afford a present satisfaction. And that remote good and evil have such effect upon us daily experience bears witness: we flatter ourselves often with distant hopes, and shudder at future dangers; we contemplate with pleasure the prospect of enjoyments afar off, and look with horror upon misfortunes before they come. Suppose a person, in whose knowledge and veracity you could fully confide, should say to you, Sir, you shall continue in plenty and the possession of everything you can desire to-day and tomorrow, but the third day your estate shall be seized, your children carried into bondage, and your body afflicted with painful distempers: would not the news fill you with a cruel anxiety? On the other hand, had you been tormented with the gout for a long while, and after having tried many remedies to no purpose had lost all hopes of relief, should you receive the like assurance that in two days' time you should be set at ease and perfectly cured: should not you feel an exhilarating joy that would overpower the pangs of your distemper? And the like happens proportionably upon the prospect of anything useful or detrimental, pleasurable or troublesome, in a lower degree.

7. This presentiment of the future makes the great privilege of human nature; for were we void of it we should have nothing but appetite to follow, like the brute creatures: but our concern for the morrow creates another appetite which prompts us to escape mischiefs that must be guarded against beforehand, and pursue great advantages that require much time and labour to attain. It likewise lengthens our pleasures beyond their natural measure, for enjoyment generally holds only for a little moment, but expectation, hope, and successful pursuit, often supply us with a constant fund of delight for a long season. But on the other hand, it is attended with some inconveniences, by tormenting us sometimes with unavoidable evils before they come near us, and making us tremble at imaginary dangers that would never have fallen upon us.

And these derivative satisfactions fluctuate as much as the original: for we do not always find equal relish in the same enjoyment, nor does the prospect of it always appear in colours equally vivid. Neither can we observe any other rule in this change of colours than that they generally heighten upon the nearer approach of the enjoyment. But the very prospect of an attainable good, or an avoidable evil, commonly proves satisfactory; therefore, however it may sometimes happen otherwise, for the most part we continue in a state of enjoyment, in some degree or other, during the pursuit of a benefit we hope to acquire, or avoidance of a mischief we can easily ward off. Whence comes the saying, Hope makes the heart glad.

8. Fifthly, I shall take notice that satisfaction always attracts, and uneasiness always repels; and either of them operates according to the present occasion. If some advantage invites, we set ourselves instantly to pursue it; if a greater starts up in view, we quit the former and run after the latter: if mischief approaches, we set ourselves to prevent it: and while it continues to hang over us, we continue our efforts to keep it aloof. Therefore to me it seems that both satisfaction and uneasiness have a like efficacy to make us either change or adhere to our measures, as occasion shall require. But Mr. Locke ascribes the change of action solely to uneasiness, and the continuance of it to satisfaction[1]; it behoves me to give my reasons for departing from so great an authority.

I shall allege first, that, properly speaking, there is no such thing as a continuance of action, all our perceptions and all our volitions being transient and momentary. What we term a continuance is indeed only a repetition of successive perceptions and volitions of the same kind: just as a spout continues to run while it pours forth innumerable drops without any interval between. So if you stare at the same picture for half an hour together, the sight comes by successive rays of light affecting your eyes in the same manner, and the perceptions raised

[1] In *Essay*, Book II, Chapter XXI, 29. Ed.

thereby, although exactly similar, are individually distinct. And if you keep pointing with a stick for the same time, successive volitions hold up your hand, for should you forbear to repeat them, your arm would fall instantly to your side.

But waving this nicety, let us consider a series of motions, all proceeding upon one plan and with the same design, as a continuance of action: yet I think one may produce instances wherein we depart from our design, and change our measures without being driven by the lash of uneasiness. Suppose a man sitting down to his harpsichord intending to play through an opera of Corelli: in the midst of his diversion enters a messenger to tell him, that, if he will come away directly to the minister, he may be instated in a considerable preferment he had long wished and ardently sought for. Is it uneasiness or joy that makes him leave his music and run to catch up his hat? Suppose a company of young folks agreeably entertained in dancing; somebody tells them of a fine fire-work just going to be played off in a neighbouring garden: I will not ensure they shall not all run instantly to the window. When their curiosity a little abates and before the sight begins to cloy, some one puts them in mind of their dancing, perhaps the rest take the admonition and they run back to their sport as hastily as they quitted it. Surely this is a change of action and a departure from the plan laid down for the employment of the night: yet I appeal to any gentleman or lady, who may have experienced such an incident, whether they feel the least spice of uneasiness either in breaking off their diversion or returning to it again. On the other hand, suppose a man travelling through a lonely forest infested with a gang of desperate villains, who murder all they meet; he sees them coming towards him, and has but just time to jump into a stinking bog, where he can hide his head behind a little bush: the rogues halt at a small distance from him, where they sit chattering perhaps an hour or two, all which time I suppose he will hardly quit his lurking hold. Now what is it holds him to this continuance of action? is it satisfaction? He sees none and expects none by sticking up to the shoulders in dirt and nastiness. Is it any other than the uneasy dread of falling into their hands, where he can expect nothing but misery and destruction?

9. But I am so averse to differing from Mr. Locke, that whenever I cannot bring my notions to tally with his, I hunt about for all expedients to reconcile them, so that I may hold my own consistently with those he entertains. And such expedient is most likely to be found by observing upon the unsteadiness and variableness of language. The most careful, as well as the giddy, use their words in various significations. Your men of close application, though taking their terms from the common language, find themselves under a necessity of recasting them in a mould of their own, to fit them for purposes that were not wanted in the usual intercourses of life: and sometimes the moulds

they severally use differ from one another in some little particular. What if this should be the case between Mr. Locke and myself? Might we not then think the same at bottom, while we express ourselves by opposite sides of a contradiction? Perhaps, what he calls a continuance of action I should call a continuance of courses; and so there is no repugnance, because we are not talking of the same thing.

Now in order to understand what I mean by courses, please to take notice that we have each of us a set of views, aims, and desires, leading us into those courses of behaviour which fill up the employment of our lives; and though we may frequently step aside out of one track into another, we still continue to pursue courses of the same set. The word carries this sense in common conversation when we speak of virtuous or vicious courses: nor is a man reckoned to alter his courses because he quits the exercise of one virtue, or gratification of one vicious appetite, for that of another, as opportunity occurs. Neither does every turning after other pursuits at intervals make a discontinuance of the first: for some are of such a nature as not to be completed but by returning to the work at distant seasons with large gaps and spaces intervening. Thus a man may continue a course of physic though he dispatches business, takes diversions, and does many things between whiles. Therefore Mr. Locke would probably say of the man that left his harpsichord to get a place, that he had two desires directing his courses, the love of music, and of money or honour, and when the latter drew him away from the former, here was no change of measures, but the continuance of a pursuit he had long since been engaged in. The dancers were following a course of pleasure which kept them on in the same road, how much soever particular objects might vary. That the poor traveller was held in his quagmire by self-preservation, which is a main principle influencing us in the course of our lives, and which we never throw aside until some hard pressure of fortune shall make us uneasy with our being.

And that Mr. Locke had these courses in view appears manifest from the instances he makes use of in support of his assertion; which are that of "an idle fellow whom you shall not move to industry, convince him never so much of the advantage plenty has over poverty, make him see and own never so plainly that the handsome conveniences of life are better than nasty penury, so long as he can content himself with the latter and finds no uneasiness in it. And of a worldling, who, though never so well persuaded of the advantages of virtue, that it is as necessary to a man who has any great aims, as food to life, yet enters not upon any action in pursuit of this confessed greater good until he hungers and thirsts after righteousness, and feels an uneasiness in the want of it." [1]

Now I shall not deny that we seldom, if ever, fail to continue our

1 Tucker is here paraphrasing Locke. See *Essay*, Book II, Chapter XXI, 35. Ed.

courses of action so long as they prove satisfactory, nor change them until they become insipid and cloy, or lead into inconveniences that gives us a disgust of them. Neither can you well reclaim a man from vicious courses by the offer of satisfaction, for you have none to propose that will be such to him: the pleasure and ease of virtue arise from the practice of it, and he who has never practised it will see nothing inviting in it. Therefore you must begin with him by representing the mischievous tendency of his evil doings, and if you can bring him to a dread and abhorrence of them, which shall make him uneasy under the apprehension of them, you may prevail upon him to change his measures. There are, indeed, besides the satisfaction your proficients in virtue feel in every exercise of it, certain rewards and fruits that any man would desire, but these operate at first by the uneasiness they create in the want of them. For when a man has taken a resolution of purchasing those rewards, the solicitations of old habits will frequently draw him back into his old courses, upon which the uneasiness and vexation of having failed in his resolution may drive him to renew it again, and while he adheres, the uneasiness of denying his other desires still torments him: so that he must remain in a state of uneasiness while the change is making, and until it be completed by the old habits entirely losing their vigour. Which makes good the observation of ancient and modern ages, that the paths of virtue are thorny and rugged at their entrance, but lead into a pleasant and delightful country.

10. Thus, though I have represented action in a different light from Mr. Locke, we must not therefore be thought to differ in substance, but in our manner of handling it. For though I do not pretend to a clearer, perhaps I may to a more microscopic eye: I consider action more minutely, endeavouring to analyze it into its primary parts. Now the shape and other circumstances belonging to the parts may vary greatly from those of the whole. Look upon your table, and you see it round or square, or of some other regular form: hold your eye near the wood, and you will perceive it waving in veins, or running in longitudinal fibres: the little particles composing it attract and cohere strongly to one another, but the table neither attracts nor coheres to the paper, the ink-bottle, nor the penknife you lay upon it. So if a habit of drinking be taken as one action, it may always be continued so long as a man can satisfy himself in the practice, and always broken off as soon as the uneasiness of a gout, or other mischief brought upon him thereby, shall exceed his fondness for the liquor: and yet the single acts whereof that large action consists may spring from satisfaction or uneasiness, indifferently, as either happens to present. For he may change his bottle either because he dislikes that standing before him, or because he pleases himself with the thought of tasting another sort; and he may stay some time at the tavern for the

pleasure of the company, and continue there after that pleasure ceases, to avoid the uneasiness of going home, where he will not know what to do with himself.

Since then, nature has furnished me with a microscope, why should I not accept her favour, for she bestows not the slightest of her gifts in vain? The Temple of Knowledge cannot be built without the concurrent labours of many artificers working with various qualifications. Who then shall blame me for making such use as I can of my little talent in pursuing minute discoveries that persons of larger views overlook? Should I fail of doing any good service myself, somebody else may turn them to better advantage: for it is no uncommon thing in the sciences, as well as arts and manufactures, to see one man prepare materials for another to work up. However, if my health and spirits hold, I shall strive hard but I will make some texture out of my materials that a man shall find convenient for his service, without sending it to another operator to be finished.

11. I hope matters are pretty well accommodated with Mr. Locke in regard to the difficulty before mentioned; but I do not know how I shall come off with him upon another point, where he speaks of the uneasiness of desire, and makes desire constantly accompanied with uneasiness.[1] I can go with him half way, so far as to admit that desire often creates us cruel uneasinesses, and that the smart of their wounds rises in proportion to the intenseness of our desire. But this happens only when desire meets with a disappointment; when two incompatible desires urge strongly at once, both of which cannot be gratified; when some hindrance checks or at least retards desire. For while desire runs on smoothly in its course towards attainment, while we want nothing besides the object we pursue, while no bar stands across the way, nor difficulty occurs to check our speed, for my part I can see nothing but continual satisfaction accompanying the progress.

I may say with Mr. Dryden, "Old as I am, for lady's love unfit, The power of beauty I remember yet." [2] I still bear in mind the days of my courtship, which in the language of all men is called a season of desire; yet, unless I strangely forget myself, it proved to me a season of satisfaction too. But, says Mr. Locke, it is better to marry than to burn, where we may see what it is that chiefly drives men into a conjugal life. This, for aught I know, might be the motive with some men, who, being of an unsociable and undomestic turn, can see nothing good in matrimony, but submit to it as a lesser evil delivering them from a greater. And I can excuse an old bachelor for entertaining so despicable a notion of a state he never experienced the pleasures of himself. Others it may be make their engagements too hastily, and then would break them off again through the shame of doing a foolish

1 In *Essay*, Book II, Chapter XXI, 32. Ed.
2 *Cymon and Iphigenia, from Boccace*, 1–2. Ed.

thing, till the smart of their burnings becomes intolerable, and drives them headlong into the matrimonial net. But this, thanks to my stars, was not my case: my own judgment, upon mature deliberation, and the approbation of my friends, gave leave for desire to take its course. I might feel some scorchings in my youthful days when it would have been imprudent to quench them, and while the object of desire lay at an undiscernible distance: but as the prospect drew nearer, and desire had license to begin its career, it had no more the fierceness of a furnace, but became a gentle flame, casting forth a pleasing exhilarating warmth. Perhaps I might meet with some little rubs in the way, that gave me disturbance: if my fair one spake a civil word to any tall, well-bred young fellow, I might entertain some idle apprehensions lest he should supplant me. When I took a hackney coach to visit her, if we were jammed in between the carts, perhaps I might fret and fume, and utter many an uneasy Pish; but as soon as we got through the stop, though desire abated not, every shadow of uneasiness fled away. As near as I can remember, during the whole scene, desire, close attended by satisfaction, directed all my steps, and occupied all my moments: it awaked with me in the morning, and was the last idea swept away by sleep: it invigorated me in business, it heightened my diversions, it gave me life when in company, and entertained me with delightful reflections when alone. Nor did it fail of accompanying me to the altar, where, laying aside its sprightliness and gaiety, as unsuitable to the solemnity of the occasion, it became more calm and decent, exhibiting the prospect of an agreeable companion, who should double the enjoyments and alleviate the troubles of life; who should ease me from the burthen of household cares, and assist me in bringing up a rising family; whose conversation should be a credit to me abroad, and a continual feast to me at home. Nor yet did possession put an end to desire, which found fresh fuel to keep it alive from time to time, in mutual intercourses of kindness and hearty friendship, in communication of interests, counsels and sentiments; and could often feed upon the merest trifles. How often, having picked up some little piece of news abroad, has desire quickened my pace to prattle over it at home! How often, upon hearing of something curious in the shops, have I gone to buy it with more pleasure than the keenest sportsman goes after his game! Thus desire, leading delight hand in hand, attended us for many years, still retaining its first vigour, although a little altered in shape and complexion; until my other half was torn from me. Then indeed desire left me, for it had nothing now to rest upon, and with it fled joy, delight, content, and all those under desires that used to put me upon the common actions of the day; for I could like nothing, find amusement in nothing, and care for nothing: and in their stead succeeded melancholy, tastelessness, and perpetual restlessness. And though I called in all my philosophy to rescue me from this disconsolate condition, it could not relieve me presently, but had a long struggle before it could get the better of nature.

12. I doubt not there are many persons in the world, who having been as happily paired, could read the account here given of myself as feelingly as ever I wrote it. As for your determined bachelors or injudicious husbands who have married only for money, or for beauty, or for a frolic, or for a bedfellow, or for they did not well know why, though they may think me romantic, yet I suppose they have had desires of their own of some sort of other; either of raising a fortune, or of preferment, or of building, or of gardening, or of sports, or of dress, or of acquisitions in learning, which have engaged them in long pursuits. And I believe we shall all give in our verdict unanimously upon the positive evidence of our own several experience, That our desires have furnished us with the greatest parts of our enjoyments in life; and that desire, so long as it can move unsuccessfully without rub or disappointment, without wanting fuel to feed it, and without pain or unlucky accidents intervening, has supplied us with a continual fund of satisfaction. But when desire grows languid for want of fresh matter to work upon, when it cannot, like a wanton bird, hop about from twig to twig, from bush to bush, continuing its play, then the time hangs heavy upon our hands: when it meets with crosses or delays, when it rises to impatience, or is of such a nature as to require an immediate gratification that cannot be had; then indeed vexation and uneasiness find a ready entrance.

That the uneasiness Mr. Locke found in desire, proceeds from some of those causes, may appear by the examples he produces in proof of it. Desire, says he, deferred, makes the heart sick.[1] Leave out the participle Deferred, and the rest of the sentence will not hold true. Change it for another, and we may lay down the contrary as a maxim; for desire promoted makes the heart glad. Therefore desire is not in its own nature a state of uneasiness, nor unless rendered so by disappointment or delay. Give me children, says Rachael, or I die; but this was not till after a long course of barrenness she began to despair of having any; when Joseph was coming, we hear no more of such exclamations, yet I suppose she still continued to desire it might prove a boy. Where he speaks of the uneasiness of hunger and thirst, surely he must have in his thoughts the cravings of a person almost dying with either, rather than the common returns of appetite at stated seasons during health. I speak only for myself: when I sit down to dinner I feel no uneasiness in being hungry, but rather rejoice at having a good appetite, from whence I expect a better relish to my victuals than any sauces could give them. How do other people fare upon the like occasion? If on coming home from a journey in hot weather, you find yourself faintish and droughty, and call for a glass of wine and water,

[1] *Ibid*. Ed.

have you not a pleasure in seeing the wine pour from the bottle or sparkle in the glass, even before you bring it to your mouth? And does not this pleasure arise from your desire? for you would feel it no longer on the like prospect after having fully quenched your thirst. Pretty bottle, says Sganarelle, how sweet are thy little glug glugs! how envied would be my lot wert thou to keep always full for all my pourings! Desire then gave the glugs their sweetness, for Sganarelle was in a state of desire, not of fruition, when he solaced himself with their music, the liquor having not yet entered his lips; nor was there I suppose anything very harmonious in the sound, or any other charm besides the assurance of his bottle being full, and the means of accomplishing his desire abundantly at hand.

Could uneasiness alone determine the Will, how wretched must the condition of mankind appear! For the Will never ceases working from morning till night: we are always a doing, but should have nothing to do unless to deliver ourselves from uneasinesses following close upon one another's heels. Human life from beginning to end would be nothing but a restless endeavour to throw off an evil we could never totally remove, and would exhibit one continued scene of uninterrupted uneasiness. But, kind nature be praised! our condition is not quite so forlorn and comfortless. We have our hours, and those of activity too, wherein we can employ ourselves with satisfaction and delight: and since in those pleasurable seasons we do not stand idle, there must be something else besides uneasiness capable of urging us to action.

13. Mr. Locke it seems once held that ancient, and till his time universally received opinion, That good, the greater good, understood and apprehended to be such, determined the Will: he first discovered that it was always something present, and no distant good, that gave the turn to our activity; for which I acknowledge myself and the world greatly obliged to him; for an important and leading discovery it was, as it has let us more than anything into the secret springs of human action. But since new discoveries are seldom perfected at once, may I be permitted to offer at an improvement, and add, that present satisfaction, as well as present uneasiness is capable of performing the office. I know that distant good does often operate by the uneasy want we have of it, by the shame, the vexation, the regret, we feel in slipping our opportunity of gaining it, but it has likewise a quality of throwing a sensible satisfaction upon every step we take in advancing towards it. Which latter I conceive wants not efficacy, especially in those who have a strong attachment to virtue and prudence, or, as Mr. Locke expresses it, who hunger and thirst after righteousness, any more than the former, to determine volition: and according as the one or the other actuates our motions, we pursue the object of our desires through the flowery meads of delight, or the thorny paths of trouble and self-denial.

14. But it may be said that, according to my own doctrine (§ 8), satisfaction and uneasiness are not so incompatible but the one may move us while the other possesses us: therefore why may not uneasiness be the sole incitement constantly spurring to action, without necessarily rendering our motions uneasy, while we can keep it aloof by continual efforts to escape it? I do not forget what I have there laid down, that one may fly uneasiness without being in a state of suffering; for the prospect of the next ensuing moment moves us to action, but the feel of the present denominates our condition: now one may have the prospect of a very different sort of ground from that one stands upon. Delightful is it, says Lucretius, to stand upon firm land and see the mariners tossing and toiling in a tempestuous sea. Delightful to behold the bloody scenes of war spread over a spacious field without sharing in the danger yourself. Not because there is any pleasure in seeing others tormented, but because the prospect of evils from which yourself are exempt is delightful. Nor I suppose would your delight be the less if you were to do something towards escaping the danger, provided you had certain and easy means at hand for effecting your escape: were you on board the fleet, but stepping into a boat that should land you safe before the storm began to rage; or in the army, and mounting an easy pad that should carry you far enough out of harm's way before the battle joined. But where Locke treats of the uneasiness giving birth to our actions, I cannot understand him of the prospect but of very uneasiness itself; which to my thinking cannot consist with a state of enjoyment, but must necessarily, according to the degree of it, throw the mind into a state of suffering so long as it continues and as often as it returns. For to the question, What determines the Will? he answers, Some uneasiness a man is at present under. So that it is not timely caution against an approaching mischief, but the pressure of uneasiness actually felt, that alone suffices to set us at work: and this equally the same, whether the avoidance of evil or attainment of distant good be the object of our endeavours. For, says he, there is a desire of ease from pain, and another of absent positive good, in which latter also the desire and uneasiness is equal: as much as we desire any absent good, so much we are in pain for it. Now whether the prospect of absent attainable good does always fill us with a painful want and uneasiness, I have some reasons to doubt: but shall defer giving them until I have gone through my next observation, which may render what I have to say upon this point more easily intelligible.

15. For my sixth remark I shall lay down, That satisfaction and uneasiness often beget and introduce each other: the bare escape from pain gives a sensible pleasure, and the loss of any great pleasure grieves us: whatever affects us strongly, of either kind, generally leaves its contrary behind. In time to come, says Eneas, we shall find

entertainment in reflecting on the hardships we now undergo. For past sufferings, not likely to return, are often a feast to the mind; and past pleasures we can no longer enjoy, remembered with regret. A man just recovered from a fever, finds enjoyment in the very deliverance from his disease; he can pass the day agreeably, though with his servants only about him, in a manner he would have thought insipid, lonely, and irksome, at another time; for he satisfies himself with ease, and wants nothing further to divert him. Thus a great deal of our good springs out of evil; we should often rust in idleness, and feel the time heavy upon our hands, were it not for pain, difficulty, and danger, which rouse us to action; and though they make us smart for the present, repay us abundantly afterwards by affording a greater satisfaction in having surmounted them, than they gave us trouble in surmounting.

On the other hand, suppose a man provided with plenty of all conveniences, and means of ordinary amusement, and fully contented with his present situation: yet tell him of some high diversion going forward in the neighbourhood which he must not partake of, and you may perhaps raise a want in him that shall vitiate all his other enjoyments, and throw him into a state of disquiet and uneasiness. For I shall never deny that strong desires do frequently raise an uneasy want of the object they fasten upon; nor that this does sometimes prevail where the satisfaction of advancing towards the object would not: but I conceive this is not always the case, but that desire sometimes operates by the satisfaction of pursuing, and sometimes by the uneasiness of wanting, the thing desired. If a lazy fellow has some acquisition greatly to his liking proposed, he may make a few faint motions at first, and please himself with the prospect of possessing it, but his indolence puts him off from day to day from using any significant endeavours; he then begins to reflect with himself, finds the completion of his wishes no nearer than at first setting out; this raises an uneasy want of them, which grows greater and greater by degrees, till at last it overpowers his slothfulness, and makes him set his hand in good earnest to the plough.

16. That uneasiness is the motive in most of those instances mentioned by Mr. Locke I shall readily agree, and might produce others wherein uneasiness does the work, although pleasure in the eye of the world runs away with the credit of it; for many times it is not easy to discern which of the two determined the Will. Your debauchees, your triflers, and very fashionable people, who make pleasure their sole employment, I doubt not find delight in it at first; but pleasure too often repeated abates of its relish, and at length becomes wholly insipid: yet still they run on the same round of diversions, thinking they follow pleasure all the while, and so indeed they do, though not with satisfaction, but for want of something else to amuse them, or through the cravings of an unnatural appetite brought upon them by custom.

Follow them to their clubs, and you may hear them sing without joy, laugh without being pleased, and thrum over the same jests till they grow threadbare. View them in their routs, and they run on the same roll of compliments and common expressions, talking incessantly without having anything to say. Peep upon them at their toilets, and you will perceive dress to be a labour undergone to avoid appearing hideous and out of mode among company. Some real satisfactions they may have when anything new or unexpected engages their fancy: but chiefly I believe in going on the way to their parties, which is a kind of business, being an action undertaken not for its own sake, but for some end: they may then rejoice at having thrown off the insupportable burden of time, and escaped the misery of staying at home alone, or may flatter themselves with the same relish in their diversions they used formerly to enjoy; for delusive expectations will satisfy the mind so long as the delusion holds. Thus the cloven-footed tyrant inveigles the unwary with exorbitant wages at first, but having once bound them to his service, by rendering them unfit for any other, he shortens their allowance, giving them no more than just enough to persuade them they earn something, and for the most part lashes them through his drudgery with scourges, or pinches them with his iron claws.

Now let us do justice on all sides, and confess honestly that the virtuous man does not always find delight in the practice of his virtues. There is a joy, a complacence of mind which I hope every one of us feels upon acting right: but there is likewise a shame, a vexation, a compunction, upon acting wrong: and this latter often serves to keep us steady in our good courses when the other would have failed. Could we behold virtue naked, says Plato, we should find her so divinely charming that we could never like anything else: but virtue is a modest virgin, she will not let you see her naked until you are wedded to her; she displays a hand, an arm, a cheek, at a time, as you get further into her familiarity. Therefore how much soever young admirers may be smitten with her at first sight, while covered with her veil, this like all sudden desires cannot hold its vigour: but the solicitations of passion or old vicious habits will draw them from their pursuit, unless the general persuasion of her being a consummate beauty shall raise a want of her acquaintance that may overpoise all uneasiness beside. As for those who are become intimate with the lovely creature, they may see so much of her beauties, and retain such a taste of her sweetness, as shall fill them with a warm and steady delight, sufficient to make them surmount difficulties and troubles with pleasure, and if I may so say, render uneasiness itself perfectly easy. I can imagine it possible in theory, that a man may have so strong a relish for the practice of virtue, as may make his condition happy under the greatest pain; that he may look upon all present sufferings as nothing for the exceeding weight of glory that lies in store hereafter. For I know any strong desire has power sometimes to pluck out the sting of pain; I have experienced it myself in little complaints, such as an aching corn or a grumbling tooth, which though I have felt, I have despised and not wished to remove when eager in the pursuit of something greatly to my fancy. But I much question whether the acquisition of so strong a desire as shall keep a man easy in Phalaris's bull, be practicable among the sons of Adam: it is a great matter if we can raise inclination enough to carry us through common difficulties and troubles without being hurt by them. Therefore, unless we had an abhorrence of vice, and felt a want of virtue when absent, as well as a delight in her company when present, we should make very little advance in our progress towards her.

Thus the lives of all men, the virtuous and the vicious alike, though not in equal proportion, are checquered; not only with respect to the vicissitudes of health and distemper, success and disappointment, favours and frowns of fortune attending them, but also to the motives of joy or vexation, content or disquiet, spurring on alternately to action. Desire, like a smiling angel, and its bastard offspring Want, like the knight of the ill-favoured face, direct our conduct by turns. While some idle passion passing by holds desire in chat, the other jumps into the box; as soon as the intruder can be got rid of the rightful coachman resumes his seat. While he holds the reins we roll smoothly and currently along, feasting our eyes upon the gladsome prospect before us; but when his deputy drives, clouds of noisome dust obstruct our view, we feel the carriage jolt and hobble, tossing us to and fro, and knocking our joints perpetually against the sides. For according as desire or want actuate our motions, we are in a state of enjoyment or a state of suffering: and this whether our object be some distant good, or the removal from approaching evil.

17. Now after what has been laid down under this sixth remark, nobody will expect me to controvert with Mr. Locke, that desire often begets uneasiness, and how much we desire an absent positive good, so much we are in pain for it: but this I apprehend never happens until something obstructs our advances towards the good desired. Want does not come before, nor does the child use to be older than the parent. We cannot be said to want what we may have when we please, or are in the ready way to obtain, yet we desire it, or else we should not proceed in the way. Some desires do not tend to immediate gratification: if a man, fond of hunting, meets with friends who propose a match for the next day, he may desire to make one among them, and give orders to his servant relative thereto, without any want of the diversion, which, were it offered, he would not choose to go upon directly, nor until he had prepared himself by a good night's rest for the fatigue. What we possess we cannot be thought to want, though we may desire the continuance of it; but that is for our future

occasions, not to remove any present uneasiness. Every man having just received his last year's income, desires I suppose to receive his next also, but he does not want it, nor had he it in hand, and were a prudent man, would he make use of it for his expenses of the current year. We all desire life and health, and do many things for their preservation; but while in vigour, peace, and plenty, what want do we feel of either? Can we never choose a food because it is wholesome, nor take an agreeable exercise to mend our constitution, unless driven by approaching sickness, or affrighted by the king of terrors staring us in the face? We all desire the fresh air we breathe, but must we never walk into the fields to enjoy a purer draught, until almost suffocated by the smoke of town?

18. Besides, although every considerable desire may have its opposite want, and either of them be capable of inciting us to action, when we seek for the motive we must consider what actually operated. For the mind may have many motives in store which do not always enter the scale, and when they do not, have no share in weighing down the balance. Whatever other folks might do, Mr. Locke, I dare say, would agree with me, that an action can be ascribed to no motive that was not present in the thought or imagination at the time of acting. A man goes to the playhouse thinking only to see the play, and there meets with an intimate acquaintance, in whose conversation he takes great delight. Perhaps he did not know the other would be there; perhaps he had heard it last week, but utterly forgot it again: amusement then was his motive; the meeting his friend had no share in his motion; although, had that occurred to his thoughts, he would have gone ten times more readily. Therefore, to discover the true spring of action, it is not enough to know that want is capable of performing the office of a spring, but we must examine whether we had such want in view at the instant of bestirring ourselves. The hard student, says Mr. Locke, will not leave his studies for the pleasures of appetite, but when hunger begins to make him uneasy, then away he goes to remove it. But is this the case with every student? When I have been staring all the morning at the light of nature, till I have stared myself almost blind, I find my spirits want recreation: I then throw aside my papers sometimes before dinner; the veriest trifle suits my purpose best: the philosopher can loll out at window like Miss Gawkey, to see the wheelbarrow trundle, or the butcher's dog carry the tray, and is perfectly contented with his situation as being fittest for the present occasion. Presently the bell rings, and down run I into the parlour. Now did Whitefield and Wesley endeavour to stop me, bellowing out their exhortations to abstinence, self-denial, and mortification, possibly I might fret a good deal, and the uneasiness of wanting my dinner urge me to exert all my might in brushing by them. But by good luck they do not honour me with their acquaintance, nor have I any of their

revelations commanding me to austerities: so that the thought of starving, or of what I should suffer by missing a meal, never once enters into my head, and therefore cannot be the motive actuating my motions.

But neither does it appear to me universally true, that how much we desire absent good so much we are in pain for it. There are many little goods weighty enough to turn the mental scale, but not strong enough to give us pain. We have numberless gentle desires continually prompting us to common actions, yet too feeble to beget any off-spring. When these prompt us, if the object can be readily come at, it is very well: if not, we give ourselves no further concern, nor think it worth any trouble to procure; we feel no want, no pain, nor disappointment, in the miss of it. Sometimes I walk to and fro in my garden in the country, intending only to ruminate on some trifle or other; perhaps I espy a peach that looks ripe and inviting, and I reach out my hand to pluck it. Should my gardener tell me, Sir, I thought to have reserved that for the company you expect tomorrow, or should any other little reason occur to stop me, I should forbear; but if nothing intervenes, I go on to complete my purpose. Now, when I reflect on the state of my mind on such occasions, and examine mine ideas with the closest application of the microscope, as well when I gratify my fancy as when I restrain it, I cannot discern the least pain, or want, or uneasiness imaginable: and therefore crave leave to conclude that something else, besides want and uneasiness, is capable of determining me to the use of my powers.

19. Whence then comes it that Mr. Locke and I entertain so different notions concerning desire? For we are both careful plodding folks; not used to do things hastily, but sifting our thoughts, and weighing our words before we deal them out. Is the difference owing to the microscopic make of mine eye, that sees minuter goods, smaller actions, slenderer desires, than other people? or is there some fallacy, some equivocation, some various use of language, that keeps us asunder? Perhaps what I take for desire, while successful in its career, he may call joy or hope, or by some other name. Perhaps all that we do in pursuit of the same object, though I should think it a series of distinct actions, and distinct volitions, he may consider as one action, and one determination of the Will, which, while retaining its full vigour, and the purpose not completed, we do not depart from to make a new determination until pressed by some urgent want or uneasiness. Thus, if your hard student determines at breakfast to study so many hours, and then take an airing abroad, while he turns over his books, or when he throws them aside, here is no determination made of the Will, for that was done once for all in the morning: nor can you draw him from his plan before the determined time by any solicitations of pleasure; but should his head ache, or his stomach cry cupboard, the

uneasiness of that might drive him into a new course of action different from that he had determined upon before. I wish somebody would help us to a clue to guide through this labyrinth, and bring us together again; for I am never better satisfied with myself than when travelling in his company. In the mean while, though I reverence his authority beyond that of all others, whether ancient or modern, in matters relating to human nature, yet he will excuse me for adhering to my own judgment until it shall be altered by better information; for he, I am sure, would be the last man in the world to impose an authority upon anybody, or desire to draw followers by any other force than the conviction of their own judgment. Yet I still hope the difference is not a variance of sentiment, but of expression, or of the manner wherein we consider the same subject; and that we travel the same road, though by different branches. But as one cannot go on currently in any other way than that one is acquainted with, I shall continue to proceed in my own track, trusting that we shall quickly be found walking hand in hand again, and speaking almost the same language.

20. In the seventh place, let it be noted, that neither satisfaction nor uneasiness ever enter the mind without some other sensation or idea to introduce them. For as you cannot have the pleasure of sweetness without putting something sweet into your mouth, nor the delight of a prospect without having some delightful prospect to look upon, so neither can you procure satisfaction without seeing or hearing, or contemplating or reflecting, on something satisfactory. And that the satisfaction is something distinct from the concomitant ideas, appears manifest, because it may be separated from them: for the same object, presenting in the same shape and features, affects us variously, being sometimes alluring and at other times insipid. One may be extremely desirous of seeing a particular play, but being disappointed this week, may not care a farthing for it the next, according as one happens to be differently disposed: the play is the same, the actors the same, and the opportunities the same with those you wished for before, nor can you find any other difference than only the relish. This makes good what I observed before, that all motives are compound ideas, for though satisfaction be the only ingredient weighing in the scale, others are necessary to serve as a vehicle for conveying it to the mind.

21. The eighth particular relating to satisfaction follows naturally from the last: for if we cannot have satisfaction but by applying some vehicle to convey it, it behoves us to look out for the proper vehicles containing the desired ingredient within them. Nature makes up the mixtures herself, nor have we any hand in the composition: sugar has its sweetness, gall its bitterness, success its joy, and disappointment its vexation, by her provision: we can neither alter nor diminish the relish of things by our own power. Sometimes she shifts her ingredients, taking out satisfaction and leaving the vehicle insipid, or substituting

uneasiness in its room: but even these changes of taste are of her making, being effected by the variable nature of our palates disposed to different viands at different times, nor can we help ourselves or restore them at pleasure to their former state, but must take objects as we find them, according to the pressing disposition either of our body or mind. This nobody will deny, nor say that when salt has lost its savour we have wherewith to salt it; or that we can always raise the same fondness we had for a particular diversion the other day, or make nothing of a fatigue we used to undergo with cheerfulness.

22. Thus far we go on currently, without opponent or contradiction; but in this divided disputatious world one must not expect to travel any road long without a check. There are people, namely, your sticklers for indifferency of Will, who pretend that nature has left some of her vehicles empty, indifferent to receive either satisfaction or uneasiness as we please to sprinkle it upon them, or mingled up others so loosely that we can pick out the vivifying ingredient, and throw in its opposite, thus changing the quality of a motive, and rendering that satisfactory which was naturally distasteful. Not that they deny volition always follows the last act of the understanding; but, say they, we have a certain degree of power to give colours to our ideas, and control the understanding, so as to make it pronounce sentence against the clearest decision of judgment, or strongest solicitation of passion.

Here I have the pleasure of returning into my old alliance again, and joining forces with Mr. Locke, whom I find as little inclined to this notion of indifferency as myself. Those he had to deal with, it seems, had delivered themselves so obscurely concerning this antecedent indifference, as they called it, that he could not tell where they placed it: whether, between the thought and judgment of the understanding, and the decree of the will, where there appears no room for anything, or before the former, which is a state of darkness exhibiting no object whereon to exercise our power. But by a book not extant in his time, Dr. King upon the Origin of Evil, and his profound commentator,[1] I can discern where they place this supposed indifference, to wit, between the thought and judgment of the understanding; that is, between the action being proposed, and the preference of that action, or its forbearance: and the matter according to their representation stands thus. The mind sits in judgment between several objects offered to her option; arguments occur in favour of either, and unexceptionable evidences are produced; she sees plainly which has the strongest cause, yet gives judgment for the weakest, by virtue of her arbitrary power. Or some council makes a motion of course, which never used to be denied, and which there is no reason for denying; nevertheless she will reject it, merely because she will. So the province of indiffer-

---

[1] Edmund Law (1703–1787), Bishop of Carlisle, whose annotated translation of William King's *De Origine Mali* appeared in London, 1731. Ed.

ence lies between the trial and the judgment, which the understanding pronounces by particular direction from the Will, annexing the idea of best to that which had it not before, and this the understanding having discerned, gives judgment accordingly: and that idea the will annexes by her own sole authority, after full cognizance of the cause, without regard to the merits, and uninfluenced by any motive at all. But there is really no motive inducing the mind to annex this idea, if any such power she has; for acting upon our ideas is an act, as well as acting upon our limbs, and she does not choose to enter upon action of any kind, unless for some end proposed, or to obtain some effect she conceives will prove satisfactory. Nor must we take understanding here in the vulgar sense for the judgment of reason, but for every discernment of the perceptive faculty, including the suggestions of fancy, and impulses of passion; which may start up unawares, and whisper the judge in the ear, just before giving sentence, although they had not spoken a word during the whole course of the trial.

Your abettors of indifference, being solemn folks, deal altogether in general terms and abstract reasonings: but to my thinking, the abstract is seen clearest in the concrete, for ideas fluctuate in our reflection, nor can we hold them long in the same state. If you would judge between two oranges you have seen a little while ago, which is the deeper coloured, you will think sometimes the one, and sometimes the other: but set them close together and fix your eye upon them, this will keep your idea of both steady, so that you may quickly perceive which is the redder and which the paler. Therefore I wish they had given us instances of some particular actions, wherein they apprehended this privilege of indifference is exerted; but since they have thought it below their dignity, or unbecoming their gravity, I shall attempt to do it for them, and if I can hit upon proper samples to their mind, we shall not rest in speculation alone, but shall see by experience whether, in actions esteemed the most indifferent, there is not some motive actually prevailing upon us to perform them.

23. But I must observe by the way, that the trial above described, is a very complex action, consisting of many single acts, each of which must have its several volition and several end in view, following one another so close, that there is nowhere room for the power of indifferency to interfere. But as the gentlemen we have to deal with seem unprovided with a microscope, I shall not trouble them with minute objects nor such as cannot be discerned with the naked eye; and therefore shall present them with larger actions, suitable to their organs, and consider the whole compound as one body.

Since then, they place the merit of their behaviour in the right use of this power of indifferency, one may expect to find the effects of it most apparent in the most arduous exercises of virtue. Suppose then a good man, solicited by temptations, attacked by threatenings, urged by tortures, to betray his country, yet he bravely resists all opposition: but has he not a thorough persuasion of the advantages of well doing; has he not a strong desire of fulfilling his duty, and a vehement abhorrence of treachery? These must move him to take up his resolution, and support him in going through with it: for another who had not such motives, or had them in a lower degree, would undoubtedly decline the task, or fail upon trial. If they should urge that all men have the like motives, would they but listen to them: those who allege this, must have a different idea of motives from that we have given before, and overlook the distinction between a motive and a good reason for doing a thing. For how reasonable soever it may be to act right, yet to him who does not discern the expedience, or can satisfy himself in the foregoing it, and feel no uneasiness in the want of it, it is no motive at all.

What will they say of the perfect wise man, would not he, if there were any such, adhere to the dictates of his judgment without deviating in a single instance? Yet he, I suppose, proceeds in all his measures upon the motive of their rectitude. So long as the matter remained doubtful, he would remain indifferent to either side, and would all that while suspend his action: but the moment expedience became manifest, his indifference would vanish, nor would he delay the determination of his Will. What will they say of those imperfect wise men we have upon earth? Have they not a quick sense of honour, and love of right conduct? And are they not therefore good and deserving because this motive influences the greatest part of their actions, and because they cannot behold villainy and meanness with indifference? Do the judicious and the worthy less enjoy or less use this most noble privilege of human nature than the gay, the giddy, and the thoughtless, whose conduct is much more unaccountable, who frequently act upon no visible motive at all, or run counter to the weightiest?

Why do they ever exhort us to this or that kind of behaviour, or to make a right use of our privilege? Does not this imply an opinion that they may prevail upon us thereby to give a right turn to our indifference? Therefore indifference it seems may be operated upon by exhortation, and may as well be carried on by the same through the execution of its purpose. But what are exhortations besides the suggestion of motives to do a thing? which were needless if we might do the same without any motive at all; and useless if actions performed upon motives had no morality in them, nor any action were valuable unless for so much of it as proceeded from our power of indifference.

Most probably the notion of this power took rise from an inaccuracy of thought occasioned by an inaccuracy of language. Desire, says Mr. Locke, so constantly accompanies our actions that it is frequently taken for Will, and confounded with it in our discourses. I have observed in a former place, that Will and pleasure are reputed synonymous terms, nor would it be thought a different question should one ask, Will you have such a thing? or Do you desire or please to have it? The preference of one thing above another, either in our judgment or inclination, is often styled the choice of our Will: and when some authority or obligation compels us to do the thing we dislike, we call it acting unwillingly, or against our Will. It would be hard to produce an instance of any man going through with an arduous undertaking, without having it strongly at heart, without a desire of the work to be completed thereby, or without feeling a want of it, upon being obstructed in his progress. I would ask the champions for indifference, whether, when they have made a wrong use of their power, (for possibly they may trip once in a while,) they do not feel a shame, a vexation, a disappointment, in reflecting thereupon; which could not well happen, if they had no desire of improving their opportunities. But this desire, which often has an efficacy to overpower the strongest motives, they confound with the Will, and finding nothing previous in the thought that should give birth to it, they suppose it self-begotten, and thence wisely conclude the Will has a power of determining itself, and of infusing satisfaction into that, which nature had mingled up with uneasiness. There is a desire, having no other object than the restraint of desire: for men virtuously inclined find their passions and appetites perpetually drawing them aside out of their road: this gives them a jealousy of such intruders, and when desires solicit strongly, although not urging to any thing mischievous or improper, yet they will not comply merely because they will not let their passions get the mastery over them, nor acquire a strength too great to be resisted at other times. Now this desire of restraining desire, our profound speculatists mistake again for the Will, to which, therefore, they attribute a power of controlling desire, without aid of any counter-weight whatsoever, and of making an election, like the King by a congê d'elire, in virtue of its royal prerogative.

24. Let us next turn to the abusers of their privilege. A man is urged to some useful attainment: you make him sensible of the good fruits dependant upon it, so as to raise in him some desire of gathering them: you convince him there is nothing difficult in the pursuit, nothing irksome, nothing thwarting his other inclinations, yet you cannot get him to stir. But is there not some secret passion, some habit, some humour, some averseness to trouble, that lies in the way? If you cannot presently discover the rub, it does not follow there is none; for the heart of man is deceitful above all things, containing many springs unknown, even to the owner. But if you have any knowledge of human nature and intimacy with the person, it is ten to one but you may discern the obstacle, which you find to be something that acts as a powerful motive upon him, though it might weigh nothing with your-

self. Since then, upon closer examination, you can generally distinguish a motive where there appeared none before, it may be presumed there is one when it escapes your search: therefore those instances of wrong management are too uncertain a foundation to build the doctrine of indifferency upon.

But now and then you shall meet with persons, who being recommended to do something advantageous to themselves, which they would have liked well enough, and been fond of, had it first occurred to their own thoughts, yet reject it out of mere crossness: the more you urge them with motives, the stronger they set themselves against it. But consider whether the bare having of their Will is not an engaging motive with most men. Liberty of itself is sweet, and to have the command of our motions without control, what we all in some measure desire. This desire, when excessive, is thought owing to a perverseness of Will, which can run contrary to all motives, either of expedience or inclination; but it may generally be traced to another source: for obstinate people are either such as have been constantly humoured by those about them, or else persons of shallow understanding. Fools are credulous at first, till having been frequently deceived, they contract a jealousy of all mankind, and see no chance of obtaining anything they like, unless by rejecting whatever shall be proposed by another. Besides, there is a kind of honour in doing as we will: and honour operates as a mighty incentive to action. But you will ask, do I conceive there is any honour in persisting obstinately to do just as we will, without regard to motives dissuading us from it? Truly I cannot answer the question so generally proposed, but must give my opinion disjunctively. When done in opposition to passion, danger, fatigue, or pain, which we will not suffer to drive us from anything we have a mind to, I applaud it highly: when in contradiction to good advice or the suggestions of reason, I censure it as highly. For tenaciousness, even of a resolution taken for opposition sake, serves either to good or bad purposes: when to the former, it is called steadiness and bravery; when to the latter, perverseness and obstinacy. But whether you, or I, or the world, allow it to be honour, or no, there are those who certainly esteem it such; like the miser in Horace, who, being hissed by the populace, applauded himself at home in counting over his bags; as appears manifestly by the shame and vexation they feel upon failing of their Will, and the triumph and exultation they express upon prevailing.

Were the Will indifferent to all motives, and could give itself the turn without any previous cause influencing it thereto, all our actions, those of them at least that are moral, must remain absolutely contingent. How then can we depend upon any man that he will keep this or that tenor of conduct? Yet we daily repose a full confidence in one man, because we know he will deal honestly by us, and refuse it to another who we know would betray us. Oh! say they, the one has acquired a rectitude, and the other a perverseness of will. What do they mean by this rectitude and perverseness of will? A perverseness of mind I can understand, when satisfaction or desire fixes upon pernicious or deceitful views, and continually moves the Will to pursue them. If they will allow this to be a perverseness of will, I have no objection: but then this depends upon a quality in the Will to follow desire starting up perpetually to the thought, and he who has this desire stronger than any other, cannot remain indifferent whether he shall gratify it, or no. Other perverseness, I know none, but were there any other it must equally destroy indifference, for we see this perverseness once contracted determines the Will afterwards to act perversely as often as opportunity shall offer: so the will remains no longer at liberty to follow or reject the instigations of perverseness, nor is it the less bound for having brought the thraldom upon itself; as a man who sells himself to the plantations is no less a servant, than the felon transported by judgment of law.

25. Thus the doctrine of indifferency, canvassed narrowly, contradicts and overthrows itself; for if indifferency be a privilege inherent in human nature, it can never depart from us, for we cannot lose our nature while we continue to be men. Then, although the Will should have given itself a perverseness, it might as well give itself a rectitude again, and vice versa, as often as it pleased without any previous cause or motive: and the behaviour of men would be totally uncertain and unsteady, for we should act right or wrong, prudently or foolishly, just as indifference happened to take the turn. But if indifferency, by I know not what magic, can control itself and persevere in the turn it has once taken, then we have our independency upon prior causes only upon some few occasions, that is, when we are to enter upon a new course of action, which having once determined, we proceed therein mechanically, like a ball put in motion, by virtue of the impulse first imparted. If this be the case, and merit or demerit extend no further than while the Will can act independently, why do your indifferencists ever punish for acts done in consequence of a perverseness already contracted? As soon as the perverseness appears, they ought to examine the degree of it, and appoint a punishment adequate thereto, which the party having suffered, has paid his penalty, and remains no longer obnoxious to the law: his independency is now gone, and nothing happening during its absence, can upon their principles be imputed to his account. Nevertheless, we find them forward enough to punish again for subsequent offences, proceeding from a perverse turn of will, visible many years before. Will they plead that the power of indifferency is a limited power, and that the Will may give itself so strong a determination, as it cannot afterwards resist by its own strength, therefore they throw in the terrors of punishment in

counterbalance, to bring the weights so nearly equal, that the power of indifferency may suffice to turn the scale? Let them have a care how they allege this, because it will tear up the main foundation whereon they build their doctrine of indifference, namely, that without it there could be no demerit, and consequently no room for punishment: for here we see there is room for punishment, which may be lawfully inflicted, not solely with reference to past offences, but also as a necessary remedy to prevent the commission of them for the future. If they give us this inch, perhaps we may take an ell, and show by parity of reason, that the justice of rewards and punishments may remain in full extent, although there should be no such power as that of indifference.

What do they mean by a determination of the Will carrying us through a long course of behaviour? Do they conceive volition a permanent act, extending to a long series of performances? Surely they never reflected with themselves upon the operation of their own Wills, nor the manner of their own motions. We have it upon Mr. Locke's authority that the mind is capable of but one determination to one action at once[1]: and his judgment stands confirmed by daily experience. Successive volitions keep us incessantly in play; each performs its several act, and has the sole direction of our powers for the present moment, both themselves and their effects being instantaneous and transitory, nor does one operate by any force received from a former. Whatever we may will to-day to do to-morrow, we shall perform or omit, according as we shall then be in the mind: for the actions of to-morrow depend upon the morrow's volitions, which are determined either by some motive occurring at the time, or else by the power of indifferency then exerted. Therefore, to talk of the Will by a single act giving birth to many successive motions, and casting a perverseness upon itself that shall continue for days, months, and years, is talking unintelligibly; the continuance of a thing in its own nature momentary, being a contradiction in terms.

Were indifferency a privilege appendant to human nature, one would think all men should possess it in equal degree: but we see the same temptations overcome some men which others can resist, although both strive equally against them. Must we not then ascribe their different success either to the variety of colours wherein the same objects appear to different minds, or to the various strength of other motives they have to oppose against them? I know an old gentleman, who, being pressed by his physicians to go out in his chariot every day, as the only thing capable of relieving him in his infirmities, acknowledged the expedience of their advice, and wished to follow it, yet could never muster up resolution enough to do as he desired. What now was become of his power of indifference, which was supposed

1 See *Essay*, Book II, Chapter, XXI, 36. Ed.

able to control any motives, but could not here act in concurrence with the weightiest? Yet he could choose for himself upon other occasions, and act rightly when tempted to the contrary: and could even go out when he fancied something of moment called him. May we not then look out for some secret motive to account for this difference of behaviour? He had been a man of business, unused to stir, unless upon some affair of importance, and had contracted an aversion to your idle jaunts, taken for amusement only, as fit for none but women and triflers; therefore could not brook his mind to descend to them, although they were become matters of moment, by being necessary to his health.

26. Hitherto we have considered important actions, such as are undertaken with deliberation and design, or upon some distant purpose in prospect. We will now take a view of sudden and trifling motions, which scarce seem to have any motive inducing us to them, and therefore may be thought to proceed from the sole power of the Will. But there needs no great sagacity to observe, that the very want of employment creates an uneasiness, and almost every exertion of our activity affords a small degree of satisfaction, which, whatever first starts up to the fancy, prompts us to pursue. Whoever will take the trouble to watch men in their idle hours, will find a certain regularity in things done without regard to any rule: some habit acting uniformly sets them for the most part at work. For though different persons amuse themselves differently in an infinite variety of ways, each adheres steadily to his own kind of amusement, and acts most in character when he thinks of it least. Therefore, one man whistles, another sings, another dances, another plays with his fingers, when he has nothing else to do. Which shows that the Will has not an indifference, even with regard to trifles, but catches, from time to time, at such little motives as custom has taught to rise most readily in the imagination. One may discern the like causes in those bye motions which fill up the vacant spaces of time during our engagement in some earnest pursuit; when we set ourselves to think intensely, few of us leave our limbs entirely at rest, but give them various employment for every little interval while thought stops, and until it can find an issue; some play with their buttons, some twist their knee-strings, or rub the table, or kick their leg to and fro, or practise some innocent trick they have fallen into by accident, or catched by imitation from somebody else. Now in times of study or business, the determination of the Will tends solely towards the principal end we labour to attain; the power of indifferency is all exerted that way: yet we see any idle habit can give a motion of its own to the Will, which, like a cord drawn to the stretch by a mighty force, may notwithstanding be bent to this side, or that, by the slightest lateral pressure.

Even in cases where the objects proposed to our option appear indifferent, as well to judgment as inclination, and the Will seems to determine by arbitrary power, because there is nothing else to give the preference; yet a prying eye may discover some latent motive that escaped the general notice. Suppose you call upon a friend just after dinner, before the bottles and glasses are removed. He asks, Will you take a glass of wine with us? Thank you, Sir, I do not care if I do. Shall I help you to red or white? Any that you have upon the table. Here are both. That that stands next your hand. See both bottles stand equally near. Why, then, white if you please. This little dialogue, happening frequently between friends, exhibits as much indifference as the mind of man can well be in; for we suppose neither wine disagreeing with your stomach, or displeasing to your palate, you had drank as much as you cared for before you came out, but a glass extraordinary will do you no harm, yet you are willing to be sociable, and therefore accept his offer, but civility makes you refer the choice of your wine to him, and the same civility prompts you afterwards to choose that which will give him the least trouble: but finding this will not do, and perceiving that further compliments would be troublesome, you take the first that occurs; for you cannot pronounce the words White and Red together, and as you want to end the dispute, whichever comes quickest to the tongue's end, is therefore fittest to relieve you from this want.

Why should choice be deemed an act of the will, when the understanding many times presents a choice ready made, without staying for the will to assist in the production? An ambassador, making his public entry, throws out money among the populace: a porter, scrambling among the crowd, spies a half-crown and a sixpence lying upon the ground: he can get either, but has not time for both, so he takes up the half-crown, not for any preference thrown upon it by his will, but from his knowledge that this piece will go five times as far at market as the other. Many times the will acts without any choice at all: a man hears a sudden cry of fire; he starts up instantly from his seat, and runs to see what is the matter. The alarm banishes all other ideas; he has not a thought of anything else he would not choose to do, nor even of forbearance from all kind of action. The wanton sallies of fancy proceed more from thoughtlessness than wrong election: ideas come in one by one without a competitor, and the mind follows the present whimsey, for want of seeing the inexpedience or impropriety attending it. Can this be called a choice? which in the very nature of it implies a judgment between several things, and a preference of one above another: but when one object only lies in view, there can be no preference, nor can one choose, but take that which alone is presented.

27. But I find there are persons of all characters in the interests of indifference. Those of a humourous turn, not being good at argument,

endeavour to ridicule our doctrine of motives, by putting the case of
an ass placed between two bundles of excellent hay, both equally alluring to his sense, who, they say, must starve in the midst of plenty,
for want of being able to prefer either. It is no uncommon thing for
wit to outrun discretion; therefore I would caution these jokers to
beware how they anger their solemn friends of their own persuasion.
For if the beasts cannot live without a power of indifferency, what
becomes of the noble privilege peculiar to human nature? It is rather a
benefit we share in common with our brethren asses, who, by the right
use of it, may merit as glorious rewards as ourselves. But we contem-
plative folks are not to be jested out of our notions; nor shall I scruple
to own that their supposition is true in theory: and so it would have
been, had they put the case of a sharpened pole, ten feet long, set
upright upon a marble pavement, with the centre of gravity directly
over the point, which would remain for ever in that posture, if nothing
meddled with it. But I question whether such experiments be practicable: let them try, if they can, to place the ass, the pole, or their own
mind, in such a situation. Should the beast shake his head ever so
little, this may bring it nearer to one bundle, which will make the scent
of that become the stronger: the least breath of air, or brush of a fly's
wing is enough to throw down the pole: and imagination continually
supplies us with motives, either great or small, either of judgment or
fancy, sufficient to put the mental balance in motion.

Of the two, I believe instances of such an inability to act for
want of motives, more likely to be met with in men than asses: I
myself have met with them in my time. I remember once calling upon
a friend in the Temple, to take a walk: we came down stairs presently,
and then began to talk of the course we should steer. I found him
irresolute, but would not interpose, having a curiosity to see the
event: the business was whether we should go to the Park, or to Is-
lington: we had no particular call to either, and both appeared equally
agreeable. I believe we stood a full quarter of an hour in the court,
before he could determine; for he was a man of gravity, used to weigh
his motives carefully, and had rejected the impulses of fancy, until
they had entirely lost their force: so he had nothing to sway with him,
for you may suppose there could be no weighty reasons for preferring
one tour before the other. Where now was his power of indifferency,
which had he possessed in the lowest degree, might have helped him
out at this dead lift?

Such hesitancies as these are weeds of the richest soils, being most
frequently found in serious, considerate, and industrious tempers: but
they will grow in more barren grounds. I have been pestered with
them upon my own estate in former days, till I found out the secret of
nourishing a crop of fancies, in those spots which judgment would not
cover. I endeavour first to take direction from my reason; but if that

has no commands, I give up the reins to fancy; if fancy presents me with double objects, I toss up, cross, or pile, rather than lose time in hesitating: for employment upon any motive, the best to be had, is better than no employment at all. I never could reap any service in those cases from indifference, for, so long as that lasts, I can do nothing at all: nor could I ever remove it unless by suggesting something expedient, or amusing to my imagination, which might urge me to bestir myself.

28. Thus have we examined every species of action, trifling and momentous, sudden and deliberate, fantastic and judicious, in search of an indifference to the preponderancy of motives, but in vain: nor is indifference anywhere to be found, unless in a suspension of action, while the motives hang doubtful, and the mind waits until some of them shall preponderate. I think now we may fairly conclude the mind enjoys no such privilege as this boasted power of indifferency. Nor would it be a valuable privilege if we had it: for as the turns it takes must be absolutely contingent, depending upon no prior cause, there is an even chance it might turn as well to our detriment as our advantage: nor could we ever pursue a plan, or lay our measures surely, or complete any long work, for want of a sufficient dependence upon our own behaviour, or that of other persons; for the hazard of wrong elections disconcerting our schemes, would discourage us from attempting anything. Should you send for a surgeon to bleed you tomorrow, you could never depend upon his attendance; profit, credit, duty, his adherence to his profession, may urge him to come, but these operate only as motives, and neither you nor he can tell but his will tomorrow, by virtue of its arbitrary power, may annex the idea of best to the refusal or his assistance. Nobody can pretend here that the motives are so strong as to exceed the power of his will to control them: for certainly he may stay at home if he will, nor will his legs or his chariot bring him without some act of his will to order their motion.

29. But is it never in a man's power to change the pleasantness or unpleasantness, that is, the satisfaction or uneasiness accompanying any sort of action? Yes, says Mr. Locke, it is plain in many cases he can.[1] One may change the displeasingness or indifferency in actions into pleasure and desire, by doing what lies in one's power towards effecting it. A due consideration will do it in some cases, and practice, application, and custom in most.—But he nowhere says it may be done by mere dint of volition, or otherwise than by the use of proper means, which means must lie within our reach or we cannot procure the change. Is your tea bitter? You may sweeten it by putting in a knob of sugar: but not if there be no sugar in the dish. Does your meat taste insipid? You may give it a relish by sprinkling a little salt:

[1] *Essay*, Book II, Chapter XXI, 69. Ed.

but not if the salt have lost its savour. So, should you feel an averseness to labour, you may conquer it by contemplating the credit of industry, or shame of idleness; or the good fruits expected from your labours: but not if you have no value for reputation, nor desire of any particular benefit, attainable by diligence greater than your love of indolence.

For I look upon it as an invariable rule, that you can never bring a man into the liking of anything disagreeable, unless by means of something he already likes appearing connected therewith, or attainable solely thereby. Bread or tobacco, says Mr. Locke, may be neglected, when shown useful to health, because of an indifference or disrelish to them: reason and consideration at first recommends and begins their trial, and use finds, or custom makes them pleasant. That this is so in virtue too, is very certain. Thus, in his opinion, our very virtues derive from other sources than the power of indifference. But if bread appears insipid, tobacco nauseous, or virtue disagreeable to the present taste, no man can render them otherwise or suddenly alter his palate, solely by willing it.

With respect to ourselves, indeed, we have another expedient for changing the state of our motives, by that command we have in some measure over our organs both of sensation and reflection. For as we can turn our eyes upon any object of the scene before us, and shut them against the light, or wink when it strikes too strongly upon them; so we can close the organs of reflection, bringing particular ideas to our notice, and thereby throw the course of thought into another channel: or, where we cannot entirely dam up the passage, we may sometimes obstruct it, thereby reducing the current to a smaller stream. This way we can, and very frequently do, alter the colour of our motives, by throwing a stronger attention upon them, or by removing, or obscuring their competitors. But when we take the latter method, it is no impeachment of the efficacy of motives that they do not strike when you shut your eyes upon them, or discern them faintly; nor mark of absolute power in the Will that is forced to thrust out of sight, a motive which it could not resist: and when the former, it is the reflection, not the Will, that adds colour to the motive. For, as when you put sugar into your mouth, it is the sugar, not yourself, that affects your palate with sweetness, notwithstanding you put it in yourself: so when you throw a strong attention upon some particular idea, it is the state of your organs, not your Will, that heightens its colours, although you put them into that state by an act of your Will. Certain it is, we do sometimes pluck up a resolution to surmount a pain, a labour, a danger, without suggesting fresh reasons to encourage us; and this I take to be done by some such method as that above spoken of; for earnest, eager resolution is a kind of temporary passion, brought upon us by our own procurement, and it is well known we may work ourselves up by degrees into almost any passion, by dwelling upon ideas, fomenting it without admission of others. Upon these occasions, I conceive the mind raises an extraordinary motion in some parts of the animal circulation, which then runs more rapidly than while under command in the service of our ordinary purposes. For it seems apparent from the quick violent starts of motion, the ferment of spirits, the solicitous turn of countenance, usual in times of vigorous resolution, that the body bears no inconsiderable share in the business.

30. This power over the organs I take to be indeed the grand privilege of human nature, for I can discern nothing of it in the brute creation. It is true our notions concerning them amount at most only to conjecture, for we know not certainly what passes within them, nor in what manner they proceed to action. Remembrance, fancy, and some degree of knowledge, cannot well be denied them; unless you suppose them mere machines, which, though perhaps it cannot be demonstratively disproved, there is not the least shadow of positive evidence to prove that they are: but their ideas come up uncalled, being occasioned, for the most part, either by sensible objects, or the motions of their animal juices, or particular state of their bodies: nor can I discern any such thing as voluntary reflection, or any control of fancy belonging to them; which therefore remains the peculiar property of man. From hence spring all our virtues, all our rules of prudence, all our measures of conduct; and upon this principally, though not entirely, stands the justice of reward and punishment; for we reward and punish the beasts, to bring them thereby to do something we like, or deter them from something we dislike. If our opponents will accept of this power in lieu of their indifferency, as equally serviceable to all useful purposes, they are heartily welcome, but I cannot allow them that both are the same thing. For indifferency implies a power in the will, or furnishing the idea of Best out of its own store and by its own sole authority, without recourse to any contrivance or artifice to obtain it. And because a man may give the preference between two objects proposed to his option, either by suggesting considerations, recommending the one and dissuading the other, or by throwing a stronger attention upon one and withholding it from the other, it no more shows an indifferency of the Will, or a power of annexing Best to what appears Worst in the judgment, than because one may make a pebble outshine a diamond, either by covering them with different kinds of paint; or, by diminishing the light falling upon the latter, and increasing that upon the former, it shows an indifferency in the eye, or a power of annexing lustre to objects naturally obscure.

31. Besides, whoever will diligently examine the state of his mind, when he gives this supposed arbitrary preference, will always find opposite desires accosting him at those times, to one of which he har-

bours a secret prepossession or favour, therefore practises every art to make that prevail in his imagination: and this alike in the right or the wrong exercises of his power. If pleasure, profit, or resentment, solicit to act, and the still voice of conscience whispers to forbear: one man has a love of virtue which he cannot easily forego, therefore he suppresses all instigations of passion that might draw him aside, for he will not suffer his beloved and valued object to be wrested from him; or fortifies himself in his desire, by considerations proper for that purpose, or the earnest contemplation of what he used always to behold with delight; another man has a favourite inclination which he longs to gratify, but reason puts in her negative: therefore he stifles the cries of reason, or turns a deaf ear against them, lest they should importune him too much; or hunts for any excuses or palliations he can muster up; or casts a wistful look upon his darling, whom he is unwilling to leave, and contemplates so long until all other ideas are banished out of his thought. Thus, in reality, the preference is already given, before we enter upon the act, whereby we fancy ourselves conferring it; nor was the mind indifferent whether such act should be performed or no: and the subsequent determination or idea of Best thrown into the doubtful scale, comes from the means used to effect it, not from the Will. But if you ascribe it to the Will because that applies the means, you might with better reason ascribe it to the predominant inclination, because that puts the Will upon making such application. For whatever the Will does towards annexing the idea of Best, even supposing it to do the business without employing any other means than its own inherent power; nevertheless, it acts herein ministerially, not authoritatively, but in service of the favourite desire, to which therefore the credit and merit of the performance belongs.

32. What has been said concerning the methods and organs employed in bringing about a determination of the mind, accounts for the limitation of that power, and the difficulty attending the exercise of it; for our organs can perform their office for a certain time, but no longer. A man may walk a mile with pleasure, but when he has walked five, he may find it fatiguing; nor perhaps can he walk twenty at all, because his legs tire long before. So he may hold up a weight at arm's length for some time; but cannot keep in that posture for ever, for the muscles of his arm will grow weary. The same may be said of satiety, which proceeds from an alteration in our organs, as weariness does from an alteration in the state of our muscles. We may like venison prodigiously for a day or two, but should be terribly cloyed had we nothing else to feed upon during the whole season: for the palate being over-clogged, no longer receives the flavour in the same manner as before. This of course limits our power to that proportion of labour the instruments we have to serve us are capable of bearing, and confines our activity to that compass of time whereto the relish of things

may extend. But I know of no labour, no difficulty, no satiety, in pure acts of the mind: we are never tired of commanding so long as our limbs and organs are not tired of executing: we will from morning to night without intermission, and without trouble; and though our employments often fatigue and nauseate, let but some new desire give play to a quite different set of organs, and the mind runs after it with as much freshness and eagerness as if it had never done anything. Upon coming home quite wearied down with a long journey, a man may give orders for his conveniences and refreshments to be brought him, perhaps with more ease and relish than he had in first mounting his horse. After a long morning spent in hard study, we could easily find volition enough to continue the work, but that our head aches, our spirits fail, and nature can no longer bear the fatigue; wherefore labour of mind is as often called labour of brain, and more truly belongs to the latter than the former. Even at night, when all kind of action becomes irksome, it is not the Will but the eye that draws straws, for the mind does not desire to sleep so long as the body can hold awake. What then should limit our power with respect to anything we can do by barely willing it? Why do we ever strive to exert such power and fail in the attempt? or why do we succeed at one time and fail at another? A man may as easily will to walk a hundred miles as one, or to lift up the house as to take up his slipper, if he can believe himself able; every one sees why he cannot do either, namely, from the deficiency of his strength: but what the Will has once performed, it then had strength to perform; what then is become of this strength, that it cannot perform the same again? Does the Will grow feeble and vigorous by turns, like the muscles, upon labour or rest? If we assign for cause, that the Will used some medium before which now is wanting, the difference may be accounted for much better than by any variation of strength in the Will itself.

History informs us that Mutius Scevola held his hand in the fire till it was burnt to the bone; therefore burning was susceptible of the idea of Best: why then could not you and I pluck up the like resolution? But perhaps we can annex the idea to some objects he could not. One man can restrain his appetite of meats and drinks, but cannot refuse the offers of ambition: another can reject all temptations of unlawful gain, but cannot resist the impulses of anger. Is there then a strong and a weak side in the Will? or are the Wills of men cast in different moulds? One may readily conceive how the various degrees of resolution may arise from the strength of spirits, texture of brain, habit, education, or turn of imagination, but from the constitution or mould of the Will it seems inexplicable. When we take up a strong resolution, we find pains and difficulty in keeping it, and often faint in the midway after having made a very good beginning. A pain or trouble that a man has borne patiently for a while, shall sometimes fairly overcome him without growing stronger, merely by tiring him out. This, not to repeat what I have said before of the effects visible upon the body, shows that there are organs or nerves employed upon those occasions which require labour to keep them upon the stretch, and can serve us no longer than to a certain period, but may acquire strength, like our limbs, by constant use and practice.

33. After all, the very expression of a power belonging to the Will, when used in philosophical discourses, will not bear a strict examination. Will, in the vulgar sense, stands for a pressing inclination, or strong conviction of judgment, to which we may properly enough ascribe the power of making labour pleasant and difficulties easy. But if we go into the land of abstraction and study the language current there, what must we understand by Will but the turn of the mind's activity? The mind has power to move our limbs and organs of reflection, but none of them will move by the bare possession of this power unless it be directed some particular way, and this direction we call our Will: therefore our actions all depend upon the Will: such as our volitions are, such will they be. So the wind has power to drive the clouds or ships along, but there being such a force in winds avails nothing unless it be turned to some particular point of the compass: therefore the courses of the vessel depend upon the turn of the wind, for it cannot get into port while the wind sets a contrary way. Now to talk of a power of the turn of the power of the wind would be accounted mere jargon: and how much better is it to contend for a power of the turn of the power of the mind? Yet have we been talking and arguing all along in that style, nor could do otherwise: for one must speak like other folks if one would speak to be understood, and this may plead our excuse. For custom has a despotic authority in matters of language, so far as to render even nonsense and absurdity reputable by turning them into propriety of speech.

34. Is there then no liberty at all in human action? no freedom of Will? Are we under a constant necessity, and our motions all brought upon us by the cogency of causes, without our intervention or power to control? By no means: neither Mr. Locke nor I ever dreamt of such a notion. As for necessity, I cannot be suspected of inclining to that, since the little conference I had with Doctor Hartley upon the road. For freedom of action, Mr. Locke strongly asserts it; but we both apprehend it to consist in our being so circumstanced as that action will follow or not upon our willing to do it or forbear: nor will our present opposers, I believe, controvert this point with us. When upon using our endeavours towards something lying within the compass of our natural powers, some obstacle would prevent their taking effect, then is our liberty gone: when no such hindrance intervenes but that we shall effect our purpose, or not, according as we try for it or forbear, then are we free; and nevertheless so for being influenced thereto

by consideration of judgment or instigation of fancy. He that relieves
a family in distress gives his money freely, although he does it upon
motives of charity or compassion or particular kindness, and would
have kept his money in his pocket had he not had those or any other
inducements whatever to part with it. He that goes to stir his fire is not
at liberty while anybody holds back his hand, but the moment they let
him alone, his liberty returns, and he acts freely, though he falls a
poking for the sake of warming himself: and even though he should
resolve to bear the cold in his toes till he can bear it no longer, still
when he puts forth his hand to relieve himself it is his own free act, for
the poker would not have stirred of itself had not he meddled with it,
neither would the muscles of his arm have operated to extend it without some act of the mind to begin their motion.

35. As to freedom of Will, how much soever Mr. Locke may seem
to reject it in words, where he declares liberty as little applicable to
Will as swiftness to sleep or squareness to virtue,[1] yet I do not apprehend him denying it in substance, nor that he would count me hetero-
dox for holding what I take to be generally understood by freewill.
For I conceive the exercise of this to be only a particular species of
action performed in raising up ideas or fixing them in the mind, which
shall determine us to such volitions as we want. And this we may and
do practise every day of our lives: we determine upon things beforehand and execute them punctually, we form resolutions for difficult
undertakings, we collect reasons to support us in them, we fortify ourselves with motives, we inculcate them deep in our imagination, and
afterwards find they produce the effect we expected. Thus we have a
power over our future volitions, and in respect of that power, are
capable either of liberty or restraint. For if any obligation or compul-
sion prevents us from exerting this power, or any prevailing dread or
inclination obstructs so that it cannot take effect, though we still remain at liberty to act, we are not at liberty to will as we desire: if no
such obstruction or hindrance lies in the way, we are perfectly free
both to will and to do. And after the determination made, our liberty
still remains to change it by the like methods whereby we established
it at first, though we shall never employ them unless we happen to
view the matter in a different light from that we saw it in before. Nor
is liberty the less for our being prompted to use it this way or that by
reasons or motives inducing us thereto. But here we must distinguish
between want of liberty and want of power: for our title to freedom
accruing to us only in respect of our power, we can be capable either
of liberty or restraint no further than our power extends. He that goes
to push down a stone wall fails in his attempt through a defect of
strength, not of liberty, provided you do not restrain him from thrust-
ing and shoving against it as long as he pleases. So we may attempt in

1 *Essay,* Book II, Chapter XXI, 14. Ed.

vain to overcome the terror of any great pain or danger, without an impeachment of our free will. None of us but may, if he will, thrust his hand into burning coals like Scevola, for the hand will undoubtedly obey the orders of the mind, should she so direct; but we cannot bring our mind to such a pitch of resolution, because we have not command enough over our imagination, nor motives in store sufficient to overbalance the smart of the fire. Yet nothing hinders us from trying, therefore we are at liberty to exert such power over our will as we have; and if any strong desire incite us, we shall employ our organs of imagination however inadequate to the task, so long as we can retain any hope of prevailing, there being no encouragement to try where we are sure to fail of success. For there is a manifest difference between the two cases; where some secret reluctance prevents us from using our best endeavours to bring the mind into a right temper, and where we set about it heartily and in good earnest, but want strength to compass our design.

Therefore I am not for expunging the term freewill out of our vocabulary, nor against exhorting men to raise their wills to a proper pitch, when some laborious enterprise is to be gone upon. But there is no occasion to trouble them with niceties concerning their manner of going to work, for though they have not the power of indifferency to determine their Will without the use of means, yet if you can once stir up in them an unreserved desire of exerting themselves, they will hit upon the proper means, without knowing what they be: just as we move our limbs by touching the nerve leading to each particular muscle, without knowing what nerves we have, or where they lie. The common notions of liberty serve well enough for the common uses of life; and were it possible totally to eradicate them, there must ensue a total stagnation of business and cessation of all activity whatever: for nobody would stir a finger, nor resolve upon any future measures of conduct, if he conceived himself not at liberty either to act or will otherwise than necessity should urge him. They may contain some inconsistencies which men of plain sense do not see, and so never perplex themselves therewith, nor yet suffer any inconveniences from this their want of discernment. The young lady spoken of some time ago, who stayed away from the ball because her aunt disapproved of it, could say she had a good Will to go, and forbore much against her Will, yet declare in the next breath that she might have gone if she would, but chose to stay at home, because she would not disoblige the old gentlewoman. She saw no contradiction in these expressions, nevertheless appears to have been a sensible girl by this instance of self-denial, and I doubt not had discretion enough to gratify her inclinations, or restrain them, whenever either were most proper: and this perhaps without having ever heard of the terms Velleity and Volition; nor had anybody done her a kindness that had taught her them, for she could not have conducted herself better, had she known them ever so well.

TUCKER'S WRITINGS

The Light of Nature Pursued has not been reprinted since 1848, although it was popular enough to go into an American edition in 1831. The work has had its scattered enthusiasts. Among them was William Hazlitt who, knowing of no "work in the shape of a philosophical treatise that contains so much good sense so agreeably expressed," produced anonymously in 1807 An Abridgment of the Light of Nature Pursued (London). The essay on free will is not available except in the original printing, but "Man in Quest of Himself" is in Metaphysical Tracts by English Philosophers of the Eighteenth Century, edited by Samuel Parr (London, 1837).

WRITINGS ON TUCKER

Very little of consequence has been published on Tucker. By far the best and longest discussion is in the two chapters devoted to him by Ernest Albee, A History of English Utilitarianism (London, 1901). Tucker's appeal, style, and views on theology and ethics are discussed at some length by Leslie Stephen in History of English Thought in the Eighteenth Century, 2 vol. (London, 1881). There are a few pages characterizing Tucker's contributions to philosophy in Sir James Mackintosh, Dissertation on the Progress of Ethical Philosophy (Edinburgh, 1838). A fuller and more interesting treatment is given by James Seth in English Philosophers and Schools of Philosophy (London and New York, 1912).

THOMAS REID

1710–1796

Thomas Reid, the first well-known exponent of the Scottish philosophy of Common Sense but not its founder, was born into the family of a minister of the Church of Scotland. Their home was near Aberdeen, and it being thought that the boy "would turn out to be a man of good and well wearing parts," he was sent there in 1722 to study classics at Marischal College. His philosophy instructor was George Turnbull, a man whose influence on Reid's own views was considerable although unacknowledged. After his graduation in 1726, Reid studied privately for the ministry, and was licensed to preach in 1731. He was appointed librarian at Marischal College two years later, holding the post until 1736, when he resigned in order to tour England. On his return the next year he became a country minister outside Aberdeen, and married in 1740.

During his tenure of fifteen years as minister, Reid read and wrote philosophy, stimulated by reading Hume's *Treatise*. In 1748 he published his first paper, "An Essay on Quantity, occasioned by reading a Treatise in which Simple and Compound Ratios are applied to Virtue and Merit," an attack on what he took to be the application of mathematical formulae to ethical questions by Francis Hutcheson. Reid was elected professor of philosophy at King's College, Aberdeen, in 1752, lecturing on mathematics and physics in addition to logic and ethics. He remained there until 1764, when, on Adam Smith's resignation, he became professor of moral philosophy at Glasgow. Reid held this position for the rest of his life, although he retired from university duties in 1780 in order to prepare his lectures for publication. He survived his wife and four children, but Dugald Stewart, his student at Glasgow and later his friend, says that even at the age of eighty-six Reid's faculties, except for his memory and hearing, "appeared as vigorous as ever," and that he still maintained his interest in science and mathematics.

Reid's published writings on philosophy are considerable in volume. "An Essay on Quantity," which was intended as an answer to some remarks made by Hutcheson in his *Inquiry into the Origin of our Ideas of Beauty and Virtue,* was followed by *An Enquiry into the Human Mind on the Principles of Common Sense* (1764), *A Brief Account of Aristotle's Logic* (1774), *Essays on the Intellectual Powers of Man* (1785), and *Essays on the Active Powers of Man* (1788). In addition, Reid wrote a short account of the University of Glasgow. His letters and his four philosophical orations have been published since his death. He also wrote some unpublished papers, including two on Priestley's materialism and "Priestley's Account of Hartley's Theory of the Human Mind."

Reid thought—and his followers have agreed with him—that his own contribution lay in his examination and exposure of Descartes' theory of ideas, especially as it was developed by Hume into a skeptical attack on our claims to have knowledge of the real world. Reid's conclusion was that neither perception nor conception takes place with the aid of intermediary objects called "ideas," and that, in consequence, there can be no question whether such "ideas" resemble any property of any external object. From the time of the publication of the *Inquiry,* in which Reid first put forward the view, critics have divided sharply on the question of the merit of Reid's interpretation of Descartes, Locke, and Hume. Many critics have said that even if Reid is correct on this point, his own doctrine of suggestion neither differs from the views of Hume nor copes with the problems Hume failed to meet.

More interesting to us nowadays, as the selections given here are intended to show, are Reid's attempts to draw a distinction between sensation and perception—he was among the first to do so seriously—his attempts to show what is wrong with Hartley's explanatory hypotheses, and to state the "first principles of contingent truths." These latter are the principles of common sense, those statements of our ordinary experience which we are forced to admit as true. Reid is not quite clear why denials of such statements are self-defeating; he oscillates between thinking of common sense as sound practical sense and as inescapable necessary beliefs. On this point, as on others, Reid began a long line of controversy. His supporters have included Dugald Stewart, Victor Cousin, Sir William Hamilton, C. S. Peirce, and G. E. Moore; his critics, Joseph Priestley, Thomas Brown, and J. S. Mill. In America, Italy, and France of the nineteenth century, Reid was widely read and widely influential: in American universities he exerted a considerable influence either directly or through people like James McCosh; in Italy through Antonio Rosmini; and in France through Théodore Jouffroy's translation and the writing of Pierre Royer-Collard and Cousin. Few British philosophers have become as well known abroad as has Reid; perhaps because so few have combined a reliance on innate principles of common sense, an adherence to the Christian religion, antiskepticism, and a devotion to the inductive precepts of Francis Bacon.

SELECTIONS FROM

An Inquiry Into the Human Mind on the Principles of Common Sense*

*

CHAPTER V

OF TOUCH

I. *Of heat and cold:* The senses which we have hitherto considered, are very simple and uniform, each of them exhibiting only one kind of sensation, and thereby indicating only one quality of bodies. By the ear we perceive sounds, and nothing else; by the palate, tastes; and by the nose, odours: these qualities are all likewise of one order, being all secondary qualities: whereas by touch we perceive not one quality only, but many, and those of very different kinds. The chief of them are heat and cold, hardness and softness, roughness and smoothness, figure, solidity, motion, and extension. We shall consider these in order.

As to heat and cold, it will easily be allowed that they are secondary qualities, of the same order with smell, taste, and sound. And, therefore, what hath been already said of smell, is easily applicable to them; that is, that the words *heat* and *cold* have each of them two significations; they sometimes signify certain sensations of the mind, which can have no existence when they are not felt, nor can exist anywhere but in a mind or sentient being; but more frequently they signify a quality in bodies, which, by the laws of nature, occasions the sensations of heat and cold in us: a quality which, though connected by custom so closely with the sensations, that we cannot without difficulty separate them; yet hath not the least resemblance to it, and may continue to exist when there is no sensation at all.

The sensations of heat and cold are perfectly known; for they neither are, nor can be, anything else than what we feel them to be; but

---

* In *Essays on the Active Powers of the Human Mind,* Vol. I, Thomas Tegg and Son (London, 1843).

the qualities in bodies which we call *heat* and *cold,* are unknown. They are only conceived by us, as unknown causes or occasions of the sensations to which we give the same names. But though common sense says nothing of the nature of these qualities, it plainly dictates the existence of them; and to deny that there can be heat and cold when they are not felt, is an absurdity too gross to merit confutation. For what could be more absurd, than to say, that the thermometer cannot rise or fall unless some person be present, or that the coast of Guinea would be as cold as Nova Zembla, if it had no inhabitants?

It is the business of philosophers to investigate, by proper experiments, and induction, what heat and cold are in bodies. And whether they make heat a particular element diffused through nature, and accumulated in the heated body, or whether they make it a certain vibration of the parts of the heated body; whether they determine that heat and cold are contrary qualities, as the sensations undoubtedly are contrary, or that heat only is a quality, and cold its privation; these questions are within the province of philosophy; for common sense says nothing on the one side or the other.

But whatever be the nature of that quality in bodies which we call *heat,* we certainly know this, that it cannot in the least resemble the sensation of heat. It is no less absurd to suppose a likeness between the sensation and the quality, than it would be to suppose, that the pain of the gout resembles a square or a triangle. The simplest man that hath common sense, does not imagine the sensation of heat, or any thing that resembles that sensation, to be in the fire. He only imagines, that there is something in the fire, which makes him and other sentient beings feel heat. Yet as the name of *heat,* in common language, more frequently and more properly signifies this unknown something in the fire, than the sensation occasioned by it, he justly laughs at the philosopher who denies that there is any heat in the fire, and thinks that he speaks contrary to common sense.

II. *Of hardness and softness:* Let us next consider hardness and softness; by which words we always understand real properties or qualities of bodies, of which we have a distinct conception.

When the parts of a body adhere so firmly, that it cannot easily be made to change its figure, we call it *hard;* when its parts are easily displaced, we call it *soft.* This is the notion which all mankind have of hardness and softness: they are neither sensations, nor like any sensation; they were real qualities before they were perceived by touch, and continue to be so when they are not perceived: for if any man will affirm that diamonds were not hard till they were handled, who would reason with him?

There is, no doubt, a sensation by which we perceive a body to be hard or soft. This sensation of hardness may easily be had, by pressing one's hand against the table, and attending to the feeling that ensues, setting aside, as much as possible, all thought of the table and its qualities, or of any external thing. But it is one thing to have the sensation, and another to attend to it, and *make it a distinct object of reflection*. The first is very easy; the last, in most cases, extremely difficult.

We are so accustomed to use the sensation as a sign, and to pass immediately to the hardness signified, that, as far as appears, it was never made an object of thought, either by the vulgar or philosophers; nor has it a name in any language. There is no sensation more distinct, or more frequent; yet it is never attended to, but passes through the mind instantaneously, and serves only to introduce that quality in bodies which, by a law of our constitution, it suggests.

There are indeed some cases wherein it is no difficult matter to attend to the sensation occasioned by the hardness of a body; for instance, when it is so violent as to occasion considerable pain: then nature calls upon us to attend to it, and then we acknowledge that it is a mere sensation, and can only be in a sentient being. If a man runs his head with violence against a pillar, I appeal to him, whether the pain he feels resembles the hardness of the stone; or if he can conceive any thing like what he feels to be in an inanimate piece of matter.

The attention of the mind is here entirely turned towards the painful feeling; and, to speak in the common language of mankind, he feels nothing in the stone, but feels a violent pain in his head. It is quite otherwise when he leans his head gently against the pillar; for then he will tell you that he feels nothing in his head, but feels hardness in the stone. Hath he not a sensation in this case as well as in the other? Undoubtedly he hath: but it is a sensation which nature intended only as a sign of something in the stone; and, accordingly, he instantly fixes his attention upon the thing signified; and cannot, without great difficulty, attend so much to the sensation as to be persuaded that there is any such thing, distinct from the hardness it signifies.

But however difficult it may be to attend to this *fugitive* sensation, to stop its rapid progress, and to disjoin it from the external quality of hardness, in whose shadow it is apt immediately to hide itself; this is what a philosopher by pains and practice must attain, otherwise it will be impossible for him to reason justly upon this subject, or even to understand what is here advanced. For the last appeal, in subjects of this nature, must be to what a man feels and perceives in his own mind.

It is indeed strange, that a sensation which we have every time that we feel a body hard, and which, consequently, we can command as often, and continue as long as we please, a sensation as distinct and determinate as any other, should yet be so much unknown, as never to have been made an object of thought and reflection, nor to have been honoured with a name in any language; that philosophers, as well as the vulgar, should have entirely overlooked it, or confounded it with that quality of bodies which we call *hardness,* to which it hath not the least similitude. May we not hence conclude, that the knowledge of the human faculties is but in its infancy? That we have not yet learned to attend to those operations of the mind of which we are conscious every hour of our lives? That there are habits of inattention acquired very early, which are as hard to be overcome as other habits? For I think it is probable, that the novelty of this sensation will procure some attention to it in children at first; but being nowise interesting in itself, as soon as it becomes familiar, it is overlooked, and the attention turned solely to that which it signifies. Thus, when one is learning a language, he attends to the sounds; but when he is master of it, he attends only to the sense of what he would express. If this is the case, we must become as little children again, if we will be philosophers: we must overcome this habit of inattention which has been gathering strength ever since we began to think; a habit, the usefulness of which, in common life, atones for the difficulty it creates to the philosopher in discovering the first principles of the human mind.

The firm cohesion of the parts of a body, is no more like that sensation by which I perceive it to be hard, than the vibration of a sonorous body is like the sound I hear: nor can I possibly perceive, by my reason, any connexion between the one and the other. No man can give a reason, why the vibration of a body might not have given the sensation of smelling, and the effluvia of bodies affected our hearing, if it had so pleased our Maker. In like manner, no man can give a reason why the sensations of smell, or taste, or sound, might not have indicated hardness, as well as that sensation which, by our constitution, does indicate it. Indeed (1) no man can conceive any sensation to *resemble* any known quality of bodies. Nor (2) can any man show, by any good argument, that all *our sensations might not have been as they are,* though no body, nor quality of body, had ever existed.

Here then is a phenomenon of human nature, which comes to be resolved. Hardness of bodies is a thing that we conceive as distinctly, and believe as firmly, as anything in nature. We have no way of coming at this conception and belief, but by means of a certain sensation of touch, to which hardness hath not the least similitude; nor can we, by any rules of reasoning, infer the one from the other. The question is, how we come by this (1) conception and (2) belief?

First, as to the *conception:* shall we call it an idea of sensation, or of reflection? The last will not be affirmed; and as little can the first, unless we will call that an idea of sensation which hath no resemblance to any sensation. So that the origin of this idea of hardness, one of the most common and most distinct we have, is not to be found in all our systems of the mind: not even in those which have so copi-

ously endeavoured to deduce all our notions from sensation and reflection.

But, *secondly,* supposing we have got the conception of hardness,
how come we by the *belief* of it? Is it self-evident, from comparing the
ideas, that such a sensation could not be felt, unless such a quality of
bodies existed? No. Can it be proved by probable or certain arguments? No, it cannot. Have we got this belief then by tradition, by
education, or by experience? No, it is not got in any of these ways.
Shall we then throw off this belief, as having no foundation in reason?
Alas! it is not in our power; it triumphs over reason, and laughs at all
the arguments of a philosopher. Even the author of the "Treatise of
Human Nature," though he saw no reason for this belief, but many
against it, could hardly conquer it in his speculative and solitary moments; at other times he fairly yielded to it, and confesses that he
found himself under a necessity to do so.

What shall we say then of this *conception,* and this *belief,* which are
so unaccountable and untractable? I see nothing left, but to conclude,
that, by an *original principle of our constitution,* a certain sensation of
touch both suggests to the mind the conception of hardness, and creates the belief of it: or, in other words, that this sensation is a natural
sign of hardness. And this I shall endeavour more fully to explain.

III. *Of natural signs:*   As in artificial signs there is often neither
similitude between the sign and thing signified, nor any connexion that
arises necessarily from the nature of the things; so it is also in natural
signs. The word *gold* has no similitude to the substance signified by it;
nor is it in its own nature more fit to signify this than any other substance: yet, by habit and custom, it suggests this and no other. In like
manner, a sensation of touch suggests hardness, although it hath neither similitude to hardness, nor, as far as we can perceive, any necessary connexion with it. The difference betwixt these two signs lies only
in this, that, in the first, the suggestion is the effect of *habit* and custom; in the second, it is not the effect of habit, but of the *original
constitution* of our minds.

It appears evident from what hath been said on the subject of language, that there are natural signs, as well as artificial; and particularly, that the thoughts, purposes, and dispositions of the mind, have
their natural signs in the features of the face, the modulation of the
voice, and the motion and attitude of the body: that without a natural
knowledge of the connexion between these signs, and the things signified by them, language could never have been invented, and established
among men: and that the fine arts are all founded upon this connexion, which we may call *the natural language of mankind*. It is now
proper to observe, that there are different orders of natural signs, and
to point out the different classes into which they may be distinguished,

that we may more distinctly conceive the relation between our sensations and the things they suggest, and what we mean by calling sensations signs of external things.

The *first class of natural signs* comprehends those whose connexion with the thing signified is established by nature, but discovered only by experience. The whole of genuine philosophy consists in discovering such connexions, and reducing them to general rules. The great Lord Verulam had a perfect comprehension of this, when he called it *an interpretation of nature.* No man ever more distinctly understood or happily expressed the nature and foundation of the philosophic art. What is all we know of mechanics, astronomy, and optics, but connexions established by nature, and discovered by experience or observation, and consequences deduced from them? All the knowledge we have in agriculture, gardening, chemistry, and medicine, is built upon the same foundation. And if ever our philosophy concerning the human mind is carried so far as to deserve the name of science, which ought never to be despaired of, it must be by observing facts, reducing them to general rules, and drawing just conclusions from them. What we commonly call natural *causes* might, with more propriety, be called natural *signs,* and what we call *effects,* the things signified. The causes have no proper efficiency or causality, as far as we know; and all we can certainly affirm is, that nature hath established a constant conjunction between them and the things called their effects; and hath given to mankind a disposition to observe those connexions; to confide in their continuance, and to make use of them for the improvement of our knowledge, and increase of our power.

A *second class is* that wherein the connexion between the sign and thing signified is not only established by nature, but *discovered to us by a natural principle, without reasoning or experience.* Of this kind are the natural signs of human thoughts, purposes, and desires, which have been already mentioned as the natural language of mankind. An infant may be put into a fright by an angry countenance, and soothed again by smiles and blandishments. A child that has a good musical ear, may be put to sleep or to dance, may be made merry or sorrowful, by the modulation of musical sounds. The principles of all the fine arts, and of what we call *a fine taste,* may be resolved into connexions of this kind. A fine taste may be improved by reasoning and experience; but if the first principles of it were not planted in our minds by nature, it could never be acquired. Nay, we have already made it appear, that a great part of this knowledge, which we have by nature, is lost by the disuse of natural signs, and the substitution of artificial in their place.

A *third class of natural signs* comprehends those which, though we never before had any notion or conception of the thing signified, do suggest it, or conjure it up, as it were, by a natural kind of magic, and at once give us a conception, and create a belief of it. I showed formerly, that our sensations suggest to us a sentient being or mind to which they belong: a being which hath a permanent existence, although the sensations are transient and of short duration: a being which is still the same, while its sensations and other operations are varied ten thousand ways: a being which hath the same relation to all that infinite variety of thoughts, purposes, actions, affections, enjoyments, and sufferings, which we are conscious of, or can remember. The conception of a mind is neither an idea of sensation nor of reflection; for it is neither like any of our sensations, nor like any thing we are conscious of. The first conception of it, as well as the belief of it, and of the common relation it bears to all that we are conscious of, or remember, is suggested to every thinking being, we do not know how.

The notion of hardness in bodies, as well as the belief of it, are got in a similar manner; being by an original principle of our nature annexed to that sensation which we have when we feel a hard body. And so naturally and necessarily does the sensation convey the notion and belief of hardness, that hitherto they have been confounded by the most acute inquirers into the principles of human nature, although they appear, upon accurate reflection, not only to be different things, but as unlike as pain is to the point of a sword.

It may be observed, that as the first class of natural signs I have mentioned, is the foundation of true philosophy, and the second, the foundation of the fine arts, or of taste; so the last is the foundation of *common sense;* a part of human nature which hath never been explained.

I take it for granted, that the notion of hardness, and the belief of it, is first got by means of that particular sensation, which, as far back as we can remember, does invariably suggest it; and that if we had never had such a feeling, we should never have had any notion of hardness. I think it is evident, that we cannot, by reasoning from our sensations, collect the existence of bodies at all, far less any of their qualities. This hath been proved by *unanswerable arguments* by the Bishop of Cloyne, and by the author of the "Treatise of Human Nature." [1] It appears as evident, that this connexion between our sensations and the conception and belief of external existences cannot be produced by habit, experience, education, or any principle of human nature that hath been admitted by philosophers. At the same time it is a fact, that such sensations are invariably connected with the conception and belief of external existences. Hence, by all rules of just reasoning, we must conclude, that this connexion is the effect of our

1 See Berkeley's *The Principles of Human Knowledge,* Sections 18–20, 86–88, and *Three Dialogues Between Hylas and Philonous,* Dialogue I, last section. For Hume's arguments see the *Treatise,* Book I, Part II, Section VI, and, in particular, Part IV, Section II. Ed.

constitution, and ought to be considered as an original principle of human nature, till we find some more general principle into which it may be resolved.

IV. *Of hardness, and other primary qualities.* Further I observe, that hardness is a quality, of which we have as clear and distinct a conception as of any thing whatsoever. The cohesion of the parts of a body with more or less force, is perfectly understood, though its cause is not: we know what it is, as well as how it affects the touch. It is therefore a quality of a quite different order from those secondary qualities we have already taken notice of, whereof we know no more naturally, than that they are adapted to raise certain sensations in us. If hardness were a quality of the same kind, it would be a proper inquiry for philosophers, what hardness in bodies is? and we should have had various hypotheses about it, as well as about colour and heat. But it is evident that any such hypothesis would be ridiculous. If any man should say, that hardness in bodies is a certain vibration of their parts, or that it is certain effluvia emitted by them which affect our touch in the manner we feel; such hypotheses would shock common sense; because we all know, that if the parts of a body adhere strongly, it is hard, although it should neither emit effluvia, nor vibrate. Yet at the same time, no man can say, but that effluvia, or the vibration of the parts of a body, might have affected our touch in the same manner that hardness now does, if it had so pleased the Author of our nature: and if either of these hypotheses is applied to explain a secondary quality, such as smell, or taste, or sound, or colour, or heat, there appears no manifest absurdity in the supposition.

V. *The distinction betwixt primary and secondary qualities hath had several revolutions.* Democritus and Epicurus, and their followers, maintained it. Aristotle and the Peripatetics abolished it. Des Cartes, Malebranche, and *Locke, revived it,* and were thought to have put it in a very clear light. But Bishop Berkeley again discarded this distinction, by such proofs as must be convincing to those that hold the received doctrine of ideas. Yet, after all, *there appears to be a real foundation for it* in the principles of our nature.

What hath been said of hardness, is so easily applicable, not only to its opposite, softness, but likewise to roughness and smoothness, to figure and motion, that we may be excused from making the application, which would only be a repetition of what hath been said. All these, by means of certain corresponding sensations of touch, are presented to the mind as real external qualities; the conception and the belief of them are invariably connected with the corresponding sensations, by an original principle of human nature. Their sensations have no name in any language; they have not only been overlooked by the vulgar, but by philosophers; or if they have been at all taken notice of, they have been confounded with the external qualities which they suggest.

VI. *Of extension:*   It is further to be observed, that hardness and softness, roughness and smoothness, figure and motion, do all suppose extension, and cannot be conceived without it; yet I think it must, on the other hand, be allowed, that if we had never felt any thing hard or soft, rough or smooth, figured or moved, we should never have had a conception of extension: so that there is good ground to believe, that the notion of extension could not be prior to that of other primary qualities; so it is certain that it could not be posterior to the notion of any of them, being necessarily implied in them all.

Extension, therefore, seems to be a quality *suggested* to us, by the very same suggestions which suggest the other qualities above mentioned. When I grasp a ball in my hand, I perceive it at once hard, figured, and extended. The feeling is very simple, and hath not the least resemblance to any quality of body. Yet it suggests to us three primary qualities perfectly distinct from one another, as well as from the sensation which indicates them. When I move my hand along the table, the feeling is so simple, that I find it difficult to distinguish it into things of different natures; yet it immediately suggests hardness, smoothness, extension, and motion, things of very different natures, and all of them as distinctly understood as the feeling which suggests them.

We are commonly told by philosophers, that we get the idea of extension by feeling along the extremities of a body, as if there was no manner of difficulty in the matter. I have sought, with great pains I confess, to find out how this idea can be got by feeling, but I have sought in vain. Yet it is one of the clearest and most distinct notions we have; nor is there any thing whatsoever, about which the human understanding can carry on so many long and demonstrative trains of reasoning.

The notion of extension is so familiar to us from infancy, and so constantly obtruded by every thing we see and feel, that we are apt to think it obvious how it comes into the mind; but upon a narrower examination, we shall find it utterly inexplicable. It is true we have feelings of touch, which every moment *present extension to the mind;* but how they come to do so is the question; for *those feelings do no more resemble extension,* than they resemble justice or courage: nor can the existence of extended things be inferred from those feelings by any rules of reasoning; so that the feelings we have by touch, can neither explain how we get the notion, nor how we come by the belief of extended things.

What hath imposed upon philosophers in this matter is, that the feelings of touch, which *suggest primary qualities, have no names,* nor

are they ever reflected upon. They pass through the mind instantaneously, and serve only to introduce the notion and belief of external
things, which by our constitution are connected with them. They are
natural signs, and the mind immediately passes to the thing signified,
without making the least reflection upon the sign, or observing that
there was any such thing. Hence it hath always been taken for
granted, that the ideas of extension, figure, and motion, are ideas of
sensation, which enter into the mind by the sense of touch, in the
same manner as the sensations of sound and smell do by the ear and
nose. The sensations of touch are so connected by our constitution
with the notions of extension, figure, and motion, that philosophers
have mistaken the one for the other, and never have been able to
discern that they were not only distinct things, but altogether unlike.
However, if we will reason distinctly upon this subject, we ought to
give names to those feelings of touch; we must accustom ourselves to
attend to them, and to reflect upon them, that we may be able to
disjoin them from, and to compare them with the qualities signified or
suggested by them.

The habit of doing this is *not to be attained without pains and
practice;* and till a man hath acquired this habit, it will be impossible
for him to think distinctly, or to judge right upon this subject.

Let a man press his hand against the table; *he feels it hard.* But
what is the meaning of this? The meaning undoubtedly is, that he hath
a certain feeling of touch, from which he concludes, without any reasoning, or comparing ideas, that there is something external really
existing, whose parts stick so firmly together, that they cannot be displaced without considerable force.

There is here a feeling, and a conclusion drawn from it, or some
way suggested by it. In order to compare these, we must view them
separately, and then consider by what tie they are connected, and
wherein they resemble one another. The hardness of the table is the
conclusion, the feeling is the medium by which we are led to that
conclusion. Let a man attend distinctly to this medium, and to the
conclusion, and he will perceive them to be as unlike as any two
things in nature. The one is a sensation of the mind, which can have
no existence but in a sentient being; nor can it exist one moment
longer than it is felt: the other is in the table, and we conclude, without any difficulty, that it was in the table before it was felt, and continues after the feeling is over. The one implies no kind of extension,
nor parts, nor cohesion; the other implies all these. Both indeed admit
of degrees, and the feeling, beyond a certain degree, is a species of
pain; but adamantine hardness does not imply the least pain.

And as the feeling hath no similitude to hardness, so neither can
our reason perceive the least tie or connexion between them; nor will
the logician ever be able to show a reason why we should conclude

hardness from this feeling, rather than softness, or any other quality whatsoever. But in reality all mankind are led by their constitution to conclude hardness from this feeling.

The sensation of heat, and the sensation we have by pressing a hard body, are equally feelings; nor can we by reasoning draw any conclusion from the one, but what may be drawn from the other: but *by our constitution* we conclude from the first *an* obscure or *occult quality,* of which we have only this relative conception, that it is something adapted to raise in us the sensation of heat; from the second, we conclude a quality of which we have a *clear* and distinct *conception,* to wit, the hardness of the body.

VII. *Of extension:* To put this matter in another light, it may be proper to try whether from sensation alone we can collect any notion of extension, figure, motion, and space. I take it for granted, that a blind man hath the same notion of extension, figure, and motion, as a man that sees; that Dr. Saunderson[1] had the same notion of a cone, a cylinder, and a sphere, and of the motions and distances of the heavenly bodies, as Sir Isaac Newton.

As sight, therefore, is not necessary for our acquiring those notions, we shall leave it out altogether in our inquiry into the first origin of them: and shall suppose a blind man, by some strange distemper, to have lost all the experience, and habits, and notions he had got by touch; not to have the least conception of the existence, figure, dimensions, or extension, either of his own body, or of any other; but to have all his knowledge of external things to acquire anew, by means of sensation and the power of reason, which we suppose to remain entire.

We shall *first* suppose his body fixed immoveably in one place, and that he can only have the feelings of touch, by the application of other bodies to it. Suppose him first to be pricked with a pin: this will, no doubt, give a smart sensation: he feels pain; but what can he infer from it? Nothing, surely, with regard to the existence or figure of a pin. He can infer nothing from this species of pain, which he might not as well infer from the gout or sciatica. Common sense might lead him to think that this pain had a cause; but whether this cause was body or spirit, extended or unextended, figured or not figured, he could not possibly, from any principles he is supposed to have, form the least conjecture. Having had formerly no notion of body or of extension, the prick of a pin could give him none.

Suppose *next* a body not pointed, but blunt, is applied to his body with a force gradually increased until it bruises him. What has he got by this, but another sensation, or train of sensations, from which he

---

1 Nicholas Saunderson (1682–1739) lost his eyes in infancy from smallpox but, nevertheless, became Lucasian professor of mathematics at Cambridge University and a Fellow of the Royal Society. Ed.

will be able to conclude as little as from the former? A schirrous tumor in any inward part of the body, by pressing upon the adjacent parts, may give the same kind of sensation as the pressure of an external body, without conveying any notion but that of pain, which surely hath no resemblance to extension.

Suppose, *thirdly,* that the body applied to him touched a larger or a lesser part of his body. Could this give him any idea of its extension or dimensions? To me it seems impossible that it should, unless he had some previous notion of the dimensions and figure of his own body, to serve him as a measure. When my two hands touch the extremities of a body, if I know them to be a foot asunder, I easily collect that the body is a foot long; and if I know them to be five feet asunder, that it is five feet long: but if I know not what the distance of my hands is, I cannot know the length of the object they grasp; and if I have no previous notion of hands at all, or of distance between them, I can never get that notion by their being touched.

Suppose, *again,* (4) that a body is drawn along his hands or face while they are at rest. Can this give him any notion of space or motion? It no doubt gives a new feeling; but how it should convey a notion of space or motion to one who had none before, I cannot conceive. The blood moves along the arteries and veins, and this motion, when violent, is felt; but I imagine no man, by this feeling, could get the conception of space or motion, if he had it not before. Such a motion may give a certain succession of feelings, as the cholic may do; but no feelings, nor any combination of feelings, can ever resemble space or motion.

Let us *next* (5) suppose that he makes some instinctive effort to move his head or his hand; but that no motion follows, either on account of external resistance or of palsy. Can this effort convey the notion of space and motion to one who never had it before? Surely it cannot.

Last of all, (6) let us suppose that he moves a limb by instinct, without having had any previous notion of space or motion. He has here a new sensation, which accompanies the flexure of joints, and the swelling of muscles. But how this sensation can convey into his mind the idea of space and motion, is still altogether mysterious and unintelligible. The motions of the heart and lungs are all performed by the contraction of muscles, yet give no conception of space or motion. An embryo in the womb has many such motions, and probably the feelings that accompany them, without any idea of space or motion.

Upon the whole, it appears that our philosophers have imposed upon themselves and upon us, in pretending *to deduce from sensation* the first origin of our notions of *external existences,* of space, motion, and extension, and all the primary qualities of body, that is, the qualities whereof we have the most clear and distinct conception. These qualities do not at all tally with any system of the human faculties that hath been advanced. They have no resemblance to any sensation, or to any operation of our minds; and therefore *they cannot be ideas either of sensation or of reflection.* The very conception of them is irreconcilable to the principles of all our philosophic systems of the understanding. The belief of them is no less so.

VIII. *Of the existence of a material world:* It is beyond our power to say, when or in what order we came by our notions of these qualities. When we trace the operations of our minds as far back as memory and reflection can carry us, we find them already in possession of our imagination and belief, and quite familiar to the mind: but how they came first into its acquaintance, or what has given them so strong a hold of our belief, and what regard they deserve, are no doubt very important questions in the philosophy of human nature.

Shall we, with the Bishop of Cloyne, serve them with a quo warranto, and have them tried at the bar of philosophy, upon the statute of the ideal system? Indeed, in this trial they seem to have come off very pitifully. For although they had very able counsel, learned in the law, *viz.*, Des Cartes, Malebranche, and Locke, who said every thing they could for their clients, the Bishop of Cloyne, believing them to be aiders and abettors of heresy and schism, prosecuted them with great vigour, fully answered all that had been pleaded in their defence, and silenced their ablest advocates, who seem, for half a century past, to decline the argument, and to trust to the favour of the jury rather than to the strength of their pleadings.

Thus, the wisdom of *philosophy* is set in opposition to the *common sense* of mankind. The first pretends to demonstrate *à priori,* that there can be no such thing as a material world; that sun, moon, stars, and earth, vegetable and animal bodies, are and can be nothing else but sensations in the mind, or images of those sensations in the memory and imagination; that, like pain and joy, they can have no existence when they are not thought of. The last can conceive no otherwise of this opinion, than as a kind of metaphysical lunacy; and concludes that too much learning is apt to make men mad; and that the man who seriously entertains this belief, though in other respects he may be a very good man, as a man may be who believes that he is made of glass, yet surely he hath a soft place in his understanding, and hath been hurt by much thinking.

This opposition betwixt philosophy and common sense is apt to have a very unhappy influence upon the philosopher himself. He sees human nature in an odd, unamiable, and mortifying light. He considers himself, and the rest of his species, as born under a necessity of believing ten thousand absurdities and contradictions, and endowed with such a pittance of reason as is just sufficient to make this unhappy discovery: and this is all the fruit of his profound speculations.

Such notions of human nature tend to slacken every nerve of the soul, to put every noble purpose and sentiment out of countenance, and spread a melancholy gloom over the whole face of things.

If this is wisdom, let me be deluded with the vulgar. I find something within me that recoils against it, and inspires more reverent sentiments of the human kind, and of the universal administration. Common sense and reason have both one Author,—that Almighty Author, in all whose other works we observe a consistency, uniformity, and beauty, which charm and delight the understanding: there must therefore be some order and consistency in the human faculties, as well as in other parts of his workmanship. A man that thinks reverently of his own kind, and esteems true wisdom and philosophy, will not be fond, nay, will be very suspicious, of such strange and paradoxical opinions. If they are false, they disgrace philosophy; and if they are true, they degrade the human species, and make us justly ashamed of our frame.

To what purpose is it for philosophy to decide against common sense in this or any other matter? The belief of a material world is older, and of more authority, than any principles of philosophy. It declines the tribunal of reason, and laughs at all the artillery of the logician. It retains its sovereign authority in spite of all the edicts of philosophy, and reason itself must stoop to its orders. Even those philosophers who have disowned the authority of our notions of an external material world, confess that they find themselves under a necessity of submitting to their power.

Methinks, therefore, it were better to make a virtue of necessity; and since we cannot get rid of the vulgar notion and belief of an external world, to reconcile our reason to it as well as we can: for if reason should stomach and fret ever so much at this yoke, she cannot throw it off; if she will not be the servant of common sense, she must be her slave.

In order, therefore, to reconcile reason to common sense in this matter, I beg leave to offer to the consideration of philosophers these two observations. *First.* That in all this debate about the existence of a material world, it hath been taken for granted on both sides, that this same *material world,* if any such there be, must be *the express image of our sensations;* that we can have no conception of any material thing which is not like some sensation in our minds; and particularly that the sensations of touch are images of extension, hardness, figure, and motion. Every argument brought against the existence of a material world, either by the Bishop of Cloyne, or by the author of the "Treatise of Human Nature," supposeth this. If this is true, their arguments are conclusive and unanswerable: but, on the other hand, if it is not true, there is no shadow of argument left. Have those philosophers, then, given any solid proof of this hypothesis, upon which the whole weight of so strange a system rests? No. They have not so much as attempted to do it. But because ancient and modern philosophers have agreed in this opinion, they have taken it for granted. But let us, as becomes philosophers, lay aside authority; we need not surely consult Aristotle or Locke, to know whether pain be like the point of a sword. I have as clear a conception of extension, hardness, and motion, as I have of the point of a sword; and, with some pains and practice, I can form as clear a notion of the other sensations of touch, as I have of pain. When I do so, and compare them together, it appears to me clear as daylight, that the former are not of kin to the latter, nor resemble them in any one feature. They are as unlike, yea, as certainly and manifestly unlike, as pain is to the point of a sword. It may be true that those sensations first introduced the material world to our acquaintance; it may be true that it seldom or never appears without their company: but for all that, they are as unlike as the passion of anger is to those features of the countenance which attend it.

So that, in the sentence those philosophers have passed against the material world, there is an error personæ. Their proof touches not matter, or any of its qualities, but strikes directly against an idol of their own imagination, a material world made of ideas and sensations, which never had nor can have an existence.

Secondly. The very *existence of our conceptions of extension,* figure, and motion, since they are neither ideas of sensation or reflection, *overturns the whole ideal system* by which the material world hath been tried and condemned: so that there hath been likewise in this sentence an error juris.

It is a very fine and a just observation of Locke, that as no human art can create a single particle of matter, and the whole extent of our power over the material world consists in compounding, combining, and disjoining the matter made to our hands; so in the world of thought, the materials are all made by nature, and can only be variously combined and disjoined by us. So that it is impossible for reason or prejudice, true or false philosophy, to produce one simple notion or conception, which is not the work of nature and the result of our constitution. The conception of extension, motion, and the other attributes of matter, cannot be the effect of error or prejudice; it must be the work of nature. And the power of faculty by which we acquire those conceptions must be something different from any power of the human mind that hath been explained, since it is neither sensation nor reflection.

This I would therefore humbly propose as an experimentum crucis, by which the ideal system must stand or fall; and it brings the matter to a short issue: extension, figure, motion, may, any one or all of them, be taken for the subject of this experiment. Either they are ideas of sensation, or they are not. If any one of them can be shown to be an idea of sensation, or to have the least resemblance to any sensation, I lay my hand upon my mouth, and give up all pretence to reconcile reason to common sense in this matter, and must suffer the ideal scepticism to triumph. But if, on the other hand, they are not ideas of sensation, nor like to any sensation, then the ideal system is a rope of sand, and all the laboured arguments of the sceptical philosophy against a material world, and against the existence of every thing but impressions and ideas, proceed upon a false hypothesis.

If our philosophy concerning the mind be so lame with regard to the origin of our notions of the clearest, most simple, and most familiar objects of thought, and the powers from which they are derived, can we expect that it should be more perfect in the account it gives of the origin of our opinions and belief? We have seen already some instances of its imperfection in this respect: and perhaps that same nature which hath given us the power to conceive things altogether unlike to any of our sensations, or to any operation of our minds, hath likewise provided for our belief of them, by some part of our constitution hitherto not explained.

Bishop Berkeley hath proved, beyond the possibility of reply, that we cannot by reasoning infer the existence of matter from our sensations: and the author of the "Treatise of Human Nature" hath proved no less clearly that we cannot by reasoning infer the existence of our own or other minds from our sensations.[1] But are we to admit nothing but what can be proved by reasoning? Then we must be sceptics indeed, and believe nothing at all. The author of the "Treatise of Human Nature" appears to me to be but a half-sceptic. He hath not followed his principles so far as they lead him: but after having, with unparalleled intrepidity and success, combated vulgar prejudices, when he had but one blow to strike, his courage fails him, he fairly lays down his arms, and yields himself a captive to the most common of all vulgar prejudices, I mean the belief of the existence of his own impressions and ideas.

I beg therefore to have the honour of making an addition to the sceptical system, without which I conceive it cannot hang together. I affirm that the belief of the existence of impressions and ideas is as little supported by reason as that of the existence of mind and bodies. No man ever did or could offer any reason for this belief. Des Cartes took it for granted, that he thought, and had sensations and ideas: so have all his followers done. Even the hero of scepticism hath yielded this point, I crave leave to say, weakly and imprudently. I say so, because I am persuaded that there is no principle of his philosophy that obliged him to make this concession. And what is there in impressions and ideas so formidable, that this all-conquering philosophy, after triumphing over every other existence, should pay homage

[1] See Hume's *Treatise,* Book I, Part IV, Section VI. Ed.

to them? Besides, the concession is dangerous: for belief is of such a nature, that if you leave any root, it will spread; and you may more easily pull it up altogether than say, Hitherto shalt thou go, and no further; the existence of impressions and ideas I give up to thee: but see thou pretend to nothing more. A thorough and consistent sceptic will never, therefore, yield this point; and while he holds it, you can never oblige him to yield any thing else.

To such a sceptic I have nothing to say; but of the semi-sceptics I should beg to know why they believe the existence of their impressions and ideas. The true reason I take to be, because they cannot help it; and the same reason will lead them to believe many other things.

All reasoning must be from first principles, and for first principles no other reason can be given but this, that, by the *constitution of our nature,* we are under a necessity of assenting to them. Such principles are parts of our constitution, no less than the power of thinking: reason can neither make nor destroy them; nor can it do any thing without them: it is like a telescope, which may help a man to see further, who hath eyes; but without eyes a telescope shows nothing at all. A mathematician cannot prove the truth of his axioms, nor can he prove anything, unless he takes them for granted. We cannot prove the existence of our minds, nor even of our thoughts and sensations. A historian, or a witness, can prove nothing, unless it is taken for granted that the memory and senses may be trusted. A natural philosopher can prove nothing, unless it is taken for granted that the course of nature is steady and uniform.

How or when I got such first principles, upon which I build all my reasoning, I know not; for I had them before I can remember: but I am sure they are parts of my constitution, and that I cannot throw them off. That our thoughts and sensations must have a subject, which we call *ourself,* is not therefore an opinion got by reasoning, but a natural principle. That our sensations of touch indicate something external, extended, figured, hard or soft, is not a deduction of reason, but a natural principle. The belief of it, and the very conception of it, are equally parts of our constitution. If we are deceived in it, we are deceived by Him that made us, and there is no remedy.

I do not mean to affirm, that the sensations of touch do from the very first suggest the same notions of body and its qualities, which they do when we are grown up. Perhaps nature is frugal in this, as in her other operations. The passion of love, with all its concomitant sentiments and desires, is naturally suggested by the perception of beauty in the other sex. Yet the same perception does not suggest the tender passion, till a certain period of life. A blow given to an infant, raises grief and lamentation; but when he grows up, it as naturally stirs resentment, and prompts him to resistance. Perhaps a child in the womb, or for some short period of its existence, is merely a sentient being: the faculties, by which it perceives an external world, by which it reflects on its own thoughts, and existence, and relation to other things, as well as its reasoning and moral faculties, do possibly unfold themselves by degree; so that it is inspired with the various principles of common sense, as with the passions of love and resentment, when it has occasion for them.

IX. *Of the systems of philosophers concerning the senses:* All the systems of philosophers about our senses and their objects have split upon this rock, of *not distinguishing* properly *sensations,* which can have no existence but when they are felt, *from the things suggested by them.* Aristotle, with as distinguishing a head as ever applied to philosophical disquisitions, confounds these two; and makes every sensation to be the form, without the matter, of the thing perceived by it. As the impression of a seal upon wax has the form of the seal, but nothing of the matter of it; so he conceived our sensations to be impressions upon the mind, which bear the image, likeness, or form of the external thing perceived, without the matter of it. Colour, sound, and smell, as well as extension, figure, and hardness, are, according to him, various forms of matter: our sensations are the same forms imprinted on the mind, and perceived in its own intellect. It is evident from this, that Aristotle made no distinction between primary and secondary qualities of bodies, although that distinction was made by Democritus, Epicurus, and others of the ancients.

Des Cartes, Malebranche, and Locke, revived the distinction between primary and secondary qualities. But they made the *secondary qualities* mere *sensations,* and the *primary* ones *resemblances* of our sensations. They maintained, that colour, sound, and heat, are not anything in bodies, but sensations of the mind: at the same time, they acknowledged some particular texture or modification of the body, to be the cause or occasion of those sensations; but to this modification they gave no name. Whereas, by the vulgar, the names of colour, heat, and sound, are but rarely applied to the sensations, and most commonly to those unknown causes of them; as hath been already explained. The constitution of our nature leads us rather to attend to the things signified by the sensation, than to the sensation itself, and to give a name to the former rather than to the latter. Thus we see, that with regard to secondary qualities, these philosophers thought with the vulgar, and with common sense. Their paradoxes were only an abuse of words. For when they maintain as an important modern discovery, that there is no heat in the fire, they mean no more, than that the fire does not feel heat, which every one knew before.

With regard to primary qualities, these philosophers erred more grossly: they indeed believed the existence of those qualities; but they did not at all attend to the sensations that *suggest* them, which having no names, have been as little considered as if they had no existence. They were aware, that figure, extension, and hardness, are perceived by means of sensations of touch; whence they rashly concluded, that these sensations must be images and resemblances of figure, extension, and hardness.

The received *hypothesis of ideas* naturally led them to this conclusion; and indeed could not consist with any other; for according to that hypothesis, external things must be perceived by means of images of them in the mind; and what can those images of external things in the mind be, but the sensations by which we perceive them?

This however was to draw a conclusion from a hypothesis against fact. We need not have recourse to any hypothesis to know what our sensations are, or what they are like. By a proper degree of reflection and attention we may understand them perfectly, and be as certain that they are not like any quality of body, as we can be, that the toothache is not like a triangle. How a sensation should instantly make us conceive and believe the existence of an external thing altogether unlike to it, I do not pretend to know; and when I say that the one suggests the other, I mean not to explain the manner of their connexion, but to express a fact, which every one may be conscious of; namely, that, by a law of our nature, such a conception and belief constantly and immediately follow the sensation.

Bishop Berkeley gave new light to this subject, by showing, that the qualities of an inanimate thing, such as matter is conceived to be, cannot resemble any sensation; that it is *impossible to conceive any thing like the sensations of our minds, but the sensations of other minds.* Every one that attends properly to his sensations must assent to this; yet it had escaped all the philosophers that came before Berkeley: it had escaped even the ingenious Locke, who had so much practised reflection on the operations of his own mind. So difficult it is to attend properly even to our own feelings. They are so accustomed to pass through the mind unobserved, and instantly to make way for that which nature intended them to signify, that it is extremely difficult to stop, and survey them; and when we think we have acquired this power, perhaps the mind still fluctuates between the sensation and its associated quality, so that they mix together, and present something to the imagination that is compounded of both. Thus in a globe or cylinder, whose opposite sides are quite unlike in colour, if you turn it slowly, the colours are perfectly distinguishable, and their dissimilitude is manifest; but if it is turned fast, they lose their distinction, and seem to be of one and the same colour.

No succession can be more quick than that of tangible qualities to the sensations with which nature has associated them: but when one has once acquired the art of making them separate and distinct objects of thought, he will then clearly perceive, that the maxim of Bishop

Berkeley above mentioned is self-evident; and that the features of the face are not more unlike to a passion of the mind which they indicate, than the sensations of touch are to the primary qualities of body.

But let us observe what use the Bishop makes of this important discovery: why, he concludes, that we can have no conception of an inanimate substance, such as matter is conceived to be, or of any of its qualities; and that there is the strongest ground to believe that there is no existence in nature but minds, sensations, and ideas: if there is any other kind of existences, it must be what we neither have nor can have any conception of. But how does this follow? Why thus: we can have no conception of any thing but what resembles some sensation or idea in our minds; but the sensations and ideas in our minds can resemble nothing but the sensations and ideas in other minds; therefore, the conclusion is evident. This argument, we see, leans upon two propositions. The last of them the ingenious author hath indeed made evident to all that understand his reasoning, and can attend to their own sensations: but the first proposition he never attempts to prove; it is taken from the doctrine of ideas, which hath been so universally received by philosophers, that it was thought to need no proof.

We may here again observe, that this acute writer argues from a *hypothesis* against *fact,* and against the common sense of mankind. That we can have no conception of any thing, unless there is some impression, sensation, or idea, in our minds which resembles it, is indeed an opinion which hath been very generally received among philosophers; but it is neither self-evident, nor hath it been clearly proved: and therefore it had been more reasonable to call in question this doctrine of philosophers, than to discard the material world, and by that means expose philosophy to the ridicule of all men who will not offer up common sense as a sacrifice to metaphysics.

We ought, however, to do this justice both to the Bishop of Cloyne and to the author of the "Treatise of Human Nature," to acknowledge, that their conclusions are justly drawn from the doctrine of ideas, which has been so universally received. On the other hand, from the character of Bishop Berkeley, and of his predecessors Des Cartes, Locke, and Malebranche, we may venture to say, that if they had seen all the consequences of this doctrine, as clearly as the author before mentioned did, they would have suspected it vehemently, and examined it more carefully than they appear to have done.

The theory of ideas, like the Trojan horse, had a specious appearance both of innocence and beauty; but if those philosophers had known that it carried in its belly death and destruction to all science and common sense, they would not have broken down their walls to give it admittance.

That we have clear and distinct conceptions of extension, figure, motion, and other attributes of body, which are neither sensations, nor like any sensation, is a fact of which we may be as certain, as that we have sensations. And that all mankind have a fixed belief of an external material world, a belief which is neither got by reasoning nor education, and a belief which we cannot shake off, even when we seem to have strong arguments against it, and no shadow of argument for it, is likewise a fact, for which we have all the evidence that the nature of the thing admits. These facts are phenomena of human nature, from which we may justly argue against any hypothesis, however generally received. But to argue from a hypothesis against facts, is contrary to the rules of true philosophy.

CHAPTER VI

OF SEEING

XX. *Of perception in general:* Sensation and the perception of external objects by the senses, though very different in their nature, have commonly been considered as one and the same thing. The purposes of common life do not make it necessary to distinguish them, and the received opinions of philosophers, tend rather to confound them: but without attending carefully to this distinction, it is impossible to have any just conception of the operations of our senses. The most simple operations of the mind admit not of a logical definition: all we can do is to describe them, so as to lead those who are conscious of them in themselves, to attend to them, and reflect upon them: and it is often very difficult to describe them so as to answer this intention.

The same mode of expression is used to denote sensation and perception; and therefore we are apt to look upon them as things of the same nature. Thus, *I feel a pain; I see a tree:* the first denoteth a *sensation,* the last a *perception.* The grammatical analysis of both expressions is the same: for both consist of an active verb and an object. But if we attend to the thing signified by these expressions, we shall find that in the first, the distinction between the act and the object is not real, but grammatical; in the second, the distinction is not only grammatical but real.

The form of the expression, *I feel pain,* might seem to imply that the feeling is something distinct from the pain felt; yet, in reality, there is no distinction. As *thinking a thought,* is an expression which could signify no more than *thinking,* so *feeling a pain* signifies no more than *being pained.* What we have said of pain is applicable to every other mere sensation. It is difficult to give instances, very few of our sensations having names; and where they have, the name being common to the sensation, and to something else which is associated with it. But when we attend to the sensation by itself, and separate it from other things which are conjoined with it in the imagination, it appears to be something which can have no existence but in a sentient mind, no distinction from the act of the mind by which it is felt.

Perception, as we here understand it, hath always an object distinct from the act by which it is perceived; an object which may exist whether it be perceived or not. I perceive a tree that grows before my window; there is here an object which is perceived; and an act of the mind by which it is perceived; and these two are not only distinguishable, but they are extremely unlike in their natures. The object is made up of a trunk, branches and leaves; but the act of the mind by which it is perceived, hath neither trunk, branches, nor leaves. I am conscious of this act of my mind and I can reflect upon it; but it is too simple to admit of an analysis, and I cannot find proper words to describe it. I find nothing that resembles it so much as the remembrance of the tree, or the imagination of it. Yet both these differ essentially from perception; they differ likewise one from another. It is in vain that a philosopher assures me that the imagination of the tree, the remembrance of it, and the perception of it, are all one, and differ only in degree of vivacity. I know the contrary; for I am as well acquainted with all the three, as I am with the apartments of my own house. I know this also, that the perception of an object implies both a conception of its form, and a belief of its present existence. I know, moreover, that this belief is not the effect of argumentation and reasoning; it is the immediate effect of my constitution.

I am aware that this belief which I have in perception, stands exposed to the strongest batteries of *scepticism*. But they make no great impression upon it. The sceptic asks me, Why do you believe the existence of the external object which you perceive? This belief, Sir, is none of my manufacture; it came from the mint of nature; it bears her image and superscription; and if it is not right, the fault is not mine: I even took it upon trust, and without suspicion. Reason, says the sceptic, is the only judge of truth, and you ought to throw off every opinion and every belief that is not grounded on reason. Why, Sir, should I believe the faculty of reason more than that of perception? they came both out of the same shop, and were made by the same artist; and if he puts one piece of false ware into my hands, what should hinder him from putting another?

Perhaps the sceptic will agree to distrust reason, rather than give any credit to perception. For, says he, since by your own concession, the object which you perceive, and that act of your mind by which you perceive it, are quite different things, the one may exist without the other; and as the object may exist without being perceived, so the perception may be without an object. There is nothing so shameful in a philosopher as to be deceived and deluded; and therefore you ought to resolve firmly to withhold assent, and to throw off this belief of external objects, which may be all delusion. For my part, I will never attempt to throw it off; and although the sober part of mankind will not be very anxious to know my reasons, yet if they can be of use to any sceptic, they are these:—

First, Because it is not in my power: why then should I make a vain attempt? It would be agreeable to fly to the moon, and to make a visit to Jupiter and Saturn: but when I know that nature has bound me down by the law of gravitation to this planet which I inhabit, I rest contented, and quietly suffer myself to be carried along in its orbit. My belief is carried along by perception, as irresistibly as my body by the earth. And the greatest sceptic will find himself to be in the same condition. He may struggle hard to disbelieve the informations of his senses, as a man does to swim against a torrent; but ah! it is in vain. It is in vain that he strains every nerve, and wrestles with nature, and with every object that strikes upon his senses. For after all, when his strength is spent in the fruitless attempt, he will be carried down the torrent with the common herd of believers.

Secondly, I think it would not be prudent to throw off this belief, if it were in my power. If nature intended to deceive me, and impose upon me by false appearances, and I, by my great cunning and profound logic, have discovered the imposture; prudence would dictate to me in this case, even to put up with this indignity done me, as quietly as I could, and not to call her an impostor to her face, lest she should be even with me in another way. For what do I gain by resenting this injury? You ought at least not to believe what she says. This, indeed, seems reasonable, if she intends to impose upon me. But what is the consequence? I resolve not to believe my senses. I break my nose against a post that comes in my way; I step into a dirty kennel; and after twenty such wise and rational actions, I am taken up and clapped into a madhouse. Now I confess I would rather make one of the credulous fools whom nature imposes upon, than of those wise and rational philosophers who resolve to withhold assent at all this expense. If a man pretends to be a sceptic with regard to the informations of sense, and yet prudently keeps out of harm's way as other men do, he must excuse my suspicion, that he either acts the hypocrite, or imposes upon himself. For if the scale of his belief were so evenly poised, as to lean no more to one side than to the contrary, it is impossible that his actions could be directed by any rules of common prudence.

Thirdly, Although the two reasons already mentioned are perhaps two more than enough, I shall offer a third. I gave implicit belief to the informations of nature by my senses, for a considerable part of my life, before I had learned so much logic as to be able to start a doubt concerning them. And now, when I reflect upon what is past, I do not find that I have been imposed upon by this belief. I find, that without it I must have perished by a thousand accidents. I find, that without it I should have been no wiser now than when I was born. I should not even have been able to acquire that logic which suggests these sceptical doubts with regard to my senses. Therefore, I consider this instinctive belief as one of the best gifts of nature. I thank the Author of my being who bestowed it upon me, before the eyes of my reason were opened, and still bestows it upon me to be my guide, where reason leaves me in the dark. And now I yield to the direction of my senses, not from instinct only, but from confidence and trust in a faithful and beneficent Monitor, grounded upon the experience of his paternal care and goodness.

In all this, I deal with the Author of my being, no otherwise than I thought it reasonable to deal with my parents and tutors. I believed by instinct whatever they told me, long before I had the idea of a lie, or thought of the possibility of their deceiving me. Afterwards, upon reflection, I found they had acted like fair and honest people who wished me well. I found, that if I had not believed what they told me, before I could give a reason of my belief, I had to this day been little better than a changeling. And although this natural credulity hath sometimes occasioned my being imposed upon by deceivers, yet it hath been of infinite advantage to me upon the whole; therefore I consider it as another good gift of nature. And I continue to give that credit, from reflection, to those of whose integrity and veracity I have had experience, which before I gave from instinct.

There is a much greater similitude than is commonly imagined, between the testimony of nature given by our senses, and the testimony of men given by language. The credit we give to both is at first the effect of instinct only. When we grow up, and begin to reason about them, the credit given to human testimony is restrained and weakened by the experience we have of deceit. But the credit given to the testimony of our senses, is established and confirmed by the uniformity and constancy of the laws of nature.

Our perceptions are of two kinds: some are natural and original; others acquired, and the fruit of experience. When I perceive that this is the taste of cyder, that of brandy; that this is the smell of an apple, that of an orange; that this is the noise of thunder, that the ringing of bells; this the sound of a coach passing, that the voice of such a friend; these perceptions, and others of the same kind, are not original, they are acquired. But the perception which I have by touch of the hardness and softness of bodies, of their extension, figure, and motion, is not acquired, it is original.

In all our senses, the acquired perceptions are many more than the original, especially in sight. By this sense we perceive originally the visible figure and colour of bodies only, and their visible place: but we learn to perceive by the eye, almost every thing which we can perceive by touch. The original perceptions of this sense, serve only as signs to introduce the acquired.

The signs by which objects are presented to us in perception, are the language of nature to man; and as in many respects it hath great affinity with the language of man to man, so particularly in this, that both are partly natural and original, partly acquired by custom. Our original or natural perceptions are analogous to the natural language of man to man, of which we took notice in the fourth chapter; and our acquired perceptions are analogous to artificial language, which, in our mother-tongue, is got very much in the same manner with our acquired perceptions, as we shall afterwards more fully explain.

Not only men, but children, idiots, and brutes, acquire by habit many perceptions which they had not originally. Almost every employment in life hath perceptions of this kind, that are peculiar to it. The shepherd knows every sheep of his flock, as we do our acquaintance, and can pick them out of another flock, one by one. The butcher knows by sight the weight and quality of his beeves and sheep before they are killed. The farmer perceives by his eye, very nearly, the quantity of hay in a rick, or of corn in a heap. The sailor sees the burthen, the build, and the distance of a ship at sea, while she is a great way off. Every man accustomed to writing, distinguishes his acquaintance by their handwriting, as he does by their faces. And the painter distinguishes, in the works of his art, the style of all the great masters. In a word, acquired perception is very different in different persons, according to the diversity of objects about which they are employed, and the application they bestow in observing them.

Perception ought not only to be distinguished from sensation, but likewise from that knowledge of the objects of sense which is got by reasoning. There is *no reasoning in perception,* as hath been observed. The belief which is implied in it, is the effect of *instinct.* But there are many things with regard to sensible objects which we can infer from what we perceive; and such conclusions of reason ought to be distinguished from what is merely perceived. When I look at the moon, I perceive her to be sometimes circular, sometimes horned, and sometimes gibbous. This is simple perception, and is the same in the philosopher and in the clown: but from these various appearances of her enlightened part, I infer that she is really of a spherical figure. This conclusion is not obtained by simple perception, but by reasoning. Simple perception has the same relation to the conclusions of reason drawn from our perceptions, as the axioms in mathematics have to the propositions. I cannot demonstrate, that two quantities which are equal to the same quantity, are equal to each other; neither can I demonstrate, that the tree which I perceive exists. But, by the constitution of my nature, my belief is irresistibly carried along by my apprehension of the axiom; and, by the constitution of my nature, my belief is no less irresistibly carried along by my perception of the tree. All reasoning is from principles. The first principles of mathematical reasoning are mathematical axioms and definitions; and the first principles of all our reasoning about existences, are our perceptions. The first principles of every kind of reasoning are given us by nature, and are of equal authority with the faculty of reason itself, which is also the gift of nature. The conclusions of reason are all built upon first principles, and can have no other foundation. Most justly, therefore, do such principles disdain to be tried by reason, and laugh at all the artillery of the logician, when it is directed against them.

When a long train of reasoning is necessary, in demonstrating a mathematical proposition, it is easily distinguished from an axiom, and they seem to be things of a very different nature. But there are some propositions which lie so near to axioms, that it is difficult to say, whether they ought to be held as axioms, or demonstrated as propositions. The same thing holds with regard to perception, and the conclusions drawn from it. Some of these conclusions follow our perceptions so easily, and are so immediately connected with them, that it is difficult to fix the limit which divides the one from the other.

Perception, whether original or acquired, implies no exercise of reason, and is common to men, children, idiots, and brutes. The more obvious conclusions drawn from our perceptions by reason, make what we call *common understanding;* by which men conduct themselves in the common affairs of life, and by which they are distinguished from idiots. The more remote conclusions which are drawn from our perceptions by reason, make what we commonly call *science* in the various parts of nature, whether in agriculture, medicine, mechanics, or in any part of natural philosophy. When I see a garden in good order, containing a great variety of things of the best kinds, and in the most flourishing condition, I immediately conclude from these signs, the skill and industry of the gardener. A farmer, when he rises in the morning, and perceives that the neighbouring brook overflows his field, concludes that a great deal of rain hath fallen in the night. Perceiving his fence broken, and his corn trodden down, he concludes that some of his own or his neighbours' cattle have broke loose. Perceiving that his stable-door is broke open, and some of his horses gone, he concludes that a thief has carried them off. He traces the prints of his horses' feet in the soft ground, and by them discovers which road the thief hath taken. These are instances of common understanding, which dwells so near to perception, that it is difficult to trace the line which divides the one from the other. In like manner, the science of nature dwells so near to common understanding, that we cannot discern where the latter ends and the former begins. I perceive that bodies lighter than water swim in water, and that those which are heavier sink. Hence I conclude, that if a body remains wherever it is put under water, whether at the top or bottom, it is precisely of the same weight with water. If it will rest only when part of it is above water, it is lighter than water. And the greater the part above water is, compared with the whole, the lighter is the body. If it had no gravity at all, it would make no impression upon the water, but stand wholly above it. Thus every man, by common understanding, has a rule by which he judges of the specific gravity of bodies which swim in water; and a step or two more leads him into the science of hydrostatics.

All that we know of nature, or of existences, may be compared to a tree, which hath its root, trunk, and branches. In this tree of knowledge, perception is the root, common understanding is the trunk, and the sciences are the branches.

SELECTIONS FROM

Essays On the Intellectual Powers of Man*

*

ESSAY II

CHAPTER III

HYPOTHESES CONCERNING THE NERVES AND BRAIN

III. What Newton only proposed as a matter to be inquired into, Dr. Hartley conceived to have such evidence, that, in his "Observations on Man," he has deduced, in a mathematical form, a very ample system concerning the faculties of the mind, from the doctrine of vibrations, joined with that of association.

His notion of the vibrations, excited in the nerves, is expressed in propositions 4 and 5, of the first part of his "Observations on Man." "Proposition 4, External objects impressed on the senses, occasion first in the nerves on which they are impressed, and then in the brain, vibrations of the small, and, as one may say, infinitesimal medullary particles. Prop. 5, The vibrations mentioned in the last proposition are excited, propagated, and kept up, partly by the æther, that is, by a very subtile elastic fluid; partly by the uniformity, continuity, softness, and active powers of the medullary substance of the brain, spinal marrow, and nerves."

* Thomas Tegg and Son (London, 1843).

The modesty and diffidence with which Dr. Hartley offers his system to the world, by desiring his reader "to expect nothing but hints and conjectures in difficult and obscure matters, and a short detail of the principal reasons and evidences in those that are clear; by acknowledging, that he shall not be able to execute, with any accuracy, the proper method of philosophising, recommended and followed by Sir Isaac Newton; and that he will attempt a sketch only for the benefit of future inquirers," seem to forbid any criticism upon it. One cannot, without reluctance, criticise what is proposed in such a manner, and with so good intention; yet, as the tendency of this system of vibrations is to make all the operations of the mind mere mechanism, dependent on the laws of matter and motion; and as it has been held forth by its votaries, *as in a manner demonstrated,* I shall make some remarks on that part of the system which relates to the impressions made on the nerves and brain in perception.

It may be observed in general, that Dr. Hartley's work consists of a chain of propositions, with their proofs and corollaries, digested in good order, and in a scientific form. A great part of them, however, are, as he candidly acknowledges, conjectures and hints only; yet these are mixed with the propositions legitimately proved, without any distinction. Corollaries are drawn from them, and other propositions grounded upon them, which, all taken together, make up a system. A system of this kind resembles a chain, of which some links are abundantly strong, others very weak. The strength of the chain is determined by that of the weakest links; for if they give way, the whole falls to pieces, and the weight, supported by it, falls to the ground.

IV. Philosophy has been in all ages adulterated by hypotheses; that is, by systems built partly on facts, and much upon conjecture. It is pity that a man of Dr. Hartley's knowledge and candour should have followed the multitude in this fallacious track, after expressing his approbation of the proper method of philosophising, pointed out by Bacon and Newton. The last considered it as a reproach, when his system was called his hypothesis; and says, with disdain of such imputation, "Hypotheses non fingo." [1] And it is very strange, that Dr. Hartley should not only follow such a method of philosophising himself, but that he should direct others in their inquiries to follow it. So he does in Proposition 87, Part I.,[2] where he deduces rules for the ascertainment of truth, from the rule of false in arithmetic, and from the art of deciphering; and in other places.

---

[1] "I frame no hypotheses": *Mathematical Principles of Natural Philosophy,* Book III, General Scholium to Proposition XLII. On the interpretation of this remark see F. Cajori's edition of the *Principles* (Berkeley, 1947), Appendix, note 55, pp. 671–76. Ed.

[2] Chapter III, Section II; reprinted in the present volume. Ed.

As to the vibrations and vibratiuncles, whether of an elastic æther, or of the infinitesimal particles of the brain and nerves, there may be such things for what we know; and men may rationally inquire whether they can find any evidence of their existence; but while we have no proof of their existence, to apply them to the solution of phenomena, and to build a system upon them, is, what I conceive, we call, building a castle in the air.

V. When men pretend to account for any of the operations of nature, the causes assigned by them ought, as Sir Isaac Newton has taught us, to have two conditions, otherwise they are good for nothing. *First,* They ought to be true, to have a real existence, and not to be barely conjectured to exist, without proof. *Secondly,* They ought to be sufficient to produce the effect.[1]

As to the existence of vibratory motions in the medullary substance of the nerves and brain, the evidence produced is this: *First,* It is observed, that the sensations of seeing and hearing, and some sensations of touch, have some short duration and continuance. *Secondly,* Though there be no direct evidence that the sensations of taste and smell, and the greater part of these of touch, have the like continuance; yet, says the author, analogy would incline one to believe, that they must resemble the sensations of sight and hearing in this particular. *Thirdly,* The continuance of all our sensations being thus established, it follows, that external objects impress vibratory motions on the medullary substance of the nerves and brain; because no motion, besides a vibratory one, can reside in any part for a moment of time.

This is the chain of proof; in which the first link is strong, being confirmed by experience; the second is very weak; and the third still weaker. For other kinds of motion, besides that of vibration, may have some continuance, such as rotation, bending or unbending of a spring, and perhaps others which we are unacquainted with; nor do we know whether it is motion that is produced in the nerves, it may be pressure, attraction, repulsion, or something we do not know. This, indeed, is the common refuge of all hypotheses, that we know no other way in which the phenomena may be produced, and therefore they must be produced in this way. There is, therefore, no proof of vibrations in the infinitesimal particles of the brain and nerves.

VI. It may be thought that the existence of an elastic vibrating æther stands on a firmer foundation, having the authority of Sir Isaac Newton. But it ought to be observed, that although this great man had formed conjectures about the æther near fifty years before he died, and had it in his eye during that long space as a subject of inquiry; yet it does not appear that he ever found any convincing proof of its existence, but considered it to the last as a question whether there be such

---

[1] See the *Principles*, Book III, "Rules of Reasoning in Philosophy." Ed.

an æther or not. In the premonition to the reader, prefixed to the second edition of his Optics,[1] anno 1717, he expresses himself thus with regard to it: "Lest any one should think that I place gravity among the essential properties of bodies, I have subjoined one question concerning its cause; a question, I say, for I do not hold it as a thing established." If, therefore, we regard the authority of Sir Isaac Newton, we ought to hold the existence of such an æther as a matter not established by proof, but to be examined into by experiments; and I have never heard that, since his time, any new evidence has been found of its existence.

But, says Dr. Hartley, "supposing the existence of the æther and of its properties to be destitute of all direct evidence, still, if it serves to account for a great variety of phenomena, it will have an indirect evidence in its favour by this means." [2] There never was an hypothesis invented by an ingenious man which has not this evidence in its favour. The Vortices of Des Cartes, the Sylphs and Gnomes of Mr. Pope, serve to account for a great variety of phenomena.

VII. When a man has, with labour and ingenuity, wrought up a hypothesis into a system, he contracts a fondness for it, which is apt to warp the best judgment. This, I humbly think, appears remarkably in Dr. Hartley. In his preface, he declares his approbation of the method of philosophising recommended and followed by Sir Isaac Newton; but having first deviated from this method in his practice, he is brought at last to justify this deviation in theory, and to bring arguments in defence of a method diametrically opposite to it. "We admit," says he, "the key of a cipher to be a true one, when it explains the cipher completely." I answer, To find the key requires an understanding equal or superior to that which made the cipher. This instance, therefore, will then be in point, when he who attempts to decipher the works of nature by a hypothesis, has an understanding equal or superior to that which made them. The votaries of hypotheses have often been challenged to show one useful discovery in the works of nature that was ever made in that way. If instances of this kind could be produced, we ought to conclude, that Lord Bacon and Sir Isaac Newton have done great disservice to philosophy, by what they have said against hypotheses. But if no such instance can be produced, we must conclude, with those great men, that every system which pretends to account for the phenomena of nature by hypotheses or conjecture, is spurious and illegitimate, and serves only to flatter the pride of man with a vain conceit of knowledge which he has not attained.

The author tells us, "that any hypothesis that has so much plausibility as to explain a considerable number of facts, helps us to digest

---

[1] In Advertisement II of the fourth edition, reprinted by Dover (New York, 1952). Ed.

[2] *Observations on Man,* Chapter I, Section I, Prop. V. Ed.

these facts in proper order, to bring new ones to light, and to make experimenta crucis for the sake of future inquirers." [1]

Let hypotheses be put to any of these uses as far as they can serve; let them suggest experiments, or direct our inquiries; but let just induction alone govern our belief.

"The rule of false affords an obvious and strong instance of the possibility of being led, with precision and certainty, to a true conclusion from a false position. And it is of the very essence of algebra, to proceed in the way of supposition." [2]

This is true; but, when brought to justify the accounting for natural phenomena by hypotheses, is foreign to the purpose. When an unknown number, or any unknown quantity, is sought, which must have certain conditions, it may be found in a scientific manner, by the rule of false, or by algebraical analysis; and, when found, may be synthetically demonstrated to be the number or the quantity sought, by its answering all the conditions required. But it is one thing to find a quantity which shall have certain conditions; it is a very different thing to find out the laws by which it pleases God to govern the world, and produce the phenomena which fall under our observation. And we can then only allow some weight to this argument in favour of hypotheses, when it can be shown, that the cause of any one phenomenon in nature has been, or can be found, as an unknown quantity is, by the rule of false, or by algebraical analysis. This, I apprehend, will never be, till the era arrives which Dr. Hartley seems to foretell, "when future generations shall put all kinds of evidences and inquiries into mathematical forms; and, as it were, reduce Aristotle's ten Categories, and Bishop Wilkins' forty Summa Genera, to the head of quantity alone, so as to make mathematics, and logic, natural history, and civil history, natural philosophy, and philosophy of all other kinds, coincide *omni ex parte.*" [1]

VIII. Since Sir Isaac Newton laid down the rules of philosophising in our inquiries into the works of nature, many philosophers have deviated from them in practice; perhaps few have paid that regard to them which they deserve. But they have met with very general approbation, as being founded in reason, and pointing out the only path to the knowledge of nature's works. Dr. Hartley is the only author I have met with who reasons against them, and has taken pains to find out arguments in defence of the exploded method of hypothesis.

Another condition which Sir Isaac Newton requires in the causes of natural things assigned by philosophers, is, that they be sufficient to account for the phenomena. Vibrations and vibratiuncles of the medullary substance of the nerves and brain, are assigned by Dr. Hartley

---

[1] *Ibid.* Ed.
[2] *Ibid.* Ed.
[3] In Chapter III, Section II, Prop. LXXXVII, reprinted in the present volume. Ed.

to account for all our sensations and ideas, and, in a word, for all the operations of our minds. Let us consider very briefly how far they are sufficient for that purpose.

IX. *It would be injustice to this author to conceive him a materialist.*—He proposes his sentiments with great candour, and they ought not to be carried beyond what his words express. He thinks it a consequence of his theory, that matter, if it can be endued with the most simple kinds of sensation, might arrive at all that intelligence of which the human mind is possessed. He thinks that his theory overturns all the arguments that are usually brought for the immateriality of the soul, from the subtilty of the internal senses, and of the rational faculty; but he does not take upon him to determine whether matter can be endued with sensation or no. He even acknowledges, that matter and motion, however subtilly divided and reasoned upon, yield nothing more than matter and motion still; and therefore he would not be any way interpreted so as to oppose the immateriality of the soul.

X. *Origin of the operations of the mind, according to Hartley's theory.*—It would, therefore, be unreasonable to require that his theory of vibrations should, in the proper sense, account for our sensations. It would, indeed, be ridiculous in any man to pretend, that thought of any kind must necessarily result from motion, or that vibrations in the nerves must necessarily produce thought, any more than the vibrations of a pendulum. Dr. Hartley disclaims this way of thinking, and therefore it ought not to be imputed to him. All that he pretends is, that, in the human constitution, there is a certain connexion between vibrations in the medullary substance of the nerves and brain, and the thoughts of the mind; so that the last depend entirely upon the first, and every kind of thought in the mind arises in consequence of a corresponding vibration, or vibratiuncle in the nerves and brain. Our sensations arise from vibrations, and our ideas from vibratiuncles, or miniature vibrations; and he comprehends, under these two words of *sensations* and *ideas,* all the operations of the mind.

But how can we expect any proof of the connexion between vibrations and thought, when the existence of such vibrations was never proved? The proof of their connexion cannot be stronger than the proof of their existence: for, as the author acknowledges, that we cannot infer the existence of the thoughts from the existence of the vibrations, it is no less evident, that we cannot infer the existence of vibrations from the existence of our thoughts. The existence of both must be known before we can know their connexion. As to the existence of our thoughts, we have the evidence of consciousness; a kind of evidence that never was called in question. But as to the existence of vibrations in the medullary substance of the nerves and brain, no proof has yet been brought.

All therefore we have to expect from this hypothesis, is, that, in vibrations considered abstractly, there should be a variety in kind and degree, which tallies so exactly with the varieties of the thoughts they are to account for, as may lead us to suspect some connexion between the one and the other. If the divisions and subdivisions of thought be found to run parallel with the divisions and subdivisions of vibrations, this would give that kind of plausibility to the hypothesis of their connexion, which we commonly expect even in a mere hypothesis; but we do not find even this.

For, to omit all those thoughts and operations which the author comprehends under the name of *ideas,* and which he thinks are connected with vibratiuncles; to omit the perception of external objects, which he comprehends under the name of *sensations;* to omit the sensations, properly so called, which accompany our passions and affections, and to confine ourselves to the sensations which we have by means of our external senses, we can perceive no correspondence between the variety we find in their kinds and degrees, and that which may be supposed in vibrations.

We have five senses, whose sensations differ totally in kind. By each of these, excepting perhaps that of hearing, we have a variety of sensations, which differ specifically, and not in degree only. How many tastes and smells are there which are specifically different, each of them capable of all degrees of strength and weakness? Heat and cold, roughness and smoothness, hardness and softness, pain and pleasure, are sensations of touch that differ in kind, and each has an endless variety of degrees. Sounds have the qualities of acute and grave, loud and soft, with all different degrees of each. The varieties of colour are many more than we have names to express. How shall we find varieties in vibrations corresponding to all this variety of sensations which we have by our five senses only?

XI. *One case in which Hartley's theory explains the phenomena:* I know two qualities of vibrations in an uniform elastic medium, and I know no more. They may be quick or slow in various degrees, and they may be strong or weak in various degrees; but I cannot find any division of our sensations that will make them tally with those divisions of vibrations. If we had no other sensations but those of *hearing,* the theory would answer well; for sounds are either *acute* or *grave,* which may answer to *quick* or *slow* vibrations; or they are loud or soft, which answer to strong or weak vibrations. But then we have no variety of vibrations corresponding to the *immense variety of sensations* which we have by sight, smell, taste, and touch.

XII. Dr. Hartley has endeavoured to find out other two qualities of vibrations; to wit, that they may primarily affect one part of the brain or another, and that they may vary in their direction, according as they enter by different external nerves; but these seem to be added to make a number: for, as far as we know, vibrations in an uniform elastic substance, spread over the whole, and in all directions. However, that we may be liberal, we shall grant him four different kinds of vibrations, each of them having as many degrees as he pleases. Can he or any man reduce all our sensations to four kinds? We have five senses, and by each of them a variety of sensations, more than sufficient to exhaust all the varieties we are able to conceive in vibrations.

Dr. Hartley, indeed, was sensible of the difficulty of finding vibrations to suit all the variety of our sensations. His extensive knowledge of physiology and pathology could yield him but a feeble aid; and therefore he is often reduced to the necessity of heaping supposition upon supposition, conjecture upon conjecture, to give some credibility to his hypothesis; and, in seeking out vibrations which may correspond with the sensations of one sense, he seems to forget that those must be omitted which have been appropriated to another.

XIII. Philosophers have accounted in some degree for our various sensations of sound, by the vibrations of elastic air. But it is to be observed, *first,* That we know that such vibrations do really exist; and, *secondly,* That they tally exactly with the most remarkable phenomena of sound. We cannot, indeed, show how any vibration should produce the sensation of sound. This must be resolved into the will of God, or into some cause altogether unknown. But we know, that as the vibration is strong or weak, the sound is loud or soft. We know, that as the vibration is quick or slow, the sound is acute or grave. We can point out that relation of synchronous vibrations which produces harmony or discord, and that relation of successive vibrations which produces melody: and all this is not conjectured, but proved by a sufficient induction. This account of sounds, therefore, is philosophical; although, perhaps, there may be many things relating to sound that we cannot account for, and of which the causes remain latent. The connexions described in this branch of philosophy are the work of God, and not the fancy of men.

XIV. *This theory may be rejected, since its first principles still require proof:* If any thing similar to this could be shown in accounting for all our sensations by vibrations in the medullary substance of the nerves and brain, it would deserve a place in sound philosophy. But, (1) when we are told of vibrations in a substance, which *no man could ever prove* to have vibrations, or to be capable of them; when such imaginary vibrations are brought to account for all our sensations, though (2) we can perceive no correspondence, in their *variety of kind and degree,* to the variety of sensations; the connexions described in such a system, are the creatures of human imagination, not the work of God.

The rays of light make an impression upon the optic nerves; but they make none upon the auditory or olfactory. The vibrations of the air make an impression upon the auditory nerves; but none upon the optic or the olfactory. The effluvia of bodies make an impression upon the olfactory nerves; but make none upon the optic or auditory. No man has been able to give a shadow of reason for this. While this is the case, is it not better to confess our ignorance of the nature of those impressions made upon the nerves and brain in perception, than to flatter our pride with the conceit of knowledge which we have not, and to adulterate philosophy with the spurious brood of hypotheses?

ESSAY III

CHAPTER VII

THEORIES CONCERNING MEMORY

II. *Peripatetic theory of memory defective.*—This ancient theory of the cause of memory is defective in two respects: *first,* If the cause assigned did really exist, it by no means accounts for the phenomenon: and, *secondly,* There is no evidence, nor even probability, that that cause exists.

It is probable, that in perception some impression is made upon the brain as well as upon the organ and nerves, because all the nerves terminate in the brain, and because disorders and hurts of the brain are found to affect our powers of perception when the external organ and nerve are sound; but we are totally ignorant of the nature of this impression upon the brain: it can have no resemblance to the object perceived, nor does it in any degree account for that sensation and perception which are consequent upon it. These things have been argued in the second Essay, and shall now be taken for granted, to prevent repetition.

If the impression upon the brain be insufficient to account for the perception of objects that are present, it can as little account for the memory of those that are past.

So that if it were certain, that the impressions made on the brain in perception remain as long as there is any memory of the object; all that could be inferred from this is, that, by the laws of nature, there is a connexion established between that impression, and the remembrance of that object. But how the impression contributes to this remembrance, we should be quite ignorant; it being impossible to discover how thought of any kind should be produced, by an impression on the brain, or upon any part of the body.

To say that this impression is memory, is absurd, if understood literally. If it is only meant that it is the cause of memory, it ought to be shown how it produces this effect, otherwise memory remains as unaccountable as before.

III. If a philosopher should undertake to account for the force of gunpowder, in the discharge of a musket, and then tell us gravely, that the cause of this phenomenon is the drawing of the trigger, we should not be much wiser by this account. As little are we instructed in the cause of memory, by being told that it is caused by a certain impression on the brain. For supposing, that impression on the brain were as necessary to memory as the drawing of the trigger is to the discharge of the musket, we are still as ignorant as we were how memory is produced; so that, if the cause of memory, assigned by this theory, did really exist, it does not in any degree account for memory.

Another defect in this theory is, that there is no evidence, nor probability that the cause assigned does exist; that is, that the impression made upon the brain in perception *remains after the object is removed.*

IV. *Five suppositions necessary to the support of this theory.*— That impression, whatever be its nature, is caused by the impression made by the object upon the organ of sense, and upon the nerve. Philosophers suppose, without any evidence, (1) that when the object is removed, and the impression upon the organ and nerve ceases, the impression upon the *brain* continues, and is permanent; that is, that when the cause is removed the effect continues. The brain surely does not appear more fitted to retain an impression than the organ and nerve.

But granting that the impression upon the brain continues after its cause is removed, its effects ought to continue while it continues; that is, the *sensation and perception* should be as permanent as the impression upon the brain, which is supposed to be their cause. But here again the philosopher makes a second supposition, with as little evidence, but of a contrary nature, to wit, (2) that, *while the cause remains, the effect ceases.*

If this should be granted also, *a third* must be made, (3) That the *same cause,* which at first produced sensation and perception, does afterwards produce *memory;* an operation essentially different, both from sensation and perception.

A *fourth* supposition must be made, (4) That this cause, though it be permanent, *does not produce its effect at all times;* it must be like an inscription which is sometimes covered with rubbish, and on other occasions made legible: for the memory of things is often interrupted for a long time, and circumstances bring to our recollection what had been long forgot. (5) After all, many things are remembered *which were never perceived by the senses,* being no objects of sense, and therefore, which could make no impression upon the brain by means of the senses.

Thus, when philosophers have piled one supposition upon another, as the giants piled the mountains, in order to scale the heavens, all is to no purpose, memory remains unaccountable; and we know as little how we remember things past, as how we are conscious of the present.

But here, it is proper to observe, that although impressions upon the brain give no aid in accounting for memory, yet it is very probable, that, in the human frame, memory is dependent on some proper state or temperament of the brain.

Although the furniture of our memory bears no resemblance to any temperament of brain whatsoever, as indeed it is impossible it should, yet nature may have subjected us to this law, that a certain constitution or state of the brain is necessary to memory. That this is really the case, many well-known facts lead us to conclude.

It is possible, that, by accurate observation, the proper means may be discovered of preserving that temperament of the brain which is favorable to memory, and of remedying the disorders of that temperament. This would be a very noble improvement of the medical art. But if it should ever be attained, it would give no aid to understand how one state of the brain assists memory, and another hurts it.

I know certainly, that the impression made upon my hand by the prick of a pin occasions acute pain. But can any philosopher show how this cause produces the effect? The nature of the impression is here perfectly known; but it gives no help to understand how that impression affects the mind; and if we knew as distinctly that state of the brain which causes memory, we should still be as ignorant as before how that state contributes to memory. We might have been so constituted, for anything that I know, that the prick of a pin in the hand, instead of causing pain, should cause remembrance; nor would that constitution be more unaccountable than the present.

V. *Limit to the investigation of the connexion between mind and body.*—The body and mind operate on each other, according to fixed laws of nature; and it is the business of a philosopher to discover those laws by observation and experiment. But, when he has discovered them, he must rest in them as facts, whose cause is inscrutable to the human understanding.

Mr. Locke, and those who have followed him, speak with more reserve than the ancients, and only incidentally, of impressions on the brain as the cause of memory, and impute it rather to our retaining in our minds the ideas, got either by sensation or reflection.

This, Mr. Locke says, may be done two ways: "*First,* by keeping the idea for some time actually in view, which is called *contemplation. Secondly,* by the power to revive again in our minds those ideas, which, after imprinting, have disappeared, or have been, as it were, laid out of sight; and this is memory, which is, as it were, the storehouse of our ideas."

To explain this more distinctly, he immediately adds the following observation: "But our ideas being nothing but actual perceptions in the mind, which cease to be anything, when there is no perception of them, this laying up of our ideas in the repository of the memory, signifies no more but this, that the mind has a power, in many cases, to revive perceptions which it once had, with this additional perception annexed to them, that it has had them before; and in this sense it is, that our ideas are said to be in our memories, when indeed they are actually nowhere; but only there is an ability in the mind, when it will, to revive them again, and, as it were, paint them anew upon itself, though some with more, some with less, difficulty, some more lively, and others more obscurely." [1]

VI. *Locke's account of memory does not make us understand how we remember and have ideas of the past.*—In this account of memory, the repeated use of the phrase, *as it were,* leads one to judge that it is partly figurative; we must therefore endeavour to distinguish the figurative part from the philosophical. The first being addressed to the imagination, exhibits a picture of memory, which, to have its effect, must be viewed at a proper distance, and from a particular point of view. The second being addressed to the understanding, ought to bear a near inspection, and a critical examination.

The analogy between memory and a repository, and between remembering and retaining, is obvious, and is to be found in all languages, it being very natural to express the operations of the mind by images taken from things material. But in philosophy we ought to draw aside the veil of imagery, and to view them naked.

When therefore memory is said to be a repository or storehouse of ideas, where they are laid up when not perceived, and again brought forth as there is occasion, I take this to be popular and rhetorical. For the author tells us, that when they are not perceived, they are nothing, and nowhere, and therefore can neither be laid up in a repository, nor drawn out of it.

But we are told, "That this laying up of our ideas in the repository of the memory signifies no more than this, that the mind has a power to revive perceptions, which it once had, with this additional perception annexed to them, that it has had them before." This, I think, must be understood literally and philosophically.

But it seems to me as difficult to revive things that have ceased to be anything, as to lay them up in a repository, or to bring them out of it. When a thing is once annihilated, the same thing cannot be again produced, though another thing *similar* to it may. Mr. Locke, in another place,[2] acknowledges, that the same thing cannot have two beginnings of existence; and that things that have different beginnings are not the same, but diverse. (1) From this it follows, that an ability to revive our ideas or perceptions, after they have ceased to be, can

---

[1] *An Essay Concerning Human Understanding,* Book II, Chapter X, 1–2. Ed.
[2] In *Essay,* Book II, Chapter XXVII, 1. Ed.

signify no more but an ability to create new ideas or perceptions *similar* to those we had before.

(2) They are said "to be revived, with this additional perception, that we have had them before." This, surely, would be a fallacious perception, since they could not have two beginnings of existence; nor could we believe them to have two beginnings of existence. We can only believe, that we had formerly ideas or preceptions *very like* to them, though not identically the same. But whether we perceive them to be the same, or only like to those we had before, this perception, one would think, *supposes a remembrance* of those we had before, otherwise the similitude or identity could not be perceived.

(3) Another phrase is used to explain this reviving of our perceptions. "The mind, as it were, paints them anew upon itself." There may be something figurative in this; but making due allowance for that, it must imply, that the mind, which paints the things that have ceased to exist, *must have the memory of what they were,* since every painter must have a copy either before his eye, or in his imagination and memory.

These remarks upon Mr. Locke's account of memory are intended to show, that his system of ideas gives no light to this faculty, but rather tends to darken it; as little does it make us understand *how* we remember, and by that means have the certain knowledge of things past.

Every man knows what memory is, and has a distinct notion of it: but when Mr. Locke speaks of a power to revive in the mind those ideas, which, after imprinting, have disappeared, or have been, as it were, laid out of sight, one would hardly know this to be memory, if he had not told us. There are other things which it seems to resemble at least as much. I see before me the picture of a friend. I shut my eyes, or turn them another way; and the picture disappears, or is, as it were, laid out of sight. I have a power to turn my eyes again towards the picture, and immediately the perception is revived. But is this memory? no surely; yet it answers the definition as well as memory itself can do.

VII. *Incautious use of the term "perception."*—We may observe, that the word perception is used by Mr. Locke in too indefinite a way, as well as the word idea.

Perception, in the chapter upon that subject, is said to be the first faculty of the mind exercised about our ideas. Here we are told, that ideas are nothing but perceptions: yet I apprehend it would sound oddly to say, that perception is the first faculty of the mind exercised about perception; and still more strangely to say, that ideas are the first faculty of the mind exercised about our ideas. But why should not ideas be a faculty as well as perception, if both are the same?

Memory is said to be a power to revive our perceptions. Will it not follow from this, that every thing that can be remembered is a perception? If this be so, it will be difficult to find any thing in nature but perceptions.

Our ideas, we are told, are nothing but actual perceptions; but in many places of the Essay, ideas are said to be the objects of perception, and that the mind, in all its thoughts and reasonings, has no other immediate object which it does or can contemplate but its own ideas. Does it not appear from this, either that Mr. Locke held the operations of the mind to be the same thing with the objects of those operations, or that he used the word idea sometimes in one sense and sometimes in another, without any intimation, and probably without any apprehension of its ambiguity? It is an article of Mr. Hume's philosophy, that there is no distinction between the operations of the mind and their objects. But I see no reason to impute this opinion to Mr. Locke. I rather think, that, notwithstanding his great judgment and candour, his understanding was entangled by the ambiguity of the word idea, and that most of the imperfections of his Essay are owing to that cause.

Mr. Hume saw farther into the consequences of the common system concerning ideas than any author had done before him. He saw the absurdity of making every object of thought double, and splitting it into a remote object, which has a separate and permanent existence, and an immediate object, called an idea or impression, which is an image of the former, and has no existence, but when we are conscious of it. According to this system, we have no intercourse with the external world, but by means of the internal world of ideas, which represents the other to the mind.

He saw it was necessary to reject one of these worlds as a fiction, and the question was, Which should be rejected? Whether all mankind, learned and unlearned, had feigned the existence of the external world without a good reason? or whether philosophers had feigned the internal world of ideas, in order to account for the intercourse of the mind with the external? Mr. Hume adopted the first of these opinions, and employed his reason and eloquence in support of it.

Bishop Berkeley had gone so far in the same track as to reject the material world as fictitious; but it was left to Mr. Hume to complete the system.

.   .   .   .   .

XI. *The theory of ideas leads to scepticism as regards both our memory and our senses.*—The same difficulty with regard to *memory* naturally arises from the system of ideas: and the only reason why it was not observed by philosophers, is, because they give less attention to the memory than to the senses: for since ideas are things *present,* how can we, from our having a certain idea presently in our mind, conclude that an event *really* happened ten or twenty years ago corresponding to it?

There is the same need of arguments to prove, that the ideas of memory are pictures of things that really did happen, as that the ideas of sense are pictures of external objects which now exist. In both cases, it will be impossible to find any argument that has real weight. So that this hypothesis leads us to absolute scepticism, with regard to those things which we most distinctly remember, no less than with regard to the external objects of sense.

XII. *Hume more consistent than Berkeley.*—It does not appear to have occurred either to Locke or to Berkeley, that their system has the same tendency to overturn the testimony of memory as the testimony of the senses.

Mr. Hume saw farther than both, and found this consequence of the system of ideas perfectly corresponding to his aim of establishing universal scepticism. His system is therefore more consistent than theirs, and the conclusions agree better with the premises.

But if we should grant to Mr. Hume, that our ideas of memory afford no just ground to believe the past existence of things which we remember, it may still be asked, how it comes to pass that perception and memory are accomplished with belief, while bare imagination is not? Though this belief cannot be justified upon his system, it ought to be accounted for as a phenomenon of human nature.

This he has done, by giving us a new theory of belief in general; a theory which suits very well with that of ideas, and seems to be a natural consequence of it, and which at the same time reconciles all the belief that we find in human nature to perfect scepticism.

What then is this belief? It must either be an idea, or some modification of an idea; we conceive many things which we do not believe. The idea of an object is the same, whether we believe it to exist, or barely conceive it. The belief adds no new idea to the conception; it is therefore nothing but a modification of the idea of the thing believed, or a different manner of conceiving it. Hear himself:

XIII. *Hume's definition of belief.*—"All the perceptions of the mind are of two kinds, impressions and ideas, which differ from each other only in their different degrees of force and vivacity. Our ideas are copied from our impressions, and represent them in all their parts. When you would vary the idea of a particular object, you can only increase or diminish its force and vivacity: if you make any other change upon it, it represents a different object or impression. The case is the same as in colours. A particular shade of any colour may acquire a new degree of liveliness or brightness, without any other variation: but when you produce any other variation, it is no longer the same shade or colour. So that as belief does nothing but vary the manner in which we conceive any object, it can only bestow on our ideas an additional force and vivacity. An opinion, therefore, or belief, may be most accurately defined *a lively idea, related to or associated with a present impression."* [1]

This theory of belief is very fruitful of consequences, which Mr. Hume traces with his usual acuteness, and brings into the service of his system. A great part of his system indeed is built upon it; and it is of itself sufficient to prove what he calls his hypothesis, "that belief is more properly an act of the sensitive than of the cogitative part of our natures."

It is very difficult to examine this account of belief with the same gravity with which it is proposed. It puts one in mind of the ingenious account given by Martinus Scriblerus of the power of syllogism, by making the *major* the male, and the *minor* the female, which being coupled by the middle *term,* generate the conclusion. There is surely no science in which men of great parts and ingenuity have fallen into such gross absurdities as in treating of the powers of the mind. I cannot help thinking, that never anything more absurd was gravely maintained by any philosopher, than this account of the nature of belief, and of the distinction of perception, memory, and imagination.

The belief of a proposition is an operation of mind of which every man is conscious, and what it is, he understands perfectly, though, on account of its simplicity, he cannot give a logical definition of it. If he compares it with the strength or vivacity of his ideas, or with any modification of ideas, they are so far from appearing to be one and the same, that they have not the least similitude.

That a strong belief and a weak belief differ only in degree, I can easily comprehend; but that belief and no belief should differ only in degree, no man can believe who understands what he speaks: for this is in reality to say that something and nothing differ only in degree, or that nothing is a degree of something.

XIV. *Its absurdity.*—Every proposition that may be the object of belief, has a contrary proposition that may be the object of a contrary belief. The ideas of both, according to Mr. Hume, are the same, and differ only in degrees of vivacity. That is, *contraries differ only in degree;* and so pleasure may be a degree of pain, and hatred a degree of love. But it is to no purpose to trace the absurdities that follow from this doctrine, for none of them can be more absurd than the doctrine itself.

Every man knows perfectly what it is to see an object with his eyes, what it is to remember a past event, and what it is to conceive a thing which has no existence. That these are quite different operations of his mind, he is as certain as that sound differs from colour, and both from taste; and I can as easily believe that sound, and colour, and

[1] In *A Treatise of Human Nature,* Book I, Part III, Section VII. Ed.

taste, differ only in degree, as that seeing, and remembering, and imagining, differ only in degree.

Mr. Hume, in the third volume of his "Treatise of Human Nature," is sensible that his theory of belief is liable to strong objections, and seems, in some measure, to retract it; but in what measure, it is not easy to say. He seems still to think that belief is only a modification of the idea, but that vivacity is not a proper term to express that modification. Instead of it he uses some analogical phrases to explain that modification, such as "apprehending the idea more strongly, or taking faster hold of it."

There is nothing more meritorious in a philosopher than to retract an error upon conviction; but in this instance I humbly apprehend Mr. Hume claims that merit upon too slight a ground: for I cannot perceive that the apprehending an idea more strongly, or taking faster hold of it, expresses any other modification of the idea than what was before expressed by its strength and vivacity, or even that it expresses the same modification more properly. Whatever modification of the idea he makes belief to be, whether its vivacity, or some other without a name, to make perception, memory, and imagination, to be the different degrees of that modification, is chargeable with the absurdities we have mentioned.

Before we leave this subject of memory, it is proper to take notice of a distinction which Aristotle makes between memory and reminiscence, because the distinction has a real foundation in nature, though in our language I think we do not distinguish them by different names.

XV. *Three degrees of memory.*—Memory is a kind of habit which is not always in exercise with regard to things we remember, but is ready to suggest them when there is occasion. The most perfect degree of this habit is, when *the thing presents itself to our remembrance spontaneously,* and without labour, as often as there is occasion. A second degree is, when the thing is forgot for a longer or shorter time, even when there is occasion to remember it, *yet at last some incident brings it to mind without any search. A* third degree is, *when we cast about and search for what we would remember,* and so at last find it out. It is this last, I think, which Aristotle calls reminiscence, as distinguished from memory.*

XVI. *Difficulty as to reminiscence answered.*—*Reminiscence,* therefore, includes a will to recollect something past, and a search for it. But here a difficulty occurs. It may be said, that what we will to remember we must conceive, as there can be no will without a conception of the thing willed. A will to remember a thing, therefore, seems to imply that we remember it already, and have no occasion to search

---

* "If it (the idea) be sought after by the mind, and with pain and endeavour found and brought again in view, 'tis *Recollection.*" Locke, Book II, Chapter XIX, Section I. [See *On Memory and Reminiscence,* Chapter II. Ed.]

for it. But this difficulty is easily removed. When we will to remember a thing, we must remember *something relating to it,* which gives us a relative conception of it; but we may, at the same time, have no conception what the thing is, but only what relation it bears to something else. Thus, I remember that a friend charged me with a commission to be executed at such a place; but I have forgot what the commission was. By applying my thought to what I remember concerning it, that it was given by such a person, upon such an occasion, in consequence of such a conversation, I am led, in a train of thought, to the very thing I had forgot, and recollect distinctly what the commission was.

XVII. *The memory of brutes different from that of men.*—Aristotle says, that brutes have not reminiscence, and this I think is probable; but, says he, they have memory. It cannot, indeed, be doubted but they have something very like to it, and in some instances in a very great degree. A dog knows his master after long absence. A horse will trace back a road he has once gone as accurately as a man; and this is the more strange, that the train of thought which he had in going must be reversed in his return. It is very like to some prodigious memories we read of, where a person, upon hearing a hundred names or unconnected words pronounced, can begin at the last, and go backwards to the first, without losing or misplacing one. Brutes certainly may learn much from experience, which seems to imply memory.

Yet I see no reason to think that brutes measure time as men do, by days, months, or years, or that they have any distinct knowledge of the interval between things which they remember, or of their distance from the present moment. If we could not record transactions according to their dates, human memory would be something very different from what it is, and perhaps resemble more the memory of brutes.

ESSAY IV

CHAPTER I

OF CONCEPTION, OR SIMPLE APPREHENSION IN GENERAL

I. *Logicians give a* quasi *definition of simple apprehension.*—CONCEIVING, imagining, apprehending, understanding, having a notion of a thing, are common words used to express that operation of the understanding, which the logicians call *simple apprehension.* The having an idea of a thing, is in common language used in the same sense, chiefly I think since Mr. Locke's time.

Logicians define simple apprehension to be the bare conception of a thing without any judgment or belief about it. If this were intended for a strictly logical definition, it might be a just objection to it, that conception and apprehension are only synonymous words; and that we may as well define conception by apprehension, as apprehension by conception; but it ought to be remembered, that the most simple operations of the mind cannot be logically defined. To have a distinct notion of them, we must attend to them as we feel them in our own minds. He that would have a distinct notion of a scarlet colour, will never attain it by a definition; he must set it before his eye, attend to it, compare it with the colours that come nearest to it, and observe the specific difference, which he will in vain attempt to define.

Every man is conscious that he can conceive a thousand things, of which he believes nothing at all; as a horse with wings, a mountain of gold; but although conception may be without any degree of belief, even the weakest belief cannot be without conception. He that believes, must have some conception of what he believes.

Without attempting a definition of this operation of the mind, I shall endeavour to explain some of its properties; consider the theories about it; and take notice of some mistakes of philosophers concerning it.

II. *First characteristic property of conception.*—1. It may be observed, that conception enters as an ingredient in every operation of the mind: our senses cannot give us the belief of any object, without giving some conception of it at the same time: no man can either remember or reason about things of which he hath no conception: when we will to exert any of our active powers, there must be some conception of what we will to do: there can be no desire nor aversion, love nor hatred, without some conception of the object: we cannot feel pain without conceiving it, though we can conceive it without feeling it. These things are self-evident.

In every operation of the mind, therefore, in every thing we call thought, there must be conception: when we analyse the various operations either of the understanding or of the will, we shall always find this at the bottom, like the "caput mortuum" of the chemists, or the "materia prima" of the Peripatetics; but though there is no operation of mind without conception, yet it may be found naked, detached from all others, and then it is called simple apprehension, or the bare conception of a thing.

As all the operations of our mind are expressed by language, every one knows that it is one thing to understand what is said, to conceive or apprehend its meaning, whether it be a word, a sentence, or a discourse; it is another thing to judge of it, to assent or dissent, to be persuaded or moved. The first is simple apprehension, and may be without the last, but the last cannot be without the first.

III. *Second characteristic property of conception.*—2. In bare conception there can neither be truth nor falsehood, because it neither affirms nor denies. Every judgment, and every proposition by which judgment is expressed, must be true or false; and the qualities of true and false, in their proper sense, can belong to nothing but to judgments, or to propositions which express judgment. In the bare conception of a thing there is no judgment, opinion, or belief included, and therefore it cannot be either true or false.

IV. *Conceptions may be true or false in one particular sense.*—But it may be said, Is there any thing more certain than that men may have true or false conceptions, true or false apprehensions, of things? I answer, That such ways of speaking are indeed so common, and so well authorised by custom the arbiter of language, that it would be presumption to censure them. It is hardly possible to avoid using them. But we ought to be upon our guard that we be not misled by them, to confound things which, though often expressed by the same words, are really different. We must therefore remember what was before observed, Essay I. chap. i. That all the words, by which we signify the bare conception of a thing, are likewise used to signify our *opinions* when we wish to express them with modesty and diffidence. And we shall always find, that, when we speak of true or false conceptions, we mean true or false opinions. An opinion, though ever so wavering, or ever so modestly expressed, must be either true or false; but a bare conception, which expresses no opinion or judgment, can be neither.

If we analyse those speeches, in which men attribute truth or falsehood to our conceptions of things, we shall find in every case, that there is some opinion or judgment implied in what they call conception. A child conceives the moon to be flat, and a foot or two broad; that is, this is his opinion: and when we say it is a false notion, or a false conception, we mean that it is a false opinion. He conceives the city of London to be like his country village; that is, he believes it to be so, till he is better instructed. He conceives a lion to have horns; that is, he believes that the animal which men call a lion, has horns. Such opinions language authorises us to call conceptions; and they may be true or false. But bare conception, or what the logicians call simple apprehension, implies no opinion, however slight, and therefore can neither be true nor false.

V. *Of true and false ideas.*—What Mr. Locke says of ideas (by which word he very often means nothing but conceptions) is very just, when the word idea is so understood, book ii. chap. xxxii. sect. 1: "Though truth and falsehood belong in propriety of speech only to propositions, yet ideas are often termed true or false, (as what words are there that are not used with great latitude, and with some deviation from their strict and proper signification;) though I think, that when ideas themselves are termed true or false, there is still some secret or tacit proposition, which is the foundation of that denomination; as we shall see, if we examine the particular occasions wherein they come to be called true or false; in all which we shall find some kind of affirmation or negation, which is the reason of that denomination: for our ideas being nothing but bare appearances, or perceptions in our minds, cannot properly and simply in themselves be said to be true or false, no more than a simple name of any thing can be said to be true or false."

It may be here observed by the way, that in this passage, as in many others, Mr. Locke uses the word *perception,* as well as the word *idea,* to signify what I call conception, or simple apprehension. And in his chapter upon perception, book ii. chap. ix. he uses it in the same sense. "Perception," he says, "as it is the first faculty of the mind, exercised about our ideas; so it is the first and simplest idea we have from reflection, and is by some called thinking in general. It seems to be that which puts the distinction betwixt the animal kingdom and the inferior parts of nature. It is the first operation of all our faculties, and the inlet of all knowledge into our minds."

VI. *Locke confounds perception and conception.*—Mr. Locke has followed the example given by Des Cartes, Gassendi, and other Cartesians, in giving the name of *perception* to the bare conception of things: and he has been followed in this by Bishop Berkeley, Mr. Hume, and many late philosophers, when they treat of ideas. They have probably been led into this impropriety, by the common doctrine concerning ideas, which teaches us, that conception, perception by the senses, and memory, are only different ways *of perceiving ideas in our own minds.* If that theory be well founded, it will indeed be very difficult to find any specific distinction between conception and perception. But there is reason to distrust any philosophical theory, when it leads men to corrupt language, and to confound, under one name, operations of the mind, which common sense and common language teach them to distinguish.

I grant that there are some states of the mind, wherein a man may confound his conceptions with what he perceives or remembers, and mistake the one for the other; as, in the delirium of a fever, in some cases of lunacy and of madness, in dreaming, and perhaps in some momentary transports of devotion, or of other strong emotions, which cloud his intellectual faculties, and for a time carry a man out of himself, as we usually express it.

Even in a sober and sound state of mind, the memory of a thing may be so very weak, that we may be in doubt whether we only dreamed or imagined it.

It may be doubted, whether children, when their imagination first begins to work, can distinguish what they barely conceive from what they remember. I have been told by a man of knowledge and observation, that one of his sons, when he began to speak, very often told lies with great assurance, without any intention, as far as appeared, or any consciousness of guilt. From which the father concluded, that it is natural to some children to lie. I am rather inclined to think, that the child had no intention to deceive, but mistook the rovings of his own fancy, for things which he remembered. This, however, I take to be very uncommon, after children can communicate their sentiments by language, though perhaps not so in a more early period.

Granting all this, if any man will affirm, that they whose intellectual faculties are sound, and sober, and ripe, cannot with certainty distinguish what they perceive or remember, from what they barely conceive, when those operations have any degree of strength and distinctness, he may enjoy his opinion; I know not how to reason with him. Why should philosophers confound those operations in treating of ideas, when they would be ashamed to do it on other occasions? To distinguish the various powers of our minds, a certain degree of understanding is necessary: and if some, through a defect of understanding, natural or accidental, or from unripeness of understanding, may be apt to confound different powers, will it follow that others cannot clearly distinguish them?

To return from this digression, into which the abuse of the word perception by philosophers has led me, it appears evident that the bare conception of an object, which includes no opinion or judgment, can neither be true nor false. Those qualities, in their proper sense, are altogether inapplicable to this operation of the mind.

VII.—*Illustration of conception.*—3. Of all the analogies between the operations of body and those of the mind, there is none so strong and so obvious to all mankind as that which there is between *painting,* or other plastic arts, and the power of conceiving objects in the mind. Hence in all languages, the words by which this power of the mind and its various modifications are expressed are analogical, and borrowed from those arts. We consider this power of the mind as a plastic power, by which we form to ourselves images of the objects of thought.

In vain should we attempt to avoid this analogical language, for we have no other language upon the subject; yet it is dangerous, and apt to mislead. All analogical and figurative words have a double meaning; and, if we are not very much upon our guard, we slide insensibly from the borrowed and figurative meaning into the primitive. We are prone to carry the parallel between the things compared farther than it will hold, and thus very naturally to fall into error.

To avoid this as far as possible in the present subject, it is proper to attend to the dissimilitude between conceiving a thing in the mind, and painting it to the eye, as well as to their similitude. The similitude strikes and gives pleasure. The dissimilitude we are less disposed to observe. But the philosopher ought to attend to it, and to carry it always in mind, in his reasonings on this subject, as a monitor, to warn him against the errors into which the analogical language is apt to draw him.

When a man paints, there is some work done, *which remains when his hand is taken off, and continues to exist, though he should think no more of it.* Every stroke of his pencil produces an effect, and this effect is different from his action in making it; for it remains and continues to exist when the action ceases. The action of painting is one thing, the picture produced is another thing. The first is the cause, the second is the effect.

VIII. *This analogy defective.*—Let us next consider what is done when he only conceives this picture. He must have conceived it before he painted it: for this is a maxim universally admitted, that every work of art must first be conceived in the mind of the operator. What is this conception? It is an act of the mind, a kind of thought. This cannot be denied. But does it produce any effect besides the act itself? Surely common sense answers this question in the negative: for every one knows, that it is one thing to conceive, another thing to bring forth into effect. It is one thing to project, another to execute. A man may think for a long time what he is to do, and after all do nothing. Conceiving as well as projecting or resolving, are what the schoolmen called *immanent* acts of the mind, which produce nothing beyond themselves. But painting is a *transitive* act, which produces an effect distinct from the operation, and this effect is the picture. Let this therefore be always remembered, that what is commonly called the image of a thing in the mind is no more than the act or operation of the mind in conceiving it.

That this is the common sense of men who are untutored by philosophy, appears from their language. If one ignorant of the language should ask, What is meant by conceiving a thing? we should very naturally answer, That it is having an image of it in the mind; and perhaps we could not explain the word better. This shows, that conception, and the image of a thing in the mind, are synonymous expressions. The image in the mind, therefore, is not the object of conception, nor is it any effect produced by conception as a cause. It is conception itself. That very mode of thinking, which we call conception, is by another name called an image in the mind.

Nothing more readily gives the conception of a thing than the seeing an image of it. Hence, by a figure common in language, conception is called an image of the thing conceived. But to show that it is not a real but a metaphorical image, it is called an image in the mind. We know nothing that is properly in the mind but thought; and when any thing else is said to be in the mind, the expression must be figurative, and signify some kind of thought.

I know that philosophers very unanimously maintain, that in conception there is a real image in the mind, which is the immediate object of conception, and distinct from the act of conceiving it. I beg the reader's indulgence to defer what may be said for or against this philosophical opinion to the next chapter; intending in this only to explain what appears to me to belong to this operation of mind, without considering the theories about it. I think it appears from what has been said, that the common language of those who have not imbibed any philosophical opinion upon this subject, authorizes us to understand *the conception of a thing, and an image of it in the mind,* not as two different things, but as two different expressions, to signify one and the same thing; and I wish to use common words in their common acceptation.

IX. *Its true extent.*—4. Taking along with us what is said in the last article, to guard us against the seduction of the analogical language used on this subject, we may observe a very strong analogy, not only between conceiving and painting in general, but between the different kinds of our conceptions, and the different works of the painter. (1) He either makes fancy pictures, or (2) he copies from the painting of others, or (3) he paints from the life; that is, from real objects of art or nature which he has seen. I think our conceptions admit of a division very similar.

X. *Peculiarity of the first kind of conceptions.*—*First,* there are conceptions which may be called fancy pictures. They are commonly called creatures of fancy, or of imagination. They are not the copies of any original that exists, but are originals themselves. Such was the conception which Swift formed of the island of Laputa and of the country of the Lilliputians; Cervantes of Don Quixote and his squire; Harrington of the government of Oceana; and Sir Thomas More of that of Utopia. We can give names to such creatures of imagination, conceive them distinctly, and reason consequentially concerning them, though they never had an existence. They were conceived by their creators, and may be conceived by others, but they never existed. *We do not ascribe the qualities of true or false to them,* because they are not accompanied with any belief, nor do they imply any affirmation or negation.

Setting aside those creatures of imagination, there are other conceptions, which may be called copies, because they have an original or archetype to which they refer, and with which they are believed to agree; *and we call them true or false conceptions,* according as they agree or disagree with the standard to which they are referred. These are of two kinds, which have different standards or originals.

The *first* kind is analogous to pictures taken from the life. We have conceptions of *individual things* that really exist, such as the city of London, or the government of Venice. Here the things conceived are the originals; and our conceptions are called true when they agree with the thing conceived. Thus, my conception of the city of London is true when I conceive it to be what it really is.

XI. *Peculiarity of the second kind.*—*Individual things which really exist,* being the creatures of God, (though some of them may receive their outward form from man,) he only who made them knows their whole nature; we know them but in part, and therefore *our conceptions of them must in all cases be imperfect and inadequate;* yet they may be true and just, as far as they reach.

XII. *Of the third kind.*—The *second* kind is analogous to the copies which the painter makes from pictures done before. Such I think are the conceptions we have of what the ancients called *universals;* that is, of things which belong or may belong to many individuals. These are kinds and species of things; such as, man, or elephant, which are species of substances; wisdom, or courage, which are species of qualities; equality, or similitude, which are species of relations. It may be asked, from what original are these conceptions formed? and when are they said to be true or false?

It appears to me, that the original from which they are copied, that is, the thing conceived, is the conception or meaning which other men who understand the language affix to the same words.

Things are parcelled into kinds and sorts, not by nature, but by men. The individual things we are connected with, are so many, that to give a proper name to every individual would be impossible. We could never attain the knowledge of them that is necessary, nor converse and reason about them, without sorting them according to their different attributes. Those that agree in certain attributes are thrown into one parcel, and have a general name given them, which belongs equally to every individual in that parcel. This common name must therefore signify those attributes which have been observed to be common to every individual in that parcel, and nothing else.

That such general words may answer their intention, all that is necessary is, that those who use them should affix the same meaning or notion, that is, the same conception to them. The common meaning is the standard by which such conceptions are formed, and they are said to be true or false, according as they agree or disagree with it. Thus, my conception of felony is true and just, when it agrees with the meaning of that word in the laws relating to it, and in authors who understand the law. The meaning of the word is the thing conceived; and that meaning is the conception affixed to it by those who best understand the language.

XIII. *Two modes of expressing an individual.*—An individual is expressed in language (1) either by a proper name, or (2) by a general word joined to such circumstances as distinguish that individual from all others; if it is unknown, it may, when an object of sense and within reach, be pointed out to the senses; when beyond the reach of the senses, it may be ascertained by a description, which, though very imperfect, may be true and sufficient to distinguish it from every other individual. Hence it is, that, in speaking of individuals, we are very little in danger of mistaking the object, or taking one individual for another.

Yet, as was before observed, our conception of them is always inadequate and lame. They are the creatures of God, and there are many things belonging to them which we know not, and which cannot be deduced by reasoning from what we know: they have a real essence, or constitution of nature, from which all their qualities flow; but this essence our faculties do not comprehend: they are therefore incapable of definition; for a definition ought to comprehend the whole nature or essence of the thing defined.

Thus, Westminster bridge is an individual object; though I had never seen or heard of it before, if I am only made to conceive that it is a bridge from Westminster over the Thames, this conception, however imperfect, is true, and is sufficient to make me distinguish it, when it is mentioned, from every other object that exists. The architect may have an adequate conception of its structure, which is the work of man; but of the materials, which are the work of God, no man has an adequate conception; and therefore, though the object may be described, it cannot be defined.

XIV. *General conceptions adequate, and agree with the thing conceived.*—Universals are always expressed by general words: and all the words of language, excepting proper names, are general words; they are the signs of general conceptions, or of some circumstance relating to them. These general conceptions are formed for the purpose of language and reasoning; and the object from which they are taken, and to which they are intended to agree, is the conception which other men join to the same words; *they may therefore be adequate, and perfectly agree with the thing conceived.* This implies no more than that men who speak the same language may perfectly agree in the meaning of many general words.

Thus mathematicians have conceived what they call a plane triangle. They have defined it accurately; and when I conceive it to be a plane surface, bounded by three right lines, I have both a true and an adequate conception of it. There is nothing belonging to a plane triangle which is not comprehended in this conception of it, or deducible from it by just reasoning. This definition expresses the whole essence of the thing defined, as every just definition ought to do; but this essence is only what Mr. Locke very properly calls a nominal essence; it is a general conception formed by the mind, and joined to a general word as its sign.

If all the general words of a language had a precise meaning, and were perfectly understood, as mathematical terms are, all verbal disputes would be at an end, and men would never seem to differ in opinion, but when they differ in reality; but this is far from being the case. The meaning of most general words is not learned like that of mathematical terms, by an accurate definition, but by the experience we happen to have, by hearing them used in conversation. From such experience we collect their meaning by a kind of induction; and as this induction is for the most part lame and imperfect, it happens that different persons join different conceptions to the same general word; and though we intend to give them the meaning which use, the arbiter of language, has put upon them, this is difficult to find, and apt to be mistaken, even by the candid and attentive. Hence, in innumerable disputes, men do not really differ in their judgments, but in the way of expressing them.

XV. *Three kinds of conceptions.*—Our conceptions, therefore, appear to be of three kinds: they are either the conceptions of individual things, the creatures of God; or they are conceptions of the meaning of general words; or they are the creatures of our own imagination; and these different kinds have different *properties* which we have endeavoured to describe.

.   .   .   .   .

ESSAY VI

CHAPTER V

THE FIRST PRINCIPLES OF CONTINGENT TRUTHS

I. "Surely," says Bishop Berkeley, "it is a work well deserving our pains, to make a strict inquiry concerning the first principles of knowledge; to sift and examine them on all sides." What was said in the last chapter, is intended both to show the importance of this inquiry, and to make it more easy.

But, in order that such an inquiry may be actually made, it is necessary that the first principles of knowledge be distinguished from other truths, and presented to view, that they may be sifted and examined on all sides. In order to this end, I shall attempt a detail of those I take to be such, and of the reasons why I think them entitled to that character.

If the enumeration should appear to some redundant, to others deficient, and to others both; if things, which I conceive to be first principles, should to others appear to be vulgar errors, or to be truths which derive their evidence from other truths, and therefore not first principles; in these things every man must judge for himself. I shall rejoice to see an enumeration more perfect in any or in all of those respects; being persuaded, that the agreement of men of judgment and candour in first principles, would be of no less consequence to the advancement of knowledge in general, than the agreement of mathematicians in the axioms of geometry has been to the advancement of that science.

II. *All truths reducible to two classes.*—The truths that fall within the compass of human knowledge, whether they be self-evident, or deduced from those that are self-evident, may be reduced to two classes. They are either necessary and immutable truths, whose contrary is impossible; or they are contingent and mutable, depending upon some effect of will and power, which had a beginning, and may have an end.

That a cone is the third part of a cylinder of the same base and the same altitude, is a necessary truth. It depends not upon the will and power of any being. It is immutably true, and the contrary impossible. That the sun is the centre, about which the earth, and the other planets of our system, perform their revolutions, is a truth; but it is not a necessary truth. It depends upon the power and will of that Being who made the sun and all the planets, and who gave them those motions that seemed best to him.

III. *Of the mode of expressing necessary truths.*—If all truths were necessary truths, there would be no occasion for different tenses in the verbs by which they are expressed. What is true in the present time, would be true in the past and future; and there would be no change or variation of any thing in nature.

We use the present tense in expressing necessary truths; *but it is only because there is no flexion of the verb which includes all times.* When I say that three is the half of six, I use the present tense only; but I mean to express not only what now is, but what always was, and always will be; and so every proposition is to be understood by which we mean to express a necessary truth. Contingent truths are of another nature. As they are mutable, they may be true at one time, and not at another; and therefore the expression of them must include some point or period of time.

If language had been a contrivance of philosophers, they would probably have given some flexion to the indicative mood of verbs, which extended to all times past, present, and future; for such a flexion only would be fit to express necessary propositions, which have no relation to time. But there is no language, as far as I know, in which such a flexion of verbs is to be found. Because the thoughts and discourse of men are seldom employed about *necessary truths,* but commonly about such as are *contingent;* languages are fitted to express the last rather than the first.

IV. *The distinction of truths into abstract and concerning real existences, not coincident with that of necessary and contingent.*—The distinction commonly made between abstract truths, and those that express matters of fact, or real existences, coincides in a great measure, but not altogether, with that between necessary and contingent truths. The necessary truths that fall within our knowledge are for the most part abstract truths. We must except the existence and nature of the Supreme Being, which is necessary. Other existences are the effects of will and power. They had a beginning, and are mutable. Their nature is such as the Supreme Being was pleased to give them. Their attributes and relations must depend upon the nature God has given them; the powers with which he has endowed them; and the situation in which he hath placed them.

V. *No contingent truth inferred from necessary principles.*—The conclusions deduced by reasoning from first principles, will commonly be necessary or contingent, according as the principles are from which they are drawn. On the one hand, I take it to be certain, that whatever can, by just reasoning, be inferred from a principle that is necessary, must be a necessary truth, and that no contingent truth can be inferred from principles that are necessary.

Thus, as the axioms in mathematics are all necessary truths; so are all the conclusions drawn from them; that is, the whole body of that science. But from no mathematical truth can we deduce the existence of anything; not even of the objects of the science.

VI. *But* one *necessary truth from contingent principles.*—On the other hand, I apprehend there are very few cases in which we can, from principles that are contingent, deduce truths that are necessary. I can only recollect one instance of this kind, namely, that, from the existence of things contingent and mutable, we can infer the existence of an immutable and eternal cause of them.

As the minds of men are occupied much more about truths that are contingent than about those that are necessary, I shall first endeavour to point out the principles of the former kind.

1. *First,* then, I hold, as a first principle, the existence of everything of which I am *conscious.*

Consciousness is an operation of the understanding of its own kind, and cannot be logically defined. The objects of it are our present pains, our pleasures, our hopes, our fears, our desires, our doubts, our thoughts of every kind; in a word, all the passions, and all the actions and operations of our own minds, while they are present. We may remember them when they are past; but we are conscious of them only while they are present.

When a man is conscious of pain, he is certain of its existence; when he is conscious that he doubts, or believes, he is certain of the existence of those operations.

But the irresistible conviction he has of the reality of those operations is not the effect of reasoning; it is immediate and intuitive. The existence therefore of those passions and operations of our minds, of which we are conscious, is a first principle, which nature requires us to believe upon her authority.

If I am asked to prove that I cannot be deceived by consciousness; to prove that it is not a fallacious sense; I can find no proof. I cannot find any antecedent truth from which it is deduced, or upon which its evidence depends. It seems to disdain any such derived authority, and to claim my assent in its own right.

If any man could be found so frantic as to deny that he thinks, while he is conscious of it; I may wonder, I may laugh, or I may pity him, but I cannot reason the matter with him. We have no common principles from which we may reason, and therefore can never join issue in an argument.

VII. *The existence of any thing of which we are conscious, a principle universally admitted.*—This, I think, is the only principle of common sense that has never directly been called in question. It seems to be so firmly rooted in the minds of men, as to retain its authority with the greatest sceptics. Mr. Hume, after annihilating body and mind, time and space, action and causation, and even his own mind, acknowledges the reality of the thoughts, sensations and passions of which he is conscious.

No philosopher has attempted by any hypothesis to account for this consciousness of our own thoughts, and the certain knowledge of their real existence which accompanies it. By this they seem to acknowledge, that this at least is an original power of the mind; a power by which we not only have ideas, but original judgments, and the knowledge of real existence.

I cannot reconcile this immediate knowledge of the operations of our own minds with Mr. Locke's theory, that all knowledge consists in perceiving the agreement and disagreement of ideas. What are the ideas, from whose comparison the knowledge of our own thoughts results? Or what are the agreements or disagreements which convince a man that he is in pain when he feels it?

Neither can I reconcile it with Mr. Hume's theory, that to believe the existence of anything, is nothing else than to have a strong and lively conception of it; or, at most, that belief is only some modification of the idea which is the object of belief. For not to mention, that propositions, not ideas, are the object of belief; in all that variety of thoughts and passions, of which we are conscious, we believe the existence of the weak as well as of the strong, the faint as well as the lively. No modification of the operations of our minds disposes us to the least doubt of their real existence.

* VIII. *Criterions.*—As therefore the *real existence of our thoughts,* and of all the *operations* and feelings of our own minds, (1) is believed by all men: (2) as we find ourselves incapable of doubting it, and (3) as incapable of offering any proof of it, it may justly be considered as a first principle, or dictate of common sense.

But although this principle rests upon no other, a very considerable and important branch of human knowledge rests upon it.

IX. *A knowledge of the operations of our minds rests on a firm basis.*—For from this source of consciousness is derived all that we know, and indeed all that we can know, of the structure, and of the powers of our own minds; from which we may conclude, that *there is no branch of knowledge that stands upon a firmer foundation;* for surely no kind of evidence can go beyond that of consciousness.

How does it come to pass then, that in this branch of knowledge there are so many and so contrary systems? so many subtile controversies that are never brought to an issue, and so little fixed and determined? Is it possible that philosophers should differ most where they have the surest means of agreement? where every thing is built upon a species of evidence which all men acquiesce in, and hold to be the most certain?

This strange phenomenon may, I think, be accounted for, if we distinguish between *consciousness and reflection,* which are often improperly confounded.

The first is common to all men at all times, but is insufficient of itself to give us clear and distinct notions of the operations of which we are conscious, and of their mutual relations, and minute distinctions. The second, to wit, attentive reflection upon those operations, making them objects of thought, surveying them attentively, and examining them on all sides, is so far from being common to all men, that it is the lot of very few. The greatest part of men, either through want of capacity, or from other causes, never reflect attentively upon the operations of their own minds. The habit of this reflection, even in those whom nature has fitted for it, is not to be attained without much pains and practice. We can know nothing of the immediate objects of sight, but by the testimony of our eyes; and I apprehend, that if mankind had found as great difficulty in giving attention to the objects of sight, as they find in attentive reflection upon the operations of their own minds, our knowledge of the first might have been in as backward a state as our knowledge of the last.

But this darkness will not last for ever. Light will arise upon this benighted part of the intellectual globe. When any man is so happy as to delineate the powers of the human mind as they really are in nature, men that are free from prejudice, and capable of reflection, will

* Vide Section XXXII, of this chapter.

recognise their own features in the picture; and then the wonder will be, how things so obvious could be so long wrapped up in mystery and darkness; how men could be carried away by false theories and conjectures, when the truth was to be found in their own breasts if they had but attended to it.

2. Another first principle, I think, is, That the thoughts of which I am conscious, are the thoughts of a being which I call *myself,* my *mind,* my *person.*

The thoughts and feelings of which we are conscious are continually changing, and the thought of this moment is not the thought of the last; but something which I call myself, remains under this change of thought. This self has the same relation to all the successive thoughts I am conscious of, they are all my thoughts; and every thought which is not my thought, must be the thought of some other person.

If any man asks a proof of this, I confess I can give none; there is an evidence in the proposition itself which I am unable to resist. Shall I think, that thought can stand by itself without a thinking being? or that ideas can feel pleasure or pain? My nature dictates to me that it is impossible.

And that nature has dictated the same to all men, appears from the structure of all languages: for in all languages men have expressed thinking, reasoning, willing, loving, hating, by personal verbs, which from their nature require a person who thinks, reasons, wills, loves, or hates. From which it appears, that men have been taught by nature, to believe that thought requires a thinker, reason a reasoner, and love a lover.

.   .   .   .   .

XIV. 4. Another first principle is our own *personal identity* and continued existence, as far back as we remember any thing distinctly.

This we know immediately, and not by reasoning. It seems, indeed, to be a part of the testimony of memory. Every thing we remember has such a relation to ourselves, as to imply necessarily our existence at the time remembered. And there cannot be a more palpable absurdity than that a man should remember what happened before he existed. He must therefore have existed as far back as he remembers any thing distinctly, if his memory be not fallacious. This principle, therefore, is so connected with the last mentioned, that it may be doubtful whether both ought not to be included in one. Let every one judge of this as he sees reason. The proper notion of identity, and the sentiments of Mr. Locke on this subject, have been considered before under the head of memory.

XV. 5. Another first principle is, That those things do really exist which we distinctly perceive by our *senses,* and are what we perceive them to be.

It is too evident to need proof, that all men are by nature led to give implicit faith to the distinct testimony of their senses, *long before they are capable of any bias from prejudices of education or of philosophy.*

How came we at first to know that there are certain beings about us whom we call father, and mother, and sisters, and brothers, and nurse? Was it not by the testimony of our senses? How did these persons convey to us any information or instruction? Was it not by means of our senses?

It is evident we can have no communication, no correspondence or society with any created being, but by means of our senses. And until we rely upon their testimony, we must consider ourselves as being alone in the universe, without any fellow-creature, living or inanimate, and be left to converse with our own thoughts.

XVI. *The knowledge of other spirits rejected, unintentionally, by the Berkleians.*—Bishop Berkeley surely did not duly consider, that it is by means of the material world that we have any correspondence with *thinking beings,* or any knowledge of their existence, and that by depriving us of the material world, he deprived us at the same time of family, friends, country, and every human creature; of every object of affection, esteem or concern, except ourselves.

The good Bishop surely never intended this. He was too warm a friend, too zealous a patriot, and too good a Christian, to be capable of such a thought. He was not aware of the consequences of his system, and therefore they ought not to be imputed to him; but we must impute them to the system itself. It stifles every generous and social principle.

When I consider myself as speaking to men who hear me, and can judge of what I say, I feel that respect which is due to such an audience. I feel an enjoyment in a reciprocal communication of sentiments with candid and ingenious friends, and my soul blesses the Author of my being, who has made me capable of this manly and rational entertainment.

But the Bishop shows me, that this is all a dream; that I see not a human face; that all the objects I see, and hear, and handle, are only the ideas of my own mind; ideas are my only companions. Cold company, indeed! Every social affection freezes at the thought!

But, my Lord Bishop, are there no minds left in the universe but my own?

Yes, indeed: it is only the material world that is annihilated; every thing else remains as it was.

This seems to promise some comfort in my forlorn solitude. But do I see those minds? No. Do I see their ideas? No. Nor do they see me or my ideas. They are then no more to me than the inhabitants of

Solomon's isles, or of the moon; and my melancholy solitude returns. Every social tie is broken, and every social affection is stifled.

This dismal system, which, if it could be believed, would deprive men of every social comfort, a very good Bishop, by strict and accurate reasoning, deduced from the principles commonly received by philosophers concerning ideas. The fault is not in the reasoning, but in the principles from which it is drawn.

All the arguments urged by Berkeley and Hume against the existence of a material world are grounded upon this principle, That we do not perceive external objects themselves, but certain images or ideas in our own minds. But this is no dictate of common sense, but directly contrary to the sense of all who have not been taught it by philosophy.

.   .   .   .   .

XXV. 8. Another first principle relating to existence is, that there is life and intelligence in our fellow-men with whom we converse.

As soon as children are capable of asking a question, or of answering a question, as soon as they show the signs of love, of resentment, or of any other affection, they must be convinced that those with whom they have this intercourse are intelligent beings.

It is evident they are capable of such intercourse long before they can reason. Every one knows, that there is a social intercourse between the nurse and the child before it is a year old. It can, at that age, understand many things that are said to it.

It can, by signs, ask and refuse, threaten and supplicate. It clings to its nurse in danger, enters into her grief and joy, is happy in her soothing and caresses, and unhappy in her displeasure. That these things cannot be without a conviction in the child that the nurse is an intelligent being, I think must be granted.

Now I would ask how a child of a year old comes by this conviction? Not by reasoning surely, for children do not reason at that age. Nor is it by external senses, for life and intelligence are not objects of the external senses.

By what means, or upon what occasions nature first gives this information to the infant mind, is not easy to determine. We are not capable of reflecting upon our own thoughts at that period of life, and before we attain this capacity, we have quite forgot how or on what occasion we first had this belief; we perceive it in those who are born blind, and in others who are born deaf; and therefore nature has not connected it solely either with any object of sight, or with any object of hearing. When we grow up to the years of reason and reflection, this belief remains. No man thinks of asking himself what reason he has to believe that his neighbour is a living creature. He would be not a little surprised if another person should ask him so absurd a question; and perhaps could not give any reason which would not equally prove a watch or a puppet to be a living creature.

But, though you should satisfy him of the weakness of the reasons he gives for his belief, you cannot make him in the least doubtful. This belief stands upon another foundation than that of reasoning; and therefore, whether a man can give good reasons for it or not, it is not in his power to shake it off.

XXVI. *We are convinced of the existence of intelligence in others.* —Setting aside this natural conviction, I believe the best reason we can give, to prove that other men are living and intelligent, is, that *their words and actions indicate like powers of understanding as we are conscious of in ourselves.* The very same argument applied to the works of nature, leads us to conclude, that there is an intelligent Author of nature, and appears equally strong and obvious in the last case as in the first; so that it may be doubted whether men, by the mere exercise of reasoning, might not as soon discover the existence of a Deity, as that other men have life and intelligence.

The knowledge of the last is absolutely necessary to our receiving any improvement by means of instruction and example; and, without these means of improvement, there is no ground to think that we should ever be able to acquire the use of our reasoning powers. This knowledge, therefore, must be antecedent to reasoning, and therefore must be a first principle.

It cannot be said, that the judgments we form concerning life and intelligence in other beings are *at first* free from error. But the errors of children in this matter lie on the safe side; they are prone to attribute intelligence to things inanimate. These errors are of small consequence, and are gradually corrected by *experience* and ripe *judgment*. But the belief of life and intelligence in other men, is absolutely necessary for us before we are capable of reasoning; and therefore the Author of our being hath given us this belief antecedently to all reasoning.

XXVII. 9. Another first principle I take to be, that certain features of the countenance, sounds of the voice, and gestures of the body, indicate certain thoughts and dispositions of mind.

That many operations of the mind have their natural signs in the countenance, voice, and gesture, I suppose every man will admit. "Omnis enim motus animi," says Cicero, "suum quemdam habet a naturâ vultum, et vocem, et gestum." [1] The only question is, whether we understand the signification of those signs, by the constitution of our nature, by a kind of natural perception similar to the perceptions of sense; or whether we gradually learn the signification of such signs from experience, as we learn that smoke is a sign of fire, or that the

[1] "To every passion of the mind Nature has given its own particular look, tone of voice, and bearing." *De Oratore,* III, 57.216. Ed.

freezing of water is a sign of cold? I take the first to be the truth.

It seems to me incredible, that the notions men have of the expression of features, voice, and gesture, are entirely the fruit of experience. Children, almost as soon as born, may be frighted and thrown into fits by a threatening or angry tone of voice. I knew a man who could make an infant cry, by whistling a melancholy tune in the same or in the next room; and again, by altering his key, and the strain of his music, could make the child leap and dance for joy.

It is not by experience surely that we learn the expression of music; for its operation is commonly strongest the first time we hear it. One air expresses mirth and festivity; so that, when we hear it, it is with difficulty we can forbear to dance. Another is sorrowful and solemn. One inspires with tenderness and love; another with rage and fury.

> Hear how Timotheus' varied lays surprise,
> And bid alternate passions fall and rise;
> While at each change, the son of Lybian Jove
> Now burns with glory, and then melts with love.
> Now his fierce eyes with sparkling fury glow,
> Now sighs steal out, and tears begin to flow.
> Persians and Greeks, like turns of nature found,
> And the world's victor stood subdued by sound.[1]

It is not necessary that a man have studied either music or the passions, in order to his feeling these effects. The most ignorant and unimproved, to whom Nature has given a good ear, feel them as strongly as the most knowing.

The countenance and gesture have an expression no less strong and natural than the voice. The first time one sees a stern and fierce look, a contracted brow, and a menacing posture, he concludes that the person is inflamed with anger. Shall we say, that, previous to experience, the most hostile countenance has as agreeable an appearance as the most gentle and benign? This surely would contradict all experience; for we know that an angry countenance will fright a child in the cradle. Who has not observed, that children, very early, are able to distinguish what is said to them in jest from what is said in earnest, by the tone of the voice, and the features of the face? They judge by these natural signs, even when they seem to contradict the artificial.

If it were by experience that we learn the meaning of features, and sound, and gesture, it might be expected that we should recollect the time when we first learnt those lessons, or, at least, some of such a multitude.

Those who give attention to the operations of children, can easily discover the time when they have their earliest notices from experience, such as that flame will burn, or that knives will cut. But no man

---

[1] Pope, *Essay on Criticism*, lines 374–81. Ed.

is able to recollect in himself, or to observe in others, the time when the expression of the face, voice, and gesture, were learned.

Nay, I apprehend that it is impossible that this should be learned from experience.

XXVIII. *The connexion between the expression of the countenance, &c., and the thoughts of the mind, not first derived from experience.*—When we see the sign, and see the thing signified always conjoined with it, experience may be the instructor, and teach us how that sign is to be interpreted. But how shall experience instruct us when we see the sign only, when the thing signified is invisible? Now this is the case here; the thoughts and passions of the mind, as well as the mind itself, are invisible, and therefore their connexion with any sensible sign *cannot be first discovered by experience;* there must be some earlier source of this knowledge.

Nature seems to have given to men a faculty or sense, by which this connexion is perceived. And the operation of this sense is very analogous to that of the external senses.

When I grasp an ivory ball in my hand, I feel a certain sensation of touch. In the sensation there is nothing external, nothing corporeal. The sensation is neither round nor hard; it is an act or feeling of the mind, from which I cannot, by reasoning, infer the existence of any body. But, by the constitution of my nature, the sensation carries along with it the conception and belief of a round hard body really existing in my hand.

In like manner, when I see the features of an expressive face, I see only figure and colour variously modified. But, by the constitution of my nature, the visible object brings along with it the conception and belief of a certain passion or sentiment in the mind of the person.

In the former case, a sensation of touch is the sign, and the hardness and roundness of the body I grasp is signified by that sensation. In the latter case, the features of the person is the sign, and the passion or sentiment is signified by it.

The power of natural signs, to signify the sentiments and passions of the mind, is seen (1) in the signs of *dumb persons,* who can make themselves to be understood in a considerable degree, even by those who are wholly inexperienced in that language.

It is seen in the traffic which has been frequently carried on between (2) *people that have no common acquired language.* They can buy and sell, and ask and refuse, and show a friendly or hostile disposition by natural signs.

It was seen still more in the (3) *actors among the ancients* who performed the *gesticulation* upon the stage, while others recited the words. To such a pitch was this art carried, that we are told Cicero and Roscius used to contend whether the orator could express any thing by words which the actor could not express in dumb show by gesticulation; and whether the same sentence or thought could not be acted in all the variety of ways in which the orator could express it in words.

But the most surprising exhibition of this kind, was that of the pantomimes among the Romans, who acted plays, or scenes of plays, without any recitation, and yet could be perfectly understood.

And here it deserves our notice, that although it required much study and practice in the pantomimes to excel in their art; yet it required neither study nor practice in the spectators to understand them. It was a natural language, and therefore understood by all men, whether Romans, Greeks, or barbarians, by the learned and the unlearned.

Lucian relates,[1] that a king, whose dominions bordered upon the Euxine sea, happening to be at Rome in the reign of Nero, and having seen a pantomime act, begged him of Nero, that he might use him in his intercourse with all the nations in his neighbourhood: "For," said he, "I am obliged to employ I don't know how many interpreters, in order to keep a correspondence with neighbours who speak many languages, and do not understand mine; but this fellow will make them all understand him."

For these reasons, I conceive, it must be granted, not only that there is a connexion established by Nature between certain signs in the countenance, voice, and gesture, and the thoughts and passions of the mind; but also, that, *by our constitution,* we *understand* the meaning of those signs, and from the sign conclude the existence of the thing signified.

XXIX. 10. Another first principle appears to me to be, That there is a certain *regard due to human testimony* in matters of fact, and even to human authority in matters of opinion.

Before we are capable of reasoning about testimony or authority, there are many things which it concerns us to know, for which we can have no other evidence. The wise Author of nature hath planted in the human mind a propensity to rely upon this evidence before we can give a reason for doing so. This, indeed, puts our judgment almost entirely in the power of those who are about us, in the first period of life; but this is necessary both to our preservation and to our improvement. If children were so framed, as to pay no regard to testimony or to authority, they must, in the literal sense, perish for lack of knowledge. It is not more necessary that they should be fed before they can feed themselves, than that they should be instructed in many things before they can discover them by their own judgment.

But when our faculties ripen, we find reason to check that propensity to yield to testimony and to authority, which was so necessary and so natural in the first period of life. We learn to reason about the

[1] In "Of Pantomime," 64. Ed.

regard due to them, and see it to be a childish weakness to lay more stress upon them than reason justifies. Yet, I believe, to the end of life, most men are more apt to go into this extreme than into the contrary; and the natural propensity still retains some force.

The natural principles, by which our judgments and opinions are regulated before we come to the use of reason, seem to be no less necessary to such a being as man, than those natural instincts which the Author of nature hath given us to regulate our actions during that period.

XXX. 11. There are many events depending upon *the will of man,* in which there is a self-evident probability, greater or less, according to circumstances.

There may be in some individuals such a degree of phrenzy and madness, that no man can say what they may or may not do. Such persons we find it necessary to put under restraint, that, as far as possible, they may be kept from doing harm to themselves or to others. They are not considered as reasonable creatures, or members of society. But, as to men who have a sound mind, we depend upon a certain degree of regularity in their conduct; and could put a thousand different cases, wherein we could venture, ten to one, that they will act in such a way, and not in the contrary.

If we had no confidence in our fellow men that they will act such a part in such circumstances, it would be impossible to live in society with them: for that which makes men capable of living in society, and uniting in a political body under government, is, that their actions will always be regulated in a great measure by the common principles of human nature.

It may always be expected, that they will regard their own interest and reputation, and that of their families and friends; that they will repel injuries, and have some sense of good offices; and that they will have some regard to truth and justice, so far at least as not to swerve from them without temptation.

It is upon such principles as these, that all political reasoning is grounded. Such reasoning is never demonstrative; but it may have a very great degree of probability, especially when applied to great bodies of men.

XXXI. 12. The last principle of contingent truths I mention, is, that, in the *phenomena of nature,* what is to be, will probably be like to what has been in similar circumstances.

We must have this conviction as soon as we are capable of learning any thing from experience; for all experience is grounded upon a belief that the future will be like the past. Take away this principle, and the experience of an hundred years makes us no wiser with regard to what is to come.

This is one of those principles, which, when we grow up and observe the course of nature, we can confirm by reasoning. We perceive that nature is governed by fixed laws, and that if it were not so, there could be no such thing as prudence in human conduct; there would be no fitness in any means to promote an end; and what, on one occasion, promoted it, might as probably, on another occasion, obstruct it.

But the principle is necessary for us before we are able to discover it by reasoning, and therefore is made a part of our constitution, and produces its effects before the use of reason.

This principle remains in all its force when we come to the use of reason; but we learn to be more cautious in the application of it. We observe more carefully the circumstances on which the past event depended, and learn to distinguish them from those which were accidentally conjoined with it.

In order to this, a number of experiments, varied in their circumstances, is often necessary. Sometimes a single experiment is thought sufficient to establish a general conclusion. Thus, when it was once found, that in a certain degree of cold, quicksilver became a\ hard and malleable metal, there was good reason to think, that the same degree of cold will always produce this effect to the end of the world.

I need hardly mention, that the whole fabric of natural philosophy is built upon this principle, and, if it be taken away, must tumble down to the foundation.

Therefore the great Newton lays it down as an axiom, or as one of his laws of philosophizing, in these words, "Effectuum naturalium ejusdem generis easdem esse causas." [1] This is what every man assents to as soon as he understands it, and no man asks a reason for it. It has therefore the most genuine marks of a first principle.

It is very remarkable, that although all our expectation of what is to happen in the course of nature is derived from the belief of this principle, yet no man thinks of asking what is the ground of this belief.

Mr. Hume, I think, was the first who put this question; and he has shown clearly and invincibly, that it is neither grounded upon reasoning, nor has that kind of intuitive evidence which mathematical axioms have. It is not a necessary truth.

XXXII. *The three tests of first principles repeated.*—He has endeavoured to account for it upon his own principles. It is not my business at present to examine the account he has given of this universal belief of mankind; because, whether his account of it be just or not, (and I think it is not,) yet, as (1) this belief is universal among mankind, and (2) is not grounded upon any antecedent reasoning, but (3) upon the constitution of the mind itself, it must be acknowledged to be a first principle, in the sense in which I use that word.*

---

[1] "Natural effects of the same kind have the same causes." *Principles,* Book III, "Rules of Reasoning in Philosophy," Rule II. Ed.

* Vide Section VIII, of this chapter. [Reprinted in the present volume. Ed.]

I do not at all affirm, that those I have mentioned are all the first principles from which we may reason concerning contingent truths. Such enumerations, even when made after much reflection, are seldom perfect.

REID'S WRITINGS

The standard edition of Reid's *Works* remains that of Sir William Hamilton, first published in Edinburgh (1846), and often reprinted. It contains almost all Reid's writings, but the double column pages of small print make reading very difficult. *Philosophical Orations,* delivered at King's College (1753–62), was edited by W. R. Humphries and first published (in Latin) Aberdeen (1937). They are sketches of some of the main doctrines of the *Inquiry.* Some previously unpublished letters of Reid to Lord Kames have been edited by Ian Ross in *Texas Studies in Literature and Language,* Vol. VII (1965). Reid's critical manuscripts on Priestley's views are outlined in James McCosh, *The Scottish Philosophy,* Appendix III (London, 1875). *Essays on the Intellectual Powers of Man* has been abridged by A. D. Woozley (London, 1941). The editor supplies a useful introduction and some interesting notes, but the omissions in the text are not well marked.

WRITINGS ON REID

Reid's views were much discussed throughout the nineteenth century and the literature on him is extensive. Some of it is listed in *A Bibliography of David Hume and of Scottish Philosophy* by T. E. Jessop (London and Hull, 1938). The fullest critical accounts of Reid in English are Hamilton's notes to his edition of Reid; Hamilton's defence of Reid against Brown in "Philosophy of Perception" (1830), a review of the French edition of Reid's *Works,* reprinted in *Discussions on Philosophy and Literature,* Sir William Hamilton (London, 1852); A. C. Fraser, *Thomas Reid* (Edinburgh and London, 1898); H. Laurie, *Scottish Philosophy* (Glasgow, 1902); James McCosh, *The Scottish Philosophy;* A. Seth, *Scottish Philosophy* (Edinburgh and London, 1899); J. F. Ferrier, "Reid and the Philosophy of Common Sense" (1847)—a review of the Hamilton edition, reprinted in Ferrier's *Lectures on Greek Philosophy and Other Philosophical Remains,* Vol. II (Edinburgh and London, 1866); G. H. Lewes, *A Biographical History of Philosophy* (London and New York, 1845–46); S. A. Graves, *The Scottish Philosophy of Common Sense* (Oxford, 1960); H. M. Bracken, "Introduction" to Reid's *Philosophical Works,* reprint of Hamilton edition (Hildesheim, 1967).
There is a short but valuable discussion of Reid's distinction between sensation and perception in D. W. Hamlyn, *Sensation and Perception* (London, 1961), and some remarks on Reid's relation to Moore in *G. E. Moore* by Alan White (Oxford, 1958). In "Thomas Reid's Theory of Sensation," *Philosophical Review,* Vol. LXIX, 1960, T. J. Dugan interestingly argues that Reid's account is self-contradictory unless "belief" is given a special sense. Reid's ethical views are taken up in D. D. Raphael, *The Moral Sense* (Oxford, 1947). For his theory of suggestion see P. G. Winch, "The Notion of 'Suggestion' in Thomas Reid's Theory of Perception," *The Philosophical Quarterly,* Vol. III (1953). Of the continental works cited by Jessop, perhaps

the most recent and readily available are: M. F. Sciacca, *La Filosofia di Tommaso Reid,* 3rd edition (Milan, 1963); and the essay on Reid in T. T. Segerstedt, *The Problem of Knowledge in Scottish Philosophy* (Lund, 1935). There is also a long article by M. Chastaining, "Reid, la philosophie du sense commun et le problème de la connaissance d'autrui," *Revue Philosophique,* Vol. CXLIV (1954). For the Scottish intellectual background to Reid's thought, and to the other Scottish philosophers as well, see G. Bryson, *Man and Society: the Scottish Inquiry of the Eighteenth Century* (Princeton, 1945).

JOSEPH PRIESTLEY

1733–1804

Born in Yorkshire near Leeds, Priestley was adopted at the age of nine by a well-to-do Calvinist aunt because his widowed father was "encumbered with a large family." In poor health as a schoolboy, Priestley taught himself a considerable number of languages, as well as mathematics and physics. By the time he entered Daventry Academy—a university for religious nonconformists, since they were barred from taking an Oxford or Cambridge degree—Priestley was interested in philosophy and intended for the ministry. At Daventry he read Locke, and Anthony Collins' *Inquiry Concerning Human Liberty* (1714). From the latter he learned of the "necessarian doctrine" and he became a determinist in 1754. He was also introduced to Hartley's *Observations on Man,* a book which greatly influenced his own views for the remainder of his life.

Between 1755, when he began assisting in the ministry, until his ordination in 1762, Priestley also tutored in many subjects, started his scientific experiments, wrote papers, and published the first of his many books, *The Rudiments of English Grammar* (1761). He married in 1762. Within four years he was made a Fellow of the Royal Society for his historical work, and had become friendly with Benjamin Franklin as a result of their joint interest in electricity. After 1770 Priestley's scientific research turned toward chemistry. From 1773 to 1780 the Earl of Shelburne employed him as his parliamentary librarian and supervisor of his son's education. Priestley used this excellent opportunity to good advantage. In addition to his experiments on gases, he wrote most of his philosophical works during this period.

After leaving Shelburne, Priestley moved to Birmingham, where he was supported, in part, by subscriptions from friends. His circle included James Watt, Josiah Wedgwood, and Erasmus Darwin. He continued with his scientific research, wrote extensively on ecclesiastical history, agitated for the abolition of the slave trade, and engaged in political controversy with Edmund Burke on the course of the

French Revolution. After his house was burnt in 1791, by enemies of the Revolution, Priestley moved to London; and after the emigration of his three sons to America, he followed in 1794, settling at Northumberland, Pennsylvania. His wife died two years later. Priestley's religious writings from this time until his death are very extensive. He also wrote defending the doctrine of phlogiston, and he attempted to establish Unitarianism in America. In neither respect was he successful. However, both John Adams and Thomas Jefferson were sympathetic and he was still remembered in England. On the day of his death his friends there had just succeeded in raising a large annual subscription for him.

Priestley's contributions to philosophical writing consist of five works: *An Examination of the Scotch Philosophers* [on Reid, James Beattie and James Oswald] (1774); *Hartley's Theory of the Human Mind* (1775); *Disquisitions Relating to Matter and Spirit* (1777); *The Doctrine of Philosophical Necessity Illustrated* (1777); *A Free Discussion of the Doctrines of Materialism and Philosophical Necessity, In a Correspondence between Dr. Price and Dr. Priestley* (1778). In the preface to *The Doctrine of Philosophical Necessity Illustrated,* Priestley says that he originally intended it as an appendix on praise and blame to his *Disquisitions.* In considering the views of Richard Price, however, he was led to write on the will, thence to other topics, and so finally to produce a separate volume. Similarly, the correspondence between Price and Priestley printed in *A Free Discussion* grew out of Price's replies, by personal letters, to Priestley's *Disquisitions* and *The Doctrine of Philosophical Necess*ity.

In the Introduction to *A Free Discussion* Priestley summarizes his position. He says that "the doctrine of the pre-existence of Christ" is "the point to which all that I have written tends; it being the capital inference that I make from the doctrines of materialism, penetrability of matter, and necessity." The inference that Priestley wishes to draw, contrary to grammatical appearances, is that Christ is not divine, that there is no separate soul, and that the resurrection of the dead is of body and soul together. His argument—necessary to such resurrection —for materialism and, in particular, for matter as being capable of displaying mental properties, draws support, he thinks, from Boscovich, the Jesuit physicist, who argued that matter is not inert but a center of force, not impenetrable but possessed of a power of attraction and repulsion. Priestley's objections to free will have a similar theological basis. For if "we suppose the mind *not* to be determined by motives, in that very degree do rewards and punishments lose their effect"; God could not foresee the effects of the motives under which he places men, and thus not every event would turn out as God wishes —"in the greatest possible happiness of his creation."

It has been said by Basil Willey that Priestley, like Hartley, represents "that typically English phenomenon of the period, 'the holy alliance between science and religion.' " When we dissolve the even closer alliance of that period—the alliance between philosophy and religion—Priestley does not come off badly. His criticism of Reid's theory of ideas was echoed long afterward without acknowledgement, his materialism has recently taken on new life as the identity theory of mind, and his determinism is strange today only in being religiously motivated. As a man of unusual all-around ability, Priestley turned his hand to philosophy when it seemed to be required. But, as the following selections indicate, Priestley was no mere amateur in the defense of his views. Indeed, his discussions with Price are a model of late-eighteenth-century controversy, a model both in the fairness and lucidity of the writers and, also, in their agreement on which issues are important to them.

SELECTIONS FROM

*An Examination of Dr. Reid's Inquiry into the Human Mind on the Principles of Common Sense, Dr. Beattie's Essay on the Nature and Immutability of Truth, and Dr. Oswald's Appeal to Common Sense in Behalf of Religion**

*

SECTION VI

MR. LOCKE'S DOCTRINE NOT SO FAVOURABLE
TO BERKLEY'S THEORY AS DR. REID'S

It is by an evident abuse and perversion of Mr. Locke's doctrine that Dr. Reid pretends that it is favourable to Bishop Berkley's notion of there being no material world; when, in reality, our author's own principles are much more favourable to that notion than Mr. Locke's.

'If,' says he, p. 42, 'impressions and ideas are the only objects of thought, then heaven and earth, and body and spirit, and every thing

* 2nd edition, J. Johnson, London, 1775.

you please, must signify only impressions and ideas, or they must be words without any meaning.' [1]

But it was never supposed by Mr. Locke, or any other advocate for ideas, that they were more than the *immediate* object of our thoughts, the things of which we are properly speaking *conscious,* or that we know in the *first instance.* From them, however, we think we can *infer* the real existence of other things, from which those ideas are derived; and then we can reason about those *objects,* as well as about the *ideas* themselves. In fact, ideas being only the signs of external things, we reason about the external things themselves, without ever attending to the ideas which represent them, and even without knowing that there are any such things in the mind, till we come to reflect upon the subject. In like manner, a person may see perfectly without ever thinking of his eyes, or indeed knowing that he has any such organs.

Mr. Locke would not, indeed, pretend to such an absolute *demonstration* of the reality of an external world as Dr. Reid pleads for; but neither is that strict demonstration necessary. It is quite sufficient if the supposition be the easiest hypothesis for explaining the origin of our ideas. The evidence of it is such that we allow it to be barely possible to doubt of it; but that it is as certain as that two and two make four, we do not pretend.

Strongly attached as our author is to this material world of ours, let us see whether his own system, in other respects, be sufficiently adapted to it. Now it appears to me that his notions of *mind, ideas,* and *external objects,* are such as are hardly compatible with one another, that he puts an impassable gulph between them, so as intirely to prevent their connection or correspondence; which is all that the bishop could wish in favour of his doctrine.

'I take it for granted,' says Dr. Reid, p. 381, 'upon the testimony of common sense, that my mind is a substance, that is, a permanent subject of thought, and my reason convinces me that it is an unextended and invisible substance; and hence I infer that there cannot be in it any thing that resembles extension.' [2] But with equal appearance of truth he might infer that the mind cannot be *affected* by any thing that has extension; for how can any thing act upon another but by means of some common property? Though, therefore, the divine being has thought proper to create an external world, it can be of no proper use to give us sensations or ideas. It must be he himself that impresses our minds with the notices of external things, without any *real instrumentality* of their own; so that the external world is quite a superfluity in the creation. If, therefore, the author of all things be a *wise* being, and have made nothing in vain, we may conclude that this external

1 *An Inquiry into the Human Mind* (Edinburgh, 1764), Chapter II, Section VI. Ed.
2 *Inquiry,* Chapter VII, 5. Ed.

world, which has been the subject of so much controversy, can have no existence.

If then we wish to preserve this external world, which is very convenient for many purposes, we must take care to entertain notions of mind and ideas more compatible with it than those of Dr. Reid.

Our author's fallacious argument from the want of resemblance between our ideas and external objects leads him into many difficulties. It makes him, in several respects, allow too much to Dr. Berkley, and to come nearer to him than he is aware. And in spite of his aversion to the union, and of every thing that he can do or say, their common principles will bring them together. 'Our sensations,' he says, p. 305, 'have no resemblance to external objects, nor can we discover by our reason any necessary connection between the existence of the former and that of the latter.' [1] 'No man,' says he, p. 85, 'can shew by any good argument, that all our sensations might not have been as they are, though no body or quality of body had ever existed.' [2] He even says, p. 304, 'that when we consider the different attributes of *mind* and *body,* they seem to be so different, and so unlike, that we can find no handle by which one may lay hold of the other.' [3]

According to our author, therefore, Berkley's theory is at least *possible;* and if, as he says, p. 117, 'sensations and ideas in our minds can resemble nothing but sensations and ideas in other minds,' [4] it may well appear *probable* that they are transferred (as Malebranche, I think, supposes) immediately from the divine mind to ours, without any real agency of a material world. If I could admit Dr. Reid's premises, I think I could hardly help drawing this conclusion from them; especially as nothing can be pleaded for the existence of this same material world, but a mere *unaccountable persuasion* that it *does* exist. This persuasion Dr. Reid says arises from a branch of his new common sense. But if I cannot discover or imagine any *end* or *reason* why it should exist; common sense, in its old and familiar acceptation, would tell me that it does not exist at all.

SECTION VII

A SOPHISM OF MR. HUME'S IN PURSUANCE OF BERKLEY'S THEORY ADOPTED BY DR. REID

Our author, struck with a panic fear of scepticism, has been no less

---

[1] *Inquiry,* Chapter VI, Section XXI. Ed.
[2] *Inquiry,* Chapter V, Section II. Ed.
[3] *Inquiry, Ibid.* Ed.
[4] *Inquiry,* Chapter V, Section VIII, reprinted in this volume. Ed.

misled and thrown off his guard by the dangerous sophisms of Mr. Hume, than by the innocent ones of Bishop Berkley.

'The *new system,'* by which he means that of Descartes and Locke, &c. he says, p. 369, 'admits only of the principles of common sense as a first principle, and pretends by strict argumentation to deduce all the rest from it. That our thoughts, our sensations, and every thing of which we are conscious has a real existence is admitted in this system as a first principle, but every thing else must be made evident by the light of reason. That the rational issue of this system is scepticism, with regard to every thing excepting the existence of our ideas, and their necessary relations, which appear upon comparing them, is evident. For ideas being the only objects of thought, and having no existence but when we are conscious of them, it necessarily follows, that there is no object of our thought which can have a continued and permanent existence. Body and spirit, cause and effect, time and space, to which we were wont to ascribe an existence independent of our thought, all are turned out of existence by this short dilemma. Either these things are ideas of sensation or reflection, or they are not. If they are ideas of sensation or reflection, they can have no existence but when we are conscious of them. If they are not ideas of sensation or reflection, they are words without any meaning.' p. 373.[1]

From this pitiful sophism, advanced by Mr. Hume, and deemed unanswerable by Dr. Reid, have been derived to us all the instinctive principles contained in this curious treatise. For being determined at all adventures to maintain the reality of body and spirit, cause and effect, time and space, &c. and the old theory of the mind not being, in his opinion, sufficient for the purpose, a new one must be found; and if nothing else can be had, still the good things above mentioned must be retained, though we can say nothing in their favour but *they are so because they are so,* which is Dr. Reid's common sense, and his short irrefragable argument.

But if, instead of such a *plenary assurance* as only this new common sense promises, he would have been content with a *reasonable degree of evidence* for the reality of all the things above mentioned, the old hypothesis would have been quite sufficient. It suits every case of sensations and ideas; and therefore, according to the received rules of philosophizing, has a just claim to be admitted.

That *mind* exists I have the very same reason to believe as I have that *body* exists; since it is only by that name that I distinguish that to which certain powers and properties, of which I am conscious, as *perception, memory, will,* &c. belong.

I am surprised that it should have been so readily admitted, that even ideas have no existence but when we are conscious of them. We

---

[1] This is a condensation of several passages, *Inquiry,* Chapter VII, 2. Ed.

have just the same reason to believe the identity of an idea as that of a tree, that of any external body, or that of our own minds themselves. The idea that I have of my wife or child to-day as much resembles the idea I had of them yesterday, though some hours of sound sleep have intervened, as my house of to-day resembles my house of yesterday. In this case I only judge by the resemblance of my ideas of it; and if the ideas of my house yesterday and to-day were not the same, I should have no medium by which to prove the identity of the house.

PRIESTLEY'S WRITINGS

Priestley wrote so much on so many different subjects—theological, scientific, educational, historical, political, and philosophical—that there exists no standard edition of all his writings. Most of his nonscientific work is collected in *The Theological and Miscellaneous Works of Joseph Priestley*, Edited by J. T. Rutt, 25 vol. in 26 (London, 1817–32). This includes all his philosophical writings. They are not otherwise available except in early editions. *A Bibliography of Joseph Priestley* by R. E. Crook (London, 1966), attempts to list all Priestley's publications; it also lists many works relating to him. A very good selection of Priestley's work, with a helpful introduction, is given in *Priestley's Writings on Philosophy, Science, and Politics*, Edited by J. A. Passmore (New York, 1965).

WRITINGS ON PRIESTLEY

The literature on Priestley is vast, but almost none of it concerns his philosophical views. Rutt's edition of Priestley's *Works* was reviewed on publication by James Martineau. His essay, still of some interest, was reprinted long after in his *Essays, Reviews, and Addresses*, Vol. I (London, 1890). There is a useful chapter on Priestley in Basil Willey's *The Eighteenth-Century Background* (London, 1940). Only a small part of it, however, is devoted to Priestley's philosophy. In Leslie Stephen's *English Thought in the Eighteenth Century*, 2 vol. (London, 1876), there is some discussion of Priestley's ecclesiastical history and of his political writing, but only passing unfavorable reference to his philosophical doctrines. S. A. Grave's *The Scottish Philosophy of Common Sense* (Oxford, 1960), contains scattered passages on Priestley which are well worth reading. The short article on Priestley in *The Encyclopedia of Philosophy* (New York and London, 1967), is by J. A. Passmore, and it is the best modern treatment. The only book which treats Priestley's doctrines at length remains: *Hartley und Priestley, die Begründer des Assoziationismus in England* (Halle, 1882).

JOSEPH PRIESTLEY
AND RICHARD PRICE

1 7 2 3 – 1 7 9 1

Like his close friend Joseph Priestley, Price was the son of a Calvinist minister, and again like Priestley, he went to a dissenting college. After leaving the Fund Academy in London, Price became a companion and personal chaplain to a man of means; he combined this with acting as Presbyterian minister to various congregations in the London area. In 1756 he inherited some money. During the next year he married, and also wrote his only independent book on philosophy, *A Review of the Principal Questions and Difficulties in Morals.* In the following years, while settled as a minister in London, Price studied philosophy and mathematics to such effect that he was made a Fellow of the Royal Society in 1765 for his work on the theory of probability. He met Hume, Franklin, Priestley, and Lord Shelburne at this period, Shelburne acting as friend in power to him, and he to Priestley.

In 1767 Price, in addition to his religious works, wrote a reply to Hume on miracles; in 1769 he wrote on the increase in population; in 1770 on the calculations used by insurance societies; and a year later on the national debt. These writings made him well known. But in 1776 he became famous for his pamphlet attacking the British government's policy of war with America. He was given the freedom of the city of London, asked for his financial advice by the American Congress, and invited to become a citizen of the United States. Yale College gave him an LL.D. in 1783. Three years later, after his wife's death, his health began to fail. However, his sermon of 1789 "On the Love of Our Country," supporting the French Revolution, drew as its reply Burke's *Reflections on the Revolution in France.* Price died in 1791, while his views on social finance were still sought by both the British and French governments, before the conservative political reaction in Britain gathered momentum. His funeral sermon was preached by his fellow Unitarian, Joseph Priestley.

If we exclude Price's essay on miracles and his exchange of letters with Priestley in *A Free Discussion,* we are left with the *Review of*

Morals as Price's only substantial work on philosophy. It was first published in 1758, and corrected, revised, and enlarged in the third edition of 1787, with a slightly different title.

Price is important in the history of British ethics as an opponent of Hutcheson and Hume. As against their view that moral judgments are based on and refer to feelings, Price argued that our judgments of right and wrong arise from the understanding; they refer to the real qualities of actions. Price's interest in epistemology and metaphysics is the result of his desire "to trace the obligations of virtue up to the truth and nature of things." Because his opponents support their ethical views by the claim that every simple idea is derived from an impression either of introspection or sensation, Price discusses, in the first chapter of the *Review of Morals,* whether there is an additional source of simple ideas. He goes on to argue that the understanding is such a source. Later, in Chapter V, he tries to rebut the skeptical view that our faculties may be "so constituted, as unavoidably to deceive us in all our apprehensions?" Can we know this is not so? Price's reply to skepticism is that: "Doubting supposes evidence; and there cannot, therefore, be any such thing as doubting, whether evidence itself is to be regarded. A man who doubts of the veracity of his faculties, must do it on their own authority." This kind of doubt, then, is self-destructive or paradoxical. Not all Price's points are as neat as this; but in the selections offered here he both displays his considerable abilities as a philosopher and expresses himself on topics he nowhere else takes up.

SELECTIONS FROM

A *Free Discussion* of *the Doctrines of Materialism and Philosophical Necessity, in a Correspondence Between Dr. Price and Dr. Priestley**

*

PART II *OF THE HUMAN MIND*

OF THE NATURE OF MIND OR SPIRIT
THE FIRST COMMUNICATION
BY DR. PRICE, WITH DR. PRIESTLEY'S ANSWERS

Dr. Price.—In the Disquisitions,[1] (Vol. III. pp. 250, 292,) it is asserted, that ideas are certainly divisible. This seems to me very absurd. It would be as proper to assert ideas to be hard or round. The idea of an object is the apprehension, view, or notion of it; and how can this be divisible? Perception is a single and indivisible act. The object perceived may be divisible; but the *perception* of it by the mind cannot be so.

Answer.—What appears to Dr. Price to be *very absurd,* I cannot help thinking, after the most deliberate review, to be very certain and very clear. What correspondence can there be between an idea and its archetype, if the archetype consist of parts, and the idea have no parts? He seems to have been misled, by not distinguishing between the *power,* or rather the *act* of perception, and the thing (i. e. the *idea*) perceived. The object of perception he acknowledges to be divisible, but *the perception of it by the mind* cannot be so. True, because perception is either a faculty or an act of a faculty, to which divisibility is not applicable; but the thing about which the perceptive power is employed (which is not the object itself, but the idea or representation of it in the mind) must be as divisible as the archetype of that idea. If the mind be a simple and indivisible substance, it cannot be possessed of more than a single idea, and that the idea of something to which division is not applicable. However, I do not see why Dr. Price should object to a *repository of divisible ideas* in a mind

---

* *The Theological and Miscellaneous Works of Joseph Priestley,* Vol. IV, Edited by J. T. Rutt (London, 1817–32).

1 *Disquisitions Relating to Matter and Spirit,* by Joseph Priestley (London, 1777). Ed.

which he supposes to be actually extended, and consequently to have room enough for that purpose.

Dr. Price.—Disquisitions, (Vol. III. pp. 254, &c. 276, &c.). *Mr. Baxter,* and other ingenious men, have undoubtedly said a great deal that is very groundless about the union of the body to the soul; its being a clog; its leaving the soul more capable of exerting its powers when separated from it, &c. Were all that has been said on these subjects true, there would be no occasion for a resurrection. Nay, it would be a calamity, not a benefit. A false philosophy has, in this instance, contradicted nature and experience, as well as revelation. Thus far I agree entirely with Dr. Priestley; but some of the objections in Sect. VI. (Vol. III. p. 252,) have little weight with me, and cannot easily be answered on any hypothesis. If it must be taken for granted that brutes, or the sentient principles in brutes, are annihilated at death, as seems to be hinted sometimes by Dr. Priestley, I am afraid it will not easily be believed that the same is not true of men. And if true, there will be a complete end of us: a resurrection will be a contradiction. But it will come in my way to say more to this purpose.

Answer.—My only reason for not supposing that *brutes* will not survive the grave is, that there is no hint of it in revelation, where only it is that we are informed that *men* will rise again. It may, however, be true, though we have not been informed of it, and the analogy between men and other animals, makes it not very improbable.

Dr. Price.—Disquisitions, (Vol. III. p. 259.) Dr. Priestley here, and throughout a great part of this work, argues on the supposition, that according to the ideas of modern metaphysicians, spirit can have no relation to place, and is incapable of being present any where. This seems to me a mistake. I do not know what modern metaphysicians Dr. Priestley means, except the Cartesians. I am certain Dr. Clarke, and some others of the best modern writers, did not entertain these ideas of spirit. It is a maxim that cannot be disputed, that *time* and *place* are necessary to the existence of all things. Dr. Clarke has made use of this maxim, to prove that infinite space and duration are the essential properties of the Deity[1]; and I think he was right. Sir Isaac Newton thought in the same way, as appears from some passages at the end of his *Principia,* and in the queries at the end of his *Optics.* As far, therefore, as Dr. Priestley combats a notion of spirit that implies it has no relation to space, and exists no where, he combats an absurdity and contradiction which deserves no regard. What the nature is of the relation of spirit to place, or in what *manner* it is present in space, I am utterly ignorant. But I can be sure that, if it exists at all, it must exist *somewhere,* as well as in *some time.*

[1] Samuel Clarke (1675–1729) published his *Demonstration* in 1705–06, and *A Letter to Dodwell* in 1706; the exchange with Anthony Collins arose from the latter. The Leibniz-Clarke correspondence was published by Clarke in 1717. See his *Works* (London, 1738–42). Ed.

Dr. Clarke was not for excluding expansion from the idea of immaterial thinking substances. See his *First Defence of an Argument to prove the Immateriality and Natural Immortality of the Soul,* in answer to *Collins.* Has Dr. Priestley read this controversy; or has he read the chapter on a Future State, with which *Butler's* Analogy begins? If he had, I fancy he would have writ differently in some parts of this book. Dr. Clarke is, without all doubt, the best and ablest of all writers, on the subjects of the Immateriality and Natural Immortality of the Soul, and also on *Liberty* and *Necessity.* What he says on these subjects in his *Demonstration of the Being and Attributes of God,* is but inconsiderable, compared with what he has said in his *Answer to Dodwell,* his *Controversies with Collins,* and the *Letters* between *him and Leibnitz.*[1]

I think it of little consequence, whether it *can* or *cannot* be determined, whether the subject of consciousness and thought in man is matter, if by matter is meant not solid extension, but an unknown something that has a relation to place; and it was hardly worth while to write a book to prove this.

Matter is incapable of consciousness and thought, not because it is *extended,* but because it is *solid,* and, as such, inert and capable of being divided without being annihilated.

Solid extension, and *perception, thought, volition,* &c. are totally different things; and it is just as clear that the latter cannot be the figure, motion and arrangement of the parts of the former, as that any one thing cannot *be* another; that a square, for instance, cannot *be,* or be *made to be,* sound or colour. Our ideas of *figured, extended, solid substances,* and of *conscious, perceiving, thinking substances,* are, according to Mr. Locke's observation, equally clear and distinct. It seems, therefore, very unreasonable to confound them, or to talk of superadding one of them to the other.

Dr. Clarke makes use of the instance of *space,* to prove that there is no necessary connexion between extension and discerptibility. *Moveantur partes spatii de locis suis et movebuntur de seipsis. Newton's Princip. Lib.* I. *Schol. Defin.*8.[2]

Answer.–If, as Dr. Clarke supposes, spirits have real extension, they must be of some shape, and therefore their relation to space cannot be a thing of which we are *utterly ignorant.* We may not know *where* they are, or *how much space* they occupy, (whether, for instance, *more* or *less* than the bodies they belong to,) but they must occupy *some space* as well as bodies.

I will farther observe, that if, according to Dr. Clarke, the Divine Being has infinite extension, and finite spirits a limited one, they must mutually penetrate each other; and these spiritual substances being of

---

1 In *A Demonstration of the Being and Attributes of God.* Ed.

2 "Suppose those parts of space to be moved out of their places, and they will be moved out of themselves." Ed.

the same nature, the difficulty attending it must be just as great as that which attends the mutual penetration of material substances.

I have carefully read all Dr. Clarke's metaphysical works, but thought it sufficient to quote his *Demonstration,* as the *best known* of all his writings, and containing a summary of his strongest arguments on all the topics that I have had occasion to discuss. I have also read *Butler's Analogy,* but this work does not stand so high with me as it does with Dr. Price. I did not think that, with respect to any thing that I have written, it was at all necessary to consider any passages of Dr. Clarke's other writings, or any of Butler's; but if Dr. Price thinks otherwise, I will give particular attention to any thing, in either of them, that he shall be pleased to point out to me.

Dr. Price admits, that if matter be not solid and impenetrable, it may be capable of thought, but wonders that I should have written a book to prove this. My book was not written to prove this, but to prove that, whatever matter be, *thinking* is the result of a modification of it, or that this faculty does not belong to an invisible substance, different from the body, which I apprehend to have been the source of the greatest corruptions of the system of revelation. Effectually to explode this notion, originally borrowed from Heathenism, and thereby to discharge from Christianity many enormous errors that now disfigure it, and make it appear absurd in the present enlightened age of philosophy, appears to me to be rendering it the most important of all services. Whether I have in any measure *succeeded,* such, if I know my own heart, have been my views in writing both the *Disquisitions* themselves, and this defence of them.

I wish Dr. Price would inform me what is the connexion between, *a capacity of consciousness,* and *being indivisible without being annihilated.* Also, if spirits be extended, and something more than space, whether they may not be divisible and discerptible, as well as matter?

Dr. Hartley has shewn that all the faculties of the human mind may be the result of vibration, except that of *simple perception;* but this, though *different* from the other known properties of matter, may not be *incompatible* with them. The facts alleged in Sect. IV. (Vol. III. p. 242,) do, I apprehend, prove, that according to the established rules of philosophizing, it is a property that must *in fact* belong to the brain, whether we ever be able to conceive *how* it results from the structure of the brain, or not. In my opinion there is just the same reason to conclude that the brain *thinks,* as that it is *white* and *soft.*

Though Mr. Locke was of opinion that our ideas of thinking substances are as distinct as those of solid ones, he was likewise of opinion, that, for any thing that we know to the contrary, thinking *may* be the mere property of a solid substance.

Dr. Clarke should have shewn not only that *extension,* but that *a capacity of motion from place to place* is not necessarily connected with discerptibility. It appears to me very clear, that if a spirit be a thing that is extended and moveable, one part of it may be conceived to be moved, and the other part left behind, whether the property of *consciousness* would be destroyed in consequence of it, or not.

Dr. Price.—In the Disquisitions, Dr. Priestley says, that "it is even demonstrable that matter is infinitely divisible." (Vol. III. p. 270.) Can he say that the being he calls *himself* is likewise infinitely divisible? What would be the result of such a division? Would it not be an infinite number of *other* beings? But does not this imply a contradiction? Can there be such a thing as *half* a self? Or can the being I call *myself* be split into two *others?* Impossible! This would not be to *divide,* but to *annihilate* me. And the truth is, that in this case division cannot be imagined without annihilation. In another place Dr. Priestley intimates, that matter consists of *indivisible points,* (p. 233). How then can it be infinitely divisible?

Answer.—The matter of which I consist may be divisible, though the *actual* division of it might so disarrange the parts of it, that the property of thinking (which is the result of a particular modification of them) would be destroyed. A whole brain may think, but half a brain may be incapable of it. I see no sort of difficulty in this case. Also, may not an extended spirit be conceived to be divided without annihilation, as well as an extended solid substance? To the imagination it is equally easy.

Dr. Price.—Disquisitions. *The "percipient power may as well belong to one system as to one atom."* (Vol. III. p. 286.) See likewise the answer to the fourth objection. *I am one person, but it does not follow that I cannot be divided: a sphere is one thing, but it does not follow that it consists of indivisible materials* (p. 263). But if matter consists of *indivisible points* (as is said in p. 233), and the soul is matter, then the soul consists of indivisible materials. But not to insist on this. Can any one believe of *himself* that he is one thinking being only as a great number of bodies forming a sphere are one sphere? If this is true, he must be either the parts themselves that compose the sphere; and if so, he is a *multitude* of beings; or he must be their *sphericity;* and if so, he is nothing but an *order* or *relation* of parts, and can never remain the same any longer than that order is preserved. As any change in the surface of a sphere would destroy the sphericity, and convert it into some other figure, so would any change in that *order* of parts which constitutes *myself,* destroy *me,* and convert me into some *other person.*

Answer.—If I say that matter consists of indivisible points, I use a common expression, though perhaps not a correct one. But as every sensible part of matter consists of an *infinity* of such points, it is plain that the substance can never be exhausted by any division. To infer from this, that the soul (consisting of matter) consists of an indivisible substance, seems to me to be a play upon words.

If a thinking being be a material substance of a particular texture and form, as I define it, it cannot follow, as is here asserted, that it is *a mere order or relation of parts.* A disarrangement of this texture would destroy all *power of thought,* but would not make *another person.*

Dr. Price.—Disquisitions. *"It must be impossible to say a priori, whether a single particle or a system of matter be the proper seat"* of *perception, but fact proves the latter.* (Vol. III. p. 285.) If a system of matter is the seat of perception, then the system is the percipient being. But the percipient being is *one.* A system consists of *many* beings.

It is inconceivable to me how any person can think that many substances united can be one substance, or that all the parts of a system can perceive, and yet no single part be a percipient being.

Answer.—A system, though consisting of many beings or things, is nevertheless but *one system.* A brain, though consisting of many parts, is but one brain; and where can be the difficulty of conceiving that no single part of a brain should be a whole brain, or have the properties of a whole brain?

.   .   .   .   .

Dr. Price.—If I understand what is said in the beginning of Sect. XVII. (Vol. III. p. 328,) on *Personal Identity,* the drift of it is to shew that a being may be the same with a *former* being, though their *substances,* and consequently all their *properties,* are different. It is likewise implied, that the men who are to be raised from death, will be the same with the men who have existed in this world, *only* as a river is called the same, because the water, though different, has followed other water in the same channel; or, as a forest is called the same, because the present trees, though new, have been planted and grown up on the same spot, in the room of other trees which had been cut down and consumed. Did I believe this to be all the identity of man hereafter, I could not consider myself as having any concern in a future state.

The assertion that the man or the agent may be the same, though his substance, or every component part of him, is different, appears to me very extraordinary indeed. I am a different person from my neighbour, though organized in the same manner, because the organized matter is different. If, therefore, man after the resurrection will be, not only a different system of matter, but also a system of matter differently organized, and placed in a different world, what will there be to make him the same with man in this world? I think, therefore, that Dr. Priestley should, by all means, keep to what he advances towards the conclusion of this 17th Section, (p. 335). It is essential to his scheme to maintain the resurrection of the *same body,* or that the very matter that composes man at death, will be collected at the resurrection, and compose him again in another world, and for ever.

But what am I saying? Man a composition of substances! It is utterly impossible. The thinking substance would then be not *one being,* but a *multitude;* nor is it possible to evade this consequence, without denying that the soul is a substance, or any thing more than a modification of a substance, or an arrangement and order of the parts of substances. Can this be true? Is the subject of thought and perception; is what every one calls *himself;* not *a being,* and *one being;* but a mere result from the figure, motion, and order of a system of material beings? In short, if the soul is material, it must certainly be one of the primary atoms of matter. No where else in the corporeal world can we find any thing like that unity and substantiality which belong to the soul of man; and if it is an atom, it must have existed from the first creation of matter, unless there are new atoms created every time an animal is generated.

Answer.—In Sect. XVII. I professedly speculate upon principles that are not my own. It is intended to prove, that there may be such an *identity of person,* as will be a foundation for future *expectation, obligation,* &c., though every particle of the man should be changed. The reasoning in this Section I must take the liberty to say, I do not think to be invalidated by Dr. Price's remarks, though to him it appears so very extraordinary.

The remainder of this remark has been obviated again and again in the course of my work, and also in the preceding parts of this. What I call *myself* is an organized system of matter. It is not therefore, myself, but my *power of thought,* that is properly termed the result of figure, motion, &c.

Dr. Price.—Disquisitions. *What is there in the matter that composes my body, that should attach me to it, more than to the matter that composes "the table on which I write?"* (Vol. III. p. 331.) This is a surprising question from Dr. Priestley. If the matter which composes my body is myself, I certainly have as much reason to prefer it to the matter of a table, as I have to prefer *myself* to a *table.* To assert, as Dr. Priestley does, that the matter of the body is the soul, and at the same time to suppose, as he does, in this 17th Section, that the soul may remain the same, though the whole matter of the body is changed, appears to me indeed so apparently inconsistent, that I cannot help suspecting I must greatly misunderstand him. Should he say, that the soul is not strictly the *matter* of the body, but the *organization* of that matter; this, as I have already observed more than once, is

making the soul a modification, an order and juxta-position and connexion of parts, and not a *being,* or *substance.* But is it possible to
conceive of any thing more substantial than the soul? Can there be a
being in nature, if the sentient principle, the subject that feels pleasure
and pain, that thinks and reasons, and loves and hates, is not a *being?*
Suppose it, however, if you can, to be merely the organization of the
body; would not a change in the matter of the body make *another*
body? And would not *another* body make *another* soul, though the
same organization should be preserved? If not, then may not I and Dr.
Priestley be the same man, since the organization of our bodies is the
same, and only the matter different? Would not, in short, any number
of living bodies be one soul, one sentient principle, supposing their
organization the same?

Answer.—The beginning of this remark relates to the speculation
above-mentioned, which goes upon other principles than my own. To
the question at the end of the remark, viz. "Would not any number of
living bodies be one soul, one sentient principle, supposing their organization the same?" I answer, that different systems of matter, organized exactly alike, must make different beings, who would feel and
think exactly alike in the same circumstances. Their minds, therefore,
would be exactly *similar,* but *numerically different.*

Dr. Price.—Disquisitions, (Vol. III. p. 309). It seems to be hinted
here, that the soul, after death, is as little of a substance (that is, as
truly nothing) as matter would be without extension. It is added, *"If
together with the opinion of the entire cessation of thought they will
maintain the real existence of the soul, it must be for the sake of
hypothesis only, and for no real use whatever."* Does Dr. Priestley
then really mean that the soul loses its existence at death?

How can it be said to be of no use to maintain the existence of the
soul after death, when without this, a resurrection must be impossible?

Answer.—I say, that they who maintain the cessation of thought
after death, cannot maintain the separate existence of the soul, except
for the sake of an hypothesis, and for no real *use* whatever, for this
plain reason, that, during this entire cessation of thought, the soul is,
in fact, of no use, no phenomena indicating that any such thing exists.
Had not the persons who maintain such an insensible state of the soul,
believed a resurrection of the body, they would naturally have concluded that the soul, or the thinking part of man, *ceased to be,* because
its existence would never more be manifested by any *effect.*

How is it true, that there can be no resurrection, unless there be a
soul distinct from the body? If the soul be the same thing with the
body, or a part of the body, may not the body, or this part of it, rise
again without the aid of *another substance?* On the contrary, I think
that a resurrection, properly so called, (because this can be only a

resurrection of something that *had been dead,* viz. the body) is manifestly useless, upon the supposition of there being a soul distinct from the body; it being upon this hypothesis, the soul, and not the body, that is the seat of all perception, and the source of all action.

.   .   .   .   .

Dr. Price.—Disquisitions. "All the exertions—of the soul—are as much produced by *sensations and ideas* as any effect in nature can be said to be produced by its proper cause." They have "properly an impelling force." They are "moving powers." (Vol. III. p. 289.) An idea, therefore, is an *agent,* and the soul is passive under its action in the same manner as a ball is passive when impelled by another. But what is an idea? Nothing but a *perception* or *judgment* of the mind, that is, of the being that acts. How can this impel? What can it be more than the *occasion* of action?

There must be somewhere a *self-moving power.* For one thing cannot move another, and that another *in infinitum.* And if there is one self-moving power in nature, why may there not be many?

Answer.—*Dr. Price* should distinguish between a *perception* or *judgment,* which is an *act* of *the mind,* and the *idea* perceived and judged of by the mind, which must be different from the *mind itself,* or any of its *acts.* I maintain that ideas, whatever they be, have a proper *impelling power,* because men are invariably impelled to action in consequence of them; but as to a *self-motive power,* I deny that man has any such thing, for the reasons that are alleged in the *Treatise on Necessity.*[1]

Dr. Price.—Upon the whole, it may perhaps be possible to convince me that there is no such thing as *matter,* and *Dr. Priestley* has contributed a little to it; but I cannot be convinced that there is no such thing as *spirit,* meaning by spirit such a thinking intelligent nature as I feel myself to be. I am indeed full of darkness about myself; but in the midst of this darkness I am taught the following particulars by an irresistible consciousness which will not suffer me to doubt:

1. That I am a *being* or a *substance,* and not a *property,* or a mere *configuration of parts.*

2. That I am *one being,* and not *many* beings, or a *system.*

3. That I am a *voluntary agent,* possessed of powers of *self-motion,* and not a passive instrument.

4. That my senses and limbs, my eyes, hands, &c., are *instruments* by which I act and receive information; and not *myself,* or *mine* and not *me.*

---

[1] See *The Doctrine of Philosophical Necessity Illustrated.* (*Appendix to Disquisitions.*) Sections I–VI. Reprinted in *Priestley's Writings on Philosophy, Science, and Politics,* edited by J. A. Passmore (New York, 1965). Ed.

Answer.—If, by *spirit, Dr. Price* means nothing more than a thinking and an intelligent substance, I have the same consciousness of it that he has. I also believe with him that I am a *being* or *substance;* also that I am a *single being,* and a *voluntary agent,* though not possessed of a self-motive power; and that my limbs and senses are instruments by which I act, and not *myself* or *me.* So that, if these be all the essential articles of *Dr. Price's* faith, and he seems to enumerate them as such, we are very nearly agreed, though in *words* we have differed so widely.

QUERIES BY DR. PRICE

1. Is not the *soul,* or what I call *myself,* a being or substance, and not merely a mode or accident?

2. Does the soul lose its existence at death, or, am I, the subject of thought, reason, consciousness, &c., to be annihilated?

3. If I am to lose my existence at death, will not my resurrection be the resurrection of a non-entity, and therefore a contradiction?

4. If I am not to lose my existence at death, may it not be properly said that I am *naturally immortal?*

Answer.—I consider myself as a being consisting of what is called matter, disposed in a certain manner. At death the parts of this material substance are so disarranged, that the powers of perception and thought, which depended upon that arrangement, cease. At the resurrection they will be re-arranged, in the same, or a similar manner, as before, and consequently the powers of perception and thought will be restored. But this will require a miraculous interposition of Divine power, and therefore it cannot be said that thinking beings are *naturally* immortal, (i. e. as thinking beings,) though the parts that compose them are so.

THE SECOND COMMUNICATION

CONTAINING DR. PRICE'S OBSERVATIONS ON THE REPLIES TO THE
FIRST COMMUNICATION, WITH DR. PRIESTLEY'S SECOND REPLIES

OF THE NATURE OF MIND OR SPIRIT
OBSERVATIONS ON DR. PRIESTLEY'S REPLY, P. 36

When the eye is destroyed we cannot see. So likewise when the brain is destroyed we cannot reason. If from hence it follows that it is the brain that reasons, why should it not also follow that it is the eye that sees? From the dependence of actual sensations and thought on the brain, we have, I think, no more reason to conclude that the brain is the mind, than a savage who had never heard the music of a harpsichord, and did not see the hand that played upon it, would have to conclude, that it played on itself, and was *the* musician; because he could trace all the sounds to the instrument, and found that when the strings were out of order, the music was disturbed or destroyed.

What experience teaches us, is, that the *exercise* of the mental powers *depends* on the brain and the nerves; not that the mind *is* the brain and the nerves. Common sense exclaims against such a conclusion as much as against concluding that there is pain in the point of a sword. We are sure the mind cannot be the brain, because the brain is an assemblage of beings. The mind is *one* being. Nothing seems to me more unphilosophical in this case than to rest our ideas on the organ, and to confound it with the being whose organ it is. This, I have said, is like thinking that a musical instrument plays on itself. But to go higher. It is not unlike resting our ideas in this visible world, and supposing it the same with that Deity who made, and actuates, and governs it. The laws of nature seem to terminate in matter. But is it philosophical, in order to avoid multiplying causes, to conclude they have no other cause than matter itself; and, with the French philosophers, to make *nature* the only Deity? In short, I am fully of opinion, that if that *mass of flesh and blood* which we call the *brain,* (no one part of which, or part of any part, touches another,) may be that sentient and intelligent being we call the *mind;* then that mass of corporeal substances which we call the *world,* may be *God;* and it must be unphilosophical to search farther than *itself* for its cause. Dr. Priestley, I know, is far from being sensible of this; but such indeed is the tendency of his principles and manner of reasoning. The very foundation of this atheistical conclusion is totally subverted by the demonstration which, I think, I have given, that the laws which govern matter, or its attractions and repulsions, are not the actions or properties of matter itself, but effects of the constant operation of a higher cause.

ANSWER, BY DR. PRIESTLEY

I cannot help expressing some surprise that my reasoning on this subject should not seem to be understood, and that such strange conclusions should be drawn from it. If, upon examination, nothing could be *found,* or *reasonably conjectured,* to move the strings of the harpsichord, it would be philosophical to conclude, that the cause of the music that came from it was *within itself.* But when we open it, and see the strings to be moved in such a manner as similar strings are never known to be moved but by *human means,* there is reason to conclude, from analogy, that these strings also are moved, though we do not see *how,* by the same, or a similar cause.

In like manner, when we see the parts of which the universe consists, to be arranged in such a manner, as, from analogy, we have reason to believe, that no other than an intelligent being could arrange them, we conclude that an intelligent being, visible or invisible, *has* arranged them.

I conclude, that there is nothing *within* the brain itself that is the cause of perception, because, for any thing that I know, perception may be the *property* of that material, as well as of any supposed immaterial substance; the relation of *perception* to *material* or *immaterial* substances being equally unknown. If the faculty of *playing could* be supposed to belong to the harpsichord, it would be unphilosophical to inquire for any *concealed musician;* so also if the power of arranging and moving the component parts of the universe *could* belong to themselves, it would be unphilosophical to inquire for a superintending mind, or God. But it is denied that the laws of nature do *seem* to terminate in the visible parts of the universe.

For the same reason that perception is ascribed to some immaterial substance within the brain, it seems to me that attraction ought to be ascribed to some immaterial substance within the earth, the sun, &c., because, according to Dr. Price, *attraction* is a power quite foreign to the nature of matter, as well as *perception*.

Dr. Price.—Observations on Dr. Priestley's *Reply,* pp. 36, 37. I had said that it is very absurd to imagine that ideas are divisible. Dr. Priestley here says, that after the most deliberate review, the contrary is very clear to him. Others must judge. What is the *idea* of an object? Is it not the *notion* or *conception* of the object? A line is infinitely divisible. Is the mind's *idea* or *conception* of a line, also infinitely divisible? But, I find *Dr. Priestley* thinks ideas to be the bodies themselves in miniature, which they represent, or models and delineations of external objects, distinct from the mind, but contained in it, like maps and globes in a chamber. And I suppose he will go so far as to ascribe all the properties of bodies to them, and particularly attraction and repulsion; and maintain, that in volition they act upon and impel the mind containing them, as one body acts upon and impels another. The bare representation of such an opinion seems sufficient to confute it. But if not, it must be in vain to argue about it.

Answer.—If ideas be nothing distinct from the mind, or modifications of the mind, varying as their archetypes vary, a mind *with ideas,* and a mind without *ideas,* would be the same thing; and if the ideas of compound objects be not compounded things, and consist of as many parts as the objects of which they are the ideas, I am unable to conceive any thing about ideas. That motions, or volitions of the mind, do depend upon ideas, or, in other words, that the mind is *influenced* or *acted upon* by them, is a certain *fact,* whether the representation confute itself or not. No person acquainted with the principles of *Hart-*

ley's Theory, can be at a loss to know what I suppose ideas to be, and in what manner they operate.

.   .   .   .   .

THE SECOND COMMUNICATION
ON THE DOCTRINE OF NECESSITY

OBSERVATIONS ON DR. PRIESTLEY'S ANSWERS TO THE QUERIES IN P. 65, BY DR. PRICE

In order to bring the dispute between me and Dr. Priestley as much to a point as possible, and to discover how far we *agreed* and *differed,* I sent to him, after my first communication, on the nature of matter and spirit, and the immortality of the soul, the following queries:

1. Can any thing act on another without being *present* to it?

2. Can, therefore, matter act on other matter without contact and impulse?

3. Is not the *soul,* or what I call *myself,* a *being* or *substance;* and not merely a *mode* or *property?*

4. Does the soul lose its existence at death? Or am I, the subject of thought, reason, consciousness, &c. to be then annihilated?

5. If I am to lose my existence at death, will not my resurrection be the resurrection of a non-entity; and therefore impossible?

6. If I am not to lose my existence at death, may it not be properly said that I am naturally immortal?

7. Do we not necessarily ascribe our volitions or actions to ourselves?

8. Do we not determine ourselves?

9. If we do not determine ourselves, are we not deceived when we ascribe our actions to ourselves; and, for that reason, reckon ourselves accountable for them?

10. Does it follow from its being certain, in any instance, that we shall determine ourselves in a particular way, that we do not, in that instance, determine ourselves at all?

In answer to these queries, I wished for no more than a simple affirmation or negation; thinking it would be a matter of some curiosity, should it appear that our minds were so differently framed, as that one of us would write a *yes* where the other would write a *no.* But I find that we are more nearly agreed than I expected. To the two first queries, Dr. Priestley has given no direct answer; but what he has said in different places, seems to imply that he would agree with me in answering them in the negative. The 3d query he has, in p. 50, answered, as I should, in the affirmative; and the 4th and 6th in the negative. It appears, however, I think, that I had some reason for expecting that he would not grant the soul to be a *substance;* much less *one single substance.* For the obvious inference from hence, is, that the soul cannot be, either any system of substances, or the *organization* of any system; and, therefore, not such an assemblage of substances as the brain, or the organization of the brain.

To the 7th query it appears also (see p. 65), that he answers in the affirmative, and yet that to the 8th he answers in the negative. In other words, he acknowledges that we necessarily ascribe our determinations to ourselves, but denies that we do *really* determine ourselves; asserting, in answer to the 9th query, that we are deceived when we imagine that our volitions are not produced by a cause foreign to our wills, and *on that account* believe ourselves responsible for them; all self-determination being impossible, and *accountableness* or liableness to punishment being only the connexion which Divine wisdom, in order to produce the greatest ultimate good, has established between certain *voluntary* though *necessary* actions and certain sufferings.

In several passages in my *Review of Morals* (pp. 301–304, and pp. 349–352, 2d edit.), I have stated, in the best manner I am able, the question concerning Liberty and Necessity. Dr. Priestley, in his second volume, Sect. V. and VI. (Vol. III. pp. 480–492,) has replied to what I have said in most of those passages, with *candour* and *ability:* but I cannot say that I think he has done it with *success.* He seems to misunderstand me, and, therefore, I will endeavour to give a more distinct account of my ideas on this subject. If they are wrong, I shall rejoice to see them proved to be so. If they are right, it will be easy to form a judgment of all Dr. Priestley's arguments in his second volume, and to determine how far we *agree* and *differ.*

After Dr. Clarke, I define Liberty to be "a power to act," or "a power of *self-motion* or self-determination." On this definition I would make the following observations:

1. That liberty is common to all *animals,* as well as to all *reasonable beings;* every animal, as such, possessing powers of *self-motion* or *spontaneity.*

2. There are no *degrees* of liberty, because there is no medium between *acting* and *not acting,* or between possessing self-motive powers and not possessing them.

3. The liberty now defined is possible. One thing cannot move another, and that another *in infinitum.* Somewhere or other there must exist a power of beginning motion, that is, of *self-motion.* This is no less certain than that, since one thing cannot produce another, and that another *in infinitum,* there must be a *first* cause.

This argument seems to me decisive, not only for the *possibility,* but the *actual existence* of liberty. But farther. We are conscious of it in ourselves. I can say nothing to convince a person who will declare that he believes *his* determinations do not originate *with himself,* or that he has no power of moving or determining himself. It is another question, whether he moves himself *with* or *without* a regard to *motives*. Asserting self-determination with a regard to motives, (and no one ever yet asserted the contrary,) is asserting *self-determination,* and, therefore, it is the same with asserting liberty. Dr. Priestley often says, that self-determination implies an effect without a cause. But this cannot be justly said. Does it follow that because I am *myself* the cause, there is no cause?

4. This definition implies, that in our volitions, or determinations, we are not *acted upon. Acting* and being *acted upon* are incompatible with one another. In whatever instances, therefore, it is truly said of us that we *act,* in those instances we cannot be *acted upon.* A being in receiving a change of its state, from the exertion of an adequate force, is not an *agent.* Man, therefore, would not be an *agent,* were all his volitions derived from any force, or the effects of any mechanical causes. In this case it would be no more true that he ever acts, than it is true of a ball that it *acts* when *struck* by another ball. But the main observation I would make is the following:

5. "The liberty now defined is consistent with acting with a regard to motives." This has been already intimated; but it is necessary it should be particularly attended to and explained.

Supposing a power of self-determination to exist, it is by no means necessary that it should be exerted without a regard to any end or rule. On the contrary, it can never be exerted without some view or design. Whoever acts, means to do somewhat. This is true of the lowest reptile, as well as of the wisest man. The power of determining ourselves, by the very nature of it, wants an *end* and *rule* to guide it; and no probability, or certainty, of its being exerted agreeably to a rule, can have the least tendency to infringe or diminish it. All that should be avoided here, is, the intolerable absurdity of making our reasons and ends in acting the physical *causes* or *efficients* of action. This is the same with ascribing the action of walking, not to the feet (or the power which moves the feet), but to the eye, which only *sees the way.* The perception of a reason for acting, or the judgment of the understanding, is no more than seeing the way. It is the eye of the mind, which informs and directs; and whatever *certainty* there may be that a particular determination will follow, such determination will be the *self-determination* of the mind, and not any change of its state stamped upon it, over which it has no power, and in receiving which, instead of being an *agent,* it is merely a *passive subject* of agency.

In a word. There is a distinction here of the last importance, which must never be overlooked. I mean the distinction so much insisted on by Dr. Clarke, between the *operation* of *physical causes,* and the *influence* of *moral reasons.* The views or ideas of beings may be the *account* or *occasions* of their acting; but it is a contradiction to make them the *mechanical efficients* of their actions. And yet I suspect that Dr. Priestley will avow this to be his opinion. Ideas he makes to be divisible and extended. He ascribes an impulsive force to them; and asserts that they act by mechanical laws on the mind, as one material substance acts upon another. See his *Replies,* pp. 36, 49, 53; and the *Disquisitions* (Vol. III. p. 250).

In order better to explain the distinction I have mentioned, I will beg leave to give an account of the following particulars, in which it appears to me that *physical* and *moral* causes differ.

1. The one are *beings;* the others are only the *views* of beings.

2. The one always *do,* and the other *may* produce a certainty of event. But the certainties in these two cases differ essentially. It is, for instance, *certain* that a man dragged along like a piece of timber, will follow the superior force that acts upon him. It may be also *certain,* that a man invited by the hope of a reward, will follow a guide. But who sees not that these certainties, having different foundations, are of a totally different nature? In both cases the man might in common speech be said to *follow;* but his following in the one case, however certain in event, would be *his own* agency: in the other case, it would be the agency of *another.* In the one case, he would really *follow;* but in the other case, being dragged, he could not properly be said to *follow.* In the one case, superior power moves him; in the other, he moves himself. In short, to ascribe a necessary and physical efficiency to motives, is (as Dr. Clarke has observed), the same with saying, that *an abstract notion can strike a ball.*

3. The certainty of event arising from the operation of *physical* causes is always equal and invariable; but the certainty of event arising from *moral* causes, that is, from the views and perceptions of beings, admits of an infinite variety of degrees, and sometimes passes into *probability* and *contingency.*

Supposing contrary reasons equally balanced in the mind, it may be *uncertain* how a being will act. If, for instance, a temptation to an act of wickedness comes in the way of a man whose love of virtue is nearly equal to the strength of his passions, it may be doubtful which way he will determine. If his love of virtue exceeds the influence of passion, there will be a *probability* of his acting virtuously, proportioned to the degree in which the love of virtue prevails within him: and it may be so prevalent as to make it *certain* that he will always follow his perceptions of virtue.

4. In the operation of physical causes, it is always implied that there is not in any sense a power to produce, or a possibility of producing, any other effect than that which is produced; but the contrary

is true of effects dependent on the wills, and occasioned by the views of free agents. A benevolent man will *certainly* relieve misery when it falls in his way; but he has the *power* of not relieving it. On the contrary, a stone thrown from the hand *must* move. There is no sense in which it can be said, that it possesses the power of not moving in the precise direction in which it is thrown. The reason of this is, that the benevolent man *acts:* the stone only *suffers.* Were the determination to give relief in the former case, and the motions of the stone in the latter, both alike *sufferances* (if I may so speak), or both effects of a force which could not be resisted, they would be both alike void of all merit. A man at the bottom of St. Paul's *will* not jump *up:* a man at the top *will* not jump *down.* Both events may be *certain.* But a man at the bottom *cannot* jump up: a man at the top *can* jump down. And if in common speech we should say, in the latter case, that a man at the top *cannot* jump down, we should speak figuratively and improperly; meaning only that he certainly *will* not. . . .

SECTION III
OF THE DOCTRINE OF NECESSITY

On this subject Dr. Price refers me to the decisions of what he calls *common sense,* or the notions of the vulgar, (p. 93). These I have observed, as far as they go, are uniformly in favour of the doctrine of necessity. For if men were properly interrogated, they would admit all that I require in order to a proper demonstration of the doctrine; though, not being used to reflection, they do not *pursue* or even *apprehend* the consequences. See my *Treatise on Necessity,* Vol. III. p. 505.

As to the consistency of the *popular language* with the doctrine of necessity, I have again and again made observations upon it, which I think it unnecessary to repeat, in answer to the conclusion of Dr. Price's note, p. 98.

Dr. Price says, that he "cannot conceive of a more groundless assertion," than "that the doctrine of liberty implies that a man in acting wickedly or virtuously, acts without a motive," (p. 94). But after putting a case in which he supposes motives to be exactly equal, viz. the combination of *passion* and *interest* on one side, and of *conscience* and *duty* on the other, he makes liberty to consist in our possessing *a power of making either of them the motive that shall prevail.*

Now it appears to me to require very little power of analyzation to see that before the mind can decide to which of the motives it shall give this preference, it must form a previous, real and most serious *determination,* and that this previous determination requires a motive as much as the final determination itself, especially as Dr. Price expressly acknowledges that "it is nonsense to deny the influence of motives, or to maintain that there are no fixed principles and ends by which the will is guided," (p. 95). In the case above mentioned I have the choice of two things, viz. either to give the preponderance to the *motives of interest,* or to *those of duty,* which, being by supposition exactly equal, are themselves out of the question, and therefore cannot at all contribute to the decision. Now this being a real determination of the mind, it must, by Dr. Price's own confession, require some motive or other.

This argument I own is quite new to me, and therefore I presume that it is, in part, the *new matter* which Dr. Price observes (p. 85) is contained in these *Additional Observations;* but I know he will excuse my frankness if I tell him, that it appears to me to be the last retreat of the doctrine of philosophical liberty, and not at all more tenable than any of those out of which it has been already driven. For when *all argument* fails, he will hardly take refuge in the *common sense* of my Scotch antagonists. I could say more on the subject of this new idea of *the mind choosing the motive on which it will decide,* but I think what I have now said may be sufficient.

I would take this opportunity of observing that if the motives, in the case above-mentioned, be not of a *moral* nature, (and since both the motive of *interest* on one side, and that of *duty* on the other, are expressly excluded, every thing else of a moral nature seems to be excluded along with them) the determination cannot with propriety be denominated *moral,* or be said to be either *virtuous* or *vicious.*

Dr. Price, on this occasion, supposes that a strict equality of motives is a very common case. I answer that we are, indeed, sometimes sensible of it, but that then the determination always remains in suspense. For it appears to me that, if we give attention to the state of our minds, we shall see reason enough to conclude that we never come to an actual determination without a sufficient preponderance of motive. And if we consider that the force of a motive depends upon *the state of the mind* to which it is presented, as well as upon what it is in itself, that the state of mind is in perpetual fluctuation, and that the point of light in which we view the same thing is continually varying, we shall not be at all surprised that, in ordinary cases, when nothing of much consequence is depending, we determine with such readiness, and from motives so evanescent, that we are not able to trace the progress of our thoughts, so as distinctly to recollect the real causes of our choice, after the shortest interval of time. If it were possible to make a balance which should support a thousand pounds' weight, and yet turn with one thousandth part of a grain, would it be any wonder that a person should not be able easily to bring it to an equipoise? But what is even this to the exquisite structure of the mind?

Dr. Price acknowledges, as above, that "it is nonsense to deny the influence of motives, or to maintain that there are no fixed principles and ends by which the will is guided;" but at the same time he says "that this nonsense is scarcely equal to that of confounding *moral* with *physical causes,*" (p. 95). Now if what I have said on this subject both in my *Treatise on Necessity,* and in my *Letter to Dr. Horsley*[1] be not satisfactory, I shall despair of ever being able to give satisfaction with respect to any thing. I will even grant moral and physical causes to be as different, in their nature and operation, as Dr. Price himself can possibly suppose them to be; but if they be really *causes,* producing *certain effects,* that is, if we be so constituted, as that one definite determination shall always follow a definite state of mind, it must be true that, without a miracle, no volition, or action, could have been otherwise than it *has been, is,* or *is to be;* and this is all that, as a necessarian, I contend for. If any person can please himself with calling this *liberty,* or the result of the *mind's determining itself,* I have no sort of objection, because these are mere *words* and *phrases.* . . .

PRICE'S WRITINGS

A *Review of the Principal Questions in Morals,* 3rd edition (London, 1787), has been Edited by D. D. Raphael (Oxford, 1948). *A Free Discussion of the Doctrines of Materialism and Philosophical Necessity* (London, 1778), is available only in early printings or in Rutt's edition of Priestley's *Works,* Vol. IV. *Four Dissertations,* of which only the fourth, "On the Importance of Christianity, the Nature of Historical Evidence, and Miracles" is of philosophical interest, appeared in five editions in London between 1767 and 1811.

WRITINGS ON PRICE

The literature on Price's philosophy is not large and all of it is chiefly concerned with his ethical views. The *Introduction* to Raphael's edition of the *Review of Morals* has a short but very useful section on Price's epistemology. In the same author's *The Moral Sense* (London, 1947), the chapter on Price contains much interesting discussion of the theory of knowledge which Price supported. There are two books in English on Price's ethics: *The Moral Philosophy of Richard Price* by L. Aqvist (Lund, 1960), and *Reason and Virtue* by A. S. Cua (Athens, Ohio, 1966). The former, though concerned with some of the epistemological questions dealt with by Price, uses an irritatingly formal apparatus. The latter book contains a straightforward chapter on Price's theory of knowledge. Of the few articles on Price as philosopher, that by W. H. F. Barnes, "Richard Price: A Neglected Eighteenth-Century Moralist," *Philosophy,* Vol. XVII (1942), attempts to arouse interest in Price's ethics. In "The indefinability and simplicity of Rightness in Richard Price's

[1] Reprinted in Volume IV of Priestley's *Works,* edited by J. T. Rutt (London, 1817–1832). Ed.

Review of Morals," Philosophy and Phenomenological Research, Vol. XIV
(1953–54), B. Peach considers Price's remarks on similarity of meaning. In
the same issue there is a rejoinder by H. D. Aiken, "The Ultimacy of Rightness in Richard Price's Ethics: A Reply to Mr. Peach." There is a counter-
rejoinder by Peach, "History of Philosophy as Justifiable Interpretation: A
Reply to Henry Aiken," in the same Journal, Vol. XVI (1955–56). *The Problem of Knowledge in Scottish Philosophy* (Lund, 1935), by T. T. Segerstedt,
discusses, in the essay on Reid, the relation of his epistemological views to
those of Price.

DUGALD STEWART

1753–1828

As the son of the Professor of Mathematics at the University of Edinburgh, Stewart was well placed to inherit, as he did, Reid's title to the leadership of the Scottish school of Common Sense philosophy. At school he interested himself in the Latin classics. At Edinburgh University, which he entered in 1765, Stewart studied Greek, mathematics, and philosophy. In particular, he read Reid's *Inquiry* and became a life-long supporter of that writer's views. In 1771–72, Stewart attended Reid's lectures in Glasgow, thus beginning a friendship with him that lasted for many years. Stewart returned to Edinburgh in 1772 in order to share the lecturing duties of his ailing father, and from 1775 to 1778 they were joint professors. In the latter year he also took over the moral philosophy lectures of Adam Ferguson, who was absent in America on a government mission. Two years later Ferguson resigned and Stewart obtained his Chair, lecturing on all branches of philosophy, on politics, rhetoric, and political economy.

Always a political liberal, Stewart welcomed the onset of the French Revolution. Three years after the death of his first wife in 1787, he remarried, and his second wife made their home a social and intellectual center for the liberal thinkers of the period, aided by the fact that many English students, no longer able to go to the Continent because of the disturbances there, were attracted to Edinburgh. Stewart's intellectual and moral influence on young men of ability was great. Not only was his character much admired, but he was thought to show "eloquence in his very spitting." His students and friends included the most distinguished public figures of the next few decades: Sydney Smith, Francis Horner, Sir Walter Scott, James Mill, Sir James Mackintosh, and the Lords Brougham, Cockburn, Dudley, Jeffrey, Palmerston, and Russell. When the Whigs came to power in 1806, Stewart was given a handsome sinecure. But by 1809 his always poor health had become worse, and he arranged to have his student Thomas Brown take over his duties as conjoint Professor while Stewart himself retired to the country in order to prepare his lectures for publication. This arrangement lasted until Brown's death in 1820, although Stewart disapproved of Brown's later attacks on Reid's philosophy. Despite a stroke in 1820, Stewart, with his daughter's help, worked on his lectures until his death eight years later. His friends, who were both numerous and appreciative, raised a monument to him in Edinburgh.

Stewart's philosophical writings consist, to a very large extent, of his university lectures reworked for publication. His books suffer, therefore, from the vices of the fascinating lecturer. They contain a wide variety of airs and graces which no longer appeal, and a cascade of examples, allusions, repetitions, and footnotes which conceal rather than clarify his argument. Even more irritating, perhaps, Stewart's books are full of threats and promises which are so highly qualified and refer to such a distant portion of his future argument that their fulfillment is unrecognizable. These defects can also be found in the lectures of Reid and Brown; but in them the manner is far less ornate and the matter more substantial. The result in the case of all three men, and Stewart in particular, is that the quality of their work is much improved by rigid selection.

Stewart's first book was Vol. I of *Elements of the Philosophy of the Human Mind* (1792). Thereafter, he published: *Outlines of Moral Philosophy* (1793) as a text book for his students; *Philosophical Essays* (1810) on the systems of Locke, Berkeley, Priestley, and Horne Tooke; Vol. II of the *Elements* (1814) from which all the present selections are taken; *A General View of the Progress of Metaphysical, Ethical and Political Philosophy Since the Revival of Letters* (1816–21), a collection of articles which appeared as supplements to the fourth and fifth editions of the *Encyclopaedia Britannica; The Philosophy of the Active and Moral Powers of Man,* 2 vol. (1828). Stewart also wrote lengthy accounts of the life and work of both Adam Smith (1794) and Reid (1802). Among his other writings are *Lectures on Political Economy,* unpublished until 1856 but first delivered in 1800.

Stewart, more than Reid himself, was the first academic expounder of Reid's philosophy. In the hands of the former, however, Reid's principles of common sense are rechristened "fundamental laws of belief." Stewart distinguishes, as Reid did not, between the premises used in an argument and its presuppositions—those beliefs whose truth is taken for granted in the statement of the argument. This is an interesting point because the injunction against treating the principle of inference of an inductive argument as one of its premises was later emphasized by Lewis Carroll in his treatment of the paradox of Achilles and the tortoise. In general, Stewart's remarks on reasoning, deduction, and induction relieve him of the charge that he was merely a fluent follower of Reid. On these topics his comments are a considerable advance on the doctrine of Reid, and they present Stewart at the very respectable height of his abilities.

Stewart was first translated into French by his friend Pierre Prévost, and later by Jouffroy. Through their advocacy, as well as Royer-Collard's and Victor Cousin's (philosopher and sometime minister of public instruction), Stewart's views, like those of Reid and Brown, were given wide and long-lived circulation in France. At home, Sir William Hamilton considered himself the natural heir to many of Stewart's principles; and if they had not met with such strong competition from both utilitarianism and the rising influence of Kant, they might have lasted as far into the nineteenth century in Britain as they did in the denominational colleges of North America.

SELECTIONS FROM

Elements of the Philosophy
of the Human Mind *

*

CHAPTER I

FUNDAMENTAL LAWS OF BELIEF

. . . At present I shall only add, to what Mr. Locke has so well stated,[1] that even in *mathematics* it cannot with any propriety be said, that the axioms are the foundation on which the science rests, or the first principles from which its more recondite truths are deduced. Of this I have little doubt that Locke was perfectly aware; but the mistakes which some of the most acute and enlightened of his disciples have committed in treating of the same subject, convince me, that a further elucidation of it is not altogether superfluous. With this view I shall here introduce a few remarks on a passage in Dr. Campbell's *Philosophy of Rhetoric*,[2] in which he has betrayed some misappre-

---

* Vols. II and III, in *The Collected Works of Dugald Stewart,* Edited by Sir William Hamilton, Edinburgh, 1854.

[1] *Essay*, Book IV, Chapter VII, Section XI, 2–3. Ed.

[2] London and Edinburgh, 1776. Reprinted and Edited by L. F. Bitzer (Carbondale, Ill., 1963). Ed.

hensions on this very point, which a little more attention to the hints already quoted from the *Essay on Human Understanding* might have prevented. These remarks will, I hope, contribute to place the nature of axioms, more particularly of mathematical axioms, in a different and clearer light than that in which they have been commonly considered.

"Of intuitive evidence," says Dr. Campbell, "that of the following propositions may serve as an illustration:—'One and four make five.' 'Things equal to the same thing are equal to one another.' 'The whole is greater than a part;' and, in brief, all *axioms* in arithmetic and geometry. These are, in effect, but so many different expositions of our own general notions taken in different views. Some of them are no more than definitions, or equivalent to definitions. To say 'One and four make *five,*' is precisely the same thing as to say, 'We give the name of *five* to one added to four.' In fact, they are all in some respects reducible to this axiom, 'Whatever is, is.' I do not say they are deduced from it, for they have in like manner that original and intrinsic evidence which makes them, as soon as the terms are understood, to be perceived intuitively. And if they are not thus perceived, no deduction of reason will ever confer on them any additional evidence. Nay, in point of time, the discovery of the less general truths has the priority, not from their superior evidence, but solely from this consideration, that the less general are sooner objects of perception to us. . . . But I affirm, that though not deduced from that axiom, they may be considered as particular exemplifications of it, and coincident with it, inasmuch as they are all implied in this, that the properties of our clear and adequate ideas can be no other than what the mind clearly perceives them to be.

"But in order to prevent mistakes, it will be necessary further to illustrate this subject. It might be thought that, if axioms were propositions perfectly identical, it would be impossible to advance a step, by their means, beyond the simple ideas first perceived by the mind. And it must be owned, if the predicate of the proposition were nothing but a repetition of the subject, under the same aspect, and in the same or synonymous terms, no conceivable advantage could be made of it for the furtherance of knowledge. Of such propositions, for instance, as these—'Seven are seven,' 'Eight are eight,' and 'Ten added to eleven are equal to ten added to eleven,' it is manifest that we could never avail ourselves for the improvement of science. Nor does the change of the term make any alteration in point of utility. The propositions, 'Twelve are a dozen,' 'Twenty are a score,' unless considered as explications of the words *dozen* and *score,* are equally insignificant with the former. But when the thing, though in effect coinciding, is considered under a different aspect; when what is single in the subject is divided in the predicate, and conversely; or when what is a whole in the one, is regarded as a part of something else in the other; such propositions lead to the discovery of innumerable and apparently remote relations. One added to four may be accounted no other than a definition of the word *five,* as was remarked above. But when I say, 'Two added to three are equal to five,' I advance a truth which, though equally clear, is quite distinct from the preceding. Thus, if one should affirm, 'Twice fifteen make thirty,' and again, 'Thirteen added to seventeen make thirty,' nobody would pretend that he had repeated the same proposition in other words. The cases are entirely similar. In both cases, the same thing is predicated of ideas which, taken severally, are different. From these, again, result other equations, as 'One added to four are equal to two added to three,' and 'Twice fifteen are equal to thirteen added to seventeen.'

"Now, it is by the aid of such simple and elementary principles, that the arithmetician and algebraist proceed to the most astonishing discoveries. Nor are the operations of the geometrician essentially different. . . ." [1]

I have little to object to these observations of Dr. Campbell, as far as they relate to arithmetic and to algebra; for in these sciences, all our investigations amount to nothing more than to a comparison of different expressions of the same thing. Our common language, indeed, frequently supposes the case to be otherwise; as when an equation is defined to be, "A proposition asserting the equality of two quantities." It would, however, be much more correct to define it, "A proposition asserting the equivalence of two expressions of the same quantity;" for algebra is merely a *universal arithmetic;* and the names of numbers are nothing else than collectives, by which we are enabled to express ourselves more concisely than could be done by enumerating all the units that they contain. Of this doctrine, the passage now quoted from Dr. Campbell shews that he entertained a sufficiently just and precise idea.

But if Dr. Campbell perceived that arithmetical equations, such as "one and four make five," are no other than definitions, why should he have classed them with the axioms he quotes from Euclid, "That the whole is greater than a part," and that "Things equal to the same thing are equal to one another;"—propositions which, however clearly their truth be implied in the meaning of the terms of which they consist, cannot certainly, by any interpretation, be considered in the light of definitions at all analogous to the former? The former, indeed, are only explanations of the relative import of particular names; the latter are universal propositions, applicable alike to an infinite variety of instances.

Another very obvious consideration might have satisfied Dr. Campbell, that the simple arithmetical equations which he mentions do not

[1] *Philosophy of Rhetoric,* Book I, Chapter V, Section I.

hold the same place in that science which Euclid's axioms hold in geometry. What I allude to is, that the greater part of these axioms are equally essential to all the different branches of mathematics. That "the whole is greater than a part," and that "things equal to the same thing are equal to one another," are propositions as essentially connected with our arithmetical computations as with our geometrical reasonings; and therefore, to explain in what manner the mind makes a transition, in the case of numbers, from the more simple to the more complicated equations, throws no light whatever on the question *how* the transition is made, either in arithmetic or in geometry, from what are properly called axioms, to the more remote conclusions in these sciences.

The very fruitless attempt thus made by this acute writer to illustrate the importance of axioms as the basis of mathematical truth, was probably suggested to him by a doctrine which has been repeatedly inculcated of late, concerning the grounds of that peculiar evidence which is allowed to accompany mathematical demonstration. "All the sciences (it has been said) rest ultimately on first principles, which we must take for granted without proof; and whose evidence determines, both in kind and degree, the evidence which it is possible to attain in our conclusions. In some of the sciences, our first principles are intuitively certain, in others they are intuitively probable; and such as the evidence of these principles is, such must that of our conclusions be. If our first principles are intuitively certain, and if we reason from them consequentially, our conclusions will be demonstratively certain; but if our principles be only intuitively probable, our conclusions will be only demonstratively probable. In mathematics, the first principles from which we reason are a set of axioms which are not only intuitively certain, but of which we find it impossible to conceive the contraries to be true: and hence the peculiar evidence which belongs to all the conclusions that follow from these principles as necessary consequences."

To this view of the subject Dr. Reid has repeatedly given his sanction, at least in the most essential points; more particularly, in controverting an assertion of Locke's, that "no science is, or hath been, built on *maxims*."—"Surely," says Dr. Reid, "Mr. Locke was not ignorant of geometry, which hath been built upon maxims prefixed to the *Elements,* as far back as we are able to trace it. But though they had not been prefixed, which was a matter of utility rather than necessity, yet it must be granted, that every demonstration in geometry is grounded either upon propositions formerly demonstrated, or upon self-evident principles." [1]

1 *Essays on Intellectual Powers,* p. 647, 4th edition. [See p. 467 of Reid's *Philosophical Works,* Vol. I, Edited by Sir William Hamilton (Edinburgh, 1846). It gives the corresponding pagination of the 1785 edition to which Stewart is referring in these selections. Ed.]

On another occasion he expresses himself thus:—"I take it to be certain, that whatever can, by just reasoning, be inferred from a principle that is necessary, must be a necessary truth. Thus, as the axioms in mathematics are all necessary truths, so are all the conclusions drawn from them; that is, the whole body of that science." [1]

That there is something fundamentally erroneous in these very strong statements with respect to the relation which Euclid's axioms bear to the geometrical theorems which follow, appears sufficiently from a consideration which was long ago mentioned by Locke—that from these axioms it is not possible for human ingenuity to deduce a single inference. "It was not," says Locke, "the influence of those maxims which are taken for principles in mathematics, that hath led the masters of that science into those wonderful discoveries they have made. Let a man of good parts know all the maxims generally made use of in mathematics, never so perfectly, and contemplate their extent and consequences as much as he pleases, he will by their assistance, I suppose, scarce ever come to know that 'the square of the hypothenuse in a right angled triangle, is equal to the squares of the two other sides.' The knowledge that 'the whole is equal to all its parts,' and, 'if you take equals from equals, the remainders will be equal,' helped him not, I presume, to this demonstration: And a man may, I think, pore long enough on those axioms, without ever seeing one jot the more of mathematical truths." [2] But surely, if this be granted, and if, at the same time, by the first principles of a science be meant those fundamental propositions from which its remoter truths are derived, the axioms cannot, with any consistency, be called the First Principles of Mathematics. They have not (it will be admitted) the most distant analogy to what are called the First Principles of Natural Philosophy; to those general facts, for example, of the gravity and elasticity of the air, from which may be deduced, as consequences, the suspension of the mercury in the Torricellian tube, and its fall when carried up to an eminence. According to this meaning of the word, the principles of mathematical science are, *not* the axioms, but the *definitions;* which definitions hold, in mathematics, precisely the same place that is held in natural philosophy by such general facts as have now been referred to.[3]

---

[1] *Essays on Intellectual Powers*, p. 577. See also pp. 560, 561, 606.

[2] *Essay on Human Understanding*, Book IV, Chapter XII, Section XV.

[3] In order to prevent cavil, it may be necessary for me to remark here, that, when I speak of mathematical axioms, I have in view only such as are of the same description with the *first nine* of those which are prefixed to the *Elements* of Euclid; for, in that list. it is well known, that there are several which belong to a class of propositions altogether different from the others. That "all right angles (for example) are equal to one another;" that "when one straight line falling on two other straight lines, makes the two interior angles on the same side less than two right angles, these two straight lines, if produced, shall meet on the side where are the two angles less than two right

From what principle are the various properties of the circle derived, but from the definition of a circle? From what principle the properties of the parabola or ellipse, but from the definitions of these curves? A similar observation may be extended to all the other theorems which the mathematician demonstrates: And it is this observation, (which, obvious as it may seem, does not appear to have occurred in all its force, either to Locke, to Reid, or to Campbell,) that furnishes, if I mistake not, the true explanation of the peculiarity already remarked in mathematical evidence.

The prosecution of this last idea properly belongs to the subject of mathematical demonstration, of which I intend to treat afterwards. In the meantime, I trust that enough has been said to correct those misapprehensions of the nature of axioms, which are countenanced by the speculations, and still more by the phraseology, of some late eminent writers. On this article, my own opinion coincides very nearly with that of Mr. Locke—both in the view which he has given of the nature and use of axioms in geometry, and in what he has so forcibly urged concerning the danger, in other branches of knowledge, of attempting a similar list of *maxims,* without a due regard to the circumstances by which different sciences are distinguished from one another. With Mr. Locke, too, I must beg leave to guard myself against the possibility of being misunderstood in the illustrations which I have offered of some of his ideas; and for this purpose, I cannot do better than borrow his words. "In all that is here suggested concerning the little use of axioms for the improvement of knowledge, or dangerous use in undetermined ideas, I have been far enough from saying or intending they should be laid aside, as some have been too forward to charge me. I affirm them to be truths, self-evident truths; and so cannot be laid aside. As far as their influence will reach, it is in vain to endeavour, nor would I attempt to abridge it. But yet, without any injury to truth or knowledge, I may have reason to think their use is not answerable to the great stress which seems to be laid on them, and I may warn men not to make an ill use of them, for the confirming themselves in error." [1]

After what has been just stated, it is scarcely necessary for me again to repeat, with regard to mathematical axioms, that although

---

angles;" are manifestly principles which bear no analogy to such barren *truisms* as these: "Things that are equal to one and the same thing are equal to one another;" "If equals be added to equals, the wholes are equal;" "If equals be taken from equals, the remainders are equal." Of these propositions, the two former (the 10th and 11th axioms, to wit, in Euclid's list) are evidently theorems which, in point of strict logical accuracy, ought to be demonstrated; as may be easily done with respect to the first, in a single sentence. That the second has not yet been proved in a simple and satisfactory manner, has been long considered as a sort of reproach to mathematicians; and I have little doubt that this reproach will continue to exist, till the basis of the science be somewhat enlarged, by the introduction of one or two new definitions, to serve as additional principles of geometrical reasoning.

[1] Locke's *Essay,* Book IV, Chapter VII, Section XIV.

they are not the *principles* of our reasoning, either in arithmetic or in geometry, their truth is supposed or implied in all our reasonings in both; and, if it were called in question, our further progress would be impossible. In both of these respects, we shall find them analogous to the other classes of primary or elemental truths which remain to be considered.

Nor let it be imagined, from this concession, that the dispute turns merely on the meaning annexed to the word *principle*. It turns upon an important question of fact,—Whether the theorems of geometry rest on the *axioms,* in the same sense in which they rest on the *definitions?* or, (to state the question in a manner still more obvious,) Whether axioms hold a place in geometry at all analogous to what is occupied in natural philosophy, by those sensible phenomena which form the basis of that science? Dr. Reid compares them sometimes to the one set of propositions, and sometimes to the other. If the foregoing observations be just, they bear no analogy to either.

Into this indistinctness of language Dr. Reid was probably led in part by Sir Isaac Newton, who, with a very illogical latitude in the use of words, gave the name of *axioms* to the *laws of motion,* and also to those general experimental truths which form the ground-work of our reasonings in catoptrics and dioptrics. For such a misapplication of the technical terms of mathematics some apology might perhaps be made, if the author had been treating on any subject connected with moral science; but surely in a work entitled *Mathematical Principles of Natural Philosophy,* the word *axiom* might reasonably have been expected to be used in a sense somewhat analogous to that which every person liberally educated is accustomed to annex to it, when he is first initiated into the elements of geometry.

The question to which the preceding discussion relates is of the greater consequence, that the prevailing mistake with respect to the nature of mathematical axioms, has contributed much to the support of a very erroneous theory concerning mathematical evidence, which is, I believe, pretty generally adopted at present—that it all resolves ultimately into the perception of *identity;* and that it is this circumstance which constitutes the peculiar and characteristical cogency of mathematical demonstration.

Of some of the other arguments which have been alleged in favour of this theory, I shall afterwards have occasion to take notice. At present it is sufficient for me to remark, (and this I flatter myself I may venture to do with some confidence, after the foregoing reasonings,) that in so far as it rests on the supposition that all geometrical truths are ultimately derived from Euclid's axioms, it proceeds on an assumption totally unfounded in fact, and indeed so obviously false, that nothing but its antiquity can account for the facility with which it continues to be admitted by the learned.

[SUBSECTION] II.—CONTINUATION OF THE SAME SUBJECT

The difference of opinion between Locke and Reid, of which I took notice in the foregoing part of this Section, appears greater than it really is, in consequence of an ambiguity in the word *principle,* as employed by the latter. In its proper acceptation, it seems to me to denote an assumption, (whether resting on fact or on hypothesis,) upon which, as a *datum,* a train of reasoning proceeds; and for the falsity or incorrectness of which no logical rigour in the subsequent process can compensate. Thus the gravity and the elasticity of the air are *principles of reasoning* in our speculations about the barometer. The equality of the angles of incidence and reflexion; the proportionality of the sines of incidence and refraction, are *principles of reasoning* in catoptrics and in dioptrics. In a sense perfectly analogous to this, the *definitions* of geometry (all of which are merely *hypothetical*) are the *first principles* of reasoning in the subsequent demonstrations, and the basis on which the whole fabric of the science rests.

I have called this the *proper* acceptation of the word, because it is that in which it is most frequently used by the best writers. It is also most agreeable to the literal meaning which its etymology suggests, expressing the original point from which our reasoning sets out or commences.

Dr. Reid often uses the word in this sense, as, for example, in the following sentence already quoted: "From three or four axioms, which he calls *regulæ philosophandi,* together with *the phenomena observed by the senses, which he likewise lays down as first principles,* Newton deduces, by strict reasoning, the propositions contained in the third book of his *Principia,* and in his *Optics.*"

On other occasions, he uses the same word to denote those *elemental* truths (if I may use the expression) which are virtually taken for granted or assumed in every step of our reasoning, and without which, although no *consequences* can be directly inferred from them, a train of reasoning would be impossible. Of this kind, in mathematics are the *axioms,* or (as Mr. Locke and others frequently call them) the *maxims;* in physics, a belief of *the continuance of the Laws of Nature;* in all our reasonings, without exception, a belief in *our own identity,* and in *the evidence of memory.* Such truths are the *last elements* into which reasoning resolves itself when subjected to a metaphysical analysis, and which no person but a metaphysician or a logician ever thinks of stating in the form of propositions, or even of expressing verbally to himself. It is to truths of this description that Locke seems in general to apply the name of *maxims;* and, in this sense, it is unquestionably true, that no science (not even geometry) is founded on maxims as its first principles.

In one sense of the word *principle,* indeed, maxims may be called principles of reasoning; for the words *principles* and *elements* are sometimes used as synonymous. Nor do I take upon me to say that this mode of speaking is exceptionable. All that I assert is, that they cannot be called *principles of reasoning,* in the sense which has just now been defined; and that accuracy requires that the word on which the whole question hinges, should not be used in both senses in the course of the same argument. It is for this reason that I have employed the phrase *principles of reasoning* on the one occasion, and *elements of reasoning* on the other.

It is difficult to find unexceptionable language to mark distinctions so completely foreign to the ordinary purposes of speech; but, in the present instance, the line of separation is strongly and clearly drawn by this criterion—that from *principles of reasoning* consequences may be deduced; from what I have called *elements of reasoning,* none ever can.

A process of logical reasoning has been often likened to a chain supporting a weight. If this similitude be adopted, the *axioms* or *elemental truths* now mentioned may be compared to the successive concatenations which connect the different links immediately with each other; the *principles* of our reasoning resemble the hook, or rather the beam, from which the whole is suspended.

The foregoing observations, I am inclined to think, coincide with what was, at bottom, Mr. Locke's opinion on this subject. That he has not stated it with his usual clearness and distinctness, it is impossible to deny; at the same time I cannot subscribe to the following severe criticism of Dr. Reid:—

"Mr. Locke has observed, 'That intuitive knowledge is necessary *to connect* all the steps of a demonstration.' [1]

"From this, I think, it necessarily follows, that in every branch of knowledge we must make use of truths that are intuitively known, in order to *deduce from them* such as require proof.

"But I cannot reconcile this with what he says, (section 8th of the same chapter): 'The necessity of this intuitive knowledge in every step of scientifical or demonstrative reasoning, gave occasion, I imagine, to that mistaken axiom, that all reasoning was *ex præcognitis et præconcessis,* which how far it is mistaken I shall have occasion to shew more at large when I come to consider propositions, and particularly those propositions which are called *maxims,* and to shew that it is by a mistake that they are supposed to be the foundation of all our knowledge and reasonings.' " [2]

The distinction which I have already made between *elements* of reasoning, and *first principles* of reasoning, appears to myself to throw much light on these apparent contradictions.

[1] *Essay,* Book IV, Chapter 2, Section I. Ed.
[2] *Essays on Intellectual Powers,* p. 643, 4th edition.

That the seeming difference of opinion on this point between these two profound writers, arose chiefly from the ambiguities of language, may be inferred from the following acknowledgment of Dr. Reid, which immediately follows the last quotation:—

"I have carefully examined the chapter on *Maxims* which Mr. Locke here refers to, and though one would expect, from the quotation last made, that it should run contrary to what I have before delivered concerning first principles, I find only two or three sentences in it, and those chiefly incidental, to which I do not assent." [1]

Before dismissing this subject, I must once more repeat, that the doctrine which I have been attempting to establish, so far from degrading *axioms* from that rank which Dr. Reid would assign them, tends to identify them still more than he has done with the exercise of our reasoning powers; inasmuch as, instead of comparing them with the *data,* on the accuracy of which that of our conclusion necessarily depends, it considers them as the *vincula* which give coherence to all the particular links of the chain; or (to vary the metaphor) as *component elements,* without which the faculty of reasoning is inconceivable and impossible.

SECTION II—OF CERTAIN LAWS OF BELIEF, INSEPARABLY CONNECTED WITH THE EXERCISE OF CONSCIOUSNESS, MEMORY, PERCEPTION, AND REASONING

1. It is by the immediate evidence of consciousness that we are assured of the *present existence* of our various sensations, whether pleasant or painful; of all our affections, passions, hopes, fears, desires, and volitions. It is thus, too, we are assured of the *present existence* of those thoughts which, during our waking hours, are continually passing through the mind, and of all the different effects which they produce in furnishing employment to our intellectual faculties.

According to the common doctrine of our best philosophers,[2] it is by the evidence of *consciousness* we are assured that we ourselves exist. The proposition, however, when thus stated, is not accurately true; for our own existence (as I have elsewhere observed)[3] is not a direct or immediate object of consciousness, in the strict and logical meaning of that term. We are conscious of sensation, thought, desire, volition; but we are not conscious of the existence of Mind itself; nor would it be possible for us to arrive at the knowledge of it, (supposing us to be created in the full possession of all the intellectual *capacities*

---

1 *Essays on Intellectual Powers,* p. 643, 4th edition.

2 See, in particular, Campbell's *Philosophy of Rhetoric.* [Book I, Chapter V, Part II, p. 37 in Bitzer edition. Ed.]

3 *Philosophical Essays,* 4th edition, p. 7 (infra, Vol. V.) [In Stewart's *Works,* Edited by Hamilton (Edinburgh, 1854). *Philosophical Essays* was first published in 1810. Ed.]

which belong to human nature,) if no impression were ever to be made on our external senses. The moment that, in consequence of such an impression, a sensation is excited, we learn two facts at once, —the existence of the sensation, and our own existence as sentient beings;—in other words, the very first exercise of consciousness necessarily implies a belief, not only of the present existence of what is felt, but of the present existence of *that* which feels and thinks: or (to employ plainer language) the present existence of that being which I denote by the words *I* and *myself*. Of these facts, however, it is the former alone of which we can properly be said to be conscious, agreeably to the rigorous interpretation of the expression. A conviction of the latter, although it seems to be so inseparable from the exercise of consciousness, that it can scarcely be considered as posterior to it in the order of *time,* is yet (if I may be allowed to make use of a scholastic distinction) posterior to it in the order of *nature;* not only as it supposes consciousness to be already awakened by some sensation, or some other mental affection; but as it is evidently rather a judgment accompanying the exercise of that power, than one of its immediate intimations concerning its appropriate class of internal phenomena. It appears to me, therefore, more correct to call the belief of our own existence a concomitant or accessory of the exercise of consciousness, than to say, that our existence is a fact falling under the immediate cognizance of consciousness, like the existence of the various agreeable or painful sensations which external objects excite in our minds.

2. That we cannot, without a very blameable latitude in the use of words, be said to be *conscious* of our personal identity, is a proposition still more indisputable; inasmuch as the very idea of personal identity involves the idea of *time,* and consequently presupposes the exercise not only of *consciousness,* but of *memory.* The belief connected with this idea is implied in every thought and every action of the mind, and may be justly regarded as one of the simplest and most essential elements of the understanding. Indeed, it is impossible to conceive either an intellectual or an active being to exist without it. It is, however, extremely worthy of remark, with respect to this belief, that, universal as it is among our species, nobody but a metaphysician ever thinks of expressing it in words, or of reducing into the shape of a proposition the truth to which it relates. To the rest of mankind, it forms not an object of knowledge; but a condition or supposition, necessarily and unconsciously involved in the exercise of all their faculties. On a part of our constitution, which is obviously one of the last or primordial elements at which it is possible to arrive in analyzing our intellectual operations, it is plainly unphilosophical to suppose, that any new light can be thrown by metaphysical discussion. All that can be done with propriety, in such cases, is to state the fact.

And here, I cannot help taking notice of the absurd and inconsistent attempts which some ingenious men have made, to explain the gradual process by which they suppose the mind to be led to the knowledge of its own existence, and of that continued identity which our constitution leads us to ascribe to it. How (it has been asked) does a child come to form the very abstract and metaphysical idea expressed by the pronoun *I* or *moi?* In answer to this question, I have only to observe, that when we set about the explanation of a phenomenon, we must proceed on the supposition that it is possible to resolve it into some more general law or laws with which we are already acquainted. But, in the case before us, how can this be expected, by those who consider that all our knowledge of mind is derived from the exercise of reflection; and that every act of this power implies a conviction of our own existence as reflecting and intelligent beings? Every theory, therefore, which pretends to account for this conviction, must necessarily involve that sort of paralogism which logicians call a *petitio principii;* inasmuch as it must resolve the thing to be explained into some law or laws, the evidence of which rests ultimately on the assumption in question. From this assumption, which is necessarily implied in the joint exercise of consciousness and memory, the philosophy of the human mind, if we mean to study it analytically, must of necessity set out; and the very attempt to dig deeper for its foundation, betrays a total ignorance of the logical rules, according to which alone it can ever be prosecuted with any hopes of success.

It was, I believe, first marked by M. Prévost[1] of Geneva, (and the remark, obvious as it may appear, reflects much honour on his acuteness and sagacity,) that the inquiries concerning the mind, founded on the hypothesis of the *animated statue*—inquiries which both Bonnet and Condillac professed to carry on analytically—were in truth altogether synthetical. To this criticism it may be added, that their inquiries, in so far as they had for their object to explain the origin of our belief of our own existence, and of our personal identity, assumed, as the principles of their synthesis, facts at once less certain and less familiar than the problem which they were employed to resolve.

Nor is it to the metaphysician only that the ideas of identity and of personality are familiar. Where is the individual who has not experienced their powerful influence over his imagination, while he was employed in reflecting on the train of events which have filled up the past history of his life; and on that internal world, the phenomena of which have been exposed to his own inspection alone? On such an occasion, even the wonders of external nature seem comparatively insignificant; and one is tempted, (with a celebrated French writer,) in contemplating the spectacle of the universe, to adopt the words of the Doge of

[1] Pierre Prévost (1751–1839), physicist and philosopher, published *Des signes envisagés relativement a leur influence sur la formation des idées* (Paris, 1800), and *Essais de philosophie* (Geneva, 1804). Ed.

Genoa, when he visited Versailles—"Ce qui m'étonne le plus ici, c'est de m'y voir." [1]

3. The belief which all men entertain of the existence of the material world, (I mean their belief of its existence independently of that of percipient beings,) and their expectation of the continued uniformity of the laws of nature, belong to the same class of ultimate or elemental laws of thought, with those which have been just mentioned. The truths which form their objects are of an order so radically different from what are commonly called *truths,* in the popular acceptation of that word, that it might perhaps be useful for logicians to distinguish them by some appropriate appellation, such, for example, as that of *metaphysical* or *transcendental* truths. They are not *principles* or *data* (as will afterwards appear) from which any consequence can be deduced; but form a part of those original *stamina* of human reason, which are equally essential to all the pursuits of science, and to all the active concerns of life.

4. I shall only take notice farther, under this head, of the confidence which we must necessarily repose in the evidence of memory, (and, I may add, in the continuance of our personal identity,) when we are employed in carrying on any process of deduction or argumentation,—in following out, for instance, the steps of a long mathematical demonstration. In yielding our assent to the conclusion to which such a demonstration leads, we evidently trust to the fidelity with which our memory has connected the different links of the chain together. The reference which is often made, in the course of a demonstration, to propositions formerly proved, places the same remark in a light still stronger; and shews plainly that, in this branch of knowledge, which is justly considered as the most certain of any, the authority of the same laws of belief which are recognised in the ordinary pursuits of life, is tacitly acknowledged. Deny the evidence of memory as a ground of certain knowledge, and you destroy the foundations of mathematical science as completely as if you were to deny the truth of the axioms assumed by Euclid.

The foregoing examples sufficiently illustrate the nature of that class of truths which I have called *Fundamental Laws of Human Belief,* or *Primary Elements of Human Reason.* A variety of others, not less important, might be added to the list; but these I shall not at present stop to enumerate, as my chief object, in introducing the subject here, was to explain the common relation in which they all stand to deductive evidence. In this point of view, two analogies, or rather coincidences, between the truths which we have been last considering, and the mathematical axioms which were treated of formerly, immediately present themselves to our notice.

---

[1] D'Alembert, *Apologie de l'Etude.* [See *Oeuvres de D'Alembert* (reprinted at Geneva, 1967), Vol. IV, p. 5. Ed.]

1. From neither of these classes of truths can any direct inference be drawn for the farther enlargement of our knowledge. This remark has been already shewn to hold universally with respect to the axioms of geometry; and it applies equally to what I have called Fundamental Laws of Human Belief. From such propositions as these—*I exist; I am the same person to-day that I was yesterday; the material world has an existence independent of my mind; the general laws of nature will continue, in future, to operate uniformly as in time past*—no inference can be deduced, any more than from the intuitive truths prefixed to the *Elements* of Euclid. Abstracted from other *data,* they are perfectly barren in themselves; nor can any possible combination of them help the mind forward one single step in its progress. It is for this reason that, instead of calling them, with some other writers, *first principles,* I have distinguished them by the title of *fundamental laws of belief;* the former word seeming to me to denote, according to common usage, some *fact,* or some *supposition,* from which a series of consequences may be deduced.

If the account now given of these *laws of belief* be just, the great argument which has been commonly urged in support of their authority, and which manifestly confounds them with what are properly called *principles of reasoning,* is not at all applicable to the subject; or at least does not rest the point in dispute upon its right foundation. If there were no first principles, (it has been said,) or in other words, if a reason could be given for everything, no process of deduction could possibly be brought to a conclusion. The remark is indisputably true; but it only proves (what no logician of the present times will venture to deny) that the mathematician could not demonstrate a single theorem, unless he were first allowed to lay down his definitions; nor the natural philosopher explain or account for a single phenomenon, unless he were allowed to assume, as acknowledged facts, certain general laws of nature. What inference does this afford in favour of that particular class of truths to which the preceding observations relate, and against which the ingenuity of modern sceptics has been more particularly directed? If I be not deceived, these truths are still more intimately connected with the operations of the reasoning faculty than has been generally imagined; not as the *principles* (ἀρχαί) from which our reasonings set out, and on which they ultimately depend, but as the necessary *conditions* on which every step of the deduction tacitly proceeds; or rather (if I may use the expression) as essential elements which enter into the composition of reason itself.

2. In this last remark I have anticipated, in some measure, what I had to state with respect to the *second* coincidence alluded to, between mathematical axioms, and the other propositions which I have comprehended under the general title of *fundamental laws of human belief.* As the truth of axioms is virtually presupposed or implied in

the successive steps of every demonstration, so, in every step of our reasonings concerning the order of Nature, we proceed on the supposition, that the laws by which it is regulated will continue uniform as in time past; and that the material universe has an existence independent of our perceptions. I need scarcely add, that, in all our reasonings whatever, whether they relate to necessary or to contingent truths, our own personal identity, and the evidence of memory, are virtually taken for granted. These different truths all agree in this, that they are essentially involved in the exercise of our rational powers; although, in themselves, they furnish no *principles* or *data* by which the sphere of our knowledge can, by any ingenuity, be enlarged. They agree farther in being tacitly acknowledged by all men, learned or ignorant, without any formal enunciation in words, or even any conscious exercise of reflection. It is only at that period of our intellectual progress when scientific arrangements and metaphysical refinements begin to be introduced, that they become objects of attention to the mind, and assume the form of propositions.

In consequence of these two analogies or coincidences, I should have been inclined to comprehend, under the general title of *axioms,* all the truths which have been hitherto under our review, if the common usage of our language had not, in a great measure, appropriated that appellation to the axioms of mathematics; and if the view of the subject which I have taken, did not render it necessary for me to direct the attention of my readers to the wide diversity between the branches of knowledge to which they are respectively subservient.

I was anxious also to prevent these truths from being all identified, in point of logical importance, under the same name. The fact is, that the one class (in consequence of the relation in which they stand to the demonstrative conclusions of geometry) are comparatively of so little moment, that the formal enumeration of them was a matter of choice rather than of necessity; whereas the other class have unfortunately been raised, by the sceptical controversies of modern times, to a conspicuous rank in the philosophy of the human mind. I have thought it more advisable, therefore, to bestow on the latter an appropriate title of their own; without, however, going so far as to reject altogether the phraseology of those who have annexed to the word *axiom* a more enlarged meaning than that which I have usually given to it. Little inconvenience, indeed, can arise from this latitude in the use of the term; provided only it be always confined to those ultimate laws of belief, which, although they form the first elements of human reason, cannot with propriety be ranked among the principles from which any of our scientific conclusions are deduced.

Corresponding to the extension which some late writers have given to *axioms,* is that of the province which they have assigned to *intuition;* a term which has been applied, by Dr. Beattie and others, not only to the power by which we perceive the truth of the axioms of geometry, but to that by which we recognise the authority of the fundamental laws of belief, when we hear them enunciated in language. My only objection to this use of the word is, that it is a departure from common practice; according to which, if I be not mistaken, the proper objects of intuition are propositions analogous to the axioms prefixed to Euclid's *Elements.* In some other respects, this innovation might perhaps be regarded as an improvement on the very limited and imperfect vocabulary of which we are able to avail ourselves in our present discussions.

To the class of truths which I have here called *laws of belief,* or *elements of reason,* the title of *principles of common sense* was long ago given by Father Buffier,[1] whose language and doctrine concerning them bears a very striking resemblance to those of some of our later Scottish logicians. This, at least, strikes me as the meaning which these writers *in general* annex to the phrase, although all of them have frequently employed it with a far greater degree of latitude. When thus limited in its acceptation, it is obviously liable, in point of scientific accuracy, to two very strong objections, both of which have been already sufficiently illustrated. The first is, that it applies the appellation of *principles* to laws of belief from which no inference can be deduced; the second, that it refers the origin of these laws to Common Sense.[2] Nor is this phraseology more agreeable to popular use than to logical precision. If we were to suppose an individual, whose conduct betrayed a disbelief of his own existence, or of his own identity, or of the reality of surrounding objects, it would by no means amount to an adequate description of his condition to say, that he was destitute of *common sense.* We should at once pronounce him to be destitute of *reason,* and would no longer consider him as a fit subject of discipline

---

1 According to Locke, we have the knowledge of our own existence by *intuition;* of the existence of God by *demonstration;* and of other things by *sensation.*—Book IV, Chapter IX, Section 2.

This use of the word *intuition* seems to be somewhat arbitrary. The reality of our own existence is a truth which bears as little analogy to the axioms of mathematics, as any other primary truth whatever. If the province of *intuition,* therefore, be extended as far as it has been carried by Locke in the foregoing sentence, it will not be easy to give a good reason why it should not be enlarged a little farther. The words *intuition* and *demonstration,* it must not be forgotten, have both of them an etymological reference to the sense of seeing; and when we wish to express, in the strongest terms, the most complete evidence which can be set before the mind, we compare it to the light of noon-day;—in other words, we compare it to what Mr. Locke here attempts to degrade, by calling it *the evidence of sensation.* [In *Traité des premières vérités* (1724); translated as *First Truths* (London, 1780). The "striking resemblance" is discussed in *The Scottish Philosophy of Common Sense* by S. A. Grave (Oxford, 1960). Ed.]

2 See the preceding part of this section, with respect to the word *principle;* and the account of Reid's life (infra, Vol. IX), for some remarks on the proper meaning of the phrase *common sense.* [Stewart's account of Reid's life appears in Vol. I of Hamilton's edition of Reid's *Works* and in Vol. IX of Hamilton's edition of Stewart's *Works.* Ed.]

or of punishment. The former expression, indeed, would only imply that he was apt to fall into absurdities and improprieties in the common concerns of life. To denominate, therefore, such laws of belief as we have now been considering, *constituent elements of human reason,* while it seems quite unexceptionable in point of technical distinctness, cannot be justly censured as the slightest deviation from our habitual forms of speech. On the same grounds, it may be fairly questioned, whether the word *reason* would not, on some occasions, be the best substitute which our language affords for *intuition,* in that enlarged acceptation which has been given to it of late. If not quite so definite and precise as might be wished, it would be at least employed in one of those significations in which it is already familiar to every ear; whereas the meaning of *intuition,* when used for the same purpose, is stretched very far beyond its ordinary limits. And in cases of this sort, where we have to choose between two terms, neither of which is altogether unexceptionable, it will be found much safer to trust to the context for restricting in the reader's mind what is too general, than for enlarging what use has accustomed us to interpret in a sense too narrow.

I must add, too, in opposition to the high authorities of Dr. Johnson and Dr. Beattie, that for many years past, *reason* has been very seldom used by philosophical writers, or, indeed, by correct writers of any description, as synonymous with the power of reasoning. *To appeal to the light of human reason from the reasonings of the schools,* is surely an expression to which no good objection can be made, on the score either of vagueness or of novelty. Nor has the etymological affinity between these two words the slightest tendency to throw any obscurity on the foregoing expression. On the contrary, this affinity may be of use in some of our future arguments, by keeping constantly in view the close and inseparable connexion which will be afterwards shewn to exist between the two different intellectual operations which are thus brought into immediate contrast.

.   .   .

CHAPTER II

REASONING AND DEDUCTION

SECTION III
OF MATHEMATICAL DEMONSTRATION

[SUBSECTION] I—OF THE CIRCUMSTANCE ON WHICH DEMONSTRATIVE
EVIDENCE ESSENTIALLY DEPENDS

The peculiarity of that species of evidence which is called demonstrative, and which so remarkably distinguishes our mathematical
conclusions from those to which we are led in other branches of science, is a fact which must have arrested the attention of every person
who possesses the slightest acquaintance with the elements of geometry. And yet I am doubtful if a satisfactory account has been hitherto
given of the circumstances from which it arises. Mr. Locke tells us,
that "what constitutes a demonstration is intuitive evidence at every
step;" and I readily grant, that if, in a single step, such evidence
should fail, the other parts of the demonstration would be of no value.
It does not, however, seem to me that it is on this consideration that
the demonstrative evidence of the conclusion depends—not even
when we add to it another which is much insisted on by Dr. Reid—
that, "in demonstrative evidence our first principles must be intuitively certain." The inaccuracy of this remark I formerly pointed out
when treating of the evidence of axioms, on which occasion I also
observed, that the first principles of our reasonings in mathematics are
not *axioms,* but *definitions.* It is in this last circumstance (I mean the
peculiarity of reasoning from *definitions*) that the true theory of
mathematical demonstration is to be found, and I shall accordingly
endeavour to explain it at considerable length, and to state some of
the more important consequences to which it leads.

That I may not, however, have the appearance of claiming in behalf
of the following discussion, an undue share of originality, it is necessary for me to remark, that the leading idea which it contains has been
repeatedly started, and even to a certain length prosecuted by different
writers, ancient as well as modern; but that, in all of them, it has been
so blended with collateral considerations, altogether foreign to the
point in question, as to divert the attention both of writer and reader,
from that single principle on which the solution of the problem hinges.
The advantages which mathematics derives from the peculiar nature
of those relations about which it is conversant, from its simple and

definite phraseology, and from the severe logic so admirably displayed in the concatenation of its innumerable theorems, are indeed immense, and well entitled to a separate and ample illustration, but they do not appear to have any necessary connexion with the subject of this section. How far I am right in this opinion, my readers will be enabled to judge by the sequel.

It was already remarked, in the first chapter of this part, that whereas, in all other sciences, the propositions which we attempt to establish express facts real or supposed—in mathematics, the propositions which we demonstrate only assert a connexion between certain suppositions and certain consequences. Our reasonings, therefore, in mathematics, are directed to an object essentially different from what we have in view, in any other employment of our intellectual faculties, —not to ascertain *truths* with respect to actual existences, but to trace the logical filiation of consequences which follow from an assumed *hypothesis*. If from this *hypothesis* we reason with correctness, nothing, it is manifest, can be wanting to complete the evidence of the result; as this result only asserts a necessary connexion between the supposition and the conclusion. In the other sciences, admitting that every ambiguity of language were removed, and that every step of our deductions were rigorously accurate, our conclusions would still be attended with more or less of uncertainty, being ultimately founded on principles which may or may not correspond exactly with the fact.[1]

Hence it appears that it might be possible, by devising a set of arbitrary definitions, to form a science which, although conversant about moral, political, or physical ideas, should yet be as certain as geometry. It is of no moment whether the definitions assumed correspond with facts or not, provided they do not express impossibilities, and be not inconsistent with each other. From these principles, a series of consequences may be deduced by the most unexceptionable reasoning; and the results obtained will be perfectly analogous to mathematical propositions. The terms *true* and *false* cannot be applied to them, at least in the sense in which they are applicable to propositions relative to facts. All that can be said is, that they are or are not connected with the definitions which form the principles of the science; and therefore, if we choose to call our conclusions *true* in the one case, and *false* in the other, these epithets must be understood merely to refer to their connexion with the *data,* and not to their correspondence with things actually existing, or with events which we

---

[1] This distinction coincides with one which has been very ingeniously illustrated by M. Prévost in his *Philosophical Essays.* See his remarks on those sciences which have for their object *absolute truth,* considered in contrast with those which are occupied only about *conditional or hypothetical truths.* Mathematics is a science of the latter description; and is, therefore, called by M. Prévost a *science of pure reasoning.*—*Essais de Philosophie,* Vol. II, p. 9, *et seq.* See also his *Mémoire sur les Signes.* Paris, Baudoin, 1800; pp. 15–16. In what respects my opinion on this subject differs from his, will appear afterward.

expect to be realized in future. An example of such a science as that which I have now been describing, occurs in what has been called by some writers *theoretical mechanics;* in which, from arbitrary hypotheses concerning physical laws, the consequences are traced which *would* follow, if such was really the order of nature.

In those branches of study which are conversant about moral and political propositions, the nearest approach which I can imagine to a hypothetical science, analogous to mathematics, is to be found in a code of municipal jurisprudence; or rather might be conceived to exist in such a code, if systematically carried into execution, agreeably to certain general or fundamental principles. Whether these principles should or should not be founded in justice and expediency, it is evidently possible, by reasoning from them consequentially, to create an artificial or conventional body of knowledge, more systematical, and at the same time, more complete in all its parts, than, in the present state of our information, any science can be rendered, which ultimately appeals to the eternal and immutable standards of truth and falsehood, of right and wrong. This consideration seems to me to throw some light on the following very curious parallel which Leibnitz has drawn (with what justness I presume not to decide) between the works of the Roman civilians and those of the Greek geometers. Few writers, certainly, have been so fully qualified as he was to pronounce on the characteristical merits of both.

"I have often said that, after the writings of geometricians, there exists nothing which, in point of force and of subtlety, can be compared to the works of the Roman lawyers. And as it would be scarcely possible, from mere intrinsic evidence, to distinguish a demonstration of Euclid's from one of Archimedes or of Apollonius, (the style of all of them appearing no less uniform than if reason herself was speaking through their organs,) so also the Roman lawyers all resemble each other like twin-brothers; insomuch that, from the style alone of any particular opinion or argument, hardly any conjecture could be formed with respect to the author. Nor are the traces of a refined and deeply meditated system of natural jurisprudence anywhere to be found more visible, or in greater abundance. And even in those cases where its principles are departed from, either in compliance with the language consecrated by technical forms, or in consequence of new statutes or of ancient traditions, the conclusions which the assumed hypothesis renders it necessary to incorporate with the eternal dictates of right reason, are deduced with the soundest logic, and with an ingenuity which excites admiration. Nor are these deviations from the law of nature so frequent as is commonly imagined." [1]

I have quoted this passage merely as an illustration of the analogy

[1] Leibnitii *Opera* (Dutensii), Vol. IV, p. 254. [Vol. IV, p. iii, pp. 267–68. Sir William Hamilton.]

already alluded to, between the systematical unity of mathematical science, and that which is *conceivable* in a system of municipal law. How far this unity is exemplified in the Roman code, I leave to be determined by more competent judges.

As something analogous to the hypothetical or conditional conclusions of mathematics may thus be fancied to take place in speculations concerning moral or political subjects, and actually does take place in theoretical mechanics; so, on the other hand, if a mathematician should affirm, of a general property of the circle, that it applies to a particular figure described on paper, he would at once degrade a geometrical theorem to the level of a fact resting ultimately on the evidence of our imperfect senses. The accuracy of his reasoning could never bestow on his proposition that peculiar evidence which is properly called *mathematical,* as long as the fact remained uncertain, whether all the straight lines drawn from the centre to the circumference of the figure were mathematically equal.

These observations lead me to remark a very common misconception concerning mathematical definitions, which are of a nature essentially different from the definitions employed in any of the other sciences. It is usual for writers on logic, after taking notice of the errors to which we are liable in consequence of the ambiguity of words, to appeal to the example of mathematicians, as a proof of the infinite advantage of using, in our reasonings, such expressions only as have been carefully defined. Various remarks to this purpose occur in the writings both of Mr. Locke and of Dr. Reid. But the example of mathematicians is by no means applicable to the sciences in which these eminent philosophers propose that it should be followed; and, indeed, if it were copied as a model in any other branch of human knowledge, it would lead to errors fully as dangerous as any which result from the imperfections of language. The real fact is, that it has been copied much more than it ought to have been, or than would have been attempted, if the peculiarities of mathematical evidence had been attentively considered.

That in mathematics there is no such thing as an ambiguous word, and that it is to the proper use of definitions we are indebted for this advantage, must unquestionably be granted. But this is an advantage easily secured, in consequence of the very limited vocabulary of mathematicians, and the distinctness of the ideas about which their reasonings are employed. The difference, besides, in *this* respect, between mathematics and the other sciences, however great, is yet only a difference in degree, and is by no means sufficient to account for the essential distinction which every person must perceive between the irresistible cogency of a mathematical demonstration, and that of any other process of reasoning.

From the foregoing considerations it appears, that in mathematics, definitions answer two purposes; first, To prevent ambiguities of language; and secondly, To serve as the principles of our reasoning. It appears further, that it is to the latter of these circumstances (I mean to the employment of hypotheses instead of facts, as the data on which we proceed) that the peculiar force of demonstrative evidence is to be ascribed. It is however only in the *former* use of definitions, that any parallel can be drawn between mathematics and those branches of knowledge which relate to facts; and therefore it is not a fair argument in proof of their *general* utility, to appeal to the unrivalled certainty of mathematical science—a pre-eminence which that science derives from a source altogether different, though comprehended under the same name, and which she will for ever claim as her own exclusive prerogative.

Nor ought it to be forgotten, that it is in pure mathematics alone that definitions can be attempted with propriety at the outset of our investigations. In most other instances, some previous discussion is necessary to shew, that the definitions which we lay down correspond with facts; and, in many cases, the formation of a just definition is the end to which our inquiries are directed. It is very judiciously observed by Mr. Burke, in his *Essay on Taste*, that "when we define, we are in danger of circumscribing nature within the bounds of our own notions, which we often take up by hazard, or embrace on trust, or form out of a limited and partial consideration of the object before us, instead of extending our ideas to take in all that nature comprehends, according to her manner of combining. We are limited in our inquiry by the strict laws to which we have submitted at our setting out."

The same author adds, that "a definition may be very exact, and yet go but a very little way towards informing us of the nature of the thing defined;" and that, "in the order of things, a definition (let its virtue be what it will) ought rather to follow than to precede our inquiries, of which it ought to be considered as the result." [1]

From a want of attention to these circumstances, and from a blind imitation of the mathematical arrangement, in speculations where facts are involved among the principles of our reasonings, numberless errors in the writings of philosophers might be easily traced. The subject is of too great extent to be pursued any further here; but it is well entitled to the examination of all who may turn their thoughts to the reformation of logic. That the ideas of Aristotle himself, with respect to it, were not very precise, must, I think, be granted, if the following statement of his ingenious commentator be admitted as correct.

"Every general term," says Dr. Gillies, "is considered by Aristotle as the abridgment of a definition; and every definition is denominated

[1] See p. 12 of "Introduction on Taste" (1759), in *A Philosophical Enquiry into the Origin of our Ideas of the Sublime and Beautiful*, Edited by J. T. Boulton (London, 1958). Ed.

by him a *collection,* because it is the result always of observation and comparison, and often of many observations and of many comparisons." [1]

These two propositions will be found, upon examination, not very consistent with each other. The first, "That every general term is the abridgment of a definition," applies, indeed, admirably to mathematics, and touches with singular precision on the very circumstance which constitutes (in my opinion) the peculiar cogency of mathematical reasoning. But it is to mathematics that it applies exclusively. If adopted as a logical maxim in other branches of knowledge, it would prove an endless source of sophistry and error. The second proposition, on the other hand, "That every definition is the result of observation and comparison, and often of many observations and many comparisons;" however applicable to definitions of natural history, and of other sciences which relate to *facts,* cannot, in one single instance, apply to the definitions of geometry, inasmuch as these definitions are neither the result of observations nor of comparisons, but the *hypotheses* or first principles on which the whole science rests.

If the foregoing account of demonstrative evidence be just, it follows that no chain of reasoning whatever can deserve the name of a *demonstration* (at least in the mathematical sense of that word) which is not ultimately resolvable into hypotheses or definitions. It has been already shrewn, that this is the case with geometry; and it is also manifestly the case with arithmetic, another science to which, in common with geometry, we apply the word mathematical. The simple arithmetical equations $2 + 2 = 4$; $2 + 3 = 5$, and other elementary propositions of the same sort, are (as was formerly observed) mere *definitions;* perfectly analogous, in this respect, to those at the beginning of Euclid; and it is from a few fundamental principles of this sort, or at least from principles which are essentially of the same description, that all the more complicated results in the science are derived.

To this general conclusion, with respect to the nature of mathematical demonstration, an exception may perhaps be, at first sight, apprehended to occur in our reasonings concerning geometrical *problems;* all of these reasonings (as is well known) resting ultimately upon a particular class of principles called *postulates,* which are commonly understood to be so very nearly akin to *axioms,* that both might, without impropriety, be comprehended under the same name. "The definition of a postulate," says the learned and ingenious Dr. Hutton, "will nearly agree also to an axiom, which is a self-evident theorem, as a postulate is a self-evident problem." [2] The same author, in another

---

[1] Gillies's *Aristotle,* Vol. I, p. 92, 2nd edition. [*Aristotle's Ethics and Politics,* trans. and edited by John Gillies (London, 1797); 2nd edition (1804). Ed.]

[2] *Mathematical Dictionary,* Art. *Postulate.* [Charles Hutton, *A Mathematical and Philosophical Dictionary* (London, 1795–96). Ed.]

part of his work, quotes a remark from Dr. Barrow, that "there is the same affinity between postulates and problems, as between axioms and theorems." [1] Dr. Wallis, too, appears from the following passage to have had a decided leaning to this opinion:—"According to some, the difference between axioms and postulates is analogous to that between theorems and problems; the former expressing truths which are self-evident, and from which other propositions may be deduced; the latter, operations which may be easily performed, and by the help of which more difficult constructions may be effected." He afterwards adds, "This account of the distinction between postulates and axioms seems not ill adapted to the division of mathematical propositions into problems and theorems. And, indeed, if both postulates and axioms were to be comprehended under either of these names, the innovation would not, in my opinion, afford much ground for censure." [2]

In opposition to these very high authorities, I have no hesitation to assert, that it is with the *definitions* of Euclid, and not with the *axioms,* that the *postulates* ought to be compared, in respect of their logical character and importance; inasmuch as all the *demonstrations* in plane geometry are ultimately founded on the former, and all the *constructions* which it recognises as legitimate, may be resolved ultimately into the latter. To this remark it may be added, that, according to Euclid's view of the subject, the problems of geometry are not less hypothetical and speculative than the theorems; the possibility of drawing a *mathematical* straight line, and of describing a *mathematical* circle, being assumed in the construction of every problem, in a way quite analogous to that in which the enunciation of a theorem assumes the *existence* of straight lines and of circles corresponding to their *mathematical* definitions. The reasoning, therefore, on which the solution of a problem rests, is not less *demonstrative* than that which is employed in proof of a theorem. Grant the possibility of the three operations described in the postulates, and the correctness of the solution is as mathematically certain, as the truth of any property of the triangle or of the circle. The three postulates of Euclid are, indeed, nothing more than the definitions of a circle and a straight line thrown into a form somewhat different; and a similar remark may be extended to the corresponding distribution of propositions into theorems and problems. Notwithstanding the many conveniences with which this distribution is attended, it was evidently a matter of choice rather than of necessity; all the truths of geometry easily admitting of being moulded into either shape, according to the fancy of the mathematician. As to the *axioms,* there cannot be a doubt (whatever opinion may be entertained of their utility or of their insignificance) that they stand precisely in the same relation to both classes of propositions.

---

[1] Ibid., Art. *Hypothesis.*
[2] *Wallisii Opera,* Vol. II, pp. 667, 668. [John Wallis, *Opera mathematica* (Oxford, 1693–99). Ed.]

[SUBSECTION] II—CONTINUATION OF THE SUBJECT.—HOW FAR IT IS
TRUE THAT ALL MATHEMATICAL EVIDENCE IS RESOLVABLE INTO
IDENTICAL PROPOSITIONS

I had occasion to take notice, in the first section of the preceding
chapter, of a theory with respect to the nature of mathematical evidence, very different from that which I have been now attempting to
explain. According to this theory (originally, I believe, proposed by
Leibnitz) we are taught, that all mathematical evidence ultimately resolves into the perception of identity; the innumerable variety of propositions which *have* been discovered, or which *remain* to be discovered in the science, being only diversified expressions of the simple
formula, $a = a$. . . .

As this account of mathematical evidence appears to me quite irreconcilable with the scope of the foregoing observations, it is necessary, before proceeding farther, to examine its real import and
amount; and what the circumstances are from which it derives that
plausibility which it has been so generally supposed to possess.

That all mathematical evidence resolves ultimately into the perception of identity, has been considered by some as a consequence of
the commonly received doctrine, which represents the axioms of Euclid as the *first principles* of all our subsequent reasonings in geometry. Upon this view of the subject I have nothing to offer, in addition
to what I have already stated. The argument which I mean to combat
at present is of a more subtile and refined nature; and, at the same
time, involves an admixture of important truth, which contributes not
a little to the specious verisimilitude of the conclusion. It is founded
on this simple consideration, that the geometrical notions of *equality*
and of *coincidence* are the same; and that, even in comparing together
spaces of different figures, all our conclusions ultimately lean, with
their whole weight, on the imaginary application of one triangle to
another;—the object of which imaginary application is merely to *identify* the two triangles together, in every circumstance connected both
with magnitude and figure.

Of the justness of the assumption on which this argument proceeds,
I do not entertain the slightest doubt. Whoever has the curiosity to
examine any one theorem in the elements of plane geometry, in which
different spaces are compared together, will easily perceive that the
demonstration, when traced back to its first principles, terminates in
the fourth proposition of Euclid's first book: a proposition of which
the proof rests entirely on a supposed application of the one triangle
to the other. In the case of equal triangles which differ in figure, this
expedient of ideal superposition cannot be directly and immediately
employed to evince their equality; but the demonstration will nevertheless be found to rest at bottom on the same species of evidence. In

illustration of this doctrine, I shall only appeal to the thirty-seventh proposition of the first book, in which it is proved that triangles on the same base, and between the same parallels, are equal; a theorem which appears, from a very simple construction, to be only a few steps removed from the fourth of the same book, in which the supposed application of the one triangle to the other is the only medium of comparison from which their equality is inferred.

In general, it seems to be almost self-evident, that the equality of two spaces can be demonstrated only by shewing, either that the one might be applied to the other, so that their boundaries should exactly coincide, or that it is possible, by a geometrical construction, to divide them into compartments in such a manner, that the sum of parts in the one may be proved to be equal to the sum of parts in the other, upon the principle of superposition. To devise the easiest and simplest constructions for attaining this end, is the object to which the skill and invention of the geometer is chiefly directed.

Nor is it the geometer alone who reasons upon this principle. If you wish to convince a person of plain understanding, who is quite unacquainted with mathematics, of the truth of one of Euclid's theorems, it can only be done by exhibiting to his eye operations exactly analogous to those which the geometer presents to the understanding. A good example of this occurs in the sensible or experimental illustration which is sometimes given of the forty-seventh proposition of Euclid's first book. For this purpose, a card is cut into the form of a right angled triangle, and square pieces of card are adapted to the different sides; after which, by a simple and ingenious contrivance, the different squares are so dissected, that those of the two sides are made to cover the same space with the square of the hypothenuse. In truth, this mode of comparison by a superposition, actual or ideal, is the only test of equality which it is possible to appeal to; and it is from this (as seems from a passage in Proclus to have been the opinion of Apollonius) that, in point of logical rigour, the *definition* of geometrical equality should have been taken. The subject is discussed at great length, and with much acuteness as well as learning, in one of the mathematical lectures of Dr. Barrow,[1] to which I must refer those readers who may wish to see it more fully illustrated.

I am strongly inclined to suspect, that most of the writers who have maintained that all mathematical evidence resolves ultimately into the perception of identity, have had a secret reference, in their own minds, to the doctrine just stated, and that they have imposed on themselves, by using the words *identity* and *equality* as literally synonymous and convertible terms. This does not seem to be at all consistent, either in point of expression or of fact, with sound logic. When

[1] Isaac Barrow, *Lectiones Mathematicae, 1664–66*, Lecture V. In *Mathematical Works,* Edited by W. Whewell (Cambridge, 1860). Ed.

it is affirmed (for instance) that, "if two straight lines in a circle inter-
sect each other, the rectangle contained by the segments of the one is
equal to the rectangle contained by the segments of the other;" can it
with any propriety be said, that the relation between these rectangles
may be expressed by the formula $a = a$? Or, to take a case yet
stronger, when it is affirmed, that "the area of a circle is equal to that
of a triangle having the circumference for its base, and the radius for
its altitude;" would it not be an obvious paralogism to infer from this
proposition, that the triangle and the circle are one and the same
thing? In this last instance, Dr. Barrow himself has thought it necessary, in order to reconcile the language of Archimedes with that of
Euclid, to have recourse to a scholastic distinction between *actual* and
potential coincidence;[1] and, therefore, if we are to avail ourselves of
the principle of *superposition,* in defence of the fashionable theory
concerning mathematical evidence, we must, I apprehend, introduce a
correspondent distinction between *actual and potential identity.* . . .

Granting, for the sake of argument, that all mathematical propositions may be represented by the formula $a = a,$ it would not therefore
follow, that every step of the reasoning leading to these conclusions
was a proposition of the same nature; and that to feel the full force of
a mathematical demonstration, it is sufficient to be convinced of this
maxim, that *every thing may be truly predicated of itself;* or, in plain
English, that *the same is the same.* A paper written in cypher, and the
interpretation of that paper by a skilful decypherer, may, in like manner, be considered as, to all intents and purposes, one and the same
thing. They are so, in fact, just as much as one side of an algebraical
equation is the same thing with the other. But does it therefore follow
that the whole evidence upon which the art of decyphering proceeds,
resolves into the perception of identity?

It may be fairly questioned, too, whether it can, with strict correctness, be said even of the simple arithmetical equation $2 + 2 = 4,$ that
it may be represented by the formula $a = a.$ The one is a proposition
asserting *the equivalence of two different expressions;*—to ascertain
which equivalence may, in numberless cases, be an object of the highest importance. The other is altogether unmeaning and nugatory, and
cannot, by any possible supposition, admit of the slightest application
of a practical nature. What opinion, then, shall we form of the proposition $a = a,$ when considered as the representative of such a *formula*
as the binomial theorem of Sir Isaac Newton? When applied to the
equation $2 + 2 = 4,$ (which, from its extreme simplicity and familiarity, is apt to be regarded in the light of an axiom,) the paradox does
not appear to be so manifestly extravagant; but, in the other case, it
seems quite impossible to annex to it any meaning whatever. . . .

---

[1] *Ibid.* Ed.

Next to geometry and arithmetic, in point of evidence and certainty, is that branch of general physics which is now called mechanical philosophy;—a science in which the progress of discovery has been astonishingly rapid, during the course of the last century; and which, in the systematical concatenation and filiation of its elementary principles, exhibits every day more and more of that logical simplicity and elegance which we admire in the works of the Greek mathematicians. It may, I think, be fairly questioned, whether in this department of knowledge, the affectation of mathematical method has not been already carried to an excess; the essential distinction between mechanical and mathematical truths being, in many of the physical systems which have lately appeared on the Continent, studiously kept out of the reader's view, by exhibiting both, as nearly as possible, in the same form. A variety of circumstances, indeed, conspire to identify in the imagination, and, of consequence, to assimilate in the mode of their statement, these two very different classes of propositions; but as this assimilation (besides its obvious tendency to involve experimental facts in metaphysical mystery) is apt occasionally to lead to very erroneous logical conclusions, it becomes the more necessary, in proportion as it arises from a *natural* bias, to point out the causes in which it has originated, and the limitations with which it ought to be understood.

The following slight remarks will sufficiently explain my general ideas on this important article of logic:—

1. As the study of the mechanical philosophy is in a great measure inaccessible to those who have not received a regular mathematical education, it commonly happens, that a taste for it is, in the first instance, grafted on a previous attachment to the researches of pure or abstract mathematics. Hence a natural and insensible transference to physical pursuits of mathematical habits of thinking; and hence an almost unavoidable propensity to give to the former science that systematical connexion, in all its various conclusions, which, from the nature of its first principles, is essential to the latter, but which can never belong to any science which has its foundations laid in facts collected from experience and observation.

2. Another circumstance which has co-operated powerfully with the former in producing the same effect, is that proneness to simplification which has misled the mind, more or less, in all its researches; and which, in natural philosophy, is peculiarly encouraged by those beautiful analogies which are observable among different physical

phenomena;—analogies, at the same time, which, however pleasing to the fancy, cannot always be resolved by our reason into one general law. In a remarkable analogy, for example, which presents itself between the equality of action and re-action in the collision of bodies, and what obtains in their mutual attractions, the coincidence is so perfect, as to enable us to comprehend all the various facts in the same theorem; and it is difficult to resist the temptation which this theorem seems to offer to our ingenuity, of attempting to trace it in both cases, to some common principle. Such trials of theoretical skill I would not be understood to censure indiscriminately; but, in the present instance, I am fully persuaded, that it is at once more unexceptionable in point of sound logic, and more satisfactory to the learner to establish the fact, in particular cases, by an appeal to experiment; and to state the law of action and re-action in the collision of bodies, as well as that which regulates the mutual tendencies of bodies towards each other, merely as general rules which have been obtained by induction, and which are found to hold invariably, as far as our knowledge of nature extends.

An additional example may be useful for the illustration of the same subject. It is well known to be a general principle in mechanics, that when, by means of any machine, two heavy bodies counterpoise each other, and are then made to move together, the quantities of motion with which one descends, and the other ascends perpendicularly, are equal. This equilibrium bears such a resemblance to the case of two moving bodies stopping each other, when they meet together with equal quantities of motion, that, in the opinion of many writers, the cause of an equilibrium in the several machines is sufficiently explained, by remarking, "that a body always loses as much motion as it communicates." Hence it is inferred, that when two heavy bodies are so circumstanced, that one cannot descend without causing the other to ascend at the same time, and with the same quantity of motion, both of these bodies must necessarily continue at rest. But this reasoning, however plausible it may seem to be at first sight, is by no means satisfactory; for (as Dr. Hamilton has justly observed [1]) when we say, that one body *communicates* its motion to another, we must suppose the motion to exist, *first* in the one, and *afterwards* in the other; whereas, in the case of the machine, the ascent of the one body cannot, by any conceivable refinement, be ascribed to a communication of motion from the body which is descending at the same moment; and, therefore, (admitting the truth of the general law which obtains in the collision of bodies,) we might suppose, that in the machine, the superior weight of the heavier body would overcome the lighter, and cause it to move upwards with the same quantity of motion with

[1] See *Philosophical Essays*, by Hugh Hamilton, D.D., Professor of Philosophy in the University of Dublin, p. 135, *et seq.* 3d edition (London, 1772).

which itself moves downwards. In perusing a pretended demonstration of this sort, a student is dissatisfied and puzzled; not from the difficulty of the subject, which is obvious to every capacity, but from the illogical and inconclusive reasoning to which his assent is required.

3. To these remarks it may be added, that even when one proposition in natural philosophy is logically deducible from another, it may frequently be expedient, in communicating the elements of the science, to illustrate and confirm the consequence, as well as the principle, by experiment. This I should apprehend to be proper, wherever a consequence is inferred from a principle less familiar and intelligible than itself; a thing which must occasionally happen in physics, from the complete incorporation (if I may use the expression) which, in modern times, has taken place between physical truths, and the discoveries of mathematicians. The necessary effect of this incorporation was, to give to natural philosophy a mathematical form, and to systematize its conclusions, as far as possible, agreeably to rules suggested by mathematical method.

In pure mathematics, where the truths which we investigate are all co-existent in point of time, it is universally allowed, that one proposition *is said* to be a consequence of another, only with a reference to our established arrangements. Thus all the properties of the circle might be as rigorously deduced from any one general property of the curve, as from the equality of the radii. But it does not therefore follow, that all these arrangements would be equally convenient: on the contrary, it is evidently useful, and, indeed, necessary, to lead the mind, as far as the thing is practicable, from what is simple to what is more complex. The misfortune is, that it seems impossible to carry this rule universally into execution: and, accordingly, in the most elegant geometrical treatises which have yet appeared, instances occur, in which consequences are deduced from principles more complicated than themselves. Such inversions, however, of what may justly be regarded as the natural order, must always be felt by the author as a subject of regret; and, in proportion to their frequency, they detract both from the beauty and from the didactic simplicity of his general design.

The same thing often happens in the elementary doctrines of natural philosophy. A very obvious example occurs in the different demonstrations given by writers on mechanics, from the resolution of forces, of the fundamental proposition concerning the lever; demonstrations in which the proposition, even in the simple case when the directions of the forces are supposed to be parallel, is inferred from a process of reasoning involving one of the most refined principles employed in the mechanical philosophy. I do not object to this arrangement as illogical; nor do I presume to say that it is injudicious. I would only suggest the propriety, in such instances, of confirming and illustrating the conclusion, by an appeal to experiment; an appeal which, in natural philosophy, possesses an authority equal to that which is generally, but very improperly, considered as a mathematical demonstration of physical truths. In pure geometry, no reference to the senses can be admitted, but in the way of illustration; and any such reference in the most trifling step of a demonstration, vitiates the whole. But, in natural philosophy, all our reasonings must be grounded on principles for which no evidence but that of sense can be obtained; and the propositions which we establish differ from each other only as they are deduced from such principles immediately, or by the intervention of a mathematical demonstration. An experimental proof, therefore, of any particular physical truth, when it can be conveniently obtained, although it may not always be the most elegant or the most expedient way of introducing it to the knowledge of the student, is as rigorous and as satisfactory as any other; for the intervention of a process of mathematical reasoning can never bestow on our conclusions a greater degree of certainty than our principles possessed.

I have been led to enlarge on these topics by that unqualified application of mathematical method to physics, which has been fashionable for many years past among foreign writers; and which seems to have originated chiefly in the commanding influence which the genius and learning of Leibnitz have so long maintained over the scientific taste of most European nations. In an account, lately published, of the *Life and Writings of Dr. Reid*,[1] I have taken notice of some other inconveniences resulting from it, still more important than the introduction of an unsound logic into the elements of natural philosophy; in particular, of the obvious tendency which it has to withdraw the attention from that unity of design which it is the noblest employment of philosophy to illustrate, by disguising it under the semblance of an eternal and necessary order, similar to what the mathematician delights to trace among the mutual relations of quantities and figures.

The consequence has been, (in too many physical systems,) to level the study of nature, in point of moral interest, with the investigations of the algebraist; an effect, too, which has taken place most remarkably where, from the sublimity of the subject, it was least to be expected—in the application of the mechanical philosophy to the phenomena of the heavens. But on this very extensive and important topic I must not enter at present.

In the opposite extreme to the error which I have now been endeavouring to correct, is a paradox which was broached, about twenty years ago, by the late ingenious Dr. Beddoes; and which has since been adopted by some writers, whose names are better entitled, on a

[1] In Stewart's *Works*, Hamilton edition, Vol. IX. Ed.

question of this sort, to give weight to their opinions. By the partisans of this new doctrine it seems to be imagined that, so far from physics being a branch of mathematics,—mathematics, and more particularly geometry, is in reality only a branch of physics. "The mathematical sciences," says Dr. Beddoes, "are sciences of experiment and observation, founded solely on the induction of particular facts; as much so as mechanics, astronomy, optics, or chemistry. In the kind of evidence there is no difference, for it originates from perception in all these cases alike; but mathematical experiments are more simple, and more perfectly within the grasp of our senses, and our perceptions of mathematical objects are clearer." [1]

A doctrine essentially the same, though expressed in terms not quite so revolting, has been lately sanctioned by Mr. Leslie; and it is to *his* view of the argument that I mean to confine my attention at present. "The whole structure of geometry," he remarks, "is grounded on the simple comparison of triangles; and all the fundamental theorems which relate to this comparison, derive their evidence from the *mere* superposition of the triangles themselves; a mode of proof which, in reality, is nothing but an ultimate appeal, though of the easiest and most familiar kind, to external observation." And, in another passage: "Geometry, like the other sciences which are not concerned about the operations of mind, rests ultimately on external observations. But those ultimate facts are so few, so distinct and obvious, that the subsequent train of reasoning is safely pursued to unlimited extent, without ever appealing *again* to the evidence of the senses." [2]

Before proceeding to make any remarks on this theory, it is proper to premise, that it involves two separate considerations, which it is of material consequence to distinguish from each other. The first is, that extension and figure (the subjects of geometry) are qualities of body which are made known to us by our external senses alone, and which actually fall under the consideration of the natural philosopher as well as of the mathematician. The second, that the whole fabric of geometrical science rests on the comparison of triangles, in forming which comparison, we are ultimately obliged to appeal (in the same manner as in establishing the first principles of physics) to a sensible and experimental proof.

1. In answer to the first of these allegations, it might perhaps be sufficient to observe, that in order to identify two sciences, it is not enough to state that they are both conversant about the same objects; it is necessary farther to shew, that, in both cases, these objects are considered in the same point of view, and give employment to the

1 Thomas Beddoes, *Observations on the Nature of Demonstrative Evidence* (London, 1793), p. 5. Ed.

2 *Elements of Geometry and of Geometrical Analysis,* p. 453. [By John Leslie (Edinburgh, 1809). Ed.]

same faculties of the mind. The poet, the painter, the gardener, and the botanist, are all occupied in various degrees and modes with the study of the vegetable kingdom; yet who has ever thought of confounding their several pursuits under one common name? The natural historian, the civil historian, the moralist, the logician, the dramatist, and the statesman, are all engaged in the study of man, and of the principles of human nature; yet how widely discriminated are these various departments of science and of art! how different are the kinds of evidence on which they respectively rest! how different the intellectual habits which they have a tendency to form! Indeed, if this mode of generalization were to be admitted as legitimate, it would lead us to blend all the objects of science into one and the same mass; inasmuch as it is by the same impressions on our external senses, that our intellectual faculties are, in the first instance, roused to action, and all the first elements of our knowledge unfolded.

In the instance, however, before us, there is a very remarkable specialty, or rather singularity, which renders the attempt to identify the objects of geometrical and of physical science, incomparably more illogical than it would be to classify poetry with botany, or the natural history of man with the political history of nations. This specialty arises from certain peculiarities in the metaphysical nature of those *sensible qualities* which fall under the consideration of the geometer; and which led me, in a different work, to distinguish them from other sensible qualities, (both primary and secondary,) by bestowing on them the title of *mathematical affections of matter*.[1] Of these mathematical affections (*magnitude* and *figure*) our first notions are no doubt derived (as well as of hardness, softness, roughness, and smoothness) from the exercise of our external senses; but it is equally certain, that when the notions of magnitude and figure have once been acquired, the mind is immediately led to consider them as attributes of space no less than of body; and (abstracting them entirely from the other sensible qualities perceived in conjunction with them) becomes impressed with an irresistible conviction, that their existence is necessary and eternal, and that it would remain unchanged if all the bodies in the universe were annihilated. It is not our business here to inquire into the origin and grounds of this conviction. It is with the *fact* alone that we are concerned at present; and this I conceive to be one of the most obviously incontrovertible which the circle of our knowledge embraces. Let those explain it as they best can, who are of opinion, that all the judgments of the human understanding rest ultimately on observation and experience.

Nor is this the only case in which the mind forms conclusions concerning space, to which those of the natural philosopher do not bear

[1] *Philosophical Essays*, pp. 94–95, 4th edition (*infra*, Vol. V.) [In Stewart's *Works*, Hamilton edition, Vol. V. Ed.]

the remotest analogy. Is it from experience we learn that space is infinite? or, (to express myself in more unexceptionable terms,) that no limits can be assigned to its immensity? Here is a fact extending not only beyond the reach of our personal observation, but beyond the observation of all created beings; and a fact on which we pronounce with no less confidence, when in imagination we transport ourselves to the utmost verge of the material universe, than when we confine our thoughts to those regions of the globe which have been explored by travellers. How unlike those general laws which we investigate in physics, and which, how far soever we may find them to reach, may still, for anything we are able to discover to the contrary, be only contingent, local, and temporary!

It must indeed be owned, with respect to the conclusions hitherto mentioned on the subject of space, that they are rather of a metaphysical than of a mathematical nature, but they are not, on that account, the less applicable to our purpose; for if the theory of Beddoes had any foundation, it would lead us to identify with physics the former of these sciences as well as the latter; at least, all that part of the former which is employed about space or extension—a favourite object of metaphysical as well as of mathematical speculation. The truth however is, that some of our metaphysical conclusions concerning space are more nearly allied to geometrical theorems than we might be disposed at first to apprehend; being involved or implied in the most simple and fundamental propositions which occur in Euclid's *Elements*. When it is asserted, for example, that "if one straight line falls on two other straight lines, so as to make the two interior angles on the same side together equal to two right angles, these two straight lines, though indefinitely produced, will never meet;" is not the boundless immensity of space tacitly assumed as a thing unquestionable? And is not a universal affirmation made with respect to a fact which experience is equally incompetent to disprove or to confirm? In like manner, when it is said, that "triangles on the same base, and between the same parallels, are equal," do we feel ourselves the less ready to give our assent to the demonstration, if it should be supposed, that the one triangle is confined within the limits of the paper before us, and that the other standing on the same base, has its vertex placed beyond the sphere of the fixed stars? In various instances, we are led with a force equally imperious, to acquiesce in conclusions which not only admit of no illustration or proof from the perceptions of sense, but which at first sight are apt to stagger and confound the faculty of imagination. It is sufficient to mention, as examples of this, the relation between the hyperbola and its asymptotes; and the still more obvious truth of the infinite divisibility of extension. What analogy is there between such propositions as these, and that which announces that the mercury in the Torricellian tube will fall, if carried up to the top of a mountain; or that the vibrations of a pendulum of a given length will be performed in the same time, while it remains in the same latitude? Were there in reality that analogy between mathematical and physical propositions which Beddoes and his followers have fancied, the equality of the square of the hypothenuse of a right angled trangle to the squares described on the two other sides, and the proportion of 1, 2, 3, between the cone and its circumscribed hemisphere and cylinder, might, with fully as great propriety, be considered in the light of physical phenomena, as of geometrical theorems: Nor would it have been at all inconsistent with the logical unity of his work, if Mr. Leslie had annexed to his *Elements of Geometry,* a scholium concerning the final causes of circles and of straight lines, similar to that which, with such sublime effect, closes the *Principia* of Sir Isaac Newton.

2. It yet remains for me to say a few words upon that superposition of triangles which is the ground-work of all our geometrical reasoning concerning the relations which different spaces bear to one another in respect of magnitude. And here I must take the liberty to remark, in the first place, that the fact in question has been stated in terms much too loose and incorrect for a logical argument. When it is said, that "all the fundamental theorems which relate to the comparison of triangles, derive their evidence from the *mere* superposition of the triangles themselves," it seems difficult, or rather impossible, to annex to the adjective *mere* an idea at all different from what would be conveyed, if the word *actual* were to be substituted in its place, more especially when we attend to the assertion which immediately follows, that "this mode of proof is, in reality, nothing but an ultimate appeal, though of the easiest and most familiar kind, to *external observation.*" But if this be, in truth, the sense in which we are to interpret the statement quoted above, (and I cannot conceive any other interpretation of which it admits,) it must appear obvious, upon the slightest reflection, that the statement proceeds upon a total misapprehension of the principle of *superposition;* inasmuch as it is not to an actual or *mere* superposition, but to an imaginary or ideal one, that any appeal is ever made by the geometer. Between these two modes of proof the difference is not only wide, but radical and essential. The one would indeed level geometry with physics, in point of evidence, by building the whole of its reasonings on *a fact* ascertained by mechanical measurement; the other is addressed to the understanding, and to the understanding alone, and is as rigorously conclusive as it is possible for demonstration to be.

That the reasoning employed by Euclid in proof of the fourth proposition of his first book is completely *demonstrative,* will be readily granted by those who compare its different steps with the conclusions to which we were formerly led, when treating of the nature of mathematical demonstration. In none of these steps is any appeal made to *facts* resting on the evidence of sense, nor indeed to any *facts* whatever. The constant appeal is to the *definition* of equality. "Let the triangle A B C," says Euclid, "be applied to the triangle D E F; the point A to the point D, and the straight line A B to the straight line D E; the point B *will* coincide with the point E, because *A B is equal to D E*. And A B coinciding with D E, A C *will* coincide with D F, *because the angle B A C is equal to the angle E D F.*" A similar remark will be found to apply to every remaining step of the reasoning, and therefore the reasoning possesses the peculiar characteristic which distinguishes mathematical evidence from that of all the other sciences—that it rests wholly on *hypotheses* and *definitions,* and in no respect upon any statement of *facts,* true or false. The ideas indeed of extension, of a triangle, and of equality, presuppose the exercise of our senses. Nay, the very idea of *superposition* involves that of *motion,* and, consequently, (as the parts of space are immovable,) of *a material triangle.* But where is there anything analogous in all this, to those *sensible facts* which are the principles of our reasoning in physics; and which, according as they have been accurately or inaccurately ascertained, determine the accuracy or inaccuracy of our conclusions? The *material* triangle itself, as conceived by the mathematician, is the object, not of sense, but of intellect. It is not an actual *measure,* liable to expansion or contraction, from the influence of heat or of cold; nor does it require, in the ideal use which is made of it by the student, the slightest address of hand or nicety of eye. Even in explaining this demonstration, for the first time, to a pupil, how slender soever his capacity might be, I do not believe that any teacher ever thought of illustrating its meaning by the actual application of the one triangle to the other. No teacher, at least, would do so, who had formed correct notions of the nature of mathematical science.

If the justness of these remarks be admitted, the *demonstration* in question must be allowed to be as well entitled to the name, as any other which the mathematician can produce; for as our conclusions relative to the properties of the circle (considered in the light of hypothetical theorems) are not the less rigorously and necessarily true, that no material circle may anywhere exist corresponding exactly to the definition of that figure, so the proof given by Euclid of the fourth proposition would not be the less demonstrative, although our senses were incomparably less acute than they are, and although no material triangle continued of the same magnitude for a single instant. Indeed, when we have once acquired the ideas of equality and of a common measure, our mathematical conclusions would not be in the least affected, if all the bodies in the universe should vanish into nothing.

To many of my readers, I am perfectly aware, the foregoing remarks will be apt to appear tedious and superfluous. My only apology for the length to which they have extended is, my respect for the talents and learning of some of those writers who have lent the sanction of their authority to the logical errors which I have been endeavouring to correct; and the obvious inconsistency of these conclusions with the doctrine concerning the characteristics of mathematical or demonstrative evidence, which it was the chief object of this section to establish.

SECTION IV
OF OUR REASONINGS CONCERNING PROBABLE OR CONTINGENT TRUTHS

[SUBSECTION] I—NARROW FIELD OF DEMONSTRATIVE EVIDENCE.—OF DEMONSTRATIVE EVIDENCE, WHEN COMBINED WITH THAT OF SENSE, AS IN PRACTICAL GEOMETRY; AND WITH THOSE OF SENSE AND OF INDUCTION, AS IN THE MECHANICAL PHILOSOPHY.—REMARKS ON A FUNDAMENTAL LAW OF BELIEF, [EXPECTATION OF THE CONSTANCY OF NATURE,] INVOLVED IN ALL OUR REASONINGS CONCERNING CONTINGENT TRUTHS

If the account which has been given of the nature of demonstrative evidence be admitted, the province over which it extends must be limited almost entirely to the objects of pure mathematics. A science perfectly analogous to this in point of evidence may, indeed, be conceived (as I have already remarked) to consist of a series of propositions relating to moral, to political, or to physical subjects; but as it could answer no other purpose than to display the ingenuity of the inventor, hardly anything of the kind has been hitherto attempted. The only exception which I can think of occurs in the speculations formerly mentioned, under the title of *theoretical mechanics.*

But if the field of mathematical demonstration be limited entirely to hypothetical or conditional truths, whence (it may be asked) arises the extensive and the various utility of mathematical knowledge in our physical researches, and in the arts of life? The answer, I apprehend, is to be found in certain peculiarities of those objects to which the suppositions of the mathematician are confined; in consequence of which peculiarities, real combinations of circumstances may fall under the examination of our senses, approximating far more nearly to what his definitions describe, than is to be expected in any other theoretical process of the human mind. Hence a corresponding coincidence between his abstract conclusions, and those facts in practical geometry and in physics which they help him to ascertain.

For the more complete illustration of this subject, it may be observed, in the first place, that although the peculiar force of that reasoning which is properly called *mathematical,* depends on the circumstance of its principles being *hypothetical,* yet if, in any instance, the supposition could be ascertained as actually existing, the conclusion might, with the very same certainty, be applied. If I were satisfied, for example, that in a particular circle drawn on paper, all the *radii* were exactly equal, every property which Euclid has demonstrated of that curve might be confidently affirmed to belong to this diagram. As the thing however here supposed is rendered impossible by the imperfection of our senses, the truths of geometry can never, in their practical applications, possess *demonstrative* evidence; but only that kind of evidence which our organs of perception enable us to obtain.

But although, in the practical applications of mathematics, the *evidence* of our conclusions differs essentially from that which belongs to the truths investigated in the theory, it does not therefore follow that these conclusions are the less important. In proportion to the accuracy of our *data* will be that of all our subsequent deductions; and it fortunately happens, that the same imperfections of sense which limit what is physically attainable in the former, limit also, to the very same extent, what is practically useful in the latter. The astonishing precision which the mechanical ingenuity of modern times has given to mathematical instruments has, in fact, communicated a nicety to the results of practical geometry, beyond the ordinary demands of human life, and far beyond the most sanguine anticipations of our forefathers.

This remarkable, and indeed singular coincidence of propositions purely hypothetical, with facts which fall under the examination of our senses, is owing, as I already hinted, to the peculiar nature of the *objects* about which mathematics is conversant; and to the opportunity which we have (in consequence of that *mensurability* which belongs to all of them) of adjusting, with a degree of accuracy approximating nearly to the truth, the *data* from which we are to reason in our practical operations, to those which are assumed in our theory. The only affections of matter which these objects comprehend are extension and figure; affections which matter possesses in common with space, and which may, therefore, be separated in fact, as well as abstracted in thought, from all its other sensible qualities. In examining, accordingly, the relations of *quantity* connected with these affections, we are not liable to be disturbed by those physical *accidents* which, in the other applications of mathematical science, necessarily render the result, more or less, at variance with the theory. In measuring the height of a mountain, or in the survey of a country, if we are at due pains in ascertaining our data, and if we reason from them with mathematical strictness, the result may be depended on as accurate within very narrow limits; and as there is nothing but the incorrectness of our data by which the result can be vitiated, the limits of possible error may themselves be assigned. But, in the simplest applications of mathematics to mechanics or to physics, the abstractions which are necessary in the theory must always leave out circumstances which are essentially connected with the effect. In demonstrating, for example, the property of the lever, we abstract entirely from its own weight, and consider it as an inflexible mathematical line;—suppositions with which the fact cannot possibly correspond, and for which, of course, allowances (which nothing but physical experience can enable us to judge of) must be made in practice.

Next to *practical geometry,* properly so called, one of the easiest applications of mathematical theory occurs in those branches of optics which are distinguished by the name of catoptrics and dioptrics. In these, the physical principles from which we reason are few and precisely definite, and the rest of the process is as purely geometrical as the *Elements* of Euclid.

In that part of astronomy, too, which relates solely to the phenomena, without any consideration of physical causes, our reasonings are purely geometrical. The *data,* indeed, on which we proceed, must have been previously ascertained by observation; but the inferences we draw from these are connected with them by mathematical demonstration, and are accessible to all who are acquainted with the theory of spherics.

In *physical* astronomy, the law of gravitation becomes also a principle or *datum* in our reasonings; but as in the celestial phenomena, it is disengaged from the effects of the various other causes which are combined with it near the surface of our planet, this branch of physics, as it is of all the most sublime and comprehensive in its objects, so it seems, in a greater degree than any other, to open a fair and advantageous field for mathematical ingenuity.

In the instances which have been last mentioned, the evidence of our conclusions resolves ultimately not only into that of sense, but into another law of belief formerly mentioned;—that which leads us to expect the continuance, in future, of the established order of physical phenomena. A very striking illustration of this presents itself in the computations of the astronomer, on the faith of which he predicts, with the most perfect assurance, many centuries before they happen, the appearances which the heavenly bodies are to exhibit. The same fact is assumed in all our conclusions in natural philosophy; and something extremely analogous to it in all our conclusions concerning human affairs. They relate, in both cases, not to necessary connexions, but to *probable* or *contingent* events, of which (how confidently soever we may expect them to take place) the failure is by no means perceived to be impossible. Such conclusions, therefore, differ essentially from those to which we are led by the demonstrations of pure mathematics, which not only command our assent to the theorems they establish, but satisfy us that the contrary suppositions are absurd. . . .

CHAPTER IV

LOGIC OF INDUCTION

[SUBSECTION] II—USE AND ABUSE OF HYPOTHESIS IN PHILOSOPHICAL INQUIRIES.—DIFFERENCE BETWEEN GRATUITOUS HYPOTHESES, AND THOSE WHICH ARE SUPPORTED BY PRESUMPTIONS SUGGESTED BY ANALOGY.—INDIRECT EVIDENCE WHICH A HYPOTHESIS MAY DERIVE FROM ITS AGREEMENT WITH THE PHENOMENA.—CAUTIONS AGAINST EXTENDING SOME OF THESE CONCLUSIONS TO THE PHILOSOPHY OF THE HUMAN MIND

As some of the reasonings in the former part of this section may, at first sight, appear more favourable to the use of Hypotheses than is consistent with the severe rules of the Inductive Logic, it may not be superfluous to guard against any such misapprehensions of my meaning, by subjoining a few miscellaneous remarks and illustrations.

The indiscriminate zeal against hypotheses, so generally avowed at present by the professed followers of Bacon, has been much encouraged by the strong and decided terms in which, on various occasions, they are reprobated by Newton.[1] But the language of this great man, when he happens to touch upon logical questions, must not always be too literally interpreted. It must be qualified and limited, so as to accord with the exemplifications which he himself has given of his general rules. Of the truth of this remark, the passages now alluded to afford a satisfactory proof; for, while they are expressed in the most unconditional and absolute terms, so many exceptions to them occur in his own writings, as to authorize the conclusion, that he expected his readers would of themselves be able to supply the obvious and necessary comments. It is probable that, in these passages, he had more particularly in his eye the Vortices of Descartes.

"The votaries of hypotheses," says Dr. Reid, "have often been challenged to shew one useful discovery in the works of nature that was ever made in that way."[2] In reply to this challenge, it is sufficient, on

---

[1] "Hypotheses non fingo. Quicquid enim ex phenomenis non deducitur hypothesis vocanda est, et hypotheses, seu metaphysicae, seu physicae, seu qualitatum occultarum, seu mechanicae, in philosophia experimentali locum non habent." See the general *Scholium* at the end of the *Principia*. ["I frame no hypotheses. Whatever is not deduced from the phenomena is to be called an hypothesis, and hypotheses, whether metaphysical or physical, whether of occult qualities or mechanical, have no place in experimental philosophy." See F. Cajori's remarks on this passage in his edition of Newton's *Mathematical Principles of Natural Philosophy* (Berkeley, 1947), Appendix, note 55, pp. 671–76. Ed.]

[2] *Essays on the Intellectual Powers of Man*, p. 88, 4th edition. In another part of the same volume, the following assertion occurs: "Of all the discoveries that have been made concerning the inward structure of the human body, never one was made by

the present occasion, to mention the theory of Gravitation and the Copernican system. Of the former we have the testimony of Dr. Pemberton, that it took its first rise from a conjecture or hypothesis suggested by *analogy;* nor, indeed, could it be considered in any other light, till that period in Newton's life, when, by a calculation founded on the accurate measurement of the earth by Picard, he evinced the coincidence between the law which regulates the fall of heavy bodies, and the power which retains the moon in her orbit. The Copernican system, however, furnishes a case still stronger, and still more directly applicable to our purpose, inasmuch as the only evidence which the author was able to offer in its favour, was the advantage which it possessed over every other hypothesis, in explaining with simplicity and beauty all the phenomena of the heavens. In the mind of Copernicus, therefore, this system was nothing more than a hypothesis;—but it was a hypothesis conformable to the universal *analogy* of nature, always accomplishing her ends by the simplest means. "C'est pour *la simplicité,*" says Bailly, "que Copernic replaça le soleil au centre du monde; c'est pour elle que Kepler va détruire tous les épicycles que Copernic avoit laissés subsister: peu de principes, de grands moyens en petit nombre, des phénomènes infinis et variés, voilà le tableau de l'univers." [1]

According to this view of the subject, the confidence which we repose in Analogy rests ultimately on the Evidence of Experience, and hence an additional argument in favour of the former method of investigation, when cautiously followed, as well as an additional proof of the imperceptible shades by which Experience and Analogy run into each other.

Nor is the utility of hypothetical theories confined to those cases in which they have been confirmed by subsequent researches; it may be equally great where they have completely disappointed the expectations of their authors. Nothing, I think, can be juster than Hartley's remark, that "any hypothesis which possesses a sufficient degree of plausibility to account for a number of facts, helps us to digest these facts in proper order, to bring new ones to light, and to make *experimenta crucis* for the sake of future inquirers." [2] Indeed it has probably been in this way that most discoveries have been made; for al-

---

conjecture. . . . The same thing may be said with justice of every other part of the works of God, wherein any real discovery has been made. Such discoveries have always been made by patient observation, by accurate experiments, or by conclusions drawn by strict reasoning from observations and experiments; and such discoveries have always tended to refute, but not to confirm, the theories and hypotheses which ingenious men had invented."—Ibid. p. 49.

[The first passage is from Essay II, Chapter III; the second is from Essay I, Chapter III, Ed.]

[1] *Histoire de l'Astronomie Moderne,* Vol. II, p. 2. [J. S. Bailly (Paris, 1779–82). Ed.]

[2] *Observations on Man,* Chapter I, Prop. V.

though a knowledge of facts must be prior to the formation of a legitimate theory, yet a hypothetical theory is generally the best guide to the knowledge of connected and of useful facts.

The first conception of a hypothetical theory, it must always be remembered, (if the theory possesses any plausibility whatever,) presupposes a general acquaintance with the phenomena which it aims to account for; and it is by reasoning synthetically from the hypothesis, and comparing the deductions with observation and experiment, that the cautious inquirer is gradually led, either to correct it in such a manner as to reconcile it with facts, or finally to abandon it as an unfounded conjecture. Even in this latter case, an approach is made to the truth in the way of *exclusion;* while, at the same time, an accession is gained to that class of associated and kindred phenomena, which it is his object to trace to their parent stock.

In thus apologizing for the use of hypotheses, I only repeat in a different form the precepts of Bacon, and the comments of some of his most enlightened followers. "The prejudice against hypotheses which many people entertain," says the late Dr. Gregory, "is founded on the equivocal signification of a word. It is commonly confounded with theory;—but a hypothesis properly means the supposition of a principle of whose existence there is no proof from experience, but which may be rendered more or less probable by facts which are neither numerous enough, nor adequate to infer its existence. When such hypotheses are proposed in the modest and diffident manner that becomes mere suppositions or conjectures, they are not only harmless, but even necessary for establishing a just theory. *They are the first rudiments or anticipations of Principles.* Without these there could not be useful observation, nor experiment, nor arrangement, because there could be no motive or principle in the mind to form them. Hypotheses then only become dangerous and censurable, when they are imposed on us for just principles; because, in that case they put a stop to further inquiry, by leading the mind to acquiesce in principles which may as probably be ill as well founded." [1]

Another eminent writer has apologized very ingeniously, and I think very philosophically, for the hypotheses and conjectures which are occasionally to be found in his own works. The author I mean is Dr. Stephen Hales, who, in the preface to the second volume of his *Vegetable Statics,*[2] has expressed himself thus:—

"In natural philosophy we cannot depend on any mere speculations of the mind; we can only reason with any tolerable certainty from proper data, such as arise from the united testimony of many good and credible experiments.

"Yet it seems not unreasonable, on the other hand, though not far

---

[1] *Lectures on the Duties and the Qualifications of a Physician.* [John Gregory (London, 1772). Ed.]

[2] See *Statical Essays,* Vol. II, "Haemastaticks" (London, 1733). Ed.

to indulge, to carry our reasonings a little farther than the plain evidence of experiments will warrant; for since at the utmost boundaries of those things, which we clearly know, a kind of twilight is cast on the adjoining borders of *Terra Incognita,* it seems reasonable, in some degree, to indulge conjecture *there;* otherwise we should make but very slow advances, either by experiments or reasoning. For new experiments and discoveries usually owe their first rise only to lucky guesses and probable conjectures; and even disappointments in these conjectures often lead to the thing sought for."

To these quotations I shall add two short extracts from Dr. Hooke, (the contemporary, or rather the predecessor, of Newton), whose acute and original remarks on this subject reflect the greater credit on his talents, that they were published at a period when the learned body, of which he was so illustrious an ornament, seem plainly to have been more disposed to follow the letter of some detached sentences, than to imbibe the general spirit of Bacon's logic.

"There may be use of method in the collecting of materials, as well as in the employment of them; for there ought to be some end and aim; some predesigned module and theory; some purpose in our experiments. And though this society have hitherto seemed to avoid and prohibit preconceived theories and deductions from particular and seemingly accidental experiments, yet I humbly conceive, that such, if knowingly and judiciously made, are matters of the greatest importance, as giving a characteristic of the aim, use, and signification thereof; and without which many, and possibly the most considerable particulars are passed over without regard and observation.[1]

"Where the *data* on which our ratiocinations are founded are uncertain, and only conjectural, the conclusions or deductions therefrom can at best be no other than probable, but still they become more and more probable, as the consequences deduced from them appear, upon examinations by trials and designed observations, to be confirmed by fact or effect. So that the effect is that which consummates the demonstration of the invention; and the theory is only an assistant to direct such an inquisition, as may procure the demonstration of its existence or non-existence."[2]

As an illustration of this last remark, Hooke mentions his anticipation of Jupiter's motion upon his axis, long before he was able, by means of a good telescope, to ascertain the fact. A much more remarkable instance, however, of his philosophical sagacity, occurs in his anticipation of that theory of the planetary motions, which, soon after, was to present itself, with increased and at length demonstrative evidence, to a still more inventive and powerful mind. This conjecture

---

[1] Robert Hooke's *Posthumous Works,* Edited by Richard Waller (London, 1705), p. 280. Ed.
[2] *Ibid.,* p. 537.

(which I shall state in his own words) affords, of itself, a decisive reply to the undistinguishing censures which have so often been bestowed on the presumptuous vanity of attempting, by means of hypotheses, to penetrate into the secrets of nature.

"I will explain (says Hooke, in a communication to the Royal Society in 1666) a system of the world very different from any yet received. It is founded on the three following positions:—

"1. That all the heavenly bodies have not only a gravitation of their parts to their own proper centre, but that they also mutually attract each other within their spheres of action.

"2. That all bodies having a simple motion, will continue to move in a straight line, unless continually deflected from it by some extraneous force, causing them to describe a circle, an ellipse, or some other curve.

"3. That this attraction is so much the greater as the bodies are nearer. As to the proportion in which those forces diminish by an increase of distance, I own I have not discovered it, although I have made some experiments to this purpose. I leave this to others, who have time and knowledge sufficient for the task."

The argument in favour of Hypotheses might be pushed much farther, by considering the tentative or *hypothetical* steps by which the most cautious philosophers are often under the necessity of proceeding, in conducting inquiries strictly experimental. These cannot be better described than in the words of Boscovich, the slightest of whose logical hints are entitled to peculiar attention. "In some instances, observations and experiments at once reveal to us all that we wish to know. In other cases, we avail ourselves of the aid of *hypotheses;—by which word, however, is to be understood, not fictions altogether arbitrary, but suppositions conformable to experience or to analogy.* By means of these, we are enabled to supply the defects of our *data,* and to conjecture or divine the path to truth; always ready to abandon our hypothesis, when found to involve consequences inconsistent with fact. And, indeed, in most cases, I conceive this to be the method best adapted to physics; a science in which the procedure of the inquirer may be compared to that of a person attempting to decypher a letter written in a secret character; and in which legitimate theories are generally the slow result of disappointed essays, and of errors which have led the way to their own detection." [1]

Nor is it solely by the erroneous results of his *own* hypotheses, that the philosopher is assisted in the investigation of truth. Similar lights are often to be collected from the errors of his predecessors; and hence it is, that accurate histories of the different sciences may justly be ranked among the most effectual means of accelerating their future

[1] *De Solis ac Lunae Defectibus* (London, 1760), pp. 211–12. ["An Attempt to Prove the Motion of the Earth by Observations," reprinted in *Early Science in Oxford,* Vol. VIII, by R. T. Gunther (Oxford, 1931), p. 28. Ed.]

advancement. It was from a review of the endless and hopeless wan-
derings of preceding inquirers, that Bacon inferred the necessity of
avoiding every beaten track; and it was this which encouraged him—
with a confidence in his own powers amply justified by the event—to
explore and to open a new path to the mysteries of nature: *Inveniam
viam, aut faciam.* In this respect, the maturity of reason in the *species*
is analogous to that in the *individual;* not the consequence of any
sudden or accidental cause, but the fruit of reiterated disappointments
correcting the mistakes of youth and inexperience. "There is no subject," says Fontenelle, "on which men ever come to form a reasonable
opinion, till they have once exhausted all the absurd views which it is
possible to take of it. What follies," he adds, "should we not be repeating at this day, if we had not been anticipated in so many of them
by the ancient philosophers!" Those systems, therefore, which are
false, are by no means to be regarded as altogether useless. That of
Ptolemy, (for example,) as Bailly has well observed,[1] is founded on a
prejudice so natural and so unavoidable, that it may be considered as
a necessary step in the progress of astronomical science; and if it had
not been proposed in ancient times, it would infallibly have preceded,
among the moderns, the system of Copernicus, and retarded the period of its discovery.

In what I have hitherto said in defence of the method of hypothesis,
I have confined myself entirely to its utility as an organ of investigation; taking all along for granted, that, till the principle assumed has
been fairly inferred as a law of nature, from undoubted facts, none of
the explanations which it affords are to be admitted as legitimate theories. Some of the advocates for this method have, however, gone
much farther, asserting, that if a hypothesis be sufficient to account
for all the phenomena in question, no other proof of its conformity to
truth is necessary. "Supposing," says Dr. Hartley, "the existence of
the æther to be destitute of all direct evidence, still, if it serves to
explain and account for a great variety of phenomena, it will, by this
means, have an indirect argument in its favour. Thus, we admit the
key of a cypher to be a true one, when it explains the cypher completely; and the decypherer judges himself to approach to the true key,
in proportion as he advances in the explanation of the cypher; and *this*
without any direct evidence at all."[2] On another occasion he observes, that "Philosophy is the art of *decyphering* the mysteries of
nature; and that every theory which can explain all the phenomena,
has the same evidence in its favour, that it is possible the key of a
cypher can have from its explaining that cypher."[3] . . .

1 In *Histoire de l'Astronomie Moderne,* Vol. I. Ed.

2 *Observations on Man,* Vol. I, pp. 15–16, 4th edition. [Chapter I, Section I,
Prop. V (London, 1801). Ed.]

3 *Ibid.* Vol. I, p. 350. [Chapter III, Section II, Prop. 87; reprinted in the present
volume. Ed.]

In reply to Hartley's comparison between the business of the philosopher and that of the decypherer, Dr. Reid observes, that "to find the key requires an understanding equal or superior to that which made the cypher. This instance, therefore," he adds, "will *then* be in point, when he who attempts to decypher the works of nature by a hypothesis, has an understanding equal or superior to that which made them." [1]

This argument is not stated with the author's usual correctness in point of logic; inasmuch as the first proposition contrasts the sagacity of the decypherer with that of the contriver of the *cypher;* and the second, with that of the author of the *composition* decyphered. Nor is this all. The argument proceeds on the supposition that, if the task of the scientific inquirer be compared to that of the decypherer, the views of the Author of Nature may, with equal propriety, be compared to those of the inventor of the cypher. It is impossible to imagine that this was Hartley's idea. The object of true philosophy is, in no case presumptuously to divine an alphabet of *secret* characters or cyphers, purposely employed by infinite Wisdom to *conceal* its operations; but, by the diligent study of facts and analogies legible to all, to discover the key which infinite Wisdom has itself prepared for the interpretation of its own laws. In other words, its object is to concentrate and to cast on the unknown parts of the universe, the lights which are reflected from those which are known.

In this instance, as well as in others where Reid reprobates hypotheses, his reasoning uniformly takes for granted, that they are wholly arbitrary and gratuitous. "If a thousand of the greatest wits," says he, "that ever the world produced, were, *without any previous knowledge in anatomy,* to sit down and contrive how, and by what internal organs, the various functions of the human body are carried on—how the blood is made to circulate, and the limbs to move—they would not, in a thousand years, hit upon anything like the truth." Nothing can be juster than this remark; but does it authorize the conclusion, that, to an experienced and skilful anatomist, conjectures founded on analogy, and on the consideration of *uses,* are of no avail as media of discovery? The logical inference, indeed, from Dr. Reid's own statement, is not against anatomical conjectures in general, but against the anatomical conjectures of those who are ignorant of anatomy. . . .

But although I do not think that Reid has been successful in his attempt to refute Hartley's argument, I am far from considering that argument as sound or conclusive. My chief objections to it are the two following:—

1. The cases compared are by no means parallel. In that of the *cypher* we have *all* the facts before us, and if the key explains them,

1 *Essays on the Intellectual Powers,* p. 88.

we may be certain that nothing can directly contradict the justness of our interpretation. In *our physical researches,* on the other hand, we are admitted to see only a few detached sentences extracted from a volume, of the size of which we are entirely ignorant. No hypothesis, therefore, how numerous soever the facts may be with which it tallies, can completely exclude the possibility of exceptions or limitations hitherto undiscovered.

It must, at the same time, be granted, that the probability of a hypothesis increases in proportion to the number of phenomena for which it accounts, *and to the simplicity of the theory by which it explains them;*—and that, in some instances, this probability may amount to a moral certainty. The most remarkable example of this which occurs in the history of science is, undoubtedly, the Copernican system. I before observed, that at the period when it was first proposed, it was nothing more than a hypothesis, and that its only proof rested on its conformity in point of simplicity, to the general economy of the Universe. "When Copernicus," says Mr. Maclaurin, "considered the form, disposition, and motions of the system, as they were then represented after Ptolemy, he found the whole void of order, symmetry, and proportion; like a piece," as he expresses himself, "made up of parts copied from different originals, which, not fitting each other, should rather represent a monster than a man. He therefore perused the writings of the ancient philosophers, to see whether any more rational account had ever been proposed of the motions of the Heavens. The first hint he had was from Cicero, who tells us, in his Academical Questions, that Nicetas, a Syracusian, had taught that the earth turns round on its axis, which made the whole heavens appear to a spectator on the earth to turn round it daily. Afterwards, from Plutarch he found that Philolaus, the Pythagorean, had taught that the earth moved annually round the sun. He immediately perceived, that by allowing these two motions, all the perplexity, disorder, and confusion he had complained of in the celestial motions, vanished; and that instead of these, a simple regular disposition of the orbits, and a harmony of the motions appeared, worthy of the great Author of the world." [1]

Of the truth of this hypothesis, the discoveries of the last century have afforded many new proofs of a direct and even demonstrative nature; and yet, it may be fairly questioned, whether to Copernicus and Galileo, the analogical reasoning, stated in the preceding quotation, did not of itself appear so conclusive as to supersede the necessity of any farther evidence. The ecclesiastical persecutions which the latter encountered in defence of his supposed heresy, sufficiently evinces the faith which he reposed in his astronomical creed.

---

[1] *Account of Newton's Philosophical Discoveries,* p. 45, 2d edition. [Colin Maclaurin (London, 1750). Ed.]

It is, however, extremely worthy of remark, with respect to the Copernican system, that it affords no illustration whatever of the justness of Hartley's logical maxim. The Ptolemaic system was not demonstrably *inconsistent* with any phenomena known in the sixteenth century; and consequently, the presumption for the new hypothesis did not arise from its exclusive coincidence with the facts, but from the simplicity and beauty which it possessed as a theory. The inference to be deduced from it is, therefore, *not* in favour of hypothesis in general, but of hypothesis sanctioned by analogy.

The fortunate hypothesis of a Ring encircling the body of Saturn, by which Huygens accounted, in a manner equally simple and satisfactory, for a set of appearances which for forty years had puzzled all the astronomers of Europe, bears in all its circumstances a closer resemblance than any other instance I know of to the key of a cypher. Of its *truth* it is impossible for the most sceptical mind to entertain any doubt, when it is considered that it not only enabled Huygens to explain all the *known* phenomena, but to predict those which were afterwards to be observed. This instance, accordingly, has had much stress laid upon it by different writers, particularly by Gravesande and Le Sage.[1] I must own, I am somewhat doubtful if the discovery of a key to so limited and insulated a class of optical facts, authorizes any valid argument for the employment of mere hypotheses, to decypher the complicated phenomena resulting from the general laws of nature. It is, indeed, an example most ingeniously and happily selected, but would not perhaps have been so often resorted to, if it had been easy to find others of a similar description.

2. The chief objection, however, to Hartley's comparison of the theorist to the decypherer is, that there are few if any physical hypotheses, which afford the *only* way of explaining the phenomena to which they are applied; and therefore, admitting them to be perfectly consistent with all the known facts, they leave us in the same state of uncertainty, in which the decypherer would find himself, if he should discover a variety of keys to the same cypher. Descartes acknowledges that the same effect might, upon the principles of his philosophy, admit of manifold explanations, and that nothing perplexed him more than to know which he ought to adopt in preference to the others. "The powers of nature," says he, "I must confess are so ample, that no sooner do I observe any particular effect, than I immediately perceive that it may be deduced from *my* principles in a variety of different ways; and nothing in general appears to me more difficult, than to

---

[1] Gravesande, *Introd. ad Philosoph.*, sects. 979, 985.—*Opuscules* de Le Sage, Premier Mémoire, sect. 25. The latter writer mentions the theory in question, as a hypothesis which received no countenance whatever from the analogy of any preceding astronomical discovery. [Willem Gravesande, *Introductio ad Philosophiam, metaphysicam et logicam continens* (Leiden, 1736). Ed.]

ascertain by which of these processes it is really produced." [1] The same remark may (with a very few exceptions) be extended to every hypothetical theory which is unsupported by any collateral probabilities arising from experience or analogy; and it sufficiently shews how infinitely inferior such theories are, in point of evidence, to the conclusions obtained by the art of the decypherer. The principles, indeed, on which this last art proceeds, may be safely pronounced to be nearly infallible.

In these strictures upon Hartley, I have endeavoured to do as much justice as possible to his general argument, by keeping entirely out of sight the particular purpose which it was intended to serve. By confining too much his attention to this, Dr. Reid has been led to carry, farther than was necessary or reasonable, an indiscriminate zeal against every speculation to which the epithet *hypothetical* can in any degree be applied. He has been also led to overlook the essential distinction between hypothetical inferences from one department of the Material World to another, and hypothetical inferences from the Material World to the Intellectual. It was with the view of apologizing for inferences of the latter description, that Hartley advanced the logical principle which gave occasion to the foregoing discussion; and therefore, I apprehend, the proper answer to his argument is this:—Granting your principle to be true in all its extent, it furnishes no apology whatever for the Theory of Vibrations. If the science of mind admit of any illustration from the aid of hypotheses, it must be from such hypotheses alone as are consonant to *the analogy of its own phenomena*. To assume, as a fact, the existence of analogies between these phenomena and those of matter, is to sanction that very prejudice which it is the great object of the inductive science of mind to eradicate.

I have repeatedly had occasion, in some of my former publications, to observe, that the names of almost all our mental powers and operations are borrowed from sensible images. Of this number are intuition; the discursive faculty; attention; reflection; conception; imagination; apprehension; comprehension; abstraction; invention; capacity; penetration; acuteness. The case is precisely similar with the following terms and phrases, relative to a different class of mental phenomena; —inclination; aversion; deliberation; pondering; weighing the *motives*

---

[1] *Dissertatio de Methodo*. In the sentence immediately following, Descartes mentions the general rule which he followed, when such an embarrassment occurred. "Hinc aliter me extricare non possum, quàm si rursus aliqua experimenta quæram; quæ talia sint, ut eorum idem non sit futurus eventus, si hoc modo quam si illo explicetur." The rule is excellent, and it is only to be regretted, that so few exemplifications of it are to be found in his writings. ["I cannot disentangle myself from this except by looking once again for some experiments; and those must be of such a kind that their outcome will not be the same, if it is to be explained by the one method, as it will be if it is to be explained by the other." See *The Philosophical Works of Descartes*, trans. by E. S. Haldane and G. R. T. Ross (Cambridge, 1931), Vol. I, p. 121, for the passage. Ed.]

of our actions; yielding to that *motive* which is the strongest;—expressions (it may be remarked in passing) which, when employed, without a very careful analysis of their import, in the discussion concerning the liberty of the will, gratuitously prejudge the very point in dispute, and give the semblance of demonstration to what is in fact only a series of identical propositions, or a sophistical circle of words.[1]

That to the apprehensions of uneducated men such metaphorical or analogical expressions should present *the images* and *the things typified,* inseparably combined and blended together, is not wonderful; but it is the business of the philosopher to conquer these casual associations, and, by *varying* his metaphors, when he cannot completely lay them aside, to accustom himself to view the phenomena of thought in that naked and undisguised state in which they unveil themselves to the powers of consciousness and reflection. To have recourse, therefore, to the analogies suggested by popular language, for the purpose of *explaining* the operations of the mind, instead of advancing knowledge, is to confirm and to extend the influence of vulgar errors.

After having said so much in vindication of analogical conjectures as steps towards physical discoveries, I thought it right to caution my readers against supposing, that what I have stated admits of any application to analogical theories of the human mind. Upon this head, however, I must not enlarge farther at present. In treating of the inductive logic, I have studiously confined my illustrations to those branches of knowledge in which it has already been exemplified with indisputable success; avoiding, for obvious reasons, any reference to sciences in which its utility still remains to be ascertained.

[SUBSECTION] III—SUPPLEMENTAL OBSERVATIONS ON THE WORDS
INDUCTION AND ANALOGY, AS USED IN MATHEMATICS

Before dismissing the subjects of *Induction* and *Analogy,* considered as methods of reasoning in Physics, it remains for me to take some slight notice of the use occasionally made of the same terms in pure Mathematics. Although, in consequence of the very different natures of these sciences, the induction and analogy of the one cannot fail to differ widely from the induction and analogy of the other, yet, from the general history of language, it may be safely presumed, that this application to both of a common phraseology, has been suggested

---

1 "Nothing," says Berkeley, "seems more to have contributed towards engaging men in controversies and mistakes with regard to the nature and operations of the mind, than the being used to speak of those things in terms borrowed from sensible ideas. For example, the will is termed the *motion* of the soul. This infuses a belief that the mind of man is as a ball in motion, impelled and determined by the objects of sense, as necessarily as that is by the stroke of a racket."—*Principles of Human Knowledge.* [Section 144. Ed.]

by certain *supposed* points of coincidence between the two cases thus brought into immediate comparison.

It has been hitherto, with a very few if any exceptions, the universal doctrine of modern as well as of ancient logicians, that "no mathematical proposition can be proved by induction." To this opinion Dr. Reid has given his sanction in the strongest terms; observing, that "although in a thousand cases it should be found by experience that the area of a plane triangle is equal to the rectangle under the base and half the altitude, this would not prove that it must be so in all cases, and cannot be otherwise, which is what the mathematician affirms." [1]

That some limitation of this general assertion is necessary, appears plainly from the well-known fact, that *induction* is a species of evidence on which the most scrupulous reasoners are accustomed, in their mathematical inquiries, to rely with implicit confidence; and which, although it may not *of itself* demonstrate that the theorems derived from it are *necessarily* true, is yet abundantly sufficient to satisfy any reasonable mind that they hold *universally*. It was by induction (for example) that Newton discovered the algebraical *formula* by which we are enabled to determine any power whatever, raised from a binomial root, without performing the progressive multiplications. The formula expresses a relation between the exponents and the co-efficients of the different terms, which is found to hold in all cases, as far as the table of powers is carried by actual calculation; —from which Newton inferred, that if this table were to be continued *in infinitum,* the same *formula* would correspond equally with every successive power. There is no reason to suppose that he ever attempted to prove the theorem in any other way; and yet there cannot be a doubt that he was as firmly satisfied of its being *universally* true, as if he had examined all the different demonstrations of it which have since been given. Numberless other illustrations of the same thing might be borrowed, both from arithmetic and geometry.

Into what principles, it may be asked, is the validity of such a proof in mathematics ultimately resolvable?—To me it appears to take for granted certain general logical maxims, and to imply a secret process of legitimate and conclusive reasoning, though not conducted agreeably to the rules of mathematical demonstration, nor perhaps formally expressed in words. Thus, in the instance mentioned by Dr. Reid, I shall suppose that I have first ascertained experimentally the truth of the proposition in the case of an equilateral triangle; and that I afterwards find it to hold in all the other kinds of triangles, whether isosceles, or scalene, right-angled, obtuse-angled, or acute-angled. It is impossible for me not to perceive, that this property having no connexion with any of the particular circumstances which discriminate

[1] *Essays on the Intellectual Powers,* p. 615, 4th edition.

different triangles from each other, *must* arise from something common to all triangles, and *must* therefore be a universal property of that figure. In like manner, in the *binomial theorem,* if the formula correspond with the table of powers in a variety of particular instances, (which instances agree in no other respect, but in being powers raised from the same binomial root,) we must conclude—and I apprehend that our conclusion is perfectly warranted by the soundest logic—that it is *this* common property which renders the theorem true in all these cases, and consequently, that it *must necessarily* hold in every other. Whether on the supposition that we had never had any previous experience of demonstrative evidence, we should have been led, by the mere inductive process, to form the idea of *necessary truth,* may perhaps be questioned; but the slightest acquaintance with mathematics is sufficient to produce the most complete conviction, that whatever is *universally* true in that science, must be true *of necessity;* and, therefore, that a universal and a necessary truth are, in the language of mathematicians, synonymous expressions. If this view of the matter be just, the evidence afforded by mathematical induction must be allowed to differ radically from that of physical; the latter resolving ultimately into our instinctive expectation of the laws of nature, and consequently never amounting to that demonstrative certainty which excludes the possibility of anomalous exceptions. . . .

Although, therefore, the mathematician, as well as the natural philosopher, may, without any blameable latitude of expression, be said to reason by *induction,* when he draws an inference from the known to the unknown, yet it seems indisputable, that in all such cases he rests his conclusions on grounds essentially distinct from those which form the basis of experimental science.

The word *analogy,* too, as well as *induction,* is common to physics, and to pure mathematics. It is thus we speak of the analogy running through the general properties of the different conic sections, with no less propriety than of the analogy running through the anatomical structure of different tribes of animals. In some instances these mathematical analogies are collected by a species of *induction;* in others, they are inferred as consequences from more general truths, in which they are included as particular cases. Thus, in the curves which have just been mentioned, while we content ourselves (as many elementary writers have done) with deducing their properties from mechanical descriptions on a plane, we rise experimentally from a comparison of the propositions which have been separately demonstrated with respect to each curve, to more comprehensive theorems, applicable to all of them; whereas, when we begin with considering them in their common origin, we have it in our power to trace from the source, both their generic properties, and their specific peculiarities. The satisfaction arising from this last view of the subject can be conceived by those alone who have experienced it; although I am somewhat doubtful whether it be not felt in the greatest degree by such as, after having risen from the contemplation of particular truths to other truths more general, have been at last conducted to some commanding station, where the mutual connexions and affinities of the whole system are brought at once under the range of the eye. Even, however, before we have reached this vantage-ground, the contemplation of the analogy considered merely as a *fact,* is pleasing to the mind; partly from the mysterious wonder it excites, and partly from the convenient generalization of knowledge it affords. To the experienced mathematician this pleasure is farther enhanced, by the assurance which the analogy conveys, of the existence of yet undiscovered theorems, far more extensive and luminous than those which have led him, by a process so indirect, so tedious, and comparatively so unsatisfactory to his general conclusions.

In this last respect, the pleasure derived from analogy in mathematics resolves into the same principle with that which seems to have the chief share in rendering the analogies among the different departments of nature so interesting a subject of speculation. In both cases, a powerful and agreeable *stimulus* is applied to the curiosity, by the encouragement given to the exercise of the inventive faculties, and by the hope of future discovery which is awakened and cherished. As the analogous properties (for instance) of the conic sections point to some general theorems of which they are corollaries; so the analogy between the phenomena of Electricity and those of Galvanism irresistibly suggests a confident, though vague, anticipation of some general physical law comprehending the phenomena of both, but differently modified in its sensible results by a diversity of circumstances. Indeed, it is by no means impossible, that the pleasure we receive even from those analogies which are the foundation of poetical metaphor and simile, may be found resolvable, in part, into the satisfaction connected with the *supposed* discovery of truth, or the *supposed* acquisition of knowledge; the faculty of imagination giving to these illusions a momentary ascendant over the sober conclusions of experience; and gratifying the understanding with a flattering consciousness of its own force, or at least with a consolatory forgetfulness of its own weakness.

STEWART'S WRITINGS

Stewart's works were first collected in a Cambridge edition of 1829, but the standard one now is that in eleven volumes, Edited by Sir William Hamilton (Edinburgh, 1854–58), and completed after his death by John Veitch who also contributed a memoir of Stewart (1860). The *Works* was reprinted (Edinburgh, 1877). Some of the individual titles, like the *Outlines* and the *Elements,* went through many printings before 1880; all the books have languished since then. About fifty pages of selections, mostly from *Active and Moral Powers* and the *Elements* have been reprinted in *The Scottish Moralists,* Edited by Louis Schneider (Chicago, 1967).

WRITINGS ON STEWART

Perhaps the oldest criticism of Stewart in English that is still worth reading is the chapter on him in Sir James Mackintosh's *Dissertation on the Progress of Ethical Philosophy* (Edinburgh, 1837). The fullest treatment of him is probably that in *The Scottish Philosophy* by James McCosh (London, 1875); it is marred, however, by McCosh's attempts to correct his subject's philosophy. In *The English Utilitarians,* Vol. I (London, 1900), Leslie Stephen discusses Stewart at length. *Scottish Philosophy* by H. Laurie (Glasgow, 1902), contains a short but helpful chapter on Stewart, and there is much interesting discussion of him scattered through *The Scottish Philosophy of Common Sense* by S. A. Grave (Oxford, 1960). The few pages on Stewart as psychologist in *Brett's History of Psychology,* Edited by R. S. Peters (London, 1953), are of more interest than their brevity would suggest. T. E. Jessop's book, *A Bibliography of David Hume and of Scottish Philosophy* (London and Hull, 1938), lists additional early commentators, most of them merely of historical importance. An exception is T. T. Segerstedt's *The Problem of Knowledge in Scottish Philosophy* (Lund, 1935); it contains an essay on Stewart. In *The Democratic Intellect,* G. E. Davie provides a wealth of information about the intellectual and university life of nineteenth-century Scotland. Stewart, like Brown and Ferrier, receives considerable attention.

THOMAS BROWN

1778–1820

Thomas Brown, like so many other Scottish philosophers, was the son of a Calvinist minister. The family moved to Edinburgh after the father's early death, and the son went to school there and, later, in London. He returned to Edinburgh University in 1792, read Stewart's *Elements,* and attended his lectures in the following year. In 1796 Brown was enrolled as a Law student but changed to medicine a few years later, graduating in 1803 with a thesis on sleep. While still at the University, Brown was a prominent member of a literary group which included Sydney Smith, Francis Horner, Lord Brougham and Francis Jeffrey—the founders, in 1802, of the *Edinburgh Review*. Brown contributed a review of a French book on Kant to the second issue.

Somewhat earlier, at the age of eighteen, Brown read Erasmus Darwin's *Zoonomia* (1794) and corresponded with the author. Two years afterward Brown published *Observations on Zoonomia,* a book which was well received by critics. By 1805 Brown had published several volumes of poetry, and more importantly, the first edition of *Observations on Cause and Effect*. This book arose from a quarrel over John Leslie, a candidate for the vacant chair of mathematics at Edinburgh. Leslie, although well known for his experimental work on meteorology and heat, was said to be disqualified because he was a supporter of Hume's theory of causation. Brown set out to justify Leslie by examining Hume's views in detail. In 1806 Brown became a medical partner of Gregory, the well-known physician. Though an earlier attempt to obtain the chair of rhetoric for Brown at Edinburgh University had been unsuccessful, he assisted Stewart in the lectures on moral philosophy from 1808–10, and in 1810, as a result of Stewart's efforts and much enthusiasm among students and the educated public, Brown was elected to be joint professor with the ailing Stewart. The four volumes of *Lectures on the Philosophy of the Human Mind,* published after Brown's death in 1820, were all written in the first two years of his professorship and not revised later.

Brown, although widely popular for his lecturing abilities, lived with his mother and sisters and did not marry. His health was always poor, and a few years after the death of his mother he became seriously ill and went to London. He died there, before the printer had been able to issue either his *Lectures* or four volumes of collected poetry.

During his lifetime Brown published three volumes on philosophy. The first was *Observations on the Zoonomia of Erasmus Darwin* (1798); the second was *Observations on the Nature and Tendency of the Doctrine of Mr. Hume Concerning the Relation of Cause and Effect* (1805). This book grew from being little more than a pamphlet in its first edition to a work of over five hundred pages in its third edition, but with a shortened title (1818). The last volume on philosophy that Brown himself prepared was *Sketch of a System of the Philosophy of the Human Mind* (1820). This was intended as a textbook. After his death Brown's unrevised lectures were seen through the press by his friends.

John Stuart Mill said of Brown that he was an active and fertile thinker who would have been even better if he "had been better read in the writings of previous thinkers." This remark fits oddly with Sir William Hamilton's complaint that Brown appropriated "to himself the observations of others, and in particular those of Destutt Tracy, that we irresistibly infer the existence of the external world from our immediate consciousness of our mental states." But if we leave questions of scholarship and plagiarism aside, it is clear that the present neglect of Brown is largely undeserved. His attempt to sketch the outlines of a nonphysiological theory of the human mind are full of interest. He gives, for example, a detailed account of how our knowledge of extended and resistant objects in the world is due "not to our organ of touch, but to our muscular frame . . . as forming a distinct organ of sense." He derives our knowledge of length in various directions from the sensations we have when contracting certain muscles over a period of time, and he traces our belief in the existence of an external world to the inescapable operation of two factors: our assumption that every change has a cause, and the principle of association by which conceptions and feelings are constructed into the world of events, objects, and relations with which we are familiar.

Brown, like Reid, spent much of his time trying to find a way around the skeptical conclusions bequeathed by Hume. But since Brown agreed with Hume that mental experience should be studied as scientifically as our physical experience, Brown's remarks on such topics as the distinction between hypotheses and theories, on consciousness as being merely the "whole series of states of the mind," and on the metaphorical use of the word "ideas" might well belong to contemporary discussion. Again, his *Observations* remains the classic statement of causation as invariable sequence, a view often mistakenly ascribed to Hume. And on those points where Brown corrects Hume, as in the case of causal belief arising after single sequences, our present view is closer to that of Brown.

The distinguished psychologist, Alexander Bain, was much influenced by Brown's writings on touch and the muscular sense. Other psychologists in the nineteenth century took over Brown's classification of the secondary laws of association. But perhaps Brown's most important influence was on James Mill, and through him on his son, John Stuart Mill. Indeed, Brown's philosophy and his criticisms of Reid form the centerpiece of a famous controversy in the middle nineteenth century, that between the supporters of the learned Sir William Hamilton, then recently dead, and the utilitarian logician, John Stuart Mill. The controversy arose from the publication of Mill's *An Examination of Sir William Hamilton's Philosophy* (1865). In this book Mill attacked Hamilton's belief that we have a direct intuition of the reality of matter and of its primary qualities like extension, solidity, and figure. Mill defended Brown's view "that matter is suggested to us only as an unknown something, all whose attributes, as known or conceived by us, are resolvable into affections of our senses."

Observations on the Nature and Tendency of the Doctrine of Mr. Hume Concerning the Relation of Cause and Effect *

*

CAUSAL RELATION AND ITS ORIGIN IN EXPERIENCE

. . . A *cause* may be defined *the object, or event,*[1] *which immediately precedes any change, and which, existing again in similar cir-*

---

* 2nd edition, Mundell and Son (Edinburgh, 1806), pp. 45–80, 100–06, 121–42.

[1] The word *event* might, in strictness of language, be omitted, and is retained only in compliance with a popular distinction: for an event is nothing more than the sudden existence of an object in those particular circumstances *in which alone* it precedes some other object. When it precedes it, in all circumstances, even the vulgar think only of *the object itself,* in their reference of causation. Thus, as the sun is never visible without an increase of heat, they have no hesitation in saying, that *the sun* is a cause of heat. But, when it is only in certain circumstances that

cumstances, will be always immediately followed by a similar change. Priority in the sequence observed, and invariableness of antecedence in the future sequences supposed, are the elements which constitute the idea of a cause. By a conversion of terms, we obtain a definition of the correlative *effect*.[1]

It may be stated as the first proposition of Mr. Hume's theory, that *the relation of cause and effect cannot be discovered a priori*. In every case, the second phenomenon must have been previously witnessed: for there is nothing in the first appearance of any object, which can lead us to predict the appearance of a particular object, rather than of

---

one object precedes another, we almost lose sight of the object itself, and transfer the causation to some *term*, expressive merely of that change of circumstances, by which the object begins to exist in its particular state of antecedence. It is *the explosion* of gun-powder, not the mere existence of the gaseous product in its state of high elasticity, that we assign, in common language, as the cause of the violent concussion, to which the elasticity gives rise. To consider *an event*, rather than *an object*, as the cause of any change, is, however, only to go back an additional step in our reference, and to ascribe the effect, not to those circumstances immediately preceding it, which, in scholastic language, are termed *the proximate cause*, but to the circumstances immediately preceding that proximate cause.

To the universal *priority* of causes, there is, in name at least, one apparent exception, in the mode of considering the phenomena of the world, in relation to the supposed will of the Supreme Being; as the term is then assigned, not to the prior, but to the subsequent, event. The *final cause* of any thing is the good which *follows* it. Thus, as adversity rouses and exercises the heroic qualities of mind in the sufferer, and the benevolent qualities in those who are witnesses of his suffering, a philosophic optimist considers the production and strengthening of those virtues, as the final cause of every physical evil. But it is evident, that, even in this application of the term, the real implied cause is prior; and it is only from a double metonymy, that it appears to be subsequent. The two events observed by us are, in the expression, placed for those circumstances, which we suppose to have preceded them in the divine mind; and we mean only, that *the consideration* of that virtue, which adversity would tend to produce, was the cause of that divine *volition*, by which adversity exists. It is in relation to the Deity alone, that the phrase is at all intelligible; and, in relation to his design, that good, which we term the final cause, and not the instrumental evil, which, to our observation appears to precede it, was in truth the prior circumstance.

1 'Similar objects,' says Mr. Hume, 'are always conjoined with similar. Of this we have experience. Suitably to this experience, therefore, we may define a cause to be *an object, followed by another, and where all the objects, similar to the first, are followed by objects similar to the second. Or, in other words, where, if the first object had not been, the second never had existed.*' [*An Enquiry Concerning Human Understanding*, Section VII, Part II, p. 60. Ed.] This last circumstance, if very rigidly examined, is not admissible into a just definition of a cause; as it excludes the possible agency of co-existing objects, which separately might have been able to produce the existence or appearance of the second object. With the possibility, in many cases, of such co-existence, even our present very limited knowledge of the phenomena of nature, has made us sufficiently acquainted. A hand, for example, may hold a piece of iron, and may approach a loadstone with it, in exactly the same direction, and with exactly the same velocity, as that with which the iron, if free, would itself have approached it. In this case, it is evident, that, whether we regard the motion as produced by the hand, or by the loadstone, *the first object might not have been, and yet the second might have existed.* The addition or omission of this circumstance, is, however, of no essential consequence to the theory of causation, which depends only on the invariableness of the sequence; and I have, therefore, ventured to omit it, in the definition which I have given.

any other, as immediately successive. Were this anticipation possible, all men would be equally philosophers, and all would be philosophers at birth. A lucky chance converted the magnet into something more than an ugly stone. It is by experience alone we know, that a spark, like that which falls and is extinguished on a heap of sand, will raise a heap of gunpowder into an irresistible conflagration. It is by experience alone we know, that the sight of wretchedness will cause in one bosom no emotion, while it melts another into pity, that almost equals in sorrow the grief which it deplores. Without that experience, we might with equal reason have imagined, that the spark would have been extinguished on the gunpowder, and that pain, unfelt by ourselves, would in others have excited no emotion.

Of the truth of this first proposition, instances may be given, as numerous and various as the phenomena of nature. The preceding are taken from mind, as well as from matter, to shew, as far as actual knowledge is concerned, the exact similarity of both cases. In the latter case, indeed, we may often seem to have, *a priori,* a knowledge of succeeding events; as motions are made in apparent adaptation to circumstances that are about to follow, before the existence of those circumstances can have been learned from experience. By what complicated muscular action is the first food of life acquired! Yet we have no reason to imagine, that an infant, who is for the first time applied to his mother's breast, has any idea of the milky stream that is to flow, when he forms his little vacuum for its reception. The necessary motions are the result of an instinct, unerring, because it is not left to the capricious accidents of human knowledge, and provident and perfect, because it is arranged by the highest wisdom. Wherever *knowledge* is concerned, however, it follows the same laws, whether in matter or in mind. That the desire of moving his arm will be followed by its motion, is not known to the swaddled babe, and is believed by the impotent paralytic. The pleasure which the contemplation of works of intellectual excellence inspires, has never entered into the imagination of the illiterate. The passions of love, ambition, avarice, are *felt* by the lover, the hero, the miser; by others their nature is *learned* from description, in the same manner as we acquire our knowledge of the serpents and tigers of the East. We think, indeed, that the phenomena of mind are less dependent on experience, than those of matter, because the greater number of emotions, and even of passions, are, in some degree, known to us so early, that we have forgotten the time when the experience was acquired; while the external world presents to us a never-ending series of new objects, and at once, by their permanence, keeps our memory alive, and impresses on it the difficulty of discovery, by the complicated apparatus which it obliges us to use. Yet, uniform as the mental phenomena in most circumstances must be, how different, even as to many of these, would be the predictions of individuals of different ages and countries! No Roman would have scrupled to foretel, that the combat of gladiators, which was to be exhibited on the morrow, would be witnessed with delight, by the most gentle and delicate of the virgins of Rome. To a Briton, unacquainted with that mixture of barbarism and civilization, such an assertion would seem not less absurd, than if it had predicted a change in the well-known order of material phenomena. What is called knowledge of the world, is knowledge of the human mind; and, when the address, and nice discrimination, of one who has spent a long life in scenes of business, are contrasted with the artlessness of a child, or even with the simplicity of a retired philosopher, it is impossible for us not to feel, that, like all other knowledge, that of our intellectual and moral frame is dependent on experience.

So different, however, has the nature of succession been considered, in the phenomena of mind and of matter, that on this difference has been founded a theory of power, which has met with very general acceptance. It has been asserted, that from mind alone we derive our idea of power; and that the idea, acquired by the consciousness of our own exertion, is *transferred* to the apparent changes of external matter. But, *unless we suppose the idea of power to have been otherwise acquired,* what we call *exertion,* is nothing more than the sequence of muscular motion to desire, as magnetism is the sequence of the motion of iron to the approach of a loadstone. We have, in each case, *two* phenomena, but we have no more; and we as little ascribe *desire* to the loadstone, as we suppose the approach of a loadstone to have preceded our muscular motion. If we say that we ascribe, not *desire,* but *power,* to the loadstone, we beg the question: for power, which has a relation to future cases, as well as to the present, is something more than the mere sequence of desire and motion, which is all that took place in exertion; and, if from one sequence any inference may be made, as to the *recurrence* of sequences, it may be made as much from the motion of iron, as from the motion of a limb. If what we feel be transferred, it is evidently *desire* which we feel. Till the muscular motion has taken place, it is desire alone; or, if we suppose, that, even before the first exertion, there is an instinctive expectation of the result, it is only desire, combined with belief, that the motion will follow; it is afterwards desire, combined with the knowledge that a muscular motion has been its consequence, and with belief that it will again be followed by the motion: but neither is the combination of belief and desire *transferred* to the loadstone, nor, after magnetism has been observed, is there less knowledge of *it* too, as a past event, nor less expectation of it as a future consequence. In both cases, indeed, as will afterwards appear, the inference, as to future similarity of event, is made from one general principle: but it is a principle common to all sequences, and which, we have every reason to believe, would operate in the same manner, though man were wholly incapable of muscular exertion.

It is, perhaps, even too much authority, which Mr. Hume gives to this error, when he allows, that the *animal nisus,* which we experience, enters very much into the vulgar idea of power. It is more probable, that the feeling of this animal nisus, though derived from cases in which the exertion has eventually succeeded, enters largely into the vulgar idea of restraint, or want of power. But, that the great and general error should have been adopted by philosophers, is peculiarly unaccountable; as it is impossible to attend to the common language of the science of mind, without perceiving its innumerable derivations from the analogies of matter. The phenomena of mind succeed each other in a certain order; the phenomena of matter also have their peculiar order: but, were we to judge, by the language of each, from which of the two sequences our idea of power is derived, the probability would seem on the side of the latter. It is only in poetry, that wishes and volitions are given to inanimate objects, while, even in common conversation, we never speak of the desires and passions of the soul, without a series of metaphors, taken from the objects around us. And, indeed, when we consider, not the language only, but the very thoughts and abstractions, of which theories are made, we discover innumerable attempts to materialize every operation of the mind, but very few attempts to spiritualize the operations of matter. How much have we heard, of images, and impulses, and traces in the sensorium, of vibrations, and vibratiuncles, of animal spirits, electricity, and galvanism! There is scarcely a single new generalization of those phenomena of matter which have been long familiar to us, or a single power in matter inferred from the observation of new phenomena, which has not been immediately seized by philosophers, and applied to mind; as if it were the great business of metaphysical science, to systematize the slight analogies of metaphor, and as if those internal processes, of which we are conscious, could be simplified, by the interposition of additional processes, of which we are not conscious, and which are themselves equally inexplicable, as the phenomena, which they are adduced to explain.

ANTHROPOMORPHISM

That there is in the nature of man a tendency to animate and personify every object around him, has indeed been sometimes urged, as a proof of the general belief of the immediate agency of mind, in all the changes of the material world. Planets, it is contended, have had their regent spirits; and Oreads, Dryads, and Naiads, have formed a part of popular mythology. In such cases of supposed belief, however, there is often nothing but a mere figure of rhetoric, or a gay pomp of worship itself almost rhetorical, which may be considered as little more than a very lively prosopopœia. But, even in those cases of real belief, in which the personification has not arisen from allegory and poetic embellishment, it is easy to trace the source of the supposed agency: for the nymphs of classical superstition, like the fays, and other shadowy beings, of our own local mythology, are usually represented, rather as inhabitants of certain districts, over which they preside, and in which they occasionally appear, when any great part is to be performed, than as connecting and carrying on all the regular and uniform natural processes, which are exhibited to our daily view. It is only where great and unusual phenomena occur, and no visible cause is discerned, that the immediate agency of spirits is supposed. It is a *dignus vindice nodus,* and a god is therefore introduced, because mind, which is the only power that is itself altogether invisible, furnishes the only *analogy* to which recourse can be had. When sounds, therefore, are heard from the mountain, the grove, or the stream, while around the hearer no blast is stirring; when a voice of many thunders cries aloud, and fire flashes from clouds, which, the very moment before, were one gloomy stilness, it is not wonderful, that the heart and knee of man should fall prostrate, as in the presence of a mighty spirit. But this belief is only the result of an analogical reasoning, which, in a certain stage of physical science, is irresistible, and differs not, in the slightest degree, from a thousand other reasonings of analogy in physics, in which the cause supposed is not spiritual but material. It is confined to certain cases, in which *the analogy of life* is more striking than any other, and is very different from that general theory, which ascribes a supposed living power to the production of every change. The Roman, who heard Jupiter in the sky, and acknowledged that he reigned, saw and recognised an endless succession of material causes, in the more common spontaneous changes of nature, and in the daily arts of life; and while in the public field of exercise he drove the ball, or watched it, as it fell and rebounded from the earth, he never once imagined, that a god was at all concerned in the operation.

The most probable source of the error, as relating, not merely to cases of inferred analogy, but to every instance of change in matter, is the continuance of apparent rest in bodies, when not under the influence of a manifest *external* force. The rock, which, many ages ago, was swept from the mountain's side, remains still, in the same spot of the valley which received it, and is scarcely distinguishable from the fragments, which the desolation of yesterday has spread around it: while the locomotive power of animals, as exerted by fits of longer or shorter duration, renders visible to us the beginnings of motion from absolute rest; the whole train of vital changes being composed, partly of motions, which are visible, and partly of affections of mind, which are invisible, and the invisible affections being neglected by us, in our consideration of the visible motions, which appear at intervals only, though, in reality, they are parts of one continuous sequence. It has thus been usual, to term matter *inert,* as if capable only of *continuing* changes, and to distinguish mind as alone active, and capable of *beginning* changes. But this assumption of a quality to mind instead of favouring, by a new and striking distinction, the pure doctrine of immaterialism, tends only to furnish its antagonists with a ground of triumph, by permitting them to suppose, that they have shewn a complete similarity of the principles of mind and matter, when they have shewn nothing but the falsehood of one asserted difference. It is enough, to maintain, that *mind* is that which is sentient, and that we have no reason to suppose, that our sensations have any common nature with their unknown external causes, the separate existence of which, however, though undemonstrated, and undemonstrable, we feel it impossible not to believe. But, when we have admitted the existence of *matter,* as the external cause of the sensations of *mind,* we are not justified by induction, in affirming, that any created matter is less capable of beginning changes, than any created mind. All is only a continuance of changes, and often of mutual changes. If, without the intervention of matter, thought arise after thought, and passion after passion, as often, without the intervention of mind, does the motion of a few small particles of matter produce in other masses a long series of elemental motions. If mind often act upon matter, as often does matter act upon mind; and though matter cannot begin a change of itself, when all the preceding circumstances have continued the same, as little, when all the preceding circumstances continue the same, is such a change possible in mind. It does not perceive, without the occurrence of an object to be perceived, nor will, without the suggestion of some object of desire. The truth is, that certain changes of mind invariably precede certain other changes of mind, and certain changes of matter certain other changes of matter, and also that certain changes of mind invariably precede certain changes of matter, and certain changes of matter invariably precede certain changes of mind. To say, that mind produces *motion* in matter, while matter cannot produce *motion* in mind, is but an abuse of language: for it might, in like manner, be said, that mind is inert, because it cannot produce, in itself, or in other minds, that painful *sensation* of heat, which is immediately produced by the contact of a burning mass; or that many of the most powerful chemical solvents are inert, while another solvent alone is active, because from the use of that one solvent alone a particular product can be derived. The changes, produced by mind in matter, are indeed more obvious to the perception of others, and more directly measurable, than the changes, produced by matter in mind; but it is the simple production of a change, not the nature of the change produced, which is essential to the argument. Even the apparent rest of matter is action, rather than repose. The *particles* of the quiescent mass are all attracting, and attracted, repelling, and repelled; and even the smallest indistinguishable element is modifying, by its joint instrumentality, the planetary motions of our system, and is performing a part, which is perhaps essential to the harmony of the whole universe of worlds.

WILL AND DESIRE AS CAUSES

The distinction which has been made of volitions and desires is another circumstance, which has in part contributed to the mistake. The number of desires, of which the mind is susceptible, are as various, as the objects of good. Of these, however, only a certain number terminate in some direct and immediate motion, and are called *volitions;* while those, which have no such direct and immediate termination, have the simple denomination of *desires.* Thus we are said to *desire* wealth, and to *will* the motion of our hand; but, if the motion of our hand had not followed our desire of moving it, we should then have been said, not to will, but to desire its motion. The distance, or the *immediate attainableness* of the good, is thus the sole difference: but, as the words are at present used, they have served to produce a belief, that of *the same immediate good* there is both a desire and a volition; that the volition which moves the hand, for example, is something different from the mere desire of moving it, the one particular motion being preceded by two affections of mind, a volition and a desire. Of this double affection, however, we have no consciousness, the desire of moving a limb, in the usual circumstances of health, being always directly followed by its motion, whatever interval of opposition there may have been, in the *motives,* or *desires of more distant good,* which preceded *the desire of the particular muscular motions,* as means of obtaining that distant good. It is indeed only in such desires, as have no direct termination in motion, that the equilibrium and pause of motives is conceivable. The voluptuary may balance his love of pleasure with his love of health, and the ambitious man his love of power with his love of ease and security, because the desires of pleasure, and of health, and of power, and of ease, may separately exist without any immediate and invariable effect, suggesting occasionally different objects of thought according to the casual associations of ideas: but, in the free and healthy state of the body, to desire the motion of our hand is to move it. The volition which moves a muscle, considered, without reference to the muscle, as an affection of the mind alone, differs not more from the desire of any trifling object of distant enjoyment, than the desire of ease differs from the desire of power; and the only difference is, that what we call a volition is followed immediately by some affection of our body, and what we call a desire is followed immediately by some other affection of our mind. It is not in any quality of our desires, therefore, but in *that arrangement in the order of nature, by which certain corporeal changes follow certain desires,* that the distinction of volitions and desires is founded; and the particular volition precedes its particular muscular motion, in no other manner, than any other change, material or mental precedes the change, which is second to it in the order of sequence. But, though it is thus apparent that our volitions are only short desires, which necessarily are not lasting, because they are immediately followed by the attainment of their object, it is not difficult to trace the circumstances, which have led the vulgar, and even philosophers, to consider the two affections of mind, as essentially distinct. One of the chief circumstances is the confidence, which, in the case of voluntary motion, is combined with the desire. We desire wealth, and do not believe that it will follow: We desire the motion of our hand, and know that the motion will follow. The volition, therefore, is desire *combined with belief of immediate sequence:* yet the belief does not arise from any peculiar circumstance in the desire itself, but merely from the experience of the order of sequence, by which the desire has terminated in the particular motion; and in the case of sudden palsy, in which no motion follows this compound of desire and belief, the compound itself is exactly the same. The term *will* is not denied to be a convenient term, for distinguishing those desires, *which have instant termination in the muscular motion that is their object,* from those *which relate to objects not directly and immediately attainable, and therefore not accompanied with the belief of direct and immediate attainment:* but still it must not be forgotten, that the mental part of the sequence, which exists in our consciousness alone, is a desire, that differs not from our other desires, more than those others mutually differ. Another circumstance, which has contributed in a very important degree, to the mistake, is the universal habit of confounding the desire which immediately precedes muscular motion, with those other desires, by which it may have been itself preceded, and of considering the will in the process of comparison, as *co-existing* with the opposite desires, not simply as that desire, which *follows* the perception and belief of the greater good. We are hence often said inaccurately, to will in opposition to our desire, as if in the process there were only two affections of mind, a desire and a volition, so essentially different in their nature, that the will was the choice of what was not desirable. Thus, if any one be compelled to support a weight in his outstretched arm, under fear of a more painful punishment if he should draw it back, he will soon experience a degree of fatigue that is almost insupportable; and, if he continue to keep his arm extended, he will be said, in the common language of philosophers, to *will* the very pain, which he cannot be supposed to *desire*. But the *direct object of his desire* is not the motion of his arm; it is simply relief from pain: and the *direct object of his continued will* is not the continuance of pain, but simply the extension of his arm. He *knows* indeed that relief from pain will be immediately procured, by drawing back his arm; but he knows also, that a severer punishment will follow that motion: and therefore, preferring the less pain to the greater, he *directly* desires or wills the continued extension of his arm. If the *direct* object of his desire were not relief from pain, but actual muscular motion of his arm, there can be no doubt, that the motion of his arm would immediately ensue. The error of philosophers thus evidently consists, in not distinguishing, with sufficient accuracy, the separate sequences of events, in a complicated process. 'With regard to our own actions,'—says Dr. Reid,—'we may desire what we do not will, and will what we do not desire; nay, what we have a great aversion to. A man athirst has a strong desire to drink, but, for some particular reason, he determines not to gratify his desire. A judge, from a regard to justice, and to the duty of his office, dooms a criminal to die, while, from humanity or particular affection, he desires that he should live. A man for health may take a nauseous draught, for which he has no desire but a great aversion. Desire therefore, even when its object is some action of our own, is only an incitement to will, but it is not volition. The determination of the mind may be not to do what we desire to do.' In all these instances adduced by Dr. Reid, his mistake consists in neglecting or forgetting that part of the process, in which there is a real opposition of desires, and supposing an opposition, in another part of the process, in which there really is none: for, in not one of the instances, is there the smallest opposition in that particular desire, which must, according to his own system, be denominated by him *the will*. The determination of the mind never is, and never can be, to *do* what we do not desire to do. When we take a nauseous draught, there is a dislike, indeed, of the sensation which follows the motion, but there is no dislike of *the motion itself, which alone depends upon our will,* and which is desired by us, not from any *love* of the *disagreeable* sensation which follows it, for that would be an absurd contradiction of terms, but from our greater dislike of that continuance of bad health, which we suppose to be the probable consequence of omitting the motion. The desire of moving the hand and the muscles of deglutition is a desire, as much separate and different from the dislike of bad health, as from the dislike of the draught. It is a new desire, arising from the belief of less evil, in one of two unavoidable evils. In like manner, a judge, who condemns a criminal to death, when, if he yielded to his humanity alone, he would spare him, does not will a single *action,* which he is not desirous of performing, whatever opposition there may have been in those desires, of which his will is not a part, but only the consequence. He has a desire of saving from death an unfortunate individual; he has a desire of the public good, and of acting in a manner worthy of his high station: both these desires exist previously to those that are termed his volitions, by which alone he dooms the criminal to death; the volitions arising only from the belief of a greater good, in the same manner, as the desire of fame arises from the contemplation of fame, or any other desire from the contemplation of its object. That the will is a desire following another desire, is true: but it has that circumstance in common with many other desires, which are not considered as involving any peculiar determination, the desire of ease perhaps inducing immediately the desire of wealth, and the desire of fame, the ambition of power. Nor is it of any consequence to the distinction, that those muscular contractions, in which our volitions terminate, are objects of trifling good in themselves, and are desired, only as means of obtaining a more distant but greater good: for this circumstance, also, our volitions have in common with many of our other desires. He is indeed a miser of no vulgar proficiency in avarice, who loves gold for its own sake alone: and, though the love of fame be not that sole and universal passion, which it has been described by the satirist, we may be assured, that at least the greater number of the objects of our apparently selfish and luxurious desires, which have no reference to the happiness of our fellow creatures, and which are sought by us in all the restless business of our lives, and changed and renewed, with an ever-varying desire of elegance and comfort, as if for our own personal enjoyment, are valued by us, not for the little direct enjoyment, which we are to receive from them, but for the means, which they seem to offer, of increasing, at however dear a cost, our estimation in the respect and regard of the society in which we live.

For the sake of simplicity and conciseness, I have confined the argument to those manifest and indisputable volitions, which precede muscular motion. I am not ignorant, that what has been termed *the will* is supposed to possess an empire over the affections of the mind, as well as over the subject muscles, and therefore not to terminate uniformly in the production of *motion:* but the same arguments, which are applicable to the motions of muscles, are applicable also to those supposed volitions, which precede certain thoughts. *The will* is in truth only another name for *desire;* and we are not conscious, in such cases, first of desire, and afterwards of volition, but only of desire more or less permanent and lively. If the will had the power, which it is supposed to exercise, over the course of thought, it must consist, either in causing the existence of an idea, which would not otherwise have arisen, or in preventing the existence of an idea, which would have arisen, in the order of spontaneous association. To will *directly* the existence of a particular idea is surely to have that idea already present. To will *directly* its non-existence is a contradiction in terms; as the very will implies the existence of the idea; and the liveliness of such a desire would tend only to make the idea more lively, or rather would imply its peculiar liveliness. It is admitted, indeed, by many, that we have no such direct influence; but still they affirm, that we have it in our power, to will ideas *indirectly,* by calling up other ideas, which we know to be connected with them: yet the supposed indirect will is nothing but the existence of desire, attended by the usual ideas of association, or it is another expression of that direct volition of an idea, which is confessed to be impossible. Thus, if I wish to remember a piece of news, which was communicated to me by a friend, I am said to *call up* the ideas which I know to have been associated with it in place and time, the idea of the person, of the spot, of the attitude, of the other circumstances which were the subject of conversation: but to will the existence of any one of those ideas is to will the idea directly; and, if I can will the idea of the person, or of the spot, without any idea of the person, or of the spot, implied in my volition, I may as readily will at once the unknown idea, which is the object of my search. Indirect volition is, therefore, exactly the same thing, as direct volition; or rather it is a series of direct volitions, and cannot therefore be adduced, with the view of getting rid of any inconsistencies, which may be implied in the direct volition of a particular idea unknown to us. The true and simple theory of the recollection is to be found in the permanence of the desire, and the natural order of the associated ideas. A desire, which passes away, without the suggestion of any ideas associated with its object, is by every one allowed to be a simple desire; but, if it be of any considerable duration, during which such associated ideas arise, its name is immediately changed, and it is termed a volition. In the case of recollection already instanced, I do not *call up* the ideas of the person, the spot, the attitude, and the various circumstances communicated to me: but I have a desire of remembering something which was told me by my friend, at a certain time; and the spot, the attitude, the circumstances, rise according to the usual order of association. The remembrance of these suggests the idea of something said at the time. If it suggest that particular part of the conversation which is wished, the desire of course ceases with the gratification of it. If it suggest any other part of it, the desire continuing keeps before me the idea of the person and the place, and allows all the ideas naturally associated to arise, till I either remember what I wish, or the wish itself die away, in the hopelessness of gratification, or in the occurrence of new objects. In like manner, we are sometimes said voluntarily to banish disagreeable reflections. To banish them *directly* is evidently impossible: but, knowing that one idea awakes by association another, we may voluntarily take up a book, with the hope of being led by it into a new order of thoughts, or give ourselves to any occupation, which may induce trains of its own. In all this, there is nothing but the first step, which can be considered as voluntary; for, when the new train has begun, it has already relieved us, without our will: and that we have that will or desire, which precedes the muscular actions necessary for taking up a book, and fixing our eyes on its pages, is not denied. We are said indeed, also, to *attend* to the book. *Attention* is merely *the lively and permanent desire of those ideas, which we expect to rise immediately*. We are led to believe, that there is a peculiar volition in it, different from the mere desire; because, when we attend to any particular object, our attention seems to us to *exclude* every foreign idea: but the nonexistence of foreign ideas does not arise from any will attempting to exclude them, which would in truth imply their existence, but from the simple fact, that no foreign ideas are associated with the object of the peculiar desire. That desire of perusing the pages of the book in our hands, which is termed our *attention* to it, is associated with the book itself, more than with any other book, or any other subject of thought; and it is not wonderful, therefore, that the attention should be uninterrupted, as long as the object of desire is not fully attained. Sometimes, indeed, the ideas, which the pages suggest, awake other ideas, so lively, as to occupy us with the temporary reverie: but our attitude, and still more the sight of the book itself, recal our original desire; and, in spite of such occasional distractions, we continue to peruse our volume, till the desire of perusing it, which constitutes our attention, be either overcome by some stronger desire, or terminate in the final and complete gratification of our curiosity. The attention of composition is exactly of the same kind. It is only the desire of immediately writing on a certain subject, which, being of course associated with the ideas connected with that subject, more than with any other ideas, that are not connected with the subject, seems to exclude those foreign ideas, merely because it does not suggest them. When, however, they occasionally occur, the feeling of the posture in which we sit, and the sight of the implements of writing, and of the books and other objects before us, being more vivid than the common ideas of memory, recal us speedily to our original design, and, therefore, to the ideas connected with that design; and we finish our composition, without the intervention of any other phenomena of mind, than the permanent desire of writing on the subject, the occurrence of the usual ideas of association, and that sense of their truth or falsehood, their propriety or impropriety, which depends only on the co-existence of the ideas, and is altogether independent of our desire. It is unnecessary, to carry this examination, through all the supposed instances of voluntary command of thought. The argument would be, in all, exactly the same kind. A desire which does not pass away, without suggesting ideas of association, and which is accompanied with the belief, or hope, that its object will speedily follow, is all which, in such cases, we shall be able to discover.

The various circumstances of supposed difference in our desires and volitions, we may therefore conclude, are not such as establish any essential distinction. *The will* is a *desire,* of the same class with our other desires, and is a term of use only to denote the belief of immediate attainment, as combining with desire, a belief, however, which is not involved in the desire itself, but arises from the observed fact, that a certain motion has immediately followed it. The belief of the essential difference of volition has, however, contributed very largely to the false theory of the idea of power, which supposes it to be derived exclusively from the changes produced by the mind: for, as all, of which we are originally conscious in volition, is the mere wish of something future, which is common to all our desires, we believe, that what remains in it, and distinguishes it, must be something very mysterious, and very great, to which it is easy to attach, in a peculiar manner, the name of *connection,* or *force,* or *power,* or any other name, which scholastic philosophers may have devised.

The idea of power, we may therefore conclude, is not derived from the invariable connection of certain motions with our will, or from any other phenomena of mind, more than from the common phenomena, of matter, both which furnish trains of sequences, that differ, only as their own respective sequences differ among themselves. The very feeling of power, or of connection, if it were to arise, as is asserted, from our consciousness of the operations of our mind, would be itself only a new part of a more complicated mental sequence. In neither case can the antecedent alone, without experience, inform us of that which is to follow; and therefore the first proposition of Mr. Hume's theory must be admitted, that *the relation of cause and effect cannot be discovered a priori.*

.   .   .   .   .

CAUSES AS INVARIABLE SEQUENCE

The belief, that something stronger, than mere precession however certain and similar, is implied in *power,* and in all the synonimous expressions of agency and production, has arisen, in a great measure, from our habit of applying sequence, and other similar terms, rather to the successions of phenomena which are past, than to those which are to come. In the past, we have known casual, as well as uniform sequences; and, as the peculiar circumstance of uniformity is comprehended with proximity in the single word *cause,* we are accustomed, for conciseness, to adopt that word alone, or some other single word of the same meaning, when the great circumstance of invariableness is meant to be strongly expressed, and to apply the terms of mere succession, only to those events, in which we have no regard to uniformity of order, and in which the successions, therefore, may have been altogether casual. *Cause* and *sequence* thus assume to our mind an appearance of opposition, rather than of similarity. When, however, in our speculations on the connections of events, we reduce *cause,* by analytic definition, to its two elements of immediate priority and invariableness, we are obliged, as we cannot use any of those single words which are exactly tautologous, to revert to the use of the term *sequence,* and to qualify it by some appropriate adjective. Yet the influence of the former habit of opposition still remains; and therefore, on the first enunciation of the proposition, that cause and effect are but a species of sequence, we feel a sort of discrepancy, in the words *cause* and *sequence,* which the mere addition of the adjective *invariable* is not able to remove. Our hesitation, in part also, arises from want of sufficient attention to the difference of *uniform* and *invariable* antecedence. *Uniform* antecedence, which has reference to the past only, does not imply the idea of power; but *invariable* antecedence, which has reference, not merely to the past, but to *every future case,* is the most exact definition, which can be given, of power. *Of this we have an accurate conception, and of more than this we have no conception:* for, though we speak metaphorically of a bond connecting events, we do not mean to assert, that we have knowledge of the actual existence of a third intermediate object; as this would only transfer a supposed difficulty, from one object to another, and leave, between the new antecedent and its consequent, an invariableness of sequence, as inexplicable as before. It is, in truth, *not as expressing more than invariableness of sequence,* but merely *as being the strongest figurative expression of invariableness of sequence,* that *bond,* and its various synonimes, have been introduced into the popular philosophy of cause and effect: for the only circumstance, in which two bodies, bound together, differ from two similar bodies, which are not bound together, is, that in the former case the appearance of one of the bodies is a mark of the immediate appearance of the other, in future time as well as in the present, while, in the latter case, any casual vicinity, that is perceived by us, may be broken by the slightest accident of the next moment. A strict examination of our own feelings must be confessed to furnish, in a case of this kind, the most satisfactory evidence. We believe, that we have no direct power over the motion of our heart; because the wish to quicken or retard its motion is not followed by an increased or diminished velocity of circulation: but we are convinced, that we have in health a direct power over the muscles of our arm; because we believe, that the desire of moving it will be always followed by its motion, when there is no foreign obstacle to impede it. The desire and the motion are immediately successive; and the belief of the invariableness of this succession of the motion to our desire constitutes the belief of our muscular power. Let those, who contend for it, as implying invariableness of sequence, but as involving also something more mysterious as essential to the belief, separate in their mind the circumstances involved, and imagine an individual, such as their antagonists represent the whole human race, so constituted, that, *without the presence of the mysterious circumstance supposed,* the motion of his muscles is immediately and invariably successive to his desire of moving them: according to their supposition, this anomalous being, though he be admitted to possess experience of the past immediate sequence of the motion to his desire, and complete assurance, that the sequence will be always the same, can still have no greater belief, that he has *power* over his own muscles, than that he has *power* over the motions of the planetary system, since he is, by supposition, destitute of that, which they contend to be essential to the idea of power; yet it is surely impossible for us to imagine, that, in such circumstances, no belief of power would be felt by him, or, indeed, that he is, in any respect, constituted differently from his brethren of mankind. That power is creation, no one supposes. Though innumerable successions of causes and effects have taken place, the particles, which constitute the present world, are, we have every reason to believe, exactly the same particles, which constituted the world at the time of its creation. Certain particles, however, have often changed their place, and have always followed the change of place of certain other particles. This is merely uniform, or *unvaried,* sequence. But he who, in addition to this, believes in *invariable,* as well as uniform, sequence, believes, by the very force of the term which he uses, that the past antecedent will always be followed by the past consequent, or, in other words, that, when the circumstances are the same, the former change *never can take place without being followed by the second.* Events which are *invariable* cannot be considered as loose and casual; for these are the very qualities to which invariableness is opposed: They are *causes* and *effects,* in the strictest sense of those terms. In what their invariableness consists, it is absurd to inquire; as it is absurd to inquire, in what the mutual attractions of the particles of matter consist. We believe, in the latter case, that a body *is* heavy; we believe, in the former case, that the body *will always be* heavy; and with the nature of the attraction, or with the nature of the *perpetual similarity* of the attraction, no experiment nor reasoning can ever make us more intimately acquainted. To attempt to account for them, by the assertion of *an operating principle* in *causes,* is to be satisfied with a change of sound, when, as far as that change is significant and intelligible, the idea is the same: for, if it be difficult to comprehend invariableness of proximity, as attached to the word *cause,* it is equally difficult to comprehend it, as attached to the words *operating principle.* We should not think highly of the philosophy of him, who should flatter himself, that he had thrown much light on the *gravity* of bodies, by asserting, that it consists in their *weight:* and *an operating principle* in a *cause* is tautology, equally inelegant, and equally unsatisfactory. It is like a *sweet-making principle* in *sweetness,* and *a principle in redness* which *makes it red:* redness, sweetness, invariableness of antecedence, are all which can be understood.

.   .   .   .   .

CAUSES AND SINGLE CONJUNCTIONS

The fourth proposition of Mr. Hume's theory is, that *the relation of cause and effect is believed to exist between objects, only after their customary conjunction is known to us.* The belief, he maintains, does not arise in our mind after a single instance of sequence, but after repeated instances of the same sequence; for it is not on one observation, nor on one result of experiment, that we rely, when we have full confidence, that we have discovered a cause. But, is it not obvious, that Mr. Hume derives his argument from a state of the mind, very different from that, in which the first trains of events were observed by us? Among so many unconnected, but *co-existing* phenomena, as are perpetually taking place around us, it is impossible, that, in the multitude of trains of sequences, the parts of one train alone should be always observed by us; and the mind, therefore, even though originally led to believe *causation,* or invariable similarity in every sequence, must soon be rendered doubtful of its first belief, when, from the confusion of parts of trains, the expected sequence is found to be different. If, as Mr. Hume confesses, no experience of the past, however long and certain, entitle us to infer a future similarity of result, in the unknown time before us, with any greater evidence to our reason, than may be drawn from the first single instance of sequence, the probability is, that the original belief is not dependent on experience. At whatever stage of observation our belief begin, whether at the first or the thousandth succession of the same events, the belief itself must still be intuitive; for the propositions, *B has once succeeded A,* and *B will for ever succeed A,* are not more different than the propositions, *B has a thousand times succeeded A,* and *B will for ever succeed A.* The belief, also, at whatever stage it begin, must be allowed to be capable of being counteracted in particular cases; for we often cease to believe in causes, the reality of which has for years formed a part of our philosophic creed. The only question then seems to be, whether the belief, equally intuitive on both suppositions, arise at one stage of observation or at another; and as, on both suppositions, the mature mind, often expecting and often deceived, but deceived always less frequently as the same succession has been more frequently observed, would learn to feel the value of experience, and to withhold its complete assent, till that important confirmation should be given, it is evident, that, on the feelings of advanced years, little reliance can be placed in the question. We have thus perhaps, at best, only a comparison of probabilities; but the probabilities are surely much stronger on that side, which asserts the feeling of sequence to be *originally* followed with the belief of power, or invariable future similarity. Does the number of believed causes increase with our years? Do we not rather remember a time, when, *if without contrary experience,* we had a tendency to combine, as necessarily consecutive, the most loose and unconnected events? The effect of age seems to have been, not to[1]

---

[1] The argument, as stated above, was written, when my knowledge of Mr. Hume's theory was derived solely from his Essays, the work which he himself desires to be 'regarded as alone containing his philosophical sentiments and principles.' Since the publication of the first edition of these Observations, I have had the curiosity, to examine that part of THE TREATISE OF HUMAN NATURE, Mr. Hume's original work, which relates to the question of cause and effect; and, though, as it was not sanctioned by its author's later judgment, I do not feel myself entitled to consider it in the light even of a legitimate commentary on that exposition of his system, which he has delivered in his Essays, it may perhaps be permitted me, to make occasional reference to it in a note. At the same time, I beg it to be understood, that the occasional remarks are made by me, only in illustration of my own view of the subject, and not as furnishing any just additional confutation of those doctrines of his maturer reflection, which alone Mr. Hume has acknowledged.

The objection, arising from the belief of causation after single sequences, seems to have struck himself. Instead of denying the fact, however, which indeed would have been impossible, he admits it, and endeavours to reconcile it with his system. ' 'Tis certain,'—he says—'that not only in philosophy, but even in common life, we may attain the knowledge of a particular cause merely by one experiment, provided it be made with judgment, and after a careful removal of all foreign and superfluous circumstances.' TREATISE, Vol. I, p. 186. [*Treatise* (London, 1739), Book I, Part III, Section VIII. Ed.] He does not furnish us with any mode, however, of determining, *what are the foreign and superfluous circumstances.* The truth is, that the superfluous circumstances are merely those, of which we have had contrary experience having observed them before, without the succession of the effect: and, when the complex sequence is stripped of these, *it becomes exactly of the same kind, as the first sequence observed by us, when we had no experience either of essential or of superfluous circumstances.* If by one observation, provided it be made with judgment, we can attain the knowledge of a particular cause, we can attain it, only as being led to believe causation, in the prior of two events, where there is no contrary experience; and, if we be led to believe it, in such circumstances, the observation of sequence must have been originally and immediately accompanied with the belief of causation. It is not from the experience of custom, that we form our conclusion; for all, which that experience tells us, *is not that A is the cause of X,* which is the real phenomenon considered, but merely that B and C, which co-exist with A, are not the cause of X, but are foreign and superfluous circumstances, since they have been often observed before, without the succession of X. The argument, by which Mr. Hume endeavours to systematize this anomaly, is truly singular, when considered in relation to that very nice scepticism, on which his own system is founded. He acknowledges, that the connection of the ideas of the increase, but to diminish, the number of our convictions, by shewing us, that many events, which we considered as necessarily antecedent of others, have not been followed by them. When we mix two substances, before uncombined, and a peculiar product appears, what is the state of our mind? Do we consider the mixture and the product, as two loose phenomena, unconnected, as completely, as the appearance of the new chemical substance in our vessel, and the appearance of a friend, who accidentally enters our appartment at the moment? It is this state of mind alone, which can be reconciled with Mr. Hume's supposition; but it is surely not the state of mind of the chemist. He believes the product to be the *effect* of the mixture, or, if he have not absolute assurance, the want of conviction *arises only from the doubts which are suggested by his past experience.* The accidental changes of temperature, the impurity of the substances used, the presence of air, or of other foreign matters, in the vessel, and the peculiar affinities of the vessel itself, occur to him *as causes* which may have modified the result. To these he turns his attention. By some possible variation of these, he believes, that the event may possibly be different; but, were he certain, that all these circumstances would for ever be the same, he would have no doubt, that the resulting product also would for ever be the same. The exact similarity of all circumstances being supposed, his conviction, after one experiment, would be, in every respect, as complete, as after a thousand repetitions. It is not necessary, to be a practised experimentalist, to have felt this confutation of Mr. Hume's theory. In the common circumstances of life, how often have we felt a struggle, between our tendency to conjoin events, and the past experience, which shews us that they have no necessary connection? It is a struggle, like that which we feel with another very strong principle of

---

first and second objects of a sequence is not habitual, after one experiment, but contends, that the connection is comprehended in another, which has been previously acquired by habit. 'The difficulty,'—he observes—'will vanish, if we consider, that though we are here suppos'd to have had only one experiment of a particular effect, yet we have many millions to convince us of this principle, *that like objects, placed in like circumstances, will always produce like effects;* and as this principle has established itself by a sufficient custom, it bestows an evidence and firmness on any opinion, to which it can be apply'd.' [*Ibid. Treatise.* Ed.] The sophism of this argument consists in the different meanings, which may be attached to the phrase *like objects.* It may signify *the many like objects,* of which we have had customary experience, or it may signify ALL *like objects,* of which we have had no customary experience. In the former sense only, can it be said, that we have millions of experiments to convince us of the truth of the principle asserted; but in the latter sense only, can it be of any aid to Mr. Hume. The experience of a million sequences cannot go beyond a million sequences; and, though we may know, that A has been a million times followed by X, and B by Y, we are not entitled, on Mr. Hume's own strict principles of scepticism, to infer from these dissimilar sequences, that C, of the priority of which we have had no customary experience, is the cause of Z. It surely would be no very great extension of this concession, to suppose, that A, which has a million times preceded X, would, if it existed again, be again followed by X; and, if the legitimacy of this inference be admitted, all the force of Mr. Hume's scepticism on the relation of cause and effect is immediately destroyed.

belief, when we look through an optical instrument, on a landscape that is familiar to us. The church, and the lake, and its hanging wood, appear to us indeed to be near; but we have a stronger conviction, from past experience, that they are far off: and we do not hasten, as if he were before us, to meet the friend, whom we see approaching at the very end of our telescope. Did *one train of phenomena alone* take place in nature, it is probable, that our conviction would be in every case undoubting; but we learn, from varied disappointment, that innumerable trains are taking place together, and we feel a want of certainty,—*but it is in this only,* that we are ignorant, *to which of the trains the particular phenomenon belongs.* The very knowledge, that there are separate trains of phenomena, is itself one of the strongest proofs, that the belief of causation is immediate. It is seldom that one simple sensation exists; or, rather, no sensation is entirely simple. Various objects at the same moment affect us, and form an aggregate, which is, probably, at no other period exactly the same. If, therefore, the return of antecedents and consequents, exactly similar, were necessary, before any belief could arise, it never would arise; as, if there was no presumption that A, which once before succeeded X, would succeed it again, more than B, or C, which we had never before observed to succeed X, it would be impossible, when X, Y, Z, were, at one moment, producing A, B, C, to determine, of which part of the aggregate the renewed A was the consequence. The analysis and distribution depend only on the belief, or presumption, which followed the observation of the first sequence. Without this, the mixed sequence would be as loose as before; and hence, the very supposition, that custom has any effect in determining our belief, is an avowal, that a previous anticipation existed. Even with all the doubts, which the experience of many years has given us, we never hesitate, in simpler cases, in which we less suspect concurring trains, to believe, where, according to Mr. Hume, belief is impossible. The organ of taste, for instance, is of easy limitation, with little chance of the admixture of foreign bodies. When a new fruit is presented to us, and we apply it to that organ, though altogether deprived of the aid of customary connection, and therefore, according to Mr. Hume, incapable of forming any opinion, but that of casual sequence, we have no scruple in ascribing the new sensation to the new object, and we say, that it is sweet, or acid, or bitter. The epicure, who relishes a new ragout, knows well that the source of his pleasure is in the dish before him, and, if he wish to enjoy it again, it is to that dish alone he returns, though twenty new objects be around it. We pluck a flower, which we have never before seen; we are sensible of a disagreeable odour; and we throw away the flower, as if from it the odour arose. The boy, who for the first time catches a bee, and is astonished to feel its sting, does not wait for a second and third application of the poison, before he learn to fear it in future. Whether his belief be consistent with reason, is not the inquiry. It has been already admitted, that the similarity of future events is not a conclusion of reason, derived from the perceived agreement of propositions, but is a single unconnected proposition, believed, not judged, that rises in the mind, inevitably, and with irresistible conviction. Whether true or false, the belief is in these cases felt, and it is felt without even the possibility of a perceived customary conjunction. Would Mr. Hume himself have considered the sequences as purely accidental? He owns, that, 'when a child has felt the sensation of pain from touching the flame of a candle, he will be careful not to put his hand near any candle:' [1] yet the child, even though old enough, to have acquired an accurate knowledge of the places of objects, and thus to be certain that it is the candle which is burning him, should, in such circumstances, think no more of removing his finger from the flame, than of shaking off the bandage of his foot. As the question is not concerning the justness of belief, but concerning the period of its rise, there is one case, which may be considered, as almost decisive of it. We often see a phenomenon, for the first time, without having attended to the particular circumstances, which preceded it. If it be the experience of custom alone, which can give us that belief of connection, by which we denominate a change an *effect,* we are, in this case, not merely without a customary sequence; we have not even a single case of it. Yet there is no one, who does not believe the change to be *an* effect, as completely as if he had witnessed every preceding circumstance. On this one point he is in no suspense, and waits, only to discover *what* object, in the uniform and regular order of succession, was its correlative cause. Are we then to assert, that all phenomena, before repeated experience of their particular conjunctions, appear to us equally loose, and that the supposition of a peculiar connection can in no instance arise, till the observed conjunction has been customary? Do not all the circumstances of our belief rather support the contrary opinion, that a peculiar connection may be supposed, even after a single sequence; that, as innumerable trains of phenomena are taking place together, and mingling in our observation, the *primary* effect of experience has been, not to increase, but to weaken, our belief of the connection of events, by presenting to us, as a regular train of consequents, irregular portions of different co-existing trains; that, our expectation of uniformity being thus often disappointed, a habit of doubt has arisen, and the *secondary* influence of experience begins to operate, which, by shewing us the customary successions of events, though it give us not our first notion of the connection of trains of phenomena, informs us, with greater certainty, to which, of many co-existing trains, a particular phenomenon belongs; that hence the belief of connection, which, according to Mr. Hume, should, in every case,

[1] *Enquiry,* Section IV, Part II, p. 33. Ed.

depend on the number of observations, and on nothing more, is more or less early, according to the nature of the particular phenomena observed, as these furnish greater or less room for imagining a number of concurring trains, being immediate, or almost immediate, where the new sequence is simple, and of longer suspense, where the sequence is complex.

If the preceeding reasoning be just, the error of Mr. Hume evidently consists, not in affirming too much, but in affirming too little: for, if any succession of events can suggest the expectation of future similarity, there is surely nothing in the frequent recurrence of the succession, which can diminish the expectation. It may not be greater, after it has been often confirmed, but it certainly cannot be less; and the theory is therefore objectionable, only as confining, to sequences that have been often observed, a belief, which, originally at least, is common to them with other sequences. Yet, by a singular mistake, Mr. Hume has been censured by his opponents, as if his affirmation had been too large. Thus, it has been maintained, that there are cases of uniform succession, in which the belief of causation is never felt, since, from the very commencement of our existence,[1] day has succeeded night in endless return, without any supposition arising, that night is the cause of day. But it should be remembered, that *day* and *night* are not words which denote two particular phenomena, but are words invented by us to express long series of phenomena. What various appearances of nature, from the freshness of the first morning beam, to the last languor of the evening sky, changing with the progress of the seasons, and dependent on the accidents of temperature, and vapour, and wind, are included in every day! These are not one, because the word which expresses them is one; and it is the believed relation of single events, not the arbitrary combinations of language, which Mr. Hume professes to explain. If, therefore, there be any force in the objection, it must be shewn, that, notwithstanding the customary conjunction, we do not believe the relation of cause and effect to exist, between the successive *pairs* of that multitude of events, which we denominate night and day. What then are the great events included in those terms? If we consider them philosophically, they are the series of positions in relation to the sun, at which the earth arrives, in the course of its diurnal revolution; and, in this view, there is surely no one, who doubts, that the motion of the earth, immediately before sun-rise, is the cause of the position, which renders that glorious luminary visible to us. If we consider the phenomena of night and day, in a

---

[1] 'The third argument is, that what we call a cause, is only something antecedent to, and always conjoined with the effect.—It is sufficient here to observe, that we may learn from it that night is the cause of day; and day the cause of night: for no two things have more constantly followed each other since the beginning of the world.' Reid, on the Intellectual Powers, Essay vi, chap. 6. [See Reid's *Works*, Vol. I, Hamilton edition, p. 457. Ed.]

more vulgar sense, they include various degrees of darkness and light, with some of the chief changes of appearance in the heavenly bodies. Even in this sense, there is no one who doubts, that the rising of the sun is the cause of the light which follows it, and that its setting is the cause of the subsequent darkness. That darkness and light mutually produce each other, they do not believe: and, if they did believe it, their belief, instead of confirming the truth of Mr. Hume's theory, would prove it to be false; as it would prove the relation of cause and effect to be supposed, where there has been no customary connection. How often, during a long and sleepless night, does the sensation of darkness exist, without being followed by the sensation of light! We perceive the gloom;—we feel our own position in bed, or some bodily or mental pain, which prevents repose;—innumerable thoughts arise, at intervals, in our mind, and with these the perception of gloom is occasionally mingled, without being followed by the perception of light. At last light is perceived, and, as mingled with all our occupations and pleasures, is perceived innumerable times during the day, without having, for its immediate consequence, the sensation of darkness. Can we then be said, to have an uniform experience of the conjunction of the two sensations? Do they not rather appear to follow each other loosely and variously, like those irregular successions of events, which we denominate accidental? In the vulgar, therefore, as well as in the philosophic sense of the terms, the recurrence of day and night furnishes no valid objection to Mr. Hume's theory.

The general conclusion, accordingly, to which we are led, on the fourth proposition, is, that the experience of customary succession is not necessary to the belief of future similarity of sequence; but that, where, from a supposed concurrence of separate trains of phenomena, any doubt is felt, the influence of the experience of customary succession is always to diminish the doubt.

·   ·   ·   ·   ·

SELECTIONS FROM

Lectures on the Philosophy of the Human Mind *

*

LECTURE VIII

ON HYPOTHESIS AND THEORY

. . . That *hypotheses,* in that wide sense of the word which implies every thing conjectural, are without use in philosophy, it would be

* Vol. I and II. W. and C. Tait, 4 vol. (Edinburgh, 1820).

absurd to affirm, since every inquiry may, in that wide sense, be said to presuppose them, and *must always* pre-suppose them if the inquiry have any object. They are of use, however, not as *superseding* investigation, but as *directing* investigation to certain objects,—not as telling us, *what we are to believe,* but as pointing out to us *what we are to endeavour to ascertain.* An hypothesis, in this view of it, is nothing more than a reason for making *one* experiment or observation rather than *another;* and it is evident, that, without some reason of this kind, as experiment and observations are almost infinite, inquiry would be altogether profitless. To make experiments, at random, is not to *philosophize;* it becomes philosophy, only when the experiments are made *with a certain view;* and to make them, with any particular view, is to suppose the presence of something, the operation of which they will tend either to prove or disprove. When Torricelli, for example,— proceeding on the observation previously made, by Galileo, with respect to the limited height to which water could be made to rise in a pump,—that memorable observation, which demonstrated, at last, after so many ages of errors, what ought not for a single moment to have required to be demonstrated; the absurdity of the horror of a void ascribed to nature—when, proceeding in this memorable observation, Torricelli made his equally memorable experiment with respect to the height of the column of mercury supported in an inverted tube, and found, on comparison of their specific gravities, the columns of *mercury* and *water* to be exactly equiponderant, it is evident that he was *led* to the experiment with the mercury by the *supposition,* that the rise of fluids *in vacuo* was occasioned by some counterpressure, exactly equal to the weight supported, and that the column of mercury, therefore, should be *less* in height than the column of water, in the exact inverse ratio of their specific gravities, *by which* the counterpressure was to be sustained. To conceive the air, which was then universally regarded as essentially *light,* to be not *light* but *heavy,* so as to press on the *fluid* beneath, was, at that time, to make as bold a *supposition* as *could* be made. It was, indeed, a temporary hypothesis, even when it led to that experimental demonstration of the fact, which proved it for ever after not to be *hypothetical.*

An hypothesis, then, in the first stage of inquiry, far from being *inconsistent* with sound philosophy, may be said to be *essential* to it. But it is essential *only in this first stage,* as suggesting what is afterwards to be verified or disproved; and, when the experiments or observations to which it directs us do not verify it, it is no longer to be entertained, *even as an hypothesis.* If we observe a phenomenon, which we never have observed before, it is absolutely impossible for us, *not* to think of the *analogous* cases which we may have seen; since they are suggested by a principle of association, which is as truly a part of our constitution, as the *senses* with which we perceived the phenomenon itself; and, if any of these analogies strike us as remarkably coincident, it is equally impossible for us not to *imagine,* that the cause, which we knew in that former instance, *may* also be present in this analogical instance, and that they *may,* therefore, both be reduced to the same class. To stop here, and, from this mere analogy, to infer positive identity of the causes, and to follow out the possible consequences, in innumerable applications, would be to do, as many great artists in systematizing have done. What a philosopher, of sounder views, however, would do, in such a case, is very different. He would assume, indeed as *possible,* or perhaps as *probable,* the existence of the supposed cause. But he would assume it, only to direct his examination of its reality, by investigating, as far as he was able, from past experience, what the circumstances would have been, in every respect, *if* the cause supposed had been actually present; and, even if these were all found to be exactly coincident, though he would think the presence of the cause *more probable,* he would be very far from considering it as *certain,* and would still endeavour to *lessen* the *chances* of fallacy, by watching the circumstances, should they again recur, and varying them, by experiment, in every possible way. . . .

While I wish to caution you against a fondness for hypotheses, by shewing you, not merely that they are *liable to error,*—for inquiry, *of every kind,* must be so in some degree,—but that, in truth, they leave the real difficulty of the succession of the observed consequents to the observed antecedents *as great as before,* and only add, to the supposed difficulty of explaining *one* sequence, the necessity of explaining a *sequence additional,*—I must remark, at the same time, that what is commonly termed *theory,* in opposition to *hypothesis,* is far from being *so* different from it as is commonly represented,—at least, in the very wide application which is usually made of it. We are told, by those who lay down rules of philosophizing, that the object of philosophy is, to observe particulars, and, from these, to frame *general laws,* which may, again, be applied to the explanation of particulars; and the view which is thus given of the real province of philosophy is undoubtedly a just one;—but there is an ambiguity in the language which may deceive you, and with respect to which, therefore, it is necessary for you to be on your guard. *If,* by the term *general law,* be meant the agreement in some common circumstances of a number of events observed, there can be no question that we proceed *safely* in framing it, and that what we have already found in *a number of events,* must be applicable *to that number of events;* in the same manner, as, after combining in the term *animal* the circumstances in which a *dog,* a *horse,* a *sheep* agree, we cannot err in applying the term *animal* to a *dog,* a *horse,* a *sheep.* But the only particular to which, in this case, we can, *with perfect confidence,* apply a *general law,* are *the very particulars* that have been before observed by us. If it be understood as *more*

general than the circumstances observed, and, therefore, capable of
being applied with perfect certainty to the explanation of new phenomena, we evidently, to the extent in which the general law is applied *beyond* the circumstances *observed,* proceed on *mere supposition,* as truly, as in any hypothesis which we could have framed; and
though the supposition may be more and more certain, in proportion
to the number of cases thus generalized, and the absence of any circumstance which can be supposed, in the new case, to be inconsistent
with it, it never can amount to actual certainty. Let us take, for example, one of the most striking cases of this sort. That bodies tend to
each other, *in all circumstances,* with a force increasing directly as
their quantities, and inversely as the squares of their distances, may
seem in the highest degree probable indeed, from the innumerable
facts observed on our globe, and in the magnificent extent of the planetary movements; but it cannot be said to be certain at all distances, in
which we have never had an opportunity of making observations,—as
it seems to be verified in the heights of our atmosphere, and in the
distances of the planets, in their orbits, from the sun, and from each
other. It is not necessary, however, to refer, for possible exceptions, to
spaces that are beyond our observation; since, on the surface of our
own earth, there is abundant evidence, that the law does *not* hold
universally. Every quiescent mass that is capable of greater compression, and of which the particles, therefore, before that compression,
are not in absolute contact, shews sufficiently, that the principle of
attraction, which, of itself, would have brought them into actual contact, must have ceased to operate, while there was still a space between the particles that would have allowed its free operation; and, in
the phenomena of *elasticity,* and *impulse in general,* it has not merely
ceased, but is actually reversed,—the bodies which, at all visible distances, exhibited a reciprocal *attraction,* now exhibiting a reciprocal
repulsion, in consequence of which they mutually fly off, as readily as
they before approached,—that is to say, the tendency of bodies *to*
each other being converted into a tendency *from* each other, by a
mere change of distance, so slight as to be almost inappreciable.
When a ball rebounds from the earth, toward which it moved rapidly
before, and the gravitating tendency is thus evidently reversed, without the intervention of any foreign force, what eye, though it be aided
by all the nicest apparatus of optical art, can discover the lines which
separate those infinitesimal differences of proximity, at which the particles of the ball still continue to gravitate toward the earth, and are
afterwards driven *from* it in an opposite direction;—yet the phenomenon itself is a sufficient proof, that in these spaces, which seem, to our
organs of sense, so completely the same, that it is absolutely impossible for us to distinguish them, the reciprocal tendencies of the particles of the ball and of the earth are as truly opposite, as if the laws of

gravitation had, at the moment at which the rebound begins, been reversed through the whole system of the universe.

It is, indeed, scarcely possible to imagine a more striking proof of the danger of extending, with too great certainty, a general law, than this instant conversion of *attraction* into *repulsion,* without the addition of any new bodies, without any change in the nature of the bodies themselves, and a change of their circumstances so very slight, as to be absolutely indistinguishable, but for the opposite motions that result from it, with a change of their circumstances. After observing the gravity of bodies, at all heights of our atmosphere, and extending our survey through the wide spaces of our solar system,—computing the tendency of the planets to the sun, and their disturbing forces, as they operate on each other,—and finding the resulting motions exactly to correspond with those which we had predicted by theory;—in these circumstances, after an examination so extensive, if we had affirmed, *as an universal law of matter,* that, at all distances, bodies tend toward each other, we should have considered the wideness of the induction, as justifying the affirmation; and yet, even in this case, we find, on the surface of our earth, in the mutual shocks of bodies, *and in their very rest,* sufficient evidence, that, in making the universal affirmation, we should have reasoned falsely. There is no theory, then, which, if applied to the *explanation* of new phenomena, is not, to a certain degree, conjectural; because it must proceed on the supposition, that what was true in certain circumstances, is true also in circumstances that have not been observed. It admits of certainty, only when it is applied to *the very substances observed—in the very circumstances observed*—in which case, it may be strictly said to be nothing more than the application of a general *term* to the particulars, which we have before agreed to comprehend in it. Whatever is more than this is truly *hypothetical,*—the difference being, that we commonly give the name of *hypothesis* to cases, in which we suppose the intervention of some *substance,* of the existence of which, as present in the phenomenon, we have no direct proof, or of some additional quality of a substance before unobserved—and the name of *theory* to cases, which do not suppose the existence of any substance, that is not actually observed, or of any *quality* that has not been actually observed, but merely the continuance, in certain *new* circumstances, of tendencies observed in other circumstances. Thus, if a planet were discovered revolving in the space which separates the orbits of any two planets at present known, were we to suppose of matter, in this new situation, that it would be subject to the *same exact law of gravitation,* to which the other planets were known to be subject, and to predict its place in the heavens, at any time, according to this law, we should be said to form a theory of its motions; as we should not take for granted, any new quality of a substance, or the existence of any substance, which was not evidently present, but only of *tendencies* observed before in other circumstances,—analogous indeed, but not absolutely the same. We should be said to form an *hypothesis* on the subject, if, making the same prediction, as to its motions, and place in the heavens, at any given time, we were to ascribe the centripetal tendency, which confines it within its orbit, to the impulse of ether, or to any other mechanical cause. The terms, however, I must confess, though the distinction which I have now stated would be, in all cases, a very convenient one, are used very loosely, not in conversation merely, but in the writings of philosophers,—an *hypothesis* often meaning nothing more than a *theory,* to which we have *not* given our assent,—and a *theory, an hypothesis* which we have adopted, or still more, *one* which we have formed ourselves.

A *theory,* then, even in that best sense, to which I wish it accurately confined, as often as it ventures *a single hair-breadth* beyond the line of former observation, *may* be wrong, as an *hypothesis* may be wrong. But, in a *theory,* in this sense of it, there are both less risk of error, and less extensive evil from error, than in an hypothesis. There is less risk of error, because we speak only of the properties of bodies, *that must be allowed actually to exist;* and the evil of error is, for the same reason, *less extensive,* since it must be confined to this single point; whereas, if we were to imagine falsely the presence of some third substance, our supposition might involve as many errors, as that substance has qualities; since we should be led to suppose, and expect, some or all of the *other* consequences, which usually attend it, when really present.

.   .   .   .   .

LECTURE XI

ON CONSCIOUSNESS

In the systems of philosophy, which have been most generally prevalent, especially in this part of the Island, consciousness has always been classed as one of the intellectual powers of the mind, differing from its other powers, as these mutually differ from each other. It is accordingly ranked by Dr Reid, as separate and distinct, in his Catalogue of the Intellectual Powers; and he says of it, that "it is an operation of the understanding *of its* own kind, and cannot be logically defined. The objects of it are our present pains, our pleasures, our hopes, our fears, our desires, our doubts, our thoughts of every kind, —in a word, all the passions, and all the actions and operations of our own minds, while they are present." [1] And in various parts of his works, which it would be needless to quote, he alludes to its radical difference from the other powers of the mind, as if it were a point on which there could be no question. To me, however, I must confess, it appears, that this attempt to *double,* as it were, our various feelings, by making them not to *constitute our consciousness,* but *to be the objects of it,* as of a distinct intellectual power, is not a faithful statement of the phenomena of the mind, but is founded, partly on a confusion of thought, and still more on a confusion of language. Sensation is not the *object* of consciousness different from itself, but a *particular sensation* is the *consciousness of the moment;* as a particular *hope,* or *fear,* or *grief,* or *resentment,* or simple *remembrance,* may be the *actual consciousness of the next moment.* In short, if the mind of man, and all the changes which take place in it, from the first feeling with which life commenced, to the last with which it closes, could be made *visible* to any other thinking being, *a certain series of feelings alone,* that is to say, a certain number of successive states of the mind, would be distinguishable in it, forming, indeed, a variety of sensations, and thoughts, and passions, as momentary *states* of the mind, but all of them existing individually, and successively to each other. To suppose the mind to exist in two different states, in the same moment, is a manifest absurdity. To the whole series of states of the mind, then, whatever the individual momentary successive states may be, I give the name of our *consciousness,*—using that term, not to express any new state additional to the whole series, (for to that, which is already *the whole,* nothing can be added, and the mind, as I have already said, cannot be conceived to exist at once in two different states,) but merely as a short mode of expressing the wide variety of our feelings; in the same manner, as I use any other generic word, for expressing briefly the individual varieties comprehended under it. There are not sensations, thoughts, passions, *and also consciousness,* any more than there is *quadruped* or *animal,* as a separate being, to be added to the wolves, tygers, elephants, and other living creatures, which I include under those terms.

The fallacy of conceiving consciousness to be something different from the feeling, which is said to be *its object,* has arisen, in a great measure, from the use of the personal pronoun *I,* which the conviction of our *identity,* during the various feelings, or temporary consciousnesses of different moments, has led us to employ, as significant of our permanent *self,* of that being, which is conscious, and *variously* conscious, and which continues, after these feelings have ceased, to be the subject of other consciousness, as transient as the former. *I* am *con-*

[1] *Essays on the Intellectual Powers* (Edinburgh, 1785), Essay VI, Chapter V, 1. Reprinted in the present volume. Ed.

scious of a certain feeling, really means, however, no more than this —*I feel in a certain manner*, or, in other words, *my mind exists in that state* which constitutes a certain feeling;—the mere *existence of that feeling*, and not any additional and distinguishable feeling that is to be termed *consciousness*, being all which is essential to the state of my mind, at the particular moment of sensation; for a pleasure, or pain, of which we are not conscious, is a pleasure or pain, that, in reference to us at least, has no existence. But when we say, *I am conscious* of a *particular feeling*, in the usual paraphrastic phraseology of our language, which has no mode of expressing, *in a single word*, the *mere existence* of a feeling, we are apt, from a prejudice of grammar, to separate the sentient *I* and the *feeling* as *different*,—not different, as they really are, *merely in this respect*, that the *feeling* is one momentary and changeable state of the permanent *substance I*, that is, capable of existing also, at other moments, in other states,—but so *radically different*, as to justify our classing the feeling, in the relation of an *object*, to that sentient principle which we call *I*,—and an object to it, not in retrospect only, as when the feeling is *remembered*, or when it is viewed in relation to other remembered feelings,—but in the very moment of the *primary* sensation itself; as if there could truly be two distinct states of the same mind, at that same moment, one of which states is to be termed *sensation*, and the other different state of the same mind to be termed *consciousness*.

To estimate more accurately the effect, which this reference to self produces, let us imagine a human being to be born with his faculties perfect as in mature life, and let us suppose a sensation to arise for the first time in his mind. For the sake of greater simplicity, let us suppose the sensation to be of a kind as little complex as possible; such, for example, as that which the fragrance of a rose excites. If, immediately after this first sensation, we imagine the sentient principle to be extinguished, what are we to call that feeling, which filled and constituted the brief moment of life? It was a simple sensation, and nothing more; and if only we say, that the sensation has existed,—whether we say, or do not say, that the mind was conscious of the sensation,—we shall convey precisely the same meaning; the *consciousness of the sensation* being, in that case, only a tautological expression of the *sensation itself*. There will be, in this first momentary state, no separation of *self* and the *sensation*,—no little proposition formed in the mind, *I feel*, or *I am conscious of a feeling;* but the *feeling* and the *sentient I* will, for the moment, be the same. It is this simple feeling, and this alone, which is the whole consciousness of the first moment; and no reference can be made of this to a *self*, which is independent of the temporary *consciousness;* because the knowledge of *self*, as distinct from the particular feeling, implies the remembrance of former feelings,—of feelings, which, together with the present, we ascribe to *one* thinking principle,—recognizing the *principle, the self, the one,* as the *same,* amid all its transient diversities of consciousness.

Let us now, then, instead of supposing life, as in the former case, to be extinguished immediately after the first sensation, suppose another sensation to be excited, as for instance that which is produced by the sound of a flute. The mind either will be completely absorbed in this new sensation, without any subsequent remembrance,—in which case *the consciousness of the sensation,* as in the case of the fragrance that preceded it, will be only another more paraphrastic expression of the simple *sensation*—or the remembrance of the former feeling will arise. If the remembrance of the former feeling arise, and the two different feelings be considered by the mind at once, it will *now,* by that irresistible law of our nature, which impresses us with the conviction of our identity, conceive the *two* sensations, which it recognizes as different in themselves, to have yet belonged to the *same being,*— that being, to which, when it has the use of language, it gives the name of *self,* and in relation to which it speaks, as often as it uses the pronoun *I.*—The notion of *self,* as the lasting subject of successive transient feelings, being *now, and not till now,* acquired, through the remembrance of *former* sensations or temporary diversities of consciousness, the mind will often again, when other new sensations may have arisen, go through a similar process, being not merely affected with the particular momentary sensation, but remembering other prior feelings, and identifying it with them, in the general designation of self. In these circumstances the memory of the past will often mingle with and modify the present; and, *now* indeed, to form the verbal proposition, *I am conscious of a particular sensation,*—since the very word *I* implies that this remembrance and identification *has* taken place,—may be allowed to express *something more than the mere existence of the momentary sensation:* for it expresses also that the mind, which now exists in the state of this particular sensation, *has formerly existed in a different state.* There is a remembrance of former feelings, and a belief that the present and the past have been states of one substance. But this belief, or, in other words, this remembrance of former feelings, is so far from being essential to every thought or sensation, that innumerable feelings every moment arise, without any such identification with the past. They are *felt,* however, for this is necessarily implied in their existence; but they exist, *as transient thoughts or sensations only,* and the *consciousness,* which we have of them, in these circumstances, is nothing more, than *the thoughts or sensations themselves,* which could not be *thoughts* or *sensations* if they were not *felt.*

In the greater number of our successions of momentary feelings, then, when *no* reference is made to former states of the mind, the consciousness is obviously nothing more than the simple momentary feeling itself as it begins and ceases; and *when* there *is* a reference to former states of the mind, we discover on analysis only a remembrance, like all our other remembrances, and a feeling of common relation of the past and the present affection of the mind to one permanent subject. It is the belief of our continued identity which involves this particular feeling of relation of past and present feelings; and consciousness, in this sense of the term, is only a word expressive of that belief.

That the fragrance of a rose, the sound of a flute, and in general all the other objects of sense, might have excited *precisely the same immediate sensations* as at present, Doctor Reid admits, *though* the belief of our personal identity had *not* been impressed upon us; for he ascribes this belief to an *instinctive principle only,* and acknowledges, that there is nothing *in our sensations themselves,* from which any such inference could be drawn by reason. If, then, this instinctive belief of identity had *not* been, as at present, a natural law of human thought,—operating irresistibly on the remembrance of our different feelings, we should have had no notion of *self,* of *me,* the sentient and thinking being, who exists at the present moment, and who existed before the present moment:—and what, then, would have been the consciousness, accompanying, and different from, our sensations, when they merely flashed along the mind and vanished? The most zealous defender of consciousness, as a separate intellectual power, must surely admit, that, *in such circumstances,* it would have been nothing more than *sensation* itself. It is the belief of our *identity* only, which gives us the notion of *self,* as the subject of *various* feelings, and it is the notion of *self,* as the *subject* of *various former feelings,* which leads us to regard the consciousness of the moment, as different from the sensation of the moment; because it suggests to us those former feelings, which truly were different from it, or at least that *subject mind,* which unquestionably existed before the present sensation.

If it be said that the faculty of consciousness is nothing more than this reference to the past, and consequent belief of identity, we may, in that case, very safely admit its existence; though the classification of it, as a peculiar *intellectual power,* would in that case be a most singular anomaly in arrangement, and would involve a very absurd, or at least a very *awkward* use of a term. To assert this signification of it, however, would be to admit every thing for which I have contended. But it certainly is not the sense, which has been attached to it by philosophers; and indeed, in *this* sense, *consciousness,* instead of having for its objects, as Doctor Reid says, *all* "our present pains, our pleasures, our hopes, our fears, our desires, our doubts, our thoughts of every kind; in a word, all the passions, and all the actions and operations of our own mind, while they are present," would be limited to the comparatively *few,* of which the consideration of our personal identity forms a part. In far the greater number of our feelings, as I have already said, the sensation dies away, almost in the moment,— not, indeed, without being enjoyed or suffered, but without any reference to self, as the subject of various feelings, or remembrance of any *prior* state of mind, as distinct from the present. The belief of our identity, is surely not the only belief that arises from an instinctive principle; and if *its* existence *entitle us,* in our systematic arrangements, *to the possession of a new intellectual power,* every *other* belief that arises instinctively from a principle of our constitution, must give us a similar title to enlarge the catalogue of our faculties. The never-failing and instant faith, by which we expect, without the slightest doubt of the similarity of the future, that events will continue to *follow* each other, in the same order as at present,—that bodies will fall to the ground, fire burn, food satisfy the craving of our appetite—that immediate intuitive principle of belief, on which all our foresight depends, and according to which we regulate our whole conduct in providing for the future,—should certainly, in that case, be ascribed by us to some peculiar intellectual power, for which it would be easy to invent a name. It is not, by any inference of our reason, we believe, that the sound of a flute which preceded the fragrance of a rose, and the fragrance of a rose which followed the sound of a flute, excited sensations that were states of the same identical mind; for there is nothing, in either of the *separate* sensations, or *in both together,* from which such an *inference* can be drawn; and yet, notwithstanding the impossibility of inferring it, we believe this, at least as strongly, as we believe any of the conclusions of our reasoning. In like manner, it is not by any inference of reason we believe, that fire will warm us to-morrow, as it has warmed us to-day; for there is nothing, in the fire of to-day, or in the sensation of warmth, considered as a mere sequence of it, from which the succession of a similar sensation to the fire of to-morrow can be inferred; yet we also rely on this future sequence, at least as strongly, as we believe any of the conclusions of our reasoning. In both cases the parallel is complete; and in both, the evidence of a *particular intellectual faculty* must consequently be alike,—*or* in *neither* is there sufficient evidence of such a power.

There is, indeed, one other sense, in which we often talk of our *consciousness of a feeling,* and a sense, in which, it must be allowed, that the consciousness *is not precisely the same as the feeling itself.* This is, when we speak of a feeling, not actually existing at present, but *past*—as when we say, that we are conscious of having seen, or heard, or done something. Such a use of the term, however, is pardonable only in the privileged looseness and inaccuracy of familiar conversation; the *consciousness,* in this case, being precisely synonimous with *remembrance* or *memory,* and not a power, different from the remembrance. The *remembrance* of the feeling, and the vivid *feeling* itself, indeed, are different. But the *remembrance,* and the *consciousness of the remembrance,* are the same—as the *consciousness of a sensation,* and the *sensation,* are the same; and to be *conscious* that we have seen or spoken to any one, is only to *remember* that we have seen or spoken to him.

Much of this very confusion with respect to memory, however, I have no doubt, has been always involved in the assertion of consciousness as a peculiar and distinct power of the mind. When we think of feelings *long past,* it is impossible for us not to be aware that our mind is then truly retrospective; and *memory* seems to us sufficient to account for the whole. But when the retrospect is of *very recent* feelings—of feelings, perhaps, that existed as distinct states of the mind, the very moment before our retrospect began, the short interval is forgotten, and we think that the primary feeling, and our consideration of the feeling, are strictly simultaneous. We have a sensation;—we look instantly back on that sensation,—such is consciousness, as distinguished from the feeling that is said to be its object. When it is anything more than the sensation, thought, or emotion, of which we are said to be conscious, it is a brief and rapid retrospect. Its object is not a *present* feeling, but a *past* feeling, as truly as when we look back, not on the moment immediately preceding, but on some distant event or emotion of our boyhood. . . .

LECTURE XXII

ON THE FEELINGS USUALLY ASCRIBED TO THE SENSE OF TOUCH—AND ANALYSIS OF THESE FEELINGS

. . . By *touch,* we are commonly said to be made acquainted with *extension, magnitude, divisibility, figure, motion, solidity, liquidity, viscidity, hardness, softness, roughness, smoothness.* These *terms,* I readily allow, are very convenient for expressing *notions* of certain forms or states of bodies, that are easily distinguishable. But, though specifically distinguishable, they admit generically of very considerable reduction and simplification. Hardness and softness, for example, are expressive only of greater or less resistance,—roughness is *irregularity* of resistance, when there are intervals between the points that resist, or when some of these points project beyond others,—smoothness is complete uniformity of resistance,—liquidity, viscidity, are expressive of certain degrees of yieldingness to our effort, which solidity excludes, unless when the effort employed is violent. All, in short, I repeat, are only different species or degrees of that which we term *resistance,* whatever it may be, which impedes our continued effort, and impedes it *variously,* as the substances without are themselves various. Such is one order, then, of the feelings commonly ascribed to the sense which we are at present considering.

To proceed to the other supposed tangible qualities, before included in our enumeration,—*figure* is the boundary of *extension,* as *magnitude* is that which it comprehends; and *divisibility,* if we consider the apparent continuity of the parts which we divide, is only *extension* under another name. If we except *motion,* therefore, which is not permanent, but accidental,—and the knowledge of which is evidently *secondary* to the knowledge which we acquire of our organs of sense, before which the objects are said to *move,*—and secondary in a much more important sense, as resulting not from any direct immediate organic state of one particular moment, but from a comparison of sensations past and present,—all the information, which we are supposed to receive primarily and directly from touch, relates to modifications of *resistance* and *extension.*

Though it is to the sense of *touch,* however, that the origin of the knowledge of these is generally ascribed, I am inclined to think, in opposition to this opinion, that, in both cases, the reference is wrongly made,—that if we had the sense of touch *only,* we should not be sensible of *resistance,* nor, I conceive, even of *extension,*—and that we seem to perceive the varieties of *extension* and *resistance* immediately by *touch* only, because the simple original tactual feeling has become representative of these, in the same manner, and for the same reason, as we seem to perceive the varieties of *distance immediately* by the *eye.* The sense of touch has unquestionably, like all our other senses, its own peculiar feelings, though, for the simple original feelings, attached to *the affections of this most extensive of organs,* we have unfortunately no name, but that which is applied in popular, and even in philosophic language, to *all* the affections of the mind. Our *joy* or *grief, hope* or *fear, love* or *hate,* I before remarked, we term *feelings,* as readily and frequently, as we use this term to express our sensations of *touch;* and that, which, however restricted in its original meaning, is *now* the *common name* of our *mental affections of every class,* has, by this extension, unfortunately, become a very unfit one, for distinguishing a *limited order* of those affections.

Whatever be the term which we may use, however, there *is,* and *must be,* a sensation *peculiar to touch, without regard to the extent or quantity of the surface impressed,*—as there is, in colour, a sensation peculiar to vision, *without regard to the extent of the portion of the retina on which the light may have fallen.* Every physical point of our *organ of touch,* when existing in a certain state, is capable of inducing in the mind a peculiar feeling, *though no other physical point of the organ were affected,*—as every physical point of the *retina, though but a single ray of light were admitted to the eye,* is capable of inducing in the mind a peculiar affection of vision; and when many such physical points are affected together, by some impressing surface, the form of which we think that we discover immediately by touch, it is from experience only that we can learn the vicinity of the physical points of our own tactual surface thus impressed, and consequently the continued extension of the object which impresses them. Before we have so much knowledge of external things, as to know even that we have any bodily organs whatever,—and it is of this state of absolute ignorance alone that we must think, as often as we speculate on the information which our senses separately afford,—when we know as little of our bodily frame, as of that material universe, of which we know nothing, we cannot, by the very terms of this supposition, know that different points of our organ of touch are affected in a certain manner—that these points are contiguous to each other—and that the mass affecting these contiguous points must consequently itself be composed of points, that are, in like manner, contiguous. We know nothing of our organs—we know nothing of any external masses—but a certain feeling is excited in our mind; and it is this simple feeling alone, whatever it may be, which constitutes the direct elementary sensation of touch, though this simple elementary sensation, like many other sensations, may afterwards be so blended with other feelings, as to become significant of them, and even to seem to involve them, as if originally and necessarily coexisting.

It is impossible for us *at present,* indeed, to have a body impressed on us, without the immediate notion of *something external and extended,*—as it is impossible for one, whose sight is perfect, to open his eyes, in the light of day, without perceiving, *as it were immediately,* the *long line* of variegated landscape, in the scenery before him:—the one impossibility is exactly equal to the other;—yet we know, in the case of vision, that all which we immediately perceive, at the very moment, when our eyes seem to comprehend the worlds of *half infinity,* in the hemisphere on which we gaze, is a small expanse of light,— *if even,* which I greatly doubt, there truly be, in our *original* perceptions of this sense, so much of extension, as is implied in the smallest possible expanse. In *touch,* in like manner, I conceive, that the *immediate sensation,* though, like *colour,* it may now seem *inseparable* from *extension* and *outness,*—if, on the authority of Berkeley, I may venture to use that barbarous but *expressive* term,—was, like colour, originally distinct from them,—that, by the mere original sensations of this organ, in short, we could as little know the existence of an impressing body, as, by the mere original sensations of vision, we could learn that such a body existed at the extremity of the room in which we sit.

In defining *sensation,* when we began our inquiry into its nature, I stated it to be *that affection of the mind, which is immediately subsequent to the affection of certain organs, induced by the action of external bodies;* and I admitted, that, in this definition, two assumptions were made,—the existence of foreign *changeable external* bodies, as *separate from the mind,*—and the existence of *organs,* also separate from the mind, and in relation to *it* truly *external,* like other bodies, but forming a permanent part of our corporeal frame, and capable of being affected, in a certain manner, by the *other* bodies, of which the existence. was assumed. As far as our analytical inquiry has yet proceeded, these assumptions are assumptions still. We have not been able to detect, in the sensations considered by us, more than in any of our internal pleasures or pains, any circumstances that seem to be indicative of a material world without. . . .

Are the *primary* sensations derived from the organ of touch, then, of such a kind as to afford us that knowledge, which they are supposed to give of things without?

Let us imagine a being, endowed with *the sense of touch,* and with every other sense and faculty of our mind, but *not* with any previous knowledge of his own *corporeal* frame, or of other *things external,*— and let us suppose a small body, of any shape, to be pressed, *for the first time,* on his open hand. Whatever feelings mere touch can give, directly of itself, would of course be the same in this case, as *now,* when our knowledge is increased, and complicated, from many other sources.

Let the body, thus impressed, be supposed to be a small *cube,* of the *same* temperature with the *hand* itself, that all consideration of *heat* or *cold* may be excluded, and the feeling produced be as *simple* as possible.

What, then, may we suppose the consequent feeling to be?

It will, I conceive, be a simple feeling of the kind of which I have already spoken, as capable of arising from the affection of a single point of our organ of touch,—a feeling that varies indeed with the quantity of pressure, as the sensation of fragrance varies with the number of the odorous particles, but *involves* as little the notion of *extension,* as that notion is involved in the mere fragrance of a violet or a rose. The connection of this original tactual feeling, however, with that of extension, is, *now,* so indissoluble, as, indeed, it could not fail to become, in the circumstance in which it has uniformly arisen, that it is almost impossible to conceive it as *separate.* We may perhaps, however, make a near approach to the conception of it, by using the *gentle gradual pressure* of a *small-pointed body,* which, in the various *slight feelings,* excited by it,—before it penetrate the cuticle, or cause any considerable pain,—may represent, in some measure, the simple and immediate effect, which pressure in any case produces, —exclusively of the associate feelings which it indirectly suggests.

Such of you, as have the curiosity to try the experiment, with any small bodies, not absolutely pointed,—such as the *head* of a pin, or any body of similar dimensions,—will be astonished to feel, how *very slightly,* if *at all,* the notion of *extension or figure* is involved in the feeling, *even after all the intimate associations of our experience;*— certainly *far less* than the notion of longitudinal distance seems to us to be involved in the immediate affections of our sense of sight. It is an experiment, therefore, which I must request you not to neglect to make.

But the pressure of such a large body, as the cube, which we have supposed to be pressed against our organ of touch, *now* awakens very different feelings. We perceive, as it were immediately, *form* and *hardness.* May not, then, the knowledge of *resistance* and *extension,* and consequently the belief of the essential qualities of *matter,*—be originally communicated by the affections of this organ?

The feeling of *resistance,*—to begin with this,— is, I conceive, to be ascribed, not to our *organ of touch,* but to our *muscular frame,* to which I have already more than once directed your attention, as forming a *distinct organ of sense;* the affections of which, particularly as existing in combination with other feelings, and modifying our judgments concerning these, (as in the case of distant vision, for example,) are not less important than those of our other sensitive organs. The sensations of this class, are, indeed, in common circumstances, so *obscure,* as to be scarcely heeded or remembered by us; but there is probably no contraction, even of a single muscle, which is not attended with some faint degree of sensation, that distinguishes it from the contractions of *other muscles,* or from *other degrees of contraction* of the same muscle. I must not be understood, however, as meaning that we are able, in this manner, by a sort of *instinctive anatomy,* to perceive and number our own muscles, and when many of them are acting together, as they usually do, to distinguish *each* from *each;* for, till we study the internal structure of our frame, we scarcely know more, than that we have *limbs* which move *at our will,* and we are altogether ignorant of the complicated *machinery* which is subservient to the volition. But each motion of the visible *limb,* whether produced by *one* or *more* of the invisible *muscles,* is accompanied with a *certain feeling,* that may be *complex,* indeed, as arising from various muscles, but which is considered by the mind as *one;* and it is this *particular feeling,* accompanying the particular *visible motion,*— whether the feeling and the invisible parts contracted be truly simple or compound,—which we distinguish from every *other feeling* accom-

panying every other *quantity of contraction*. It is as if a man, born
blind, were to walk, for the first time, in a flower garden. He would
distinguish the fragrance of one parterre from the fragrance of another, though he might be altogether ignorant of the separate odours
united in each; and might even consider as one simple perfume, what
was, in truth, the mingled product of a thousand.

Obscure as our muscular sensations are in common circumstances,
there are other circumstances,—which I pointed out to you in treating
before of this subject,—in which they make themselves abundantly
manifest. I need not refer to the *diseased state* of the muscles, in
which they become *painfully* sensible; and I will admit, that the reference to such a morbid state, in which the structure may be supposed
to be altered by the disease, would perhaps scarcely be a fair one. It is
sufficient to refer to phenomena of which every one must have been
conscious innumerable times, and which imply no *disease* nor *lasting*
difference of state. What is the feeling of *fatigue,* for example, but a
muscular feeling? that is to say, a feeling of which our muscles are as
truly the organ, as our eye or ear is the organ of sight or hearing.
When a limb has been *long* exercised, without sufficient intervals of
rest, the repetition of the contraction of its muscles is accompanied,
not with a *slight and obscure sensation,* but with one which amounts,
if it be gradually increased, to *severe pain,* and which, before it arrives
at this, has passed progressively through *various stages of uneasiness.*
Even when there has been no previous fatigue, we cannot make a
single powerful effort, at any time, without being sensible of the muscular feeling connected with this effort. . . .

When I move my arm, without resistance, I am conscious of a *certain feeling;* when the motion is *impeded,* by the presence of an *external body,* I am conscious of a *different* feeling, arising partly, indeed,
from the mere sense of touch, in the moving limb *compressed,* but not
consisting *merely* in this compression, since, when the *same pressure*
is made by a foreign force, *without any muscular effort on my part,*
my *general feeling is very different.* It is the feeling of this resistance
to our progressive effort, (combined, perhaps, with the mere tactual
feeling) which forms what we term, our feeling of *solidity* or *hardness;* and, without it, the tactual feeling would be nothing more, than
a sensation *indifferent* or *agreeable,* or *disagreeable* or *severely painful,* according to the force of the pressure, in the particular case; in the
same way, as the *matter of heat,* acting, in different degrees, on this
very *organ of touch,* and on different portions of its surface, at different times, produces all the *intermediate sensations, agreeable, disagreeable,* or *indifferent,* from the pain of *excessive cold,* to the *pain
of burning;* and produces them, *in like manner, without* suggesting the
presence of any *solid body, external to ourselves.*

Were the *cube,* therefore, in the case supposed, pressed, *for the first time,* on the hand, it would excite *a certain sensation, indeed,* but not that of *resistance,* which always implies a muscular effort that is resisted, and consequently not that of *hardness,* which is a mode of *resistance.* It would be very different, however, if we fairly made the attempt to *press against it;* for, *then,* our effort would be *impeded,* and the *consequent feeling of resistance would arise;* which, as co-existing in this case, and in every case of effort, with the particular sensation of touch, might *afterwards* be *suggested* by it, *on the simple recurrence of the same sensation of touch,* so as to excite the notion of *hardness, in the body touched,* without the *renewal of any muscular effort on our part,* in the same manner as the *angular surfaces of the cube,* if we chance to turn our eye on it, are suggested by the mere *plane* of *colour,* which it presents to our immediate vision, and which is all that our immediate vision would, of itself, have made known to us. The feeling of resistance, then, I trust, it will be admitted, and consequently of hardness, and all the other modes of resistance, is a muscular, not a tactual feeling.

But, though the *resistance* or *hardness* of the cube, as implying some *counter effort,* may not be *immediately sensible* to our superficial organ of touch, are not its *dimensions* so perceived? Its *cubical* form, it will be allowed, cannot be felt, as only one of its surfaces is supposed to be pressed upon the hand; but, is not at least this *square surface* perceived immediately? In short, does not *touch, originally* and *immediately,* convey to us the knowledge of *extension?*

With our present complete belief of external things, indeed, and especially of our organs of sense, the most important of these, the origin of our knowledge of extension, seems to us a matter of very easy explanation. The *square surface* presses on our *organ of touch,* —it affects not a *single physical point merely,* but a portion of the organ, corresponding exactly, in surface with itself; and the perception of the similar *square,* it will be said, thus immediately arises. But, in all this easy explanation, it is very strangely forgotten, that the *feeling,* whatever it may be, which the impression of the square surface produces, is not *itself the square configuration of our tactual organ, corresponding with that surface,* but the state of a very different *substance,* which is as little square, as it is round or *elliptical,* —which is, indeed, from its own *absolute simplicity, incapable* of resemblance in shape to any thing; and the resemblance of which, therefore, to the shape of the *mere organ,* is as little to be expected in the sensations of touch,—as *that other state of mind,* which constitutes the *sensation* of the *fragrance* of a rose, can be expected to resemble the shape of the *odorous particles themselves,* or the *organ* of *smell,* which is affected by them. The very knowledge which touch is supposed to give, is, in this case, most inconsistently, assumed, as existing in the mind, before the very touch which is supposed to give it. If, indeed, the mind could *know,* that a part of its external corpo-real organ *is compressed into the form of a square,* or that *another square surface is compressing that organ,* the difficulty would be at an end; for it would, *then,* most undoubtedly, have that very *knowledge of extension,* the origin of which we seek. But it is not explained, *how* the mind, which alone can have sensation or knowledge, and which certainly is not square itself, is to be made *acquainted* with the *squareness* of its *own corporeal organ,* or of the *foreign body;* nor, indeed, how the *squareness of the mere external organ* should produce this particular *affection of the mind,* more than if the organ were com-pressed into the *shape of a polygon of one thousand sides.*

Let it be supposed, that, when a small cube is pressed on the hand, one hundred physical points of the organ of touch are affected in a certain manner. We have, it is said, an immediate perception of a square surface. Let it next be supposed, that, instead of one hundred of these *continuous* points of the organ, an equal number of points, at various distances in the surface of the body, are affected in the same manner. On this supposition, it will scarcely be said, that the percep-tion of a square would arise, when there is no square, more than any other imaginable form, in the space comprehended in the pressure. Yet what difference is there, in these two cases, to a mind that is, by supposition, absolutely ignorant of every bodily organ, and conse-quently alike ignorant of the nearness or distance of the points of the organ of touch? In both cases, one hundred points, equally sensible, are affected, and are affected precisely in the same manner;—and there is truly no difference, unless we tacitly suppose the mind to be conscious of the bodily frame, and, therefore, of the continuity of certain points of the organ of touch, with the other points that are proximate to them,—a sort of knowledge, for which it would not be easy to account, and which it is impossible to conceive, without con-ceding the very point in question. A little attentive reflection on the circumstances of these two cases, will, perhaps, aid you in freeing your minds from the illusive belief, of which it may not be easy for you at first to divest yourselves,—that the continuity and similarity of shape, which are known to *us* the inquirers, are known also to that little sentient being, whose first elements of knowledge we are endeav-ouring to trace.

We are too apt to forget, in inquiries of this sort, that it is not in our organ of *touch merely,* that a certain extent of the nervous extremity of our sensorial organ is affected. This occurs, *equally, in every other organ.* In the superficial expansion of the nerves of *hearing, smell, taste,* for example, it is not a *point* merely that is affected, but *a num-ber of continuous points,* precisely, as in the superficial organ of touch; and if, therefore, the notion of *extension* in general, or of *figure,* which is *limited extension,* arose whenever a part of the nervous expansion was affected in any way, we should derive these notions as much from a *taste,* or a *smell,* or a *sound,* as from any of the configurations or affections of our organ of touch.

It is not, therefore, merely because *a certain limited part of the sensorial organ* is affected, that we have the notion of the *square surface,* in the case supposed by us: for, if *this alone were necessary,* we should have *square inches,* and *half inches,* and various other forms, rectilinear or curvilinear, of *fragrance* and *sound.*

But, it may perhaps be urged, though *all* our organs must, indeed exist equally with our organ of touch *of a certain shape* when affected, —and though the sensorial figure of our *other* organs, is *not* accompanied with any of those mental affections, which constitute the perception of angular or curvilinear figure, there is something, in *the nature of that part of the sensorial organ, which terminates on the general surface of the body,* that impresses the mind, *immediately,* with a sensation, corresponding with the *exact figure,* in which the organ may itself exist. When the *square,* therefore, in the case imagined by us, is *impressed* upon the *organ,* the mental affection which constitutes our notion of a square may immediately arise, though it would not arise from the similar squareness of our organs of smell or hearing.

In answer to this *mere supposition,* I may remark, that the sensorial organ of *touch* exists, at *every moment,* of a *certain shape,* and that we yet have no perception of this shape, so as to be able to delineate the whole extent of our *tactual* organ, in the same manner as we could delineate the *impressing square,* in the case supposed: or, if it be said, that the configuration of the organ does not excite this mental affection, in the quiescent state of the part, but only *when it is itself affected,* I may remark, that we are as little able *to delineate its figure,* when we are exposed to the action of *heat,* which yet *acts most powerfully* upon this very organ, inducing sensations, at least as vivid as those of hardness or figure.

It may still, however, be contended, for in a question of this sort I wish fairly to imagine every possible argument—it may still be contended, that, though the organ of touch has no effect, in this way, *merely as configured,* and might, *in any other configuration,* operate, *precisely in the same manner,* on the sentient mind,—still, the harmony of the bodily and mental changes is so arranged by nature, that the organic state in touch, *whatever it may be,* is immediately followed by the knowledge of the extension of the impressing body,—in the same manner as a certain state of the organ of *smell, whatever that state may be,* is immediately followed by that affection of the mind, which constitutes our sensation of the fragrance of a rose. Though this argument, in truth, rather *begs* the question, than attempts to *meet* it, let us give to it all the force which it may *claim.* The accurate determination of the point may, indeed, seem, at first, almost impossible; since, in whatever manner the seeming perception may arise, it must be admitted, that we now seem to perceive extension, *as it were immediately,* by touch; though not more immediately than in vision we seem to perceive the positions of objects in different distances before our eyes.—But there is, fortunately, at least *one test,* which the point in question still admits. *If* the apparent perception of extension by touch, be truly and originally *immediate,* and not *acquired,* like the apparent perception of *distance* in vision, so as to involve a sort of intellectual measurement or suggestion of some sort, after the primary sensation,—the perception must be *constant* and *universal,*—not confined to a *few* simple and familiar forms, which, if we can distinguish *these alone,* we may be supposed to have learned from experience, *but extending to forms of every kind;* for it would certainly be a very strange abuse of the *licence of supposition,* to imagine, that we perceive a *square immediately,* but not a *circle,* or a *circle* but not a *square,* or indeed *any other figure.* Even at present, then—though the circumstances of the trial,—when the *experience* of many years must have *exhausted so many varieties of form,* associating the notion of these with the particular tactual feeling *whatever that may be*—are surely very unfavourable to the opinion which I maintain,—*even at present,* I may safely trust to *experiment,* the determination of the question. When a body, *which we do not see,* is pressed on any part of our tactual organ, *do* we immediately *discover its form,* —*as immediately,* as we are sensible of *fragrance,* when our organ of smell is in a healthy state, and an odoriferous body is presented to it, or of *sound,* when a cannon is fired beside us? This we certainly should do, if figure were as direct an object of the sense of touch, as fragrance and sound are of the senses of smell and hearing. Even though it be a form of the simplest kind, *square, round, triangular,* that is thus pressed upon our palm, we scarcely distinguish the precise species of *figure* for a moment, and are long before we can convince ourselves, that we have perceived its *exact magnitude,* in the determination of which, after all, we shall very probably be mistaken, if we confine ourselves to the mere *intellectual measurement;* though we should even add to the immediate sensation of touch, all the *discriminating skill* of our *judgment* and *reflection.* But, if the body be *irregular in form,*—however slight the irregularity may be, and of a species that would not perplex in the slightest degree our *sense of sight,* and which certainly, therefore, should perplex as little our sense of touch, which is supposed to be still more immediately perceptive of form,— we are incapable for some time, *and I may even say are incapable altogether,* of fixing, *with precision,* its magnitude and figure—that very magnitude and figure which are yet said to be the direct objects of touch. Of this a single trial may convince any one; it is a trial which, as it seems to *me decisive,* I must request you to make. Are we then entitled to say, in the case of the square surface of the cube pressed upon our hand, that though we cannot discover *other* forms and magnitudes, we yet discover *its* extension, and consequently *its* figure, by the immediate sense of touch?—or may we not rather conclude with confidence, that what is true of other forms is true of *this* also, that it is only in consequence of more frequent experience we have *learned* as it were to distinguish, with *some* degree of certainty, the simpler forms, which, as mere forms, are not more direct objects of the sense of touch than forms the most irregular, and that without such experience, therefore, our *mere sense of touch* is incapable of informing us of the figure of bodies, *immediately,* and *originally.*

If then the knowledge of extension be *not* derived from our *immediate sense of touch,* it must be derived from some other source, which allows it to be *associated with the feelings of touch,* and *afterwards suggested by these,* in the same manner as *distant extent,* in the case of vision, is suggested by a *few slight varieties of colour.* Let us endeavour, then, *since some such source there must be,* to discover *what the source is.*

.   .   .   .   .

To the period of our *first sensations,* therefore, we *cannot* look back; and, hence, all which remains for us, in an inquiry of this kind, is to consider *the circumstances in which the infant is placed,* and to *guess,* as nearly as general analogy will allow us, the nature and the order of the *feelings,* which, in such circumstances, would arise, in a being possessing the *powers* and *susceptibilities* of man, but destitute of all the *knowledge* which man possesses.

In these first circumstances of life, the infant, of course, cannot know that he has a *bodily frame,* or a single *organ* of that frame, more than he can know, that there are other bodies in nature, that act upon his own; and we are not entitled to suppose,—however difficult it may be for us to accommodate our supposition to the true circumstances of the case, —that because *we,* the *inquirers,* know, that external bodies are pressing on his organ of touch, the little sensitive being is to have *any* knowledge, *but* of the *mental affections,* which these external bodies excite. How the knowledge of any thing more than his own mind is acquired, is, in truth, the *very* difficulty, which it is our labour to solve.

In conformity with this view, then,—when we look on the infant,— one of the most remarkable circumstances, which strike us, is its tendency to use its muscles, with almost incessant exercise, particularly the muscles of those parts, which are afterwards its principal *organs of measurement.* Its little fingers are continually *closing* and *opening,* and its little arms *extending* and *contracting.* The *feelings,* therefore,

—whatever these may be,—which attend the *progressive contraction of those parts,*—and some feeling unquestionably attends the *contraction* in all its stages,—*must* be continually arising in its mind, *beginning* and *finishing,* in *regular series,* and *varying exactly,* with the *quantity* of the *contraction.*

A *succession* of feelings, however, when *remembered* by the mind, which *looks back upon them,* we found to *involve, necessarily,* the notion of *divisibility* into separate parts, and, therefore, of length, which is only another name for *continued divisibility.* Time, in short, is to our conception, a series in constant onward progress, and cannot be conceived by us, *but as* a progressive series, of which our *separate feelings* are *parts;* the remembrance of the events of our life, whenever we take any distant retrospect of them, being like the *remembrance* of the *space,* which we have *traversed* in a journey,—*an indistinct continuity of length,*—as truly *divisible,* in our conception, into the *separate events* which we *remember,* as the *space,* which we remember to have traversed, into its separate variety of *scenes.*

Time, then, or *remembered succession,* we found to *involve,* not *metaphorically,* as is commonly said, but *truly* and *strictly,* in its very essence, the notions of *length* and *divisibility,*—the great elements of *extension;* and whatever other feelings may be *habitually* and *uniformly associated* with these, will involve, of course, these elementary notions.

The *series of muscular feelings,* of which the infant is conscious,— in incessantly closing and opening his little hand,—*must,* on these principles, be accompanied with the notion,—not, indeed, of the existence of his hand, or of any thing external,—but of a certain *length* of *succession;* and each *stage of the contraction,* by frequent renewal, gradually becomes significant of *a particular length,* corresponding with the portion of the series. When any hard body, therefore, is placed in the infant's hand,—though he cannot, indeed, have any knowledge of the *object,* or of the *hand,*—he yet feels, that he can no longer perform the accustomed contraction,—or, to speak more accurately,—since he is *unacquainted* with any *parts* that are *contracted,* he feels, that he can no longer *produce his accustomed series of feelings;* and he knows the *quantity of contraction,* which remained to be performed, or rather the *length* of the series, which remained to be felt. The place of this *remaining length* is now *supplied* by a new *feeling,* partly muscular, and partly the result of the affection of the compressed organ of touch,—and is supplied by the *same feeling,* at the *same point of the series,* as often, as he attempts to renew the contraction, while the body remains within his hand. The *tactual feeling,* therefore,—whatever it may be,—becomes, by this frequent repetition, *associated* with the notion of that particular progressive series, or length, of which it thus uniformly supplies the place; and at last becomes *representative* of this particular length, precisely in the same manner, as, in the acquired perceptions of vision, certain *shades of colour* become *representative* of *distance,* to which they have, of themselves, no resemblance or analogy whatever; and we thus *learn* to *feel length,* as we *learn* to *see* length,—not directly by the mere affections of our *tactual* or *visual organs,* but by the *associated notions* which they *suggest.*

If *time,*—as perceived by us in the continued series of our feelings, —*do* involve conceptual *length* and *divisibility,* it seems, indeed, scarcely possible, that, in the *circumstances supposed,* the *notions supposed* should not arise,—that the infant should be conscious of a *regular series* of feelings, in the contraction of its fingers and arms, and yet that *portions of this series* should not become *significant* of *various proportional lengths;*—and, if the notion of certain proportional lengths *do* truly accompany certain degrees of progressive contraction, it seems equally impossible, according to the general principles of our mental constitution, that the compound tactual and muscular *feeling,* which must arise in every case, in which any one of these degrees of contraction is impeded, should not become associated with the notion of that particular length, of which it supplies the place, so as at last to become truly representative of it.

In this manner, I endeavoured to explain to you, how our knowledge of the mere length of bodies may have been acquired, from varieties of length that are recognized as coexisting and proximate, and are felt to unite, as it were, and terminate in our sensation of resistance, which interrupts them equally, and interrupts always a greater number of the coexisting truths, in proportion to the size of the body compressed; and, in a similar manner, our notions of the *other* dimensions of bodies, which are only these varieties of length in different directions. I cannot conclude this summary, however, without recalling to your attention, a *very simple experiment,* which I requested you to make for yourselves,—an experiment, that, even in the *unfavourable* circumstances in which it must now be tried, is yet, I conceive, demonstrative of the influence of *mere time,* as an element of that complex notion, which we have been examining, when the more rapid measurements of *vision,*—which are confessedly not *original* but *acquired,*—are excluded. If, in passing our finger, with different degrees of slowness or rapidity, along the *same surface,* with our eyes shut,— even though we should previously know the exact boundaries of the extent of surface,—we feel it almost impossible *not* to believe,—and but for the contrary evidence of vision, could not have hesitated a single moment in believing,—that this extent is *greater* or *less,* according as the *time,* employed in performing *exactly the same quantity of motion,* with *exactly the same force of pressure,* on the *same quantity of our organ of touch,* may have been *greater* or *less,*—it must surely be admitted, that the notion of the *length,* which thus uniformly varies with the time, when all other circumstances are the same, is not absolutely *independent of the time,*—or it must, in like manner, be believed, that our notion of visual distance, which varies with the distribution of a few rays of light on the small expanse of the optic nerve, is yet *independent* of those faint *shades of colouring,* according to the mere varieties of which, it seems at one time to lay open to our view a landscape of many miles, and at another time to present to us, as it were before our very eyes, an object of scarcely an inch in diameter. The greater dimness, and diminished size of a few objects in the back ground of a picture, which is in itself one coloured plane of light, does not more truly seem to increase the line of distance of those objects, than, in the other case, the increased slowness of the motion of our hand along any surface, seems to lengthen the line which separates one of its boundaries from the other.

.   .   .   .   .

That *memory* is a part of our mental constitution, and that we are thus capable of thinking of a *series of feelings,* as *successive to each other,* the experience of every moment teaches us sufficiently. This succession frequently repeated, *suggests immediately,* or *implies* the notion of *length,* not *metaphorically,* as is commonly said, but as *absolutely* as extension itself: and, the *greater the number* of the successive feelings may have been, the greater does this length appear. It is *not* possible for us to look back on the years of our life, since they form truly a progressive *series,* without regarding them as a *sort of length,* which is *more distinct* indeed, the *nearer* the succession of feelings may be to the moment at which we consider them, but which, however remote, is still felt by us as *one continued length,* in the same manner, as when, after a journey of many hundred miles, we look back, in our memory, on the distance over which we have passed, we see, as it were, a long track of which *some* parts, *particularly the nearer parts,* are sufficiently *distinct,* but of which the rest seems *lost* in a sort of *distant obscurity.* The line of our long journeying—or, in other words, that almost immeasurable line of plains, hills, declivities, marshes, bridges, woods,—to endeavour to comprehend which in our thought, seems an effort as fatiguing as the very journey itself—we know well, can be *divided* into those *various parts:*—and, in like manner, the *progressive line of time*—or, in other words, the *continued succession,* of which the joy, the hope, the fragrance, the regret, the melody, the fear, and innumerable other affections of the mind, were *parts,* we feel that we can mentally *divide* into those separate portions of the train. Continuous *length* and *divisibility,* those great elementary notions of space, and of all that space contains, are thus found in *every succession of our feelings*. There is no language in which *time* is not described as long or short,—not from any metaphor —for no *mere arbitrary* metaphor can be thus *universal,* and *inevitable,* as a form of human thought—but because it is truly impossible for us to consider *succession, without this notion of progressive divisibility attached to it:* and it appears to us as absurd to suppose, that by *adding,* to our retrospect of a week, the events of the month preceding, we do not truly *lengthen* the succession, as it would be to suppose, that we do not *lengthen* the line of actual distance, by adding, to the few last stages of a long journey, the *many* stages that preceded it.

. . . . .

That which is progressive must have *parts.* Time, or succession, then involves the very notions of *longitudinal extension* and *divisibility,* and involves these, *without the notion of any thing external to the mind itself;*—for, though the mind of man had been susceptible only of *joy, grief, fear, hope,* and the other varieties of *internal feeling,* WITHOUT the possibility of being *affected by external things,* he would still have been capable of considering these feelings, as *successive* to each other, in a *long continued progression, divisible* into *separate parts.* The notions of *length,* then, and of *divisibility,* are not confined to *external things,* but are *involved,* in that very memory, by which we consider the series of the past,—not in the memory of distant events only, but in those first *successions* of feeling, by which the mind originally became conscious of its own permanence and identity. The *notion* of *time,* then, is precisely *coeval* with that of the *mind itself;* since it is implied in the knowledge of succession, by which alone, in the manner formerly explained to you, the mind acquires the knowledge of its own reality, as something more than the mere sensation of the present moment.

Conceiving the notion of *time,* therefore, that is to say of feelings past and present, to be thus one of the earliest *notions* which the infant mind can form, so as to precede its *notions* of external things, and to *involve* the notions of *length* and *divisibility,* I am inclined to *reverse* exactly the process commonly supposed; and, instead of deriving the measure of *time* from *extension,* to derive the knowledge and original measure of extension from time. That one notion or feeling of the mind may be united indissolubly with other feelings, with which it has frequently coexisted, and to which, but for this coexistence, it would seem to have no common relation, is sufficiently shown by those phenomena of vision to which I have already so frequently alluded.

In what manner, however, is the notion of *time peculiarly*

associated with the *simple sensation* of *touch,* so as to form, with it, the *perception of extension?* We are able, in the theory of *vision,* to point out the coexistence of sensations which produce the *subsequent union;* that renders the perception of distance apparently *immediate.* If a similar coexistence of the original *sensations of touch,* with the notion of *continued and divisible succession,* cannot be pointed out in the present case, the opinion, which asserts it, must be considered merely as a wild and extravagant conjecture.

The source of such a coexistence is not merely *to be found,* but is at least *as obvious,* as *that* which is universally admitted in the case of *vision.*

.   .   .   .   .

As yet, however, the only dimension of the knowledge, of which we have traced the origin, is mere length; and it must still be explained, how we acquire the knowledge of the other dimensions. If we had had but *one* muscle, it seems to me very doubtful, whether it would have been possible for us, to have associated with touch any other notion than that of mere length. But nature has made provision, for giving us a wider knowledge, in the various muscles, which she has distributed over different parts, so as to enable us to perform motions in various directions at the same instant, and thus to have coexisting series of feelings, each of which series was before considered as involving the notion of length. The infant bends one finger gradually on the palm of his hand; the finger, thus brought down, touches one part of the surface of the palm, producing a certain affection of the organ of touch, and a consequent sensation; and he acquires the notion of a certain length, in the remembered succession of the muscular feelings during the contraction:—he bends another finger; *it,* too, touches a certain part of the surface of the palm, producing a certain feeling of touch, that coexists and combines, in like manner, with the remembrance of a certain succession of muscular feelings. When both fingers move together, the coexistence of the two series of successive feelings, with each of which the mind is familiar, gives the notion of coexisting lengths, which receive a sort of unity, from the proximity in succession of the tactual feelings in the contiguous parts of the palm which they touch,—feelings, which have *before* been found to be proximate, when the palm has been repeatedly pressed along a surface, and the tactual feelings of these parts, which the closing fingers touch at the same moment, were always immediately successive,—as immediately successive, as any of the muscular feelings in the series of contraction. When a body is placed in the infant's hand, and its little fingers are bent by it as before, sometimes *one* finger only is impeded in its progress, sometimes *two,* sometimes *three,*—and he thus adds to the notion of mere length, which would have been the same, whatever number of fingers had been impeded, the notion of a certain number of proximate and coexisting lengths, which is the very notion of breadth; and with these, according as the body is larger or smaller, is combined always the tactual affection produced by the pressure of the body, on more, or fewer, of the interior parts of the palm and fingers, which had before become, of themselves, representative of certain lengths, in the manner described; and the concurrence of these three varieties of length, in the single feeling of resistance, in which they all seem to meet, when an incompressible body is placed within the sphere of the closing fingers,—however rude the notions of concurring dimensions *may* be, or rather *must* be, as at first formed,—seems at least to afford the rude elements, from which, by the frequent repetition of the feeling of resistance, together with the proximate lengths, of which it has become representative, clearer notions of the kind may gradually arise.

The progressive contractions of the various muscles which move the arms, as affording similar successions of feelings, may be considered in precisely the same light, as sources of the knowledge of extension; and, by their motion in various directions, at the same time with the motion of the fingers, they concur powerfully, in modifying, and correcting, the information received from these. The whole hand is brought, by the motion of the arm, to touch one part of the face or body; it is then moved, so as to touch another part, and, with the frequent succession of the simple feelings of touch, in these parts, is associated the feeling of the intervening *length,* derived from the sensations that accompanied the progressive contraction of the arm. But the motion is not always the same; and, as the same feeling of touch, in one part, is thus followed by various feelings of touch in different parts, with various series of muscular feelings between, the notion of length in various *directions,* that is to say, of length in various series commencing from one power, is obtained in another way. That the knowledge of extension, or, in other words, the association of the notion of succession with the simple feelings of touch, will be rude and indistinct at first, I have already admitted; but it will gradually become more and more distinct and precise: as we can have no doubt, that the perception of distance by the eye, is, in the first stages of visual association, very indistinct, and becomes clearer after each repeated trial. For many weeks or months, all is confusion in the visual perceptions, as much as in the *tactual* and *muscular.* Indeed, we have abundant evidence of this continued progress of vision, even in mature life, when, in certain professions that require nice perceptions of distance, the power of perception itself, by the gradual acquisitions which it obtains from experience, seems to unfold itself more and more, in proportion to the wants that require it. . . .

LECTURE XXV

ON THE DISTINCTION BETWEEN SENSATION AND PERCEPTION—AND
BETWEEN THE PRIMARY AND SECONDARY QUALITIES OF MATTER

My last Lecture, Gentlemen, was chiefly employed in considering
the nature of that complex process which takes place in the mind,
when we ascribe the various classes of our sensations to their various
external objects,—to the analysis of which process we were led, by the
importance which Dr Reid has attached to the distinction of *sensation* and *perception;*—a sensation, as understood by him, being the
simple feeling that immediately follows the action of an external body
on any of our organs of sense, considered merely as a feeling of the
mind; the corresponding perception being the reference of this feeling
to the external body as its cause.[1]

The distinction I allowed to be a convenient one, if the nature of
the complex process which it expresses be rightly understood. The
only question that seemed, philosophically, of importance, with respect to it, was, whether the *perception* in this sense,—the reference
of the sensation to its external *corporeal* cause,—imply, as Dr Reid
contends, a peculiar mental power, coextensive with sensation, to be
distinguished by a peculiar name in the catalogue of our faculties, or
be not merely one of the results of a more general power, which is
afterwards to be considered by us,—the *power of association,*—by
which one feeling suggests, or induces, other feelings that have formerly coexisted with it.

It would be needless to recapitulate the argument minutely, in its
relation to *all* the senses. That of smell, which Dr. Reid has himself
chosen as an example, will be sufficient for our retrospect.

Certain particles of odorous matter act on my nostrils,—a peculiar
sensation of fragrance arises,—I refer this sensation to a rose. This
reference, which is unquestionably something superadded to the original sensation itself, is what Dr Reid terms the *perception* of the *fragrant body.* But what is the reference itself, and to what source is it to
be ascribed? That we should have supposed our sensations to have
had a cause of some sort, as we suppose a cause of all our feelings
internal as well as external, may indeed be admitted. But if I had had
no other sense than that of smell,—*if I had never seen a rose,*—or,
rather, since the knowledge which vision affords is chiefly of a secondary kind, if I had *no mode of becoming acquainted* with the compound of *extension* and *resistance,* which the mere sensations of

---

[1] See *An Inquiry into the Human Mind* (Edinburgh, 1764), Chapter VI, Section
XX. Reprinted in the present volume. Ed.

smell, it is evident, are incapable of affording,—could I have made this reference of my sensation to a quality of a fragrant *body?* Could I, in short, have had more than the mere sensation itself, with that general belief of a cause of *some sort,* which is not confined to our sensations, but is common to them with all our other feelings?

By *mere smell,* as it appears to me, I could not have become acquainted with the existence of *corporeal substances,*—in the sense in which we now understand the term *corporeal,*—nor, consequently, with the *qualities* of corporeal substances; and, if so, how could I have had that *perception* of which Dr Reid speaks,—that reference to a fragrant *body,* of which, as a body, I was before in absolute ignorance? I should, indeed, have ascribed the sensation to some cause or antecedent, like every other feeling; but I could as little have ascribed it to a bodily cause, as any feeling of joy or sorrow. I refer it now *to a rose;* because, being endowed with *other* sensitive capacities, I have previously learned, from another source, the existence of *causes without,* extended and resisting,—because I have previously touched or seen a rose, when the sensation of fragrance coexisted with my visual or tactual sensation; and all which distinguishes the *perception* from the mere *sensation,* is this suggestion of former experience, which reminds me now of other feelings, with the continuance or cessation of which, in innumerable former instances, the fragrance itself also continued or ceased. The perception, in short, in smell, taste, hearing, is a *sensation suggesting, by association,* the notion of some extended and resisting substance, *fragrant, vapid, vibratory,*—a notion which smell alone, taste alone, hearing alone, never could have afforded; but which, when once received from any other source, may be suggested by these as readily as any other associate feeling that has frequently coexisted with them. To the simple primary sensations of *vision* the same remark may be applied. A mere sensation of colour could not have made me acquainted with the existence of bodies, that would resist my effort to grasp them. It is only in one sense, therefore,—that which affords us the knowledge of *resistance,*—that any thing like original *perception* can be found; and even in *this,* the process of perception, as I formerly explained to you, implies no *peculiar* power, but only common *sensations,* with *associations* and *inferences* of precisely the same kind, as those which are continually taking place in *all* our reasonings and trains of thought.

Extension and *resistance,* I need scarcely repeat, are the complex elements of what we term matter; and nothing is *matter* to our conception, or a *body,* to use the simpler synonymous term, which does not involve these elements. If we had no other sense than that of smell, and, therefore, could not have referred the sensations to any fragrant *body,* what, in Dr Reid's meaning of this term, would the supposed power of perception, in these circumstances, have been?

What would it have been, in like manner, if we had had only the sense of taste in sweetness and bitterness,—or of hearing in melody,—or of vision in colour,—without the capacity of knowing light as a material substance, or the *bodies* that *vibrated,* or the *bodies* of another kind that were *sweet* or *bitter?* It is only by the sense of *touch,* or, at least, by that class of perceptions which Dr Reid ascribes to touch,—and which, therefore, though traced by us, in part, to another source, I, for brevity's sake, comprehend under that term in our present discussion, —it is only by *touch* that we become acquainted with those elements which are essential to our very notion of a *body;* and to *touch,* therefore, in his own view of it, we must be indebted, directly or indirectly, as often as we refer the sensations of any other class to a *corporeal* cause. Even in the supposed perceptions of touch itself, however, as we have seen, the reference of our feelings to an external cause is not demonstrative of any peculiar power of the mind, to be classed separately from its other faculties. But when a body is first grasped, in infancy, by fingers that have been accustomed to *contract* without being impeded, we learn to consider the sensation as the result of a cause that is *different from our own mind,* because it breaks an accustomed series of feelings, in which all the antecedents, felt by us at the time, were such as were before uniformly followed by a different consequent, and were expected, therefore, to have again their usual consequent. The *cause* of the new sensation, which is thus believed to be something different from our sentient self, is regarded by us as something which *has parts,* and which *resists our effort,* that is to say, as an external *body;*—because the muscular feeling, excited by the object grasped, is, in the *first* place, the very feeling of that which we term resistance; and, *secondly,* because, by uniformly supplying the place of a definite portion of a progressive series of feelings, it becomes ultimately representative of that particular length of series, or number of parts, of which it thus uniformly supplies the place. Perception, then, even in that class of feelings by which we learn to consider ourselves as surrounded by substances extended and resisting, is only another name, as I have said, for the result of certain *associations* and *inferences,* that flow from other more general principles of the mind; and with respect to all our other sensations, it is only another name for the *suggestion* of these *very perceptions of touch,* or at least of the feelings, tactual and muscular, which are, by Dr Reid, ascribed to that single sense. If we had been unsusceptible of these tactual and muscular feelings, and, consequently, had never conceived the existence of any thing extended and resisting *till* the sensation of fragrance, colour, sweetness, or sound had arisen, we should, after any one or all of these sensations, have still known as little of *bodies* without, as if no sensation whatever had been excited.

The distinction, then, on which Dr Reid has founded so much, involves, in his view of it, and in the view that is generally taken of it, a false conception of the nature of the process which he describes. The two words *sensation* and *perception,* are, indeed, as I have already remarked, very convenient for expressing, in one case, the mere existence of an external feeling,—in the other case, the reference which the percipient mind has made of this feeling to an external cause. But this reference is *all,* which the *perception* superadds to the *sensation;*—and the source of the reference itself we are still left to seek, in the other principles of our intellectual nature. We have no need, however, to invent a peculiar power of the mind for producing it; since there are other principles of our nature, from which it may readily be supposed to flow,—the principle by which we are led to believe, that every new consequent, in a train of changes, must have had a new antecedent of some sort in the train,—and the principle of association, by which feelings, that have usually coexisted, suggest or become representative of each other. With these principles, it certainly is not wonderful, that when the fragrance of a rose has uniformly affected our sense of smell, as often as the flower itself was presented to us, we should ascribe the fragrance to the flower which we have seen and handled;—but though it would not be wonderful, that we should make it, it *would indeed* be wonderful, if, with these principles, we *did not* make that very reference, for which Dr Reid thinks it necessary to have recourse to a peculiar faculty of perception.

Such, then, is the view, which I would take of that distinction of *sensation* and *perception,* which Dr Reid, and the philosophers who have followed him, and many of the philosophers, too, that preceded him,—for the distinction, as I have said, is far from being an original one,—have understood in a *different* sense; in consequence, as I cannot but think, of a defective analysis of the mental process, which constitutes the *reference* of our feelings of this class to *causes* that are *without.*

There is another distinction, which he has adopted from the philosophers that preceded him, and which forms an important part of his system of perception,—a distinction, that is just to a certain extent,— though not to the full extent, and in the precise manner, in which he and other writers have maintained;—and with respect to which, therefore, it will be necessary to point out to you, how far I conceive it to be safely admissible. I allude to the division, which has been formed of the *primary* and *secondary* qualities of matter.

"Every one knows that extension, divisibility, figure, motion, solidity, hardness, softness, and fluidity, were by Mr. Locke called *primary qualities of body;* and that sound, colour, taste, smell, and heat or cold, were called *secondary qualities*. Is there a just foundation for this distinction? Is there any thing common to the primary, which belongs not to the secondary? And what is it?

"I answer, That there appears to me to be a real foundation for the distinction; and it is this: That our senses give us a direct and a distinct notion of the primary qualities, and inform us what they are in themselves; but of the secondary qualities, our senses give us only a relative and obscure notion. They inform us only, that they are qualities that affect us in a certain manner, that is, produce in us a certain sensation; but as to what they are in themselves, our senses leave us in the dark.

"The notion we have of primary qualities is direct, and not relative only. A relative notion of a thing, is, strictly speaking, no notion of the thing at all, but only of some relation which it bears to something else.

"Thus gravity sometimes signifies the tendency of bodies towards the earth; sometimes it signifies the cause of that tendency: When it means the first, I have a direct and distinct notion of gravity: I see it, and feel it, and know perfectly what it is; but this tendency must have a cause: We give the same name to the cause; and that cause has been an object of thought and of speculation. Now what notion have we of this cause, when we think and reason about it? It is evident, we think of it as an unknown cause, of a known effect. This is a relative notion, and it must be obscure; because it gives us no conception of what the thing is, but of what relation it bears to something else. Every relation which a thing unknown bears to something that is known, may give a relative notion of it; and there are many objects of thought, and of discourse, of which our faculties can give no better than a relative notion.

"Having premised these things to explain what is meant by a relative notion, it is evident, that our notion of primary qualities is not of this kind; we know what they are, and not barely what relation they bear to something else.

"It is otherwise with secondary qualities. If you ask me, what is that quality or modification in a rose which I call its smell, I am at a loss to answer directly. Upon reflection I find, that I have a distinct notion of the sensation which it produces in my mind. But there can be nothing like to this sensation in the rose, because it is insentient. The quality in the rose is something which occasions the sensations in me; but what that something is, I know not. My senses give me no information upon this point. The only notion, therefore, my senses give is this, That smell in the rose is an unknown quality or modification, which is the cause or occasion of a sensation which I know well. The relation which this unknown quality bears to the sensation with which nature hath connected it, is all I learn from the sense of smelling; but this is evidently a relative notion. The same reasoning will apply to every secondary quality.

"Thus I think it appears, that there is a real foundation for the distinction of primary from secondary qualities; and that they are distinguished by this, that of the primary we have by our senses a direct and distinct notion; but of the secondary only a relative notion, which must, because it is only relative, be obscure; they are conceived only as the unknown causes or occasions of certain sensations with which we are well acquainted." [1]

Though, as I have explained to you fully, in my former Lectures, we should not,—at least in far the greater number of our sensations, —have considered them, originally, as proceeding from *external causes,* we yet, after the acquisitions of knowledge, with which the first years of our life enrich us, believe, that there is an external cause of all our sensations,—of smells and tastes, as much as of those feelings of the mind, which constitute our notions of extension and resistance. But the difference, in these cases, is, that though we *learn,* by experience of certain successions or coexistences of feelings, to refer to a *corporeal* cause our sensations of fragrance, and various other species of sensations, there is nothing in the sensation of fragrance itself, or in the other analogous sensations, of which I speak, that might not indicate as much a cause directly spiritual, as a cause like that to which we at present give the name of *body,*—while the very notion of *extension* and *resistance* combined, seems necessarily to indicate a material cause, or rather is truly that which constitutes our very notion of *matter.*

We believe, indeed, that our sensations of *fragrance, sweetness, sound,* have *causes of some sort,* as truly as we believe, that our feelings of *extension* and *resistance* have a cause, or causes of some sort; but if we have previously given the name of matter, with direct reference to the *one* set of effects, and *not with* direct reference to the other, it necessarily *follows,* that, in relation to matter, as often as we speak or think of it, the qualities which correspond with the one set of effects, that have led us to use that name, must be regarded by us as primary, and the others, which may, or may not coexist with these, only as secondary. An external *body* may, or may not be fragrant, because fragrance is not one of the qualities previously included by us in our definition of a *body;* but it *must* be *extended,* and present an obstacle, to our compressing force, because these *are* the very qualities, which we *have* included in our definition, and without which, therefore, the definition must cease to be applicable to the thing defined.

If, originally, we had invented the word *matter* to denote the cause, whatever it might be, of our *sensations* of *smell,* it is very evident, that

[1] *On the Intellectual Powers,* Essay II, Chapter XVII.

fragrance would then have been to us the primary quality of *matter,* as being that which was essential to our definition of matter,—and all other qualities, by which the cause of smell might, or might not at the same time affect our other senses, would then have been *secondary* qualities only,—as being qualities compatible with our definition of matter, but not *essential* to it.

What we now term matter, however, I have repeatedly observed,— is that which we consider *as occupying space, and resisting our effort to compress it;*—and those qualities of matter may well be said to be primary, by which matter itself, as thus defined, becomes known to us,—or by the union of which, in our conception, we form the complex notion of matter, and give or withhold that name according as these qualities are present or absent. *Extension* and *resistance* are the distinguishing qualities that direct us in all our applications of the word which comprehends them. They are truly *primary* qualities, therefore; since, without our consideration of them, we never could have formed the complex notion of the substance itself, to which we afterwards, in our analysis of that complex notion, ascribe them separately as qualities;—and all the other qualities, which we may afterwards find occasion to refer *to an extended resisting substance,* must evidently be *secondary,* in reference to those qualities, without which, as previously combined in our thought, we could not have had the primary notion of the substance to which we thus secondarily refer them. If, in the case which we have already frequently imagined, of the single sense of smell, we had been absolutely unsusceptible of every other external feeling, we might, indeed, have considered our sensation as the effect of *some* cause,—and even of a cause that was different from our mind itself; but it is very evident that we could not have considered it as the effect of the presence of *matter,* at least as that term is now understood by us. If, in these circumstances,—after frequent repetition of the fragrance, as the only quality of bodies with which we could be acquainted,—we were to acquire in an instant all the other senses which we now possess,—so as to become capable of forming that *complex notion of things extended and resisting,* which is our present notion of matter, we should then, indeed, have a fuller notion of the rose, of the mere fragrance of which we before were sensible, without knowing of what it was the fragrance, and might *learn* to refer the fragrance *to the rose,* by the same coexistences of sensations which have led us, in our present circumstances, to combine the fragrance with other qualities, in the complex conception of the flower. Even then, however, though the fragrance, which was our first sensation, had truly been known to us before the other qualities, and though the sensation, therefore, would deserve the name of primary, the *reference* of this earlier feeling to the external rose as its cause, would still truly be *secondary* to the earlier reference, or rather to the earlier *combination* of *other* qualities, in one complex whole, by which we had formed to ourselves the notion of the extended and resisting rose, as a body, that admitted the subsequent reference of the delightful sensation of fragrance to be made to it, as the equal cause of these different effects.

In this sense, then, the distinction of the primary and secondary qualities of matter is just,—that, whatever qualities we refer to a *material* cause *must* be, in reference, secondary to those qualities that are essential to our very notion of the body, to which the *subsequent* reference of the other qualities is made. We have formed our definition of matter; and, as in every other definition of every sort, the qualities included in the definition, must always, in comparison of other qualities, be primary and essential, relatively to the thing defined.

Nor is this all.—It will be admitted likewise, that the qualities termed *primary,*—which alone are included in our general definitions of matter, and which are all, as we have seen, modifications of mere extension and resistance, are, even after we have learned to consider the causes of *all* our sensations as substances external to the mind, still felt by us to be external, with more clearness and vividness, than the *other* qualities, which we term *secondary.* The difference is partly, and chiefly, in the nature of the sensations themselves, as already explained to you, but depends also, I conceive, in no inconsiderable degree, on the permanence and universality of the objects which possess the primary qualities, and the readiness with which we can renew our feeling of them at will, from the constant presence of our own bodily frame, itself extended and resisting, and of the other causes of these feelings of extension and resistance, that seem to be every where surrounding us. *Tastes, smells, sounds,*—even colours, though more lasting than these—are not always before us;—but there is not a moment at which we cannot, by the mere stretching of our hand, produce at pleasure the feeling of something extended and resisting. It is a very natural effect of this difference, that the one set of causes which are always before us, should seem to us, therefore, peculiarly permanent, and the other set, that are only occasionally present, should seem almost fugitive as our sensations themselves.

In these most important respects, there *is*, then, a just ground for the distinction of the primary from the secondary qualities of bodies. They are primary in the order of our definition of matter; and they are felt by us as peculiarly permanent, independently of our feelings, which they seem at every moment ready to awake. The power of affecting us with smell, taste, sight, or hearing, may or may not be present; but the power of exciting the feelings of extension and resistance is constantly present, and is regarded by us as essential to our very notion of matter,—or, in other words, we *give* the name of *matter,* only where this complex perception is excited in us. We seem, therefore, to be constantly *surrounded* with a material world of substances extended and resisting, that is to say, a world of substances capable of exciting in us the feelings which are ascribed to the primary quality of matter;—but still the feeling of these primary qualities, which we regard as permanent, is *not* less than the feeling of the secondary qualities, a state or affection of the mind, and nothing more;—and in the one case, *as much as in the other,* in the perception of the qualities termed secondary, as much as of the qualities termed primary, the feeling, when it occurs, is the direct or immediate result of the presence of the external body with the quality of which it corresponds;—or, if there be any difference in this respect, I conceive that our feeling of fragrance, or sweetness, was, originally at least, a more immediate result of the presence of odorous or sapid particles,—than any *feeling of extension,* without the mind, was the effect of the first body which we touched.

To the extent which I have now stated, then, the *difference* of these classes of qualities may be admitted. But as to the other differences asserted, they seem to be founded on a false view of the nature of perception. I cannot discover any thing in the sensations themselves, corresponding with the primary and secondary qualities, which is direct, as Dr Reid says, in the one case, and only relative in the other. All are *relative,* in his sense of the term, and *equally* relative,—our perception of extension and resistance, as much as our perception of *fragrance* or *bitterness.* Our feeling of extension is not itself *matter,* but a feeling excited by matter. We ascribe, indeed, our sensations as effects, to external objects that excite them; but it is only by the medium of our *sensations* that these, in any case, become known to us as objects. To say that our perception of extension is not *relative,* to *a certain external cause of this perception, direct or indirect,* as our perception of fragrance is relative to a certain external cause, would be to say that our perception of extension, induced by the presence of an external cause, is not a *mental* phenomenon, as much as the perception of fragrance, but is something *more* than a state of the mind; for, if the *perception of extension* be, as *all* our perceptions and other feelings must surely be, a *mental* phenomenon, a state of *mind,* not of *matter,* the reference made of this to an external cause, must be only to *something* which is conceived *relatively* as the cause of this feeling. What matter is independently of our perception, we know not, and cannot know, for it is only by our sensations that we can have any connexion with it; and even though we were supposed to have our connexion with it enlarged, by various senses additional to those which we possess at present, and our acquaintance with it, therefore, to be far more minute, this very knowledge, however widely augmented, must itself be a *mental phenomenon,* in like manner, the reference of which, to matter, as an external cause, would still be *relative* only like our present knowledge. That the connexion of the feeling of extension, with a corporeal substance really existing without, depends on the arbitrary arrangement made by the Deity; and that all of which we are conscious might, therefore, have existed, as at present, *though no external cause had been,* Dr. Reid, who ascribes to an intuitive principle, our belief of an external universe, virtually allows; and this very admission surely implies, that the notion does not, directly and necessarily, involve the existence of any particular cause, whatever it may be in itself, by which the Deity has thought proper to produce the corresponding feeling of our mind. It is quite evident, that we cannot, in this case, appeal to experience, to inform us what sensations or perceptions are more or less direct; for experience, strictly understood, does not extend beyond the feelings of our own mind, unless in this very relative belief itself, that there are certain external causes of our feelings,—causes which it is impossible for us not to conceive as really existing, but of which we know nothing more than that our feelings, in all that wide variety of states of mind, which we express briefly by the terms sensation or perception, are made to depend on them. In the series of states in which the mind has existed, from the first moment of our life, to the present hour, the feelings of extension, resistance, joy, sorrow, fragrance, colour, hope, fear, heat, cold, admiration, resentment, have often had place; and some of these feelings, it has been impossible for us not to ascribe to a direct external cause; but there have not been in the mental series, which is all of which we can be conscious, both that feeling of the mind, which we term the perception of extension, and also body itself, as the cause of this feeling; for body, as an actual substance, cannot be a part of the consciousness of the mind, which is a different substance. It is sufficient for us to believe, that there are external causes of this feeling of the mind, permanent and independent of it, which produce, in regular series, all those phenomena that are found by us in the physical events of the universe, and with the continuance of which, therefore, our perceptions also will continue; we cannot truly suppose more, without conceiving our very notion of extension, a mental state, to be itself a body extended, which we have as little reason to suppose, as that our sensation of fragrance, another mental state, is itself a fragrant body. It is needless to prolong this discussion, by endeavouring to place the argument in new points of view. The simple answer to the question, "*Is* our notion of extension, or of the other primary qualities of matter, a phenomenon or affection of *matter* or of mind?" would be of itself sufficient; for if it be a state of the *mind,* as much as our feeling of heat or of fragrance, and a state produced by the presence of an external cause, as our sensations of heat or fragrance are produced, *then* there is no reason to suppose, that the knowledge is, in one case, more direct than in the other. In both, it is the effect of the presence of

an external cause, and in both it must be *relative only,*—to adopt Dr
Reid's phrase,—to that particular cause which produced it; the
knowledge of which cause, in the case of *extension,* as much as in the
case of *fragrance,* is nothing more than the knowledge, that there is,
without us, something which is not our mind itself, but which exists,
as we cannot but believe, permanently, and independently of our
mind, and produces, according to its own varieties, in relation to our
corporeal frame, at one time, that affection of the mind which we
denominate the perception of extension; at another time, that different
affection of the mind, which we denominate the perception of fragrance. *What it is,* as it exists in absolute independence of our perceptions, we who become acquainted with it, only by those very perceptions, know not, in either case; but we know it at least,—which is the
only knowledge important for us,—as it exists *relatively* to *us;* that is
to say, it is impossible for us, from the very constitution of our nature,
not to regard the variety of our perceptions, as occasioned by a corresponding variety of causes, external to our mind; though, even in making this reference, we must still believe our *perceptions themselves,* to
be altogether different and distinct from the external causes, whatever
they may be, which have produced them; to be, in short, phenomena
purely *mental,* and to be this *equally,* whether they relate to the primary or the secondary qualities of matter; our notion of extension, in
whatever way the Deity may have connected it with the presence of
external things, being as much a state of the mind itself, as our notion
of sweetness or sound. . . .

LECTURE XXVII

HYPOTHESIS OF THE PERIPATETICS
REGARDING PERCEPTION

. . . In the philosophy of the Peripatetics, and in all the dark ages
of the scholastic followers of that system, *ideas* were truly considered
as little images derived from objects without; and, as the word *idea*
still continued to be used after this original meaning had been abandoned, (as it continues *still,* in all the works that treat of perception,)
it is not wonderful that many of the accustomed forms of expression,
which were retained together with it, should have been of a kind that,
in their strict etymological meaning, might have seemed to harmonize
more with the theory of *ideas* as *images,* which prevailed when these
particular forms of expression originally became habitual, than with
that of *ideas* as mere *states of the mind itself;* since this is only what
has happened with respect to innumerable other words, in the trans-
mutations of meaning which they have received during the long prog-

ress of scientific inquiry. The idea, in the old philosophy, had been that, of which the presence immediately preceded the mental perception,—the direct external cause of perception; and, accordingly, it may well be supposed, that when the direct cause of perception was believed to be, not a foreign phantasm, but a peculiar affection of the sensorial organ, that word, which had formerly been applied to the supposed object, would *still* imply some reference to the organic state, which was believed to supply the place of the shadowy film, or phantasm, in being, what it had been supposed to be, the immediate antecedent of perception. *Idea,* in short, in the old writers, like the synonymous word *perception* at present, was expressive, not of one part of a process, but of two parts of it. It included, with a certain vague comprehensiveness, the *organic* change as well as the *mental,*—in the same way as *perception* now implies a certain change produced in our organs of sense, and a consequent change in the state of the mind; and hence it is surely not very astonishing, that while many expressions are found in the works of these older writers, which, in treating of ideas, have a reference to the mental part of the process of perception, other expressions are occasionally employed which relate only to the material part of the process,—since both parts of the process, as I have said, were, to a certain degree, denoted by that single word. All this might very naturally take place, though nothing more was meant to be expressed by it than these two parts of the process,—the organic change, whatever it might be, and the subsequent mental change,— without the necessary intervention of something distinct from both, such as Dr Reid supposes to have been meant by the term Idea.[1]

It is this application, to the bodily part of the process, of expressions, which he considered as intended to be applied to the *mental* part of perception, that has sometimes misled him in the views which he has given of the opinions of former philosophers. But still more frequently has he been misled, by understanding in a *literal* sense phrases which were intended in a *metaphorical* sense, and which seem so obviously metaphorical, that it is truly difficult to account for the misapprehension. Indeed, the same metaphors, on the mere use of which Dr Reid founds so much, continue still to be used in the same manner as before he wrote. We speak of *impressions on the mind,*— of ideas *bright* or *obscure, permanent* or *fading,*—of senses, that are the *inlets* to our knowledge of external things,—and of memory, in which this knowledge is *stored,*—precisely as the writers and speakers before us used these phrases; without meaning anything more, than that certain organic changes, necessary to perception, are produced by external objects,—and that certain feelings, similar to those originally excited in this manner, are afterwards renewed, with more or less permanence and vivacity, without the recurrence of the objects that

[1] See *Inquiry,* Chapter V, Section VIII, reprinted in the present volume. Ed.

originally produced them;—and to arrange all the moods and figures of logic in confutation of mere metaphors, such as I cannot but think the *images in the mind* to have been, which Dr Reid so powerfully assailed, seems an undertaking not very different from that of exposing, syllogistically and seriously, all the follies of Grecian Paganism as a system of theological belief, in the hope of converting some unfortunate poetaster or poet, who still talks, in his rhymings to his mistress, of *Cupid* and the *Graces*. . . .

The language of Mr Locke,—to begin with one of the most eminent of these,—is, unfortunately, so very figurative, when he speaks of the intellectual phenomena, (though I have no doubt that he would have avoided these figures, if he could have foreseen the possibility of their being interpreted literally), that it is not easy to show, by any single quotation, how *very* different his opinions as to perception were, from those which Dr Reid has represented them to be. The great question is, whether he believed the existence of *ideas,* as *things in the mind, separate* from *perception,* and *intermediate* between, the *organic* affection, whatever it might be, and the *mental affection;* or whether the *idea* and the *perception* were considered by him as the same. "In the perception of external objects," says Dr Reid, "all languages distinguish three things,—the *mind* that perceives,—the operation of that mind, which is called *perception,*—and the object perceived. Philosophers have introduced a *fourth thing,* in this process, which they call the *idea of the object.*" [1] It is the merit of shewing the nullity of *this supposed fourth thing,* which Dr Reid claims, and which has been granted to him, without examination. The *perception itself,* as a *state of the mind,* or, as he chooses to call it, *an operation of the mind,* he admits, and he admits also the *organic* change which precedes it. Did Mr Locke then contend for any thing more, for that *fourth thing,* the *idea,* distinct from the *perception,*—over which Dr Reid supposes himself to have triumphed? That he did *not* contend for any thing more, nor conceive the *idea* to be any thing different from the *perception itself,* is sufficiently apparent from innumerable passages, both of his Essay itself, and of his admirable defence of the great doctrines of his Essay, in his controversy with Bishop Stillingfleet.[2] He repeatedly states, that he uses the word *idea,* as synonymous with *conception* or *notion,* in the common use of those terms; his only reason for preferring it to *notion,* (which assuredly Dr Reid could not suppose to mean any thing, distinct from the mind) being, that the term *notion* seems to him better limited to a *particular class* of ideas, those which he technically terms *mixed modes.* That ideas are *not* different from perceptions, is clearly expressed by him. "To ask at

---

[1] *On the Intellectual Powers,* Essay II, Chapter XII.

[2] *Three Letters to the Lord Bishop of Worcester concerning Some passages in the Essay concerning Human Understanding* (London, 1697–99). See especially Locke's second letter. Ed.

what time a man has first any *ideas,"* he says, "is to ask when he begins to *perceive;* having *ideas* and *perception* being the same thing." [1] If he speaks of our senses, as the *inlets* to our ideas, the metaphor is surely a very obvious one; or, if any one will still contend, that what is said metaphorically must have been intended really, it must be remembered, that he uses precisely the same metaphor, in cases in which the *real* application of it is absolutely impossible, as, for example, with respect to our *perceptions* or *sensations,* and that, if we are to understand, from his use of such metaphors, that he believed the *ideas,* thus *introduced,* to be distinct from the mind, we must understand, in like manner, that he believed our *sensations* and *perceptions, introduced,* in like manner, to be also things self-existing, and capable of being admitted, at certain inlets, into the mind as their recipient. "Our senses, conversant about particular sensible objects, do *convey,"* he says, *"into the mind,* several distinct *perceptions* of things, according to those various ways wherein those objects do affect them." [2] "The senses are *avenues* provided by nature for the *reception* of *sensations."* [3] I cannot but think, that these, and the similar passages that occur in the Essay, *ought,* of themselves, to have convinced Dr Reid, that he who thus spoke of PERCEPTIONS, *conveyed into the mind,* and of *avenues provided for the reception of* SENSATIONS, might also, when he spoke of the *conveyance* of *ideas* into the mind, and of *avenues* for the reception of *ideas,* have meant nothing more than the simple external origin of those *notions,* or *conceptions,* or *feelings,* or *affections* of mind, to which he gave the name of *ideas;* especially when there is not a single argument in his Essay, or in any of his works, that is founded on the substantial reality of our ideas, as separate and distinct things in the mind. I shall refer only to one additional passage, which I purposely select, because it is, at the same time, very full of the particular figures, that have misled Dr Reid, and shews, therefore, what the true meaning of the author was, at the time at which he used these figures.

"The other way of retention, is the power to revive again in our minds those ideas, which after imprinting have disappeared, or have been as it were laid aside out of sight; and thus we do, when we conceive heat or light, yellow or sweet, the object being removed. This is memory, which is, as it were, the store-house of our ideas. For the narrow mind of man not being capable of having many ideas under view and consideration at once, it was necessary to have a repository to lay up those ideas, which at another time it might have use of. But our ideas being nothing but actual perceptions in the mind, which cease to be any thing, when there is no perception of them, this laying

1 Essay concerning Human Understanding, Book II, Chapter I, Section IX.
2 Essay concerning Human Understanding, Book II, Chapter I, Section III.
3 Section XII.

up of our ideas in the repository of the memory, signifies no more but this, that the mind has a power in many cases to revive perceptions, which it has once had, with this additional perception annexed to them, that it has had them before. And in this sense it is, that our ideas are said to be in our memories, when indeed they are actually no where, but only there is an ability in the mind when it will to revive them again, and as it were paint them a-new on itself, though some with more, some with less difficulty; some more lively, and others more obscurely." [1]

The doctrine of this truly eminent philosopher, therefore, is, that the presence of the external object, and the consequent organic change, are followed by an idea, "which is nothing but the actual perception;" and that the *laying up of these ideas* in the memory, signifies nothing more, than that the mind has, in many cases, a power to revive perceptions which it has once had. All this, I conceive, is the very doctrine of Dr Reid on the subject; and to have confuted Mr Locke, therefore, if it had been possible for him, must have been a very unfortunate confutation, as it would have been also to have confuted as completely the very opinions on the subject, which he was disposed himself to maintain.

· · · · ·

LECTURE XXVIII

ON DR. REID'S SUPPOSED PROOF OF A
MATERIAL WORLD—ON VISION—AND ANALYSIS
OF THE FEELINGS ASCRIBED TO IT

In my Lecture of yesterday, Gentlemen, we were engaged in considering the grounds of Dr Reid's claim to the honour of *detecting* and *exposing* the fallacy of the hypothesis of *ideas, as images, or things, in the mind, distinct from the mind itself,*—a claim which, though made by one who has many *other* indubitable titles to our respect and gratitude, we found, in this particular instance, to be inadmissible.

It appeared, on an examination of the original works of the eminent philosophers who preceded him for more than a century, and even of the common elementary treatises of the schools, that, though after the Peripatetic hypothesis of *species* had been universally or generally abandoned, the *language* of that hypothesis continued to subsist metaphorically,—as it continues with equal force at this moment,—it was *only metaphorically* that it did thus continue; and that when Dr Reid, therefore, conceived,—in proving ideas not to be *self-existing*

1 Essay concerning Human Understanding, Book II, Chapter X, Section II.

things, separate and distinct from the percipient mind itself,—that he was confuting what every body believed, he merely assumed as *real* what was intended as *metaphorical,* and overthrew opinions which the authors, to whom he ascribes them, would themselves have been equally eager to overthrow. But there is yet another point, connected with the theory of perception, on which he is believed to have made an important addition to our metaphysical knowledge. I allude to his supposed proof of the existence of a material world. In this, too, we shall find, that he has truly added nothing to our former knowledge; that he has left us, in short, our belief as originally felt by us, but has not supplied us with the slightest evidence in addition to the force of that original belief itself, nor given any additional strength to that very belief, which before was confessedly irresistible.

The confutation of the scepticism on this subject, it is evident, may be attempted in *two ways,*—by shewing the arguments urged by the sceptic to be *logically false;* or by opposing to them the belief itself, as of evidence either directly intuitive, or the result, at least, of other intuitions, and early and universal associations and inferences, so irresistible after the first acquisitions of infancy, as to have then all the force of intuition itself. As long as Dr Reid confines himself to the latter of these pleas, he proceeds on safe ground; but his footing is not so firm when he assails the mere logic of the sceptic,—for the sceptical argument, *as a mere play of reasoning,* admits of no reply. It is vain for him to say, that the scepticism proceeding, as he thinks, on the belief of ideas in the mind, as the direct objects of perception, must fall with these ideas; for, though the scepticism may be *consistent* with the belief of ideas as separate existences in the mind, it does not *depend,* in the slightest degree, on their existence or non-existence. We have only to change the term *ideas* into the synonymous phrase *affections or states of the mind,* and the scepticism, if not stronger, is at least in strength exactly what it was before. In the one case the sceptic will say, that we are sensible of *ideas* only, not of *external objects,* which may have *no resemblance to our ideas;* in the other case, that perception is but a state of the mind as much as any of our other feelings, and that we are conscious only of this, and other *states or affections of our mind,* which have variously succeeded each other, and not of *external objects, which themselves can be no parts of that train of mental consciousness.* Whatever weight there may be in the former of these sceptical theories, exists, I may say, even with greater force, because with greater simplicity, in the second; and the task, therefore, of proving *by logic,*—if logical proof were requisite for our belief,—the existence of a material world, would remain as laborious as before, after the fullest confutation of the system, which might suppose perception to be carried on by the medium of little images of bodies in the mind.

So far, indeed, would the confutation of this hypothesis as to perception,—even if Dr Reid had truly overthrown it,—be from *lessening* the force of the scepticism as to the existence of matter, that, of two sceptics, one believing every thing with respect to ideas which Dr Reid supposed himself to have confuted, and the other believing ideas to be mere states of his mind, there can be no question, that the *former* would be the *more* easy to be overcome, since his belief would *already* involve the existence of SOMETHING *separate from the mind;* while the other might maintain, that all of which he was conscious, was the mere series of affections of his own mind, and that beyond this consciousness he could know nothing.

Against the argument of one, who founds his very argument on his consciousness merely, and professes to have no knowledge either of little images, or of anything else beyond his consciousness, it would be as idle to urge, that *ideas are not little images in the mind,* as it would have been for a Cartesian to attempt to confute the *Newtonian system of attraction,* by a *denial of the Ptolemaic spheres.*

All that remains, then, to supply the place of logical demonstration, which would be needless where the belief is as strong as that of demonstration itself, is the paramount force of this universal and irresistible belief; and there is no fear that this can be weakened by any argument, or be less felt by him who *denies* it, than by him who asserts it. We are conscious, indeed, *only of the feelings that are the momentary states of our own mind;* but some of these it is absolutely impossible for us not to ascribe to causes that are external, and independent of us; and the *belief of a system of external things,* is one of these very *states of the mind,* which itself forms, *and will ever form,* a part of the train of our consciousness. This Mr Hume himself, the great sceptic whom Dr Reid opposes, admits as readily as Dr Reid himself:—"A Copernican or Ptolemaic, who supports each his different system of astronomy, may hope to produce a conviction, which will remain constant and durable, with his audience. A Stoic or Epicurean displays principles, which may not only be durable, but which have an effect on conduct and behaviour. But a Pyrrhonian cannot expect, that his philosophy will have any constant influence on the mind: or, if it had, that its influence would be beneficial to society. On the contrary, he must acknowledge, if he will acknowledge any thing, that all human life must perish, were his principles universally and steadily to prevail. All discourse, all action, would immediately cease; and men remain in a total lethargy, till the necessities of nature, unsatisfied, put an end to their miserable existence. It is true, so fatal an event is very little to be dreaded. Nature is always too strong for principle; and, though a Pyrrhonian may throw himself, or others, into a momentary amazement and confusion by his profound reasonings, the first and most trivial event in life will put to flight all his doubts and

scruples, and leave him the same, in every point of action and speculation, with the philosophers of every other sect, or with those who
never concerned themselves in any philosophical researches. When he
awakes from his dream, he will be the first to join in the laugh against
himself." [1] In what respect does this differ from the language of Dr
Reid himself, when he says, that "the belief of a material world is
older, and of more authority, than any principles of philosophy. It
declines the tribunal of reason, and laughs at all the artillery of the
logician." [2] Surely, if it decline the tribunal of reason, it is not by
reasoning that it is to be supported,—even though the reasoner should
have the great talents which Dr Reid unquestionably possessed.

The sceptic, and the orthodox philosopher of Dr Reid's school,
thus come precisely to the same conclusion. The creed of each, on this
point, is composed of two *propositions,* and of the *same two propositions;* the first of which is, that the existence of a system of things,
such as we understand when we speak of an external world, cannot be
proved by argument; and the second, that the belief of it is of a force,
which is paramount to that of argument, and absolutely irresistible.
The difference, and the *only* difference is, that, in asserting the same
two propositions, the sceptic pronounces the first in a *loud* tone of
voice, and the second in a *whisper,*—while his supposed antagonist
passes *rapidly* over the *first,* and dwells on the *second,* with a tone of
confidence. The negation, in the one case, and the affirmation in the
other case, are, however, *precisely the same.* To him, indeed, who
considers the *tone* only, and not the *meaning;* there may seem to be a
real strife of sentiment; but, if we neglect the *tone,* which is of no
consequence, and attend to the *meaning* only of what is affirmed and
denied by both, we shall not be able to discover even the slightest
discrepancy. There is no argument of mere reasoning that can prove
the existence of an external world; it is absolutely impossible for us
not to believe in the existence of an external world. We may call these
two propositions, then, a summary of the doctrine of Reid, or of the
doctrine of Hume, as we please; for it is truly the common and equal
doctrine of the two.

Though we have thus seen reason to deny to Dr Reid the merit
commonly ascribed to him, on the points which we have been considering, relative to the theory of perception, I trust you will not, on that
account, be insensible to the merits which he truly possessed. *He*
knows little, indeed, of the human mind, who does not know, how
compatible many errors and misconceptions are with the brightest and
most active energies of intellect. On this "Isthmus of a Middle State,"
of which Pope speaks, man, though not "reasoning but to err," is yet
subject to occasional error, even in his proudest reasonings. With all

---

1 Essays—Inquiry concerning Human Understanding, Section XII, Part 2.
2 Inquiry into the Human Mind, &c. Chapter V, Section VII.

his wisdom, he is still but "darkly wise;" and, with all the grandeur of
his being, but "rudely great."

LECTURE XLI

REDUCTION OF CERTAIN SUPPOSED
FACULTIES TO SIMPLE SUGGESTION

·   ·   ·   ·   ·

Let us now, then, apply the knowledge which we have thus acquired, and proceed to consider some of those forms of *suggestion,*
which have been ranked as distinct intellectual powers.

That, which its *greater simplicity* leads me to consider first, is what
has been termed by philosophers the *Power of Conception,* which has
been defined, *the power that enables us to form a notion* of an *absent
object of perception, or of some previous feeling of the mind.* The
definition of the supposed power is sufficiently intelligible; but is there
reason to add the power thus defined, to our other mental functions,
as a distinct and peculiar faculty?

That we have *a certain mental power, or susceptibility,* by which, in
accordance with this definition, the perception of one object may excite *the notion of some absent object,* is unquestionably true. But *this*
is the *very function* which is meant by the *power of suggestion* itself,
when stripped of the illusion as to prior association; and if the *conception* be separated from the suggestion, *nothing will remain* to constitute the power of suggestion, which is only another name for the same
power. I enter, for example, an apartment in my friend's house during
his long absence from home; I see his *flute,* or the *work of some
favourite author,* lying on his table. The mere *sight* of either of these,
awakes instantly my conception of my friend, though, at the moment,
he might have been absent from my thought. I see him again *present.*
If I look at the *volume,* I almost think that I hear him arguing strenuously for the merits of his favourite, as in those evenings of social
contention, when we have brought poets and philosophers to war
against poets and philosophers. If I look at the flute, I feel instantly a
similar illusion. I hear him again animating it with his very touch,—
breathing into it what might almost, without a metaphor, be said to be
the *breath of life,*—and giving it not *utterance* merely, but eloquence.
In these cases of simple suggestion, it is said the successive mental
states which constitute the notions of my *friend* himself, of the *arguments* which I again seem to hear and combat, of the *melodies* that
silently enchant me,—are *conceptions* indicating, therefore, a power
of the mind from which they arise, that, in reference to the effects

produced by it, may be called the *power of conception*. But, if they arise from a peculiar *power of conception,*—and if there be a *power of association* or *suggestion,* which is also concerned, how are these powers to be distinguished, and what part of the process is it which we owe to this latter power? If there were no *suggestion* of my friend, it is very evident that there could be no *conception* of my friend; and if there were no *conception* of him, it would be absurd to speak of a *suggestion,* in which *nothing was suggested.* Whether we use the term *suggestion,* or *association,* in this case, is of no consequence. Nothing more can be accurately meant by either term, in reference to the example which I have used, than the tendency of my mind, after existing in the state which constitutes the perception of the flute or volume, and of the room in which I observe it, to exist *immediately afterwards* in that different state which constitutes the conception of my friend. The laws of *suggestion* or *association* are merely the general circumstances, according to which *conceptions,* or certain other feelings, arise. There is not, in any case of suggestion, *both* a *suggestion* and a *conception,* more than there is in any case of vision, both a *vision* and a *sight.* What one *glance* is to the capacity of *vision,* one *conception* is to the capacity of *suggestion.* We may *see* innumerable objects in succession; we may *conceive* innumerable objects in succession. But we *see* them, because we are susceptible of *vision;* we conceive them, because we have that susceptibility of *spontaneous suggestion,* by which conceptions arise after each other in regular trains.

This *duplication* of a single power, to account for the production of a single state of mind, appears to me a very striking example of the influence of that *misconception,* with respect to association, which I occupied so much of your time in attempting to dissipate. If *association* and *suggestion* had been considered as *exactly synonymous,* implying merely the *successions* of *one* state of mind to *another* state of mind,—without any mysterious process of union of the two feelings *prior* to the suggestion, the attention of inquirers would, in this just and simple view, have been fixed on the single moment of the suggestion itself:—and I cannot think that any philosopher would, in this case, have contended for *two* powers, as operating together at the very same moment, in the production of the very same conception; but that *one* capacity would have been regarded as sufficient for this *one simple* effect, whether it were termed, with more immediate reference to the secondary feeling that is the *effect,* the *power of conception,* or with more immediate reference to the primary feeling which precedes it as its cause, the power of *suggestion or association.* It is very different, however, when the *conception,*—the one simple effect produced,—is made to depend, not merely on the tendency of the mind to exist in that state, at the particular moment at which the conception arises, but on some process of *association,* which may have operated at a considerable interval before; for in that case the process of association, which is supposed to have taken place at one period, must itself imply *one power,* or function of the mind, and the actual *suggestion,* or rise of the conception, at an interval afterwards, some different power or function.

With respect to the supposed *intellectual power* of *conception,* then, as distinct from the intellectual *power of association* or suggestion, we may very safely conclude, that the belief of this is founded merely on a mistake as to the nature of *associations;*—that the *power of suggestion* and the power of *conception* are the same, both being only that particular susceptibility of the mind, from which, in certain circumstances, *conceptions arise,*—or, at least, that if the power of *conception* differs from the *more general powers of suggestion,* it differs from it only as *a part* differs from the *whole,*—as the power of taking *a single step* differs from the power of *traversing a whole field,* —the *power of drawing a single* breath from the general *power of respiration,*—the *moral susceptibility* by which we are capable of forming one charitable purpose from that almost divine universality of benevolence, in a whole virtuous life, to which *every moment* is either some *exertion for good,* or *some wish for good,* which comprehends within its *sphere of* ACTION,—that has no limits but physical impossibility,—every being whom it can *instruct* or *amend,* or *relieve* or *gladden;* and, in its *sphere of generous* DESIRE, all that is *beyond* the limits of its power of *benefitting.*

The next supposed *intellectual power* to which I would call your attention, is the *power of memory.*

In treating of our *suggestions,* and consequently, as you have seen, of our *conceptions,* which are only parts of the suggested series, I have, at the same time, treated of our *remembrances,* or, at least, of the more important part of our remembrances, because our *remembrances* are nothing more than conceptions united with the notion of a certain relation of time. They are *conceptions* of the *past,* felt *as conceptions of the past,*—that is to say, felt as having a *certain relation of antecedence* to our present feeling. The remembrance is not a simple but a complex state of mind; and all which is necessary to reduce a remembrance to a mere conception, is to separate from it a part of the complexity,—that part of it which constitutes the notion of a certain relation of antecedence. We are conscious of our *present feeling,* whatever it may be; for this is, in truth, only another name for our *consciousness itself.* The moment of present time, at which we are thus conscious, is a *bright point,*—ever *moving,* and yet, as it were, ever *fixed,*—which divides the *darkness of the future* from the *twilight of the past.* It is, in short, what Cowley terms the whole of human life,—

"A weak *isthmus,* that doth proudly rise
Up betwixt two eternities." [1]

The present moment, then, though ever *fleeting,* is to us, as it were, a fixed point; and it is a point which guides us in the most important of our measurements, in our *retrospects of the past,* and our *hopes of the future.* The particular feeling of any moment before the present, as it rises again in our mind, would be a *simple conception,* if we did not think of it, either *immediately* or *indirectly,* in relation to some other feeling earlier or later. It becomes a remembrance when we combine with it this feeling of relation,—the relation which constitutes our notion of *time;*— for *time,* as far as we are capable of *understanding* it, or rather of *feeling* it, is nothing more than the varieties of this felt relation, which, in reference to one of the subjects of the relation, we distinguish by the word *before,*—in reference to the other, by the word *after.* It is a relation, I may remark, which we feel nearly in the same manner as we feel the relation which bodies bear to each other, as coexisting in space. We say of a *house,* that it is *two miles* from a particular village, half a mile from the river, a mile from the bridge, with a feeling of relation very similar to that with which we say of one event, that it occurred a month ago,—of another event, that it occurred in the memorable year of our first going to school,—of another, that it happened in our infancy. There is some *point* to which, in estimating distance of space, we refer the objects which we measure, as there is a *point of time* in the present moment, or in some event which we have before learned to consider thus relatively, to which, directly or indirectly, we refer the events of which we speak as *past* or *future,* or *more or less recent.*

If we had been incapable of considering more than *two events together,* we probably never should have invented the word *time,* but should have contented ourselves with simpler words, expressive of the simple relation of the two. But we are capable of considering a *variety of events,* all of which are felt by us to bear to that state of mind which constitutes our present consciousness, some relation of priority or subsequence,—which they seem to us to bear also reciprocally to each other;—and the *varieties* of this relation oblige us to invent a *general term* for expressing them *all.* This *general word,* invented by us for expressing *all the varieties of priority and subsequence,* is *time,* —a word, therefore, which expresses no actual reality, but only relations that are felt by us, in the objects of our conception. To think of time is not to think of any thing existing of itself, for time is not a thing but a relation; it is only to have *some conceptions of objects,* which we regard as *prior* and *subsequent;* and without the conception

---

1 Cowley's Ode on Life and Fame, Stanza I. ver. 10, 11, slightly altered.
"Vain weak-built Isthmus, that dost proudly rise
Up betwixt two eternities."—*Orig.*

of objects of some kind, *as subjects of the relation* of priority and subsequence, it is as little possible for us to imagine any *time,* as to imagine *brightness* or *dimness* without a single ray of light,—proportional magnitude without any dimensions,—or any other relation without any other subject. When the notion of *time,* then, is combined with any of our conceptions, as in memory, all which is combined with the simple *conception* is the feeling of a certain relation. To be capable of remembering, in short, we must have a capacity of the feelings which we term *relations,* and a capacity of the feelings which we term *conceptions,* that may be the subjects of the relations; but with these two powers no other is requisite,—no power of memory distinct from the *conception* and *relation* which that complex form denotes.

When I say that *time,* as *far as we are capable of understanding it,* is nothing more than a certain felt relation of certain conceptions of our own mind, I am sufficiently aware of the necessity of this qualifying clause with respect to the limits of our understanding, and of the truth of the very striking remark of St Austin on this most obscure subject, that he knew well what time was *till* he was asked about it, and that *then* he knew nothing of it.—"Quid ergo est tempus? Quis hoc facile explicuerit? Si nemo a me quærat, scio. Si quærenti explicare velim, nescio." [1]

It is truly one of those subjects, which, instead of growing clearer as we gaze upon it, grows more obscure beneath our very gaze. All of which we can be said to be *conscious,* is certainly the present moment *alone.* But of that complex state of mind, which forms to us the present moment, there are *parts* which impress us irresistibly, and beyond all the power of scepticism, with the *relation,* which, as I have already said, we term *priority,* in reference to the *one,* and *succession* or *subsequence,* in reference to the *other;* time, as felt by us, being this *relation* of the two, and *nothing more.* It is not because we have a previous notion of time that we regard objects as prior and posterior, more than we regard objects as large or small, because we have a previous notion of magnitude; but time, as a general word, is significant to us merely of the felt varieties of the relation of priority and subsequence, as magnitude is a general word, expressive of the felt varieties of comparative dimensions.

But I have already dwelt too long on a point, which I may very probably have made *darker* to you than it was before; but which, impressed as I am with the truth of St Austin's remark, I scarcely can venture to flatter myself with the hope of having made much more *distinctly* conceivable by you.

---

[1] "What, then, is time? Who can explain it easily and briefly? If no one asks me, I know. If I wish to explain it to a questioner, I do not know." Augustine, *Confessions,* Book XI, Chapter XIV. Ed.

Obscure as the relation of priority and succession may be, however, which is all that mingles with conception in our remembrance, it is still only a certain relation; and the *feeling* of this *relation* does not imply any *peculiar power,* generically distinct from that which perceives *other relations, whether clear or obscure;* unless, indeed, we should be inclined to invent a separate name of some *new* faculty of the mind for *every* relation with which the mind can be impressed, in the almost infinite variety of these feelings. Memory, therefore, is not a distinct *intellectual faculty,* but is merely *conception* or *suggestion* combined with the feeling of a particular relation,—the relation to which we give the name of *priority,* a feeling that is not essential, indeed, to the accompanying conception itself, but that admits of being combined with it, in the same manner as the relation of place, or any other relation, admits of being combined with other conceptions or perceptions. It cannot be denied, for example, that in the darkness of the night, after an interval of many years, and at the distance probably of many thousand miles, we have the faculty of *conceiving,* or of beholding again, almost with the same vividness as when we trod its steep ascent, the *mountain* which we have been accustomed perhaps to ascend in our boyhood, for the pleasure of looking down, from its topmost rock, with a sort of pride at the height which we had mastered. To behold mentally this eminence again, *without any feeling of the relation of past time,* is to have only a *conception* of the mountain. We cannot think of the mountain itself, however, even for a few moments, without thinking also of the *scene* which we have been accustomed to survey from it,—the humbler hills around, that served only to make the valley between appear *lower,* than we should otherwise have conceived it to be, and to make us feel still more proudly the height which we had attained,—the scattered villages,—the woods,—the streams, in various directions, mingling and resting in the motionless expanse of the lake. By comprehending gradually more of these objects in our mental view, we have *widened our conception,* indeed, but it is still a *conception only;* and we are not said to exercise any power distinct from that of *conception* or *suggestion.* Yet we cannot thus conceive the landscape *as a whole,* without feeling various *relations* which its parts bear to each other in space, as *near* or *distant, high* or *low,*—the wood *hanging* over the village,—the spire gleaming *through* the trees,—the brook *hurrying* down to the mill, and the narrow path-way by its side. These relations, which give unity to the scene, are relations of space only, and they do not hinder our *complex* feeling from being denominated simply a conception. So far, then, no new power is said to be concerned. If, however, in addition to all these *local* relations, we introduce but a single relation of time,—the thought of the most trifling circumstance which occurred when we last ascended the same mountain, and beheld the same scene,—though this new part of the complex feeling have risen, according to the same exact laws of suggestion, as the conception of the mere scene, the conception is then instantly said to indicate a *new power,* and what was before a conception is a conception no longer. In one sense, indeed, there is truly the operation of a *new power,* for there is a *new relation* most certainly felt; and every *relation felt* implies a power or susceptibility in the mind of *feeling this relation.* But the relations of coexistence in *space* are not less *relations* than those of *succession in time;* and *both* or *neither,* therefore, when coexisting with our conceptions, should be said to indicate a new intellectual faculty.

The state of mind, in memory, is, as I have already said, a complex one,—a *conception,* and a *feeling of relation.* But it admits of very easy *analysis* into these *two parts,* and, therefore, does not require the supposition of any *new power* to comprehend it, more than the *complex state of mind,* which results from the combination of the simple sensations of *warmth and fragrance,* requires the supposition of a new power to comprehend it, distinct from the *separate senses* to which the elementary feelings, if existing alone, would be referred. The conception, which forms one element of the *remembrance,* is referable to the *capacity of simple suggestion,* which we have been considering; the *feeling of the relation of priority,* which forms the other element of the remembrance, is referable, like all our other feelings of relation, to the *capacity of relative suggestion,* which we are afterwards to consider. It is merely as this relation of priority *is* or *is not* felt, that the state of mind, in which there is pictured some absent object or past feeling, has the name of a *conception* or the name of a *remembrance;* and that *part* of the complex whole, which is a *mere conception,* does not differ from the common products of *suggestion,* but, as we have seen, in treating of our conceptions in general, is merely a particular form, or result, of that *general power of suggestion,* which gives a second being to the whole shadowy train of our thought. Indeed, since *one of the relations,* according to which association or suggestion is said to take place, is, by every writer who treats of the laws of association, allowed to be that of *priority, or former succession in time,* it would surely have been a very singular arrangement, if the *conceptions,* arising according to this very relation, were to be held as not fairly referable to the class to which they have previously been ascribed; and that what renders them *associate* should be itself the very cause, for which, and for which alone, they are to be excluded from the class of associations.

Simple memory, then, it appears, is nothing more than a *particular suggestion,* combined with the feeling *of the relation of priority;* and all the conceptions, therefore, which it involves, arise *according to the laws which regulate suggestion in general.* The same *resemblances, contrasts, contiguities,* give rise to our *conceptions of objects,* whether we *do* or *do not* consider those objects in the *relation of priority,* which they bear to our present feeling, or to any other event. In journeying along a road which I have never passed before, some form of the varying landscape may recal to me the scenery around the home which I have left; and it suggests it equally by its *mere resemblance,* whether it recal it to me as a *simple picture,* or remind me, at the same time, that it *is* the very home which I have left, and that, as many weeks have intervened since I saw it, many weeks are likely also to pass before I see it again. . . .

LECTURE XLIII

REFUTATION OF HARTLEY'S THEORY OF ASSOCIATION

. . . . .

It is chiefly in the southern part of the island, that the hypothesis of Dr Hartley has met with followers; and his followers have generally been extravagant admirers of his philosophical genius, which, I own, seems to me to be very opposite to the genius of sound philosophy. That there is considerable acuteness, however, displayed in his work, and that it contains some successful analyses of complex feelings, I am far from denying; and, as intellectual science consists so much in the *analysis* of the *complex phenomena* of *thought,* its influence, in *this* respect, has unquestionably been of service, in promoting that *spirit of inquiry,* which, in a science that presents no attraction to the senses, is so easily laid asleep, or, at least, so readily acquiesces, as if to justify its *indolence,* in the authority of great names, and of all that is ancient in error, and venerable in absurdity. But, though the influence of his philosophy may have been of service in *this* respect, the advantage, which has, perhaps, flowed from it *in this way,* must have been inconsiderable, compared with the great evil, which has unquestionably flowed from it *in another way,* by leading the inquirer to acquiesce in remote analogies, and to adopt explanations and arrangements of the phenomena of mind,—not as they agree with the actual phenomena,—but as they chance to agree with some supposed phenomena of our *material part.* Dr Hartley, indeed, does not consider *materialism,* as a *necessary consequence* of his theory. He does not say, that the *vibrations* and *vibratiuncles* of the medullary parts of the sensorium constitute the very sensations and passions, but merely that they are changes, *necessary to every mental affection.* Yet, by adopting a supposed analogy of a particular *species of motion,* as common to all the intellectual functions,—and thus imposing the necessity of finding, or attempting to find, in every case some exact correspondence of the mental phenomena, with the varieties and combinations of this particular species of motion, he has done as much to distract the attention of the intellectual inquirer, as if he had made all the phenomena to consist of this particular notion,—and without contending for materialism, or even believing in materialism, has produced this belief in the minds of those who have adopted his general system, as effectually as if he had himself believed and contended that the soul is a cube, or a cone, or some irregular solid of many sides.

If we admit—as in sound philosophy it is impossible not to admit—the existence of *mind,* as a substance not cubical, conical, nor of many sides, regular or irregular, but one and simple, different from matter, and capable, by the affections of which it is susceptible, of existing in all those various states which constitute the whole history of our life, as sentient, and intelligent, and moral beings,—though we must allow, that its *sense of external things,* and, perhaps, some of its other susceptibilities, require certain previous sensorial changes or affections, not for constituting its feelings, but merely for giving occasion to them, as any other cause gives occasion to any other effect;—there is no reason for believing, that such changes of the material organs are necessary for *every feeling or affection of the mind,* even as the mere *occasions* on which the feelings arise. Though we were to admit this necessity, however, without any reason for admitting it, and were to think ourselves obliged, therefore, to have recourse to some analogy of matter,—we must still reject the hypothesis of *vibrations;* since, of all the corporeal changes, that could be imagined, in the soft medullary matter of the brain and nerves, *vibrations* seem the least likely,—certainly, at least, the *worst fitted* for marking accurately the nice distinctions of things. Indeed, it has always seemed to me peculiarly wonderful, that *such an hypothesis* should have been formed by a *physician,* to whom the structure of the brain and its appendages must have been familiar. If we wished to have a substance, that should *damp* and *deaden* every species of vibration, so as to prevent a single vibration from being accurately transmitted, it would not be very easy to find one better suited for this purpose, than that soft pulpy matter, which is supposed by Dr Hartley to transmit, with most exact fidelity, all the nicest divisions of infinitesimal vibratiuncles.

Of the system of *vibrations* and *vibratiuncles,* which has now fallen into merited disrepute, even with those who are inclined, in other respects, to hold in very high estimation the merits of Hartley, as an intellectual analyst, it is scarcely necessary to offer any serious confutation. The very primary facts of association or suggestion on which the whole of his metaphysical system is founded, have always appeared to me a sufficient confutation of that very hypothesis which is adduced to explain them; and as these are his favourite phenomena, on which he constantly insists, they may fairly be taken as the most suitable instances in which to examine the force of the analogy which he wishes to establish. Though the sensorium, then, were allowed to be, in almost every circumstance, the very *opposite* of what it is—to be finely elastic, and composed of chords, adapted in the best possible manner, for the nicest differences of vibrations; and though varieties, in the mere times of vibration of the same strings, were allowed to be sufficient for explaining all the infinite diversities of sensation; still the influence of that very association on which Hartley founds so much, would remain wholly unexplained. We may suppose, indeed, any two of these chords, from *accidental simultaneous impulse,* to have vibrated together; but this can be no reason, even though the accidental concurrence of vibrations should have taken place *one thousand times* at the same moment—that there should be any greater tendency in the second chord than there was originally, to vibrate, without a repetition of the primary impulse, in consequence of the mere vibration of the first. If the *chords,* or series of vibratory particles, still retain the same length and tension, the motion of the *second* may indeed be allowed to be producible indirectly, by an *impulse* given only to the *first,* if the strings *truly harmonize;* but, in this case, the motion of the *second* must have been produced in like manner, *originally,* by the *first* vibrations of the other, when external force was applied to *it* alone; and, if the two series of vibratory particles be of such a kind as *not to harmonize,* a thousand accidental coexistences or successions of their vibrations, cannot make them harmonize more than at first. *Association,* therefore, or *habit,* on such an hypothesis, would not be necessary to account for phenomena which must have taken place *equally* by the mere laws of *harmonics,* without association. If the sight of a pictured rose recal to me its *fragrance,* or the fragrance of a rose in the dark, recal to me its form and colour, it is a proof that the sensorial chords, of which the vibrations give rise to these conceptions, are of such a length as to harmonize, and to admit, therefore, of *joint* vibration from a single impulse. But, in this case, it is surely unnecessary that both the *sight* and *smell* should ever have existed before. Though I had never *seen* a rose, the mere *smell* of one in the dark should have brought before me instantly the form and colour which I never had beheld, because it should instantly have produced this particular corresponding vibration in the harmonizing strings; and, though I had never enjoyed its delightful fragrance, the mere *picture* of the flower, on paper or canvas, should have given me, in the very instant, by a similar correspondence of vibration, the knowledge of its odour.

All this, it may perhaps be said, would be very true, if the vibrations, of which metaphysical physiologists speak, were meant in their common physical sense. But, if they are *not* used in their common physical sense, *what is it* that they are intended to denote? and why is not the precise difference pointed out? Nothing can be *simpler* than the meaning of the term *vibration*—an alternate approach and retrocession of a series of particles; and if this particular species of motion be not meant, it is certainly most absurd to employ the *term,* when another term could have been adopted or invented without risk of error; or at least to employ it without stating what is distinctly meant by it, as different from the other vibrations of which we are accustomed to speak. If it be not understood in its usual meaning, and if no other meaning be assigned to the term, the hypothesis, which expresses nothing that can be understood, has not even the scanty glory of being an hypothesis. The same phenomena might, with as much philosophic accuracy, be ascribed to any other fanciful term—to the Entelecheia of Aristotle, or to the Abracadabra of the Cabalists. Indeed, they might be ascribed to either of these magnificent words with greater accuracy, because, though the words might leave us as ignorant as before, they, at least, would not communicate to us any notion *positively false.* There is certainly very little resemblance of *memory* to an *effervescence,* yet we might theorize as justly in ascribing *memory* to an *effervescence* as to a *vibration,* if we be allowed to understand both terms in a sense totally different from the common use, without even expressing what that different sense is; and if the followers of Hartley, in preferring *vibratiuncles* to little *effervescences,* profess to understand the term *vibration* as it is commonly understood, and to apply to the phenomena of association the common laws of *vibrating chords,* they must previously undertake to shew, that the phenomena of musical chords, on which they found their hypothesis, are the *reverse* of what they are known to be,—that strings of such a length and tension as to harmonize, are *not* originally capable of receiving vibrations from the motions of each other, but communicate their vibrations mutually only after they have repeatedly been touched together,—and that musical chords, of such a length and tension as to be absolutely discordant, acquire notwithstanding, when frequently touched with a bow or the finger, a tendency to harmonize, and at length vibrate together at the mere touch of one of them. *Then,* indeed, when the tendencies to vibratory motion are shewn to be precisely the reverse of what they are, the phenomena of suggestion *might* find some analogy in the phenomena of vibration; but, knowing what we know of musical chords, it is impossible to bring their phenomena to bear, in the slightest degree, on the phenomena of association,—unless, indeed, by convincing us, that, little as we know positively of the mysterious principle of suggestion, we may at least negatively have perfect knowledge, that it is *not* a *vibration* or a *vibratiuncle.*

BROWN'S WRITINGS

Observations on the Zoonomia of Erasmus Darwin (Edinburgh, 1798), seems never to have been reprinted. *Observations on Cause and Effect* (Edinburgh, 1st edition 1805, 2nd edition, enlarged, 1806), was retitled *Inquiry into the Relation of Cause and Effect* in the third and further enlarged edition of 1818. An American edition appeared in 1822 and the last edition in London (1835). The *Sketch of a System of the Philosophy of the Human Mind* (Edinburgh, 1820), came out only in the original edition. It was replaced almost immediately by *Lectures on the Philosophy of the Human Mind,* 4 vol. (Edinburgh, 1820); the *Lectures* went through twenty-one editions by 1860, but has not appeared since then.

WRITINGS ON BROWN

The chapter on Brown in *Dissertation on the Progress of Ethical Philosophy* (Edinburgh, 1837), by Sir James Mackintosh is still readable, though some portions are irrelevant to the subject. In *The Scottish Philosophy* (London, 1875), James McCosh has an informative but somewhat unsympathetic discussion of Brown. In the second volume of *The English Utilitarians* (London, 1900), Leslie Stephen gives extended treatment to Brown as "the last in the genuine line of Scottish commonsense philosophers." Henry Laurie's *Scottish Philosophy* (Glasgow, 1902), is also worth consulting. Brown's contributions to the development of associationist psychology are interestingly discussed in *A History of the Association Psychology* (New York, 1921), by H. C. Warren. There are passing references of value in S. A. Grave, *The Scottish Philosophy of Common Sense* (Oxford, 1960). In many ways, however, the fullest and liveliest treatment of Brown's views is that given by Sir William Hamilton in his long article "Philosophy of Perception" (1830), a review of Jouffroy's French edition of Reid's *Works,* reprinted in Hamilton's *Discussions on Philosophy and Literature* (London, 1853); and in the partial defense of Brown given by John Stuart Mill in his *An Examination of Sir William Hamilton's Philosophy and of the Principal Philosophical Questions Discussed in His Writings* (London, 1865). In French there is a standard and useful work: F. Rethoré, *Critique de la Philosophie de Thomas Brown* (Paris, 1863). Other references, though of minor interest, are given in T. E. Jessop's *A Bibliography of David Hume and of Scottish Philosophy* (London and Hull, 1938).

JAMES MILL

1773–1836

The distinguished father of John Stuart Mill was himself the studious son of a country shoemaker in the county of Angus, Scotland. "The tender hand of his mother reserved James exclusively for study"; and after receiving a classical education at a local grammar school, he obtained a scholarship to Edinburgh University under the patronage of Sir John and Lady Jane Stuart whose summer residence was in the neighborhood of his father's cottage. Later, James Mill became their daughter's tutor. He entered the university in 1790, studied Greek and Latin, and attended Stewart's philosophy lectures which impressed him strongly. From 1794–98 Mill was a divinity student but read much philosophy. He was licensed to preach in 1798, and did so locally while supporting himself by tutoring.

When Sir John Stuart, as a member of parliament, went to London in 1802 Mill accompanied him and began a career as a journalist. From 1803–06 Mill edited the weekly *Literary Journal,* and for a few years after 1805 the *St James Chronicle.* He married in 1805 and his eldest son, John Stuart, was born the following year. After the loss of his editorships, Mill managed a precarious living until 1808 when he began writing for the *Edinburgh Review,* started his *History of British India,* and met Jeremy Bentham with whom he quickly became close. Mill was soon a foremost member of the radical, nonreligious, social thinkers who formed Bentham's circle. With the immediate success of the *History of India* on its publication in 1818, Mill was given a good post in India House, advanced rapidly to become head of his office, and for the first time was financially comfortable. In 1821 he published *Elements of Political Economy,* the text of lectures he had produced to educate his son.

As Bentham aged, Mill took over the active leadership of the philosophical radicals, or utilitarians, as they were later called. His closest friend was the economist, David Ricardo, and his closest followers, George Grote, the historian of Greece, and John Austin, the jurist. Their views were now encouraged by two newspapers and by the series of influential articles Mill wrote between 1816 and 1823 for the supplement to the *Encyclopaedia Britannica*. The article on "Government," a summary of social utilitarianism, became the object of a famous attack by Thomas Babington Macaulay in the *Edinburgh Review* (1829). In this year, also, the *Analysis of the Phenomena of the Human Mind* appeared; Mill had worked on it during the summer holidays of the previous six years.

While maintaining a stream of essays on many aspects of social, economic, and political reform, Mill was engaged at this period in such practical affairs as helping to found University College, London, in 1825; in the preparatory work for the first Reform bill of 1832; and in arguing the case for the renewal of the East India Company's Charter in the committees of the House of Commons, 1831–33. Mill died of lung disease, as did two of his nine children. He lived long enough to see the delayed publication of his second philosophical work, *A Fragment on Mackintosh,* which was, in part, an oblique reply to the criticisms by Macaulay.

James Mill, like Price and Priestley, was a part-time philosopher; and like them he was interested in philosophy as a means of underpinning certain fundamental views to which he was committed for other reasons. In Mill's case these views were ethical. He wished, as a supporter of the greatest happiness for the greatest number, to show how this could arise from the innate tendency of each person to seek merely his own pleasure or personal happiness. It arises, he thought, by the operation of association upon sensations and ideas, the latter being simply the residual copies of the former. The particular pleasures a man pursues are determined by what they have been associated with in the past. Hence, as a matter of social policy, people can be educated in such a way that for them the mere means to their personal pleasure are inseparably associated with that pleasure. People then will pursue the social means—the happiness of all other people—to the goal of private pleasure as strenuously as they pursue that goal itself.

But by going on to use the principle of association to explain all our mental life and all our knowledge of the world, Mill did much more than argue for the principle that every man should seek the greatest happiness of the greatest number. He clearly indicated, though unawares, the explanatory limitations of the associationist doctrine. From him John Stuart Mill inherited a set of difficult and fundamental problems. And as the younger Mill's notes on these selections from the *Analysis* make clear, the father's ability to philosophically educate and stimulate his son extended well beyond James Mill's own death. The elder Mill had been chiefly influenced by the British empiricists— Hobbes, Locke, Hume, Hartley, Brown—and by their French followers, Condillac, Helvétius, Cabanis. In John Stuart Mill's inheritance of these influences they become part and parcel of contemporary philosophy in the English speaking world. For on many topics, he and they still set the terms in which we discuss these questions.

SELECTIONS FROM

Analysis of the Phenomena
of the Human Mind *

*

C H A P T E R   I X

ABSTRACTION

"I think, too, that he (Mr. Locke) would have seen the advantage of 'thoroughly weighing,' not only (as he says) 'the *imperfections* of Language;' but its *perfections* also: For the perfections of Language, not properly understood, have been one of the chief causes of the imperfections of our knowledge."
—*Diversions of Purley, by John Horne Tooke, A.M.,* i. 37.

The two cases of Consciousness, CLASSIFICATION, and ABSTRACTION, have not, generally, been well distinguished.

According to the common accounts of Classification, ABSTRACTION was included in it. When it is said, that, in order to classify, we leave out of view all the circumstances in which individuals differ, and retain only those in which they agree; this separating one portion of what is contained in a complex idea, and making it an object of consideration by itself, is the process which is named Abstraction, at least a main part of that process.

It is necessary now to inquire what are the purposes to which this separating of the parts of a complex idea, and considering and naming the separated parts by themselves, is subservient.

We have already observed the following remarkable things in the process of naming: 1, Assigning names of those clusters of ideas called objects; as man, fish; 2, Generalizing those names, so as to make them represent a class; 3, Framing adjectives by which minor classes are cut out of larger.

Those adjectives are all names of some separate portion of a clus-

* Vol. I and II. Edited by John Stuart Mill (London, 1869).

ter, and are, therefore, all instruments of abstraction, or of that separating one or more of the ingredients of a complex idea from the rest, which has received the name of Abstraction. One purpose of Abstraction, therefore, is the formation of those *subspecies,* the formation of which is required for certain purposes of speech.

These observations will be rendered familiar by examples. We say, tall man, red flower, race horse. In my complex idea of a man, or the cluster of ideas of sense to which I affix that mark, are included, certain ideas of colour, of figure, size, and so on. By the word tall, I single out a portion of those ideas, namely, the part relating to size, or rather size in one direction, and mark the separation by the sign or name. In my complex idea of a flower, colour is always one of the ingredients. By applying the adjective red, I single out this one from the rest, and point it out for peculiar consideration. The explanation is obvious, and need not be pursued in a greater number of instances.

Words of this description all denote differences; either such as mark out species from genera, or such as mark out individuals from species. Of this latter sort the number is very small; of which the reason is obvious; individual differences are too numerous to receive names, and are marked by contrivances of abridgment which will be spoken of hereafter.

To explain this notation of differences, the same examples will suffice. In the phrase "tall man," the adjective "tall" marks the difference between such a man, and "short man," or "middle-sized man." Of the genus man, tall men are one species; and the difference between them and the rest of the genus is marked by the word tall. Of the genus flower, red flowers form a species, and the difference between them and the rest of the genus is marked by the adjective red. Of the genus horse, race horse forms a species, and the difference between this species and the rest of the genus is marked by the word race.

It is of importance further to observe, that adjectives singling out ideas which are not differences, that is, ideas common to the whole class, are useless: as, tangible wood; coloured man; sentient animal. Such epithets express no more than what is expressed by the name without them.

Another thing requiring the attention of the student is the mode in which these differential adjectives are generalized. As the word man, applied first to one individual, then to another, becomes associated with every individual, and every variety of the species, and calls them all up in one very complex idea; so are these adjectives applied to one class after another, and by that means at last call up a very complicated idea. Let us take the word "black" for an example; and let us suppose that we apply this adjective first to the word man. We say "black man." But we speedily see that for the same reason for which we say black man we may say black horse, black cow, black coat, and so on. The word black is thus associated with innumerable modifications of the sensation black. By frequent repetition, and the gradual strengthening of the association, these modifications are at last called up in such rapid succession that they appear commingled, and no longer many ideas, but one. Black is therefore no longer an individual but a general name. It marks not the particular black of a particular individual; but the black of every individual, and of all individuals.[1] The same is the case with all other words of the same class. Thus I apply the word sweet, first to the lump of sugar in my mouth, next to honey, next to grapes, and so on. It thus becomes associated with numerous modifications of the sensation sweet; and when the association is sufficiently strengthened by repetition, calls them up in such close succession, that they are converted into one complex idea. We are also to remember, that the idea and the name have a mutual power over one another. As the word black calls up the complex idea, so every modification of black calls up the name; and in this, as in other cases, the name actually forms a part of the complex idea.

The next thing, which I shall observe, deserves in a high degree, the attention of the learner. In the various applications of that species of marks which we are now considering, they are associated with two distinguishable things; but with the one much more than the other. Thus, when we say black man, black horse, black coat, and so of all other black things, the word black is associated with the cluster, man, as often as black man is the expression; with the cluster horse, as often as black horse is the expression, and so on with infinite variety: but at the same time that it is associated with each of those various clusters, it is also associated with the peculiar sensation of colour which it is intended to mark. The CLUSTERS, therefore, with which it is associated, are variable; the PECULIAR SENSATION with which it is

---

[1] The example which the author has here selected of a general name, sets in a strong light the imperfection of the theory of general names, laid down by him in the preceding chapter. A name like "black," which marks a simple sensation, is an extreme case of the inapplicability of the theory. Can it be maintained that the idea called up in our minds by the word black, is an idea compounded of ideas of black men, black horses, black cows, black coats, and the like? If I can trust my own consciousness, the word need not, and generally does not, call up any idea but that of a single black surface. It is still not an abstract idea, but the idea of an individual object. It is not a mere idea of colour; it is that, combined with ideas of extension and figure, always present but extremely vague, because varying, even from one moment to the next. These vague ideas of an uncertain extension and figure, combined with the perfectly definite idea of a single sensation of colour, are, to my consciousness, the sole components of the complex idea associated with the word black. I am unable to find in that complex idea the ideas of black men, horses, or other definite things, though such ideas may of course be recalled by it.

In such a case as this, the idea of a black colour fills by itself the place of the inner nucleus of ideas knit together by a closer association, which I have described as forming the permanent part of our ideas of classes of objects, and the meaning of the class-names.—J.S.M.

associated is invariable. It is much more constantly, and therefore much more strongly associated with the SENSATION than with any of the CLUSTERS. It is at once a name of the clusters, and a name of the sensation; but it is more peculiarly a name of the SENSATION.

We have, in a preceding note, observed, that such words have been called *connotative;* and I shall find much convenience in using the term NOTATION to point out the sensation or sensations which are peculiarly marked by such words, the term CONNOTATION to point out the clusters which they mark along with this their principal meaning.

Thus the word, black, NOTES that of which black is more peculiarly the name, a particular colour; it CONNOTES the clusters with the names of which it is joined: in the expression, black man, it connotes man; black horse, it connotes horse; and so of all other cases. The ancient Logicians used these terms, in the inverse order; very absurdly, in my opinion.[1]

---

[1] The word Connote, with its substantive Connotation, was used by the old logicians in two senses; a wider, and a narrower sense. The wider is that in which, up to this place, the author of the Analysis has almost invariably used it; and is the sense in which he defined it, in a note to section 6 of his first chapter. "There is a large class of words which denote two things both together; but the one perfectly distinguishable from the other. Of these two things, also, it is observable, that such words express the one primarily as it were; the other in a way which may be called secondary. Thus white, in the phrase white horse, denotes two things, the colour and the horse; but it denotes the colour primarily, the horse secondarily. We shall find it very convenient to say, therefore, that it *notes* the primary, *connotes* the secondary signification."

This use of terms is attended with the difficulty, that it may often be disputed which of the significations is primary and which secondary. In the example given, most people would agree with the author that the colour is the primary signification; the word being associated with the objects, only through its previous association with the colour. But take the other of the two words, horse. That too is connotative, and in the same manner. It signifies any and every individual horse, and it also signifies those attributes common to horses, which led to their being classed together and receiving that common name. Which, in this case, is the primary, and which the secondary signification? The author would probably say, that in this case, unlike the other, horse is the primary signification, the attributes the secondary. Yet in this equally with the former case, the attributes are the foundation of the meaning: a thing is called a horse to express its resemblance to other horses; and the resemblance consists of the common attributes. The question might be discussed, pro and con, by many arguments, without any conclusive result. The difference between primary and secondary acceptations is too uncertain, and at best too superficial, to be adopted as the logical foundation of the distinction between the two modes of signification.

The author, however, has, throughout the preceding chapters, regarded words as *connoting* any number of things which though included in their signification, are not, in his judgment, what they primarily signify. He said, for example, that a verb notes an action, and connotes the agent (as either me, thee, or some third person), the number of agents (as one or more), the time (as past, present, or future), and three modes, "that in which there is no reference to anything preceding, that in which there is a reference to something preceding, and that in which reference is made to the will of one of the Persons." I cite this complicated case, to shew by a striking example the great latitude with which the author uses the word Connote.

But in the present chapter he follows the example of some of the old logicians in adopting a second and more restricted meaning, expressive of the peculiar con-

In using these connotative names, it is often highly convenient to drop the connotation; that is, to leave out the connoted cluster.

A mark is needed, to shew when it is meant that the connotation is dropped. A slight mark put upon the connotative term answers the purpose; and shews when it is not meant that any thing should be connoted. In regard to the word black, for example, we merely annex to it the syllable *ness;* and it is immediately indicated that all connotation is dropped: so, in sweetness; hardness; dryness; lightness. The

---

notation which belongs to all concrete general names; viz. that twofold manner of signification, by which every name of a class signifies, on the one hand, all and each of the individual things composing the class, and on the other hand the common attributes, in consideration of which the class is formed and the name given, and which we intend to affirm of every object to which we apply the name. It is difficult to overrate the importance of keeping in view this distinction, or the danger of overlooking it when not made prominent by an appropriate phrase. The word Connote, which had been employed for this purpose, had fallen into disuse. But, though agreeing with the old logicians in using the word Connote to express this distinction, the author exactly reverses their employment of it. In their phraseology, the class-name connotes the attributes: in his, it notes the attributes, and connotes the objects. And he declares that in his opinion, their mode of employing the term is very absurd.

We have now to consider which of these two modes of employing it is really the most appropriate.

A concrete general name may be correctly said to be a mark, in a certain way, both for the objects and for their common attributes. But which of the two is it conformable to usage to say that it is the name of? Assuredly, the objects. It is they that are called by the name. I am asked, what is this object called? and I answer, a horse. I should not make this answer if I were asked what are these attributes called. Again, I am asked, what is it that is called a horse? and I answer, the object which you see; not the qualities which you see. Let us now suppose that I am asked, what is it that is called black; I answer, all *things* that have this particular colour. Black is a name of all black things. The name of the colour is not black, but blackness. The name of a thing must be the name which is predicated of the thing, as a proper name is predicated of the person or place it belongs to. It is scarcely possible to speak with precision, and adhere consistently to the same mode of speech, if we call a word the name of anything but that which it is predicated of. Accordingly the old logicians, who had not yet departed widely from the custom of common speech, considered all concrete names as the names of objects, and called nothing the name of an attribute but abstract names.

Now there is considerable incongruity in saying that a word connotes, that is, signifies secondarily, the very thing which it is a name of. To connote, is to mark something along with, or in addition to, something else. A name can hardly be said to mark the thing which it is a name of in addition to some other thing. If it marks any other thing, it marks it in addition to the thing of which it is itself the name. In the present case, what is marked in addition, is that which is the cause of giving the name; the attributes, the possession of which by a thing entitles it to that name. It therefore seems more conformable to the original acceptation of the word Connote, that we should say of names like man or black that they connote humanity or blackness, and *de*note, or are names of, men and black objects; rather than, with the author of the Analysis, that they note the attributes, and connote the things which possess the attributes.

If this mode of using the terms is more consonant to propriety of language, so also is it more scientifically convenient. It is of extreme importance to have a technical expression exclusively consecrated to signify the peculiar mode in which the name of a class marks the attributes in virtue of which it is a class, and is called by the name. The verb "to note," employed by the author of the Analysis as the correlative of "to connote," is far too general to be confined to so specific

new words, so formed, are the words which have been denominated ABSTRACT; as the connotative terms from which they are formed have been denominated CONCRETE; and, as these terms are in frequent use, it is necessary that the meaning of them should be well remembered.

It is now also manifest what is the real nature of ABSTRACT terms; a subject which has in general presented such an appearance of mystery. They are simply the CONCRETE terms, with the connotation dropped. And this has in it, surely, no mystery at all.[1]

---

a use, nor does the author intend so to confine it. "To connote," on the contrary, is a phrase which has been handed down to us in this restricted acceptation, and is perfectly fitted to be used as a technical term. There is no more important use of a term than that of fixing attention upon something which is in danger of not being sufficiently taken notice of. This is emphatically the case with the attribute-signification of the names of objects. That signification has not been seen clearly, and what has been seen of it confusedly has bewildered or misled some of the most distinguished philosophers. From Hobbes to Hamilton, those who have attempted to penetrate the secret of the higher logical operations of the intellect have continually missed the mark for want of the light which a clear conception of the connotation of general names spreads over the subject. There is no fact in psychology which more requires a technical name; and it seems eminently desirable that the words Connote and Connotative should be exclusively employed for this purpose; and it is for this purpose that I have myself invariably employed them.

In studying the Analysis, it is of course necessary to bear in mind that the author does not use the words in this sense, but sometimes in a sense much more vague and indefinite, and, when definite, in a sense the reverse of this. It may seem an almost desperate undertaking, in the case of an unfamiliar term, to attempt to rectify the usage introduced by the actual reviver of the word: and nothing could have induced me to attempt it, but a deliberate conviction that such a technical expression is indispensable to philosophy, and that the author's mode of employing these words unfits them for the purpose for which they are needed, and for which they are well adapted. I fear, however, that I have rarely succeeded in associating the words with their precise meaning, anywhere but in my own writings. The word Connote, not unfrequently meets us of late in philosophical speculations, but almost always in a sense more lax than the laxest in which it is employed in the Analysis, meaning no more than *to imply*. To such an extent is this the case, that able thinkers and writers do not always even confine the expression to names, but actually speak of Things as connoting whatever, in their opinion, the existence of the Things implies or presupposes.—J.S.M.

[1] After having said that a concrete general name notes an attribute, that is, one of the sensations in a cluster, and connotes the objects which have the attribute, i.e. the clusters of which that sensation forms a part; the author proceeds to say that an abstract name is the concrete name with the connotation dropped.

This seems a very indirect and circuitous mode of making us understand what an abstract name signifies. Instead of aiming directly at the mark, it goes round it. It tells us that one name signifies a part of what another name signifies, leaving us to infer what part. A connotative name with the connotation dropped, is a phrase requiring to be completed by specifying what is the portion of signification left. The concrete name with its connotation signifies an attribute, and also the objects which have the attribute. We are now instructed to drop the latter half of the signification, the objects. What then remains? The attribute. Why not then say at once that the abstract name is the name of the attribute? Why tell us that x is *a* plus *b* with *b* dropped, when it was as easy to tell us that x is *a*?

The noticeable thing however is that if *a* stands merely for the sensation, x really is a little more than *a:* the connotation (in the author's sense of the term) of the concrete name is not *wholly* dropped in the abstract name. The term blackness, and every other abstract term, includes in its signification the existence of a black object, though without declaring what it is. That is indeed the distinction between

It hence, also, appears that there can be no ABSTRACT term without an implied CONCRETE, though cases are not wanting, in which there is much occasion for the ABSTRACT term but not much for the CONCRETE; in which, therefore, the concrete is not in use, or is supplied by another form of expression.

In irregular and capricious languages, as our own, the dropping of the connotation of the concrete terms is not marked in a uniform manner; and this requires some illustration. Thus, heavy is a concrete term, and we shew the dropping of the connotation, by the same mark as in the instances above, saying heaviness; but we have another term which is exactly the equivalent of heaviness, and frequently used as the abstract of heavy; that is, weight. Friend is a concrete, connotative term, in the substantive form. Its connotation is dropped by another mark, the syllable ship; thus, friendship; in like manner, generalship; brothership; cousinship. The syllable age is another of the marks we use for the same purpose; pilotage, parsonage, stowage.

Among concrete connotative words, we have already had full opportunity of observing that verbs constitute a principal class. Those words all NOTE some *motion* or *action;* and CONNOTE an *actor.* There is the same frequency of occasion to leave out the connotation in the case of this class of connotative words, as in other classes. Accordingly ABSTRACT terms are formed from them, as from the connotative adjectives and substantives. The infinitive mood is such an abstract term; with this peculiarity, that, though it leaves out the connotation of the *actor,* it retains the connotation of *time.*[1] It is convenient, however, to have abstract terms from the verbs, which leave out also the connotation of time; such are the substantive *amor* from *amo, timor* from *timeo,* and so on.

Verbs have not only an active but a passive form. In the passive form, it is not the *action,* but the *bearing* of the action, which is NOTED; and not the *actor,* but the *bearer* of the action, that is CON-

---

the name of an attribute, and the name of a kind or type of sensation. Names of sensations by themselves are not abstract but concrete names. They mark the type of the sensation, but they do not mark it as emanating from any object. "The sensation of black" is a concrete name, which expresses the sensation apart from all reference to an object. "Blackness" expresses the same sensation with reference to an object, by which the sensation is supposed to be excited. Abstract names thus still retain a limited amount of connotation in both the author's senses of the term—the vaguer and the more specific sense. It is only in the sense to which I am anxious to restrict the term, that any abstract name is without connotation.

An abstract name, then, may be defined as the name of an attribute; and, in the ultimate analysis, as the name of one or more of the sensations of a cluster; not by themselves, but considered as part of any or all of the various clusters, into which that type of sensations enters as a component part.—J.S.M.

[1] The infinitive mood does not always express time. At least, it often expresses it aoristically, without distinction of tense. "To love" is as abstract a name as "love," "to fear," as "fear": they are applied equally to past, present, and future. The infinitives of the past and future, as *amavisse, amaturus esse,* do, however, include in their signification a particular time.—J.S.M.

NOTED. In this case, also, there is not less frequent occasion to drop the connotation. By the simple contrivance of a slight alteration in the connotative term, the important circumstance of dropping the connotation is marked. In the case of the passive as the active form of verbs, the infinitive mood drops the connotation of the person, but retains that of the time. Other abstract terms, formed from the passive voice, leave out the connotation both of person and time. Thus from *legor,* there is *lectio;* from *optor, optatio;* from *dicor, dictio;* and so on.

It is to be remarked that the Latin mode of forming abstract terms from verbs, by the termination "tio," has been adopted to a great extent in English. A large proportion of our abstract terms are thus distinguished; as action, association, imagination, navigation, mensuration, friction, motion, station, faction, legislation, corruption, and many others.

It is also of extreme importance to mark a great defect and imperfection, in this respect, of the Latin language. Such words as *lectio, dictio, actio,* are derived with equal readiness either from the supine, *lectum, dictum, actum;* or from the participle, *lectus, dictus, actus.* The supine is *active,* the participle, *passive.* From this circumstance probably it is, that these abstract terms in the Latin language possess both the active and passive signification; and by this most unfortunate ambiguity have proved a fertile source of obscurity and confusion. This defect of the Latin language is the more to be lamented by us, that it has infected our own language; for as we have borrowed from the Latin language a great proportion of our abstract terms, we have transplanted the mischievous equivocation along with them. This ambiguity the Greek language happily avoided: thus it had πρᾶξις and πρᾶγμα, the first for the active signification of *actio,* the latter the passive.[1]

Of the abstract terms, of genuine English growth, derived from the concrete names of action, or verbs, the participle of the past tense supplied a great number, merely dropping the adjective, and assuming the substantive form. Thus, weight, a word which we had occasion to notice before, is the participle weighed, with the connotation dropped: stroke is merely struck; the *thing* struck, the connotation, being left out: thought is the past participle passive of the verb to think, and differs from the participle in nothing, but that the participle, the adjective, has the connotation; the abstract, the substantive, has it not. Whether the concrete, or the abstract, is the term employed, is in such cases always indicated by the context; and, therefore, no particular mark to distinguish them is required.

In our non-inflected language, a facility is afforded in forming a non-

---

[1] I apprehend that πρᾶγμα is not an abstract but a concrete term, and does not express the attribute of being done, but the thing done—the effect which results from the completed action.—J.S.M.

connotative from the connotative, in the active voice of verbs; because the connotative word is always distinguished by the presence of the persons of the verb, or that of some part of the auxiliary verb. The same word, therefore, answers for the abstract, as for the concrete; it being of course the abstract, when none of the marks of the concrete are present. Thus the word love, is both the verb or the connotative, and the substantive or the non-connotative; thus also fear, walk, ride, stand, fight, smell, taste, sleep, dream, drink, work, breath, and many others.

We have in English, formed from verbs, a great many abstracts or non-connotatives, which terminate in "th," as truth, health, dearth, stealth, death, strength. It may be disputed whether these words are derived from one part of the verb or another; but, in all other respects, the nature of them is not doubtful. The third person singular of the present, indicative active, ends in "th;" and, therefore, they may be said to be that part of the verb with the connotation dropped. The termination, however, of the past participle is "d," and we know that "th" and "d," are the same letter under a slight difference of articulation; and, therefore, they may just as well be derived from the past participle, and as often at least as they have a passive signification, no doubt are. Thus the verb trow, to think, has either troweth, or trowed; from one of which, but more likely from the last, we have truth: the verb to heal, has either healeth, or healed; from one of which, but more likely the last, we have health: the verb to string has stringeth, or stringed; from one of which we have strength; thus from dieth, or died, death; from stealeth, or stealed, stealth; mirth in the same manner, from a verb now out of use; so heighth, length, breadth.

It would be interesting to give a systematic account of the non-connotatives, derived from English verbs; and this ought to be done; but for the present inquiry it would be an operation misplaced. The nature of the words, and the mode of their signification, is all which here is necessary to be understood.

One grand class of connotative terms is composed of such words as the following: walking, running, flying, reading, striking; and we have seen that, for a very obvious utility, a generical name was invented, the word ACTING, which includes the whole of these specific names; and to which the non-connotative, or abstract term ACTION corresponds. There was equal occasion for a generical name to include all the specific names belonging to the other class of connotative terms; such as coloured, sapid, hard, soft, hot, cold, and so on. But language has by no means been so happy in a general name for this, as for the other class. The word SUCH, is a connotative term, which includes them all, and indeed the other class along with them; for when we apply the word SUCH to any thing, we comprehend under it all the ideas of which the cluster is composed. But this is not all which is

included under the word such. It is a relative term, and always connotes so much of the meaning of some other term. When we call a
thing *such,* it is always understood that it is such *as* some other thing.
Thus we say, John is such as James. Corresponding with our "such
as," the Latins had *talis qualis.* If we could suppose *qualis* to have
been used without any connotation of *talis, qualis* would have been
such a word as the occasion which we are now considering would have
required. The Latins did not use *qualis,* in this sense, as a general
concrete, including all the other names of the properties of objects
other than actions. But they made from it, as if used in that very
sense, a non-connotative or abstract term, the word QUALITY, which
answers the same purpose with regard to both classes, as action docs
to one of them. That is to say; it is a very general non-connotative
term, including under it the non-connotatives or abstracts of hot, cold,
hard, soft, long, short; and not only of all other words of that description, but of acting, and its subordinates also.

Quantus, is another concrete which has a double connotation like
qualis. It connotes not only the substantive with which it agrees, but
also, being a relative, the term *tantus,* which is its correlate. By dropping both connotations, the abstract QUANTITY is made; a general
term, including under it the abstracts of all the names by which the
modifications of greater and less are denominated; as large, small, a
mile long, an inch thick, a handful, a ton, and so on.

Much remains, beside what is here stated, of the full explanation of
the mode in which *talis qualis, tantus quantus,* are made conducive to
the great purposes of marking. But this must be reserved till we come
to treat of RELATIVE TERMS, in general.

We have previously observed, that one of the purposes for which
we abstract, or sunder the parts of a complex idea, marked by a general name, is, to form those adjectives, or connotative terms, which,
denoting differences, enable us to form, and to name, subordinate
classes. We now come to the next of the great purposes to which abstraction is subservient, and it is one to which the whole of our attention is due.

Of all the things in which we are interested, that is, on which our
happiness and misery depend, meaning here by things, both objects
and events, the most important by far are the successions of objects;
in other words, the effects which they produce. In reality, objects are
interesting to us, solely on account of the effects which they produce,
either on ourselves, or on other objects.

But an observation of the greatest importance readily occurs; that
of any cluster, composing our idea of an object, the effects or consequents depend, in general, more upon one part of it than another. If a
stone is *hot,* it has certain effects or consequences; if *heavy,* it has
others, and so on. It is of great importance to us, in respect to those

successions, to be able to mark discriminately the real antecedent; not the antecedent combined with a number of things with which the consequent has nothing to do. I observe, that other objects, as iron, lead, gold, produce similar effects with stone; as often as the name *hot* can, in like manner, be predicated of them. In the several clusters therefore, hot stone, hot iron, hot gold, hot lead, there is a portion, the same in all, with which, and not with the rest, the effects which I am contemplating are connected. This part is marked by the word *hot;* which word, however, in the case of each cluster, connotes also the other parts of the cluster. It appears at once, how much convenience there must be in dropping the connotation, and obtaining a word which, in each of those cases, shall mark exclusively that part of the cluster on which the effect depends. This is accomplished by the abstract or non-connotative terms, heat, and weight.

Certain alterations, also, are observed in those parts of clusters on which such and such effects depend; which alterations make corresponding alterations in the effects, though no other alteration is observable, in the cluster, to which such parts belong. Thus, if a stone is more or less hot, the effects or successions are not the same; so of iron, so of lead; but the same alteration in the same part of each of those clusters, is followed by the same effects. It is true, that we know nothing of the alteration in the cause, but by the alteration in the effects; for we only say that a stone is hotter, because it produces such other effects, either in our sensations immediately, or in the sensations we receive from other objects. It is, however, obvious that we have urgent use for the means of marking, not only the alterations in the effects, but the alterations in the antecedents. This we do, by supposing the alterations to be those of increase and diminution, and marking them by the distinction of lower and higher degrees. But, for this purpose, it is obvious that we must have a term which is not connotative; because we suppose no alteration in any part of the cluster but that which is not connoted; thus we can say, with sufficient precision, that a greater or less degree of heat produces such and such effects; but we cannot say, that a greater or less degree of hot stone, of hot iron, of hot any thing else, produces these effects.

This then, is another use, and evidently a most important use, of abstract, non-connotative terms. They enable us to mark, with more precision, those successions, in which our good and evil is wholly contained.

This also enables us to understand, what it is which recommends such and such aggregates, and not others, for classification. Those successions of objects, in which we are interested, determine the classifications which we form of them.

Some successions are found to depend upon the clusters, called objects, all taken together. Thus a tree, a man, a stone, are the antecedents of certain consequents, as such; and not on account of any particular part of the cluster.

Other consequents depend not upon the whole of the cluster, but upon some particular part: thus a tall tree, produces certain effects, which a tree not tall, cannot produce; a strong man, produces certain effects, which a man not strong cannot produce. When these consequents are so important, as to deserve particular attention, they and their antecedents must be marked. For this purpose, are employed the connotative terms marking differences. These terms enable us to group the clusters containing those antecedents into a sub-class; and NON-CONNOTATIVE or ABSTRACT terms, derived from them, enable us to speak separately of that part of the cluster which we have to mark as the precise antecedent of the consequent which is engaging our attention.

It is presumed, that these illustrations will suffice, to enable the reader to discern the real marking power of abstract terms, and also to perceive the mode of their formation.

CHAPTER XIV

NAMES REQUIRING EXPLANATION

SECTION II

RELATIVE TERMS

The explanation of Relative Terms will run to a considerable length. The mode in which they are employed as marks is peculiar; and has suggested the belief of something very mysterious in that which is marked by them. It is therefore necessary to be minute in exhibiting the combinations of ideas of which they are the names.

One peculiarity of Relative Terms, which it is necessary for us to begin with noticing, is, that they always exist in pairs. There is no relative without its correlate, either actual or implied. Thus, we have *Father* and *Son; Husband* and *Wife; Master* and *Servant; Subject* and *King;* also *High* and *Low; Right* and *Left; Antecedent* and *Consequent.*

In these cases of relative pairs, the two names are two different words; in other cases, one word serves for both names. Of this sort are the words *Brother, Sister, Cousin, Friend, Like, Equal,* and so on. When we say that John is brother, we always mean of some one else, as James, whom we also call brother. We call Jane the sister of Ann, as we call Ann the sister of Jane. When we say that A is equal to B, we signify, by the same expression, that B is equal to A; and so on.

It is always to be remembered, that, in speaking, we are only indicating our own trains; and that of course every word is a mark of some part of a train. The parts of our trains to which we give relative names, are either simple, or complex. The simple, are either the simple sensations, or the ideas of those sensations. The complex, are either those clusters of simple ideas which we call the ideas of objects, because they correspond with clustered sensations; or they are the clusters which the mind puts together arbitrarily for its own purposes.

If it is asked, why we give names in pairs? The general answer immediately suggests itself; it is because the things named present themselves in pairs; that is, are joined by association. But as many things are joined in pairs by association, which do not receive relative names, the cause may still be inquired of the classification. What is the reason that some pairs do, while many more do not, receive relative names? The cause is the same by which we are guided in imposing other names. As the various combinations of ideas are far too numerous for naming, and we are obliged to make a selection, we name those which we find it of most importance to have named, omitting the rest. It is a question of convenience, solved by experience. It will be seen more distinctly hereafter, that relative names are one of the contrivances for epitomising; and that they enable us to express ourselves with fewer words than we should be able to do without them.[1]

---

[1] No part of the Analysis is more valuable than the simple explanation here given of a subject which has seemed so mysterious to some of the most enlightened and penetrating philosophers, down even to the present time. The only difference between relative names and any others consists in their being given in pairs; and the reason of their being given in pairs is not the existence between two things, of a mystical bond called a Relation, and supposed to have a kind of shadowy and abstract reality, but a very simple peculiarity in the concrete fact which the two names are intended to mark.

In order to make quite clear the nature of this peculiarity, it will be desirable to advert once more to the double mode of signification of concrete general names, viz. that while they denote (or are names of) objects, they connote some fact relating to those objects. The fact connoted by any name, relative or not, is always of the same nature; it is some bodily or mental feeling, or some set of bodily or mental feelings, accompanying or produced by the object. But in the case of the ordinary names of objects, this fact concerns one object only, or rather only that one object and the sentient mind. The peculiarity in the case of relative names is, that the fact connoted concerns two objects, and cannot be understood without thinking of them both. It is a phenomenon in which two objects play a part. There is no greater mystery in a phenomenon which concerns two objects, than in a phenomenon which concerns only one. For example; the fact connoted by the word cause, is a fact in which the thing which is the cause, is implicated along with another thing which is the effect. The facts connoted by the word parent, and also by the word son or daughter, are a long series of phenomena of which both the parent and the child are parts; and the series of phenomena would not be that which the name parent expresses, unless the child formed a part of it, nor would it be that which the name son or daughter expresses, unless the parent formed a part of it. Now, when in a series of phenomena of any interest to us two objects are implicated, we naturally give names expressive of it to both the objects, and these are relative names. The two correlative names denote two different objects,

I. The only, or at least the principal, occasions, for naming simple sensations, or simple ideas, in pairs, seem to be these:

1. When we take them into simultaneous view, as such and such;

2. When we take them into simultaneous view, as antecedent and consequent.

II. The principal occasions on which we name the complex ideas, called objects, in pairs, are these four:

1. When we speak of them as having an order in space;

2. When we speak of them as having an order in time;

3. When we speak of them as agreeing or disagreeing in quantity;

4. As agreeing or disagreeing in quality.

III. The occasions on which we name the complex ideas of our own formation in pairs, are,

1. When we speak of them as composed of the same or different simple ideas;

2. When we speak of them as antecedent and consequent.

Whatever it may be necessary to remark, respecting relative terms, will occur in the consideration of these several cases.

I. 1. We speak of two sensations, as *Same* or *Different, Like* or *Unlike*.

These words are Relatives of the double signification; each individ-

---

the cause and the effect, or the parent and son; but though what they denote is different, what they connote is in a certain sense the same: both names connote the same set of facts, considered as giving one name to the one object, another name to the other. This set of facts, which is connoted by both the correlative names, was called by the old logicians the ground of the relation, *fundamentum relationis*. The *fundamentum* of any relation is the facts, fully set out, which are the reason of giving to two objects two correlative names. In some cases both objects seem to receive the same name; in the relation of likeness, both objects are said to be like; in the relation of equality, both are said to be equal. But even here the duality holds, on a stricter examination: for the first object (A) is not said to be like, absolutely, but to be like the second object (B); the second is not said to be like absolutely, but to be like the first. Now though "like" is only one name, "like A" is not the same name as "like B," so that there is really, in this case also, a pair of names.

From these considerations we see that objects are said to be related, when there is any fact, simple or complex, either apprehended by the senses or otherwise, in which they both figure. Any objects, whether physical or mental, are related, or are in a relation, to one another, in virtue of any complex state of consciousness into which they both enter; even if it be a no more complex state of consciousness than that of merely thinking of them together. And they are related to each other in as many different ways, or in other words, they stand in as many distinct relations to one another, as there are specifically distinct states of consciousness of which they both form parts. As these may be innumerable, the possible relations not only of any one thing with others, but of any one thing with the same other, are infinitely numerous and various. But they may all be reduced to a certain number of general heads of classification, constituting the different kinds of Relation: each of which requires examination apart, to ascertain what, in each case, the state of consciousness, the cluster or train of sensations or thoughts, really is, in which the two objects figure, and which is connoted by the correlative names. This examination the author accordingly undertakes: and thus, under the guise of explaining names, he analyses all the principal cases which the world and the human mind present, of what are called Relations between things.—J.S.M.

ual of the pair has the same name. When we say that sensation A is the "same" with sensation B, we mean that B also is the "same" with A; "different," "like," and "unlike," have the same double application.

Another ambiguity needs to be noted in the word "same." When there are *two* things, they are not the *same* thing; for "same," in the strict sense of the word, means one thing, and that only. Here it means a great degree of likeness, a sense in which, with respect to sensations and ideas, it is very frequently used.

Of two sensations, or two ideas, we, in truth, can only say, that they are like or unlike; or, that the one comes first, the other after it.

It is now necessary to attend very carefully to what happens, when we say that two sensations are like, or that they are unlike.

First of all, we have the two sensations. But what is it to have two sensations? It is merely to be conscious of a change. But to be conscious of a change in sensation, is sensation. It is an essential part of the process. Without it we should not be sentient beings. To have sensation, and not to be conscious of any change, is to have but one sensation continued. We have already seen that this is a state which seems incapable of being distinguished from that of having no sensation. At any rate, what we mean by a sentient being, is not a being with one unvaried sensation, but a being with sensations continually varied; the varying being a necessary part of the having more sensations than one; and the varying, and the being conscious of the variation, being not two things, but one and the same thing. Having *two* sensations, therefore, is not only having sensation, but the only thing which can, in strictness, be called having sensation; and the having two, and knowing they are two, which are not two things, but one and the same thing, is not only sensation, and nothing else than sensation, but the only thing which can, in strictness, be called sensation. The having a new sensation, and knowing that it is new, are not two things, but one and the same thing.[1]

---

[1] The author is here endeavouring to express the most fundamental fact of the consciousness—the necessity of change, or transition from one state to another in order to our being conscious. He approaches very near to, without exactly touching, the inference that all consciousness, all sensation, all knowledge must be of *doubles;* the state passed from and the state passed to, are equally recognised by us. Opening the eyes to the light, for the first time, we know a contrast,—a present light, a past privation—but for the one we should not have known the other. Any single thing is unknowable by us; its relative opposite is a part of its very existence.

In a former page it is stated that relative names are one of the conveniences of epitomising. This is a narrow view to take of them. They are an essential part of language; they are demanded by the intrinsic relativity of all nameable things. If we have a thing called "light," we have also another thing but for which light could not be known by us, "dark." It is expedient to have names for both elements of the mutually dependent couple. And so everywhere. Language would be insufficient for its purposes if it did not provide the means of expressing the correlative (called also the negative) of every thing named.—Bain

The case between sensation and sensation, resembles that between sensation and idea. How do I know that an idea is not a sensation? Who ever thought of asking the question? Is not the having an idea, and the knowing it as an idea, the same thing? The having without the knowing is repugnant. The misfortune is, that the word, know, has associations linked with it, which have nothing to do with this case, but which intrude themselves along with the word, and make a complexity, where otherwise there would be none.

This is a matter which deserves the greatest attention. One of the most unfortunate cases of the illusions, which the close association of ideas with words has produced, is created by ideas clinging to words when they ought to be disjoined from them, and mixing themselves by that means with the ideas under consideration, when they ought to be considered wholly distinct from them. Nothing was of more importance, than that the phenomenon, to which we are just now directing our attention, the very first ingredient in the great mental composition, should be accurately understood, and nothing mixed up with it which did not truly belong to it.

There is no doubt that in one of its senses, knowledge is synonymous with sensation. If I am asked what is my knowledge of pain? I answer, the feeling of it, the having it. The blind man has not the knowledge of colours; the meaning is, he has not the sensations: if deaf also, he is without the knowledge, that is, the sensations, of sounds: suppose him void of all other sensations, you suppose him void of knowledge. In many cases, however, we arrive at knowledge, by certain steps; by something of a process. The word, know, is most frequently applied to those cases. When we know, by mere sensation, we say we see, we hear, and so on; when we know by mere ideas, or rather ideation, if we could use such a word, we say we conceive, we think. The word know, therefore, being almost constantly joined with the idea of a process, it is exceedingly difficult, when we apply it to sensation, not to have the idea of a process at the same time; and thus exceedingly difficult to conceive that sensation, and knowing, in this case, are purely synonymous.

As the knowing I have an idea, is merely having the idea; as the having a sensation, and knowing I have a sensation; the knowing, for example, that I have the pain of the toothache, and the having that pain; are not two things, but one and the same thing; so the having a change of sensation, and knowing I have it, are not two things but one and the same thing.

Having a change, I have occasion to mark that change. The change has taken place in a train of feelings. I call the first part by one name, the last by another, and the marking of the change is effected. Suppose that, without any organ of sense but the eye, my first sensation is red, my next green. The whole process is sensation. Yet the green is not the red. What we call making the distinction, therefore, has taken place, and it is involved in the sensation.

My names, green, and red, thus applied, are absolute names. The one has no reference to the other. Suppose that after green, I have the sensations, blue, yellow, violet, white, black; and that I mark them respectively by these names. These are still absolute names. Each marks a particular sensation, and does nothing more. But, now, suppose that, after my sensations red, green, blue, &c., I have the sensation red again; that I recognise it as like the sensation I had first, and that I have a desire to mark that recognition; it remains to explain what are the steps of this process.

Having the sensation a second time needs no explanation; it is the same thing as having it the first. But what happens in recognising that it is similar to a former sensation?

Beside the *Sensation,* in this case, there is an *Idea.* The idea of the former sensation is called up by, that is, associated with, the new sensation. As having a sensation, and a sensation, and knowing them, that is, distinguishing them, are the same thing; and having an idea, and an idea, is knowing them; so, having an idea and a sensation, and distinguishing the one from the other, are the same thing. But, to know that I have the idea and the sensation, in this case, is not all; I observe, that the sensation is like the idea. What is this observation of likeness? Is it any thing but that distinguishing of one feeling from another, which we have recognised to be the same thing as having two feelings? As change of sensation is sensation; as change, from a sensation to an idea, differs from change to a sensation, in nothing but this, that the second feeling in the latter change is an idea, not a sensation; and as the passing from one feeling to another is distinguishing; the whole difficulty seems to be resolved; for undoubtedly the distinguishing differences and similarities, is the same thing; a similarity being nothing but a slight difference.[1] As change from red to green, and knowing the change, or from a sensation of sight, to one of any other of the senses, the most different, is all sensation; so change from one shade of red to another, is assuredly sensation. Its being a different shade consists in my feeling of it, that is, in my sensation.

Passing from red to red, red, red, through a succession of distinguishable shades, is one train of pure sensation: passing from red to

[1] More properly Similarity is "agreement in difference." Difference or discrimination is one thing, one element of knowledge or cognition; Similarity or agreement in difference is another thing, the second or completing element of knowledge. The two work together in closest intimacy, but they should neither be looked upon as the same fact, nor as merely a various shading of the same fact. Without difference there would be no similarity; but similarity is difference and something more. At their roots or first origins, the two processes lie in almost undistinguishable closeness; but in their developments they run wide apart. No fact or attribute is known, or mentally possessed, without the union of many shocks of difference with many shocks of identity, or agreement in difference.—Bain

green, blue, tasting, smelling, hearing, touching, is another train of pure sensation; that these are not the same trains, but different trains, consists in their being felt to be so; they would not be different, but for the feeling: and that a feeling is different, and known to be so, are not two things, but one and the same thing. Having two such trains, I want marks to distinguish them. For this purpose, I invent the words "same," "similar," and their contraries; by means of which, my object is attained. I call the parts of a train, such as the first, "same," or "similar;" those of a train like the last, "different," "dissimilar."

By these relative terms, we name the sensations in pairs. When we say, same, we mean that sensations A, and B, are the same; different, that A, and B, are different; like and unlike, the same. By these words we have four pairs of relative terms.

A.	B.
same	same
different	different
like	like
unlike	unlike.

The feeling is perfectly analogous in the case of the *ideas* of those sensations; and the naming is the same. Thus the idea of red, green, and so on, and the ideas of the different shades of red are distinguished from one another by the ideas themselves. To have ideas different and ideas distinguished, are synonymous expressions; different and distinguished, meaning exactly the same thing.

The sensations above mentioned, and their ideas, have the same absolute names: thus, red is at once the name of the sensation, and the name of the idea; green, at once the name of the sensation and the idea; sweet, at once the name of the sensation and the idea. The relative terms, it is obvious, have the same extent of application. Same, different, like, and unlike, are names of pairs of ideas, as well as pairs of sensations.

It seems, therefore, to be made clear, that, in applying to the simple sensations and ideas their absolute names, which are names of classes, as red, green, sweet, bitter; and also applying to them names which denote them in pairs, as such and such; there is nothing whatsoever but having the sensations, having the ideas, and making marks for them.[1]

---

[1] The author commences his survey of Relations with the most universal of them all, Likeness and Unlikeness; and he examines these as subsisting between simple sensations or ideas; for whatever be the true theory of likeness or unlikeness as between the simple elements, the same, in essentials, will serve for the likenesses or unlikenesses of the wholes compounded of them.

Examining, then, what constitutes likeness between two sensations (meaning two exactly similar sensations experienced at different times); he says, that to feel the two sensations to be alike, is one and the same thing with having the two sensations.

2. The only other relative terms applicable to simple sensations and ideas, are those which denote them as *Antecedent* and *Consequent*.

I have sensation red, sensation green. Why I mark them red, and green, or as "different," has already been seen. What happens in marking them as "antecedent" and "consequent" comes next to be considered.

A sensation, the moment it ceases, is gone for ever. When I have

---

Their being alike is nothing but their being felt to be alike; their being unlike is nothing but their being felt to be unlike. The feeling of unlikeness is merely that feeling of change, in passing from the one to the other, which makes them two, and without which we should not be conscious of them at all. The feeling of likeness, is the being reminded of the former sensation by the present, that is, having the idea of the former sensation called up by the present, and distinguishing them as sensation and idea.

It does not seem to me that this mode of describing the matter explains anything, or leaves the likenesses and unlikenesses of our simple feelings less an ultimate fact than they were before. All it amounts to is, that likeness and unlikeness are themselves only a matter of feeling: and that when we have two feelings, the feeling of their likeness or unlikeness is inextricably interwoven with the fact of having the feelings. One of the conditions, under which we have feelings, is that they are like and unlike: and in the case of simple feelings, we cannot separate the likeness or unlikeness from the feelings themselves. It is by no means certain, however, that when we have two feelings in immediate succession, the feeling of their likeness is not a third feeling which follows instead of being involved in the two. This question is expressly left open by Mr. Herbert Spencer, in his "Principles of Psychology;" and I am not aware that any philosopher has conclusively resolved it. We do not get rid of any difficulty by calling the feeling of likeness the same thing with the two feelings that are alike: we have equally to postulate likeness and unlikeness as primitive facts—as an inherent distinction among our sensations; and whichever form of phraseology we employ makes no difference in the ulterior developments of psychology. It is of no practical consequence whether we say that a phenomenon is resolved into sensations and ideas, or into sensations, ideas, and their resemblances, since under the one expression as under the other the resemblance must be recognised as an indispensable element in the compound.

When we pass from resemblance between simple sensations and ideas, to resemblance between complex wholes, the process, though not essentially different, is more complicated, for it involves a comparison of part with part, element with element, and therefore a previous discrimination of the elements. When we judge that an external object, compounded of a number of attributes, is like another external object; since they are not, usually, alike in all their attributes, we have to take the two objects into simultaneous consideration in respect to each of their various attributes one after another: their colour, to observe whether that is similar; their size, whether that is similar; their figure, their weight, and so on. It comes at last to a perception of likeness or unlikeness between simple sensations: but we reduce it to this by *attending* separately to one of the simple sensations forming the one cluster, and to one of those forming the other cluster, and if possible adjusting our organs of sense so as to have these two sensations in immediate juxtaposition: as when we put two objects, of which we wish to compare the colour, side by side, so that our sense of sight may pass directly from one of the two sensations of colour to the other. This act of attention directed successively to single attributes, blunts our feeling of the other attributes of the objects, and enables us to feel the likeness of the single sensations almost as vividly as if we had nothing but these in our mind. Having felt this likeness, we say that the sensations are like, and that the two objects are alike in respect of those sensations: and continuing the process we pronounce them to be either like or unlike in each of the other sensations which we receive from them.—J.S.M.

two sensations, therefore, A, and B, one first, the other following, sensation A is gone, before sensation B exists. But though *sensation* A is gone, its *idea* is not gone. Its idea, called up by association, exists along with sensation B, or the idea of sensation B. My knowing that the idea of sensation A is the idea of sensation A, is my having the idea. Having it, and knowing it, are not two things, but one and the same thing. *Having* the idea of sensation A, that is, having the idea of the immediate antecedent of sensation B, seems, also, to be the same thing with knowing it as the idea of that antecedent. Having sensation A, and after it sensation B, is mere sensation; and having the idea of sensation A, the immediate antecedent, called up by sensation B, the immediate consequent, is knowing it for that antecedent. The links of the train are three; 1, sensation A; 2, sensation B; 3, the idea of sensation A, in a certain order with B, called up by sensation B; and after this, NAMING.

The case appears mysterious, solely, from the want of words to express it clearly; and our confirmed habit of inattention to the process. Suppose, that instead of two sensations, A, and B, we have three, A, B, and C, in immediate succession. I recognise A, as the antecedent of B; B, as the antecedent of C. What is the process? The idea of sensation A, is associated with sensation B; and the idea of sensation B, is associated with sensation C. But sensation C, is not associated with the idea of sensation B solely, it is associated also with the idea of sensation A. It is associated, however, differently with the one and the other. It is associated with B immediately; it is associated with A, only through the medium of B; it calls up the idea of B, by its own associating power, and the idea of B, calls up the idea of A. This second state of consciousness is different from the first. The first is that in consequence of which B receives the name "Antecedent," and C the name "Consequent." When two sensations in a train are such, that, if one exists, it has the idea of the other along with it, by its immediate exciting power, and not through any intermediate idea; the sensation, the idea of which is thus excited, is called the antecedent, the sensation which thus excites that idea, is called the consequent.

It is evident that the terms, "antecedent," and "consequent," are not applied in consequence of sensation merely, but in consequence of sensation joined with ideas. The antecedent sensation, which is past, must be revived by the consequent sensation, which is present. It is the peculiarity of this revival which procures it the name. If revived by any other sensation, it would not have that name.

The Clock strikes three. My feelings are, three sensations of hearing, in succession. How do I know them to be three successive sensations? The process in this instance does not seem to be very difficult to trace. The clock strikes one; this is pure sensation. It strikes two; this is a sensation, joined with the idea of the preceding sensation, and the idea of the feeling (also sensation), called change of sensation, or passage from one sensation to another. After two, the clock strikes three; there is, here, sensation, and a double association; the third stroke is sensation; that is associated immediately with the idea of the second, and through the idea of the second, with the idea of the first. It is observable, that these successive associations soon cease to afford distinct ideas; they hardly do so beyond the second stage. When the clock strikes, we may have distinct ideas of the strokes, as far as three, hardly farther; we must then have recourse to NAMING, and call the strokes, four, five, six, and so on: otherwise we should be wholly unable to tell how often the clock had struck.

In the preceding pairs of relative terms, we have found only one name for each pair. Thus, when we say of A and B, that A is similar to B, we say also, that B is similar to A. We have now an instance of a pair of relative terms, consisting not of the same, but of different names. If we call A antecedent, we call B consequent. The first class were called by the ancient logicians, synonymous, the second heteronymous; we may call them more intelligibly, single-worded, and double-worded, relatives.[1]

---

[1] The next relation which the author examines is that of succession, or Antecedent and Consequent. And here again we have one of the universal conditions to which all our feelings or states of consciousness are subject. Whenever we have more feelings than one, we must have them either simultaneously or in succession; and when we are conscious of having them in succession, we cannot in any way separate or isolate the succession from the feelings themselves. The author attempts to carry the analysis somewhat farther. He says that when we have two sensations in the order of antecedent and consequent, the consequent calls up the idea of the antecedent; and that this fact, that a sensation calls up the idea of another sensation directly, and not through an intermediate idea, *constitutes* that other sensation the antecedent of the sensation which reminds us of it—is not a *consequence* of the one sensation's having preceded the other, but is literally all we mean by the one sensation's having preceded the other. There seem to be grave objections to this doctrine. In the first place, there is no law of association by which a consequent calls up the idea of its antecedent. The law of successive association is that the antecedent calls up the idea of the consequent, but not conversely; as is seen in the difficulty of repeating backwards even a form of words with which we are very familiar. We get round from the consequent to the antecedent by an indirect process, through the medium of other ideas; or by going back, at each step, to the beginning of the train, and repeating it downwards until we reach that particular link. When a consequent directly recalls its antecedent, it is by synchronous association, when the antecedent happens to have been so prolonged as to coexist with, instead of merely preceding, the consequent.

The next difficulty is, that although the direct recalling of the idea of a past sensation by a present, without any intermediate link, does not take place from consequent to antecedent, it does take place from like to like: a sensation recalls the idea of a past sensation resembling itself, without the intervention of any other idea. The author, however, says, that "when two sensations in a train are such that if one exists, it has the idea of the other along with it by its immediate exciting power, and not through any intermediate idea; the sensation, the idea of which is thus excited, is called the antecedent, the sensation which thus excites that idea is called the consequent." If this therefore were correct, we should give the names of antecedent and consequent not to the sensations which really are so, but to those which recall one another by resemblance.

Thirdly and lastly, to explain antecedence, *i.e.* the succession between two feel-

II. Having shewn what takes place in naming simple SENSATIONS, and simple IDEAS, in pairs, both as such and such, and as antecedent and consequent, we come to the second case of relative terms, that of naming the clusters, called EXTERNAL OBJECTS, in pairs. The principal occasions of doing so we have said are four.

1. When we speak of them, as they exist in the synchronous order, that is, the order in space, we use such relative terms as the following: high, low; east, west; right, left; hind, fore; and so on.

It is necessary to carry along with us a correct idea of what is meant by synchronous order, that is, the order of simultaneous, in contradistinction to that of successive, existence. The synchronous order is much more complex than the successive. The successive order is all, as it were, in one direction. The synchronous is in every possible direction. The following seems to be the best mode of conceiving it.

Take a single particle of matter as a centre. Other particles may be aggregated to it, in the line of every possible radius; and as the radii diverge, and other lines, tending to the centre, may be continually interposed, to any number, particles may be aggregated in those numberless directions. They may also be aggregated in those directions to a less or a greater extent. And they may be aggregated to an equal extent in every direction; or to a greater extent in some of the directions, a less extent in others. In the first case of aggregation they compose a globe; in the last, any other shape.

Every one of the particles in this aggregate, has a certain order; first with respect to the centre particle; next with respect to every other particle. This order is also called, the Position of the particle. In such an aggregate, therefore, the positions are innumerable. It is hence observable, that position is an exceedingly complex idea; for the position of each of those particles is its order with respect to every one of the other innumerable particles; it includes, therefore, innumerable ingredients. Hence it is not wonderful that, while viewed in the lump, it should seem obscure and mysterious.

Of positions, thus numberless, it is a small portion only that have names. Bulk is a name for an aggregate of particles, greater, or less. Figure is only a modification, or case, of bulk; it is more or fewer particles in such and such directions.

These things being explained, it now remains to shew, of what

---

ings, by saying that one of the two calls up the idea of the other, that is to say, is followed by it, is to explain succession by succession, and antecedence by antecedence. Every explanation of anything by states of our consciousness, includes as part of the explanation a succession between those states; and it is useless attempting to analyse that which comes out as an element in every analysis we are able to make. Antecedence and consequence, as well as likeness and unlikeness, must be postulated as universal conditions of Nature, inherent in all our feelings whether of external or of internal consciousness.—J.S.M.

copies of sensations, peculiarly combined, the complex ideas in question are composed.

The simplest case of position, or synchronous order, is that of two or more particles in one direction. Let us take the particle, conceived as the centre particle, in a preceding supposition, and let us aggregate to it a number of particles, all in the direction of a single radius, one by one. We have first the centre particle, and one other, in juxta-position. This is the simplest case of synchronous order, and this is the simplest of all positions. Let us next aggregate a second particle; we have now the centre particle, and two more. The position of the first of the aggregated particles with respect to the centre particle is contact, or juxta-position; that of the second is not juxta-position, but position at the distance of a particle; the next which is aggregated, is at the distance of two; the next of three particles, and so on, to any extent.

Particles thus aggregated, all in the direction of a single radius from the first, constitute a line of less or greater length, according to the number of aggregated particles.

Line is a word of great importance; because it is by that, chiefly, we express ourselves concerning synchronous order; or frame names for positions. Now it happens, that Line has a duplicity of meaning, most unfortunate, because it has confounded two meanings, which it is of the highest importance to preserve distinct.

We have already remarked the distinction between concrete, and abstract, terms; and explained wherein the difference of their signification consists. We have also observed, that though in very many cases, the concrete term, and the abstract term, are different words, as good and goodness, true and truth, there are many others in which the concrete and abstract terms are the same; and this is the case, unhappily, with the word Truth itself, which is used in the concrete sense, as well as the abstract. Thus we call a proposition, a Truth; in which phrase, the word Truth, means "True Proposition;" and in this sense we talk of eternal truths, meaning, Propositions, always true. "Property," is another word, which is sometimes concrete, sometimes abstract. Thus, a man calls his horse, his field, his house, his property. In such phrases the word is concrete. He also says, he has a property in such and such things. In these phrases, it is abstract.

Of this ambiguity, the word Line is an instance. It is applied as well to what we call a physical line, as to what we call a mathematical line. In the first case, it is a concrete, or connotative term; in the second case, it is an abstract or non-connotative term. Let us then conceive clearly the two meanings. The purest idea of a physical line, is that which we have already formed; the aggregate of particle after particle, in the direction of a radius. When this aggregate of particles in this order is called a line, the word, line, is connotative; it marks or notes the *direction,* but it also marks or connotes the *particles;* it means the particles and the direction both; it is, in short, the *concrete* term. When it is used as the *abstract* term, the connotation is left out. It marks the direction without marking the particles.

It is here necessary to call to mind, that abstract terms derive their meaning wholly from their concretes; and that by themselves they have absolutely no meaning at all. I know a green tree, a sweet apple, a hard stone, but greenness without something green, hardness without something hard, are just nothing at all.

The same, in its abstract sense, is the case with line, though we have not words by which we can convey the conception with equal clearness. If we had an abstract term, separate from the concrete, the troublesome association in question would have been less indissoluble, and less deceptive. If we had such a word as Lineness, or Linth, for example, we should have much more easily seen, that our idea is the idea of the physical line; and that linth without a line, as breadth without something broad, length without something long, are just nothing at all.[1]

What are, then, the sensations, the ideas of which, in close association, we mark by the word line?

Though it appears to all men that they see position, length, breadth, distance, figure; it is nevertheless true, that what appear, in this manner, to be sensations of the eye, are Ideas, called up by association. This is an important phenomenon, which throws much light upon the darker involutions of human thought.

The sensations, whence are generated our ideas of synchronous order, are from two sources; they are partly the sensations of touch,

1 This conception of a geometrical line, as the abstract, of which a physical line is the corresponding concrete, is scarcely satisfactory. An abstract name is the name of an attribute, or property, of the things of which the concrete name is predicated. It is, no doubt, the name of some part, some one or more, of the sensations composing the concrete group, but not of those sensations simply and in themselves; it is the name of those sensations regarded as belonging to some group. Whiteness, the abstract name, is the name of the colour white, considered as the colour of some physical object. Now I do not see that a geometrical line is conceived as an attribute of a physical object. The attribute of objects which comes nearest to the signification of a geometrical line, is their length: but length does not need any name but its own; and the author does not seem to mean that a geometrical line is the same thing as length. He seems to have fallen into the mistake of confounding an abstract with an ideal. The line which is meant in all the theorems of geometry I take to be as truly concrete as a physical line; it denotes an object, but one purely imaginary; a supposititious object, agreeing in all else with a physical line, but differing from it in having no breadth. The properties of this imaginary line of course agree with those of a physical line, except so far as these depend on, or are affected by, breadth. The lines, surfaces, and figures contemplated by geometry are abstract, only in the improper sense of the term, in which it is applied to whatever results from the mental process called Abstraction. They ought to be called ideal. They are physical lines, surfaces, and figures, idealized, that is, supposed hypothetically to be perfectly what they are only imperfectly, and not to be at all what they are in a very slight, and for most purposes wholly unimportant, degree.—J.S.M.

and partly those of which we have spoken under the name of muscular sensations, the feelings involved in muscular action.[1]

A line, we have said, is an order of particles, contiguous one to another, in the direction of a radius from one particle. Let us begin from this one particle, and trace our sensations. One particle may be an object of touch; it may be felt, as we call it, and nothing more; it may, at the same time, give the sensation of resistance, which we have already described as a feeling seated in the muscles, just as sound is a feeling in the ear. Resistance, is force applied to force. What we feel, is the act of the muscle. Without that, no resistance. This state of consciousness is, in reality, what we mark by the name. It is, at the same time, a state of consciousness not a little obscure; because we habitually overlook many of the sensations of which it is composed; because it is, in itself, very complex; and because it is entangled with a number of extraneous associations.

We have already remarked the habit we acquire of not attending to the sensations which are seated in the muscles, of attending only to the occasions of them, and the effects of them; that is, their antecedents, and consequents; overlooking the intermediate sensations. In marking, therefore, or assigning our names, it seems to be rather the occasions and effects, the antecedents and consequents, than the sensations themselves, which are named. The word resistance is thus the name of a very complex idea. It is the name; first, of the feelings which we have when we say we feel resistance; secondly, of the occasions, or antecedents, of those feelings; and, thirdly, of their consequents. The feelings intermediate between the antecedents and consequents, are themselves complex. There are two kinds of sensations included in them; the sensation of touch, and the muscular sensations; and there is something more. When we move a muscle, we Will to move it. This state of consciousness, the Will to move it, is part of the feeling of the motion. What that state of consciousness, called the Will, is, we have not yet explained. At present we speak of it merely as an element in the compound. Of what elements it is itself compounded we shall see hereafter. In the idea of resistance, then, there is the will to move the muscles, the sensations in the muscles, the occasion or antecedent of those feelings, and the effects or consequents of them. And there is the common complexity attending all generical terms, that of their including all possible varieties.

[1] In attaining the ideas of synchronous order, which is another name for Space, or the Extended World, sight is a leading instrumentality. It is by sight more than by any other sense that we get somewhat beyond the strict limits of the law of the successiveness of all our perceptions. Although we can *distinctly* see only a limited spot at one instant, we can couple with this a vague perception of an adjoining superficies. This is an important sign of co-existence, as contrasted with succession, and enters with various other signs into the very complex notion of the author's synchronous order, otherwise called the Simultaneous or Co-existing in Space.— Bain

These things being explained, the learner will now be able to trace, without error, the formation of one of the most important of all our ideas, that of resistance, or pressure. We touch one thing, butter, for instance; it yields to the finger, after a slight pressure; that is, a certain feeling of ours. The will to move the muscles, and the sensations in the muscles, are both included in that feeling; but, for shortness, we shall speak of them, through the present exposition, under one name, as the feelings or sensations in the muscles. As we call the butter yellow, on account of a feeling of sight; odorous, on account of a feeling of smell; sapid, on account of a feeling of taste; so we call it soft, on account of a feeling in our muscles. We touch a stone, as we touched the butter, and it yields not, after the strongest pressure we can apply. As we called the butter soft, on account of one muscular feeling, we call the stone hard, on account of another. The varieties of these feelings are innumerable. Only a small portion of them have received names. The feeling upon pressure of butter, is one thing; of honey, another; of water, another; of air, another; of flesh, one thing; of bone, another. We mark them as we can, by the terms soft, more soft, less soft; hard, more hard, less hard, and so on. We have great occasion, however, for a word which shall include all these different words. As we have "coloured" to include all the names of sensations of sight; "touch" all the names of sensations of touch, and so on; we invent the word "resisting," which includes all the words, soft, hard, and so on, by which any of the sensations of pressure are denoted.

Such, then, are the feelings which we are capable of receiving from the particle with which we may suppose a line of particles to commence. These feelings, in passing along the line, we should receive in succession from each, if the tactual sense were sufficiently fine to distinguish particles in contact from one another. It has not, however, this perfection. Even sight cannot distinguish minute intervals. If a red-hot coal is whirled rapidly round, though the coal is present at only one part of the circle at each instant, the whole is one continuous red. If the seven prismatic colours are made to pass rapidly in order before the eye, they appear not distinct colours, but one uniform white. In like manner, in passing from one to another, in a line of particles, there is no feeling of interval; there is the feeling we call continuity; that is, absence of interval.

The sensations, then, the ideas of which combined compose the idea which we mark by the word line, may thus be traced. The tactual feeling, and the feeling of resistance, derivable from every particle, attend the finger in every part of its progress along the line. What is there besides? To produce the progress of the finger, there is muscular action; that is to say, there are the feelings combined in muscular action. That we may exclude extraneous ideas as much as possible, let us suppose, that, when a person first makes himself acquainted with a line, he has the sense of touch, and the muscular sensations, without any other sense. He has one state of feeling, when the finger, which touches the line, is still; another, when it moves. He has also one state of feeling from one degree of motion, another from another. If he has one state of feeling from the finger carried along, as far as it can extend, he has another feeling when it is only carried half as far, and so on.

It is extremely difficult to speak of these feelings precisely, or to draw by language those who are not accustomed to the minute analysis of their thoughts, to conceive them distinctly; because they are among the feelings, as we have before remarked, which we have acquired the habit of not attending to, or rather, have lost the power of attending to.

It is certain, however, that by sensation alone we become acquainted with lines; that in every different contraction of the muscles there is a difference of sensation; and that of the tactual feeling, and the feelings of the contracted muscles, all the feelings which constitute our knowledge of a line are composed.

As, after certain repetitions of a particular sensation of sight, a particular sensation of smell, a particular sensation of sight, and so on, received in a certain order, I give to the combined ideas of them, the name rose, the name apple, the name fire, and the like; in the same manner, after certain repetitions of particular tactual sensations, and particular muscular sensations, received in a certain order, I give to the combined ideas of them, the name Line. But when I have got my idea of a line, I have also got my idea of extension. For what is extension, but lines in every direction? physical lines, if real, tactual extension; mathematical lines, if mathematical, that is, abstract, extension.

It would be tedious to pursue the analysis of extension farther. And I trust it is not necessary; because the application of the same method to the remaining cases, appears completely obvious. Take plane surface for example. It is composed of all the lines which can be drawn in a particular plane; the idea of it, therefore, is derived from the tactual feeling, and the feeling of resistance, combined with the muscular feelings involved in the motion of the finger in every direction which it can receive on a plane.

Let us now take some of the words which, along with the synchronous order, connote objects in pairs. The names of this sort are not very numerous. High, and low, right, and left, hind, and fore, are examples. These, it is obvious, are names of the principal directions from the human body as a centre. The order of objects, the most frequently interesting to human beings, is, of course, their order with respect to their own bodies. What is over the head, gets the name of high; what is below the feet, gets the name of low; and so on. Of the pairs which are connoted by those words, the human body is always one. The words, right, left, hind, fore, when they denote the object so called, always connote the body in respect to which they are right, left, hind, fore. We have already noticed the cases in which the objects, thus named in pairs, have each a separate name, as father, son; also those in which both have the same name, as sister, brother. We have here another case, which deserves also to be particularly marked, that in which only one of them has a name. The human body, which is always one of the objects named, when we call things right, left, hind, fore, and so on, has no corresponding relative name. The reason is sufficiently obvious; this, being always one of the pair, cannot, the other being named, be misunderstood.

For the complete understanding of these words, it does not appear that any thing remains to be explained. If one line, proceeding from a central particle, be understood, every line, which can proceed from it, is also understood. If that central point be a part of the human body, it is plain that as the hand, passing along a line in a certain direction from that centre, has certain muscular actions, passing along in another direction, it has muscular actions somewhat different. When we say muscular actions somewhat different, we say muscular feelings somewhat different. Difference of feeling, when important, needs difference of naming.

A particular case of association is here to be remarked; and it is one which it is important for the learner to fix steadfastly in his memory.

We never perceive, what we call an object, except in the synchronous order. Whatever other sensations we receive, the sensations of the synchronous order, are always received along with them. When we perceive a chair, a tree, a man, a house, they are always situated so and so, with respect to other objects. As the sensations of position are thus always received with the other sensations of an object, the idea of Position is so closely associated with the idea of the object, that it is wholly impossible for us to have the one idea without the other. It is one of the most remarkable cases of indissoluble association; and is that feeling which men describe, when they say that the idea of space forces itself upon their understandings, and is necessary.

2. We come now to the case of naming OBJECTS in pairs, on account of the Successive Order.

We have had occasion to observe that there is nothing in which human beings are so deeply interested, as the Successive Order of objects. It is the successive order upon which all their happiness and misery depends; and the synchronous order is interesting to them, chiefly on account of its connection with the successive.

When we speak of objects, it is necessary to remember, that it is sensations, not ideas, to which we are then directing our attention. All our sensations, we say, are derived from objects; in other words, object is the name we give to the antecedents of our sensations. And, reciprocally, all our knowledge of objects is the sensations themselves. We have the sensations, and that is all. A knowledge, therefore, of the successive order of objects, is a knowledge of the successive order of our sensations; of all the pleasures, and all the pains, and all the feelings intermediate between pleasure and pain, of which the body is susceptible.

Of successions, that is, the order of objects as antecedent and consequent, some are constant, some not constant. Thus, a stone dropped in the air always falls to the ground. This is a case of constancy of sequence. Heavy clouds drop rain, but not always. This is a case of casual sequence.[1] Human life is deeply interested in ascertaining the constant sequences of all the objects from which human sensations are derived. The great business of philosophy is to find them out; and to record them, in the form most convenient for acquiring the knowledge of them, and for applying it.

In the successions of objects, it very often happens, that what appear to us to be the immediate antecedent and consequent, are not immediately successive, but are separated by several intermediate successions. Thus, the falling of a spark on gunpowder, and the explosion of the gunpowder, appear antecedent and consequent; but several successions in reality intervene; various decompositions, and compositions, in which, indeed, all the sequences cannot as yet be traced. Most of the successions, which we are called upon to notice and to name, are in the same situation. We fix upon two conspicuous points in a chain of successions, and the intermediate ones are either overlooked, or unknown.

Thus, we name Doctor and Patient, the two extremities of a pretty long succession of objects. The Doctor is not the immediate antecedent of any change in the patient. He is the immediate antecedent of a certain conception, of which the consequent is, writing a prescription; the consequent of this, is the sending it to the apothecary; the consequent of that, is the apothecary's reading it, and so on; the whole composing a multitudinous train. Doctor and Patient, therefore, are not only two paired names of two paired objects, but names of all the successions between the one and the other. Doctor and Patient, therefore, properly speaking, are to be considered one name, though made up of two parts. Taken together, they are the name of the complex idea of a considerable train of sequences, of which a particular man is

[1] This is surely an improper use of the word Casual. Sequences cannot be exhaustively divided into invariable and casual, or (as by the author a few pages further on) into constant and fortuitous. Heavy clouds, though they do not always drop rain, are not connected with it by mere accident, as the passing of a waggon might be. They are connected with it through causation: they are one of the conditions on which, when united, rain is invariably consequent, though it is not invariably consequent on that single condition. This distinction is essential to any system of Inductive Logic, in which it recurs at every step.—J.S.M.

one extremity, a particular man another; just as navigation is the single-worded name of the complex idea of a very long train, of which the extremities are not particularly marked. If you say, navigation from the Thames to the Ganges, you have a many-worded name, by which the extremities of this long train are particularly marked.

The relative terms, Father and Son, are obviously included in this explanation. They are the two extremities of a train of great length and intricacy, very imperfectly understood. They also, both together, compose, as may easily be seen, but one name. Father is a word which connotes Son, and whether Son is expressed or not, the meaning of it is implied. In like manner Son connotes Father; and, stripped of that connotation, is without a meaning. Taken together, therefore, they are one name, the name of the complex idea of that train of which father is the one extremity, son the other.[1]

Brother and Brother are a pair of relative terms marking a still more complex idea. Two brothers are two sons of the same Father; taken together, they are, therefore, marks of all that Son, taken twice, is capable of marking. Son, as we have just seen, always implies Father; and, taken together, they are the name of a train. The relatives, therefore, brother and brother, are the compound name; two brothers, are the name of the train marked by the term, Father and Son, taken twice, the prior extremity of the train being the same in both cases, the latter different.

The above terms, Father and Son, Brother and Brother, are imposed on account of sequences which are passed. I do not at this moment recollect any relative terms imposed on account of sequences purely future. The terms, Buyer and Seller, are sometimes, indeed, used in a sense wholly future; when they mean persons having something to buy and something to sell: but they are also used in a sense wholly passed, when they signify persons who have effected purchase and sale. We have, however, many relative terms on account of trains

[1] It seems hardly a proper expression to say that Physician and Patient, or that Father and Son, are one name made up of two parts. When one of the parts is a name of one person and the other part is the name of another, it is difficult to see how the two together can be but one name. Father and Son are two names, denoting different persons: but what the author had it in his mind to say, was that they connote the same series of facts, which series, as the two persons are both indispensable parts of it, gives names to them both, and is made the foundation or *fundamentum* of an attribute ascribed to each.

With the exception of this questionable use of language, which the author had recourse to because he had not left himself the precise word Connote, to express what there is of real identity in the signification of the two names; the analysis which follows of the various complicated cases of relation seems philosophically unexceptionable. The complexity of a relation consists in the complex composition of the series of facts or phenomena which the names connote, and which is the *fundamentum relationis*. The names signify that the person or thing, of which they are predicated, forms part of a group or succession of phenomena along with the other person or thing which is its correlate: and the special nature of that group or series, which may be of extreme complexity, constitutes the speciality of the relation predicated.—J.S.M.

which are partly passed and partly future. Thus, Lender and Borrower, are imposed partly on account of the passed train included in the contract of lending and borrowing; partly on account of the future train implied in the repayment of the money. The words Debtor and Creditor are names of the same train, partly passed and partly future.

The relative terms, Husband and Wife, are of the same class; the name of a train partly passed, to wit, that implied in entering into the nuptial contract; and partly future, to wit, all the events expected to flow out of that contract. Master and Servant are imposed, on account of a train partly passed and partly future; the train of entering into the compact of master and servant, and the train of acts which flow out of it. King and Subject are the name of a train similarly divided; first, the train which led to the will of obeying on the part of the people, the will of commanding on the part of the king; secondly, the trains which grow out of these wills.

Owner and Property are relative terms, or terms which connote one another. They also are imposed on account of a train partly passed and partly future. The part which is passed is the train implied in the circumstances of the acquisition, whether inheritance, gift, labour, or purchase. The part which is future is the train implied in the use which the owner may make of the property.

Of the terms which denote objects in successive pairs, several are very general. Thus we have antecedent and consequent, which are applicable to any parts of any train. Prior and Posterior, are nearly of the same import. First and Last, are applicable to the two extremities of any train. Second, third, fourth, and so on, are applicable to the contiguous parts of any train.

We have remarked, above, that successions of objects are to be distinguished into two remarkable kinds; that of the successions which are fortuitous, and that of the successions which are constant. Names to mark the antecedent and consequent in all constant successions, which are things of such importance to us, were found of course indispensable. Cause and Effect, are the names we employ. In all constant successions, Cause is the name of the antecedent, Effect the name of the consequent. And, beside this, it has been proved by philosophers,[1] that these names denote absolutely nothing.

It is highly necessary to be apprized, that each of the two names, Cause, and Effect, has a double meaning. They are used, sometimes in the concrete sense, sometimes in the abstract. By this ambiguity, ideas are confounded, which it is of the greatest importance to preserve distinct. When we say, the sun is the Cause of light, cause is concrete; the meaning is, that the sun always causes light. When we say that ice

[1] Chiefly by Dr. Brown, of Edinburgh, in a work entitled "Inquiry into the Relation of Cause and Effect;" one of the most valuable contributions to science for which we are indebted to the last generation.—James Mill

is the Effect of cold air, effect is concrete; the meaning is, that ice is effected by cold air. "Cause," in these cases, is merely a short name for "causing object," "Effect" a short name for "caused object." In abstract discourse, on the other hand, Cause and Effect are often used in the abstract sense, in which cases Cause means the same thing as would be meant by CAUSINGNESS; Effect, the same as would be meant by CAUSEDNESS. They are merely the connotative or concrete terms, with the connotation dropped.

As the abstract terms have no meaning, except as they refer to the concrete, it is in the concrete sense I shall always use the words Cause and Effect, unless when I give notice to the contrary.

Other terms, pairing the parts of a train, take parts more or less distant; first and last, take the most distant; father and son, take parts at a considerable distance; cause and effect, on the other hand, mean always the proximate parts. It does not, indeed, happen, that we always apply them to the proximate parts; because the intermediate sequences are often unknown, at other times overlooked. They are always, however, applied to the parts regarded as proximate. For we do not, strictly speaking, say, that any thing is the cause of a thing, when it is only the cause of another thing, which is the cause of that thing; still less, when there is a series of causes and effects, before you arrive at that which you have marked as *the* effect, because the ultimate one. In all the inquiries of philosophers into causes, it is the antecedent and consequent, really proximate, which is the object of their pursuit.

We have observed, in the case of the relative terms, applied to objects as successive, that the words, properly speaking, form but one name,—that of the complex idea of a train of less or greater length: thus, Doctor and Patient is a name; Father and Son is a name; each denoting a train of which two individuals are the principal parts. In like manner, the relative terms Cause and Effect, taken together, are but one name, the name of a short train, that of one antecedent and one consequent, regarded as proximate, and constant.

3. We have now shewn, in what manner the principal Relative Terms are applied, when we have to speak of OBJECTS as having order in Space, and when we have to speak of them as having order in Time. We proceed to shew in what manner they are applied, when we have to speak of objects as differing in Quantity, or differing in Quality; and first, as differing in Quantity.

We apply the word Quantity, in a very general manner; to things, which have the greatest diversity. Thus, we use the word quantity, when we speak of extension; we use the word quantity, when we speak of weight; we use it, when we speak of motion; we use it, when we speak of heat; we use it, in short, on almost every occasion, on which we can use the word degree. Of course, it represents not one idea, but many ideas, some of which have the greatest diversity.

The relative terms, which we co-apply with quantity, are equal, un-equal, or some particular case included under these more general terms; as, more heavy, less heavy; more strong, less strong; whole, part; and so on.

When quantity is applied to extent, it may be extent either in one, or more, or every direction; it may mean either quantity in line, quan-tity in surface, or quantity in bulk. Accordingly, we can say, equal, or unequal, lines; equal, or unequal, surfaces; equal, or unequal, bulks.

Line is the simplest case; the explanation of it will, therefore, facili-tate the rest. We have already traced the sensations, which constitute our knowledge of a line. We have seen that they are certain sensations of touch, combined with the muscular sensations involved in extend-ing the arm.

As the sensations, involved in extending the arm so far, are not the same with those which are involved in extending it farther; and as the having different sensations, and distinguishing them, are not two things, but one and the same thing;—as often as I have those two cases of sensation, I distinguish them from one another; and, distin-guishing them from one another, I require names to mark them. The first I mark, by the word, short; the other, by the word, long. As I call a line long, from extending my arm so far; that is, from the sensations involved in extending it; I call it longer from extending it farther. After experience of a number of lines, there are some which I call long, long, long, one after another, to any amount; others which I call longer, longer, longer; others which I call short, short, short; and so on.

When we have perceived the sensations, on account of which we call lines long, longer, short, shorter, we can be at no loss for the knowledge of those, on account of which we call them equal, and unequal. It is to be observed, that in applying the words long, longer, short, shorter, minute differences are not named. They cannot be named. The names would be too numerous. A general mark, however, may be invented, to show when there is even a minute difference, and when there is not. When there is not, we call the two lines equal; when there is, we call them unequal.

We shall presently see, when we come to trace the ideas, which the class of words, called numbers, are employed to mark, what distinc-tion of sensation it is which is marked by the words, one, and two. In the mean time, it is easy to see, that the case of sensation, when we trace one line, with the hand, and then another, is different from the case of sensation when we trace one line only, or even the same line twice; and this diversity needs marks to distinguish it. It is true, that in tracing one line, and then another, and marking the distinction, there is something more than sensation, there is also memory. But to this ingredient in the compound, after the explanation which has already been given of memory, it is not, at present, necessary particularly to advert.

When it is seen, what are the sensations which are marked by the terms longer and shorter, applied to a line, it will not be difficult to see what are the sensations, which are marked by the terms, part, and whole.

The terms, a part, and whole, imply division. Of course, the thing precedes the name. Men divided, before they named the act, or the consequences of the act. In the act of division, or in the results of it, no mystery has ever been understood to reside. It is of importance to remark, that the word division, in its ordinary acceptation, includes, and thence confounds, things which very much need to be distinguished. It includes the will, which is the antecedent of the act; the act itself; and the results of the act. At present we may leave the will aside; it will be explained hereafter; and, as it is not the act, but the antecedent of the act, the consideration of it is not required for the present purpose.

The act of dividing, like all the other acts of our body, consists in the contraction and relaxation of certain muscles. These are known to us, like every thing else, by the feelings. The act, as act, is the feelings; and only when confounded with its results, is it conceived to be any thing else. If it be said, that the contraction of the muscles of my arm, is something more in me than feelings, because I see the motion of my arm; it is to be observed, that this seeing, this sensation of sight, is not the act, but one of its results; the feelings of the act are the antecedent; this sensation of sight one of the consequents.

In the act of dividing a line, as in the act, already analysed, of tracing a line, there is a feeling of touch, and there is also a muscular feeling. There may be more or less of cohesion in the parts of the line; and thence, more or less of what we call muscular force, required to disunite them. Of course, what we call more or less of force, are only names for different states of feeling. The states of feeling which we mark by the term, force, being antecedent, all the rest are consequents of this antecedent. The disunion of the parts of one line is attended with a certain muscular feeling; I call the feeling a small force. That of another line is attended with a muscular feeling somewhat different; I call it a greater force; and so on. This muscular feeling, however, has various accompaniments; which are closely associated with the idea of the act, and with its name. Thus there is the sight of the line, there is the sight of the hands in the act of disruption, and there is the sight of the line after it is divided. The term division, as we have mentioned before, includes all; the muscular feeling, the sight of the line before division, and the sight of it after. I need a pair of names for the line before division, and the line after. I call the one whole, the other parts. Like other relative terms, the one of these connotes the other; whole has no meaning, but when associated with parts; parts have no meaning, but when associated with whole. Taken together; that is, whole and parts, used as one name; they mark a complex idea, consisting of three principal parts; an undivided line, the act of division, and the consequent of that antecedent, the line after division.

In the preceding exposition, it is actual division, the actual making of parts, which has been spoken of. It is observable, however, that the same language, by which we name actual division, and actual parts, is applied to conceived division, and conceived parts. Thus we talk of the parts of a line, when it is not divided, nor meant to be divided. The exposition of this, however, is easy; and there is obscurity only when the double use of the terms confounds the two cases, the division which is actual, with that which is conceived.

The division of the line may consist of one act, or of more acts than one. By the first act, it is divided into two parts; by the second into three; by the third into four, and so on. The parts of a line are so many lines. These may be equal, or unequal. But the sensations, on account of which we denominate lines equal, or unequal, have been already shewn; the equality, and inequality, therefore, of the parts of a line, need no further explanation.

When the learner conceives distinctly the sensations on account of which we apply the terms whole and parts to a line, he will not find it difficult to understand, on what account we apply them to all the modifications of extension; seeing that all these modifications are lines combined.

Thus, a plane surface is a number of straight lines, in contact, in the direction called a plane. It is of greater or less extent, according as these lines are longer or shorter from a central point; it is of one shape or another shape, according as the lines are of the same length, or of different lengths. When they are all of one length, the surface is called a circle. As they may be of different lengths in endless variety, the surface may have an endless variety of shapes, of which only a few have received names. The square is one of these names, the triangle another, the parallelogram another, and so on.

Bulk, which is the other great modification of extension, is lines from a central point in every direction. This bulk is greater or less, according as these lines are longer or shorter. The figure or shape of this bulk is different, according as the lines are of the same or different lengths. If they are of the same length, the bulk is called round, or, in one word, a sphere; sphere meaning exactly round bulk. As the lines, when they differ in length, may differ in endless ways; figures, or the shapes of bulk, are also endless, as our senses abundantly testify. Of these but a small number have received names. In this number are the cube, the cylinder, the cone. We name some shapes by referring to known objects; thus we speak of the shape of an egg, the shape of a pear, and so on.

It seems that nothing, therefore, is now wanting, to shew in what manner the relative terms, expressive of Quantity, are applied to all the modifications of extension.

After what has been said, it will not be difficult to ascertain the sensations on account of which we apply the same relative terms to cases of Weight.

Weight is the name of a particular species of pressure; pressure towards the centre of the earth. Pressure, as we have already fully seen, is the name we apply, when we have certain sensations in the muscles, just as green is the name we apply when we have a certain sensation in the eye. As green is the name of the sensation in the eye, pressure is the name of the sensation in the muscles. Pressure upwards, is one thing; pressure downwards, is another; pressure of a body, when that body is urged by another body, is one thing; pressure of a body, when it is not urged by another body, is a different thing: pressure of a body in altering the position of its parts is one thing; pressure, when there is no alteration of the position of its parts, is another thing. Of this last sort is weight, the pressure downwards, or towards the centre of the earth, of a body not urged by another body, and not altering the position of its parts.

In supporting in my hand a stone, I resist a certain pressure; in other words, have certain muscular feelings, on account of which I call the stone heavy. I support other stones, and in doing so have muscular feelings, in one case similar, in another dissimilar. In the case of similarity, I call two stones equal, meaning in weight; in the case of dissimilarity, unequal; and so I apply all the other relative terms by which quantity is expressed.

It seems unnecessary to carry this analysis into further detail. The words equal, unequal: greater, less; applied to Motion, to Heat, and other modifications of sensation, have a meaning, which in following the course so fully exemplified it cannot be difficult to ascertain.

It seems still necessary that I should say something of the word *Quantus,* from which the word Quantity is derived. *Quantus* is the correlate of *Tantus. Tantus, Quantus,* are relative terms, applicable to all the objects to which we apply the terms, Great, or Little; they are applicable, therefore, to all the modifications of extension, of weight, of heat; in short, to all modifications which we can mark as degrees.

Of two lines, we call the one *tantus,* the other *quantus.* The occasions on which we do so are, when the one is as long as the other. *Tantus,* and *Quantus,* then, in this case, mean the same thing as equal, equal. They will be found to have the same import as equal, equal, when applied also to surface, and bulk; and so in all other compatible cases.

What then, it may be asked, is the use of them? If it should appear that they were of no use, it would not be very surprising; considering by whom languages have been made; and that redundancy is frequent in them as well as defect. In the present case, however, a use is not wanting.

It is necessary to observe the artifice, to which we are obliged to have recourse, to name, and even to distinguish, the different modifications, not of kind but of degree, included under the word quantity. We are obliged to take some one object, with which we are familiar, and to distinguish other objects, as differing or agreeing with that object. Thus, we take some well-known line, the length of the foot, or the length of the arm, and distinguish and name all other lengths by that length; which can be divided or multiplied so as to correspond with them. In like manner, we take some well-known object as a standard weight, which we call, for example, a pound, and distinguish and name all other weights, as parts or multiples of that known weight.

Now it will be recognised, that, in applying the relative terms, equal, equal, or in calling two objects equal, no one of them is marked as the standard. Both are taken on the same footing. The one is equal to the other; and the other is equal to that. But when we say that one thing is *tantus, quantus* another; or one so great, as the other is great; the first is referred to the last, the *tantus* to the *quantus;* the first is distinguished and named by the last. The *quantus* is the standard.

It is this which gives its peculiar meaning to the word Quantity, and has recommended it for that very comprehensive and generical acceptation, in which it is now received.

Our word Quantity, is the Latin word *Quantitas;* and *Quantitas* is the abstract of the concrete *Quantus.* We have no English words, corresponding to *Tantus, Quantus.* We form an equivalent, by aid of the relative conjunctions; we say, So Great, As Great. But these concrete terms do not furnish abstracts; we do not say, As-greatness; in the first place, because it is an awkward expression; and in the next place, because the relative, "as," is not steady in its application, since we use "as great" not for *quantus* only, but frequently also for *tantus.* As greatness, therefore, does not readily suggest the idea of the abstract of *Quantus.*

On what account, then, is it we give to any thing the name *Quantus?* As a standard by which to name another thing *Tantus.* The thing called *Quantus,* is the previously known thing, the ascertained amount, by which we can mark and define the other amount. Leaving out the connotation of *Quantus,* which is some one individual body, *Quantitas* merely denotes such and such an amount of body. *Quantitas,* if it was kept to its original meaning, would still connote *Tantitas;* just as paternity connotes filiality. But in the case of Quantity, even this connotation is dropped; it is used not as a *relative* abstract term, but an *absolute* abstract term; and is employed as a generical name for any portion of extension, any portion of weight, of heat, or any thing else, which can be measured by a part of itself.[1]

4. After tracing the sensations and ideas, which are marked when we apply relative terms to objects, as agreeing or disagreeing in *quantity;* we have now to trace the sensations and ideas, which are marked, when we apply relative terms to objects, on account of their agreeing or disagreeing in *quality.*

First of all, the learner must take note of what he means by *Quality.* We ascribe qualities to an object on account of our sensations. We call an object green, on account of the sensation green; hard, on account of the sensation hard; sounding, on account of the sensation sounding. The names of all qualities of objects, then, are names of sensations. Are they any thing else? Yes; they are the names of our sensations, with connotation of a supposed unknown cause of those sensations. As far, however, as our knowledge goes, they are names of sensations, and nothing else. The supposed cause is never known; the effects alone are known to us.

We ascribe qualities to objects, in two cases, which require to be distinguished: on account of the sensations which we have from them primarily; on account of those which we have from them secondarily. The first we call their sensible qualities; as green, hot, hard, sweet, scented, and so on: the second we more frequently call their powers; as the power of the loadstone to draw iron, the power of water to melt sugar. In this latter case, the sensations marked are not those which are derived from the loadstone, or from water; but those which are derived from the changes in the iron, and the sugar; of which changes,

---

1 After analysing Position and Extension under the head of Relative Terms, the author now, under the same head, gives the analysis of Quantity and Quality. To what he says on the subject of Quantity it does not appear necessary to add anything. He seems to have correctly analysed the phenomenon down to a primitive element, beyond which we have no power to investigate. As Likeness and Unlikeness appeared to be properties of our simple feelings, which must be postulated as ultimate, and which are inseparable from the feelings themselves, so may this also be said of More and Less. As some of our feelings are like, some unlike, so there is a mode of likeness or unlikeness which we call Degree: some feelings otherwise like are unlike in degree, that is one is unlike another in intensity, or one is unlike another in duration; in either case one is distinguished as more, or greater, the other as less. And the fact of being more or less only means that we feel them as more or less. The author says in this case, as he had said in the other elementary cases of relation, that the more and the less being different sensations, to trace them and to distinguish their difference are not two things but one and the same thing. It matters not, since there the difference still is, unsusceptible of further analysis. The author's apparent simplification amounts only to this, that differences of quantity, like all other differences of which we take cognizance, are differences merely in our feelings; they exist only as they are felt. But (as we have already said of resemblance, and of antecedence and consequence) they must be postulated as elements. The distinction of more and less is one of the ultimate conditions under which we have all our states of consciousness.—J.S.M.

we call the loadstone, and the water, the cause. In the latter case, the train of antecedents and consequents is longer than it is in the former. When I seen an object green; there is the object, the antecedent; and myself sentient of green, the consequent. When I see a loadstone draw iron, there is the following train; the loadstone, antecedent; iron drawn, first consequent; myself seeing it drawn, second consequent. When I see water melt sugar, there is the antecedent water; sugar melting, first consequent; myself seeing it, second consequent. What I call the powers of an object, then, are its order in respect to certain of my sensations, the order of antecedence, not proximate, but more or less remote.

When I say that grass is green, I trace my sensation green, no farther than to the grass. When I say, the sugar is melting, I trace my sensations (for they are several) called sugar melting, first to the sugar, and then to the water. My word green, therefore, is the notation of a sensation, and connotation of an unknown cause; my name melting, is the notation of a compound of sensations, and connotation of two causes, an antecedent and a consequent: the first, an unkown cause in the sugar; the second, the cause of that unknown cause, namely, the water.

In speaking of the qualities of an object, it is necessary to take notice of an inaccuracy of language; which not only, as Dr. Brown has well observed, lies at the bottom of many philosophical errors, but induces men to mistake the very business of the philosopher.

The term, "quality" or "qualities of an object," seems to imply, that the qualities are one thing, the object another. And this, in some indistinct way, is, no doubt, the opinion of the great majority of mankind. Yet, the absurdity of it strikes the understanding, the moment it is mentioned. The qualities of an object are the whole of the object. What is there beside the qualities? In fact, they are convertible terms: the qualities are the object; and the object is the qualities. But, then, what are the qualities? Why, sensations, with the association of the object as the cause. And what is the association of the object as the cause? Why, the association of other sensations as antecedent. What, for example, are the smell, and colour, and other qualities of the rose? Is not each of the names of these qualities, that of the smell, for example, a connotative name, not only noting the sensation, of which it is properly the name, but connoting all the sensations of colour, of consistence, of figure, of position; to which, all combined by association, so as to form one complex idea, we give the specific name, rose, the more general name, vegetable, and the still more general name, object? When the smell of a rose is perceived by me, or the idea suggested to me, immediately all the other ideas included under the term rose, are suggested along with it, and their indissoluble union presupposed. But this belief of the previous indissoluble union of each of those sensations with all the other sensations, is all which I really mean when I refer each sensation to the rose as its cause.

If the learner has fully apprehended the ideas here premised, it will be easy for him to trace to the bottom the relative terms, which we apply to objects on account of their agreeing or disagreeing in *Quality*.

We say, that objects agree or disagree, on account of one quality, or more than one quality, that is, on account of single sensations, or combined sensations.

Let us first observe the case of one quality. We say, that a blade of grass is like the leaf of an oak, meaning, that in the quality of colour both are green; we say that the leaf of the rose-tree, is unlike the petal of the flower, meaning in colour. By these words, we name the objects in pairs; first, the pair of leaves, to each of which, we give the name, like; secondly, the leaf and the petal, to each of which, we give the name, unlike. We name the first two objects, "like," on account of the two sensations, green, and green, one of each object; we name the next two objects unlike, on account of the two sensations, green of the one, red of the other. What is done, or rather what is felt, when we give the same, or a different name, to each of two sensations, has been already so fully explained, that a bare suggestion of what has been premised, is here all that will be required.

We have two sensations, A, B. Having two sensations, and knowing them to be two sensations, that is, not one sensation, is having the sensations, and nothing more.

Why do I call one sequence of sensations, green, green; another sequence, green, red? Clearly on account of the sensations. No other explanation can be given of it, nor can be required. For the same reason for which I called the sensations of the first sequence individually, green, green, I call them both, like; and for the same reason for which I called those of the second sequence, not green, green, but green, red, I call them, unlike.

Let us next put the case of several sensations. We say, that one rose is like another. We have only to take the sensations combined under the name rose, one by one, to see that this, and the former, case, are in reality the same. The two roses are like in colour, like in smell, like in consistence, like in form, like in position. The likeness of the two roses, is a likeness not in one sensation, but in several. But the likeness of two sensations of smell, is of the same nature as the likeness of the two sensations of sight. When I call the smell, therefore, of the two roses like, it is for the same reason as I call the colour of them like, that is, the sensations. When I call the shape and consistence, and position, like, it is for the same reason still; the tactual and muscular sensations, whence the ideas are derived to which these names are annexed. In this case, however, the reason is by no means so clearly seen, first, because the sensations are complex, and secondly,

because they are of that class of sensations which we habitually overlook.

The Latin words, *Talis, Qualis,* are applied to objects in the same
way, on one account, as *Tantus, Quantus,* on another; and the explanation we gave of *Tantus, Quantus,* may be applied *mutatis mutandis,*
to the pair of relatives we have now named. *Tantus, Quantus,* are
names applied to objects on account of dimension. *Talis, Qualis,* are
names applied to objects on account of all other sensations. We apply
Tantus, Quantus, to a pair of objects when they are equal; we apply
Talis, Qualis, to a pair of objects, when they are like.

Talis, Qualis, however, express the likeness of two objects in a
manner somewhat different from the other pair of nearly equivalent
relatives, "Like," and "Like." When we call two objects Like, the one
is placed on the same footing as the other. No one of them is taken as
the standard. When we apply, *Talis, Qualis,* the case is different. One
of the objects is then the standard. The object *Qualis,* is that to which
the reference is made.

This being understood, the extensive meaning which came to be
given to the word Quality, may be easily explained. Quality is the
Latin *Qualitas,* and *Qualitas* is the abstract of *Qualis.* The meaning of
the abstract is the same with that of the concrete, the connotation
being dropped. When the word *Qualis,* is applied to an object, it notes
something about it in particular, but connotes the whole object. The
Qualitas of that object, is the something noted in particular, the connotation being dropped. As *Qualis* is applied to objects, sometimes on
account of one thing belonging to them, sometimes on account of another, *Qualitas* comes in turn to be applied to every thing in them,
requiring at any time a separate notation. *Qualitas,* when first formed
from *Qualis,* has the force of a relative, and connotes the abstract of
Talis; but in its frequent use, in marking every thing in objects, which
requires separate notation, this connotation, also, comes to be
dropped; and Quality is finally used as an absolute term, the generical
name of every thing in objects, for which a separate notation is required.[1]

[1] As in the case of Quantity, so in that of Quality, it is needless to add anything
to the author's very sufficient elucidation. I merely make the usual reserves with
respect to the use of the word Connotation. The concrete names which predicate
qualities (for of abstract relative names the author is not yet speaking) are said
by him to be the names of our sensations; green, for instance, and red. But it is
the abstract names alone which are this: the names greenness, and redness. And
even the abstract names signify something more than only the sensations: they are
names of the sensations considered as derived from an object which produces them.
The concrete name is a name not of the sensation, but of the object, of which
alone it is predicable: we talk of green objects, but not of green sensations. It
however connotes the quality greenness, that is, it connotes that particular sensation
as produced by, or proceeding from the object; as forming one of the group of
sensations which constitutes the object. This, however, is but a difference, though
a very important one, in terminology. It is strictly true, that the real meaning of

III. It was remarked at the beginning of this investigation of relative terms or names applied in pairs, that we name in pairs—1, single sensations or ideas; 2, the clusters we call objects; 3, the complex ideas we form arbitrarily for our own purposes. Having finished the consideration of the two former cases, we shall not find occasion to speak much at length upon the last.

The clusters, formed by arbitrary association, receive names in pairs, on two occasions; either,

1. When they consist of the same or different simple ideas; or,

2. When they succeed one another in a train.

1. The ideas which we put together arbitrarily are sometimes less, sometimes more, complex; for the most part, they are exceedingly complex.

Of the less complicated kinds, are such ideas as that of the unicorn, which is a horse with one straight horn growing from the middle of its forehead; the Cyclops, a gigantic man, with a single eye in the middle of his forehead; a mermaid, of which the upper part is a woman, the lower a fish; the Brobdingnagian and Lilliputian of Swift, which are men of greatly reduced, or greatly enlarged dimensions.

Of the more complicated kinds, are such ideas as those which are marked by the word Science, by the word Trade, by the word Law, by the word Religion, by the word Faith, by the words God and Devil, by the word Value, by the words Virtue, Honour, Vice, Beauty, Deformity, Space, Time, and so on.

Language has not many relative terms, applicable to ideas of this class. We speak of pairs of them as like or unlike, same or different, greater or less; and except when their order in time is to be noted, we hardly apply to them any other marks in pairs.

We say the Cyclops in Homer, and the Brobdingnagian of Swift, are unlike. We do so precisely in the same way, as we say, the rose and the lily are unlike; and the explanation which we have given of that which is distinctively marked by those terms, when applied to objects, is precisely applicable here. In the case of objects, that which is named, is, clusters of ideas;[1] in the present case, that which is named, is clusters of ideas. That one cluster has been formed in one way, another in another, makes no difference in annexing marks to the clusters when they are formed.

There is as little difficulty in tracing what is marked by the relatives, different, and same, when applied to ideas of this class. We say, the

the word is the sensations; as, in all cases, the meaning of a connotative word resides in the connotation (the attributes signified by it), though it is the name of, or is predicable of, only the objects which it denotes.—J.S.M.

[1] Say rather, in the case of objects, what is named is clusters of sensations, supplemented by possibilities of sensation. If an object is but a cluster of ideas, what is there to distinguish it from a mere thought?—J.S.M.

unicorn is different from the horse; because, to the idea of the horse it adds that of a horn growing in the middle of the forehead. In the case of very complex ideas, it is much more difficult to say, with precision, what are the added and subtracted ideas, on account of which, we apply the term, different; as when we say, the courage of Ajax was different from that of Achilles; but it is not the less certain, that it is wholly on account of ideas added and subtracted, that we so denominate the courage of the two men.

Rather more explanation is needed, to shew what is peculiarly marked by the relatives equal, unequal, greater, less, when applied to the class of arbitrarily formed complex ideas.

We have already seen, that those terms are primarily applied to what we call objects, on account of their extension; objects are equal or unequal, greater or less, in extension.

We have also seen, that in marking the extension of different objects, we are under the necessity of taking some known object as a standard, and by that object naming others. Thus, we take the foot, and say that other objects are two feet, three feet, or the half or quarter of a foot, and so on.

Having become familiar with what we call degrees of extension, we are led to employ the same mode of notation, when we come to mark analogous differences in other cases of sensation. Thus, when we perceive the weight of different heavy bodies; as the terms equal, unequal, greater, less, are applied with convenience to certain cases of extension, it appears they may be applied with equal convenience, and even precision, to cases of weight. All other sensations, having distinguishable differences, may be marked in the same way: thus sounds are more or less loud, and we speak of equal, or unequal, less or greater loudness of sound; less or greater sweetness in objects of the palate; less or greater resistance; less or greater pain; less or greater pleasure.

When the terms equal, unequal, less, greater, had been applied to simple sensations of the pleasurable kind, and their ideas; the transference of them to complex ideas, of the pleasurable or painful kind, was easy. If the less or greater sweetness of the rose and the woodbine, was a convenient notation, so was the less or greater beauty of those two flowers, the less or greater beauty of two women, the less or greater wisdom or folly, vice or virtue, of two men.

It thus appears, that, as we apply the term unlike to our complex ideas, on account of the addition and subtraction of ideas of *different* kinds, so we apply to them the term unequal, on account of the addition and subtraction of ideas of the *same* kind. Like and equal we apply, when we neither add, nor subtract.[1]

[1] In this passage the author has got as near as it is perhaps possible to get, to an analysis of the ideas of More and Less. We say there is *more* of something,

2. We apply the same relative terms to successive ideas of this class, which we apply to simple ideas, or the clusters called objects, when successive. We call them antecedent and consequent, or names equivalent; as prior, posterior; first, second; or even successive, which is a name including both antecedent and consequent.

In speaking of the relative terms applied to objects as successive, we had occasion to explain the two important terms, Cause and Effect. We found that Cause and Effect, were only other names for antecedent and consequent, in a certain set of cases. We do not use the terms, Cause and Effect, as synonymous with antecedent and consequent, in those cases in which, though the objects may be antecedent and consequent to our perception, we know not whether they are parts of the same series, or parts of two different series. Within the sphere of our observation, innumerable series of events are going on; and we are observing, first a part of one series, and then a part of another, continually. It is thus constantly happening, that those things, which are immediately antecedent and consequent to our observation, are not parts of the same series, but parts of different series; and, of course, in those antecedents and consequents, there is no constancy; they are accidental, as the course of each man's attention. This may be illustrated by many familiar instances. There may be immediately before me, a man playing on the violin, one series; another man filing a saw, a second series. My attention may pass immediately from the sight of the man playing on the violin, to the sound produced by the filing of the saw. Playing on the violin, and the disagreeable sound of the file on the saw, are thus antecedent and consequent to my attention. But, as we recognise such antecedents and consequents, as parts of different series of events, we do not call them cause and effect.

There are two cases of antecedents and consequents, even when they are parts of the same series. They may be proximate; or they may be remote; that is, parts of the series, more or fewer, may come between them. It is only to the case of the proximate parts of the same series, that the relatives, cause and effect, are properly and strictly applied. When the series, however, is the same, the intermediate links between any two remote parts are constant. Suppose a series, A, B, C,

---

when, to what there already was, there has been superadded other matter of the same kind. And when there is no actual superadding, but merely two independent masses of the same substance, we call that one the greater which produces the same impression on our senses which the other would produce if an addition were made to it. So with differences of intensity. One sweet taste is called sweeter than another because it resembles the taste which would be produced by adding more sugar: and so forth. In all these cases there is presupposed an original difference in the sensations produced in us by the greater mass and by the smaller: but according to the explanation now offered, the idea which guides the application of the terms is that of physical juxtaposition.—J.S.M.

D; as B is the immediate consequent of A, C the immediate consequent of B, and D the immediate consequent of C; when I know A and D as antecedent and consequent, without knowing the intermediate parts B, and C, there is little inaccuracy in naming A and D cause and effect; because B and C are surely intermediate, and the succession of A and D, though not immediate, is constant. We accordingly do name cause and effect parts of a series thus removed from one another, in all those cases in which the intermediate parts are either unknown to us, or habitually overlooked.

The terms Cause and Effect, thus applied to Objects as antecedent and consequent, are applied also to Thoughts as antecedent and consequent. Thus we say, that Evidence is the cause of Belief; Villany is the cause of Indignation, and so on.

Of objects, antecedent and consequent, we have observed, that innumerable series are existing at the same time; a separate series, of vegetation, for example, in every plant, of animalization in every animal, of composition and decomposition in objects without number. In the mind, however, there is but one train, not various trains at the same time; and therefore, according to the sense above applied to the terms Cause and Effect, each thought in a train is the cause of that which follows it, and each succeeding thought is the effect of that which precedes it.

But if thoughts are reciprocally Cause and Effect; that is to say, if, in trains of thought, the same antecedent is regularly followed by the same consequent, how happens it that all trains of thought are not the same? For if the ideas A, B, C, D, &c., constantly follow one another, every mind into which A may enter, goes on with B, C, D, &c., and hence all such minds should consist of the same trains, that is, should be the same.

Supposing the succession of two thoughts to have that constancy to which we apply the terms cause and effect, trains would still have that variety which we experience. Our trains consist of two distinguishable ingredients; sensations and ideas. Sensations depend upon the innumerable series of objects. They are, therefore, liable to all that variety which attends the perception of those objects. A perpetual variety in sensations produces a perpetual variety in the thoughts which are consequent upon them. The variety of sensation, is even much greater than is commonly supposed. The most active of all our sensations is the sight. But in most objects of sight there are numerous parts. Some of these are more seen, some are less seen; some not seen at all. Of these, the parts that are more seen by one man, are less seen by another; whence it is probable, that from an object of any complexity no two men ever receive precisely the same sensations. There is a striking exemplification of this, in the fact, so constantly observed, of the different manner in which different men are affected by the comparison of two countenances. To one man there appears a strong likeness, where another man cannot discover any. Of the minute particulars, on which the likeness depends, none, or an insufficient number, is embraced by the vision of the one, while the contrary is the case with that of the other.

The variety in the sensations, which mix in the trains of men, is one grand cause of the variety in the ideas, which make up or complete those trains. The variety in the order of those sensations is another cause. We have seen that ideas follow one another, in the order in which the sensations have followed. Thus, a man may be a kind father to his child. The sight of him to the child is habitually accompanied with agreeable sensations. The same man may be a severe master to his slaves. The sight of him to the slaves is habitually accompanied with painful sensations. A corresponding difference exists in the case of the ideas. When his image presents itself to the mind of the child, it is followed by a train of pleasurable ideas, corresponding to the pleasurable sensations which the child has habitually enjoyed in his presence. When his image rises to the mind of the slave, it is followed, from the contrary cause, by ideas of the contrary description.

This, then, is all which seems necessary to be said respecting the occasions on which we apply Relative Terms, and to show what it is which they distinctively mark, in the trains of our sensations and ideas.

SECTION IV

PRIVATIVE TERMS

. . . Now, then, we can easily understand what extension is in all its cases. Linear extension is the idea of a line, the connotation dropped, that is, the idea of resisting, dropped; superficial extension is the idea of a surface, the same connotation dropped; and solid extension, or bulk, is merely the idea of bulk, the connotation, or resisting, dropped. But bulk, the connotation (*i.e.* resistance) dropped, is what? The place for bulk: Position. But place is, what? A portion of SPACE; or, more correctly speaking, SPACE itself, with limitation.

We thus seem to have arrived, without any difficulty, at an exact knowledge of what is noted or marked by the word SPACE; a phenomenon of the human mind hitherto regarded as singularly mysterious. The difficulty which has been found in explaining the term, even, by those philosophers who have approached the nearest to its meaning, seems to have arisen, from their not perceiving the mode of signification of Abstract Terms; and from the obscurity of that class of sensations, a portion of which we employ the word "extended" to mark. The word "space" is an abstract, differing from its concrete, like other abstracts, by dropping the connotation. Much of the mystery, in which the idea has seemed to be involved, is owing to this single circumstance, that the abstract term, space, has not had an appropriate concrete. We have observed, that, in all cases, abstract terms can be explained only through their concretes; because they note or name a part of what the concrete names, leaving out the rest. If we were to make a concrete term, corresponding to the abstract term space, it must be a word equivalent to the terms "infinitely extended." From the ideas included under the name "infinitely extended," leave out resisting, and you have all that is marked by the abstract SPACE.[1]

In the idea of SPACE, the idea of Infinity is included. What the idea of Infinity is, needs therefore to be explained. When the word Infinite is not used metaphorically, as it is when we speak of the infinite perfections of God, in which case it is not a name for ideas, but for the want of them, it is applied only to Number, Extension, and Duration.

We increase numbers by adding one to one, one to two, and so on, without limit, giving a name to each aggregate. The association of ideas which constitutes the process has been already explained. With each number, one, two, three, four, as we go on, the idea of one more is so strongly associated, that we cannot help its existing in immediate conjunction. However high, therefore, we go in numbering, the idea of one more always forces itself upon us; and hence we say that number is infinite. That this, literally, is not true; that, indeed, it is a verbal contradiction, is obvious. Number, is something numbered; but if numbered, limited; that is, not infinite. Number is the negation of infinite; as black is the negation of white. The name infinite, in this case, is, in reality, nothing but a mark for that state of consciousness, in which the idea of one more is closely associated with every succeeding number. And Infinity, the abstract term, is the peculiar idea, without the connotation.

When we apply "infinite" to extension, we do so equally to all its three modifications, to lines, surfaces, and bulk. How we do so is

---

[1] There is great originality as well as perspicacity in the explanation here given of Space, as a privative term, expressing, when analysed, the absence of the feeling of resistance in the circumstances in which resistance is frequently felt, namely, after the sensations of muscular action and motion. The only part of the exposition to which I demur is the classing of Space among abstract terms. I have already objected to calling the word *line,* when used in the geometrical sense, an abstract term. I hold it to be the concrete name of an ideal object possessing length but not breadth. In like manner a Space may be said to be the concrete name of an ideal object, extended but not resisting. The sensations connoted by this concrete name, are those which accompany the motion of our limbs or of our body in all directions: and along with these sensations is connoted the absence of certain others, viz. of the muscular sensations which accompany the arrest of that motion by a resisting substance. This being the meaning of *a* Space, Space in general must be a name equally concrete. It denotes the aggregate of all Spaces.—J.S.M.

obvious. We know no infinite line, but we know a longer, and a longer. A line is lengthened, as number is increased, by continual additions; a line of any length, say of an inch, is increased, by the continual addition of other lengths, say of an inch. In the process, then, by which we conceive the increase of a line, the idea of one portion more, is continually associated with the preceding length; and to what extent soever it is carried, the association of one portion more, is equally close and irresistible. This is what we call the idea of infinite extension; and what some people call the *necessary* idea; which only means, that the idea of a portion more, rises necessarily, that is, by indissoluble association, so that we cannot help its rising. Infinite is the concrete term, here connoting Line; drop the connotation, you have Infinity, the abstract.

If such be the whole of what is involved in the idea of Infinity, in the case of a line; call it necessary idea, if you will; the idea of it, in the case of surface, and of bulk, is also explained; for surface, and bulk, are only lines, in such and such, or in all directions. The idea of a portion more, adhering, by indissoluble association, to the idea of every increase, in any or in all directions, is the idea of "infinitely extended," and the idea of "infinitely extended," the connotation dropped, is the idea of Infinite Space. It has been called a simple idea (so little has the real nature of it been understood); while it is thus distinctly seen, to be one of the most complex ideas, which the whole train of our conscious being presents. Extreme complexity, with great closeness of association, has this effect—that every particular part in the composition is overpowered by the multitude of all the other parts, and no one in particular stands marked from the rest; but all, together, assume the appearance of ONE. Something perfectly analogous occurs, even in sensation. If two or three ingredients are mixed, as wine and honey, we can distinguish the taste of each, and say it is compound. But if a great many are mixed, we can distinguish no one in particular, and the taste of the whole appears a simple peculiar taste.[1]

1 This explanation of the feeling of Infinity which attaches itself to Space, is one of the most important thoughts in the whole treatise; and, obvious as its truth is to a mind prepared by the previous exposition, it has great difficulty in finding entrance into other minds.

Every object is associated with some position: not always with the same position, but we have never perceived any object, and therefore never think of one, but in some position or other, relative to some other objects. As, from every position, Space extends in every direction (i.e. the unimpeded arm or body can move in any direction), and since we never were in any place which did not admit of motion in every direction from it, when such motion was not arrested by a resistance; every idea of position is irresistibly associated with extension beyond the position: and we can conceive no end to extension, because the place which we try to conceive as its end, raises irresistibly the idea of other places beyond it. This is one of the many so-called Necessities of Thought which are necessities only in consequence of the inseparableness of an association: but which, from unwillingness

This, indeed, is one great cause of the mistakes, which have been committed, in the examination of abstract ideas. We have shewn that they are all complex, and in the highest degree. Yet the greater number of them have always been treated as simple. Mr. Locke shewed that some of them, which he calls mixed modes, were undoubtedly compounded, as obligation, crime, &c. But they are no otherwise complex, than as power, quality, chance, fate, position, and space, are complex.

It is truly remarkable, how many of the cases of indissoluble association are all united in the idea of SPACE. First of all, with the idea of every object, the idea of *position* or *place,* is indissolubly united. Secondly, with the idea of position or place, the idea of *extension* is indissolubly united. Thirdly, with the idea of extension the idea of *infinity* is indissolubly united. Fourthly, by the unfortunate ambiguity of the *Copula,* the idea of *existence* is indissolubly united with SPACE, as with other abstract terms. What these several ingredients, the ideas of Position, Extension, Infinity, Existence, are composed of, we have already seen. All these, forced into combination, by irresistible association, constitute the idea of SPACE.

SECTION V

TIME

As SPACE is a comprehensive word, including all Positions, or the whole of synchronous order; so TIME is a comprehensive word, including all Successions, or the whole of successive order.

The difficulty of the exposition, in this case, consists not in the ideas; for they are clear and certain enough; but in finding expressions which will have even a chance of conveying to readers, who are not familiar with the analysis of mental phenomena, the ideas which it is my object to impart.

As all objects, considered as existing together, are said to exist in SPACE, so all objects considered as existing one after another, are said to exist in TIME.

Objects, however, are said to exist in Time, in two distinguishable cases; either when they are in constant flow; or, when they have, what we call, stability or duration. The constant passage of men, horses, vehicles, &c., in a busy and crowded street, is in Time; the permanence of St. Paul's, in its well-known position, is also in Time. If Time

to admit this explanation, men mistake for original laws of the human mind, and even regard them as the effect and proof of a corresponding necessary connexion between facts existing in Nature.—J.S.M.

mean the succession of the objects in the one case, it must mean something else in the other. It cannot mean the succession of St. Paul's. But it may mean the idea of St. Paul's, associated with the idea of other successions.

Of TIME itself we conceive, that it is never still. It is a perpetual flow of instants, of which only one can ever be present. The very idea of Time, therefore, is an idea of successions. It consists of this, and of nothing else.

But there are no real successions, save successions of objects, that is of feelings in our minds.[1] What, then, are the successions of TIME, which are the successions of nothing? To those who have thoroughly familiarized themselves with the account which we have given of abstract terms, and who can promptly and steadily conceive the mode of their signification, we can render an answer, which will be understood at once, and will be felt to be complete and satisfactory.

We have shewn, how we form the abstracts, redness, from red; sweetness, from sweet; hardness, from hard; by simply dropping the connotation of the concrete term. Thus red, always means something red; redness, is the red without the something; so of sweetness, hardness, and so forth. When the ideas are more complicated, the case is still the same. When we use the concrete, living, it always connotes something living; a living man, a living quadruped, a living bird, fish, insect, and so forth. When we use the abstract, life, we convey all that we convey by the term living, except the connotation. We say that John is healthy, James is healthy, on account of circumstances the idea of which forms a very complex idea. The concrete healthy always connotes an individual. Use the abstract, health, you have the idea without the connotation.

In applying this doctrine to the case of successions, we are ill supplied with appropriate names; and hence the difficulty of the case, both to the teacher, and the learner.

We have said that there are no real successions, but successions of objects. The tickings of my watch are successive sounds, that is, sensations. The beatings which are felt by the physician, in the artery of his patient, are successive feelings or sensations of touch.

---

[1] There is an unusual employment of language here, which if attention is not formally drawn to it, may embarrass the reader. By objects are commonly meant, those groups or clusters of sensations and possibilities of sensation, that compose what we call the external world. A single sensation, even external, and still less if internal, is not called an object. In a somewhat larger sense, whatever we think of, as distinguished from the thought itself and from ourselves as thinking it, is called an object; this is the common antithesis of Object and Subject. But in this place, the author designates as objects, all things which have real existence, as distinguished from the instants of mere Time, which, as he is pointing out, have not; and a puzzling effect is produced by his applying the name Object, in even an especial manner, to sensations: to the tickings of a watch, or the beatings of a patient's pulse.—J.S.M.

When the different particulars of a scene in which a man has been engaged, of a battle, for example, in which he has commanded, pass through his mind, there is a succession of ideas. In all these cases of the successions of sensations, or ideas, there is always one present, others past, and others to come, that is, future. Drop the connotation of "something past," "something present," "something future." You have pastness, presentness, and futureness. But pastness, presentness, and futureness, are TIME. TIME can neither be shewn, nor conceived, to be any thing else. It is a single-worded abstract, involving the meaning of these three several abstracts. The true meaning of these abstracts is clearly made out from their concretes. The precise idea, therefore, marked by the word TIME; if the meaning of these abstracts is sufficiently apprehended; is at last apparent. Nor is there any mysteriousness in it whatsoever, but that which has arisen from misapprehension of that grand department of Naming, which belongs to abstract terms; and from inattention to that class of words, which are invented to supply the place, each of them singly, of several other words.

To our conclusion, that TIME is the equivalent of Pastness, Presentness, and Futureness, combined, it may be objected, that the word Time is applicable to all the three cases; as we can say, past time, present time, and future time, all with equal propriety. This, however, is so far from being any presumption against the conclusion, that it is a clear confirmation of it; since Time, standing by itself, marks no particular case, and, in order to do so, must have another mark applied to it to limit its signification. It is only because Time marks all the cases of pastness, presentness, and futureness, that it needs the marks past, present, or future, to confine its meaning; present time being merely another name for presentness, future time, for futureness, and past time, for pastness. The same thing is seen in the case of all other abstracts. Redness is the name of a certain colour, in all its modifications, and to whatever object belonging. But by the addition of an appropriate mark, we confine its meaning to any particular case; as when we say, the redness of a rose, the redness of scarlet, and so on.

The accounts, which have been rendered of Time by different philosophers, so far as they have in them any acknowledged accuracy, are, all of them, parts, and but parts, of the analysis which we have thus been presenting. Dr. Reid says, Memory gives us the conception and belief of finite intervals of duration; and these we enlarge by our mental processes to infinity.[1] We have already seen what Memory is. It is not a faculty, as Dr. Reid supposes, which "gives" any thing; it is an idea, formed by association of the particulars of a certain train; a train of antecedents and consequents, of which the present feeling is

[1] Intellect. Powers. Essay III. Chapter V, p. 583.—James Mill

one extremity. Pastness is included under the term Memory. Memory is the name of a certain whole, and Pastness is the name of a part of that whole. Memory is a connotative term; what it notes, is the antecedence and consequence of the several parts of that which forms the chain of the remembrance; what it connotes, are the feelings themselves, the objects remembered. When what it connotes is left out, and what it notes is retained, we have the idea which is expressed by pastness.

In the chain of memory, consisting of antecedent, antecedent, antecedent, traced back to any length from the present feeling, we call that which immediately precedes the present, the nearest; the next, we call more distant; the next, more distant still; and that, between which and the present feeling the greatest number of successions intervenes, we call the most distant, also the farthest back; but the farthest back of a series of successions, is the oldest, that between which and the present time the greatest length of time has intervened. Greatest length of time, therefore, in this case, is only another name for greatest number of successions.

It has been already seen, that there is nothing in which we are so deeply interested, as an accurate knowledge of the antecedents and consequents, in the midst of which we exist. Of the different innumerable trains of antecedents and consequents which it is important for us carefully to mark, it is observed, that some succeed more quickly, some less. While the long pendulum of an eight-day clock is performing one oscillation, the short pendulum of a table-clock performs two or three.

What that is, to which we give the name of quickness, or slowness, in those successions; in other words, what is the state of consciousness which we have thus occasion to mark; has already been seen. Every succession, observed by us, is a case of sensation and memory; sensation of the consequent, memory of the antecedent. If we have observed simultaneously the oscillations of the two pendulums, mentioned above, we remember two or three antecedent oscillations of the short pendulum, before we get back to one of the long. It is a mere case, therefore, of the greater or less number of antecedents in a chain of memory, expounded in a preceding chapter.

In the knowledge, so important to us, of antecedents and consequents, it is not enough that we know what antecedents are followed by what consequents; much depends upon the quickness or slowness of the successions. It is, therefore, of the highest importance that we should have the means of marking them.

What we do is, to take some well-known case of successions, and to make that a standard, by which to ascertain the rest. We take, for example, the oscillations of a pendulum. So many of these we call a minute. So many minutes we call an hour. These minutes and hours, then, are so many oscillations, that is successions. We call them measures of time. But things are measurable only by parts of themselves; extension by extension, weight by weight, and so on. What is measured by succession, therefore, is itself nothing but succession.

Having assumed a certain case of successions as a standard, and marked it into quantities, by distinctive names, we mark or name all other successions, by the names applied to the standard case. Thus, that grand succession, on which so much of what we are interested in depends, a revolution of the earth upon its own axis, we distinguish, by the term, twenty-four hours; which we also call by the name, day; and afterwards make use of, as a standard, to mark still slower successions, such as a revolution of the moon about the earth, a revolution of the earth about the sun. In all these measurements, and expressions, of time, it is still seen, that there is nothing in reality conceived but successions.

Beside the standards, more distinctly conceived and expressed, there is always, in these estimates of time, a tacit reference to another standard, which is regarded as the unit, or minimum of time. The case here is precisely analogous to that of the unit, or minimum, of extension, which we have already observed. Our tactual, and muscular, senses are not sufficiently fine to discern objects of less than a certain magnitude. The least which they can discern is tacitly assumed as the unit of extension. Nor are any of our senses fine enough to discern successions which have more than a certain degree of rapidity. Thus, if the seven primitive colours are made to pass with a certain velocity before the eye, they do not appear separate, but blended into one continuous white. In like manner, if sounds are made to succeed one another, at first, slowly, afterwards, with greater and greater rapidity, they cannot, at last, be distinguished as different sounds, but appear as one continuous sound. In fact, this is probably the account of all sounds, which are merely effects of the vibrations in the air, and therefore pulses; but often so quick, in succession, that no interval is distinguishable, and the perception is that of a continuous sound.

The close resemblance, in this respect, between sensations and ideas, is remarkable. When sensations are brought into close conjunction they become blended, and appear, not several, but one. We have seen, in a most important case of association, that when ideas are called up together in close conjunction, they, too, cease to be distinguishable, and, being blended together, assume, even when there is the greatest complexity, the appearance, not of many ideas, but of one. Of this we have very remarkable examples, in the two cases of SPACE, and TIME. . . .

CHAPTER XXV

INTENTION

The word "intend," the concrete, seems to be employed on two occasions. 1. We are said to intend, or not to intend, certain actions of our own. 2. And we are said to intend, or not to intend, certain consequences of our own actions.

We have to examine what is the state of mind which the word designates on each of those occasions.

1. We are said to intend only a *future* action. When the action is immediate, we are not said to INTEND, but to WILL it; an action intended, is an action of ours contemplated as *future,* or certainly to be.

We have minutely analysed, on a former occasion, the state of mind which exists, when events, other than actions of our own, are contemplated as future. An association, from prior habit, exists, between antecedent and consequent, in a series of events; an association, such, that we cannot think of one of the events as existing, without thinking of the others as existing; that is, without anticipating their existence.

That this process is involved in anticipating that peculiar event, called an action of our own, cannot be doubted. The only question is, what are the circumstances from which it derives its peculiar character.

Something peculiar is imparted to it, from the very circumstance of its being an action of our own. In anticipating an action of our own, we necessarily anticipate the mental processes, which are its antecedents. Among these we necessarily anticipate what is called the act of willing. In such anticipations, the association is of that intimate character, which constitutes Belief. In anticipating an action of our own, therefore, we contemplate the act as certainly future; that is, we believe that we shall will it. But to look forward through a certain train of antecedents and consequents, the concluding part of which is a certain act, which we shall then will, and then do, is a process which apparently involves in it all that is meant by what, in this class of cases, we call Intention.

It may still, however, be objected, that the explanation thus presented, recognises, in the state of mind in question, only the ideas involved in the process called willing, with the idea of the action, and the belief that the action will take place; but that there seems to be something more than the present existence of ideas and belief, in that state of mind which we call intending, which seems to partake of the nature of willing at the moment of its existence.

There is something here of the customary illusions of language. The word "intend" is an active verb. And, wherever we use an active verb, we have the association of activity and of willing, involved in it.

That there can be nothing of willing in the case, is abundantly certain; since the will relates only to immediate acts.

It may, however, be objected, that though there is nothing of willing in the case, there is nevertheless a determination or purpose to will. A man may say, I not only believe that I shall act so and so, but I am determined that I shall act so and so.

In this objection, the words "determine," and "determination," are still but substitutes for "intend," and "intention." At most, they only mark a degree of strength in the intention. There is another expression, however, which deserves notice. A man may not only resolve to do a thing, but he may promise to do it. And the promises of men form a very important class of their actions.

After all, a Promise is in its very essence merely the *Declaration* of an *Intention*. If it be asserted that it is not only the declaration of an intention, but the declaration that nothing shall occur to hinder that intention of its effect; what is this but the declaration of another intention; the intention not to frustrate an existing intention? But this second intention is included in the first. The very existence of an intention implies the absence of any counter intention.

Why is it that a man intends? For the same reason, of course, that he wills. In willing, a certain act is contemplated as a cause of pleasure; an immediate act, and an immediate pleasure. In intending, a certain future act is contemplated as cause of a future pleasure. The idea of the pleasure and its cause, united by association, constitute the motive. In this act of anticipation, the sequence, consisting of motive as cause, action as effect, is indissoluble. In our supposed state of intention, the motive is presented to the mind as about to exist at the time in contemplation; the idea of the act as existing irresistibly follows. An act of our own anticipated by irresistible association, when the motive is immediate, is willed; when the motive is future, is intended. Intention is the strong anticipation of a future will. But every thing which strengthens the motive, that is, associates the idea of the act with that of a greater amount of good arising from it, increases the certainty of the act. A promise to perform the act strengthens the motive; in some cases exceedingly. As it is of great consequence to men in general, that promises should be performed, they take care to reward the performing of promises, to punish the non-performing of them, with their favour in the one case, their disfavour in the other. When the favour and disfavour of mankind are general, and strong, to a certain degree, they amount to the highest of all punishments, and all rewards. A promise, then, which is the *declaration* of an intention, greatly strengthens the certainty of the act, by greatly adding to the force of the motive.

2. The next case of the meaning of Intention is of easy explanation. When we will, or when we intend, an action, we either foresee, or do not foresee, certain of its consequences. In what associations the act of foreseeing or anticipating consists, we need not again explain. The question, whether a man did or did not foresee certain consequents of his acts, is of great importance in certain cases of judicature, because upon this circumstance depends the propriety of a less or greater degree of punishment, perhaps the propriety or impropriety of punishing at all.

A person administers to another person a medicine. It turns out to be poison. The person whose act the administration was, believing the drug to be salubrious, not hurtful, anticipated good consequences; in other words, intended the benefit of the patient; intending, and anticipating, here, being only two names for the same thing. He did not foresee the evil consequences; and this we commonly express by saying he did not intend them. If the person who administered the drug, instead of believing it to be a proper medicine, and anticipating from it salutary effects, knew it to be poison, anticipating from it destructive effects, he would be said to intend those effects.

It thus appears, that when a man, having certain consequences of an act in view, proceeds to the performance of the act, the having in view, or anticipating, receives, in these circumstances, the name of intention. It is a case of anticipation, anticipation in peculiar circumstances, and is marked by a peculiar name.

The consequence of an act may be such, that the person had no reason to anticipate them, or could not possibly anticipate them; or they may be such, that, though actually not foreseen, they might, with more or less of care, have been foreseen. These are questions respecting the nature of one solitary act. They are what in law are called questions of fact. The exact determination of them is essential to the right decision of the judge in the particular case; but any further consideration of them is not within the province of this inquiry.

MILL'S WRITINGS

The *Analysis of the Phenomena of the Human Mind,* 2 vol. (London, 1829), appeared in only one other edition, that Edited by J. S. Mill, with notes by A. Bain, A. Findlater, and G. Grote, 2 vol. (London, 1869). The notes are lengthy and voluble. Some critics have said those by the younger Mill are more worth reading than his father's book. *A Fragment on Mackintosh,* first published anonymously (London, 1835), is chiefly of interest in the history of ethical controversy. It is an attack on Mackintosh's criticisms of utilitarian ethics in his *The Progress of Ethical Philosophy* for the *Encyclopaedia Britannica,* 7th edition (1830). Both authors were passionate in their language, and Mill delayed publishing his reply until some years after Mackintosh's death in 1832.

WRITINGS ON MILL

A great deal has been written on James Mill, including an interesting biography by Alexander Bain, the professor of logic at Aberdeen University, distinguished psychologist, and founder of *Mind* in 1876. However, critical treatment of Mill's philosophical views is much slighter in volume. It includes the following: a sensible chapter in *English Psychology* by Th. Ribot (London, 1889); G. S. Bower's *Hartley and James Mill* (London, 1887); an informative but characteristically irritating chapter in James McCosh's *The Scottish Philosophy* (London, 1875); the substantial discussion of the *Analysis* in the volume devoted to James Mill (Vol. II) of *The English Utilitarians,* 3 vol. (London, 1900), by Leslie Stephen; a few useful pages by James Seth in *English Philosophers and Schools of Philosophy* (London, 1912); illuminating treatments in *Brett's History of Psychology,* Edited by R. S. Peters (London, 1953), and H. C. Warren's *A History of the Association Psychology* (New York, 1921); and last but important, the long and many-sided account of Mill in Elie Halévy, *The Growth of Philosophic Radicalism* (London, 1952).

JAMES FREDERICK FERRIER

1808–1864

The man who thought labor "is the standard which measures the value of truth" also produced a theory of ignorance and introduced the word "epistemology" into English. He was the son of a successful Edinburgh solicitor and was given a good classical education in Scotland and in Greenwich. For two years, 1825–26, he attended Edinburgh University, but then transferred to Magdalen College, Oxford, and graduated with an arts degree in 1831. He was admitted to the Scottish bar in the following year. However, he had become friendly with Sir William Hamilton, who later became professor of logic and metaphysics at Edinburgh, and Ferrier, under his influence, took up the study of philosophy instead of practicing law. In 1834 he went to Heidelberg for a few months to read German philosophy and literature, an interest which he retained throughout his life. He married in 1837 the daughter of his uncle, John Wilson—well known as a writer, critic, and literary philosopher under the pen name "Christopher North"—who had defeated Hamilton for the chair of Moral Philosophy at Edinburgh on the death of Thomas Brown.

Ferrier began publishing in 1838; his long series of papers "Introduction to the Philosophy of Consciousness" appeared in *Blackwood*'s magazine and immediately established a considerable reputation for him. In 1842 he was made professor of Civil History at Edinburgh, substituted for Hamilton during the latter's illness in 1844–45; and then became professor of Moral Philosophy and Political Economy at St. Andrews. There he remained for the rest of his life, although he tried unsuccessfully to obtain the Edinburgh chair resigned by his uncle in 1852, and the chair left vacant by Hamilton's death in 1856. A popular lecturer, absorbed in his university work, Ferrier seldom left St. Andrews. The book for which he has been most widely known, *Institutes of Metaphysic,* came out in 1854. Two years later Ferrier replied to some criticisms of it in *Scottish Philosophy, the Old and the New.* After his uncle's death, Ferrier edited Wilson's literary manuscripts and continued to produce his own literary pieces and translations. In 1861 he had a heart attack from which he never fully recovered, but he lectured intermittently in his own home until death.

The philosophical writings of Ferrier fall into two distinct groups. There are, first, the early papers he wrote before becoming settled at St. Andrews, and second, the published lectures resulting from his work there. The differences between the early and later publications are important. Some critics have preferred the former; and at least one of them has suggested that the intellectual isolation of St. Andrews made Ferrier's thought deteriorate in quality. To the early period belong the articles from *Blackwood*'s magazine: "Introduction to the Philosophy of Consciousness," parts I–VII; "The Crisis of Modern Speculation," (1841); the three articles reprinted here; and the long review of Hamilton's 1846 edition of Reid's *Works*, "Reid and the Philosophy of Common Sense." To the later period belong the *Institutes of Metaphysic*, the *Scottish Philosophy*—published posthumously in 1866—*Lectures on Early Greek Philosophy*, and four miscellaneous lectures dating from 1847 onward.

Ferrier was a critic of George Berkeley and Thomas Reid, a reader of Kant, and a somewhat reluctant admirer of Hegel. Some nineteenth-century Germans praised Ferrier as doing "battle against the stream of shallow empiricism which English philosophy still follows." What Ferrier did battle against in his later period was the view, descended from Locke and Hume, that all our mental states can be constructed out of two sorts of elementary units—sensations and their residual copies, ideas—with the aid of the principle of association. This view, thought Ferrier, led to the absurd conclusion that we could have no knowledge of the external world or of ourselves, since we were then forced to make the inference that our sensations and ideas had unknowable causes, external and internal. For this reason Ferrier's own theory of knowledge in the *Institutes* begins with the proposition, taken to be necessarily true, that all knowledge is also self-knowledge: "Along with whatever any intelligence knows, it must, as the ground or condition of its knowledge, have some cognisance of itself." From this Ferrier tried to produce a deductive set of necessary truths elaborating the claim that the unit of knowledge is always a mind standing in some psychological relation to an object.

However, in his earlier days, as in the writings given here, Ferrier was an ingenious empiricist who was interested in the origins of our self-knowledge. He discusses this in connection with the way in which we learn to distinguish the activity of each sense organ from the properties about which it provides information. He argues that in each case we learn to distinguish between the process of sensing and that which is sensed by using other sense organs to make the distinction. We learn to project greenness on to the grass because we can cover our eyes with our hands and make the grass disappear. From the sense of touch we learn that the presence of an eyeball is a general condition of our seeing anything. The importance of Ferrier's attempt to describe the process by which we correlate the information given by our various sense organs is undoubted. Its appreciation is hindered, although not thwarted, by the gesticulatory mannerisms of Ferrier's style—once much admired, but now seen as an unhappy side effect of his tendency to relapse from the philosophy of Scottish common sense into that of Hamiltonian metaphysics.

While Ferrier is commonly known, from his *Institutes,* as the first of the British absolute idealists, he produced no followers. It was left to the later Idealists like Edward Caird, T. H. Green, and F. H. Bradley, to do that. Ferrier's early writings were, until recently, obscured by the deficiencies of his more ambitious later work.

SELECTIONS FROM

Lectures on Greek Philosophy
and Other Philosophical Remains*

✳

BERKELEY AND IDEALISM

. . . We shall now proceed to make a few remarks on the work which stands at the head of the present article, Mr Bailey's 'Review of Berkeley's Theory of Vision,' [1] in which he endeavours "to show the unsoundness of that celebrated speculation."

Mr Bailey is favourably known to the literary portion of the community as the author of some ingenious 'Essays on the Formation and Publication of Opinions,' and he is doubtless a very clever man. But in the work before us, we must say that he has undertaken a task far beyond his powers, and that he has most signally failed, not because these powers are in themselves feeble, but because they have been misdirected against a monument—*ære perennius*—of solid and everlasting truth. The ability displayed in the execution of his work is immeasurably greater than the success with which it has been crowned.

Therefore, when we say that, in our opinion, Mr Bailey's work has

---

* Vol. II. Edited by Sir Alexander Grant and E. L. Lushington (Edinburgh and London, 1883).
[1] London, 1842. Ed.

been anything but successful in its main object, we can at the same time conscientiously recommend a careful perusal of it to those who are interested in the studies of which it treats. Its chief merit appears to us to consist in this, that it indicates with sufficient clearness the difference between the entire views advocated by Berkeley himself on the subject of vision, and the partial views which it has suited the purposes or the ability of his more timid but less cautious followers to adopt. We shall immediately have occasion to speak of the respects in which the disciples have deserted the principles of the master; but let us first of all state the precise question at issue. There is not much fault to be found with the terms in which Mr Bailey has stated it, and therefore we cannot do better than make use of his words.

"Outness," says he, p. 13, "distance, real magnitude, and real figure, are not perceived (according to Berkeley's theory) immediately by sight, but, *in the first place,* by the sense of feeling or touch; and it is from experience alone that our visual sensations come to suggest to us these exclusively tangible properties. We, in fact, see *originally* nothing but various coloured appearances, which are felt as internal sensations; and we learn that they are external, and also what distances, real magnitudes, and real figures these coloured appearances indicate, just as we learn to interpret the meaning of the written characters of a language. Thus a being gifted with sight, but destitute of the sense of touch, would have no perception of outness, distance, real magnitude, and real figure. Such is Berkeley's doctrine stated in the most general terms."

We beg the reader particularly to notice that the distance and outness here spoken of are the distance and outness of an object from the eye of the beholder; for Mr Bailey imagines, as we shall have occasion to show, that Berkeley holds that another species of outness, namely, the outness of one visible thing from other visible things, is not immediately perceived by sight. This latter opinion, however, is certainly not maintained by Berkeley, and the idea that it is so is, we think, the origin of the greater part of Mr Bailey's mistakes. The only other remark which we think it necessary to make on this exposition is, that we slightly object to the words which we have marked in italics, *"in the first place,"* for they seem to imply that outness, &c., are perceived by sight in the *second* or in the *last* place. But Berkeley holds—and in this opinion we agree with him—that they are never perceived *at all* by the sense of *sight,* properly so called. The same objection applies to the word *"originally,"* where it is said that we "see originally nothing but various coloured appearances," for it seems to imply that *ultimately* we come to *see more* than various coloured appearances. But this, following Berkeley's footsteps, we deny that we ever do. In other respects we think that the statement is perfectly correct and unobjectionable.

As a further statement and abstract of the theory, Mr Bailey proceeds to quote Berkeley's own words, in which he says "that distance or outness" (*i.e.,* outness from the eye) "is neither immediately of itself perceived by sight, nor yet apprehended and judged of by lines and angles, or anything that hath a necessary connection with it; but that it is only *suggested* to our thoughts by certain visible ideas and sensations attending vision, which, in their own nature, have no manner of similitude or relation either with distance or things placed at a distance. But, by a connection taught us by experience, they (viz., *visible ideas and visual sensations*) come to signify and suggest them (viz., *distance, and things placed at a distance*) to us after the same manner that words of any language suggest the ideas they are made to stand for. Insomuch that a man born blind, and afterwards made to see, would not at first sight think the things he saw to be without his mind, or at any distance from him." Such is an outline of the theory which Mr Bailey undertakes to controvert.

In laying the groundwork of his objections, he first of all proceeds —and we think this the most valuable observation in his book—to point out the distinction between two separate opinions which may be entertained with regard to the outness of visible objects. The one opinion is, that sight is unable to determine that visible objects are external, or at any distance *at all* from the eye: the other opinion is, that sight, though gifted with the capacity of determining that all visible objects are at *some* distance from the eye, is yet unable to determine the relative distances at which they stand towards it and towards one another. In the words of Mr Bailey, "Whether objects are seen to be external, or at *some* distance, is one question altogether distinct from the inquiry—whether objects are seen by the unassisted vision to be at *different* distances from the percipient." He then adds, "Yet Berkeley uniformly assumes them to be the same, or at least takes it for granted that they are to be determined by the same arguments." This is true enough in one sense, but Mr Bailey should have considered that if Berkeley did not make the discrimination, it was because he conceived that the opinion which maintained the absolute non-externality of visible objects (*i.e.,* of objects in relation to the organ of sight) was the only question properly at issue. The remark, however, is valuable, because Berkeley's followers, Reid, Stewart, and others, have supposed that the other question was the one to be grappled with; and, accordingly, they have not ventured beyond maintaining that the eye is unable to judge of the *different degrees* of distance at which objects may be placed from it. But the thorough-going opinion is the true one, and the followers have deserted their leader only to err, or to discover truths of no scientific value or significance whatever.

Let us now consider the general object which Berkeley had in view, and determine the proper point of sight from which his "theory of vision" should be regarded. We have already remarked that it was but the stepping-stone or prelude to those maturer and more extended doctrines of idealism in which his genius afterwards expatiated, and which have made his name famous throughout every corner of the philosophic world; and which we have endeavoured to do justice to in the preceding pages, giving a more enlarged and unobjectionable construction to their principle, and clearing, we think, at least some of the difficulties which beset his statement of it. His theory of vision may be called an essay on the idealism of the eye, and of the eye alone. It is idealism restricted to the consideration of this sense, and is the first attempt that ever was made to embody a systematic and purely speculative critique of the facts of seeing. We use the words *purely speculative* in contradistinction from geometrical and physiological critiques of the same sense; of which there were abundance in all languages, but which, proceeding on mathematical or anatomical *data,* which are entirely *tactual,* had, in Berkeley's opinion, nothing whatever to do with the science of *optics,* properly so called. Optics, as hitherto treated, that is to say, as established on mathematical principles, appeared to him to be a false science *of vision;* for this reason, that the blind were found to be just as capable of understanding and appreciating it, as those were who could see. Hence he concluded, and most justly, that the true facts of sight had been left out of the estimate, because these were, and necessarily must be, facts which no blind person could form any conception of. He accordingly determined to construct, or at least to pave the way towards the construction of, a truer theory of vision, in which these—the proper and peculiar facts of the sense—should be taken exclusively into account: and hence, passing from the mathematical and physiological method, he took up a different, and what we have called a purely speculative ground—a ground which cannot be rendered intelligible or conceivable to the blind, inasmuch as they are deficient in the sense which alone furnishes the *data* that are to be dealt with. The test by which Berkeley tried optical science was, Can the blind be brought to understand, or to form any conception of it? If they can, then the science *must* be false, for it ought to be a science of experiences from which they are entirely debarred. We should bear in mind, then, first of all, that his object in constructing his theory of vision was, leaving all geometrical and anatomical considerations out of the question, to apprehend the proper and peculiar facts of *sight*—the facts, the whole facts, and *nothing but* the facts, of that particular and isolated sense.

Now we think that Mr Bailey's leading error consists in his not having remarked the unswerving devotedness with which Berkeley follows out this aim; and hence, having failed to appreciate the singleness and unrelaxing perseverance of his purpose, he has consequently failed to appreciate the great success which has attended his endeavours. He has not duly attended or done justice to the pertinacity with which Berkeley adheres to the facts of vision cut off from all the other knowledge of which our other senses are the inlets. In studying the science of vision, the eye of his mind has not been "single"; and hence his mind has not been "full of light." He does not himself appear to have experimentally verified the pure facts of the virgin eye as yet unwedded to the touch. He has not formed to himself a clear conception of the absolute distinction between these two senses and their respective objects—a distinction upon the clear apprehension of which the whole intelligibility of Berkeley's assertions and reasonings depends.

In proof of what we aver, let us turn to the consideration of one fact which Berkeley has largely insisted on as the fundamental fact of the science. Colour, says the Bishop, is the proper and only object of vision, and the *outness* of this object (*i.e.,* its outness from the eye) is *not* perceived by sight. Upon which Mr Bailey, disputing the truth of the latter fact, remarks,—"On turning to Berkeley's essay, we find literally no arguments which specifically apply to this question; nothing but bare assertion repeated in various phrases." This is undoubtedly too true—and perhaps Berkeley is to be condemned for having left his assertion so destitute of the support of reasoning. But he saw that he had stated a fact which he himself had verified, and perhaps he did not think it necessary to prove it to those who had eyes to see it for themselves; perhaps he was unable to prove it. But, at any rate, Mr Bailey's complaint shows that he is deficient in that speculative sense which enables a man to see that to be a fact which is a fact, and to explicate its reason, even when no *rationale* of it has been given by him who originally promulgated it. This reason we shall now endeavour to supply. Let us ask, then, What do we mean when we say that a colour is *seen* to be external? We mean that it is seen to be external to *some other colour* which is before us. Thus we say that white is external to black, because we see it to be so. It is *only* when we can make a comparison between two or more colours that we can say that they are seen to be external—*i.e.,* external to each other. But if there were no colour but one before us, not being able to make any comparison, we should be unable by sight to form any judgment at all about its outness, or to say that we *saw* it to be out of anything. For what would it *be seen* to be out of? Out of the eye or the mind, you say. But you do not see the colour of the eye or of the mind—and therefore you have no ground whatever afforded you on which, instructed by the sense of sight, you can form your judgment. You have no other colour with which to compare it, and therefore, as a comparison with other colours is necessary before you can say that any one of them is *seen* to be external, you cannot predicate visible outness of it at all.

Nor does it make any difference how numerous soever the colours before you may be. You can predicate outness of them all in relation to each other; but you can predicate nothing of the sort with regard to any of them in relation to your eye or to your mind, for you have no colour of your eye or mind before you with which you can compare them, and *out* of which, in virtue of that comparison, you can say that they *visibly* exist. Doubtless, if you saw the colour of your own eye, you could then say that other visible objects, that is, other colours, were seen to be external to it. But, as you never see this, you have nothing left for it but even now to accept the fact as Berkeley laid it down, coupled with the reasoning by which we have endeavoured to explain and expiscate it. But the *touch!* Does not the touch enable us to form a judgment with respect to the outness of objects from the eye? Undoubtedly it does—as Berkeley everywhere contends. But the only question at present at issue is, Does the sight?—and the *fact* established beyond all question by the foregoing reasoning is, that it *does not.*

What makes people so reluctant and unwilling to accept this fact is, that they suppose we are requiring them to believe that visible objects, that is, colours, are not seen to be external to their own visible bodies; that, for instance, a colour, at the other end of the room, is not seen to be external to their hand, or the point of their own nose. They think that when such a colour is said not to be seen to be external to the eye, that we are maintaining that they must see it to be in close proximity to their own visible nose or eyebrows. But, in truth, we are maintaining no position so completely at variance with the fact, and we are requiring of them no such extravagant and impossible belief. As well might they conceive that we are inclined to maintain that the chairs are not seen to be external to the table. Now, on the contrary, we hold it to be an undeniable fact (and so does Berkeley), that all visible objects are seen to be external, and at a distance from one another; that objects at the end of the street, or at the end of the great ranges of astronomy, are all seen to be very far removed from the visible features of our own faces; but we deny that these objects, and our own noses among the number, are seen to be external, or at any distance at all from our own sight; simply for this reason, that our sight is unable to see itself. How can we *see* a thing to be at any distance whatsoever from a thing which we *don't* see? Suppose a person were privately to bury a guinea somewhere, and then, pointing to St. Paul's, were to ask a friend, How far is my guinea buried from that cathedral? What judgment could the person so interrogated form—what answer could he give? obviously none. The guinea might be buried under St. Paul's foundation—it might be buried at Timbuctoo. There are no *data* furnished, from which a judgment may be formed, and a reply given. In the same way, with regard to sight and its objects; the requisite *data* for a judgment are not supplied to this sense. One *datum* is given, the visible object; but the other necessary *datum* is withheld, namely, the visibleness of the organ itself. Therefore, by sight, we can form no judgment at all with respect to the distance at which objects may be placed from the organ; or perhaps it would be more proper to say, that we do form an obscure judgment, to the effect that all visible objects lie within the sphere of the eye; and that where the object is, there also is the organ which apprehends it. Or, to repeat the proof in somewhat different words, we affirm, that before sight can judge of the distance of objects from itself, or that they are distant at all, it must first *localise* both itself and the object. But it can only localise these two by seeing them, for sight can do nothing except by seeing. But it cannot see both of them; it can only see one of them. Therefore, it cannot localise both of them, and hence the conclusion is driven irresistibly home, that it can form no judgment that they are in any degree distant from one another.

Touching this point Mr Bailey puts forth an averment, which really makes us blush for the speculative capacity of our country. Speaking of the case of the young man who was couched by Cheselden,[1] he remarks, in support of his own doctrine, that visible objects are seen to be external to the sight; and in commenting on the young man's statement, that "he thought all objects whatever touched his eyes as what he felt did his skin," he remarks, we say, upon this, that it clearly proves "visible objects appeared external *even* to his body, *to say nothing of his mind.*" External *even* to his body! Surely Mr Bailey did not expect that the young man was to perceive visible things to be *in* his visible body. Surely he does not think that the hands of Berkeley's argument would have been strengthened by any such preposterous revelation. Surely he is not such a crude speculator as to imagine that the mind is *in* the body, like the brain, the liver, or the lungs; and that to bear out Berkeley's theory, it was necessary that the visible universe, of which the visible body is a part, should be seen to be in this mind internal again in its turn to the visible body. Truly this is ravelling the hank of thought with a vengeance.

Berkeley's doctrine with regard to the outness of visible objects, we would state to be this: All these objects are directly seen to be external to each other, but none of them are seen or can be seen, for the reason above given, to be external to the eye itself. He holds that the knowledge that they are external to the eye—that they possess a real and tangible outness independent of the sight—is entirely brought about by the operation of another sense—the sense of touch. He further maintains that the tactual sensations having been repeatedly ex-

---

[1] William Cheselden (1688–1752), famous as a surgeon and anatomist, published in 1728 a widely read paper of "Some Observations made by a young gentleman who was born blind . . . and was couched between 13 and 14 years of age." Ed.

perienced along with the visual sensations, which yield no such judgment, these visual sensations come at length of themselves, and in the absence of the tactual impressions, to suggest objects as external to the eye, that is, as endowed with real and tangible outness; and so perfect is the association, that the seer seems to originate out of his own native powers, a knowledge for which he is wholly indebted to his brother the toucher.

Now Mr Bailey views the doctrine in a totally different light. According to him Berkeley's doctrine is, that not only the tangible outness of objects, or their distance from the eye, is not immediately perceived by sight, but that not even their visible outness or their distance from one another is so perceived. He thinks that, according to Berkeley, the latter kind of outness is *suggested* by certain "internal feelings"—Heaven knows what they are!—no less than the former. He does not see that this "internal feeling," as he calls it, is itself the very sensation of visible outness as above explained. He seems to think that, according to Berkeley, the eye does not even see visible things to be out of one another—out of our visible bodies for example; but that the disintrication of them is accomplished by a process of suggestion. No wonder that he made dreadful havoc with the Bishop's doctrine of association. The following is his statement of that doctrine:—

"Outness is not immediately perceived by sight, but only suggested to our thoughts by certain visible ideas and sensations attending vision. Berkeley (he continues) thus in fact represents the visual perception of objects as external, to be an instance of the association of ideas. If, however, he had clearly analysed the process in question, he would have perceived the fallacy into which he had fallen. It is impossible that the law of mind, by which one thing suggests another, should produce any such effect as the one ascribed to it. Suppose we have an internal feeling A, which has never been attended with any sensation or perception of outness, and that it is experienced at the same time with the external sensation B. After A and B have been thus experienced together, they will, according to the law of association, suggest each other. When the internal feeling occurs, it will bring to mind the external one, and *vice versa*. But this is all. Let there be a thousand repetitions of the internal feeling with the external sensation, and all that can be effected will be, that the one will invariably suggest the other. Berkeley's theory, however, demands more than this. He maintains that because the internal feeling has been found to be accompanied by the external one, it will, when experienced alone, not only suggest the external sensation, but absolutely be regarded as external itself, or rather be converted into the perception of an external object. It may be asserted, without hesitation, that there is nothing in the whole operations of the human mind analogous to such a process." [1]

There certainly *is* nothing in the mental operations analogous to such a process, and just as little is there anything in the whole writings of Berkeley analogous to such a doctrine. Throughout this statement, the fallacy and the mistake are entirely on the side of Mr Bailey. The "outness" which he here declares Berkeley to hold *as suggested,* he evidently imagines to be *visible* outness: whereas Berkeley distinctly holds that visible outness is never *suggested* by sight at all, or by any "visible ideas or sensations attending vision," and that it is only *tangible* outness which is so suggested. "Sight" (says Berkeley, Works, vol. i. 147) "doth not *suggest* or in any way inform us that the *visible* object we immediately perceive exists *at a distance."* [2] What Berkeley maintains is, that vision with its accompanying sensations suggests to us another kind of outness and of objects which are invisible, and which always remain invisible, but which may be perceived by touch, provided we go through the process necessary for such a perception. He admits the immediate and unsuggested sensation of visible outness in the sense explained above—that all visible things are directly seen to be external to our visible bodies, only denying (and we think we have assigned good grounds for this denial) that any of them *are seen* to be external to our own *invisible* sight. He maintains that this direct sensation of visible outness comes through experience to suggest the perception of a different, namely, of a tangible and invisible, outness. He asserts (we shall here adopt Mr Bailey's language, with some slight variation giving *our* view of the case), that in consequence of there having been a thousand repetitions of the sensation of visible outness with the sensation of tangible outness, the one will invariably suggest the other. And his theory demands no more than this. He never maintains that because the sensation of visible outness—already explained, we beg the reader to keep in mind, as the sensation of visible objects as external to one another, but not as external to the sense perceiving them—he never maintains that because this sensation has been found to be accompanied by the sensation of tangible outness, that it will, when experienced alone, not only suggest the tangible outness, but absolutely be regarded as tangible itself, or be converted into the perception of a tangible object. He never, we say, maintains anything like this, as Mr Bailey represents him to do. It may therefore be asserted with hesitation, that there is nothing in the whole history of philosophical criticism analogous to the blunder of

[1] *A Review of Berkeley's Theory of Vision,* pp. 20–21. Ed.
[2] *Three Dialogues Between Hylas and Philonous,* "First Dialogue"; pp. 412–13 in *Works of George Berkeley,* edited by A. C. Fraser (Oxford, 1901). Ed.

his reviewer. Nothing is easier than to answer a disputant when we confute, as his, a theory of our making.

Berkeley informs us, that visual sensation, that is, the direct perception of the outness of visible things with regard to one another, having been frequently accompanied with sensations of their tactual outness and tactual magnitudes, comes at length, through the law of association, to suggest to us that they are external to the eye, although we never see them to be so; and to suggest this to us, of course as the word suggestion implies, in the absence of the tactual sensations. Thus the visual sensations which, in the absence of the tactual sensations, call up the tactual sensations, resemble a language, the words of which, in the absence of things, call up the ideas of things. Thus the word rose, in the absence of a rose, suggests the idea of that flower; and thus a visible rose, not seen as external to the eye, does, in the absence of a tangible or touched rose, suggest a tangible or touched rose as an object external to the eye. "But," says Mr Bailey, "this comparison completely fails. To make it tally, we must suppose that the audible name, by suggesting the visible flower, becomes itself a visible object." What! does he then suppose that Berkeley holds that the visible flower, by suggesting the tangible flower, becomes itself a tangible object? To make Mr Bailey's objection tell, Berkeley must be represented as holding this monstrous opinion, which he most assuredly never did.

Our limits prevent us from following either Berkeley or his reviewer through the further details of this speculation. But we think that we have pointed out with sufficient distinctness Mr Bailey's fundamental blunder, upon which the whole of his supposed refutation of Berkeley is built, and which consists in this: that he conceives the Bishop to maintain that the perception of visible outness, or the distance of objects among themselves, is as much the result of suggestion as the knowledge of tangible outness, or the distance of objects from the organ of sight. He seems to think Berkeley's doctrine to be this: that our visual sensations are mere internal feelings, in which there is originally and directly no kind of outness at all involved, not even the outness of one visible thing from another visible thing; and that this outness is in some way or other suggested to the mind by these internal feelings. "But," says he, "Berkeley's theory demands more than this; for the internal feeling not only suggests the idea of the external object, but by doing so suggests the idea, or, if I may use figure, infuses the perception of *its own* externality." And he cannot understand how this result should be produced by any process of association. But neither does Berkeley's theory demand that it should, for this "internal feeling" is itself, as we have already remarked, the direct perception of visible outness—that is to say, the outness of objects in relation, for instance, to our own visible bodies—and so far there is no suggestion at all in the case, nor any occasion for any suggestion. Suggestion comes into play when we judge that, over and above the outness of objects viewed in relation to themselves and our visible bodies, there is another kind of outness connected with these objects, namely, their outness in relation to the organ itself which perceives them; and this suggestion takes place only after we have learned, through the experience of touch, to localise that organ. Having thus indicated the leading mistake which lies at the root of Mr Bailey's attempted refutation, we shall bid adieu both to him and Berkeley, and shall conclude by hazarding one or two speculations of our own, in support of the conclusions of the latter.

How do we come to judge that objects are external to the eye as distinguished from our perception, that they are external to one another, and how do we come to judge that they possess a real magnitude quite different from their visible magnitude? These are the two fundamental questions of the Berkeleian optics; and in endeavouring to answer them, we must go to work experimentally, and strive to apprehend the virgin facts of seeing, uncombined with any other facts we may have become acquainted with from other sources. Let us suppose, then, that we are merely an eye, which, however, as it is not yet either tangible or localised, we shall call the soul, the seer. Let this seer be provided with a due complement of objects, which are mere colours in the form of houses, clouds, rivers, woods, and mountains. Everything is excluded but sight and colours. Nothing but pure seeing is the order of the day. Now, here it is obvious that the seer must pronounce itself or its organ to be precisely commensurate in extent with the things seen. It may either suppose the diameter of the landscape to be conformed to the size of its diameter, or it may suppose its diameter conformed to the size of the landscape. It is quite immaterial which it does, but one or other of these judgments it must form. The seer and the seen must be pronounced to be coextensive with one another. No judgment to a contrary effect, no judgment that the organ is infinitely disproportioned to its objects, is as yet possible. Well, we shall suppose that these objects keep shifting up and down within the sphere of the organ, growing larger and smaller, fainter and brighter in colour, and so forth. Still no new result takes place: there is still nothing but simple seeing. Until at length *one particular* bifurcated phenomenon, with black extremities at one end and lateral appendages, each of them terminating in a somewhat broad instrument, with five points of rather a pinky hue, begins to stir. Ha! what's this? This is something new; this is something very different from *seeing*. One of the objects within the sight, one of our own visual phenomena has evolved, by all that's wonderful! a new set of sensations entirely different from anything connected with vision. We will call them muscular sensations. As this is the only one of all the visual phenomena

which has evolved these new sensations, the attention of the seer is
naturally directed to its operations. Let us then attend to it particularly. It moves into close proximity with other visual objects, and here
another new and startling series of sensations ensues, sensations
which our seer never found to arise when any of the other visual phenomena came together. We will call these our sensations of touch.
The attention is now directed more particularly than ever to the proceedings of this bifurcated phenomenon. It raises one of the aforesaid
lateral appendages, and with one of the points in which it terminates,
it feels its way over the other portions of its surface. Certain portions
of this touched surface are not visible; but the seer, by calling into
play the muscular sensations, that is, by moving the upper part of this
phenomenon, can bring many of them within its sphere, and hence the
seer concludes that all of the felt portions would become visible, were
no limit put to these movements and muscular sensations. Very well.
This point, which occupies an infinitely small space among the visual
phenomena, continues its manipulating progress, until it at length
happens to rest upon a very sensitive and orbed surface, about its own
size, situated in the upper part of the bifurcated object. And now what
ensues? Speaking out of the information and experience which we
have as yet acquired, we should naturally say that merely this can
ensue; that if the point (let us now call it our finger) and the orbed
surface on which it rests are out of the sphere of sight, the seer has
nothing to do with it—that it is simply a case of touch: or if the finger
and the surface are within the sphere of sight, that then the finger will
merely hide from our view a surface coextensive with itself, as it does
in other similar instances; and that, in either case, all the other objects
of sight will be left as visible and entire as ever. But no; neither of
these two results is what ensues. What then does ensue? This astound-
ing and almost inconceivable result ensues, that the *whole* visual phenomena are suddenly obliterated as completely as if they had never
been. One very small visible point, performing certain operations
within the eye, and coming in contact with a certain surface as small
as itself, and which must also be conceived as lying within the eye, not
only obliterates that small surface, but extinguishes a whole landscape
which is visibly many million times larger than itself. If this result
were not the fact, it would be altogether incredible. From this moment, then, a new world is revealed to us, in which we find that, instead of the man and all visible objects being in the eye, the eye is in
the man; and that these objects being visibly external to the bifurcated
phenomenon, whose operations we have been superintending, and
which we shall now call *ourselves,* they must consequently be external
(although even yet they are never visibly so) to the eye also. The seer,
the great eye, within which we supposed all this to be transacted,
breaks, as it were, and falls away; while the little surface to which the

forefinger was applied, and which it covered, becomes, and from this time henceforward continues to be, our true eye. Thus, by a very singular process, do we find ourselves, as it were, within our own eye, a procedure which is rescued from absurdity by this consideration, that our eye itself, our tangible eye, is also found within the primary eye, as we may call it, which latter eye falling away when the experience of touch commences, the man and the universe which surrounds him start forth into their true place as external to the seer, and the new secondary eye, revealed by touch, becoming localised, shrinks into its true proportions, now very limited when tactually compared with the objects which fall under its inspection. And all this magical creation— all our knowledge that objects are out of the eye, and that the size of this organ bears an infinitely small proportion to the real magnitude of objects—all this is the work of the touch, and of the touch alone.[1]

Perhaps the following consideration may help the reader to understand how the sight becomes instructed by the touch. Our natural visual judgment undoubtedly is, as we have said, that the eye and the landscape which it sees are precisely coextensive with each other; and the natural conclusion must be, that whatever surface is sufficient to cover the one, must be sufficient to cover the other also. But is this found to be the case? By no means. You lay your finger on your eye, and it completely covers it. You then lay the same finger on the landscape, and it does not cover, perhaps, the hundred millionth part of its surface. Thus are the judgments and conclusions of the eye corrected and refuted by the experience of the finger, until, at length, the eye actually believes that it sees things to be larger than itself; a total mistake, however, on its part, as Berkeley was the first to show; for the object which it seems to see as greatly larger than itself, is only *suggested* by another object which is always smaller than itself. The small visible object suggests the thought of a large tangible object, and the latter it is which chiefly occupies the mind; but still it is never seen, it is merely suggested by the other object which alone is presented to the vision.

By looking through a pair of spectacles, any one may convince himself of the impossibility of our seeing the real and tangible magnitude of things, or of our seeing anything which exceeds the expansion of the retina. A lofty tower, you will say, exceeds the expansion of the retina, certainly a tangible, a *suggested* tower, does so: but does a visible, a seen tower, ever do so? Make the experiment, good reader, and you will find that it never does. Look, then, at this tower from a small distance, through a pair of spectacles, which form a sort of pro-

[1] It may, perhaps, be thought that all this information might be acquired by the simple act of closing our eyelids. But here the tactual sensations are so faint that we might be doubtful whether the veil was drawn over our eye or over the face of things. Our limits prevent us from stating other objections to which this explanation is exposed.

jected retina, not much, if at all, larger than your real retina. At first sight you will probably say that it looks about a hundred feet high, and, at any rate, that you see it to be infinitely larger than your own eye. But look again, attending in some degree to the size of your spectacle glasses, and you shall see that it does not stretch across one half, or perhaps one fourth, of their diameter. And if a fairy pencil, as Adam Smith supposes, were to come between your eye and the glass, the picture sketched by it thereon, answering in the exactest conformity to the dimensions of the tower you see, would be an image, probably not the third of an inch high, or the hundredth part of an inch broad. This is certainly not what you seem to see, but this is certainly what you *do* see. These are the dimensions into which your lofty tower has shrunk. Now is this tower, seen to be one-third of an inch high, and very much smaller than the retina, represented by the spectacles—is this tower another tower, seen to be a hundred feet high, and infinitely larger than the retina, and existing out of the mind *in rerum natura?* or is not the latter tower merely *suggested* by the former ideal one, in consequence of the great disparity which touch, and touch alone, has proved to exist between the thing seeing and the thing seen? Unquestionably the latter view of the matter is the true one; seen objects are always ideal; and always remain ideal; they have no existence *in rerum natura.* They merely suggest other objects of a real, or at least of a tangible kind, with which they have no necessary, but merely an arbitrary connection, established by custom and experience. So much upon the idealism of the eye.

In conclusion, we wish to hazard one remark on the subject of inverted images depicted on the retina. External objects, we are told, are represented on the retina in an inverted position, or with their upper parts pointing downwards. Now, in one sense this may be true, but in another sense it appears to us to be unanswerably false. Every visible object must be conceived as made up of a great number of *minima visibilia,* or smallest visible points. From each of these a cone of rays proceeds, with its base falling on the pupil of the eye. Here the rays are refracted by the humours so as to form other cones, the apices of which are projected on the retina. The cones of rays proceeding from the upper *minima visibilia* of the object are refracted into foci on the lower part of the retina, while those coming from the lower *minima* of the object are refracted into foci on the upper part of the retina. So far the matter is perfectly demonstrable; so far we have an image on the retina, the lower parts of which correspond with the upper parts of the object. But what kind of image is it, what is the nature of the inversion which here takes place? We answer that it is an image in which not one single *minimum* is *in itself* reversed, but in which all the *minima* are transposed merely in relation *to one another.* The inversion regards merely the relative position of the *minima,* and not the *minima* themselves. Thus, the upward part of each *minimum* in the object must also point upwards in the image on the retina. For what principle is there in optics or in geometry, in physiology or in the humours of the eye, to reverse it? We do not see how opticians can dispute this fact, except by saying that these *minima* have *no* extension, and consequently have neither an *up* nor a *down;* but that is a position which we think they will hardly venture to maintain. We can make our meaning perfectly plain by the following illustrative diagram—In the lines of figures,

A	B	C
1	9	6
2	ϛ	5
3	ᚹ	4
4	ε	3
5	ᴢ	2
6	I	1

let the line A be a string of six beads, each of which is a *minimum visibile,* or smallest point from which a cone of rays can come. Now, the ordinary optical doctrine, as we understand it, is, that this string of beads A falls upon the retina in an image in the form of the row of figures B; that is to say, in an image in which the bead 1 is thrown with its head downward on the retina, and all the other beads in the same way with their heads downwards. Now, on the contrary, it appears to us demonstrable, that the beads A must fall upon the retina in an image in the form of the row of figures C; that is to say, in an image in which each particular bead or *minimum* lies with its head upwards upon the retina. In the annexed scheme our meaning, and the difference between the two views, are made perfectly plain; and it is evident, that if the object were reduced to only one *minimum*—the bead 2, for instance—there would be no inversion, but a perfectly erect image of it thrown upon the retina.

Now, there are just five different ways in which the fact we have now stated may be viewed. It is either a fact notoriously announced in all or in most optical works; and if it is so, we are surprised (though our reading has not been very extensive in that way) that we should never have come across it. Or else it is a fact so familiar to all optical writers, and so obvious and commonplace in itself, that they never have thought it necessary or worth their while to announce it. But if this be the case, we cannot agree with them; we think that it is a fact as recondite and as worthy of being stated as many others that are emphatically insisted on in the science. Or else, though neither notorious nor familiar, it may have been stated by some one or by some few optical writers. If so, we should thank any one who would be kind enough to refer us to the works in which it is to be found. Or else, fourthly, it is a false fact, and admits of being demonstrably disproved. If so, we should like to see it done. Or else, lastly, it is true, and a new, and a demonstrable fact; and if so, we now call upon all optical writers, from this time henceforward, to adopt it. We do not pretend to decide which of these views is the true one. We look to Dr Brewster for a reply; for neither his, nor any other man's *rationale* of the inverted images, appears to us to be at all complete or satisfactorily made out without its admission.

MR BAILEY'S REPLY TO AN ARTICLE IN BLACKWOOD'S MAGAZINE

We have just been favoured with a pamphlet from Mr Bailey, entitled 'A Letter to a Philosopher, in Reply to some Recent Attempts to Vindicate Berkeley's Theory of Vision, and in further Elucidation of its Unsoundness.' Our article on Mr Bailey's review of Berkeley's theory, which appeared in 'Blackwood's Magazine' of June 1842, was one of these attempts. Had the author merely attacked or controverted our animadversions on his book, we should probably have left the question to its fate, and not have reverted to a subject, the discussion of which, even in the first instance, may have been deemed out of place in a journal not expressly philosophical. There is, in general, little to be gained by protracting such controversies. But, as Mr Bailey accuses us, in the present instance, of having misrepresented his views, we must be allowed to exculpate ourselves from the charge of having dealt, even with unintentional unfairness, towards one whose opinions, however much we may dissent from them, are certainly entitled to high respect and a candid examination, as the convictions of an able and zealous inquirer after truth.

In our strictures on Mr Bailey's work, we remarked, that he had represented Berkeley as holding that the eye is not directly and originally cognisant of the outness of objects in relation to each other, or of what we would call their reciprocal outness; in other words, we stated that, according to Mr Bailey, Berkeley must be regarded as denying to the eye the original intuition of space, either in length, breadth, or solid depth. It was, however, only in reference to one of his arguments, and to one particular division of his subject, that we laid this representation to his charge. Throughout the other parts of his discussion, we by no means intended to say that such was the view he took of the Berkeleian theory. Nor are we aware of having made any statement to that effect. If we did, we now take the opportunity of remarking, that we restrict our allegation, as we believe we formerly restricted it, to the single argument and distinction just mentioned, and hereafter to be explained.

In his reply, Mr Bailey disavows the impeachment *in toto.* He declares that he never imputed to Berkeley the doctrine, that the eye is not directly percipient of space in the two dimensions of length and breadth. "The perception of this kind of distance," says he, "never formed the subject of controversy with any one. . . . That we see extension in two dimensions is admitted by all."—('Letter,' p. 10.) If it can be shown that the doctrine which is here stated to be admitted by all philosophers, is yet expressly controverted by the two metaphysicians whom Mr Bailey appears to have studied most assiduously, it is, at any rate, possible that he may have overlooked, in his own writings, the expression of an opinion which has escaped his penetration in theirs. To convince himself, then, how much he is mistaken in supposing that the visual intuition of longitudinal and lateral extension is admitted by all philosophers, he has but to turn to the works of Dr Brown and the elder Mill. In arguing that we have no immediate perception of visible figure, Dr Brown not only virtually, but expressly, asserts that the sight has no perception of extension in any of its dimensions. Not to multiply quotations, the following will, no doubt, be received as sufficient:—"They (*i.e.,* philosophers) have—*I think without sufficient reason*—universally supposed that the superficial extension of *length and breadth* becomes known to us by sight originally." [1] Dr Brown then proceeds to argue, with what success we are not at present considering, that our knowledge of extension and figure is derived from another source than the sense of sight.

Mr James Mill, an author whom Mr Bailey frequently quotes with approbation, and in confirmation of his own views, is equally explicit. He maintains, in the plainest terms, that the eye has no intuition of space, or of the reciprocal outness of visible objects. "Philosophy," says he, "has ascertained that we derive nothing from the eye whatever but sensations of colour; that the idea of extension [he means in its three dimensions] is derived from sensations not in the eye, but in the muscular part of our frame." [2] Thus, contrary to what Mr Bailey affirms, these two philosophers limit the office of vision to the perception of mere colour or difference of colour, denying to the eye the original perception of extension in any dimension whatever. In their estimation, the intuition of space is no more involved in our perception of different colours than it is involved in our perception of different smells or different sounds. Dr Brown's doctrine, in which Mr Mill seems to concur, is, that the perception of superficial extension no more results from a certain expanse of the optic nerve being

[1] Brown's "Lectures," Lecture XXVIII. [Thomas Brown, *Lectures on the Philosophy of the Human Mind* (Edinburgh, 1820), Vol. II, p. 66. Ed.]
[2] Mill's "Analysis," Vol. I, p. 73. [Analysis of the Phenomena of the Human Mind (London, 1829). Ed.]

affected by a variety of colours than it results from a certain expanse of the olfactory nerve being affected by a variety of odours.[1] So much for Mr Bailey's assertion, that *all* philosophers admit the perception of extension in two dimensions.

But, of course, our main business is with the expression of his own opinion. In rebutting our charge, he maintains that "the visibility of angular distance (that is, of extension laterally) is assumed, by implication, as part of Berkeley's doctrine, in *almost* every chapter of my book."—('Letter,' p. 13.) That word *almost* is a provident saving clause; for we undertake to show that not only is the very reverse assumed, by implication, as part of Berkeley's doctrine, in the *single* chapter to which we confined our remarks, but that, in another part of his work, it is expressly avowed as the only alternative by which, in the author's opinion, Berkeley's consistency can be preserved.

At the outset of his inquiry, Mr Bailey divides his discussion into two branches: first, Whether objects are originally seen to be external, or at *any* distance at all from the sight; and, secondly, Supposing it admitted that they are seen to be external, or at *some* distance from the sight, whether they are all seen in the same plane, or equally near. It was to the former of these questions that we exclusively confined our remarks,[2] and it was in reference to it, and to an important argument evolved by Mr Bailey in the course of its discussion, that we charged him with fathering on Berkeley the doctrine which he now disavows as his interpretation of the Bishop's opinion. He further disputes the relevancy of the question about our perception of lateral extension, and maintains that distance in a direction from the percipient, or what we should call protensive distance, is the only matter in

---

[1] This reasoning of Dr. Brown's is founded upon an assumed analogy between the structure of the optic nerve, and the structure of the olfactory nerves and other sensitive nerves, and is completely disproved by the physiological observations of Treviranus, who has shown that no such analogy exists: that the ends of the nervous fibres in the retina, being elevated into distinct separate *papillæ*, enable us to perceive the extension and discriminate the position of visible bodies; while the nerves of the other senses, being less delicately defined, are not fitted to furnish us with any such perception, or to aid us in making any such discrimination. See "Müller's Physiology," translated by W. Baly, M.D., Vol. II, pp. 1073–74. [Johannes Peter Müller, *Handbuch der Physiologie des Menschen* (1833–40); London (1842). Ed.] Although the application of Treviranus's discovery to the refutation of Dr. Brown's reasoning is our own, we may remark, in justice to an eminent philosopher, that it was Sir William Hamilton who first directed our attention to the *fact* as established by that great physiologist.

[2] Mr. Bailey seems disposed to carp at us for having confined our remarks to this first question, and for not having given a more complete review of his book. But the reason why we cut short our critique is obvious; for if it be proved, as we believe it can, that objects are originally seen at *no distance whatever* from the sight, it becomes quite superfluous to inquire what appearance they would present if originally seen at *some* distance from the sight. The way in which we disposed of the first question, however imperfect our treatment of it may have been, necessarily prevented us from entering upon the second; and our review, with all its deficiencies, was thus a complete review of his book, though not a review of his complete book.

dispute; and that it is a misconception of the scope of Berkeley's essay to imagine otherwise. The relevancy of the question shall be disposed of afterwards. In the meantime, the question at issue is, Can the allegation which we have laid to Mr Bailey's charge be proved to be the fact, or not?

In discussing the first of the two questions, it was quite possible for Mr Bailey to have represented Berkeley as holding, that visible objects, though not seen to be external to the sight, were yet seen to be out of each other, or laterally extended within the organism or the mind. But Mr Bailey makes no such representation of the theory, and the whole argument which pervades the chapter in which the first question is discussed, is founded on the negation of any such extension. All visible extension, he tells us, must, in his opinion, be either plane or solid. Now he will scarcely maintain that he regarded Berkeley as holding that we perceive solid extension within the organism of the eye. Neither does he admit that, according to Berkeley, and in reference to this first question, plane extension is perceived within the organism of the eye. For when he proceeds to the discussion of the *second* of the two questions, he remarks that "we must, *at this stage* of the argument, consider the theory under examination, as representing that we see all things *originally in the same plane;*" [1] obviously implying that he had not *as yet* considered the theory as representing that we see things originally in the same plane: in other words, plainly admitting that, in his treatment of the first question, he had not regarded the theory as representing that we see things originally under the category of extension at all.

But if any more direct evidence on this point were wanted, it is to be found in the section of his work which treats of "the perception of figure." In the chapter in which he discusses the first of the two questions, he constantly speaks of Berkeley's theory as representing that "our visual sensations, or what we ultimately term visible objects, are originally mere internal feelings." The expression *mere internal feelings,* however, is ambiguous; for, as we have said, it might still imply that Mr Bailey viewed the theory as representing that there was an extension, or reciprocal outness of objects within the retina. But this doubt is entirely removed by a passage in the section alluded to, which proves that, in Mr Bailey's estimation, these mere internal feelings not only involve no such extension, but that there would be an inconsistency in supposing they did. In this section he brings forward Berkeley's assertion, "that neither solid nor plane figures are immediate objects of sight." He then quotes a passage in which the Bishop begs the reader not to stickle too much "about this or that phrase, or manner of expression, but candidly to collect his meaning from the whole sum and tenor of his discourse." And then Mr Bailey goes on

[1] "Review of Berkeley's Theory," p. 35.

to say, "Endeavouring, in the spirit here recommended, to collect the author's meaning when he affirms that the figures we see are neither plane nor solid, it appears to me to be *a part or consequence* of his doctrine already examined, which asserts that visible objects are only internal feelings." [1] We can now be at no loss to understand what Mr Bailey means, and conceives Berkeley to mean, by the expression "mere internal feelings." He evidently means feelings in which no kind of extension whatever is involved: for, in the next page, he informs us that all visual extension, or extended figure, *"must* be apprehended as either plane or solid, and that it is impossible even to conceive it otherwise." Consequently, if the figures we see are, as Berkeley says, apprehended neither as plane nor as solid, Mr Bailey, entertaining the notions he does on the subject of extension, *must* regard him as holding that they cannot be apprehended as extended at all; and accordingly such is the express representation he gives of the theory in the passage just quoted, where he says that "the doctrine of Berkeley, which affirms that the figures we see are neither plane nor solid [that is, are extended in *no* direction, according to Mr Bailey's ideas of extension], appears to him to be *a part* of the doctrine which asserts that visible objects are only internal feelings." Now if that be not teaching, in the plainest terms, that, according to Berkeley, no species of extension is implied in the internal feelings of vision, we know not what language means, and any one thought may be identical with its very opposite.

Here we might let the subject drop, having, as we conceive, said quite enough to prove the truth of our allegation that, in reference to the first question discussed, in which our original visual sensations are represented by Berkeley to be mere internal feelings, Mr Bailey understood and stated those feelings to signify sensations in which no perception of extension whatever was involved. However, as Mr Bailey further remarks that, "although Berkeley's doctrine about visible figures being neither plane nor solid, is thus consistent with his assertion that they are internal feelings, it is in itself contradictory," [2] we shall contribute a few remarks to show that while, on the one hand, the negation of extension is not required to vindicate the consistency of Berkeley's assertion, that visible objects are internal feelings, neither, on the other hand, is there any contradiction in Berkeley's holding that objects are not seen either as planes or as solids, and are yet apprehended as extended. Mr Bailey alleges that we are "far more successful in involving ourselves in subtle speculations of our own, than in faithfully guiding our readers through the theories of other philosophers." Perhaps in the present case we shall be able to thread a labyrinth where our reviewer has lost his clue, and, in spite of

1 "Review of Berkeley's Theory," p. 136.
2 "Review of Berkeley's Theory," p. 137.

the apparent contradiction by which Mr Bailey has been gravelled, we shall, perhaps, be more successful than he in "collecting Berkeley's meaning from the whole sum and tenor of his discourse."

First, with regard to the contradiction charged upon the Bishop. When we open our eyes, what do we behold? We behold points—*minima visibilia*—out of one another. Do we see these points to be in the same plane? Certainly not. If they are in the same plane, we learn this from a very different experience from that of sight. Again, do we see these points to be *not* in the same plane? Certainly not. If the points are not in the same plane, we learn this too from a very different experience than that of sight. All that we see is, that the points are out of one another; and this simply implies the perception of extension, without implying the perception either of plane or of solid extension. Thus, by the observation of a very obvious fact, which, however, Mr Bailey has overlooked, is Berkeley's assertion that visible objects are apprehended as extended, and yet not apprehended either as planes or solids, relieved from every appearance of contradiction.

It must, however, be admitted that Mr Bailey has much to justify him in his opinion that extension must be apprehended either as plane or as solid. None of Berkeley's followers, we believe, have ever dreamt of conceiving it otherwise; and, finding in their master's work the negation of solid extension specially insisted on, they leapt to the conclusion that the Bishop admitted the original perception of plane extension. But Berkeley makes no such admission. He places the perception of plane extension on precisely the same footing with that of solid extension. "We see planes," says he, "in the same way that we see solids." [1] And the wisdom of the averment is obvious; for the affirmation of plane extension involves the negation of solid extension, but this negation involves the conception (visually derived) of solid extension; but the admission of that conception, so derived, would be fatal to the Berkeleian theory. Therefore its author wisely avoids the danger by holding that in vision we have merely the perception of what the Germans would call the *Auseinanderseyn,* that is, the *asunderness,* of things—a perception which implies no judgment as to whether the things are secerned in plane or in protensive space.

With regard to the supposition that, in order to preserve Berkeley's consistency, it was necessary for him to teach that our visual sensations (colours namely), being internal feelings, could involve the perception neither of plane nor of solid extension—that is to say, of no extension at all, according to Mr Bailey's ideas—we shall merely remark that there appears to us to be no inconsistency in holding, as Berkeley does, that these colours, though originally internal to the sight, are nevertheless perceived as extended among themselves.

We shall now say a few words on the *relevancy* of the question, for

[1] Essay, Section 158.

Mr Bailey denies that this question concerning the reciprocal outness of visible objects ought to form any element in the controversy. We shall show, however, that one of his most important arguments depends entirely on the view that may be taken of this question; and that while the argument alluded to would be utterly fatal to Berkeley's theory, if the perception of reciprocal outness were denied, it is perfectly harmless if the perception in question be admitted.

Mr Bailey's fundamental and reiterated objection to Berkeley's theory is, that it requires us to hold that conceptions or past impressions derived from one sense (the touch) are not merely recalled when another sense (the sight) executes its functions, but are themselves absolutely converted into the present intuitions of that other sense. In his own words ('Review,' p. 69), the theory is said to require "a transmutation of the conceptions derived from touch into the perceptions of sight." "According to Berkeley," says he ('Review,' p. 22), "an internal feeling (*i.e.,* a visual sensation) and an external sensation (*i.e.,* a tactual sensation) having been experienced at the same time: the internal feeling, when it afterwards occurs, not only suggests the idea, but, by doing so, suggests the idea, or, if I may use the figure, infuses the perception of its own externality. Berkeley thus attributes to suggestion an effect contrary to its nature, which, as in the case of language, is simply to revive in our conception what has been previously perceived by the sense."

Now, this objection would be altogether insurmountable if it were true, or if it were a part of Berkeley's doctrine, that the sight has no original intuition of space or of the reciprocal outness of its objects—in other words, of colours out of colours; for it being admitted that the sight has ultimately such a perception, it would be incumbent on the Berkeleian to show how conceptions derived from another sense, or how perceptions belonging to another sense, could be converted into that perception. We agree with Mr Bailey in thinking that no process of association could effect this conversion; that if we did not originally see colours to be out of each other, and the points of the same colour to be out of each other, we could never so see them; and that his argument, when thus based on the negation of all original visual extension, and on the supposition that the touch is the sole organ of every species of externality, would remain invulnerable.

But, with the admission of the visual intuition of space, the objection vanishes, and the argument is shorn of all its strength. This admission relieves the theory from the necessity of maintaining that conceptions derived from touch are transmuted into the perceptions of sight. It attributes to the sight all that ever truly belongs to it—namely, the perception of colours out of one another; it provides the visual intuitions with an externality of their own, and the theory never demands that they should acquire any other; and it leaves to these visual intuitions the office of merely suggesting to the mind tactual impressions, with which they have been invariably associated in place. We say *in place;* and it will be found that there is no contradiction in our saying so when we shall have shown that it is the touch, and not the sight, which establishes a protensive interval between the organ and the sensations of vision.

Visible extension, then, or the perception of colours external to colours, being admitted, Mr Bailey's argument, if he still adheres to it, must be presented to us in this form. He must maintain that the theory requires that the objects of touch should not only be suggested by the visual objects with which they have been associated, but that they should actually be *seen*. And then he must maintain that no power of association can enable us to see an object which can only be touched —a position which, certainly, no one will controvert. The simple answer to all which is, that we never do see tangible objects, that the theory never requires we should, and that no power of association is necessary to account for a phenomenon which never takes place.

We cannot help thinking that not a little of the misconception on this subject which prevails in the writings of Mr Bailey, and, we may add, of many other philosophers, originates in the supposition that we identify vision with the eye in the mere act of seeing, and in their taking it for granted that sight of itself informs us that we possess such an organ as the eye. Of course, if we suppose that we know instinctively, or intuitively, from the mere act of seeing, that the eye is the organ of vision, that it forms a part of the body we behold, and is located in the head, it requires no conjurer to prove that we *must* have an instinctive or intuitive knowledge of visible things as larger than that organ, and, consequently, as external to it. In this case, no process of association is necessary to account for our knowledge of the distance of objects. That knowledge must be directly given in the very function and exercise of vision, as every one will admit, without going to the expense of an octavo volume to have it proved.

But we hold that no truth in mental philosophy is more incontestable than this, that the sight originally, and of itself, furnishes us with no knowledge of the eye, as we *now* know that organ to exist. It does not inform us that we have an eye at all. And here we may hazard an observation, which, simple as it is, appears to us to be new, and not unimportant in aiding us to unravel the mysteries of sensation; which observation is, that, in no case whatever, does any sense inform us of the existence of its appropriate organ, or of the relation which subsists between that organ and its objects, but that the interposition of some other sense[1] is invariably required to give us this information. This

[1] It would not be difficult to show, that as, on the one hand, *distance* is not involved in the original intuitions of sight, so, on the other hand, *proximity* is not involved in the original intuitions of touch; but that, while it is the touch which establishes an interval between the organ and the objects of sight, it is the sight

truth, which we believe holds good with regard to all the senses, is most strikingly exemplified in the case of vision, as we shall now endeavour to illustrate.

Let us begin by supposing that man is a mere "power of seeing." Under this supposition, we must hold that the periphery of vision is one and the same with the periphery of visible space; and the two peripheries being identical, of course whatever objects lie within the sphere of the one must lie within the sphere of the other also. Perhaps, strictly speaking, it is wrong to say that these objects are apprehended as internal to the sight; for the conception of internality implies the conception of externality, and neither of these conceptions can, as yet, be realised. But it is obvious what the expression *internal* means; and it is unobjectionable, when understood to signify that the Seeing Power, the Seeing Act, and the Seen Things, coexist in a synthesis in which there is no interval or discrimination. For, suppose that we know instinctively that the seen things occupy a locality separate from the sight. But that implies that we instinctively know that the sight occupies a locality separate from them. But such a supposition is a falling back upon the notion just reprobated, that the mere act of seeing can indicate its own organ, or can localise the visual phenomena in the eye—a position which, we presume, no philosopher will be hardy enough to maintain, when called upon to do so, broadly and unequivocally. The conclusion, therefore, is irresistible, that, in mere vision, the sight and its objects cling together in a union or synthesis, which no function of that sense, and no knowledge imparted to us by it (and, according to the supposition, we have, as yet, no other knowledge), can enable us to discriminate or dissolve. Where the seeing is, there is the thing seen; and where the thing seen is, there is the seeing of it.

But man is not a mere seeing animal. He has other senses besides: He has, for example, the sense of touch, and one of the most important offices which this sense performs, is to break up the identity of cohesion which subsists between sight and its objects. And how? We answer, by teaching us to associate *vision in general,* or the abstract *condition* regulating our visual impressions, with the presence of the small tangible body we call the eye, and *vision in particular,* or the individual sensations of vision (*i.e.,* colours), with the presence of immeasurably larger bodies revealed to us by touch, and tangibly external to the tangible eye. Sight, as we have said, does not inform us that its sensations are situated in the eye: it does not inform us that we have an eye at all. Neither does touch inform us that our visual sensations are located in the eye. It does not lead us to associate with the

---

which establishes *no* interval between the organ and the objects of touch. Sight thus pays back every fraction of the debt it has incurred to its brother sense. This is an interesting subject, but we can only glance at it here.

eye any of the visual phenomena or operations *in the first instance.* If it did, it would, *firstly,* either be impossible for it *afterwards* to induce us to associate them with the presence of tangible bodies distant and different from the eye: or, *secondly,* such an association would merely give birth to the abstract knowledge or conclusion, that these bodies were in one place, while the sensations suggesting them were felt to be associated with something in another place; colour would not be seen —as it is—incarnated with body: or, *thirdly,* we should be compelled to postulate for the eye, as many philosophers have done, in our opinion, most unwarrantably, "a faculty of projection," [1] by which it might dissolve the association between itself and its sensations, throwing off the latter in the form of colours over the surface of things, and reversing the old Epicurean doctrine that perception is kept up by a transit to the sensorium of the ghosts or *simulacra* of things,

> "Quæ, quasi membranœ, summo de corpore rerum
> Dereptæ, volitant ultro citroque per auras." [2]

It is difficult to say whether the hypothesis of "cast-off films" is more absurd when we make the films come from things to us as spectral effluxes, or go from us to them in the semblance of colours.

But according to the present view no such incomprehensible faculty, no such crude and untenable hypothesis is required. *Before* the touch has informed us that we have an eye, *before* it has led us to associate anything visual with the eye, it has *already* taught us to associate in place the sensations of vision (colours) with the presence of tangible objects which are not the eye. Therefore, when the touch discovers the eye, and induces us to associate vision in some way with it, it cannot be the particular sensations of vision called colours which it leads us to associate with that organ; for these have been already associated with something very different. If it be not colours, then what is it that the touch compels us to associate with the eye? We answer that it is the abstract *condition* of impressions as the general law on which all seeing depends, but as quite distinct from the particular visual sensations apprehended in virtue of the observance of that law.

Nor is it at all difficult to understand how this general condition comes to be associated with the eye, and how the particular visual sensations come to be associated with something distant from the eye: and further, how this association of the condition with one thing, and of the sensations with another thing (an association established by the touch and not by the sight), dissolves the primary synthesis of seeing and colours. It is to be observed that there are two stages in the proc-

---

[1] We observe that even Müller speaks of the "faculty of projection" as if he sanctioned and adopted the hypothesis.—See "Physiology," Vol. II, p. 1167.

[2] Lucretius, IV, 31. [Which, peeled like films from the surfaces of things, constantly flutter hither and thither through the air. *De Rerum Natura.* Ed.]

ess by which this secernment is brought about—*First,* the stage in which the visual phenomena are associated with things different from the organ of vision, the very existence of which is as yet unknown. Let us suppose, then, the function of sight to be in operation. We behold a visible object—a particular colour. Let the touch now come into play. We feel a tangible object—say a book. Now from the mere fact of the visible and the tangible object being seen and felt together, we could not associate them in place; for it is quite possible that the tangible object may admit of being withdrawn, and yet the visible object remain: and if so, no association of the two in place can be established. But this is a point that can only be determined by experience; and what says that wise instructor? We withdraw the tangible object. The visible object, too, disappears: it leaves its place. We replace the tangible object—the visible object reappears *in statu quo.* There is no occasion to vary the experiment. If we find that the visible object invariably leaves its place when the tangible object leaves its, and that the one invariably comes back when the other returns, we have brought forward quite enough to establish an inevitable association in place between the two. The two places are henceforth regarded not as two, but as one and the same.

By the aid of the touch, then, we have associated the visual phenomena with things which are *not* the organ of vision; and well it is for us that we have done so betimes, and before we were aware of the eye's existence. Had the eye been indicated to us in the mere act of seeing, had we become apprised of its existence *before* we had associated our visual sensations with the tangible objects constituting the material universe, the probability, nay the certainty, is that we would have associated them with this eye, and that then it would have been as impossible for us to break up the association between colours and the organ, as it now is for us to dissolve the union between colours and material things. In which case we should have remained blind, or as bad as blind; brightness would have been in the eye when it ought to have been in the sun; greenness would have been in the retina when it ought to have been in the grass. A most wise provision of nature it certainly is, by which our visual sensations are disposed of in the right way before we obtain any knowledge of the eye. And most wisely has nature seconded her own scheme by obscuring all the sources from which that knowledge might be derived. The light eyelids—the effortless muscular apparatus performing its ministrations so gently as to be almost unfelt—the tactual sensations so imperceptible when the eye is left to its own motions, so keen when it is invaded by an exploring finger, and so anxious to avoid all contact by which the existence of the organ might be betrayed. All these are so many means adopted by nature to keep back from the infant seer all knowledge of his own eye—a knowledge which, if developed prematurely, would have perverted the functions, if not rendered nugatory the very existence, of the organ.

But, *secondly,* we have to consider the stage of the process, in which vision is in some way associated with an object which is *not* any of the things with which the visual sensations are connected. It is clear that the process is not completed—that our task, which is to dissolve the primary synthesis of vision and its phenomena, is but half executed, unless such an object be found. For though we have associated the visual sensations (colours) with something different from themselves, still vision clings to them without a hair's-breadth of interval, and pursues them whithersoever they go. As far, then, as we have yet gone, it cannot be said that our vision is felt or known to be distanced from the fixed stars even by the diameter of a grain of sand. The synthesis of sight and colour is not yet discriminated. How, then, is the interval interposed? We answer, by the discovery of a tangible object in a different place from any of the tangible objects associated with colour; and then by associating, in some way or other, the operations of vision with this object. Such an object is discovered in the eye. Now, as has frequently been said, we cannot associate colours or the visual sensations with this eye; for these have been already disposed of otherwise. What, then, do we associate with it—and how? We find, upon experiment, that our apprehension of the various visual sensations depends on the presence and particular location of this small tangible body. We find that the whole array of visual phenomena disappear when it is tactually covered, that they reappear when it is re-opened, and so forth. Thus we come in some way to associate vision with it—not as colour, however, not as visual sensation. We regard the organ and its dispositions merely as a general condition regulating the apprehension of the visual sensations, and no more.

Thus, by attending to the two associations that occur,—the association (in place) of visual sensations with tangible bodies that *are not* the eye; and the association (in place) of vision with a small tangible body that *is* the eye— the eye regarded as the condition on which the apprehension of these sensations depends; by attending to these, we can understand how a protensive interval comes to be recognised between the organ and its objects. By means of the touch, we have associated the sensations of vision with tangible bodies in one place, and the apprehension of these sensations with a tangible body in another place. It is, therefore, impossible for the sight to dissolve these associations, and bring the sensations out of the one place where they are felt, into the other place where the *condition* of their apprehension resides. The sight is, therefore, compelled to leave the sensations where they are, and the apprehension of them where it is; and to recognise the two as sundered from each other—the sensations as separated from the organ, which they truly are. Thus it is that we would explain the origin of the perception of distance by the eye; believing firmly that the sight would never have discerned this distance without the mediation of the touch.

Rightly to understand the foregoing reasoning—indeed, to advance a single step in the true philosophy of sensation—we must divest ourselves of the prejudice instilled into us by a false physiology, that what we call our organism, or, in plain words, our body, is necessarily *the seat* of our sensations. That all our sensations come to be associated *in some way* with this body, and that some of them even come to be associated with it *in place,* is undeniable; but so far is it from being true that they are all essentially implicated or incorporated with it, and cannot exist at a distance from it, that we have a direct proof to the contrary in our sensations of vision; and until the physiologist can prove (what has never yet been proven) an *a priori* necessity that our sensations must be where our bodies are, and an *a priori* absurdity in the contrary supposition, he must excuse us for resolutely standing by the fact as we find it.

This is a view which admits of much discussion, and we would gladly expatiate upon the subject, did time and space permit; but we must content ourselves with winding up the present observations with the accompanying diagram, which we think explains our view beyond the possibility of a mistake.

$$A$$
$$Ba \qquad\qquad áC$$

Let A be the original synthesis, or indiscrimination of vision and its sensations—of light and colours. Let *á* be the visual sensations locally associated by means of the touch with the tangible bodies C *before* vision is in any way associated with B—before, indeed, we have any knowledge of the existence of B. Then let *a,* the general condition on which the sensations, *after a time,* are found to depend, and in virtue of which they are apprehended, be locally associated with B—the eye discovered by means of the touch—and we have before us what we cannot help regarding as a complete *rationale* of the whole phenomena and mysteries of vision. Now, the great difference between this view of the subject and the views of it that have been taken by *every* other philosopher, consists in this, that whereas their explanations invariably implicated the visual sensations *á* with B from the very first, thereby rendering it either impossible for them to be afterwards associated with C, or possible only in virtue of some very extravagant hypothesis—our explanation, on the contrary, proceeding on a simple observation of the facts, and never implicating the sensations *á* with B at all, but associating them with C *a primordiis,* merely leaving to be associated with B, *a,* a certain general condition that must be complied with, in order that the sensation *á* may be apprehended,—in this way, we say, our explanation contrives to steer clear both of the impossibility and the hypothesis.

We would just add by way of postscript to this article—which, perhaps, ought itself to have been only a postscript—that with regard to Mr Bailey's allegation of our having plagiarised one of his arguments, merely turning the coat of it outside in, we can assure him that he is labouring under a mistake. In our former paper, we remarked that we could not see things to be *out* of the sight, because we could not see the sight itself. Mr Bailey alleges that this argument is borrowed from him, being a mere reversal of his reasoning, that we cannot see things to be *in* the sight, because we cannot see both the sight and the things. That our argument might very naturally have been suggested by his, we admit. But it was not so. We had either overlooked the passage in his book, or it was clean out of our mind when we were pondering our own speculations. It did not suggest our argument, either nearly or remotely. Had it done so, we should certainly have noticed it, and should probably have handled both Mr Bailey's reasoning and our own to better purpose in consequence. If, notwithstanding this disclaimer, he still thinks that appearances are against us, we cannot mend his faith, but can merely repeat, that the fact is as we have stated it.

A SPECULATION ON THE SENSES

How can that which is a purely subjective affection—in other words, which is dependent upon us as a mere modification of our sentient nature—acquire, nevertheless, such a distinct objective reality, as shall compel us to acknowledge it as an independent creation, the permanent existence of which is beyond the control of all that we can either do or think? Such is the form to which all the questions of speculation may be ultimately reduced. And all the solutions which have hitherto been propounded as answers to the problem, may be generalised into these two: either consciousness is able to transcend, or go beyond itself; or else the whole pomp, and pageantry, and magnificence, which we miscall the external universe, are nothing but our mental phantasmagoria, nothing but states of our poor, finite, subjective selves.

But it has been asked again and again, in reference to these two solutions, Can a man overstep the limits of himself—of his own consciousness? If he can, then says the querist, the reality of the external world is indeed guaranteed; but what an insoluble, inextricable contradiction is here—that a man should overstep the limits of the very nature which is *his,* just because he cannot overstep it! And if he cannot, then says the same querist, then is the external universe an empty name—a mere unmeaning sound; and our most inveterate convictions are all dissipated like dreams.

Astute reasoner! the dilemma is very just, and is very formidable; and upon the one or other of its horns has been transfixed every adventurer that has hitherto gone forth on the knight-errantry of speculation. Every man who lays claim to a direct knowledge of something different from himself, perishes impaled on the contradiction involved in the assumption, that consciousness can transcend itself: and every man who disclaims such knowledge, expires in the vacuum of idealism, where nothing grows but the dependent and transitory productions of a delusive and constantly shifting consciousness.

But is there no other way in which the question can be resolved? We think that there is. In the following demonstration, we think that we can vindicate the objective reality of things—(a vindication which, we would remark by the way, is of no value whatever, in so far as that objective reality is concerned, but only as being instrumental to the ascertainment of the laws which regulate the whole process of sensation)—we think that we can accomplish this, without, on the one hand, forcing consciousness to overstep itself, and on the other hand, without reducing that reality to the delusive impressions of an understanding born but to deceive. Whatever the defects of our proposed demonstration may be, we flatter ourselves that the dilemma just noticed as so fatal to every other solution will be utterly powerless when brought to bear against it: and we conceive, that the point of a third alternative must be sharpened by the controversialist who would bring us to the dust. It is a new argument, and will require a new answer. We moreover pledge ourselves that, abstruse as the subject is, both the question and our attempted solution of it shall be presented to the reader in such a shape as shall *compel* him to understand them.

Our pioneer shall be a very plain and palpable illustration. Let A be a circle, containing within it X Y Z.

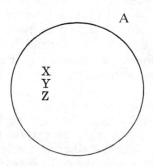

X Y and Z lie within the circle; and the question is, by what art or artifice—we might almost say by what sorcery—can they be transplanted out of it, without at the same time being made to overpass the limits of the sphere? There are just four conceivable answers to this question—answers illustrative of three great schools of philosophy, and of a fourth which is now fighting for existence.

1. One man will meet the difficulty boldly, and say—"X Y and Z certainly lie within the circle, but I believe they lie without it. *How* this should be, I know not. I merely state what I conceive to be the fact. The *modus operandi* is beyond my comprehension." This man's answer is contradictory, and will never do.

2. Another man will deny the possibility of the transference—"X Y and Z," he will say, "are generated within the circle in obedience to its own laws. They form part and parcel of the sphere; and every endeavour to regard them as endowed with an extrinsic existence, must end in the discomfiture of him who makes the attempt." This man declines giving any answer to the problem. We ask him *how* X Y and Z can be projected beyond the circle without transgressing its limits; and he answers that they never are, and never can be so projected.

3. A third man will postulate as the cause of X Y Z a transcendent X Y Z—that is, a cause lying external to the sphere; and by referring the former to the latter, he will obtain for X Y Z, not certainly a real externality, which is the thing wanted, but a *quasi-externality,* with which, as the best that is to be had, he will in all probability rest contented. "X Y and Z," he will say, "are projected, *as it were,* out of the circle." This answer leaves the question as much unsolved as ever. Or,

4. A fourth man (and we beg the reader's attention to this man's answer, for it forms the fulcrum or cardinal point on which our whole demonstration turns)—a fourth man will say, "If the circle could only be brought *within itself,* so—

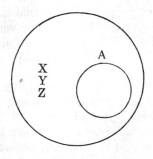

then the difficulty would disappear—the problem would be completely solved. X Y Z must now of necessity fall as extrinsic to the circle A; and this, too (which is the material part of the solution), without the limits of the circle A being overstepped."

Perhaps this may appear very like quibbling; perhaps it may be regarded as a very absurd solution—a very shallow evasion of the difficulty. Nevertheless, shallow or quibbling as it may seem, we venture to predict, that when the breath of life shall have been breathed into the bones of the above dead illustration, this last answer will be found to afford a most exact picture and explanation of the matter we have to deal with. Let our illustration, then, stand forth as a living process. The large circle A we shall call our whole sphere of sense, in so far as it deals with objective existence; and X Y Z shall be certain sensations of colour, figure, weight, hardness, and so forth, comprehended within it. The question then is, How can these sensations, without being ejected from the sphere of sense within which they lie, assume the status and the character of real independent existences? How can they be objects, and yet remain sensations?

Nothing will be lost on the score of distinctness, if we retrace, in the living sense, the footprints we have already trod in explicating the inanimate illustration. Neither will any harm be done, should we employ very much the same phraseology. We answer, then, that here, too, there are just four conceivable ways in which this question can be met.

1. The man of common sense (so called), who aspires to be somewhat of a philosopher, will face the question boldly, and will say, "I feel that colour and hardness, for instance, lie entirely within the sphere of sense, and are mere modifications of my subjective nature. At the same time I feel that colour and hardness constitute a real object, which exists out of the sphere of sense independently of me and all my modifications. *How* this should be I know not, I merely state the fact as I imagine myself to find it. The *modus* is beyond my comprehension." This man belongs to the school of Natural Realists. If he merely affirmed or postulated a miracle in what he uttered, we should have little to say against him (for the whole process of sensation is indeed miraculous). But he postulates more than a miracle—he postulates a contradiction, in the very contemplation of which our reason is unhinged.

2. Another man will deny that our sensations ever transcend the sphere of sense, or attain a real objective existence. "Colour, hardness, figure, and so forth," he will say, "are generated within the sphere of sense in obedience to its own original laws. They form integral parts of the sphere; and he who endeavours to construe them to his own mind as embodied in extrinsic independent existences must for ever be foiled in the attempt." This man declines giving any answer

to the problem. We ask, *How* can our sensations be embodied in distinct permanent realities? And he replies, That they never are and never can be so embodied. This man is an Idealist, or, as we would term him (to distinguish him from another species about to be mentioned of the same genus), an *Acosmical* Idealist; that is, an Idealist who absolutely denies the existence of an independent material world.

3. A third man will postulate as the cause of our sensations of hardness, colour, &c., a transcendent something, of which he knows nothing except that he feigns and fables it as lying external to the sphere of sense: and then, by referring our sensations to this unknown cause, he will obtain for them, not certainly the externality desiderated, but a *quasi-externality,* which he palms off upon himself and us as the best that can be supplied. This man is a *Cosmothetical* Idealist; that is, an Idealist who postulates an external universe as the unknown cause of certain modifications we are conscious of within ourselves, and which, according to his view, we never really get beyond. This species of speculator is the commonest, but he is the least trustworthy of any; and his fallacies are all the more dangerous by reason of the air of plausibility with which they are invested. From first to last he represents us as the dupes of our own perfidious nature. By some inexplicable process of association he refers certain known effects to certain unknown causes, and would thus explain to us how these effects (our sensations) come to assume, *as it were,* the character of external objects. But we know not "as it were." Away with such shuffling phraseology. There is nothing either of reference, or of inference, or of quasi-truthfulness in our apprehension of the material universe. It is ours with a certainty which laughs to scorn all the deductions of logic and all the props of hypothesis. What we wish to know is, *how* our subjective affections can *be,* not *as it were,* but in God's truth and in the strict, literal, earnest, and unambiguous sense of the words, real independent, objective existences. This is what the cosmothetical idealist never can explain and never attempts to explain.

4. We now come to the answer which the reader who has followed us thus far will be prepared to find us putting forward as by far the most important of any, and as containing in fact the very kernel of the solution. A fourth man will say, "If the whole sphere of sense could only be withdrawn *inwards,* could be made to fall somewhere *within itself,* then the whole difficulty would disappear and the problem would be solved at once. The sensations which existed previous to this retraction or withdrawal, would then of necessity fall without the sphere of sense (see our second diagram), and in doing so they would necessarily assume a totally different aspect from that of sensations. They would be real independent objects, and (what is the important part of the demonstration) they would acquire this *status* without overstepping by a hair's-breadth the primary limits of the sphere.

Were such phraseology allowable, we should say that the sphere has *understepped* itself, and in doing so has left its former contents high and dry, and stamped with all the marks which can characterise objective existences."

Now the reader will please to remark, that we are very far from desiring him to accept this last solution at our bidding. Our method, we trust, is anything but dogmatical. We merely say, that *if* this can be shown to be the case, then the demonstration which we are in the course of unfolding will hardly fail to recommend itself to his acceptance. Whether or not it is the case can only be established by an appeal to our experience.

We ask, then, Does experience inform us, or does she not, that the sphere of sense falls within, and very considerably within, itself? But here it will be asked, What meaning do we attach to the expression, that sense falls within its own sphere? These words, then, we must first of all explain. Everything which is apprehended as a sensation—such as colour, figure, hardness, and so forth—falls within the sentient sphere. To be a sensation, and to fall within the sphere of sense, are identical and convertible terms. When, therefore, it is asked, Does the sphere of sense ever fall within itself? this is equivalent to asking, Do the senses themselves ever become sensations? Is that which apprehends sensations ever itself apprehended as a sensation? Can the senses be seized on within the limits of the very circle which they prescribe? If they cannot, then it must be admitted that the sphere of sense never falls within itself, and consequently that an objective reality—*i.e.,* a reality extrinsic to that sphere—can never be predicated or secured for any part of its contents. But we conceive that only one rational answer can be returned to this question. Does not experience teach us, that much if not the whole of our sentient nature becomes itself in turn a series of sensations? Does not the sight—that power which contains the whole visible space, and embraces distances which no astronomer can compute—does it not abjure its high prerogative, and take rank within the sphere of sense—itself a sensation—when revealed to us in the solid atom we call the eye? Here it is the touch which brings the sight within, and very far within, the sphere of vision. But somewhat less directly, and by the aid of the imagination, the sight operates the same introtraction (pardon the coinage) upon itself. It ebbs inwards, so to speak, from all the contents that were given in what may be called its primary sphere. It represents itself, in its organ, as a minute visual sensation, out of, and beyond which, are left lying the great range of all its other sensations. By imagining the sight as a sensation of colour, we diminish it to a speck within the sphere of its own sensations; and as we now regard the sense as for ever enclosed within this small embrasure, all the other sensations which were its, previous to our discovery of the organ, and which are its still, are built up into a world of objective existence, *necessarily* external to the sight, and altogether out of its control. All sensations of colour are necessarily out of one another. Surely, then, when the sight is subsumed under the category of colour—as it unquestionably is whenever we think of the eye—surely all other colours must, of necessity, assume a position external to it; and what more is wanting to constitute that real objective universe of light and glory in which our hearts rejoice?

We can, perhaps, make this matter still plainer by reverting to our old illustration. Our first exposition of the question was designed to exhibit a general view of the case, through the medium of a dead symbolical figure. This proved nothing, though we imagine that it illustrated much. Our second exposition exhibited the illustration in its application to the living sphere of sensation *in general;* and this proved little. But we conceive that therein was foreshadowed a certain procedure, which, if it can be shown from experience to be the actual procedure of sensation *in detail,* will prove all that we are desirous of establishing. We now, then, descend to a more systematic exposition of the process which (so far as *our* experience goes, and we beg to refer the reader to his own) seems to be involved in the operation of seeing. We dwell chiefly upon the sense of sight, because it is mainly through its ministrations that a real objective universe is given to us. Let the circle A be the whole circuit of vision. We may begin by calling it the eye, the retina, or what we will. Let it be provided with the ordinary complement of sensations—the colours X Y Z. Now, we admit that these sensations cannot be extruded beyond the periphery of vision; and yet we maintain that, unless they be made to fall on the outside of that periphery, they cannot become real objects. How is this difficulty—this contradiction—to be overcome? Nature overcomes it, by a contrivance as simple as it is beautiful. In the operation of seeing, admitting the canvas or background of our picture to be a retina, or what we will, with a multiplicity of colours depicted upon it, we maintain that we cannot stop here, and that we never do stop here. We invariably go on (such is the inevitable law of our nature) to complete the picture—that is to say, we fill in our own eye as a colour within the very picture which our eye contains—we fill it in as a sensation within the other sensations which occupy the rest of the field; and in doing so, we of necessity, by the same law, turn these sensations out of the eye; and they thus, by the same necessity, assume the rank of independent objective existences. We describe the circumference infinitely within the circumference; and hence all that lies on the outside of the intaken circle comes before us stamped with the impress of real objective truth. We fill in the eye greatly within the sphere of sight (or within the eye itself, if we insist on calling the primary sphere by this name), and the eye thus filled in is the only eye we know anything at all about, either from the experience of sight or of touch. *How* this operation is accomplished, is a subject of but secondary moment; whether it be brought about by the touch, by the eye itself, or by the imagination, is a question which might admit of much discussion; but it is one of very subordinate interest. The *fact* is the main thing—the fact that the operation *is* accomplished in one way or another—the fact that the sense comes before itself (if not directly, yet virtually) as *one* of its own sensations—*that* is the principal point to be attended to; and we apprehend that this fact is now placed beyond the reach of controversy.

To put the case in another light. The following considerations may serve to remove certain untoward difficulties in metaphysics and optics, which beset the path, not only of the uninitiated, but even of the professors of the sciences.

We are assured by optical metaphysicians, or metaphysical opticians, that, in the operations of vision, we never get beyond the eye itself, or the representations that are depicted therein. We see nothing, they tell us, but what is delineated within the eye. Now, the way in which a plain man should meet this statement is this—he should ask the metaphysician *what* eye he refers to. Do you allude, sir, to an eye which belongs to my visible body, and forms a small part of the same; or do you allude to an eye which does not belong to my visible body, and which constitutes no portion thereof? If the metaphysician should say that he refers to an eye of the latter description, then the plain man's answer should be—that he has no experience of any such eye—that he cannot conceive it—that he knows nothing at all about it—and that the only eye which he ever thinks or speaks of, is the eye appertaining to, and situated within, the phenomenon which he calls his visible body. Is *this,* then, the eye which the metaphysician refers to, and which he tells us we never get beyond? If it be—why, then, the very admission that this eye is a part of the visible body (and what else can we conceive the eye to be?) proves that we *must* get beyond it. Even supposing that the whole operation were transacted within the eye, and that the visible body were nowhere but within the eye, still the eye which we invariably and inevitably fill in as belonging to the visible body (and no other eye is ever thought of or spoken of by us),—*this* eye, we say, must necessarily exclude the visible body, and all other visible things, from its sphere. Or, can the eye (always conceived of as a visible thing among other visible things) again contain the very phenomenon (*i.e.,* the visible body) within which it is itself contained? Surely no one will maintain a position of such unparalleled absurdity as that.

The science of optics, in so far as it maintains, according to certain physiological principles, that in the operation of seeing we never get beyond the representations within the eye, is founded on the assumption that the visible body has no visible eye belonging to it. Whereas we maintain that the only eye that we have—the only eye we can form any conception of—is the visible eye that belongs to the visible body, as a part does to a whole; whether this eye be originally revealed to us by the touch, by the sight, by the reason, or by the imagination. We maintain that to affirm we never get beyond this eye in the exercise of vision, is equivalent to asserting that a part is larger than the whole, of which it is only a part—is equivalent to asserting that Y, which is contained between X and Z, is nevertheless of larger compass than X and Z, and comprehends them both. The fallacy we conceive to be this, that the visible body can be contained within the eye, without the eye of the visible body also being contained therein. But this is a procedure which no law either of thought or imagination will tolerate. If we turn the visible body, and all visible things, into the eye, we must turn the eye of the visible body also into the eye; a process which, of course, again turns the visible body, and all visible things, *out* of the eye. And thus the procedure eternally defeats itself. Thus the very law which appears to annihilate, or render impossible, the objective existence of visible things, as creations independent of the eye—this very law, when carried into effect with a thoroughgoing consistency, vindicates and establishes that objective existence, with a logical force, an iron necessity, which no physiological paradox can countervail.

We have now probably said enough to convince the attentive reader that the sense of sight, when brought under its own notice as a sensation, either directly, or through the ministry of the touch, or of the imagination (as it is when revealed to us in its organ), falls very far, falls almost infinitely within its own sphere. Sight, revealing itself as a sense, spreads over a span commensurate with the diameter of the whole visible space; sight, revealing itself as a sensation, dwindles to a speck of almost unappreciable insignificance when compared with the other phenomena which fall within the visual ken. This speck is the organ, and the organ is the sentient circumference drawn inwards, far within itself, according to a law which (however unconscious we may be of its operation) presides over every act and exercise of vision; a law which, while it contracts the sentient sphere, throws, at the same time, into necessary objectivity every phenomenon that falls external to the diminished circle. This is the law, in virtue of which, subjective visual sensations are real visible objects. The moment the sight becomes one of its own sensations, it is restricted in a peculiar manner to that particular sensation. It now falls, as we have said, within its own sphere. Now, nothing more was wanting to make the other visual sensations real independent existences, for, *quà* sensations, they are all originally independent of each other, and the sense itself being now a sensation, they must now also be independent of it.

We now pass on to the consideration of the sense of touch.

Here precisely the same process is gone through which was observed to take place in the case of vision. The same law manifests itself here, and the same inevitable consequence follows, namely, that sensations are things, that subjective affections are objective realities. The sensation of hardness (softness, be it observed, is only an inferior degree of hardness, and therefore the latter word is the proper generic term to be employed)—the sensation of hardness forms the contents of this sense. Hardness, we will say, is originally a purely subjective affection. The question then is, How can this affection, without being thrust forth into a fictitious, transcendent, and incomprehensible universe, assume, nevertheless, a distinct, objective reality, and be (not as it were, but in language of the most unequivocating truth) a permanent existence altogether independent of the sense? We answer, that this can take place only provided the sense of touch can be brought under our notice *as itself hard.* If this can be shown to take place, then (as all sensations which are presented to us in space necessarily exclude one another, are reciprocally *out* of each other), all other instances of hardness must of necessity fall as extrinsic to that particular hardness which the sense reveals to us as its own; and, consequently, all these other instances of hardness will start into being as things endowed with a permanent and independent substance.

Now, what is the verdict of experience on the subject. The direct and unequivocal verdict of experience is, that the touch reveals itself to us as one of its own sensations. In the finger-points more particularly, and generally all over the surface of the body, the touch manifests itself not only as that which apprehends hardness, but as that which is itself hard. The sense of touch vested in one of its own sensations (our tangible bodies, namely) is the sense of touch brought within its own sphere. It comes before itself as *one* sensation of hardness. Consequently all its *other* sensations of hardness are necessarily excluded from this particular hardness; and falling beyond it, they are, by the same consequence, built up into a world of objective reality, of permanent substance, altogether independent of the sense, self-betrayed as a sensation of hardness.

But here, it may be asked, if the senses are thus reduced to the rank of sensations, if they come under our observation as themselves sensations, must we not regard them but as parts of the subjective sphere; and though the other portions of the sphere may be extrinsic to these sensations, still, must not the contents of the sphere, taken as a whole, be considered as entirely subjective, *i.e.,* as merely *ours,* and consequently must not real objective existence be still as far beyond our grasp as ever? We answer, No; by no means. Such a query implies a total oversight of all that experience proves to be the fact with regard to this matter. It implies that the senses have *not* been reduced to the rank of sensations, that they have *not* been brought under our cognisance as themselves sensations, and that they have yet to be brought there. It implies that vision has not been revealed to us as a sensation of colour in the phenomenon, the eye; and that touch has not been revealed to us as a sensation of hardness in the phenomenon, the finger. It implies, in short, that it is not the sense itself which has been revealed to us in the one case as coloured, and in the other case as hard, but that it is something else which has been thus revealed to us. But it may still be asked, How do we know that we are not deceiving ourselves? How can it be proved that it is the senses, and not something else, which have come before us under the guise of certain sensations? That these sensations are the senses themselves, and nothing but the senses, may be proved in the following manner:—

We bring the matter to the test of actual experiment. We make certain experiments *seriatim* upon each of the items that lie within the sentient sphere, and we note the effect which each experiment has upon that portion of the contents which is not meddled with. In the exercise of vision, for example, we remove a book, and no change is produced in our perception of a house; a cloud disappears, yet our apprehension of the sea and the mountains, and all other visible things, is the same as ever. We continue our experiments until our test happens to be applied to one particular phenomenon which lies, if not directly, yet virtually, within the sphere of vision. We remove or veil this small visual phenomenon, and a totally different effect is produced from those that took place when any of the other visual phenomena were removed or veiled. The whole landscape is obliterated. We restore this phenomenon, the whole landscape reappears; we adjust this phenomenon differently, the whole landscape becomes differently adjusted. From these experiments we find that this phenomenon is by no means an ordinary sensation, but that it differs from all other sensations in this, that it is the sense itself appearing in the form of a sensation. These experiments prove that it is the sense itself, and nothing else, which reveals itself to us in the particular phenomenon, the eye. If experience informed us that the particular adjustment of some other visual phenomenon (a book, for instance) were essential to our apprehension of all the other phenomena, we should, in the same way, be compelled to regard this book as our sense of sight manifested in one of its own sensations. The book would be to us what the eye now is; it would be our bodily organ: and no *a priori* reason can be shown why this might not have been the case. All that we can say is, that such is not the finding of experience. Experience points out the eye, and the eye alone, as the visual sensation essential to our apprehension of all our other sensations of vision, and we come at last to regard this sensation as the sense itself. Inveterate association leads us to regard the eye not merely as the organ, but actually as the sense of vision. We find from experience how much depends upon its possession, and we lay claim to it as a part of ourselves with an emphasis that will not be gainsaid.

An interesting enough subject of speculation would be, an inquiry into the gradual steps by which each man is led to *appropriate* his own body. No man's body is given him absolutely, indefensibly, and at once, *ex dono Dei*. It is no unearned hereditary patrimony. It is held by no *a priori* title on the part of the possessor. The credentials by which its tenure is secured to him are purely of an *a posteriori* character; and a certain course of experience must be gone through before the body can become his. The man acquires it, as he does originally all other property, in a certain formal and legalised manner. Originally, and in the strict legal as well as metaphysical idea of them, all bodies, living as well as dead, human no less than brute, are mere *waifs,* the property of the first finder. But the law, founding on sound metaphysical principles, very properly makes a distinction here between two kinds of finding. To entitle a person to claim a human body as his own, it is not enough that he should find it in the same way in which he finds his other sensations, namely, as impressions which interfere not with the manifestations of each other. This is not enough, even though, in the case supposed, the person should be the first finder. A subsequent finder would have the preference if able to show that the particular sensations manifested as this human body were essential to his apprehension of all his other sensations whatsoever. It is this latter species of finding—the finding, namely, of certain sensations as the essential condition on which the apprehension of all other sensations depends—it is this finding alone which gives each man a paramount and indisputable title to that "treasure trove" which he calls his own body. Now, it is only after going through a considerable course of experience and experiment, that we can ascertain what the particular sensations are upon which all our other sensations are dependent. And therefore were we not right in saying that a man's body is not given to him directly and at once, but that he takes a certain time, and must go through a certain process, to acquire it?

The conclusion which we would deduce from the whole of the foregoing remarks is, that the great law of *living*[1] sensation, the *rationale* of sensation as a *living* process, is this, that the senses are not merely *presentative, i.e.,* they not only bring sensations before us, but that they are *self-presentative, i.e.,* they, moreover, bring themselves be

[1] We say *living,* because every attempt hitherto made to explain sensation has been founded on certain appearances manifested in the *dead* subject. By inspecting a dead carcass we shall never discover the principle of life; by inspecting a dead eye or a camera obscura, we shall never discover the principle of vision. Yet, though there is no seeing in a dead eye, or in a camera obscura, optics deal exclusively with such inanimate materials; and hence the student who studies them will do well to remember, that optics are the science of vision, with the *fact* of vision left entirely out of the consideration.

fore us as sensations. But for this law we should never get beyond our mere subjective modifications; but, in virtue of it, we necessarily get beyond them; for the results of the law are—1st, that we, the subject, restrict ourselves to, or identify ourselves with, the senses, not as displayed in their primary sphere (the large circle A), but as falling within their own ken as sensations, in their secondary sphere (the small circle A). This smaller sphere is our own bodily frame, and does not each individual look upon himself as vested in his own bodily frame? And, 2dly, it is a necessary consequence of this investment or restriction, that every sensation which lies beyond the sphere of the senses, viewed as sensations (*i.e.,* which lies beyond the body), must be, in the most unequivocal sense of the words, a real independent object. If the reader wants a name to characterise this system, he may call it the system of *Absolute or Thoroughgoing presentationism.*

FERRIER'S WRITINGS

The *Philosophical Works,* 3 vols. (Edinburgh and London, 1875), is complete. Vols. II and III were reprinted separately in the following decade, and Vol. I contains the third edition of the *Institutes of Metaphysic,* first published in Edinburgh and London (1854), reprinted in a second edition (1856). Also in Vol. I is the essay *Scottish Philosophy, the Old and the New,* second edition; like the first edition it originally appeared at Edinburgh and London (1856). Vol. II contains the *Lectures on Early Greek Philosophy,* and Vol. III contains the articles, already listed, from *Blackwood's* magazine, the four miscellaneous lectures, and a few other pieces of no great philosophical interest. The latter include an unsent letter to Hamilton and a short biography of Hegel. The contents of these two volumes first appeared as *Lectures on Early Greek Philosophy and Other Philosophical Remains,* 2 vols., Edited by Ferrier's son-in-law, Sir Alexander Grant, and E. L. Lushington (Edinburgh and London, 1866). The lectures on Greek philosophy were intended as a simple introduction to the subject and they have been praised as meeting that purpose well. Ferrier's edition of *The Works of Professor Wilson,* 12 vols., was published in Edinburgh and London (1855–58).

WRITINGS ON FERRIER

What has been written on Ferrier is almost entirely devoted to the *Institutes of Metaphysic* rather than to his early papers on perception. John Grote's *Exploratio Philosophica* (Cambridge, 1865), contains a substantial and acute paper on the *Institutes;* and there is a good expository discussion on Ferrier's "higher philosophy" by John Tulloch in *Modern Theories in Philosophy and Religion* (Edinburgh and London, 1884). The chapter on Ferrier in *Scottish Philosophy* (Glasgow, 1902), by Henry Laurie, is a straightforward exposition of the later Ferrier. The more critical remarks in G. F. Stout's paper in *Votiva Tabella* (St. Andrews, 1911), are based on the view that Ferrier's later work is his "most valuable and characteristic." However, the few pages on Ferrier in James Seth's *English Philosophers and Schools of Philosophy* contain the comment that "Berkeley and Idealism" is "perhaps Ferrier's most perfect piece of philosophical writing." Jean Pucelle's *L'Idéalisme en Angleterre de Coleridge à Bradley* (Neuchatel, 1955), gives most of its twenty pages on Ferrier to expounding the *Institutes*. Two modern enthusiasts for the early writings of Ferrier are: Arthur Thomson who, in "The Philosophy of J. F. Ferrier," *Philosophy*, Vol. XXXIX (1964), usefully discusses and criticizes Ferrier's arguments; and G. E. Davie whose short article on Ferrier in *The Encyclopedia of Philosophy* (New York, 1967), calls attention to the neglect of him. Davie's book *The Democratic Intellect* (Edinburgh, 1961), contains a long and interesting treatment of Ferrier's role in the intellectual life of nineteenth-century Scotland. There is also a short biography: *J. F. Ferrier* by E. S. Haldane, the translator of Descartes, published at Edinburgh and London (1899). Also useful is T. T. Segerstedt's essay on Ferrier's later views; it is in *The Problem of Knowledge in Scottish Philosophy* (Lund, 1935).

INDEX

ROBERT BROWN was educated at the University of New Mexico and the University of Chicago before obtaining a Ph.D. at the University of London. He has taught at Los Angeles State College, the University of Wisconsin, and the University of Massachusetts. For some years he has been on the staff of the Institute of Advanced Studies, Australian National University, Canberra, where he is now a Senior Fellow. He has written *Explanation in Social Science* (1963), is co-editor of *Contemporary Philosophy in Australia* (1969), and has contributed extensively to philosophical journals in this country, Britain, and Australia.